# THE
# AMERICAN ALPINE
# JOURNAL

# 1998

Gardner Heaton

*Cover: Brendan Murphy and Andy Cave on the north face of Changabang.*
ROGER PAYNE

*Above: Alexander Huber and Toni Gutsch on the west face of Latok II.* THOMAS HUBER
*Right: Camp III on Nanga Parbat at dawn.* CARLOS BUHLER

# THE AMERICAN ALPINE JOURNAL

VOLUME 40          1998          ISSUE 72

## CONTENTS

The American Alpine Journal artists
John Svenson·Mike Clelland
Clay Wadman·Jim Springer
Gardner Heaton

# THE AMERICAN ALPINE JOURNAL

Christian Beckwith, *Editor*

**Advisory Board**

John E. (Jed) Williamson, *Managing Editor*; Michael Kennedy, Steven Swenson; Geoffrey Tabin, MD, and Charles Houston, MD, *Medical Advisors*; Brent Bishop and Chris Naumann, *Environmental Advisors*

**Associate Editors**

David Stevenson, *Reviews*

Frederick O. Johnson, *Club Activities*

**Translators**

Marina Heusch, *French;* Sabra Ayers, *Russian;* Alex Baer, *Italian, Spanish*; Sergei Nekhai, *Russian;* Christiane Leitinger, *German;* Bean Bowers, *Spanish;* Ilya Rapoport, *Russian*

**Indexer**

Jessica Kany

**Regional Contacts**

Charlie Sassara, *Wrangell-St. Elias*; Joe Josephson, *Canadian Rockies*; Alan Bartlett, *Sierra Nevada*; Steve Schneider, *Yosemite*; Yossi Brain, *Bolivia*; Evelio Echevarría, *South America*; Facundo Jose, *Patagonia*; Rolando Garibotti, *Argentine Patagonia*; W.H. Ruthven, *United Kingdom*; Lindsay Griffin, *United Kingdom*; Jean-Marc Clerc, *France;* Miha Peternel, *Slovenia;* Franci Savenc, *Slovenia*; Vladimir Linek, *Slovakia*; Vladimir Shataev, *C.I.S.*; Harish Kapadia, *India*; Elizabeth Hawley, *Nepal*; Asem Mustafa Awan, *Pakistan;* Josep Paytubi, *Spain*

**With additional thanks to**

Diane Henderson, Joe Reichert, Darryl Miller, Roger Robbinson, Don Serl, Stephen Koch, Norm Larson, Angus Thuermer, Jr., The Jackson Hole News, David Swift, Colleen Thompson, Dana Olsen, John Wright, Atomic Digital, Forest Dramis, Beth Wald, Renny Jackson, George Montopoli, Liana Darenskaya, Garth Willis, Peter Anderson, Ed Bice, Wendy Wilkinson, Sol, Clay Wadman, Jeff Hollenbaugh, Nick Clinch, Alison Osius, Jim and Laura McCarthy, Mark Richey, Chrissy Spinuzzi, Conrad Anker, Duane Raleigh, Christian Oberli, Jared Ogden, Johanna Merz, Carlos Buhler, Gay Roesch, Mark Newcomb, Dougald MacDonald, Arturo Bergamaschi, Roberto Mantovani, Richard Abendroth


# FRIENDS OF THE AMERICAN ALPINE JOURNAL

The following provided financial support for Volume 40 of The American Alpine Journal

Yvon Chouinard

W.L. Gore and Associates

The North Face

New York Section of the AAC

Verne and Marion Read

John Boyle

Ann Carter

Peter McGann, MD

Gregory Miller

The H. Adams Carter Endowment Fund
for The American Alpine Journal

# Preface

At the highest levels of alpinism, altitude continues to be less and less of a factor in the style climbers choose to make an ascent. This is not a new trend, but it was illustrated with an exclamation point in 1997 as climbs on Latok II, Thalay Sagar, Shipton Spire and Changabang were all put up at altitude in good style. The ascents, established by climbers who routinely climb hard at the crags as well, underscored what to expect as the frenetic evolution of mixed climbing and ever-more-difficult free and aid routes are extrapolated to the mountains in the years to come.

Not all of the year's fine routes employed superalpinism's lightweight, self-sufficient style. A Russian ascent of Makalu's west face exemplified an older style of mountaineering: fixed camps, fixed ropes, and rotating teams worked for two months to overcome one of the highest technical walls in the world. Gasherbrum IV's west face was climbed as well, by a Korean team consciously attempting to push Korean climbing to world-class standards. Like the Russians, the Koreans worked through a magnificent and much-coveted feature with fixed ropes and camps, accomplishing a first ascent that is the pinnacle of that country's short climbing history.

But of all the climbing done in 1997, one ascent stands out both for its boldness and for the recurring motif of tragedy in the story of one country's climbing. While a teammate in base camp coordinated their navigation with binoculars and radio, Slovenians Tomaž Humar and Janez Jeglič took five days to make a stunning unroped ascent of the west face of Nuptse (7925m). They had reached the west summit when a gust of wind blew Jeglič to his death, leaving Humar to descend their route in a 36-hour ordeal that nearly killed him as well. Their ascent, as their countrymen's before them, ensured the prominence of Slovenia at the edge of world alpinism, but again came at drastic price.

This serious aspect of climbing is played out over and over in the pages of this volume as friends and climbing partners recount their losses. In the spring, Russia lost one of its storied climbers when Vladimir Bashkirov, a team member of Anatoli Boukreev's during the heyday of Soviet alpinism, succumbed on Lhotse's west face to a combination of exertion at altitude and an illness contracted in Kathmandu. When approached with condolences in the fall, Boukreev replied simply: "Alpinism is alpinism." This, too, is part of climbing, as Boukreev, who died on Christmas Day while attempting a new route on Annapurna I, knew well. The deaths are hard to bear, but as they help us appreciate our own mortality they sharpen our lives and heighten our friendships. The spirit of the climbing community, intense and rich as a result, is captured by Allan Bard, who died last year while climbing the Grand Teton. "I am a wealthy man who just happens to be broke most of the time," he wrote, "but I'm in good company."

The events of May 1996 on Everest continue to ripple through climbing in myriad ways. Outside the community, the success of Jon Krakauer's book, *Into Thin Air*, and the popular large-format IMAX film, *Everest*, have brought climbing to a mainstream prominence it has not known before. Though it is a limelight cast on a single facet of the sport, it has repercussions for all of us. A higher profile means higher scrutiny. Those watching climbing today include not only armchair mountaineers but regulatory agencies as well. In the world of high-altitude mountaineering, two safety valves that might lessen the chances of future regulation (and future disasters) on the high peaks came from within the climbing community itself. In its "Recommended Code of Practice for High Altitude Guided Commercial Expeditions," the UIAA drew up guidelines for climbing and guiding the world's highest peaks. The recommendations were echoed by the ISO 8000, a consortium of 8000-meter guiding companies. Both are good efforts on the parts of climbers to undertake responsibilities themselves before outside intervention appears, and both are to be applauded.

Similar action will be necessary on other fronts as well. As we go to press, Yosemite Valley is embroiled in lawsuit as the American climbing community fights both the National Park Service and developmental interests for containment of proposed damage to the Valley's wilderness. Yosemite remains singular in world climbing, the jumping-off point for great leaps in standards and the origins of American wilderness philosophy. Its defense is an important one, for it represents a larger fight all climbers must invest in. Any loss in Yosemite will influence battles in our other parks and wilderness areas as well. In this volume we offer up a celebration of Yosemite's place in American climbing with pieces by Chris MacNamara, John Middendorf and Tom and Ryan Frost, all of whom are actively engaged in preserving our ability to participate safely in climbing. They serve as role models for the rest of us as the need for a new paradigm—that of the activist climber—emerges.

We introduce two new sections in this volume that broaden our coverage of climbing. Mountain Medicine, by Dr. Geoffrey Tabin, gives a summary of eye conditions related to high-altitude mountaineering and offers practical guidelines to the corrective medical procedures currently available. The Mountain Environment section, authored by Chris Naumann and Brent Bishop, covers efforts to reclaim and sustain mountain areas. At the same time, it underscores what is becoming central to all climbing. As Bishop notes, no longer is a summit and the survival of all team members the yardstick of success; it must, for the sake of climbing areas and our continued enjoyment of them, include every attempt to minimize our impact on the land. America, one of the developed countries with the greatest wilderness to learn from, must continue to push for an appreciation of wilderness as a finite resource in need of conservation, and climbers must continue to be the strongest proponents of sustainable wilderness practices.

Today, as national parks impose climbing-specific regulations and the National Forest Service bans the use of fixed anchors in the wilderness, the future of climbing in America is imperiled. All of us involved with climbing, from publications such as this journal to climbing companies earning money from the sport to the individuals at the end of a rope, must invest in its future. Pick your fight, but whether it be working to preserve a local crag or helping to influence national legislation, we all must take a role in safeguarding our common welfare.

And it begins, as all things do, with the individual. For inspiration, look to the mountains, and to our heritage, rich with men and women who have fought for their preservation. We are in good company. In their lessons we will find the ways to enter the next chapter in our history, one that evolves wisely in the face of our greater numbers while continuing to embrace the places we love to climb.

CHRISTIAN BECKWITH, *Editor*

# Nuptse's West Face

*Upping the ante in the Nepal Himalaya*

BY TOMAŽ HUMAR, *Planinska zveza Slovenije*

I left Slovenia for Nepal on September 10, the leader of an expedition to Pumori and Nuptse. Six days later we left the airport at Lukla and headed for the Khumbu. After a few smaller acclimitization tours, we put up a base camp beneath Pumori. Between September 29 and October 1, Janez Jeglič, Carlos Carsolio and I made a first ascent in alpine style of the northeast face of Lobuche East, encountering ice up to 85° on the 900-meter route.

Carlos, Janez, Marjan Kovač and I then turned our attention to Pumori, where, on October 9, we began up a new variation to the French Spur on the southeast face. We managed to climb 800 meters and encountered pitches up to 90°, before abandoning our attempt to help in a very difficult rescue of four Slovakian climbers who had fallen down Pumori's north face. We were able to save only one, Milos Kijonka. We returned to climb Pumori by its normal route on October 15 with Berčič Cene and Franci Kokalj, but without Carlos. The weather on both mountains had been bad every day.

From October 19 until October 25, it snowed heavily. When the bad weather was interrupted by an unexpected north wind from Tibet, the preparations for our last goal—Nuptse's west face—began.

For a month and a half—since our expedition started—our eyes have caught glimpses now and again of this ice-pyramid from which seracs keep falling without regard for any timetable. Only the old Japanese man who wants to climb Pumori comes over to see what is going on. The expression on his face as his sirdar tells him we actually are going to ascend the wall that we keep talking about all the time gives away his surprise. I have the impression they had not been taking us seriously.

After the last period of bad weather, all the expeditions, including the famous Kammerlander's expedition, abandon the valley. The favorable change of weather is our last chance for a successful outcome.

In the afternoon of October 26, Chindi makes a fire in the chorten with fragrant dry twigs. Later on, he helps Marjan, Janez and I cross the snow-covered Kumbu glacier as it is bathed in sunlight. Before nightfall, we manage to level out enough space for our tent and lie down for the night, packed like sardines.

Marjan's coughing in the morning promises no good. Pain in his lungs and a sudden illness force him to give up the dreams of the last few years. Janez and I must change our climbing tactics, and we decide to take only a kevlar static rope—"just in case."

After a painful parting with Marjan, we start off at six in the morning with heavy rucksacks and head for the base of the wall. Before reaching the first seracs, we notice a torn red crampon strap, which must have belonged to someone looking for peace on this glacier. The kevlar static rope is useful to us only here, when we are unable to find our way in the labyrinth of crevasses.

Next we enter a couloir over which hangs a huge mass of seracs. We name it the Orient Express. We both feel some very unpleasant anxiety until we climb out of the tedious funnel.

*The west face of Nuptse.* TOMAŽ HUMAR

*Janez Jeglič in the labyrinth of crevasses at the base of the face—the only time the pair would use a rope.*
Tomaž Humar

We set up our first bivouac on a plateau at 5900 meters.

A windy night and bad weather in the morning prohibit us from climbing until 11 o'clock. After four hours of climbing, we arrange our second bivouac in a crevasse at 6300 meters.

"What a bivouac!" Janez comments enthusiastically as we lie down for the night after a well-deserved supper. We are convinced we could stick it out here in bad weather for quite some time.

Our illusion of a perfect bivouac vanishes in the night the moment we hear the familiar sound of wind sweeping the wall. It makes our lives hell in the morning, when we have to dig out our tent. A narrow ice bridge and, after that, a mixed traverse to the left are enough to warm our frozen fingers. At about 11 the weather calms down; hanging on our ice axes, we can afford a quick snack. We continue climbing until three in the afternoon. We realize we will not reach the big snow ridge at 7000 meters before evening, so we dig a plateau into a steep slope, where we put up our tent.

It storms again at night, and I have a headache coming on top of that. It seems strange to me, because I believe we had acclimatised well enough on Lobuche and Pumori. I turn on the light and realize the headache is not from insufficient acclimatization but rather from our tent walls bending as they are burdened by the spindrift. The night is still pitch dark and the wind is not relenting, so we have no choice but to spend the rest of the night kneeling, leaning against the walls.

The next day, we manage to put our tent back up, but the day is lost. There is enough food; however, problems with a gas leak from the stove force us to make a decision. Because the weather forecast for the next day is favorable, we decide to try to climb the remaining 1000 meters with light rucksacks in one push. We spend the afternoon preparing for the last attempt—and cooking, cooking. . . .

"Today you are really spoiling me," says Janez, as I give him his third portion of soup, complete with ham and other delicacies. "It's about time you and Miha go climb somewhere so he can see for himself what good eating is! Wow, this is real good . . . ."

We go on filling our stomachs until evening, when, as a dessert, we receive a greeting from the setting sun.

On October 31, we get up at two o'clock, and by four, when we start climbing, I have already obeyed the call of nature twice. Before I manage to zip my trousers, spindrift fills the gap in my backside. By seven o'clock, we are at 7000 meters and Janez turns off route, climbing 200 meters to the right and scaling a rocky crest. My argument that we are just below a hidden couloir does no good until we climb back together higher up, each by his own route.

"Man, did you see where I had got myself?" Janez asks.

"I told you. . . . Well, let's just drop it."

"You feel as cold as I do?"

"Sure, Janez. Hope the sun comes out soon."

We take a few sips of tea from my piss bottle, remembering the previous night's talk with a laugh.

"Tomaž, you think this will be OK?"

"You know, Janez, we'll just rinse out our mouths. It can't hurt. Anyway, the important thing is—it flows!"

"You're right," he says—and the entire quantity of freshly made tea ends up in my emergency bottle.

After a chat by radio with Marjan, who is pleased with our quick advance, we begin up the nasty couloir, a mixture of rocks and vertical powdery snow. A bit of protection would have come in handy, but because there is no way we can protect ourselves, I instead expose myself to the sun as it makes a short appearance. Something beastly is approaching from the west and we hurry as fast as we can.

At half past 11, we contact Marjan from 7500 meters. He tells us there are lenticulars over Everest and strong wind on the ridges of Nuptse. I am much against our calling in live from the top for the Italian national television company RAI. We receive a call from Richard Pavlovski at the base, telling us we still have two or three hours to go to the summit. Janez asks me again if I could say a word for RAI.

"Janez, never mind the interview now—let's climb until 2 p.m. as agreed and, if we make it to the top, we take some shots and speed down. See what's coming in from the west. It's gonna be fucking tough!"

My teeth are chattering as Janez helps me get the snow out of my pants. My poor chilled buttocks haven't been able to melt it since morning.

"Gee, how much of it have you got here?" Janez wonders, and adds the joke of the expedition: "Hey, kitten, when the wind starts blowing upward . . . !" We both laugh, as we often have during this expedition, unaware how cruelly true the joke will shortly turn out to be.

We drink up all there is in my "emergency" bottle, eat some pieces of chocolate and head for the top.

Tears in our eyes reveal the relief when we realize we will succeed. Janez is ahead of me, and every now and then we wave to each other with our ice axes. Richard was right; there is still some way to the top. At one o'clock in the afternoon, Janez reaches the summit, looks back and waves. Just a bit more effort and it will all be over.

When I put my feet on top, Janez is not there to greet me. Instead, there are only the strong wind and footsteps leading toward the northwest summit across the south side of the ridge.

"Where is he going now?" I wonder when I see him for a second. I wait, calling after him,

*Jeglič at the second bivouac at 6300 meters.* Tomaž Humar

"Janez, Janez!"

"Maybe he went forward a bit to have a look," I guess. I follow him, though cursing mad.

"Where is he pushing himself in this weather?" I think. The wind is blowing in gusts as I reach the last footsteps—only to see the radio, turned on and upside-down on the other side of the ridge.

I break down.

"Nooo!! Janez, Janez!"

There is no trace of him. He just vanished. While asking myself how it could have happened, I call Marjan.

"Marjan, what happened, Marjan?!"

"What is it now, Tomi? Where are you?"

He was expecting me and Janez to shout with joy. Instead, I have to tell him, "Janez, Janez is gone!"

"What do you mean, gone? Gone where?"

Marjan, Peter and I try to figure out what happened. In spite of their urging to descend at once, I fear I have reached the point of no return myself.

I try to pull myself together and keep my head cool for the descent.

*The west face of Nuptse, showing the line of ascent.* Tomaž Humar

I do quite all right at the start; as soon as I draw back from the ridge to the wall, the wind is no longer a problem. I hurry to the first rocks. During the ascent, I had figured protection would be useful for this part. I lose my frozen goggles here. The day is fading away; a scary night is about to begin.

Not long after the cold chases away the last sunbeams, I become aware of my loneliness. Five days on this wall and as many sleepless nights are eating away at my forces. The cold disables my headlamp batteries and my inner light vanishes with the sun and the moon. I am in a labyrinth of ice and rock, not comprehending my actual position.

The voice from the radio keeps waking me up.

"Come on, Tomaž, don't give up! Hold on a little more. The tent must be nearby!"

My head tells me not to quit, but my body is slowly and steadily losing power. A terrible feeling! Swinging my ice axes and crampons into the hard ice becomes purely automatic, driven by the instinct for survival. I am lost, with no idea where I am or where I am going. The only important thing is to be moving. The terrible cold and tiredness push me slowly toward the edge of no return. Complete darkness swallows everything around me, and my friends' voices from the valley grow thinner and thinner. They, too, are aware that if I don't find the bivouac, the night will be mine forever—the same as it was for Janez only ten hours before.

Far below, I somehow spot a black point that could be my tent. Down in camp, Peter has the brilliant idea of sending me energy via music on the radio. I swallow a few bloody snots and get back on my feet. It seems like an eternity before I come to the troublesome steep corner, which I am forced to climb without being able to see anything. My crampons slip, leaving an insignificant scratch and the familiar smell of sulphur. Both ice axes are losing purchase. I think it is the end of the story. . . when the crampons, having hit an ice "pancake" just at the end of the steep corner, stop me with a jerk.

I take time to recover my breath, then cross about 30 meters to the tent. These last meters seem never to end. I pull open the frozen zipper on the tent and fall inside with ice axes and crampons still on. A stomachache wakes me up as green bile-like mucus spouts from my mouth. I turn over on my back just to tell the base I am safe. I can't say any more, though I would like to speak to my friends. Quiet music is all I want. I can't manage to light the stove . . . .

I doze off beside a burning candle.

At around three in the morning, I wake up in flames. Not really knowing what is going on, I instinctively start hitting the stove. At last, I somehow throw it out of the tent—that is, what is left of the tent. Immediately I fall asleep again, without even pulling the burned sleeping bag over me.

Although my friends in the valley are expecting my call in early morning, by 11 o'clock I can still barely lift my head. It takes me another hour to climb out of the tent. Unbearable thirst spurs me on either to descend 1500 meters or perish.

In spite of the wind, I make it quite quickly to the edge of the crevasse where Janez and I had our second bivouac at 6300 meters, but the small bridge that we used four days ago now is gone. Throwing myself some five meters across the edge into a snow cone below the crevasse is the only option. There is no time for guessing what could happen if I break a pick. I am also rather ill-disposed to enter such a guessing game, as I still have ahead of me the couloir into which everything that breaks off the Orient Express—our name for the mass of seracs—falls.

Vertical ice sections are draining what little force I have left. Given the hard, dinner-plating ice, my feet often grope for purchase in the air and not on the steep wall. When I have only a few meters left to the snow-cone at the end of the couloir, I hear a deafening crack above. With all my might, I drive my axes into the ice.

"Damn it," I curse. "Has the mountain let me come all this way only to finish me like a fly on a windscreen?" Then I bend my head in powerless resignation.

I take one last look above. Ice blocks are bumping into each other and breaking to pieces on the vertical walls. Pieces fall on me, causing my feet to slip twice; they break my nose, and the sharpest piece hits me on top of my head. I look up just as a spindrift avalanche comes rushing down as if to chill my overheated head.

"Holy cow—I am alive!" Adrenaline fills every inch of my body; I throw myself onto the snow-cone and rush down on my backside, back into life. I use my axes to slow down a bit and spare at least something of my coccyx. The last sunbeams say goodbye to the wall for the day while I hurry on down to the rock pillar at the side of the glacier.

I reach the crevasses at twilight, fix a piton and, wrapped in my bivouac sack, wait for Marjan. I can't afford to cross the dangerous glacier without a light. In my dreams, or rather delirium, I search for a gulp of water. Luckily, the delirium ends as my drowsing head hits the rock.

Shortly after midnight, Marjan is by my side. Stiff and frostbitten, I get to the base of the wall with his help. Two Poles, Richard Pavlovski and Jacek Maselko, are there as well, waiting for me with a full canteen.

Two days later, from the back of a litter, I glance toward Nuptse for the last time. The cold wind reminds me of the words: "Hey, kitten, when the wind starts blowing upward. . . ."

Reinhold Messner called this face a death zone. To the two of us, it was an ice dream. Unfortunately, it became the path to eternity.

SUMMARY OF STATISTICS

AREA: Nepal Himalaya

VARIOUS ASCENTS: *Talking About Tsampa* (VI 5.9 WI4, 900m) on the northeast face of Lobuche East (6119m), September 29-October 1, Tomaž Humar, Janez Jeglič, Carlos Carsolio; the normal route on Pumori, October 10-15, Humar, Jeglič, Kovač, Franci Kokalj, Cene Berčič; *Humar-Jeglič* (VI 5.7 WI5, 2500m) on the west face to Nuptse's northwest summit (7742m), Tomaž Humar and Janez Jeglič

# The West Face of Makalu

*Finding a solution to one of the Himalaya's great problems*

BY SERGEI EFIMOV

TRANSLATED BY SERGEI NEKHAI

On March 15, nine mountaineers from Ekaterinburg, Russia—Salavat Habibulin (the team leader), Alexei Bolotov, Nikolai Zhilin, Yuri Ermachek, Dmitri Pavlenko, Igor Bugachevski, Andrei Klepikov, Sergei Buchkovski (medical doctor) and Sergei Efimov (head of the expedition)—appeared once again in Kathmandu, and the expedition to climb the west face of Makalu began.

A helicopter landed in Lukla on March 28 to pick up the advance group. More than 3,000 pounds of expedition gear would have to be lowered to the 4500-meter base camp, while extra cargo was dropped at the 5300-meter advanced base camp. Given the cloudy skies, it was unclear whether the helicopter would be able to get through to base camp. The caravan with five other members of the expedition carrying the rest of the cargo had left Hille six days before and was expected to arrive in base camp a week later, about April 4.

"Let's try, Valera," I said to the pilot, deciding to take the risk rather than change the expedition plans at the outset.

The helicopter flew up into the clouds, finding its way into the valley with difficulty, and finally landed beneath the south face at 4500 meters. It took off again, this time with Salavat and Alexei aboard, and headed toward the west face. Ten minutes later, it was back. Alexei jumped out, cussing. They had not been able to land and had been forced to drop everything while still flying at a high altitude and speed.

We started setting up base camp. The same day, Salavat and Alexei went up to advanced base camp to pick up the scattered gear. It took them more than seven hours to reach ABC. Later on, after acclimatization, the same route would take only three-and-a-half hours to reach.

The 1997 Makalu West Face Expedition was the final object of a two-year Himalayan program organized under the sponsorship of the Ekaterinburg local government. The idea of the program, which was designed by the Federation of Alpinism in Ekaterinburg and supported financially by the local government, was to organize several Himalayan expeditions, building up and training a team capable of climbing Makalu's west face. The first expedition climbed the west face of Baruntse (7220m), a beautiful peak just in front of Makalu's west face. Photographs of Makalu's west face were made during the climb; later, they were used to plan the Makalu ascent route.

The route could be divided into four parts. The first part, from 5800 meters to 6100 meters, entailed reaching the top of the steep-to-overhanging glacier by going along the rock wall right of the icefall. The next stage climbed through 35-45° ice fields, reaching a bergschrund at 6500 meters. From there, a mixed section of 50-55° rock and ice leading to 7400 meters would have to be negotiated. Finally, a rock buttress connected the route to the 1971 French West Pillar route at 8000 meters. The 70-75° rock on this last part of the climb would be the most challenging part of the ascent.

When we arrived, we found the conditions on the wall different from what we had seen in the 1995 photographs. The bergschrund separating the glacier from the wall was much wider.

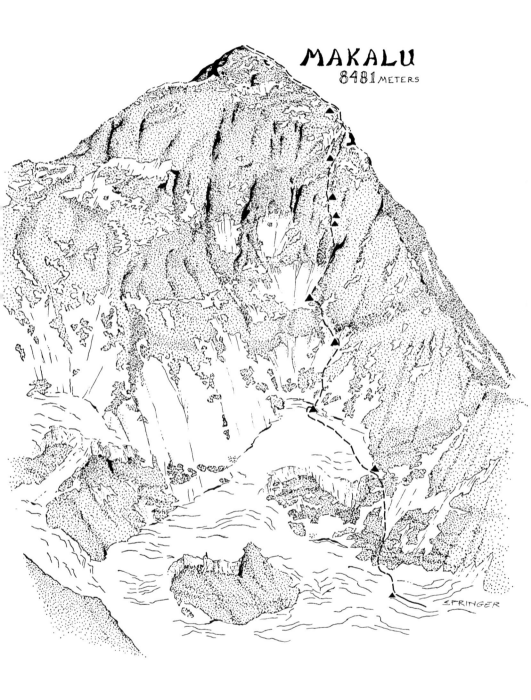

**MAKALU**

*8481* METERS

SPRINGER

*The 1997 Russian West Face route*

*The west face of Makalu.* SERGEI EFIMOV

We thought, however, that we could see a snow bridge at the upper part of the 'schrund that seemed to reach the wall. From there to the buttress, 55° ice fields brought one into the first rock belt. These smooth ice-polished rock slabs would be hard to free climb, so we chose a route that followed icy gullies across them from 6700 meters to 6800 meters. Higher, there seemed to be a passage to some black rocks at 6900 meters and then to an "S-like" rocky formation that we called "the dollar," where we planned to set up Camp V. From that point, an icy slope rose 100 meters to a 70-75° rock wall. This wall was vertical from 7400 meters to 7600 meters, then continued up to 8000 meters, where it reached the West Pillar. It was the third and greatest obstacle to a connection with the West Pillar route, and had remained untouched for the last 15 years.

On April 9, work on the wall started. While Dmitri and Andrei shuttled loads between Camp I at 5700 meters and Camp II at 6100 meters, Igor, Yuri, and I went up to the bergschrund at 6500 meters and chose a place for Camp III. The 'schrund was filled with snow and nicely protected from avalanches and rocks by a huge overhanging upper side. At this point, however, the weather was still cold and the mountain was silent. Falling snow did not accumulate on the face; rather, it came down in dry spindrift avalanches that did no harm to the mountaineers, who simply pulled up the hoods of their parkas and waited until it was over.

In the beginning, cold weather and insufficient acclimatization hampered early departures; work began each day after 9 a.m. On April 13, Dmitri overcame the first pitch above the bergschrund and fixed a rope. The next day, Igor climbed and fixed two more pitches. Meanwhile, Alexei, Nikolai and Salavat reached 7000 meters on the West Pillar for acclima-

*Jugging toward Camp IV (6700m).* SALAVAT HABIBULIN

tization. It was also a reconnaissance attempt to see whether it was possible to downclimb the West Pillar from the summit.

Later, all climbers gathered and rested at the 5300-meter ABC. After a discussion, it was decided to undertake two more pushes on the wall. The first would bring extra gear to Camp III, set up Camp IV at 7000 meters, and fix ropes between the camps. The second would reach the top of the vertical rocks at 7400 meters, then get to a snow pocket at the top of the tower at 7600 meters in order to have a look at the following rock section and assess the chances of success. It was a tough decision to make two more pushes instead of going straight for the summit, but we felt it was necessary.

On April 16, Salavat, Nikolai, Andrei and Dmitri went up from ABC. The next day, Alexei, Igor, Yuri and I followed. A storm camp was organized in the wide 'schrund, where we cached climbing gear, food and fuel, and put up two tents.

Traffic on the wall started. Groups went up, the leaders of which changed each day. The climbers headed toward the enormous rock wall of the west face, which seemed to hang over our heads. The huge scale of the wall was especially obvious as the small figures of the climbers disappeared on the icy slope leading to its base.

Everybody worried about the next two camps. Was there a place to put up a tent above 6500 meters?

Taking bivouac gear, Salavat and three others started from the Camp III 'schrund on April 20. In the evening, they radioed that they had used pieces of platforms found on the rocks (the highest point reached by a 1992 British expedition) to establish the camp. It was not a lot of room for four people, but they managed to spend a night there. (Later, Camp IV would be moved almost 100 meters lower to where Nikolai and Andrei worked an entire day cutting a

*The bergschrund camp (CIII) at 6500 meters.* Sergei Efimov

tent platform out of solid ice.)

On April 23, all the climbers gathered once again at ABC. Ropes had been fixed up to 7100 meters. We had not expected to fix that much rope and were running out, so we decided to remove three ropes below 6100 meters and one rope from the snow slope above Camp IV. I ordered 400 meters of rope from Kathmandu as well. A helicopter was to arrive on May 3; until then, we borrowed ropes from Danish and Swiss mountaineers who had attempted the normal route and who had their base camp next to ours.

On April 26, Salavat, Dmitri, Nikolai and Andrei went up again to the buttress. Salavat rested less then the other men; however, he refused to stay in Base Camp any longer, arguing that he had recovered. Two days later, Alexei, Yuri and Igor followed. They aimed to reach the "dollar" rocks and set up Camp V at 7300 meters, for which there seemed to be a place on a fluted ridge. They then would attempt to climb the buttress at 7400 meters and fix the ropes up to 7500 meters.

On April 28, Salavat and Dmitri reached 7200 meters on steep rocks, finding no place for a tent. Above was overhanging rock. The climbers felt tired and were forced to retreat to Camp IV at 6900 meters, where Nikolai and Andrei were cutting out the tent platform centimeter by centimeter through solid ice. Nikolai worked without glasses. He had set up an anchor for himself and Andrei when they started to make the platform, then called for Andrei to climb. Andrei started, then fell and hung on the rope. Nikolai was jerked by the rope and dropped his glasses, which fell on his boot. He had just bent to get them when Andrei fell again. The glasses were gone. He had to work the rest of the day without them.

The next day, Nikolai decided to go up anyway, hoping to get through the slope before the sunlight hit. But the climbers had to work until very late in the evening to get to Camp V at 7300 meters. Dmitri, the day's leader, wrote: "The climbing was nasty. I had to use my fingers for balance, but it was cold and I had to wear thin gloves. I placed one ice screw below a very smooth 20-meter wall. On and above the wall, there was no place for a belay. I had to climb ten meters to place another ice screw. It was getting late; I did not have time to think. I had to go fast to beat the darkness. I barely reached the end of the pitch.

"The others came after me. They started to make a place for the tent. I went down to get my backpack. Night was coming. My descent was horrible. My strength had left me, my backpack was heavy, I was alone with nobody to help. The others had not had enough time to set up a good platform. We were forced to spend the night sitting. We made some water, but did not bother to prepare food. Nobody could eat. When I reached the tent, I only wanted to fall down somewhere—or at least to sit a bit."

The next morning, Nikolai experienced sharp pain in his eyes and was forced to go down alone to Base Camp.

"I had to go down to Camp IV as well," wrote Dmitri, "because I felt horrible after the previous evening's climbing. Salavat and Andrei, having spent five hours chopping a place for the tent, also descended. The next group was about to pass us on their way to Camp V while we rested at Camp IV."

The plan for Salavat, Andrei and Dmitri to rest at Camp III at 6500 meters for two days while the other three were working at Camp V was changed the next morning, when Andrei discovered that his toes were frostbitten. Somehow he had not taken his boots off for two days, not even while in his sleeping bag, and he had lost track of his toes. Salavat and Dmitri followed Andrei down to Camp II at 6100 meters, where they were met by the coach, Alexandr Mikhailov and Andrei Belikov. That day, Alexei, Yuri and Andrei reached Camp V and started to move up.

"The day Salavat and I climbed back up was a horrible day," Dmitri continued. "We spent a night at 6500 meters after helping Andrei, waited in the morning snowfall, and then got an extra load at 7000 meters. When we left the 'schrund, it was almost normal weather. I was frying in the sun. I took off my clothes, leaving on only a fleece jacket. Then, just under 7300 meters, on the last fixed rope, everything changed. A snowstorm started suddenly as it sometimes does in winter on Elbrus or on Peak Pobeda. I thought I would freeze to death. I did not know how I would get up. The next day, I could not go higher, so I sat in the tent. I thought that maybe because of this our plans would be delayed. We had to stay there for four days longer than anybody else."

Alexei, Sergei and Yuri spent two days trying to reach the top of the buttress. But their attempt to go to the right failed. This part of the buttress was too hard to climb.

"I tried to reach the top of the buttress the whole day," wrote Alexei, "and then Igor tried as well. A lot of loose rocks. I thought that it was easier on the right, but we moved into polished rocks with no holds at all. Only by aiding on bolts could we do it. I took a three- or four-meter fall, worked the whole day, and finally managed to get six or seven meters up the buttress. But then, we decided to go to the left. We rappelled down, leaving pitons. Igor went left, traversing under the dihedral."

On May 3, Igor and Yuri came down from 7300 meters. That day, Dmitri and Salavat went up. First, Salavat started to continue. He aided 30 meters, going from one piton to the next. It took him almost three hours.

"During the third attempt," Alexei said, "I left with Salavat and his group to complete the part we had decided on earlier. The others were tired from following Andrei down to 6500 meters. Nikolai had burned his eyes and gone down. I was supposed to go down to bring up an extra tent. Instead, I went up and belayed Salavat as he aided the first 30 meters of the buttress. Then I belayed Dmitri."

Dmitri wrote: "Normally, somebody volunteered to be a leader, but I spent a day in the tent, because of my bad experience climbing in the snowfall. Alexei decided to go up and belay Salavat. Without his help, we would have missed two or three days and might therefore not have made the summit.

"The next day, I led. It was mixed climbing; I either used my ice-fifi or free climbed. My ice tools were no good, as the ice was too thin. Fortunately, the ice-fifi hooked on thin holds and patches of ice. Rocks alternated with ice "loaves," where I placed ice screws. Later, on our next attempt, this ice would be gone. In some places, I used stoppers; elsewhere, especially in the loose rock, pitons. Above, there was a part with some beautiful free climbing and later on, more free climbing in a clean, vertical crack. I stopped one pitch under 7600 meters, due to lack of ropes."

On May 3, the helicopter landed, bringing food, fuel, ropes and two NTV (Russian National Television Company) operators. Andrei Klepikov, whose toes were frostbitten, was flown to Kathmandu. (All his toes were ultimately saved.)

It took the men four days to rest in base camp at 4500 meters. Then, after getting to the advanced base camp and resting another two days, Igor, Nikolai and Yuri went up on May 11. They were followed two days later by Salavat, Alexei and Dmitri. The skies were clear, but a strong north wind blew for several days. Climbers were buffeted on the fixed ropes, barely able to keep balance on the steep ice below 6900 meters. Apparently, the wind had caused rockfall, for the tent at 7300 meters was found with its pole broken and punched through by rocks. Above 7300 meters, one of the fixed ropes on a hard pitch had come untied, forcing the climbers to climb the pitch again.

On May 14, Igor, Yuri and Nikolai reached the top of the buttress at 7600 meters. They had bivouac gear. Because we could see them through binoculars from Base Camp, we did not worry much. The next morning, however, they reported that they had had difficulties putting up a tent the previous night because of the wind. Below them, in Camps IV and V, the tents had been destroyed. In Base Camp, the cold north wind also was trying to destroy the tents, and the prayer flags blew almost horizontally.

Preliminary examination of the west face indicated that the crux would be in getting to the top of the buttress at 7600 meters. As it turned out, however, the climbing above was difficult as well. Only 100 to 150 meters were overcome a day. Couloirs often ended in overhangs, so it was hard to choose the correct line of ascent. The climbers radioed for directions from base camp, but it was difficult to give them from such a long ways away. Still, day after day, they reached higher altitudes and set up new bivouacs.

"There were several cool places to climb free above 7500 meters," Dmitri would write of the climbing at that point. "At 7650 meters, there was one hard pitch, then two or three more hard but beautiful pitches later on."

Going in turn, Salavat, Dmitri, Alexei and Igor came up through the buttress. Nikolai and Yuri chopped platforms for the tents. The climbers were tired. Physical and physiological loads were taking a lot of strength. Going up the fixed ropes with heavy backpacks was difficult as well, especially when they were vertical, at which point the climbers had to hang the backpacks from their harnesses to ascend.

On May 19, at 11 a.m., Alexei radioed that he had reached a snow field under the 7900-meter pillar, and that they could begin climbing unroped.

Wrote Nikolai: "It was the most memorable moment when Alexei shouted from above that the buttress was over. I remember that day more than the summit."

On May 20, six climbers went up the West Pillar on Makalu, one of the most beautiful

*In the thick of the buttress at 7500 meters.* SALAVAT HABIBULIN

8000-meter peaks in the Himalaya. The climbers were on their eighth day on the mountain and their fourth day above 7500 meters. Below and behind them were the rock buttress and icy slopes. Ahead, there remained what technically was the easiest part of the route. The west face had been conquered.

At 2 p.m., Salavat radioed to BC that they had stopped at 8150 meters because of the wind and cold and were putting up tents. He spoke hoarsely and slowly. Two hours later, he radioed again, this time from within the tent, in a normal voice. Everything was OK; they were drinking tea and warming up. Suggestions to use some oxygen were turned down. To the question, "What are your plans for tomorrow?" Salavat replied that they were going to go for the summit early in the morning. Igor confirmed this plan (their two tents were 50 meters apart).

On May 21, everyone woke up at 5 a.m. Radio communication had been arranged for that hour but nobody got on. At 6 a.m., they reported that they were getting ready.

At an altitude of more than 8000 meters, all these preparations lasted for hours. Lack of oxygen affects a person's physical and mental state. Moving and thinking gets slow, and the simplest things, such as dressing up and packing the backpack, require continuous willpower and much longer time. One has to make an effort to think and then to do something. Also, you can not dress up all together in a tight tent—so somebody starts, then the other one follows, and so on.

The climbers started to leave the tents on the ready, indifferent to who was first and who was last. The psychological tension of the wall was gone; they no longer had to belay or be belayed. Ahead was a simple route along the wide ridge, where everyone could move at their own speed, struggling only with their fatigue, indifferent to surroundings, only their subconscious pushing them to the summit.

Salavat got out first, walked to the other tent and came back. He told the departing climbers that he had to drink some tea and warm up his feet. This did not alert his friends because it had happened before on the wall, when Salavat had had to warm up his boots and feet on the gas stove.

At about 8 a.m., five people started to move up the ridge. At 9 a.m., Salavat went on the radio, but the battery was frozen and we could not hear him. I asked that he turn on the radio three times if everything was OK, one time if they needed help. Salavat answered with three signals. I said that we were on all the time and asked not to leave anybody alone on the slope on the way back. After that, nobody got on the radio. At 1:15 p.m., we saw three points moving toward the summit and then, later on, two more.

"This was a special day," wrote Alexei. "I felt as if I had extra strength. When we left the tents and got to the ridge, I became certain that we would summit. I was first, breaking through two to four inches of fresh snow. I used an old fixed rope to get up the steep part, which led to the south ridge at 8350 meters. After that, we followed a gully with deep snow. I asked Nikolai to go ahead and break trail. He had not brought his ice axe. I gave him mine, and he reached hard snow after 10 meters. I tried to go after him, but after the fresh snow, slick rock slabs appeared, and I could not move. Nikolai went ahead and did not notice. I had to wait for the others. They came, fixed a rope and we reached steep firn snow. Soon, I reached the summit."

"The summit was closer than I expected," wrote Dmitri. "Just three hillocks. Smaller than I thought. No view. Valleys in clouds. Only the west side was clear. I felt tired. I asked Yuri to clip me in and belay. Thus we downclimbed to the old fixed rope. The other men had already gone."

At 4 p.m., Igor radioed that five people had reached the summit. To our question of Salavat's whereabouts, he answered that Salavat had remained in the tent.

At 5 p.m., the radio came on. Igor tried to say something but could not. He passed the receiver to Alexei, who said that Salavat had died.

Nikolai said that Salavat got out of the tent an hour and a half after the others. He climbed up two pitches. They found him leaning against a rock as if he were resting. He was not breathing and his pupils did not react to the light. The men carried the body to the first section of level ground and buried him there. It took two and a half hours. They returned to the tents in the darkness.

The next morning, the climbers were able to leave the tents only at about 11 p.m. They took one tent with them and headed down. We monitored them with binoculars, through which we saw that one pair was far behind the other three people. Later, we learned that Igor had fallen and broken a rib. After that, he could not move very fast. There was one oxygen tank, which was given to Igor. After breathing some oxygen, he went down more quickly.

That day, all five came down to Camp VII at 7650 meters. All night, Igor breathed oxygen and the next morning felt strong enough to go down. Nikolai went first and, at 4 p.m., reached the bergschrund, where he was met by Alexandr Mikhailov and Andrei Belikov, who had come up earlier. Nikolai was certain that everybody would be there, but Yuri and Igor were at Camp VI at 7300 meters and Dmitri and Alexei even higher.

On May 23, the remaining four climbers could not get out of the tent for a long time. That day, information on the groups' movement was forwarded directly to Ekaterinburg on the satellite phone. Relatives and friends called my wife, who passed along information on the condition of the climbers.

My experience told me that the climbers were not aware of their condition, and every extra day they spent at altitude was dangerous. We could see that rappelling was going too slowly. At 4 p.m., Alexei relayed that he could not move Dmitri, who was hanging on the rope, telling everyone to leave him alone. We also learned that Alexei had dropped his sleeping bag from 7650 meters, while Yuri had dropped his backpack with sleeping bag, down parka, gas canisters and food. We realized that a night at 7300 meters might have tragic consequences. Yuri understood it as well, and decided to push through to Camp IV at 6500 meters. He was going to rappel all night if needed, because to stay at 7300 meters without warm clothes was dangerous.

Yuri reached 6500 meters at 10 p.m. Igor, Alexei and Dmitri spent the night at 7300 meters.

On May 24, the remaining three started to move at 8 a.m. Dmitri and Igor were moving very slowly. Alexei was coming last. After descending diagonally through difficult rock sections on the fixed ropes, they reached the ice. Alexei made sure that the others were moving OK, then went ahead.

When Alexei reached the 'schrund, Andrei Belikov started to climb up to bring some hot tea to the men. When rocks started to fall, he decided to stay under the overhanging roofs to wait. Dmitri passed him, and later on reached the 'schrund, but Igor was still on the buttress. Andrei decided to go up to see what happened. When he reached Igor, he saw that he was hanging on the fixed rope, dead. His left temple had been shattered by a rock. He did not have a helmet, though it later was claimed that he started to rappel with one on.

Rocks continued to fall. Andrei rushed to lower the body to the closest station and fix it with rope. The warming of the last few days had triggered massive rockfall on the wall. It was getting dangerous, and we had to leave.

On May 25, the climbers reached 5300 meters, and on May 26 everybody was at 4500 meters in Base Camp. On May 28, the expedition flew to Lukla and from there on to Kathmandu.

SUMMARY OF STATISTICS

AREA: Nepal Himalaya

NEW ROUTE: The West Face (3163m) of Makalu (8463m), March 23-May 28, 1997

PERSONNEL: Salavat Habibulin, Alexei Bolotov, Nikolai Zhilin, Yuri Ermachek, Dmitri Pavlenko, Igor Bugachevski, Andrei Klepikov, Sergei Buchkovski, Sergei Efimov

# Ship of Fools

*Twenty-five days on a Karakoram giant*

BY JARED OGDEN

S tanding at the base of Shipton Spire, Mark Synnott and I shivered silently, neither wanting to tell the other our fears or doubts about the climb we were about to begin. Our
intended route was just 500 feet to the right of the shredded remains of ropes and gear
at the base of the spire's east face, a grim reminder of Ryuji Taniguchi, the solo Japanese
climber who perished in a massive rockfall while attempting the wall two years before. His
haulbag was still 13 pitches up, constantly reminding us of how far away we were from safety. We had traveled halfway around the world to throw our best at this 4,000-foot granite tooth
that climbed out of the Trango Glacier to 19,700 feet. Its history was festooned with numerous failed attempts and one climber dead. Would this mountain ever see success?

It wasn't until the summer of 1996 that a strong North American/Australian team finally
conquered Shipton Spire. Reports came back from them about near-death experiences, horrific rockfall and a lot of dangerous loose rock. Encouragement was hard to rally out of them,
and when pried (with a crow bar) they told us there wouldn't be any other safe lines. "Be careful, mate. . . " they told us.

Mark and I confided in each other the possibility of disappointment, but we were overly
confident that we could find a safe and quality route. With an abundance of lines scoring its
faces, we knew we could find a way to the top.

T he first time I met Mark was in Jackson, New Hampshire, at the 1997 Mount
Washington Valley Ice Festival. I had heard of his prolific big-wall exploits and was
psyched finally to meet up with him for a week of ice climbing. We spent a few days
climbing together and made good friends right off. We traveled to Vermont to give slide shows
on Nameless Tower and Polar Sun Spire, big alpine walls we had climbed separately in the
past.

On one night, over countless 40-ounce beers, we talked about Shipton Spire. We figured
that it wasn't as bad as its reputation; admittedly, we also had never been there. Shipton Spire
was high on both of our Sick Lists, and the booze helped us dream. Another sufferfest was
born.

After keeping in touch through the winter, we decided to go for Shipton Spire as a two-
man team. We wanted to climb in the best style possible and would go with minimal gear —
and a minimal budget. With a summit below 6000 meters, there would be no need for an
expensive permit or all the headaches associated with a full-on expedition. Both Mark and I
were making a living (at least a meager one) off of climbing, and knew from our years of
scrapping trips together that we could knock off Shipton for four grand apiece.

With three weeks until departure, things looked set. I was picking over last details when
Mark called with the news. He had just finished the fastest time up *Lost in America* on El
Capitan.

"Wow. Congratulations, man!" I said.

*Shipton Spire, showing* Ship of Fools *(Ogden-Synnott, 1997).* MARK SYNNOTT

"Thanks. But there's something else, too."

"Oh?"

"I think I broke my ankle. It looks real bad, bro," Mark said.

Mark had fallen on a hooking section and indeed had broken his ankle. He came to visit me and to show off his cast. The doctor assured him that he would be able to climb in four weeks. Mark's enthusiasm was still indefatigable. We decided to get on with it anyway. With Mark in a cast, and me still recovering from a fractured back I had sustained in a 500-foot ride down an avalanche in February while back East, we were the most pathetic, wanna-be-alpine-big-wallers-this-summer the world over. Yet there was hope, because we wanted this more than we wanted functioning bodies. We were not going to take no for an answer.

We flew over with another bunch of wall climbers who were setting out for the Great Trango Tower's north face. They were surprised at our appearance. Mark hobbled on one leg while I tried to lift our haulbags onto the scales with a limp back. They were all laughing at us; I assume they thought it was a joke. Once we got to Rawalpindi, though, things really got into gear.

Rawalpindi has smog thicker than L.A.'s and a sweltering heat that will melt tires. We negotiated back alleyways and crowded bazaars in search of our wall food and final supplies for the trip. After bartering with shop keepers and rickshaw drivers for a few days, we were ready for the perilous journey up the Karakoram Highway. We managed to bribe the hotel clerk into selling us illegal beers for the ride. Considering the road, they would have little effect.

Our chain-smoking drivers, who looked like they were strung out on heroin, drove in a constant haze of hash smoke, swerving away from certain disaster at the last possible second. The 24-hour tour to Skardu, rife with ill humor, uncertainty, anticipation, and blaring Balti music that would drive you insane, was excruciatingly enjoyable.

In Skardu, we hired Kareem, our expedition guide/cook. Kareem was adamant that our three-person kitchen be the size of a K2 expedition's. As our budget was already overrun with complications, Mark and I refused. A snickering Pakistani isn't the greatest experience, but when Kareem began to figure out this wasn't the high-dollar sponsored trip he thought it would be, he turned cynical. Things started to look bad. Because I had a little experience in the irate-Pakistani-handling business, I played the bad guy to Mark's good guy, and we managed to cool him down. In two days' time once again we were riding the dirty roads to the Baltoro Glacier—toting a tiny expedition kitchen.

After six hours, the jeeps ground to a halt. Drivers yelled with their hands in the air: The river had washed out the road. We put together a bridge with timbers, then watched panic-stricken as our jeep edged toward the unstable booby trap. It managed to cross the torrent without mishap, and we toasted to a clear road all the way to Askole, the last real outpost of civilization before we headed on to the trail.

For three days, we hobbled and limped our way to the head of the Baltoro Glacier, from where we could see the magnificent Trango Towers for the first time. Shifting gears, we motored up to our friends at Trango base camp, then continued beyond for another two hours until we finally landed in a base camp of our own. Mark landed, literally: He was hiking in tennis shoes, slipped on a rock and reinjured his ankle. But he recovered quickly in our five-star camp. Whereas camps usually are dirty rocky outcrops suited for marmots and dryer than a windy day in Beirut, ours was different. We set up on a lush meadow five football fields wide, with a trickling brook meandering through it. Ibex often roamed about grazing on the fertile soils and climbed up blank walls without a whimper.

Three miles across the Trango Glacier and just above the confluence of the North and

South Hainablak glaciers was the elusive Shipton Spire. It rises out of the ice without hesitation; its walls looked fierce and steep. We would spend only one day in camp before we carried our first load across to the base.

It took several hours, but we found a secret passage through collapsing talus fields and over ice, and shuttled loads for two days. Back at camp, Kareem would greet us with some concoction in a warm mug, followed by slimy green gruel over burned rice accompanied by stone-infested dry chapaties—and all served with mirth and a sneer. One time, I was accosted by flying plates and profanity.

"Hey, pal, forget the tip," I snapped.

But for me to forget the pump for the MSR stove was inexcusable. Mark had to get a stove from the porters down at Trango base camp. I escaped up to the wall. Petrified of falling rock wiping out ABC, I woke from a restless night spent listening to rock shower the base and skated my way up the scree to the start of our route. Gazing up the wall, I followed a golden pillar as far as I could see. Light drizzle accompanied several days' carrying before I finally returned to camp to face Kareem's cuisine. Mark was back with our new 50-rupee, four-pound, alpine-clunker-special Pakistani stove which, as it turned out, would climb with us on the wall. We decided to send Kareem on his way.

The next morning, we exchanged savvy apologies. Kareem was happy to go on a paid four-week vacation from base camp. Now, just Mark and I faced Shipton Spire.

As Eric Shipton might have felt when he first entered the valley in 1937, Mark and I were about to forge into unknown territory, exploring where no one had ever been before. Already far from home, we now were faced with what any adventurer seeks out in life: the excitement of discovery. Ours would be climbing virgin rock on a pristine granite spire in the Karakoram.

Our first foray into this vertical world was cursed with horrible crumbling rock that instilled fear and loathing for what lay ahead. We fixed three 200-foot ropes over several days and found a suitable site for our first bivy, but the objective dangers loomed ominously overhead. We followed a crack system that lent itself to a lot of moderate free climbing with occasional nailing. For five days we stretched out our five ropes until a rain storm swarmed the Trango valley. Mark had decided to bring a down bag, and he was worried. On the first bivy, he woke up in the middle of the night to get his bivy sac.

"Hey, Jared, do you want me to grab yours?" he asked.

"No way, bro. I've got a synthetic bag. I don't need one."

Mark persisted. "Are you sure? It's really wet in here."

"Thanks, but this bag is the shit," I said, and rolled off to sleep.

I would regret it deeply later. The rain leaked into our ledge and I found myself sleeping in a pool of water, literally swimming in my sleeping bag. I kept waking Mark to tell him how wet it was (and to make sure he couldn't sleep, either) but he would just laugh and roll over, sleeping soundly and dry.

On the second night, I crawled back into my pond. Mark was brewing up when we heard the first pieces of ice hitting the fly of our ledge. When one piece put a gash in the fly, we both hit the inner wall and hunched down. As we listened to the ice and rock exploding around us and pelting the fly with greater force, we wondered if this was going to be it. I have never been more silent or still in my life. Were we going to wind up like Ryuji?

A sharp cracking sound resonated from above; we could hear something gathering speed. Mark and I were inches away from each others' face, staring into eyes full of terror. Something that sounded like a 747 jumbo jet was on its way down, creating a great wind disturbance as it thundered along. Tied into the ledge, Mark and I had nowhere to hide. We waited for the next hit. The big hit. There we were, a mere 600 feet off the ground, and who knew

*Jared Ogden on the lower headwall of* Ship of Fools. *Behind him can be seen (from left to right) Nameless Tower, The Great Trango Tower, and Hainablak Spire.* MARK SYNNOTT

how far this monster had fallen.

Then it happened.

A thousand pieces exploded all around. The force of the impact should have swept us off the wall. The debris from the impact was scattered all over our route. The biggest piece destroyed the ledge we had belayed on one pitch below; a tombstone lay imbedded in the rock and ice. The volume of ice and rock hitting the wall echoed off surrounding peaks until it quietly disappeared down the valley.

All was silent once again. Our grips eased off the cords that held up our ledge. We started to breathe as the last pellets bounced off the fly.

"Well, that wasn't very close, was it?" Mark asked.

"No. I didn't think I was going to die," I said.

We looked out of the ledge to inspect the damage. The rain was not letting up and we were looking at a long wet night with new gashes in our rain fly. Once again, we endured a miserable night.

In the morning, we decided to go down until the storm subsided. We hauled most of our gear up to the next bivy, working all day in the rain, then slogged back to base camp. With no Kareem around, we cooked up bread pockets, pizza, noodles, and desserts. The sky was clear the next day, which meant we had to go back on the wall. We only had so many days to climb; missing one could mean failure.

Both Mark and I know what it takes to set a goal and achieve it. But on a big alpine wall, each day you walk a fine line between danger and safety, survival and fun. The climber must have complete faith and confidence that the other will carry his share more than half the time, and have 110 percent determination to stay focused for long periods of time. We planned on living up on the climb for three weeks in a row. To keep up the vision and strength necessary to endure hardships greater than expected and live under miserable conditions that no one really wants to go through are the hardest parts of such a climb.

With no one knowing what we were doing, it was an unspoken fact that no one falls, no one gets injured—period. Looking back at Ryuji's haulbag and the close call of the day before, it was a test of our determination to jumar back up and commit to the wall.

We pulled our five ropes behind us and never looked back.

We had climbed 1,500 feet to a spacious ledge halfway up the pillar at 17,200 feet. While setting up the bivouac, I reached high to hang the ledge in a better position when the fly made a nasty shredding sound. Upon further inspection, I found that the entire fly had just ripped off of the suspension system, neatly sliding down to my feet in a ruined mess.

"Oh, God. That didn't really just happen, did it?" I asked.

"Don't worry," Mark replied. "It doesn't rain much here."

I felt like an idiot, but managed to sew up the fly so well that it looked better than before. It had started to get decrepit, with duct tape over horrific gashes—and now this. But the climbing ahead looked so good it didn't seem to matter. Besides, we were used to sleeping in lakes.

Blessed with warm sunny weather, I led off from the ledge we had dubbed "Fantasy Island." Stemming, hand jamming, and locking fingers up compact golden granite, I became immersed in the motions of the climbing and found it to be the greatest crack I had ever led. Closing in on 18,000 feet on the wall added a surreal effect as I struggled to get enough oxygen to keep climbing. Mark lay on the ledge, baking in the sun. Soon he was following, cooing at the quality of the climbing and the dramatic exposure. We finished two more pitches that day, one we named the Slot from Hell that Mark will never forget: a 200-foot-gash that started in a chimney, led to a ten-inch offwidth, and finished with a copperhead seam.

Fortunately, it brought us to a huge deluxe platform that would accommodate our two-man tent. The "Captain's Quarters" was so big we wandered around unroped and slept without swamis. There was even an abundance of ice for melting. We abandoned our portaledge, the barrel we had used to haul our water supply in, and other heavy items on Fantasy Island, and moved camp, dragging our ropes up behind. Gasherbrum IVs' west face now was in view, and the rugged Nameless and Great Trango Towers cast long shadows across the crumbling Trango Glacier.

The following pitches were a blend of technical wizardry, savvy, and hard free climbing. We pushed several over 200 feet to get to a stance or to make the best of each lead. Scattered clouds had begun forming, often showering us with snow or sleet by mid-day.

Each day put us closer to a ramp that led to a small col where we had decided to put our last camp. Each day, we were up at 5 a.m. and would not get back to the ledge until it was dark. The snow was blowing hard and we were tired. The constant grind wears you out, and this is when you look to your partner for encouragement. When I reached Mark's belay, we talked about resting for the afternoon. By this point, Mark's hands were constantly needing repair. In the thinner dry air, cuts take longer to heal, and after freeing a long hard pitch his hands would be bleeding again. But we decided to push on; Mark's infallible enthusiasm was contagious. We had a great day pushing our limits and freeing hard pitches in lousy weather.

With our ropes fixed to the col, we were ready to move. Storm clouds threatened the sky, but we were going for it anyway. Mark and I swapped hauling the bags each pitch. Things were running smoothly until it started to snow. By the time we got to the col, we were both exhausted and soaking wet. The last thing we wanted to do was dig out a platform for our tent, but we had no choice. With heavy arms, we patched together rocks and snow to make a pathetic platform that would only deteriorate with time.

At 18,500 feet, the nights got considerably colder than on the lower portion of the climb. Mark's cuts looked appallingly painful. Wet numb hands and fingers made climbing a gruesome task for him, and the cuts never healed. Along with wet sleeping bags, we were having the pleasure of pulling on wet plastic boots; the stench was strong enough to raise the dead. With wind and snow driving at us each day, there was never a chance to dry out, and the psychological stress proved to be as hard as the climbing.

Above our camp, a steep ridge splintered with hand cracks split the east and north faces with spectacular exposure dropping from each side. We wouldn't need to drill for the rest of the route. In deteriorating weather, Mark freed a long section of the ridge, placing cams and pitons for a belay, then rappelled down through thick fog.

Strong winds kept us pinned in our tent for the remainder of the day. Although we were out of the storm, we now had to deal with tent time. Eric Shipton sums it up perfectly in *Blank on the Map*:

> "There is a certain grim satisfaction to be derived from struggling upwards, however slowly; but the bulk of one's time is necessarily spent in the extreme squalor of a high camp. Smoking is impossible; eating tends to make you vomit; the necessity of reducing weight to a bare minimum forbids the importation of literature beyond that supplied by the labels on tins of food; sardine oil, condensed milk and treacle spill themselves all over the place; except for the briefest moments, during which one is not usually in the mood for aesthetic enjoyment, there is nothing to look at but the bleak confusion inside the tent and the scaly, bearded countenance of one's companion—fortunately the noise of the wind usually drowns out his stuffy breath."

Cooking with our hanging stove in the tent created condensation that collected on the tent walls. The snow floor melted out. It seemed there was no way to avoid being wet. After several days our tent floor, replete with holes and muddy water, looked more like a riverbed than

*Ogden on mixed ground.* MARK SYNNOTT

a floor. Mark's bivy sac seemed to keep him dry. Mine seemed to leak perpetually.

"Hey, Jared—looks like that bivy sac really works."

"Yeah. It's designed for people who like to suffer, like me," I chuckled. "Besides, I didn't really want to stay dry anyway. My bag is more comfortable when it's soggy like this."

(When the climb was over, I would give the useless-rag-of-a-bivy-sac as a tip to Kareem, telling him how well it worked. "Yeah, Kareem, this is the best one I have ever used," I lied.)

The storm continued to rage outside; when we woke, the tent was buried in snow. From Mark's last belay, we strapped on our crampons and donned ice axes for the rest of the climb. The snow was blinding, and the belayer suffered long hours tied to the anchor. The knife edge ridge splitting the mountain created dramatic 4,000-foot drops to both sides. With one ice axe in a runnel of ice and the other hooking rock, we were experiencing hard mixed climbing that was difficult to protect; 5.9 rock moves interspersed with vertical ice typified the climbing. Ahead on the ridge, three prominent rock towers impeded our passage. Finding a circuitous path through the towers was going to be dangerous. And thousands of feet off the ground, there was no room for mistake.

The first of the towers was guarded by an overhanging rock chimney and rotten snow over thin ice. Beyond it, on one of the worst days of the storm, Mark climbed up and around the ridge on to the north face to pass the second tower. The wind was so fierce I couldn't see 30 feet in front of me. For three hours, Mark battled the urge to retreat in the face of strong winds and the worst snow we had encountered. I could hear him hammering pitons into the frozen rock while I froze at the belay. I called out into the storm to see how things were going, and to keep myself from going insane from standing alone.

"How's it going, Mark?" I yelled.

"It's going," he moaned. "But I can hardly see, and I'm totally soaked."

The climbing was hard. A long unprotected traverse across mixed ground over the north face led to a steep section of crumbling rock with the consistency of kitty litter. The final unprotected 5.8 rock traverse in plastic boots across an icy vertical face over the abyss without any gear pushed Mark to the edge of his patience, but his perseverance paid off. He was in a protected alcove and had linked us through to the next ice wall leading to the final tower.

I had suffered at the belay. My feet had turned numb and I had been shivering for hours trying to stay warm. Soaking wet, I clamped on my jumars to follow the pitch.

Re-climbing the traverse made me feel sick. The exposure was unnerving; a slip would mean a long swing off the face and into the rock wall below. Nearing Mark's belay, I realized the severity of the lead and how nerve-racking it had been for him to continue in the storm. I could just make him out on a snow ledge when he started shouting at me.

I thought the rope was snagging over an edge, slowly sawing its way through, or that the belay was coming loose and we were going to fall off the wall. My head was pounding from the altitude, and adrenaline pumped through my veins as I imagined what I would look like as I tumbled down the north face. I settled down when he told me the haul bag was caught. He needed help freeing it. Suddenly, the rope jerked violently down and the haul line snapped me in the face. Pieces of protection flew out of the crusty rock just before the traverse, causing the rope to drop. I was looking at a nasty swing if the last piece ripped. I snapped.

"Goddamnit, Mark! Just wait a minute," I shouted.

"Hey, you know, I wouldn't mind hearing you say, 'Great job, bro!'" Mark said.

The climbing had been dangerous, and I should have praised his efforts, but I was scared, wet and tired. At times like these, when you have pushed yourself through a tense situation where fear and uncertainty rule your actions, you need support from your partner to keep going. I hadn't given Mark a lot of support in the past few days and it showed. Dealing with hard climbing in the face of bad weather had put me more into myself than our team effort. Both Mark and I had our uncertainties about the remaining climbing and the food, time and energy we needed to get to the top, and the storm was intimidating. I felt like an asshole and apologized. Support for each other, we both agreed, was essential to get up the face.

The following two days, we climbed past the third tower to the base of the final headwall that led to the summit ridge. A wild tyrolean traverse we called "the Northwest Passage" linked the final moves of the puzzle. We now had all five ropes fixed 1,000 feet above our bivy and were ready to go for the summit.

We looked at our food supply, then at our limp arms and shrinking stomachs. Meager rations sat in the soggy food bag as a foot of fresh snow buried our tent. We had been eating the same food for 21 days in a row. The thought of forcing down diluted soup and stale crackers ruined our appetite faster than you can say puke.

*Ogden on tricky terrain, with the summit visible above.*
MARK SYNNOTT

"You know, Kareem wasn't such a bad cook, was he?" Mark asked.

"You must be joking. I would rather eat my own vomit than his cooking," I said.

We began to dream about massive buffets and cookouts on the beach. It was time to finish the climb.

With only a few gas cartridges left, we realized we would have to push on for the summit in the storm. Four Power Bars and two liters of water made up our food for the summit push. The rack of gear was just as thin as we were: five ice screws, one set of stoppers, a small amount of camming units, two ropes we would pull up from the fixed section, headlamps, a few slings, one pack, and a few extra clothes. Nothing that wasn't necessary was coming with us.

The next morning offered no signs of good weather. We were back at our high point by 9 a.m., then climbed up steep fluted ice on the north face. Occasional rock bands and buttresses broke up the face, offering the best alpine mixed climbing either of us had ever experienced. Following long sweeping sheets of ice over compact granite and slamming in the occasional piton and ice screw belays, we climbed 600 feet to just below a long overhanging cornice on the summit ridge. The day had worn on and the fact that there was no way we were going to make the summit in the daylight made us even more committed than before. The

*Mark Synnott on summit day.* JARED OGDEN

overhang was like a heavy burden, weighing down our thoughts with unexpected bivies we had suffered in the past.

As I watched the fiery red sun set the clouded sky ablaze in an awe-inspiring display of colors, I wondered what the rest of the climb was going to be like in the dark. Mark started to tug on the rope, but there was nothing left. I yelled up that he was out of rope, but he couldn't hear. I jumared over the hideous cornice, my rope sawing through the snow that threatened to collapse on me. I followed a double-corniced ridge to Mark, who stood waist-deep in snow with no belay in sight.

"Have you been just standing there the whole time?" I asked.

"Oh, yeah. I like it when you jumar on my harness," Mark said. "Let me go put in a belay."

"Nice job on the cornice," I offered.

"Unconsolidated sugar snow under windslab without any gear is ugly to face anywhere," Mark said. "Looks like you're up, bro."

I was exhausted. The thoughts that were running through my mind didn't help. I was worried about freezing at belays and the consequences of a mistake. There was nobody for miles. We didn't have a radio to call for help. The chance of any kind of rescue was impossible. What the fuck were we doing here?

"Looks like an iced-over chimney there, huh?" I said.

"Yeah. This is pretty sick, man. We're not going to take no for an answer," Mark replied.

"OK. This looks kinda sketchy. Watch me," I said.

The spotlight from Mark's headlamp went on. I grunted up the flaring chimney, cursing the night and the cold. Up and around the chimney, the ridge came back in sight. To the right, under the cornice, dropped 4,000 feet of air to the North Hainablak Glacier. To the left, the granite slabs disappeared to the South Hainablak. In front lay the summit.

"I'm off belay, Mark," I yelled into the blackness.

"Can you see the summit?" he asked.

"Yeah. It's 100 feet away!" I was cheering.

The storm had let up enough that we could see stars. Breathing in crisp frozen air, the realization that we were going to do it settled in. When Mark caught up to me, we both shouted a victorious yell.

"Yeah baby! We got this one in the bag!" we cried.

Mark was the first to the summit. At 10:30 at night, 100 feet from my belay, I could see his head lamp higher than the top. He had to mantle onto it, it was so small. The thing really is a spire—with a tiny spot for a top, just enough to stand on without falling over. Mark downclimbed back to me and said there wasn't enough room for two. I was next.

On the summit, the walls on all sides dropped off into darkness. It was pitch black; we couldn't really see anything, but we knew what was out there. After a few moments, we knew we had to start down. The night was freezing the sweat and snow on our clothes, making them stiff. The first three rappels were more like downclimbing. The fragile cornice remained in place as we gently rapped over to a horn of rock just below. Out on the face again, it was scary not to be able to see where we had come from or where we were going. The ropes were pulling well, but if one were to get stuck, it would be a real pain in the ass.

We were dehydrated now, and starving. The cold had crept under our skin and our bones ached. Eighteen hours of non-stop climbing to 19,700 feet had taken its toll. Each time we rapped, we left a single screw, or a sling—the cams were frozen useless. While setting the belay and waiting for the next to come down, we would doze off out of sheer exhaustion. By the time we reached the bottom of the headwall, it was all we could do to continue. The ice encasing the ropes made them heavy and cumbersome to pull, then coil and toss for the next rappel. We had to re-climb sections of the ridge until we finally reached the remaining three fixed ropes that connected us to our tent.

At sunrise, we were surprised to see the sun shining on our tent just 500 feet below. By 6 a.m., after 13 rappels, we had made it back, and collapsed in the tent still wearing all our clothes and gear. Mustering up enough energy to brew water for a drink took a while, but with the sun shining on a victorious morning, we could dry some things out and relax.

The hardest part was over. We knew we only had to go down.

The haul bags were mostly empty; once back on the vertical wall, lowering them was basic. The weather began clearing, too—sort of ironic for it to clear after we made the summit, but we were looking forward to being finished.

I had a hard time trying to sleep the last night on the wall. I didn't want the climb to be over. My mind wouldn't turn off, away from the incredible experience we were on the verge of finishing. The amount of work, determination, and fun we had had on the spire was almost done. As when watching your favorite movie over and over, I was reluctant for it to end.

"Hey, Mark?" I whispered.

"Hey. Mark?" I said louder. "Are you sleeping?"

I wouldn't get a reply until morning, when I was awakened by Mark, packing.

"Jared, I need a small bag of stuff to top off this haulbag," he said.

"OK." I felt around. "Here." Knowing I just had to get some sleep, I had taken a sleeping pill at 3 a.m. In my drug-hazed semi-coma I had no idea I had just handed him every roll of film I had shot on the wall.

An hour later, we were ready to start throwing things off the wall.

"Hey, bro," Mark said. "Take a picture of this."

As I snapped photos, Mark tossed the pig. We both laughed, watching as the weighty bag quickly picked up speed on its 1,500-foot ride. Mark was chuckling like a chubby Cub Scout as the bag bounced off the wall and started a death-defying spin. Seconds later, the valley erupted into thunderous booming as the haul bag exploded into the rocks far below. We watched in delight as the contents of the bag were shredded, impaled, and projected all over the final 200 feet of the wall and onto the ground.

"Wow! That was rad!" I shouted.

"Holy shit, dude," Mark gasped. "That was sick! Did you get pictures?"

"Yeah. Those are going to be great," I said.

By the time we were 400 feet from the ground, I could tell something tragic had happened. I was rappelling down toward the remains of the haulbag when the crushed shell of a roll of film stopped me in my tracks. I lurched on the rope and found my heart skipping beats. I choked back the lump in my throat.

"Mark!" I called out frantically. "There's film down here."

"What do you mean, film?"

I continued rappelling, finding a dozen fragments of other cartridges scattered about the rocks and debris. What made the ear-curdling scream fly off my tongue was the destroyed roll I found that I had marked with tape.

It said summit day on it.

My heart was racing; I couldn't hold back the tears. Neither was to blame. After recovering what we could, we finished the final rappel in a light rain and raced for camp.

We reached camp just after dark. Kareem was nowhere to be found. We wouldn't see him for four more days.

We returned twice to the base of the wall to recover all the gear and to carry out our trash. When Kareem arrived, he was happy to see we had summitted and began the arduous task of burning rice, making tooth-breaking chapaties, and snickering at our very sight. Our days were numbered, and our porters showed up right on time. We would be praying to Allah that we would have enough money to pay the porters' wages on the way out and somehow get back home.

We left our base camp as clean and pristine as we found it, wanting the next group to find it the same way. The breathtaking views from camp, the serenity of the upper Trango Glacier, and the whole experience were very hard to say good-bye to. Our efforts, dreams and successes lay folded in the crevasses and the fissures of Shipton Spire. Our presence may hardly be noticed, but we will never forget our ride on the Ship of Fools.

SUMMARY OF STATISTICS

AREA: Pakistan Karakoram

NEW ROUTE: *Ship of Fools* (VII 5.11 A2 WI6, 1350m) on Shipton Spire (5900m), July 9-August 8, 1997, Jared Ogden and Mark Synnott

# The West Face of Latok II

*El Cap on top of Denali*

BY ALEXANDER AND THOMAS HUBER

*The west face of Latok II, showing* Tsering Mosong. ALEXANDER HUBER

*Alexander*

A ugust 13, 1995: *The four of us sit at 6600 meters on a tower on the northwest ridge of Latok II. A difficult decision must be made. For three days, we have been struggling on the ridge; the weather has been fantastic. One more bivy and we will be on the summit—except for that treacherous front of clouds, still far away in China. All of us are more or less weakened, if not on the verge of exhaustion, from the demands of the last few days. For reasons of weight, we have taken only sleeping bags for bivouacs on this alpine-style attempt. A delicate, and, on closer examination, precarious situation. The consequences of a night of storm on this exposed ridge would be fatal.*

The mountain gained a victory on us; we descended. It was our last attempt. The object of our yearning, the summit of Latok II, vanished in the mental emptiness, in the vacuum left by defeat.

For four weeks, we had been captured by the idea of reaching this summit. The last steps to the summit dug deeply into our thoughts, but we didn't succeed in converting illusion into reality. The mountain chucked us out; we reached base camp pumped and empty. But I gained new energy from this vacuum, too. The joy of having gotten off unhurt and of having spent a good time with friends made the blood run fresh again in my veins. I wouldn't be myself if such a defeat didn't spur on my ambitions even more.

Latok II was only a stage. Two years later, my dream would either be fulfilled or finally fade away as an unattainable illusion.

*Thomas*

Two years until departure. That means organizing, talking to sponsors, getting permission, going through a lot of (partly unnecessary) red tape with Pakistan, several convivial Bavarian expedition meetings and a continually changing expedition team. Markus Bruckbauer, for example, quickly decides to become a father, and it is only understandable that he turns his back on the potentially dangerous adventure. But most people remain faithful to the team.

Toni Gutsch, a quiet alpinist, but also strong and full of energy. Christian Schlesener, who is ruled by chaos but who in the mountains is capable of top achievements. Franz Fendt, an unknown mountaineer with enormous potential. Michael Graßl, a man without nerves but with a lot of experience in alpine first ascents. Bernd Geffken, the doctor of our expedition. And the two of us, Alexander and Thomas Huber. Our team, all members with strong heads, all with our own character, all wanting to breathe the air of adventure.

Two months before the departure to Pakistan, the airplane takes off, bound for San Francisco. Once again, I am standing at the foot of El Capitan, this time in order to experience the subtleties of big-wall climbing. With Conrad Anker, a big-wall specialist from sunny California, I am infected by techno fever.

Dreaming in the portaledges, 500 meters above the ground; friendship; tension; diving into a world of tricks and ploys, fear and child-like joy, two scamps who for five days creep through a jungle of hooks, heads, blades, and beaks are, in the end, immensely happy about a successful prank: *Gulf Stream*.

We talk about Latok II. Conrad is getting more and more anxious. In his eyes, a rhombus-shaped mountain, a part of the Bavarian flag at 6000 meters, a "Bavarian mountain. . . ."

"You want to?"

"Let's go!"

The day of packing in Berchtesgaden! Two thousand meters of rope, gear and equipment for a big wall at 6000 meters, plus German specialties like Nutella and bacon. Everything is packed in sacks and barrels. Absolute chaos. The cheese finds a place between the crampons, the bacon gets mixed in with the copperheads. Everything is packed to weigh 25 kilos and locked down, ready for the journey to Pakistan. All in all, 1.7 tons of luggage—hard to imagine, but, considering the duration of the expedition, necessary.

The last days before departure. . . .

Damned telephone—every ten minutes somebody calls.

"How are you?"

"All the best!"

"Come back home well. . . ."

"Have you got the gear?"

Time turns into a roller coaster, up and down, making it impossible to have a clear thought. Our brains are pumped.

My personal things are packed. Time for a last beer in The Cuckoo's Nest, my favorite pub in Berchtesgaden. The last drop, the last conversation with friends. I have a strange feeling in my stomach. We all know that this journey won't be a cakewalk, that it is high-risk. The word "last"—has it got the fatal meaning of "it is the last time," or is it just set in a timeframe? None of us will be able to answer this question. We don't look forward to dying the death of a hero in the mountains. Fear is always present, and most so when saying good-bye to friends. . . but let's go! Our adventure is waiting for us, there's no time for sentiment or tears, I try to drive those moments away. Scotty, beam me up, into the timeless space on the way to another world.

Pakistan. Islam. An absolutely male domain. Rawalpindi: a synonym for dirt, oppressive sultriness, anarchy in the streets, and bacteria that lurk everywhere waiting to clean out your stomach. The week is not a particularly easy one: Formalities have to be settled, food has to be purchased at the bazaar. For reasons of interest, the topics of conversation in the hotel room shift to "How was it, what about consistency, thin or pulpy or solid with a little liquid afterward. . . ." Though this conversation might seem imbecilic, it is decisive for success on the mountain. A severe bacterial infection now would be, at the same time, a return ticket to Germany.

After the arrival of the rest of the expedition team, we leave Rawalpindi. Before us lie 24 hours of rough riding in a bus on the Karakoram Highway—an adventure of a special kind. Relics of bus drivers who fell asleep at the wheel lie far below on the shores of the Indus River, reinforcing the picture of the Pakistanis' attitude toward life. Inshallah—God granting, we will arrive safely.

*Alexander*

June 14: The first day in base camp.I wake up with swollen eyes. I have caught it. Here, of all places. Head cold, completely. For the first two weeks, I am banished to base camp, condemned to passivity while the others transport gear, kit out the advanced base camp at the foot of the wall and get acclimatized daily to higher and higher altitudes.

I have been looking at this wall for four years. I have turned over in my bed hundreds of times, haunted by its image. And now my body refuses to cooperate. Uncertainty arises. Can my body cope with the infection? Can my body deal with the altitude at all?

Bernd, our doctor, has caught it even worse. He loses the fight against the infection and descends, leaving behind three expedition barrels full of medicine. Michael, a member of the Berchtesgaden mountain rescue team, is our last hope from a medical point of view. But after two weeks he, too, must give in to severe inflammation of the kidneys.

Inshallah—let's hope nothing more will happen.

*Thomas*

Tomorrow will be the day. The couloir. Self-doubts torture my brain. Is it a flight forward without return? Nobody will be able to answer this question for me.

Conrad, the "early bird," drags Toni and me out of our sleeping bags at 1 a.m. We make tea and quickly enjoy muesli (if you really can call it "enjoying" at that time of night). Today we will take the first step into the couloir. We don't talk much. Every one of us experiences the same oppressing tension at the thought of the most dangerous part of our expedition: climbing through this shitty snow couloir, the key to the actual wall.

We cross horizontally into the couloir, below an 800-meter rock wall. Let's just not think of the accounts of rockfall in 1995, let's just hurry away from here. But the situation does not get better. We ascend below an overhanging serac for half an hour before we can cross over to the right onto seemingly safe ground. Conrad's eyes have changed; I have never seen this expression in his face. He shouts out something, the meaning of which I don't quite catch at first—but then I understand it. It is a saying that describes the situation in the couloir rather well: "Dancing in the ballroom of death with the fat lady of faith." From now on, we will endearingly call this serac "the fat lady."

Eight hundred meters above us lurks another huge hanging glacier: The ballroom of death. The fear of gliding away into a black nothing with a loud bang is present at every step. But in spite of this fear, something draws us upward, step by step, as if up there, 1500 meters above our heads, there waits some huge treasure. We don't know what is waiting up there; probably only snow, and, weather permitting, a gigantic view of the surrounding mountains. But this highest point emits so much energy, a magnet to which we are the counterpole, that we continue our way despite the risk. Three hours later, we arrive at a comparatively safe place below an overhang of rock at 5600 meters. We dig a small plateau—space for two little tents—and forget the time. Already it is eight o'clock. We must hurry down before the couloir begins to come alive.

*Alexander*

Today, on June 24, Thomas, Conrad and Toni have already reached the balcony camp at 5600 meters. The foot of our big wall is coming closer, and my hopes of still taking an active part diminishes more and more with each meter of altitude the others gain.

*Thomas*

Over the next few days, a kind of working routine sets in among the team. Get up at 1 a.m., transport as much gear as one can to the balcony camp, go down to the glacier camp and sleep or read by day. The fear has disappeared, too. One's thoughts don't wander any longer to the danger threatening from above—they are busy with one's own body. Holding out, motivating oneself again and again, meter by meter, in order to get the 30 kilos on one's back higher up.

Conrad and I put down our loads at the balcony camp. It's starting to snow. Soon, the whole mountain is in motion: spindrift from the walls, avalanches in the couloir. We have no business staying here.

Every minute counts now; the adrenaline in our bodies chases us through the couloir. We are running, jumping over the snow slides. . . . After 30 minutes we reach safe ground before the bigger avalanches roar through the couloir.

*In the couloir at 5300 meters, with the west face looming above.* ALEXANDER HUBER

*Alexander*

During the following days, we get almost one meter of snow in base camp. We have now all come together here and stand on our marks. It is my big chance. If my body is able to cope with the infection during this spell of bad weather, then—so I hope—

*Conrad Anker penduluming to better features on pitch 16. Note popping gear.* ALEXANDER HUBER

I can make up for my delay in acclimatization.

Three days later, on July 3, I start from base camp with Toni. We stand at the beginning of the climb in the thin air of 6100 meters. My delay in acclimatization has been noticeable for the first time today. Twice I had to hand over my load to Toni while leading in the couloir; try as I might, I was not able to pump the necessary oxygen into my lungs. My brain cells have been laboring amidst oxygen deficiency for hours, and slowly but surely I'm getting drunk—intoxicated by the altitude.

Fifty carabiners, 20 friends, 30 nuts, 15 pegs, six different skyhooks, hammers, ladders—a heavily laden Christmas tree stands in the snow in front of a one-kilometer-high piece of granite. With trembling legs, I stand on the first footholds of a 6b slab with bad protection and some runouts. At last we gain the lower end of the crack system for which we have been heading. I hang from the first good protection, relaxed, my brain cells approaching a state of drunken stupor. With pegs and hammer, I toil clumsily to get over the first roof. Thank God that compared to free climbing, aid climbing is not too strenuous, and I soon recover.

After two pitches, we rappel and set up our bivy at the foot of the wall. Our first night at 6000 meters. Again and again, Toni and I wake up, gasping for air. We are not yet acclimatized and our respiratory systems react with Cheyne-Stoke breathing—no sounds for two minutes, followed by a panic-stricken struggle for oxygen. Nevertheless, the next morning Toni performs a phenomenal lead over a desperately smooth-looking roof. Rurps, knifeblades and another hook, and the first A3 pitch is finished.

During the next two days, Toni and I are replaced by Thomas and Conrad, and the two push the route up to 6450 meters before yet another front of bad weather unites us all in base camp.

July 13. Yesterday brought on more good weather. Toni and I are at the place where things are happening once again. From the end of the fixed ropes, I climb up a perfectly shaped layback flake until it runs out completely. I cross to the right, hooking on edges only a few millimeters wide, then composedly select the right hook for the next edge.

Damned hook—I hang upside down, ten meters lower. Back to square one. Again I'm at the upper end of the flake and again I cross to the right. This time, where the hook popped, I take the power drill, and with a little hole, the move is outwitted.

The next pitch is precarious, too. A delicately hooked slab is followed by a moderate hairline crack ten meters in length. The following six-meter flake is pure dynamite. Fixed at the base only by ice, it hovers above our heads completely (or so it seems) detached. No, I don't want to—no flying exercises with such unairworthy objects. Again I fall back upon the power drill and drill five small holes, thus passing the flake.

When Toni and I rappel the next day at sunset, we meet Thomas and Conrad as agreed upon. The time has come when we begin living on the wall. Thomas and Conrad have toiled all day long to haul their entire gear to 6500 meters, including portaledge, for eight days of living in the vertical dimension.

While Thomas and Conrad work on the route for the next days, the same torture awaits Toni and me. Thank God the wall is so steep and solid that we don't have any problems hauling up the haulbag—the number one enemy of big-wall climbing.

Slowly the setting sun bathes the wall in glowing red light. Down in the valley, it has long been dark; up here, the last rays of the sun still warm us. Toni and I stick our heads out of the portaledge and watch Thomas and Conrad rappel. In the evening light, this scene appears unbelievably warm, but in only a few seconds the last rays of the sun go out and deadly cold forces us into our sleeping bags.

*Thomas*

The day of the summit.

Eleven p.m. Conrad moves nervously in the portaledge.

"Another quarter of an hour, please!"

We had agreed on a 11:30 wake-up time. . . . But no chance, he is already in his plastic boots.

Four small lights move up on the fixed ropes to our turning-point at 6900 meters. In the background, 200 kilometers farther to the west, parallel to the Nanga Parbat range, the monsoon is showing its effects. A huge storm front, every second a glowing in the sky. The performance is impressive but at the same time, threatening. Have we got a chance in this weather? Will the monsoon reach the Latok range? A game with time. In one hour, everything might be over and a snow storm might sweep us off the mountain. A battle between success and defeat on the last stage to the summit.

Alexander leads. The climbing on mixed ground is harder than we have expected. To get over wafer-thin verglas on granite slabs, he works for more than an hour by the light of his headlamp. We, however, watch the weather while freezing at the belay. We are on pins and needles. Faster! If it goes on like that, we will never make it today! Maybe it is our last chance before the monsoon puts an end to this gigantic spell of good weather. Faster!

The monsoon remains at Nanga Parbat. Maybe Allah is on our side. Luckily, the climbing gets easier. Toni climbs what apparently is the last part of the ridge. There is a snow slope before us. Can it be true?

Together, we walk up the last meters to the top. Our eyes are shining. The energy, the moving force to tackle any situation, be it ever so difficult, is exploding like a volcano. The sparks get mixed up—we have done it, as a team!

And the summit is indeed "only" a little snow plateau at 7108 meters, but everybody finds his own personal treasure. A feeling of freedom, loosening the bonds in which we were caught when thinking of climbing through the west face of Latok II.

Six days later, Franz and Schlesi, too, stand on the summit of Latok II. They have climbed the northwest ridge alpine-style to the summit in a tour de force.

The success of our expedition can be described simply as thus: "A strong team was at the right place at the right time. . . ."

SUMMARY OF STATISTICS

AREA: The Karakoram range, Pakistan

NEW ROUTES: *Tsering Mosong* ("Long Life") (VII 5.10c A3, 2200m, ca. 1000m of wall, 26 pitches) on the west face of Latok II (7108m), June 12-21, 1997, Alexander Huber, Thomas Huber, Toni Gutsch, Conrad Anker; Nomadu (VI 5.10a WI5 A2, 1100m) on the Northwest Ridge of Latok II, Christian Schlesener and Franz Fendt

*Alexander Huber on the day of the summit.* THOMAS HUBER

# The West Face of Gasherbrum IV

*To the top of the Shining Wall*

BY JAE-HAG JUNG, *Corean Alpine Club*

When Sung-Dae Cho and three other Corean Alpine Club* members climbed Mount McKinley's Cassin Ridge in 1988, it was not only the first Korean ascent of the Cassin, but also the first step of the Corean Alpine Club's decade-long pursuit of big-wall climbing in the high mountains. At that time, Yosemite-style big-wall and free climbing, together with the Yosemite Decimal System, recently had been introduced to Korea, where it had spread rapidly to Korean crags. Many Korean climbers tried to learn and adapt themselves to these new ideas of climbing, which certainly pushed the limits of our climbing.

It was, however, hard to find a similar evolution in mountaineering. Most expeditions still relied on outdated siege tactics, depended on Sherpa support for ascents, and lacked any first-ascent experience. The summit mentality was that an ascent would be made by whatever means necessary; consequently, the real spirit of the challenge was diluted.

Sung-Dae, together with In-Mo Koo (who, after attending a special École Nationale de Ski et d'Alpinisme program in Chamonix in the early 1970s, almost single-handedly introduced French ice technique to Korean climbing) devised the ten-year project of big-wall climbing in the high mountains, which included establishing new routes rather than repeating established ones.

In 1990, four CAC members went to the Pamir International Camp in the Soviet Union. Heavy storms hit the region and huge avalanches buried many climbers on Pik Lenin. Nevertheless, CAC members climbed two 7000-meter peaks within a month. Both were true alpine-style and one-push efforts. All of the CAC members were high-altitude rookies. Hak-Jae Yoo summitted Peak Communism solo.

Two years later, Sung-Dae Cho went back to McKinley, aiming for the American Direct route. But the team members became involved in rescue activity in the early stages of the expedition. They carried out two dead Italian climbers, as well as American climber Mugs Stump. The CAC members then moved to Kichatna Spire without having attempted the American Direct. There, Hak-Jae Yoo, Dong-Suk Shin, and Tae-Il Han put up a new line on the east face just right of the first ascent route [See *AAJ* 1993, p. 140]. They also met Mark Bebie there and exchanged information about the Lailak and Karavshin Ak-Su regions in Kyrghyzstan. Two years later, in 1994, they went to the Pamir Alai, where Sang-Man Shin and Dong-Yun Lee climbed the 5,000-foot north face of Rocky Ak-Su in the Lailak Ak-Su valley in four days. Meanwhile, Dong-Suk Shin and Byoung-Ki Choi created a 900-meter variation to a line on the east face of Pik 4810 in the Karavshin Ak-Su.

In 1995, Sung-Dae Cho led the Corean Alpine Club GIV expedition, the crowning event of the 50th anniversary of the Corean Alpine Club. Hak-Jae Yoo and Sang-Man Shin reached 7800 meters via the Northwest Ridge, but severe frostbite forced them to retreat. In 1997, the

---

* The Corean Alpine Club was founded September 15, 1945, one month after the end of WWII. The original club name was the Chosun Alpine Club. "Chosun," the old name of the kingdom of Korea, was liberated from Japan at the end of the war. Though the new democratic country became Korea, the club retained the old name, and today remains the Corean Alpine Club.

*Gasherbrum IV's mighty west face, showing the 1997 Korean route and Camps II and III.* JAE-HAG JUNG

Corean Alpine Club Climbing Technique Committee returned to Pakistan, this time for the final goal of the program: the unclimbed west face of GIV.

The 12 expedition members arrived in Islamabad, Pakistan, on May 11. Sung-Dae Cho led the troop once again. In 1997, Hak-Jae was on the mountain again as well, though this time he certainly had a heavier burden. First of all, we had decided to tackle the West Face via the western rib. Without a doubt, it was our toughest assignment yet. Many were skeptical about our plans. The skepticism easily turned to criticism when people realized that we had only a few experienced climbers on the expedition. Four out of the 12 members were true rookies in high-altitude mountains; in other words, they had never been on a mountain higher than 2000 meters because there is no such mountain in Korea. We didn't have a fancy star climber, but we did have climbers who were eager to climb. Moreover, we had a strong team spirit, and we believed that this would be our greatest strength on such a mountain.

The cumbersome administrative procedure had been easily taken care of with the help of Liaison Officer Nauman. Two years before, Sung-Dae had a terrible experience with a nasty liaison officer who caused constant trouble from the beginning before ruining the whole expedition. Mr. Nauman, on the other hand, was a respectable Pakistan Army officer with great dignity, and also was a good trekker. We shared common interests and paid each other respect. Things went well in Islamabad, except for getting a flight to Skardu. The weather was so unpredictable that nobody knew the flight schedule. We couldn't afford to be tourists in the capital city, so we took two charter buses to Skardu via the Karakoram Highway.

The caravan went on for eight days, camping out at Goropo, Paiyu, Urdukas, Goro, and Concordia. On May 23, we set up base camp at an elevation of 4700 meters on the West Gasherbrum Glacier, with the west face of GIV looming behind us. Among the peaks that enclosed the Concordia terrain, the west face of GIV seemed the most magnificent, just as its nickname, "the shining wall," implies. The central rib of the west face previously had been attempted by at least six other parties; though none reached the top, seven alpinists were sacrificed to this deadly wall. Probably two of the foremost alpinists of their day, Wojciech Kurtyka and Robert Schauer, had successfully climbed the right side of the west face in 1985, yet they couldn't reach the summit either.

The day after we settled down at base camp, we had a ritual ceremony common among Korean climbers. We not only bowed down to the mountain god but also presented great respect to the ten ancestral climbers of the Corean Alpine Club who had been buried together in an avalanche three decades before while preparing for a Himalayan expedition.

We also went to Miroslav Svetičič's empty grave near base camp. Svetičič, a world-class climber with great potential, had attempted a solo climb of the west face at the same time Sung-Dae led his 1995 expedition. Unfortunately, Svetičič disappeared in the clouds and never returned to base camp. Sung-Dae managed to make an empty grave for Sveticic's soul, and one skillful team member engraved his name on a stainless steel plate, then hung it on a cliff near base camp. Svetičič's had been a brave attempt, and it certainly had been inspiring to the 1995 CAC GIV members.

The 1997 expedition started climbing on May 25. We got up at 3 a.m. when the stars were still sparkling in the dark sky. Sooner or later, that became the official morning call for the entire expedition. We had to move when the wall was still frozen; otherwise, it was too easy to become a victim of the falling ice and rock.

Each member packed food and equipment in his backpack and set off for Camp I. We began to ascend a huge slope covered with deep snow. Crevasses had developed at the foot of the slope. According to local people, there had been a paucity of snow during the last two years.

On May 27, we established Camp I on a vast snow plateau at 5400 meters after detouring around a huge icefall area by traversing a steep snow face. There were countless crevasses on the plateau; we were forced to set up fixed rope all the way to the camp, even though it was a flat area.

On May 30, we started to press the route through to Camp II. This was the real launch of the west face climb where most of the previous teams had struggled and failed. The vertical distance from the snow plateau of Camp I to the summit was about 2500 meters, with only two possible places to camp on the entire central rib of the west face.

By the time we established Camp I, a group of Spanish climbers aiming to climb GIV's Northwest Ridge settled in nearby. Kike de Pablo, Jose Carlos Tamayo, and Jon Lazkano—all of whom were experienced climbers in the Karakoram Himalaya—were among them. We agreed to share fixed ropes up to Camp I, and they reimbursed us. We became good neighbors, sharing food and information. Hak Jae also shared firsthand information from his 1995 experience with them. They were superb climbers, yet the demands of the mountains seemed to be a bit higher than their manpower. Besides, fortune wasn't with them at all. They were the victims of an avalanche that destroyed advanced base camp, and they also lost a tent at Camp I. They retreated shortly after setting up Camp III at 7000 meters, having simply run out of gas.

We had to ascend about 600 meters on a 70 to 80° wall to reach the tiny narrow snow ridge suitable for Camp II. We started climbing at 4 a.m., because after 10 o'clock, when the sun started shining on the wall, falling rock and chunks of snow came down like bullets. A few days later, even with our early starts, Sang-Ho Moon became the first victim hit by falling rock and was disabled for a while.

For several consecutive days, it snowed every afternoon. The leader often swam in deep snow. The climbing conditions were poor and progress was barely noticeable. We finally built Camp II by putting up a small tent on the knife-edge ridge at 6100 meters. It had been ten days since the first step to Camp II. It was the first triumph for us.

Nevertheless, a cornice collapsed the next day while Gung-Yeal Huh was trying to secure the tent with pickets. He plunged with it; Byoung-Ki Choi, who also was working on the tent and who was tied in to Gung Yeal, immediately jumped off the other side of the knife ridge. Both men hung on opposite sides of the ridge, which was about six feet wide and 25 feet long, until other team members could haul them up. The incident remained a secret for a while, because they didn't want to depress the whole expedition. But anyone who came up to Camp II found out about the danger. Tip-toe was common behavior on the CII ridge. Everybody knew that it was not a safe place, but we didn't have a choice. It was the only place to pitch the tent between Camp I and Camp III.

The section between CII to CIII was a nasty mixed route that combined steep rock faces and ridges covered by snow. There also were several overhanging chimneys that frightened us. The biggest obstacle on the route to Camp III was the Black Tower, a 100-meter obstacle that rises from the center of the precipitous ridge. We found old fixed rope and collected a CMI carabiner on the right side of the tower. There also were two expansion bolts at the last anchor point at 6400 meters, but we couldn't find a trace of further progress by previous attempts.

It took 32 days to break through to Camp III. During that period, a week-long snow storm hit the Karakoram. Camps were almost destroyed, and fixed rope was buried deep. It was a totally new mountain; we had to start again from scratch. In the meantime, two members were injured from 25-meter falls, ABC was totally blown out by a tremendous avalanche, and we had to send a mail runner to Skardu to buy supplementary rations.

As we ran out of rope and pitons, we heard that a Japanese K2 expedition had lost a member in a tragic avalanche and was withdrawing from its attempt. Sung Dae dispatched two members as a condolence. They also asked for left-over equipment, but only received some Japanese food. Meanwhile, two Spanish climbers—the Iñurrategi brothers, who have climbed seven 8000-meter peaks without oxygen or Sherpas—were on Broad Peak challenging themselves on a new route. They gave us some good rope; we also got some more from the Korean Student Federation GI/GII Expedition. The great help from these people kept us on the mountain. When we ran out of pitons while working toward Camp III, we cut snow stakes into pitons with a saw and file; Hak-Jae also placed a spoon as a piton. The

*Hak-Jae Yoo climbing above Camp III, and left, Jung-Ho Bang climbing toward the Devil's Brow.* JAE-HAG JUNG COLLECTION

climb had become much more serious than we had expected.

On July 12, Hak-Jae Yoo and Byung Ki Choi finally established Camp III at 6800 meters. We pressed on, adding speed to the climbing. We had been in the mountain for two months and the season was nearly over. The clock was ticking. We realized that we had only one chance to push to the summit. Hak-Jae Yoo proceeded about 100 meters up a mixed route on a perpendicular wall that included a 20-meter vertical and partially overhanging pitch to reach 7000 meters. A few days later, Ki-Yong Hwang joined the force to extend the route to 7200 meters. In contrast, Byung-Ki Choi and Kung-Yeal Huh had to retreat to BC because of frostbite on their toes.

The final summit team was organized by four volunteers, Hak-Jae Yoo, Dong-Kwan Kim, Jung-Ho Bang, and Ki-Yong Hwang. Except for the sub-leader, Hak-Jae, all of them were rookies in the Karakoram Himalaya, and two of them had never been higher than 2000 meters.

On the night of July 15, four members set out from CIII, the last formal camp. We planned three days to the summit and one day to get back to CIII, which meant three bivouacs. We sorted out equipment to take: 15 pitons, six ice screws, 100 meters of 5mm rope, personal bivouac gear, and a minimal amount of food and fuel. Each of us carried eight kilos of gear and equipment.

Ki-Yong and Dong-Kwan arrived at 7200 meters at 3 a.m. The wind blowing from the top was getting severe, and the weather looked uncertain. Ki-Yong and Jung-Ho started to lead, placing the last portion of the fixed rope at dawn. Suddenly, the wind was blowing in gusts, sweeping down the snow piled on the upper part of the west face. It was impossible to move; each climber was stopped in his tracks, dodging the lethal storm. Ki-Yong, who was exposed to the storm for three hours, had severe signs of frostbite on his fingers and toes and was forced to retreat.

At noon, the weather cleared out, and the three remaining men set off again. When the last man, Jung-Ho, weighted an ascender, a piton pulled, causing him to fall three to four meters. He hit a rock, breaking his goggles and cutting himself around the eye. Despite the injury, he continued climbing, and by 5 p.m., we had advanced to 7400 meters and prepared a place to bivouac by digging out a tiny snow ledge with endless drops on both sides. We secured ourselves by driving some pitons into the rock and went to sleep wearing our harnesses.

On July 17, Jung-Ho, injured but tireless, took the lead. The rock was very loose, so it was hard to find a place to put pitons. We progressed slowly but steadily. After climbing 300 meters, we were at an elevation of 7500 meters. We were lucky to find a much more satisfactory bivouac site than the previous night's. Another dangerous night passed by.

July 18. The summit day had come. It was a perfect day. The three members got up at 4 a.m. and reduced equipment to the minimum. Dong-Kwan led the team. After climbing 300 meters on the 70° snow-covered wall, we approached a place called "The Devil's Brow." Jung-Ho took over the lead and advanced another 80 meters on the icy surface.

*Ha-Jae Yoo at 7900 meters after the summit, with Masherbrum in the background.* JAE-HAG JUNG COLLECTION

We established a 30-meter pitch by traversing across the 70° wall in the two o'clock direction. All gathered at one spot for a snack. We were surprised when we looked at each other; everyone appeared nearly exhausted. Nonetheless, no one showed a white flag yet. We could barely proceed up the 60° slope of ice and snow with our beaten bodies. As we went higher, breaking trail became more difficult because the snow surface was not firm. For a moment, Hak-Jae, who was carrying the video camera, went ahead of the others to capture the scene. After advancing 100 meters, we finally reached the summit ridge. The time was 12:26 p.m. To the east, a wall formed a perpendicular drop downward; snow crowned its top along the summit ridge.

We crossed a distance of about 100 meters along the ridge toward a pinnacle in the south that was the tallest on the crest. Hak-Jae climbed to the top of the ridge to observe the east side of the mountain. He could see Camps I and II and noticed that six small pinnacles stuck out on the summit ridge of GIV. All of them appeared to be less than ten meters high. He easily distinguished the third one as the highest because the summit ridge curves around to the east.

When Hak-Jae returned from his reconnaissance, Dong-Kwan took off for the third pinnacle. He nailed two pitons into a crack and traversed in the two o'clock direction. (As we were still on the west face, the rest of the team and the Pakistani employees in Base Camp were able to watch our movement through a telescope.) Dong-Kwan arrived at the third pinnacle after traversing 30 meters along the snow wall right below the ridge. He placed a knife blade and bong-bong and used them to belay the others. At 2:27, they joined him at the belay.

Above us, there was a three-meter-high smooth rock covered by a two-meter snow cor-

*The footsteps leading to the summit shoulder, as photographed from base camp.* SUNG-DAE CHO

nice. Hak-Jae realized that we could it if we demolished the cornice before stepping on it, but it seemed too vulnerable to tackle. The danger of its collapse made the last few meters of climbing meaningless. As sub-leader of the team, he decided that was as far as we would go.

We took a few pictures and started descending right away. We rappelled until we came to the gently sloped summit ridge, and hurried down to the Devil's Brow by 3:55 p.m. After a brief break, we continued descending, and everyone returned safely to the bivouac site that we had left early that morning. We were completely exhausted, and Hak-Jae complained of frostbite on his toes. We decided to stay for another night. It was our third consecutive bivouac. At 6 o'clock the next morning, we continued our escape from the deadly mountain.

In the middle of the descent, Hak-Jae found a body at 7000 meters. It was Miroslav Svetičič.

By 11 in the morning, the summit members returned to CIII, where Gung-Yeal and Dong-Chul had been waiting to help in the return to BC. In the process of retreating, the CII cornice collapsed. Gung-Yeal was caught by a thin rope; unfortunately, he lost his backpack that contained ten rolls of film, including the summit pictures. After midnight, all members returned to BC without any summit photos. The next day, we took some pictures with a telescopic lens. The photographs clearly show footsteps going up to the summit ridge. We hope that the next climbers will find our pitons at the top of the mountain.

After the team returned to Korea, Sung-Dae and Hak-Jae were criticized by some fellow climbers for not getting to the very top of the mountain. Some were rather skeptical of the success itself because we didn't have photographic proof with someone holding a flag on the summit. We were deeply disappointed, not only because we couldn't convince them, but also because of the prevalence of disbelief amongst climbers. As the controversy has grown hotter, people seem to neglect the achievement of climbing the face. It is a clear parallel to Schauer and Kurtyka's climb on the same mountain in 1985, considered one of the most impressive climbs, even though they didn't reach the summit.

The summit was not the primary goal for us. We were there to climb the west face, which many people thought nearly impossible. We finally did it after two months' toil; all 12 members devoted themselves to the team and three summiters carried the other members' sacrifice. We could not have had success without perfect teamwork. We could not have made it to the top if there was one person missing. Although six of us were rookies in the Himalaya, every one was of the essence for the team.

If we were mere peak baggers, we could have climbed one of the 8000-meter peaks more easily. The summit priority is one of the things that still dilutes pure alpinism in the Korean climbing community. We wanted to be different, and we have done a different thing. We wonder if that's why we got such a strong reaction to our success.

SUMMARY OF STATISTICS

AREA: Karakoram Himalaya, Pakistan

NEW ROUTE: The West Face (VI 5.10 A3, 2500m) of GIV (7925m) via the West Rib, May 23-July 18, 1997 (Hak-Jae Yoo, Tong-Kwan Kim, Jung-Ho Bang)

PERSONNEL: Sung-Dae Cho, leader; Hak-Jae Yoo, sub-leader; Young-Soon Hwang, Sang-Ho Moon, Jung-Ho Bang, Tong-Kwan Kim, Ki-Yong Hwang, Dong-Chul Shin, Byoung-Ki Choi, Chan-Sung Woo, Jae-Hag Jung, Captain Nauman (L.O.), Sullaiman Sardik, cook

# A Touch Too Much?

*The first ascent of
Changabang's north face*

BY MICK FOWLER

I squatted uncomfortably over the public toilet hole in the airport customs building. It was the first full day of the trip and already diarrhea was dripping simultaneously from both buttocks. A challenging start indeed. I peered hopefully around for some toilet tissue to be faced only with a small plastic jug nestled under a floor-level tap. India's a great place, but it can come as something of a shock. Straight from the soft toilet-paper tissue world of rural England, six of us had come to climb the north face of Changabang, an objective that Roger Payne had led a trip to attempt the previous year and that we all had an overriding urge to climb.

Three of the previous year's team—Roger, his wife Julie-Ann Clyma, and Brendan Murphy—were back. In addition, there was Steve Sustad, Andy Cave and me. The plan was to climb alpine style as three independent teams of two—"alpine style" to us meaning that we would climb in one push, carrying all our equipment on our backs and, within reason, the second and the leader climbing the whole route without any jumaring or other jiggery-pokery with ropes.

A more immediate plan was that Steve Sustad and I would sign lots of forms and extract our freighted equipment from the Customs import building while Roger Payne would rush to the Indian Mountaineering Federation for the Changabang expedition's official briefing. I did not know Roger, the General Secretary of the British Mountaineering Council, that well before the trip, but already it was clear that he had a natural enthusiasm and ability at all things to do with paperwork and officialdom. Steve and I were more than happy to defer.

*The north faces of Kalanka and Changabang from the Baghini Glacier.* ROGER PAYNE

There was, however, a problem. All three of us had started the customs trail but, once Roger left us, it quickly transpired that only he had an "action" pass for the building. Steve and I had "visitor-only" passes. I couldn't understand why anyone might want to visit the Customs building, as it's not exactly a tourist attraction; so I squatted miserably amidst the inevitable time delay and confusion involved in changing my pass for one that enabled some constructive action.

Roger, though, must have a sixth sense. The day was saved by his arrival, brimming with health, confidence and paperwork just as I felt at the opposite end of the spectrum and a bureaucratic impasse seemed inevitable.

I had not been on a Payne-Clyma expedition before. Previous jaunts in the big mountains always had been on the basis of a sort of communal responsibility vaguely steered by one person. Here, though, Roger and Julie-Ann were clearly in complete control. Prior to leaving for India, I had wondered about this when Roger and I met on the crag, only to discover that we hadn't enough equipment to climb. . . . But now, organized computer lists of things to do in Delhi appeared with alarming efficiency.

In fact, in retrospect, things had been different from usual the moment we arrived at the airport. Instead of the chaos and confusion followed by the cheapest possible transport to Delhi, we were met by a luxury minibus, complete with curtains, which whisked us away to comfortable and clean pre-booked accommodation. A whole new experience for me.

And it continued. Shopping by computer list prepared in Britain, our own pre-booked minibus to Josimath, porters to order and a bus to carry them. Roger was in his element, beating even the Indian bureaucrats at their own game. The poor local magistrate was left a perplexed man. We had been told to advise him formally of our intentions and ended up sitting in his courtroom before a huge raised desk with 100 or so seats behind us. With much forelock tugging and references to "Sir," a letter detailing our plans was put before him. Roger slipped a photo of the mountain in for good measure. There was a long pause while the magistrate peered quizzically at what was before him. Eventually, he drew his very substantial frame up to full height.

"What do you want from me?" he inquired.

"Nothing," replied our bureaucratic expert.

And so the meeting ended and we were on our way. Lesser bureaucrats than Roger have been known to fail at such hurdles.

The roadhead was not really a roadhead at all, more a rest area where everyone piled out of the bus and porters queued for items such as socks, shoes and sunglasses. Personally, I'd never previously bothered with supplying such items and simply negotiated slightly higher wages instead. It had to be admitted, though, that their availability gave us an additional weapon in our efforts to maintain order. . . or perhaps it was just that Roger's porter-controlling efforts had the edge over any I'd come across before. Either way, the end result avoided the usual rush for the easiest—or lightest—looking loads, and a remarkably organized group of 35 or so porters headed off up the excellent forested tracks toward the summer village of Dunagiri and, ultimately, our base camp at just above 4500 meters.

I lay in my tent nursing my throbbing head. The Fowler body was, true to form, acclimatizing slowly. After two days at base camp, the others were bubbling with energy and talking positively about how to tackle Changabang's north face. Meanwhile, I groaned gently and faced such decisions as how many painkillers I should sensibly take.

Changabang is not visible from Base Camp, so I was spared the pleasure of seeing it until four days after arriving, by which time I felt just about ready to tackle the challenging walk to an Advanced Base Camp at about 5100 meters. The walk acted as a brutal reminder of the truly demoralizing nature of unacclimatized activity. Roger and Julie-Ann had told us to expect a six-hour walk. We arrived in the morning of our third day.

The views, though, were uplifting. Directly across the glacier from ABC, the north face of Changabang rose in an impressive steep wall, peppered with a liberal assortment of snow and ice. In places, the ice looked white, friendly and probably easy to climb. In other areas, though, a shiny green reflection revealed hard, uncompromising shields that appeared to be stuck to near-vertical ground. Try as we might, it was impossible to link up the white streaks; we were going to have to climb the white ice, green ice and rock sections in between.

"Nice to have a bit of variety," Steve assured me. I peered at the green, featureless 55° ice slopes that formed a substantial part of the lower section. They looked technically mundane but physically knackering. I declined to comment.

Acclimatizing is boring, the main aim of the game being to spend as much time "up high" as possible to get the body in a condition where it at least stands a chance of success on the real objective. Our plan was to maximize interest in this process by climbing up to a col (the Bagini Col), which we intended to cross on our planned circuitous descent from the mountain. If we felt energetic, we might even descend the far side to the Ramani Glacier (from where Joe Tasker and Pete Boardman made their generation-inspiring 1976 ascent of Changabang's north face) and leave a food dump there.

Reality proved different. Day four from Base Camp saw us wading through knee-deep snow on the upper Bagini Glacier. The temperature hovered around 40°C and the Bagini Col was 600 meters above us and a couple of horizontal miles away. . . or, at our current rate, at least another two days. As on the three previous days, we used heat exhaustion as an arguably valid excuse for bringing the day to a possibly premature close at 10 a.m. and settled down to a strenuous day of acclimatizing by lying horizontally reading books and drinking endless cups of tea. I was just slipping into full relaxation mode when the sound of heavy breathing outside attracted our attention.

Andy and Brendan were powering their way up the glacier toward us, having left Base Camp that morning. My feeling of general exhaustion deepened. The potential for demoralization is high with these young (well, under 35) fit types on a trip. I made a mental note to think about ensuring that I am surrounded by slow and unhealthy companions in the future. Much to my relief, they decided not to carry on, and we camped side by side that night, convincing each other that the snow conditions were such that the Bagini Col would be avalanche-prone. The immense amount of energy that would have to be expended to get there also seemed to be a contributing factor. As Steve explained to me, "It's important not to burn out too early on a trip."

I agreed heartedly, and spent the rest of the day snoozing gently in my sleeping bag with the occasional brew break. Every now and then, I even managed to read a few words of my book.

The acclimatization process continued in an enervating and rather unsatisfying manner. Steve and I climbed 300 meters up a rather impressive unclimbed 6500-meter peak called Dunagiri Parbat, while Andy and Brendan did likewise on a different spur of the same peak. Judging our bivy height of about 5500 meters to be high enough, Steve and I managed two nights there with general lassitude and intermittent dozing extending over the whole of the intervening day. With my youngest child not being the best sleeper, I took great pleasure in maximizing on the snoozing hours. The boredom potential was, however, increasing, and as we gradually felt a little better (my altitude headache was even moderating by now), an urge to get under way on Changabang grew stronger. We headed back to Base Camp for some decent food and a proper rest before going for it.

It was a surprise for us to find Andy and Brendan already at Base Camp. We had expected to be down first and ready to get on the face before them, but it turned out that they had coped with acclimatization and boredom even less well than we and had descended the day before. Roger and Julie-Ann also had been out acclimatizing. Later that day, they, too, arrived back at Base Camp feeling ready to begin.

We always knew that there was a number problem on this trip, but the prospect of three

*Steve Sustad, pitch one, day two.* MICK FOWLER

teams in action on the face, one behind the other, brought it into a sharp focus that was only slightly relieved when Roger and Julie-Ann decided to try a line to one side of that preferred by the rest of us.

Steve and I sat at Advanced Base peering at the face through binoculars. Andy and Brendan had been caught by the morning sun on the initial ice slopes and their progress had slowed to a crawl. We felt for them, and noted that the midday sun over Changabang is so high that even the steep north face gets it for most of the day—that is, of course, if the sun was not obscured by the incessant clouds that boiled up every afternoon and which had prompted at least some precipitation every day so far.

It was rather pleasant reclining in the tent eating excessively ("stocking up for the route," we said), chatting away and occasionally stretching for the binoculars. It was a unanimous and easily reached decision that an extra day at Advanced Base would give the others a chance to get well under way. "Best not to end up fighting over bivy ledges," as Steve put it.

And so we set off two days behind them, while Roger and Julie-Ann, following a different line, set off one day behind us. It was beginning to feel a bit crowded. We had not seen any Westerners at all since leaving Joshimath and, in all probability, there were no climbers whatsoever within a ten-mile radius, and yet there were six of us engrossed on the north face of Changabang. As lovers of adventure and isolation, the irony of the situation did not escape us.

We had food for eight days and gas for ten. I had organized "breakfast" and Steve the "evening meal." Breakfast had been easy: two small bags of muesli-type stuff looked about right for 16 servings. Steve's task was more challenging. Evening meals were to consist of mashed potatoes and noodles on alternate nights. Noodle quantities were pretty straightforward, mashed potatoes not so. The problem was that our selected supermarket's mashed-potato packets claimed to do 18 servings, whereas another similar-sized product of powder that we had been using claimed to do six servings but only lasted us for one meal. Steve decided the servings must be very small.

Day one was a potato day, and the evening found us perched on a 12-inch-wide bum ledge marveling at the mashed potatoes liberally overflowing from the huge pan of our hanging stove. Steve decanted furiously into the lid and both our mugs. It was indeed impressive that such a small quantity of powder could be turned into such a vast quantity of potatoes. Perhaps we had found the ultimate hill food? "Full of carbohydrates," Steve assured me, as I dutifully struggled with the volume, keen not to commit the ultimate Himalayan sin of not eating my full allocation of food. "Full of weight, too," I managed to comment between dry and powdery mouthfuls. I was mindful of the unwieldy weight of our sacks, about which we had both been moaning constantly.

The afternoon of our first day had been cut abruptly short by the usual pattern of heavy snowfall, which translated into a continuous stream of spindrift pouring down the groove line that we were trying to climb. In fact, without spindrift, it was a particularly nice groove line, very steep, but with only intermittent breaks in a covering of perfect white ice. It was disappointing to have to stop earlier than planned and even less satisfying to spend a very uncomfortable spindrift-ridden night perched on one buttock. But, by the morning, we had at least both recovered from the previous night's potato excess and were in a position to take advantage of the standard fine morning weather. Unfortunately, though, the rigors of the night had been such that we somehow didn't actually get going until just past 9 a.m. Inexcusable, really, when it was fully light by 5:30 a.m.

In terms of climbing time per day, day two on the face was even worse. Our late start didn't help, and by the time we completed the fourth pitch of the day, the weather was such that

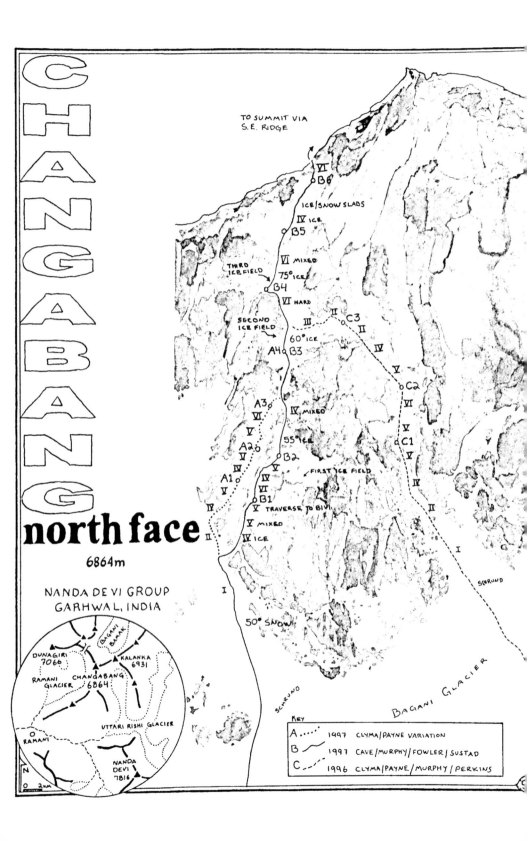

C H A N G A B A N G

# north face

6864m

NANDA DEVI GROUP
GARHWAL, INDIA

TO SUMMIT VIA
S.E. RIDGE

VI B6

ICE/SNOW SLABS

IV ICE
B5

VI MIXED
THIRD
ICE FIELD
75° ICE
B4

VI HARD

III II C3
II
SECOND
ICE FIELD

60° ICE
A4 B3

V C2
A3
VI IV MIXED
V
A2
55° ICE
IV B2
V
A1
VI
V
FIRST ICE FIELD
IV
V C1
V
V B1
V TRAVERSE TO BIVI
V MIXED
IV
IV ICE
II

II

I

SCHRUND

I

SCHRUND

50° SNOW

BAGANI GLACIER

KEY
A ..... 1997 CLYMA/PAYNE VARIATION
B ——— 1997 CAVE/MURPHY/FOWLER/SUSTAD
C – – – 1996 CLYMA/PAYNE/MURPHY/PERKINS

DUNAGIRI 7066
BAGANI BARAK
KALANKA 6931
RAMANI GLACIER
CHANGABANG 6864
UTTARI RISHI GLACIER
RAMANI
NANDA DEVI 7816
N
0    2 KM

a stop was inevitable. We sat huddled together while a three-hour fabric-flapping storm buffeted our little tent, tucked into a snow spur beneath the first of a series of three ice slopes.

Unknown to us, up above, Andy and Brendan were caught out on difficult ground in this violent weather. Brendan fell 60 feet and Andy suffered frostbite in his thumb. Meanwhile, Roger and Julie-Ann spent a character-building night standing up somewhere down to our left with their bivy bags over their heads. Relatively speaking, we were pretty comfortable.

We were now at the foot of the first of the ice fields. Photos taken the previous year showed these to have been largely snowy, but this year they glistened hard and shiny — pure calf-wrenching stuff. In fact, it seemed that it was not just the ice slopes that were very different from the previous year. Brendan had recalled never wearing his duvet on the face in 1996. This year, though, it was cold enough for me to wear mine leaving Base Camp, and not a day went by without us wearing them on the route. Global change or local anomaly?

The ice was as hard as it looked, and long, precarious wobbles on front points were wearing on both the mind and body. Steve eased the belay strain by tying his rucksack in and sitting on it with his legs dangling free. It looked very strange but seemed to work well.

A false line and a couple more interesting pitches saw us bivying at the foot of the second ice field. Unfortunately, my homemade adze had failed to stand up to the strain of the interesting pitches. I like a huge adze for tackling nasty overhanging Himalayan snow and had had one made for me back in 1995. The manufacturers warned me then that it wasn't very strong, but I suppose that after 43 pitches of hard use on Tawoche in Nepal I had become overconfident of its strength. My axe looked sort of naked without it. I kept my fingers crossed that we wouldn't come across too many overhanging powdery sections higher up.

Day four on the face consisted of another smooth slab of hard ice and a hard mixed pitch leading out on to an ice field below the steep upper third of the face. From the ice field, we could look out right to the snow rib, which marked the high point of the 1996 attempt. It looked to be a long calf-wrenching traverse away, and I felt glad that a change in ice conditions since the previous year had tempted everyone to steer clear of the 1996 line.

On arriving at ice slope three (getting tedious by now, these ice slopes), it was a both a pleasant but worrying discovery to find Andy and Brendan in situ on a tiny platform hacked out of the ice. They were about to spend their third night there.

"Thought we'd hang around a bit and enjoy the view," Brendan explained mischievously.

The truth, of course, was slightly different. The vicious storm of two days ago had caught them on the hard pitch between the ice fields. Climbing in such conditions must have been character-building, to say the least. After Brendan's fall, and a long, cold lead by Andy, they managed to squeeze into their bivy at about midnight. Andy had some frostbite damage in his fingertips and, potentially more seriously, in his thumb. Understandably, they then felt that a recovery and recuperation day was in order.

The following day, they set out on the steep upper third of the face, only to find that by the time the daily bad weather moved in they were only about 120 meters up without a hint of a bivy site in sight. Tying their ropes together, they returned to the icefield bivy. . . and had the dubious pleasure of meeting Steve and me.

I say dubious in a tongue-in-cheek way, but it is true that to a certain extent we all felt it best to be well clear of other climbers on a route like this. Too many people together increases the risk of (very) uncomfortable bivouacs, long waits on stances and stone/icefall. Another, almost inevitable, result seems to be lots of jumaring and rope antics in general, rather than climbing. Not my cup of tea at all.

Having said all this, the other side of the coin was an obvious pleasure involved in meeting friends unexpectedly and the camaraderie involved in being together. But what should we do now? Continue together, or wait for Andy and Brendan to clear the way? The decision was far from clear-cut, but both Steve and I have a strong aversion to inactive days on the mountain. The others appeared indifferent, so the decision was made. We would team up as four and proceed as best we could. As Andy and Brendan were just completing their sixth day on the face and had only eight days' food, there was, of course, another benefit in staying together and sharing our mashed-potato surplus.

And so the next morning saw Steve and me enjoying a lie-in while the others headed off. The start was, in fact, delayed by some unhealthy looking sunrise clouds, and it was midday before they reached the previous day's high point and were ready to start climbing. Steve and I dithered more as the hours ticked by. With the usual afternoon bad weather, it was unlikely that they would manage more than two or three pitches before being forced to stop. As far as we could see, that meant that they wouldn't reach a bivy ledge good enough for two, let alone four. And to make matters worse, clouds were already swirling around them in line with the trend of the bad weather arriving earlier every day.

They had taken our ropes to speed things up, so we could remove and use theirs; also, the gear was split fairly evenly between us. All in all, there was no reason why we couldn't continue as independent teams of two if we wanted to. Steve shouted up that we would stay put for the day and, in the absence of any violent objection, we prepared for a day of relaxation. Being camped on a slight arête projecting from the third ice field, we felt relatively safe from any falling debris. Little did we know how wrong this would prove to be.

The trouble with Himalayan ice climbs is that it is virtually impossible to climb pure ice without it shattering and substantial plates falling away. Naturally, they break into smaller pieces as they bounce down—but the ground that Brendan was leading on was sufficiently steep and icy for them to fall more or less sheer to the ice slope, at which point they tended to cartwheel off in any direction that they fancied.

At about 1 p.m., a particularly loud noise signaled the approach of something notably unpleasant. I was struggling to put my boots on and clear the accumulating snow that was threatening to push us off our little ledge while Steve was lying down waiting for me to get out of the way. We both pressed ourselves against the inner wall of the tent as a six-inch diameter flat piece of rock came straight through the back panel, missing Steve's head by perhaps two inches.

What to do? We were clearly not in as safe a position as we had hoped. I hurled some abuse up into the clouds and received an apologetic response—but then they were hardly throwing things at us on purpose. Practically, there was nowhere safer to move to, and we would have to grin and bear it.

The rest of the day was spent huddled against the sidewall with our helmets on. The end result was three holes in the tent, lots of adrenaline flow, but no injuries. Steve did a wonderful job sewing up the tent with a spare lurid pink bootlace that he happened to be carrying.

Somehow our "rest" day hadn't proved very relaxing, and the next morning it was hardly a refreshed-feeling team that climbed up the two ropes that the others had left. Here, though, we were comfortably on to the upper third of the face. The occasional piece of ice shot past, reminding us of the other two, but at least there was relief from the monotonous tedium of the knackering, featureless ice slopes. In fact, the ground here was much more my cup of tea: steep, thin ice runnels with lots of variety and mixed climbing. I was really beginning to enjoy myself at the time—as opposed to the Himalayan norm of retrospective pleasure. Inevitably, though, it did not last.

By 11 a.m., the "afternoon" bad weather was pouring waves of spindrift down on to us. Steve had headed off up a deepening groove system. His signals of discomfort warned me in

*Sustad on day seven.* MICK FOWLER

*Mick Fowler high on mixed ground.* STEVE SUSTAD

good time when particularly penetrating blasts of spindrift were approaching and, as ever, in such conditions our progress slowed to a crawl.

Our bivouac was such that it simply served to justify our decision not to proceed as a team of four. The ledge wasn't even big enough for the two of us in a sitting position. We hung forlornly in the flapping tent fabric dangling uncomfortably from tied-off ice screws. Midway through the night, life seemed particularly miserable. Spindrift kept pouring through a hole in the tent and blasting its way around the inside. Keeping it out of my sleeping bag while suspended from a rope tied round my waist was a challenging way to spend a few hours. Meanwhile, Steve groaned noisily next to me. He was in a bivy bag inside the tent and so was better off from the spindrift point of view, but had a less comfortable (well, even more uncomfortable) section of bum ledge than I did. I've had worse bivouacs, but an awful lot better ones, too.

By the time we had sorted ourselves out the next day, I was perhaps not feeling my best. It was, though, rather demoralizing to realize that it was already snowing hard as Steve was leading the first pitch of the day at 8:15 a.m. We managed a meager two pitches that day before the first ledge in seven days of climbing provided all the temptation we needed to pitch the tent and assess our position.

"Enjoying your holiday, Michael?"

"Most rewarding," I responded, contemplating our remaining food. This was the end of day seven from Advanced Base, so we should have had just one day's food left. Reality, though, was much more encouraging. The mashed potato surplus was such that we clearly had at least something to eat for another five to six days. The gas, too, was lasting well. There was clearly no justifiable excuse to retreat. . . and, after all, a bit of bad weather has to be expected when out on the mountain for so long.

"Onward, Stephen."

"Certainly, Michael."

As an added incentive, Roger and Julie-Ann's tent now was visible down on the ice field.

The morning dawned perfect, with superb views right across the breadth of the Himalayan chain. We could see from Tibet in the north to the Indian plains in the south—magnificent. I remember saying to Steve how lucky we were to be able to "do this kind of thing." He agreed.

We were feeling confident now and guessed the top of the face to be only 500 feet or so above us. Route-finding looked to be a bit of a problem and, sure enough, we probably followed a more difficult line than we had to. But at least we enjoyed some wonderful mixed climbing through a steep rocky band to gain an ice slope and exciting corniced exit on to the summit ridge.

And what a ridge, what a relief to be able to walk about after eight days on the face, and what a stunning view of Nanda Devi standing gloriously aloof in the middle of her forbidden (courtesy of the Indian Government) sanctuary. That afternoon, the clouds boiled up to the extent that we caught only a tantalizing glimpse of the sun-struck summit, but that alone was enough to fire the imagination.

It was a day from there to the summit and back. Andy and Brendan had been to the top that day and could be seen descending toward us, but tracks going down the ridge suggested that their tent was a little lower down. "Let's go and pitch the tent with the others," Steve suggested.

To me, the spot where we had joined the ridge looked okay for cutting out a good platform and would minimize the height gain necessary in the morning, but Steve was already off. I wondered whether to call a halt, but then it would be sensible to have a good chat with the others, and they probably would appreciate some mashed potatoes (even though I was getting pretty sick of them). I said nothing, took up some coils and prepared to follow.

Steve had been having trouble with his crampons from the word go. They balled up almost immediately on the ridge and he slipped over, stopping himself straight away. I could see he was uncharacteristically uncomfortable, though. As he continued, his heel sections balled up again after only one or two steps. I could see them slipping to one side.

Suddenly, one foot slipped away from beneath him on the balled-up snow and he fell onto his side. Braking from that position was difficult, as the still-heavy rucksack tended to pull him back. I watched with horror as he started to slide down the side of the ridge. I knew that it steepened markedly just below us and my quickly positioned ice-axe-in-the-snow belay was not really up to any serious forces. I remember glancing up at the crest. Could I jump down the other side? No, it was too far above me. I braced myself. I had managed to get a waist belay and leaned in to take the strain.

To begin with, I felt I was in with a chance. I could feel my crampon points biting home and see Steve swinging around below me. But the farther he swung, the more the slope steepened and the more the strain grew. Ultimately, I crumpled to one side and came on to the axe. I felt just a token resistance as I was dragged down. My feelings were of complete despair. All those promises to my wife and children.

"Be careful," Nicki had said when I left.

"I will," I'd replied cheerfully.

I swear I saw their faces as I fell. More than fear was a tremendous feeling that I'd let them down. I was accelerating fast now and then free falling. A huge thump winded me and I was simultaneously aware of a sharp pain across my face. Then I had stopped. I explored myself and my position cautiously. My nose was bleeding and appeared to be broken but my arms, legs and body seemed fine. The rope had wrapped itself around me in such a way that I couldn't move easily.

"Steve. You all right?"

I knew then that Steve was only ten feet away, but I couldn't squirm around to see him clearly. There was a terrible, pregnant, silence. He, too, was checking his body.

"My ribs hurt. Not feeling too good."

Steve is a tough man. I knew he would not be exaggerating. I also knew that he, like me, would be shocked, and further injuries might come to light. Untangling myself from the rope was surprisingly difficult, but it was encouraging that Steve, too, was able to free himself. We both stood there contemplating our position.

I still had an incredibly strong vision of my family, and the close call had clearly had a deep emotional impact. I could feel tears welling up in my eyes. The snow platform on which we had come to a halt was about 200 feet below the ridge, and huge. We admitted later that an early thought that we both shared was what a pain it was to have to climb straight up to the crest when we had thought the day's exertions were almost over.

Practically, of course, they were. It was already 5 p.m. and the weather was far from settled. As we gathered our thoughts, it was obvious that the only sensible thing to do was to stay put for the night and assess our position in the morning.

It was disturbing to hear Steve making nasty gurgling and groaning noises in his sleep. Had he punctured a lung or got some other internal injury? There was no way of knowing, and frankly, little I could do but keep my fingers crossed.

To begin with, things looked bad in the morning, but it soon became clear that, once upright, he was able to move around quite easily, although unable to carry much beyond his sleeping bag. Distressing as it was, we abandoned all of our non-essential equipment. Some of it was very expensive. We must have felt that the situation was serious.

The first task was to get back to the crest of the ridge which, fortunately, was approachable at one point via a 50-55° snow/ice slope. (And I thought I'd be spared any more slopes like this on the trip.) We could see the others up on the ridge and headed diagonally up to them, gratefully taking up Andy's offer of a top rope, which meant that Steve and I could climb together and we wouldn't have to waste time belaying.

And so we met for the second time on the route. This time, though, there was no doubt about it. Going up was out of the question for Steve, and the decision to join together for the descent was easily made and unanimous.

In fact, the others were having their fair share of problems, too. Their food had now effectively run out and Andy appeared to have contracted secondary frostbite in his thumb. Steve, the acknowledged frostbite expert among us (one toe gone) confided in me that he thought that Andy could well have to have it amputated at the joint.

There were two possible ways of descending: abseil the face, or descend the south side of the mountain (reputedly snow slopes, with one or two abseils) and cross two largely unknown cols to return to our Advanced Base Camp. Steve was keen to abseil/be lowered (depending on the pain), whereas the rest of us voted for the south-side descent. This involved traversing along the knife-edged col between Changabang and Kalanka and then rising up for a few hundred feet to a system of glacial steps before descending diagonally across Kalanka's huge open south face.

By that evening, we were camped at the beginning of the glacial steps. The intervening day had involved a couple of slanting abseils on hard ice and some steep bottomless powder slopes. All in all, I was encouraged. Steve was able to walk strongly and didn't seem to be as badly impaired as he had on more awkward ground. Andy's thumb hardly seemed to affect him at all.

The next day looked to be the crucial descent day. If we could get down to the Changabang glacier we would at least have two options: either descend the glacier and try to walk out via the politically "closed" Rishiganga Gorge, or follow our original and preferred plan of crossing the Shipton and Bagini Cols to get back to Advanced Base. Either way, we needed good visibility and fine weather to descend safely to the glacier.

Luck was not with us. The morning dawned with intermittent cloud, and by the time we had descended 500 meters, it was snowing heavily and was impossible to see quite where we were going. Eventually, we came to a point where we would clearly have to abseil. It looked to be the edge of the giant couloir that Andy and Brendan had seen on their summit day and which we knew we had to descend into. But, in the conditions, we could not be sure.

We placed an ice screw and I abseiled. Almost immediately, it was clear that the situation was far from ideal. I was abseiling over the lip of a large serac, hanging free and gently rotating. After 100 feet or so, I landed on 70° rock slabs and, as these were exposed to anything falling out of the rather unstable-looking serac, I scrabbled 30 feet or so to one side out of the fall line.

Looking up, it was clear that, apart from the high chance of the rope jamming, this would be a potentially dangerous abseil for anyone with broken ribs or a badly frostbitten thumb. I secured myself and shouted up that the others should move the abseil rope across 30 feet or so to a position where a relatively straightforward abseil would be possible. I then disconnected myself from the abseil rope and settled down to wait.

It was still snowing heavily and small snow slides swished past intermittently. An ominous roaring sound gave warning of something more serious. I was anchored in a shallow groove and stuck my nose as firmly into the back as it would go. Heavy snow battered my helmet and shoulders. This was a nasty one, by far the heaviest so far; I prayed that there wouldn't be anything hard and painful mixed in with the snow. It probably lasted less than a minute, but felt an awful lot longer.

Eventually, though, the pressure eased and I was able to shake off the loose snow. I was getting cold now and wanted to put my duvet on but was wary of doing so in case further avalanches came down. I decided to wait until after the next abseil—but what was going on up above? Nothing seemed to be happening. I shouted up, "What's the problem? It's fine down here."

After several increasingly insistent shouts, Andy's voice penetrated the mist. "Is Brendan with you?"

This seemed a curious question. My alarm bells rang immediately. Of course he wasn't with me—the abseil rope hadn't even been moved.

"No!"

"Oh. . . . Fucking hell. He's gone!"

Brendan had been swept off by the avalanche while moving the abseil point. My heart was in my mouth immediately. I looked down hopefully. Below me, 300 to 400 feet of 70° mixed ground gave way to a couple thousand feet of snow slopes with occasional rock steps as much as a couple hundred feet high. There was no sign of Brendan and, realistically, no chance that he would have survived.

Our abseiling proceeded carefully and quietly. There was little conversation and much feeling for Brendan, his friends and family. This was a new experience for Andy and me. . . and I think we both sensed that its impact would grow rather than diminish as the days passed. Steve remained his usual stoic, reliable self, although he, too, was clearly moved. He hadn't really known Andy or Brendan before the trip, but only 30 minutes or so before the accident had commented to me "what nice blokes" they both were.

It was dark way before we reached a bivouac spot, and mid-morning the following day before we could see the whole of the area where Brendan probably ended up. There was no

*Sustad on the upper Changabang Glacier on the walk out, with Nanda Devi in the background.*
MICK FOWLER

sign of him at all. Andy shouted hopefully, but there was no response. The sun was hitting the face and the first snow slides of the day were already coming down. I was exhausted now. I think we all were. It may well have been beyond us, but if not, it would certainly have been unjustifiably dangerous to search through avalanche debris beneath a huge hot Himalayan face. And to what purpose? The most likely end result would have been further fatalities. With a sense of reluctance and with huge sadness, we turned our backs on the face and waded through the soft snow and searing heat of the Upper Changabang Glacier to a safe tent site.

In "normal" circumstances, we would have been able to relax and walk easily down to a Base Camp the following day. Here, though, the Nanda Devi Sanctuary below us offered little in the way of security. Not visited since the early 1980s, and protected by the difficult Rishi Ganga Gorge, it was pretty clear to us that the old tracks would be extremely difficult to follow and the bridges long since swept away. Even with the track in good condition, it used to be six porter days from a Base Camp at the foot of the Changabang Glacier to the road. In our condition, and with the track unused for more than ten years, it would doubtless take even longer, and could even prove impossible. We had enough mashed potatoes for only one day, and the exit on to the road was a long, long way from our Base Camp by the Bagini Glacier. The only alternative was to follow our original plan of traversing the mountain over Shipton Col and the Bagini Col to regain the Upper Bagini glacier. This had seemed a great idea back in Britain, but now, faced with the reality of two 1,500-foot climbs, it didn't seem quite so appealing. We spent the rest of the day lying flat out in the heat, talking about Brendan and staring at the horribly lengthy slope leading up to the Shipton Col.

The next two days drifted by in a sea of exertion. Andy was walking strongly, but the snow was crusty and exhausting. Progress was erratic and uncertain. We started walking at midnight, but even so, the snow would frequently almost take our weight only to have the crust break at the last moment. The resultant jarring was clearly excruciating for Steve.

The Shipton Col showed a vertical headwall to the Ramani Glacier on the other side, which involved more abseiling than the descent from Changabang to the Changabang Glacier. The Ramani Glacier itself, where Pete Boardman and Joe Tasker had based themselves in 1976, gave four or five miles of gradual height gain before the final 1,500-foot, 45-50° slope to the Bagini Col provided a huge sting in the tail. Several times I caught myself falling asleep draped over my ice axes. This was day 13 for Steve and me and day 15 for Andy. It struck me that this was how it would all finish if one carried on to the bitter end. . . just falling asleep and not waking up again. . . no pain. . . .

The sun caught us on the Bagini Col. Previously, we had been worried about our cold feet. Now, though, the problem was the heat, which had a debilitating effect on our bodies and softened the slope horribly. We frontpointed, slipped, slithered and finally got down to the flat snow of the Upper Bagini.

Steve and I argued over the best way to descend the final 500 feet to Advanced Base. It was all feeling a bit out of control; we never argue in the mountains. Even worse, we opted to take different lines. I scraped my hands nastily slipping down a steep icy section, and Steve twisted his leg coming down a slope of soft snow covering hard ice. Ten hours after leaving the Ramani Glacier, we finally crawled into our Advanced Base Camp. . . and food, safety, contentment. The greatest adventure of my life nearly over.

Back at Base Camp, we were reunited with Roger and Julie-Ann. They had only gotten back the day before us and had had their fair share of excitement, spending 11 days in all on the face. The weather had pinned them down on the third ice field and the spindrift had been such that they even had to abort one attempt at an abseil descent and climb back up to their bivouac spot, where they then spent four days desperately trying to stop the accumulating snow from pushing their tent off the mountain.

And what do I think of it all now? Andy's thumb has made a miraculous recovery. Steve's ribs (he'd broken four in several places) have healed well. . . but Brendan will never come back. I feel the loss of life and our near-miss have complicated my emotions and soured the sense of euphoric achievement that usually accompanies a Himalayan success. But I learned a lot and experienced a lot. As an adventure, the experience was unbeatable. The mountains need not worry. I love them still.

SUMMARY OF STATISTICS

AREA: Indian Himalaya

NEW ROUTE: The North Face (1600m) of Changabang (6864m), May 23-June 6, 1997, Andy Cave and Brendan Murphy (to summit), Mick Fowler and Steve Sustad, May 25-June 6 (to summit ridge). Murphy killed on June 3.

PERSONNEL: Roger Payne, Julie-Ann Clyma, Andy Cave, Brendan Murphy, Mick Fowler, Steve Sustad

# To Thalay With Love

*Through the shale band on Thalay Sagar's north face*

BY ANDREW LINDBLADE

I woke from a dream like a frightened child, startled, thinking I was safely home. The skitter-scatter of falling ice on the ledge brought me back to reality. We were at 21,100 feet, waiting for a storm to ease; I had been drifting in and out of sleep.

Athol Whimp handed me a brew. Staring at the stormfly, I noticed my gloves hanging from a strap, frozen as if in rigor mortis by the deep cold night. I quickly unclipped them and thrust them under my legs. As my hand passed the hanging stove, its luxurious warmth served as a distinct reminder of a world left far behind. We had cast out from the ground several days back, hoping to climb the north face of Thalay Sagar directly through the notorious shale band to the summit. We talked about our progress. We were both keen to get higher and see the headwall at close quarters for the first time.

The two of us had attempted a line on the 4,950-foot face in 1996. Extreme cold and constant spindrift avalanches finally forced us to retreat from 21,500 feet. Down in Base Camp after our descent, Athol said he was coming back in '97. I stared into the cooker flame, nursing frostbitten toes that luckily had escaped circulatory shutdown. I admired his fortitude, and hoped I would want to return as well. But sitting there, I was immersed in doubt.

We went to Mt. Cook, New Zealand, in late June, getting in a couple of fine routes and a -15°C night out with no gear on the summit. After two weeks, we walked back down the Hooker Glacier, battered artillery in our packs and hammered toes in our plastics. Deep inside, I struggled with Thalay. Did I really have what it would take to succeed on the north face? We had been whipped there in '96; I remembered the desperation of staring up a massive wall that moved rapidly in and out of storm as we rigged the abseil that sealed our failure. I suffered from a lack of belief in myself.

How easily fooled one can be; how quickly the memories become devoid of pain. Back in Melbourne, the dreary weight of winter made the flanks of Thalay Sagar seem like a shimmering paradise. Running through the dark streets of the city at night, I realized that I really did want it. The desire had been moving through me ever since we walked out of base camp. I just hadn't tuned into it, letting graver concerns—like dying—dominate my mind instead.

July, 1997. As I approached Base Camp, the north face appeared over the top of the moraine wall. My eyes zoomed straight to our proposed route up the face's central couloir. Kitty Calhoun and Jay Smith had reached 20,900 feet on this line in 1996. It had been Kitty's second attempt; in 1986 she and Andy Selters spent eight days in their ledge at nearly 21,000 feet before abseiling off, starved and debilitated. Walking toward Base Camp, the sounds of the shifting glacial rock underfoot punctuated my tiny presence. Higher above me, in Base Camp, Athol and Patricia awaited my arrival. It felt strange, like amplified deja-vu, to be back.

We studied the north face through binoculars, formulating various strategies for our ascent while we acclimatized. Every time you looked up, a foreshortened Thalay looked back. During sunset, the roaring orange light would pick up detail on the face that was totally invisible at other times. Sometimes the shale headwall a kilometer above our heads looked so close

*The north face of Thalay Sagar, showing the 1997 Australian line.* JAY SMITH

you could touch it. At other times, as I walked up the glacier with another load, I'd look up to see the north face looming high above, and be struck with the sensation that we actually might stand up there on the summit snows, two little black dots in their own crazy world.

We adapted more to the thinner air each day. Patricia, the expedition doctor, took daily stats on our respiration, pulses, and blood pressure, and prepared little medical emergency bags for us in case things went ballistic on the face. From the latter half of August through the first ten days of September, the monsoon adhered to its daily cycle, snowing nearly every day—a good thing, considering we were still acclimatizing, carrying equipment up, and fine-tuning our personal gear. Some mornings were deliciously snap frozen; on others, we sank knee-deep. In between getting the 300 pounds of equipment and supplies up from Camp I, we read and threw laps on Patricia's walkman. We drank like fish. Took our Diamox. Slept. And waited.

We positioned ourselves well for launching up the face, fixing about 650 feet of line onto the icefield from a gear cache just above a 'schrund. Camp II sits on a small plateau at the edge of an icefall. The slopes between Camp II and the icefield are avalanche-prone; Jay and Kitty had been hit there while making their final abseils off the face in 1996. We met up with them on the debris the following day; they were very pleased to be alive. The slopes had ripped early this season, too, and gradually were loading up again with more and more snow. It was with committed resignation that we went up and down this section.

On September 11, we scampered down to Base Camp in swirling snow and poor visibility. The following morning dawned fine; we headed back up again, relaxed and certain. This was it—time to get the runs on the board. Patricia walked with us to the corner, where we hugged her goodbye under a serenely beautiful sky. I could see the concern in her eyes. I turned and drifted away as she said goodbye to Athol. Soon I heard Athol's ski poles on the moraine, and we cruised across, roving through the glacial desert, then up the ridge toward Camp II.

"We smoked that," said Athol as we pulled into Camp II. It was comforting to know we were well acclimatized and very fit on the day before the big effort.

When the sun began to get dim on September 13, we mobilized. At 10 p.m., we arrived at the beginning of the icefield at 18,700 feet and erected the ledge. Lying back after a hot brew, we listened as the sporadic showers of ice and spindrift fell down the face, delivering glancing blows to the ledge. We were fixing line up the final section of the icefield the next day when a piece of falling ice slammed into my left jaw with fierce intensity. It felt as though I'd been decked by the school thug. As I jumared up toward Athol, the pain gradually turning numb, I had the thought that my boyhood dreams of being a soldier were finally being fulfilled on a frozen wall in the middle of nowhere.

Leading up the final 300 feet of the icefield, my throat felt like it was cut inside, and with a mouth devoid of moisture, breathing was painful. I pulled up to meet a smooth granite wall, black and white dots glittering over a yellow blankness. I dropped down slightly and followed the toe of the wall, patiently trying to find a crack to make an anchor, scraping wherever a seam looked likely. "Fuck this," I grumbled, pulling my hood over my helmet as a shower of loose, snowy crystals made their way down the wall. Eventually, a slight fissure in the rock yielded a thin, tapered slot, good for a knifeblade. The placement was okay, but I was concerned about the rock. Together with my tools, it would have to do.

Athol jumared up, and I looked into the couloir as far as I could while catching my breath between hauling stints. Then, like a car-crash dream, it felt as if we were really doing it, slowly leaving earth, gaining momentum, moving through space. But, of course, it was nothing like space; and with a big rack to cover the options for the unknown headwall, a ledge, food and fuel, and the cold, we couldn't move like we would in the Alps.

*Andrew Lindblade at the top of the icefield at 20,000 feet.* ATHOL WHIMP

After a brief pause at the belay, Athol moved up, following the toe of the buttress for as long as possible before heading out on steep, unconsolidated snow over hard ice. He ran it out at least 150 feet before getting a screw in at the beginning of the steeper bulges. By carefully tracking the thicker ice, he avoided bottoming his tools on the granite. From my frigid, semi-hanging stance at the toe of the buttress, I watched him tie a screw off and abseil as the evening shadows lengthened.

It was a still, clear evening as we abseiled to the portaledge. Small, low clouds drifted slowly across from the Jogin peaks, evaporating by the time they reached us. In the morning we drank coffee and hot energy drinks, then dressed one after another in the 'ledge and began jumaring and hauling, throwing our body weight onto the anchor to bring up the ledge and haul bag.

We climbed on two 300-foot 8mm statics, which minimized anchors and the time it took to get them. Anchors were proving tiresome work; it often would take as long to get one in as it did to lead a pitch. Promising seams would blank out, and decent cracks always belonged to loose flakes. But eventually, after patiently scraping and searching in the right places, a placement would reveal itself. In one spot, under a build-up of ice, we found a fixed stopper from Jay and Kitty the year before.

From the end of the fixed line at 20,000 feet, Athol led up steep polished ice occasionally spread thin over granite. The haul bag and ledge hung next to me. At the end of the pitch, as Athol hauled, I helped the bag and ledge as they caught against the ice, untwisting the haul line from the other rope.

It was good to move, even if it was desperately hard work. The cold in the couloir had a great sense of permanence about it, and we crawled into the ledge at 20,500 feet on our third night like two dogs chained to our kennels during a long winter. We called this site Camp Nothing. Cold, dark and eerie, there was nothing there for us.

The next morning, after the usual three hours of melting ice and drinking, we packed the

*Looking down on the portaledge camp in the upper couloir (ca. 21,000').* Athol Whimp

ledge and headed up. We were positioned at the base of the steepest section of the couloir. Athol craned his neck and studied the line before moving up on his front points, his movement focused and committed. Within a few meters the couloir went vertical, and he grappled with rotten ice, getting only poor screws for protection. I could sense him gritting his teeth, fighting his way up a seemingly endless vertical ice ribbon, his tools occasionally blowing out on the rock at the ribbon's edge.

Finally, he spied an anchor on the left wall of the couloir. A delicate few moves left and he clipped in. As I jumared the pitch, I unweighted the rope to unclip from several sideways-tensioned pieces. A swing followed the unclipping, then another; I couldn't see anything; spindrift avalanches blasted down the couloir, creating their own vicious vortexes of wind. Somehow, eventually, I joined Athol at the anchor.

We hung there, waiting for a break in the storm. Every time we thought it'd clear up, it got worse. We shivered and beat our hands, adjusted our feet (though there's only so many ways you can put your front points in), and shook the spindrift build-up off our one-piece suits. Our hoods were up, and as I briefly glanced at Athol, I saw a determination and calmness in his eyes that I had seen before. It lent me a sincere confidence, and I burrowed my head into my shoulders. There was a lot of kick in us yet.

When things settled down a bit, Athol headed off, valiantly tackling the fluted pillars of ice that guarded the final run to the end of the couloir. My thoughts turned to Kitty and Jay higher in the couloir as I looted a couple of biners stamped "KC" and "JS" that were clipped to two ice screws. In the ledge that night, we looked at the faded, stamped impressions of their initials, marveling at the fact that there were at least two other people we knew who were crazy enough to come up here. We added ice to the pot, piece by piece, hoping they were sitting in warm cafes and climbing in the sun somewhere in America.

By the end of the day, we had established the ledge on two ice screws at 21,100 feet. We were wasted and drained by a day of being avalanched; we both nearly passed out with the first brews in our hands. We fed ice to the pot in a bid to keep drinking, and snacked on Power Bars. We couldn't muster the energy to eat anything else. We woke to the sound of spindrift ripping down the face, then drifted off to sleep again. We drank more, and, half-asleep, waited for the weather to clear.

That afternoon, we fixed 300 feet up the ice—and found ourselves at the end of the couloir. We were both slightly intoxicated as we hung on the anchor at 21,400 feet, the immense shale headwall spread out above us, the sun just dropped over the horizon. What an outrageous sight! The whole place was going off, the way mountains do, and up here, with the headwall and summit within some sort of reach, all we wanted was more good weather. We cinched our suits snug, and rapped to the portaledge.

Athol brought out a black-and-white photo of the face, and as we lay in our bags, he made calculations about our altitude and how far we had to go. Based on our progress, we thought it looked pretty good—but never underestimate a mountain. We arrived at the 21,400-foot anchor the next day and anchored the portaledge, then followed with a big brew session, chocolate and some energy bars. While Athol was sitting back in the ledge admiring the view of Base Camp and beyond, a lone rock hurtled down from above, went through the open door of the ledge, and scored him in the leg. After a pain-induced expletive, we both made the observation that he was lucky not to have been hit in the head.

We set out to fix line up to the shale band that afternoon. Earlier, Athol had fixed 150 feet up a snow ramp from the portaledge. From this point, I climbed toward a huge hanging granite tower. It was classic alpine terrain under a dark blue Himalayan sky: I moved up and slightly left on unconsolidated snow over hard ice, hoping a small gully higher up would give us an entry onto the tower. I was keen to get Athol's opinion. After reaching the end of a fantastic mixed gully, I tied the rope off on a pin and two friends and yelled for Athol to jumar.

When he joined me, we quickly decided on the best line to take. I headed off again, trying to move as fast as possible, while the sun dipped toward the horizon. I tackled a steep section of iron-hard ice, my legs screaming for it to relent. I felt utterly exhausted. A slight rest at the beginning of the ramp leading up the back of the hanging tower was cut short by the dying light. I had to move. I swung my left tool high and landed it in thin ice, the tip hard up on the rock. I couldn't get it any higher; an overhanging wall on the left prevented me from standing straight. Suddenly, as I struck a calculated blow with my right tool, it glanced off the granite, leaving my arm feeling flimsy and pathetic, and the rest of me hideously nauseated.

"Slow it down, Andy," I told myself. My crampons were scratching on the rock as I somehow managed to get a friend in a crack on the left. In the suffocating confines of the corner, snow fell in my face as I scraped around for a crack to torque a tool in. I stepped up high on my right points, waiting for something to blow out.

Finally, I slammed in a couple of friends and tied the rope off. As I began abseiling in the darkness, I looked down the vaunting abyss of the north face and saw the yellow dot of Athol's headlamp growing smaller as he descended to the portaledge.

We were at the top of the fixed line by 10 a.m. When I arrived at the anchor, Athol was racked and ready to go. He made the first few moves, his feet on solid granite, his hands on loose, slate-like shale. He soon realized he needed to cross at least two steep gully systems to gain the line leading to the final corner system. I could hear his crampons scrape over the rock as small layers of ice gave way. After negotiating some very loose, grim terrain with inadequate protection, severe rope drag forced him to belay. I started jumaring under a cloudless sky, my shivering slowly giving way to the generation of body warmth. The temperature hovered at about -20°C; even with chemical warmers in our gloves and boots, we were still freezing cold.

Athol was already shivering when I joined him at the belay, and keen to keep going. I handed him the rack as we traded words about our progress. Neither of us had the energy to say much. Athol moved into a delicate tension traverse and loose, unpredictable dry-tooling, eventually landing at a stance. The next few moves were truly horrible: An undercling on a loose block with one hand allowed him to reach high with the other before gaining a small corner in which he torqued both tools to move up. It was with luxurious relief that I heard him yell, "safe!" He had dealt with the 300 feet in one pitch—the most awesome display of climbing I'd ever seen. I knew that with that much rope out we must be very close to the snowfields.

I jumared fast, slowing down a bit for some tenuous freehanging moments with the rope over layers of breaking shale. By this stage, the ropes had taken a hammering, and I noticed as I slid the jumars up that we were into the core at a couple of spots. I pulled over the lip to see Athol with a smile on his face standing at the best belay on the wall. As I stood trying to get my breath back from 300 feet of flat-out jumaring, Athol was already away, negotiating the final chimney. We were keen to top out before dark.

We climbed the summit snowfields while snow fell in isolated patches, swirling around us at random and sliding down the snow cap in loose sheets. The world dropped away; we knew we would do it. Athol took my hand as I stepped on top, and I felt an enormous love and respect for him. We stood on the summit at 5:45 p.m., barely able to smile, snapping photos in the fading light, watching the streams of evening sunlight and fields of weightless, falling snow as they moved in and out of the beautiful scene.

We put on insulated jackets under our suits, inserted fresh hand warmers in our gloves, and started down. At the first abseil anchor, we rigged our headlamps and began descending through the inky darkness. By 10 p.m., we were inside the portaledge brewing up, swearing like crazy, immensely relieved we'd done the job. We could hardly believe our luck at not getting a rope stuck. We talked about how we'd rip through the abseiling and be off the wall the next day.

We were abseiling with the haul bag and portaledge by midday—just as a grim-looking storm boiled up on the opposite side of the glacier. A stuck rope cost us at least an hour. Spindrift began to avalanche us in the couloir, slamming us in regular, then constant, barrages. The only consolation was that we were on the way down. At one point, I nearly abseiled past Athol, who was only a few meters away, so poor was visibility and sound. When would the torture end?

As we abseiled and lowered the ledge and haulbag down the icefield and onto the lower snowslopes, darkness bled across the sky quicker than we wanted. We continued down, stripping our fixed line from the face as we went. Several times the ledge and haul bag got tangled in the chaos of rope and darkness. It would have been easy to drop the lot, but we persevered, somehow improvising when the haul bag ended up hanging short of an anchor and we couldn't hear each other, our voices suffocated by the magnitude of the snowfields. We were severely depleted; only a focused effort maintained the discipline and kept our technique wrapped tight as we descended the avalanche slopes. Camp II—and flat ground—was only an hour away.

At 9:30, we pulled into camp, staggering around like drunks. We were hardly able to stand up. I screamed out, feeling as if I were a shadow of my real self. We cranked the cookers full bore and were soon pouring mug after mug of hot liquid down our starving gullets. Even after

*In the shale band's final chimney (ca. 22,100').* ATHOL WHIMP

a week of eating energy bars, it was all we could manage to force down.

We stumbled across the glacier the following afternoon, wondering where Patricia might be, and whether Tristram and Erik had arrived. Then, in the distance, we saw Patricia on the moraine ridge. I dropped back a bit as we approached her. I heard Ath say "yes," and she jumped up and down, hugging Athol, then me.

As we walked the final hour to Base Camp, the mountain was in storm again. I thought of warmth and home, of the people I love so dearly. It brought a few tears to my eyes, but before they had a chance to dry, the wind had picked them up and carried them away.

*Andrew Lindblade, Bell (the cook) and Athol Whimp in base camp after the ascent.* PATRICIA GALANOPOULOS

SUMMARY OF STATISTICS

AREA: Indian Himalaya

NEW ROUTE: The North Face (VII 5.9 WI5, 4,950') of Thalay Sagar (22,650'), September 13-20, 1997, Athol Whimp and Andrew Lindblade

PERSONNEL: Andrew Lindblade, Athol Whimp, Patricia Galanopoulos, Tristram Whimp, Erik Pootjes

# University Peak

*The wild card of the Wrangell-St. Elias*

BY CARLOS BUHLER

**M**y eyes traced our complicated route through the last problematic crevasses. Suddenly, the peaceful silence on the glacier was interrupted by the distant whine of an approaching Supercub airplane. This hour, 11 a.m. on May 22, 1995, was the conclusion of our close shave on Mt. Bear in the Wrangell-St. Elias mountains of Alaska. Ruedi Homberger was going to live through his battle with pulmonary edema. Our pilot, Paul Claus, had been worried about us for days. We had had poor weather, and Paul had not found a sign of us where we had agreed to meet. Searching the north side of the mountain in his plane, Paul had finally found us on a different glacier. As long as these clouds didn't close back in, Paul's dad, John, would appear soon in the Supercub and fetch me off the crevasse-infested glacier we'd hung out on for the last three days of storm and cloud. Hans and Ruedi, scooped up in Paul's first plane load, would be taking saunas at the lodge by now. I took in my surroundings with one last look up the icefall we'd skied through three days earlier. This land of extraordinary mountains was beautiful. Unique. Vast. And somewhat beyond the consciousness of most climbers outside Alaska's borders.

Sitting atop my rucksack in the Supercub, legs wrapped around the seat in front of me, I crouched behind John, my pilot. I felt as though I was on a toboggan ride with my brothers when I was eight. John banked the plane to the right and we came within spittin' distance of the gigantic walls of University Peak. I strained to hear the words he yelled to me over the roar of the engine: "Wha'da ya think of the south face?"

I knew why he was asking. His son, Paul, dreamed of climbing it.

"Looks kinda exposed!" I yelled into John's ear. "The south face looks kinda. . . ." I thought about it a second longer. "Featureless!"

University Peak is the wild card mountain of the entire area north of the Chitina Glacier — perhaps of the entire Wrangell-St. Elias range. The mountain, which sits in plain view along the popular "flight corridor" for all those who pass through on their way to the more prominent summits of St. Elias and Logan, had been climbed only once. University Peak reminds me of Ama Dablam's position in Nepal's Khumbu Valley. How many climbers passing Ama Dablam's flanks on their way to Everest have secretly wished they were climbing something as beautiful and alluring as those steep and attractive lines?

The "big" peaks of the Wrangell-St. Elias Range, like the 8000ers in Asia, beckon most visitors, for they are truly among the mightiest peaks of the Western Hemisphere. These splendid challenges in Alaska and Canada that surpass 17,000 feet in altitude offer some of the finest high-altitude mountaineering anywhere. Yet University Peak (14,800') takes no second place. There are no easy lines on the mountain. There are no "walk-ups" for the inexperienced mountaineer. The rounded summit ice cap hovers 8,500 feet above the eastern and southern glaciers that drain the area. The south face sweeps abruptly upward off a level glacier to the summit, forming a massive headwall to the valley that drains the south side of the peak. The more complex east flank rises in a similar uninterrupted angle to the ice cap's hanging seracs, about 1,000 feet below the high point.

The north face is a different story, but no less puzzling. The majestic north ridge drops off the mountain with nearly the same determination as its southern counterparts, but its plunge is caught early by a rising chaos of icefalls that meet at the feature's base. These churning icebergs ultimately bring the northern and western faces's bergschrunds about 4,000 feet higher than their southern and eastern cousins. But to reach those higher bergschrunds, that is a different story! A mile or more of tangled icefalls wrapping around to the east and west would discourage all but the most determined maniacs.

And the riddle is only half-solved by the ascent line. If one is determined enough to get up one of the flanks of University Peak, a simple question remains: Where the hell would you descend?

This certainly was uppermost in my mind as I swept my eyes along the gigantic features. I looked out across the south face, feeling like I was sitting too close to the screen in one of those IMAX cinemas. . . .

But wait! What's that? We were just passing around from the east to the south when an eastern-facing rib grabbed my attention. Wow! It was attractive! My eyes followed it from the ground floor at 6,500 feet to a balcony four-fifths of the way up the mountain. The seracs that formed the balcony hung discouragingly over the face. But the rib. . . .

Then it was gone out of sight, and we were around the corner and passing the south face. John's question hung in my mind.

"There's no place to hide on the southern flank," I thought to myself as I tried to imagine a storm catching me part way up the wall. Gulp! I didn't want to think about the waves of snow that would sweep down the face in the event of even a little afternoon snow squall. Maybe one could climb it in a long day, without bivouac gear. . . . But where would you descend? Caught out on top of University Peak in a storm suddenly seemed an ugly proposition. You might have to wait for days to get down those avalanche-laden walls. I didn't even want to imagine it.

There was no need. Before I knew it, I was back behind my desk in Idaho.

A year later, back at the Ultima Thule Lodge in 1996, Charlie Sassara and I were in a position to think about University Peak again. With our friends, we had just made the first ascent of Mt. Miller in the short time of 48 hours. We were sitting around the meal table at the lodge with Paul and Ruedi, our companions from the previous day's ascent. The east flank of University Peak, and that vague memory of a line on the buttress, again came to mind.

Charlie had noticed it, too. Little had escaped his eye over the years. He had flown around the mountain umpteen times in his wanderings throughout the range. Now, however, we had time to kill before I left Alaska, and the weather was perfect.

"You'll never get up that thing, Charlie. It's too much to bite off," Paul told us. We both squirmed with his comment. Mt. Miller had been no epic, but it had been no cakewalk, either. All of us realized how lucky we'd been just getting up Miller. University's east face was many magnitudes of difficulty and commitment beyond what we'd just experienced. Not being very familiar with Alaskan climbing, I was afraid to offer a counter judgment. The descent off University still dogged my mind. The mountain had had only that one 1955 ascent of the north ridge in all its history. I still didn't understand how the mountain was laid out, much less what the first ascent had involved. I knew it couldn't have been easy since no one had repeated it in 40 years. And not for a lack of interest among the locals!

Ultimately, with Paul's blessing and assistance, we went waterfall climbing for the rest of the week. Then I was gone, and another year rolled by.

*The east face of University Peak, showing the Buhler-Sassara line of ascent.* RUEDI HOMBERGER

In the winter of 1996-97 Charlie and I made the proposal to take a closer look at University
Peak in the spring. So much depended on conditions, and our moods, that neither of us
wanted to commit early to a full-on attempt.

When spring rolled around, I joined Charlie, his wife Siri, and another Alaskan couple,
Sean and Michelle, for five fun-filled days making ski tours and the first ascent of an 11,000-
plus-foot peak we named Mt. Benkin (after Igor Benkin, the Russian who had died while
descending with me on the North Ridge of K2 nine months earlier). After a night at the Ultima
Thule Lodge, Charlie and I were eyeing the weather like coiled cobras watching a flute play-
er. Paul was visibly nervous. He now knew a lot more than we did about University Peak.

Two weeks before I flew to Alaska, Paul, Ruedi, Dave Staeheli and Danny Kost had made
the second ascent of the mountain via the first ascent line of the north ridge. Their tremendous
achievement had given them a clear understanding of the north flank. Complicated route-finding through seracs, hidden crevasses, and avalanche-laden slopes on the ridge had dogged
their climb. One of the team had disappeared into a hole so suddenly and deeply that they had
feared the worst. Fortunately, he was unhurt and they had continued their ascent. When I
asked Ruedi whether we would be able to find our way down their ascent route having never
set foot on it, he was doubtful about our chances.

Nevertheless, he penned out a diagram showing the main features of the ridge. The real
breakthrough had come with the discovery that Paul could land his Supercub on a small pocket glacier at 10,000 feet just left of the base of the north ridge. This single achievement meant
that literally days of torture in the Western Glacier's icefall could be bypassed. It was akin to
landing a plane in the Western Cwm of Everest, thus avoiding the work of the Khumbu Icefall.

The combination of their ascent of the north ridge in one long 15-hour day, and the fact
that Paul would be the pilot who would land on that hanging glacier at 10,000 feet below the
ridge to take us home, gave us a vein of hope we hadn't felt before. We might get stuck for
days trying to get down the north ridge, but if we made it somehow, we had a real good chance
of getting air-lifted out when the weather permitted, avoiding the mind-boggling icefalls that
encircled the mountain's northern flanks.

Paul, having squeezed under a blanket of clouds that did not look promising, dropped me
off first below the east face. I had visions of spending a couple of nights by myself before
Charlie could get in and grumbled at being chosen first. My worries were unnecessary, however, as Paul soon delivered Charlie to our camp, 6,000 feet beneath the towering east wall of
University.

We spent the next day trying to get a feel for the place. My memory of the rib was hazy
at best—and what I saw now was nothing like what I remembered from the air. Our rib was
really a corner of the eastern flank. While the lower part of the face appeared to be moderate
snow climbing, a nasty mixed section above a steep rock wall blocked the route about a third
of the way up. To get a closer look, we packed a load of food plus a bit of gear and skied a
mile up the cwm to the base of the face.

Finding a continuous snow gully on the far northern side of the lower rock buttress made
our day. We stomped 1,500 feet up the 45° couloir and cached our loads under a small rock
outcrop at the base of a steeper, fluted ice face.

We could clearly see that anything that broke free from the serac a vertical mile above us
would surely wipe us out. The only solution seemed to be to trend leftward toward the rib and
hope that its modest size would protect us from any falling debris.

Our descent back to glacier camp was quick and simple. For the time being, we could feel
that the lower 2,000 feet of the face were climbable and in reasonably good condition.

Never wanting to rush into things, we set off the next day with the rest of our gear at about

*Charlie Sassara at the second bivouac.* CARLOS BUHLER

noon. A mile up the glacier, Paul flew into the valley, landed, and taxied his plane to within 50 meters of us.

"Are you ready to come home now?" he grinned. "I figured you'd seen enough of that serac. I didn't want to keep you waiting around too long."

"We're just going up now. We've got four days of food, five in a pinch." We tried to sound confident. He was a little surprised with our decision.

In my mind, it was not the instability of the serac barrier 7,000 feet over our heads that hung like an ox yoke over my shoulders; it was the uncertainty of the descent on the north ridge, literally miles away from our present position. Yes, the glacier had some huge ice blocks imbedded in it—but they didn't appear to be from recent releases. And besides, we figured we could climb on the very left-hand edge of the face, thereby avoiding most of the danger of the serac band.

Was I justifying this whole climb without reason? I tried to be honest with myself. There were a dozen reasons to back out now, not the least of which was that Paul was standing there with his Supercub. But we figured we'd regret it later. Nothing was stopping us as far as the cache, and we'd learn nothing if we didn't take a real look now. Paul conveyed a few more brief details about the north ridge, then took off with the promise that he'd be back in a cou-

*Sassara at the top of the rock spur below Camp III.* CARLOS BUHLER

ple more days to see how we were doing.

I would kick myself for the next six days for not asking more questions about his splendid ascent of the north ridge three weeks before. A more thorough understanding of our proposed descent route couldn't have come from a better source.

By evening, we had cut a platform out of the largest snow fluting we could find and settled into our bivouac tent. The nearness of solid ice to the surface depressed us; our little ledge was way more work than expected and smaller than we'd hoped for. But it would get us through the night.

Sometime that evening, it began to snow heavily. By morning, we had about five fresh inches, and it was not letting up. Suddenly, those huge slopes above us were a lot more meaningful.

We began a waiting game of nerves and determination. It snowed for several more hours. Stopped. Then began again. Our snow gully was undoubtedly building up beneath us. If we decided to go down, we knew it had to be soon. If we had any chance at all to continue, it would have to stop snowing fairly quickly.

The day lulled us on. Our four- to five-day food supply didn't allow for much in the way of storm days. We ate anyway, resigned to the fact that the prospects didn't look very promising. We'd spend one more night and see what the next day brought.

I'm not sure if I was happy or not to see blue skies in the morning. It meant we would go upward; from above this bivouac, there would be far more trouble should we have to descend. It was the first of several layers of commitments we would be forced to make. As we packed up the gear, we noted that innumerable small avalanches had swept the 60° runnels to both sides of the Peruvian-style fluting we were on. "Good decision to put it here," I mused to myself. "But what if something really big cuts loose above?" I was under no illusions.

The day's climbing took us up steeply to the actual rib and across it to its less dramatic southern exposure. Several rope lengths higher, we made a 50-meter rappel off the crest of the rib to the south and continued the ascent on the flank less threatened by serac avalanches. This was the second rather committing move on the face. Climbing back up onto the rib in the event of a retreat would be troublesome. Nevertheless, we hoped that this line would avoid the majority of the rock step and severe mixed climbing we had seen from below.

A day and a half later, we realized we'd chosen correctly. At a point perhaps 1,500 feet higher than our rappel, we regained the actual knife edge of the buttress by following a steep snow band back right until it ended on mixed ground among the spectacular towers about mid-height on the face. By following the exposed rock and mixed rib, we gained the upper ice fields by the end of the fourth day. With the mixed section beneath us, the way above looked open as far as the seracs.

As promised, we had repeated visits by Paul. He brought by a variety of guests in his plane who were out for a tourist visit to the lodge. It seems that we had become the week's major sightseeing attraction. So small and insignificant did we appear against the 8,500-foot wall of the mountain that people had trouble believing we were actual living creatures until they saw us move. It must have been a shocking sight for a particular couple from Atlanta that had never been to the mountains before, much less witnessed a couple of people clinging to the side of one!

But from our perspective, it all meant one thing: So long as Paul flew in to see how we were doing, we knew the weather was basically settled. Though at times we could only hear the whine of his engine due to local cloud build-up on the mountain, the tell-tale buzz was like music to our ears. No other weather report could have been more accurate or more welcome.

By the end of the fifth day, our food supply was running low. The huge serac barrier loomed above us and stretched to our right for a quarter of a mile across a vast, 55° rock-hard ice field. It was late in the day; we were one-and-a-half pitches below the vertical ice, and it didn't look like the 250-foot barrier would offer an easy way through. Frantically, we scouted about for a place to carve a platform. The bullet-proof ice slope we were on offered no hope of chopping a ledge. It was looking like we were going to spend a night hanging from a couple of ice screws when a slight kink in the knife-edged rib brought us the gift we'd been praying for. We chopped down five feet of the rib through snow and eventually created a platform that was a good four to five feet wide.

Our evening was saved; we'd be able to rehydrate and get some rest. It looked as though we'd need it for the next bit of climbing.

It's been socked in since dawn. There's light snow falling. It looks as though the one spot we can get through the seracs is about 300 feet to the right of us. Thank God we found this place to spend the night! It looks like there's no other place whatsoever where we could have laid down. . . .

. . . Considering we don't have any food left, I feel relatively good. We ought to at least get through the steep ice and onto the summit cap today. I won't push my expectations. I just want to get through that wall of ice that's been pressing down on my mind for the past four days. . . .

. . . Snap! Ah, shit. Broke the pick off. It must be colder out than I thought. Better get Charlie's. I'll climb back to that first ice screw. . . .

. . . Damn, he's taking his time on that ice. I can't even see him in this heavy cloud. Relax,

*Sassara leading out beneath the summit serac.* CARLOS BUHLER

relax. You're going to be climbing in no time. Let him work it out. All you gotta do is jug the line. . . .

. . . Yuk. I hate being out here beneath this thing. Two million tons of ice over my head and not a place to hide. Just stay put up there, serac. Now is not the time to loosen up. . . .

. . . It's going to be hell trying to find our way up this ice cap. Tons of crevasses and me with no idea how the summit is laid out. We could wander around for days looking for the way down. I suppose we better just dig in and sit until the weather clears and we can see something. Better that than trying to pull ourselves out of some epic hole that one of us falls into. . . .

. . . This would be a terrific place to get a photo if we could see something. It's gotta be exposed on this serac. Yikes! We're 7,000 feet off the floor and there's nothing but air under my ass and a Swiss cheese wall of ice above me at a 45° overhanging angle. Please let there be some way over to the left. . . .

. . . .Must weigh about 100,000 tons. I'm going to be glad when I'm out from under this shit. . . .

. . . I can't make this move with my pack on. The axe might pull through this soft névé and bingo—I'm flying. No, nooo. Come back down. Take the pack off and don't stick your neck out here. You're too close to the top now. You'd never forgive yourself if you peeled off now. . . .

. . . Another lost hour. We don't have the time. I could get a screw in this rock-hard over-hanging ice bulge to the right. No, I don't think so—it's right over Charlie's belay. It would be just my luck to crack it with a screw placement. Damn serac ice is so brittle. I'll be lucky

*On the summit.* CHARLIE SASSARA

not to break another pick off. . . .

. . . Sound of a plane out there in the cloud. Far out—it's gotta be Paul. Far out. Hot damn. He be flyin'! Is that ever great news. This has got to be just a localized storm. Yahoo. Come on, man, break! Show him where we are. Maybe he can land that thing on the summit. Now that would be good. Hey, they do it in the Alps, don't they? I'm not proud. . . .

. . .This has got to be the top. Big place up here. Where the hell am I coming up on this thing? Where is the north ridge gonna be? This does not look simple. Big rounded ice cap. We better get the hell out of here before it socks back in completely and we're stuck up here for a week. . . .

. . . Is that a wand? Yes—a Ruedi wand! Pretty funny. It'd be great if they had it wanded all the way down.

Dream on, Buhler. . . .

. . . Afternoon light is something else up here. Big white and black piles of clouds. A bit of blue breaking through, and streaks of white beams. Incredible contrast of dark and light. Man, it coulda snowed all day. . . .

. . . Whoa! There's that engine again! He's comin' back to look for us. Dang, he must get be gettin' a deal on plane fuel! I can't believe it. Maybe he's gonna actually try and land the thing. Now that would be something to talk about. . . .

. . . Circles and circles. He's seen us. . . . Damn, he's coming in close!! Who's that? Shit, it's Ruedi! They must be off Logan. Couldn't mistake that hairdo anywhere. . . .

. . . They're comin around again. Window's open. . . something's flying out. . . . Bounce, bounce. . . one red stuff sack down the south face. Don't think I'll chase that one down. Coming again. Second attempt. Window open. That smilin' face. . . . Bingo—direct hit! Man, it's dinner! What service! Fifty feet from us and . . . holy shit—it's gonna be a great night after all. Special delivery, Alaska style. All right! Those Domino's pizza delivery boys would be

jealous. . . .

. . . Why didn't I listen to those guys more closely on the descent. I'm sooo stupid. What on earth were you thinking about? These slopes are unbelievably avalanche prone. That's all we need, to get swept off now. . . .

. . . Back up, back up. This just isn't going to go. This slope's too likely to slide. We gotta find another way down the ridge. There's gotta be another way around these ice cliffs and crevasses. . . .

. . . Let's just spend the night here. It's been enough for one day. We're still alive. How's about calling it a day. We've got fuel. We've got our air-dropped dinner . . . we got through the damn serac wall. It's pretty damn good weather considering we started up this thing a week ago. . . .

. . . That's what stuff sacks are really for: rappel anchors. Oh, yes, that looks solid. You could rap a tank off that ol' bag in the snow. . . .

. . . We're almost down now. Spectacular. Spectacular. We'd be a week trying to pick our way down either one of these icefalls. There's the smiling crevasse face on the glacier. Landing strip, extraordinaire. Can see that tent there, too. Ha, ha, ha. Food. Yes! That big curved crevasse with ice blocks looks like a smilin' face just calling us home to dinner. . . .

. . . Oh, man, I can smell those home-baked oatmeal raisin cookies already. We're gonna get down to that landing zone today! Wouldn't that be incredible if Paul came in today to check us out. But shit, it's socked in. Doubt he'd be landing in that stuff. No worries—let's just not get caught in this last 1,000-foot 35° slope. I hate these. Big 'ol traverse we're making is just about perfect to cut and release this mama. Stay close to the top; go for those seracs and blocks of ice. Maybe they'll anchor this horrendous slope. . . .

. . . Ooohh—there's a hum in the air. . . quiet. . . . Yeah! That's the Supercub!! He's comin' in to look for us. Hot shit. I think I love that guy. Too many more climbs like this and he's going to go bankrupt. Look at 'im go. Scopin' it out. Is he gonna land?

Just keep your mind on the task at hand, Buhler. Just pick the right route down off this stupid slope. . . .

. . . Look at that. I can't believe it. He's skiing toward us! Oh, yes. What a pilot. He's gonna ski over to us. All we gotta do now is get across that smilin'-shaped crevasse and we're home free. I can almost taste those home-baked cookies at the lodge melting in my mouth. Incredible seven days. . . .

**P**aul not only picked us up that afternoon and dropped us off at the Ultima Thule Lodge, but flew back into the eastern cwm of University, skied up to the base of the wall and picked up our skis. Then he and his assistant taxied down to our base camp, folded up our tent and collected our duffels. All while we were taking a sauna! By the time we were sitting down to supper, our gear, our skis, and Paul and his assistant were back at the lodge cabins.

The couple from Georgia were still there, too. And they had a lot of questions.

SUMMARY OF STATISTICS

AREA: Wrangell-St. Elias range, Alaska

NEW ROUTE: The East Face (Alaskan Grade 6-, 8,500') of University Peak (14,800'), April 29-May 5, 1997, Charlie Sassara and Carlos Buhler

# Wet and Wild in Kichatnas

*Four thousand feet of rainy big wall on Middle Triple Peak*

BY KITTY CALHOUN

K itty, something is bothering me," Jay Smith said with apprehension.

"What?"

"I've gotta go back and do that route on Middle Triple that Steve Gerberding and I tried a couple of years ago. Other climbers have been asking me about it lately. I keep telling them that the rock is choss, but they know I'm lying."

Jay clearly was uptight. He pulled some slides out of his pocket and held them up to the light.

"See that pillar? Charlie Porter did a route on it back in 1976 and that's the only time anyone has ever touched this face. Our route follows the discontinuous cracks straight up to the right of the pillar—4,000 feet of solid granite."

"Yeah. . ." I interrupted. "But ya'll nearly died trying that route before, right?"

"Well," said Jay, pulling out stacks of slide pages from the drawer. "We were climbing alpine-style and it started to rain hard. We were six pitches up and had fixed our only two ropes above. Somehow the rain worked its way into our portaledge and got us wet as dogs. Our down sleeping bags were drenched and scraps of food and pieces of clothing floated on the floor of our ledge in a puddle.

"That night, the rain stopped and the temperature plummeted. Everything, including our two ropes fixed above, became frozen in place in a thick sheet of ice. We were shivering violently but couldn't rap down until the sun came out and melted the ice off our ropes. When that finally happened, large sheets of ice came crashing down the face above."

I watched Jay re-enacting the scene, then took another look at the slides. "I'll have to think about this," I said. "I can't say I'm too psyched about the idea at the moment."

"Yeah, but we'd do it differently this time. I'd fix the bottom part of the route and always keep two free ropes with us. If we climb as two teams of two and trade leading and hauling, it may go faster. This time, I'd bring a synthetic bag."

"What's the climbing like?"

"Mostly hard aid. Pretty sustained too," he said. He didn't seem to notice that I was becoming quite sullen.

I did not have much aid-climbing experience, and I was not excited about climbing in the rain. I remembered my first aid climb in Yosemite in 1987. I sat up all night before the climb memorizing the information in Royal Robbins' *Advanced Rock Climbing*. I got stuck in lots of predicaments, but with a little creativity, I managed to get up the wall. What the hell, I thought—I'll try it and see if I like it. If I did, I knew of many other rainy big walls waiting to be climbed.

O n June 27, we flew onto the Kichatna Glacier under a clear blue sky that would last for the next nine days. After moving camp over a pass and down the next valley, we settled into a routine: an hour wandering through the icefall with gear-laden packs to the base of the wall, jumaring fixed ropes, four to seven hours per 200-foot lead, then rap down and stumble back to camp. This, on average, took 19 hours round-trip, and the next day

was a rest day while a fresh crew went to work.

On day 11, the storm arrived. First the clouds lowered, engulfing us in a white-out. Then a steady rain settled in. We had all been happy when we were climbing, but now each of us faced a long, personal battle with boredom.

Steve lay in his tent and told stories the whole time he was awake. He reminded me of the old people in the South, continuing the mostly forgotten tradition of storytelling. Like an old man on his rocking chair on the front porch, Steve would settle in with a cup of coffee and the tales would begin. One story ran into the other, and each was told with unending humor and enthusiasm.

Dan is a master craftsman. Every item still in his tent needed to be repaired or modified. When heavy-metal music was not blaring through his loudspeakers, I could hear him hammering, filing, or rustling through his possessions in search of another project.

Jay was the weatherman. His barometer provided little encouragement, so every hour on the hour, he would surf the radio stations, futilely searching for a long-range weather report.

I finished the books I brought and started to brood on the fact that I had only led one pitch so far. With four people sharing leads, nobody gets enough. I was proud of my pitch—modern A3 with lots of beaks and hooks. Still, I had a suspicion that I would not get any more hard pitches. It had taken me seven hours just to lead 200 feet.

"You want this pitch?" Jay had asked as I bumbled over the lip of a roof and tried to untangle myself from a web of slings and hardware.

"You think I can do it? What if I take too long? Is everybody gonna hate me?"

"You'll do just fine."

Easy for him to say, I thought, as I proceeded to rack up. What if these little beaks didn't hold and I took a 200-foot whipper? I started up the only seam in an ocean of flawless granite. One beak after another went in; I was starting to relax and enjoy the routine. Then the seam disappeared.

"What do I do now?" I yelled down to Jay, who was fading into dreamland.

"I guess you'll have to use hooks to get over to that little crack on your right."

I placed my first hook. I was scared.

"Do you think it will hold me?" I yelled down nervously.

"There's only one way to find out!" he yelled back, oblivious to the desperation in my voice, my sewing-machine legs, my racing heart.

"Oh God please, please, please. . . ."

I gently transferred my weight. The hook held.

Several more hook placements in a row brought me to the crack and the security of more beaks, followed by tied-off and stacked pitons. One hundred sixty-five feet into it I reached some solid placements.

"How about I put the belay here?" I yelled down.

"Is there a fixed anchor there?"

"No."

"You need to keep going until you get to our old belay," Jay yelled back.

Two hundred feet out. No old belay anchors. No solid placements, either.

"Now what, Jay?" I yelled, mentally drained after the longest lead of my life.

"Our old anchors should be there."

"Well, they aren't, so I guess I'll have to down-aid to where I can get an anchor in," I yelled, exasperated.

*The southwest faces of Nightwind Spire and Middle Triple Peak.* Ride the Lightning *joins the snow crest on Middle Triple for its final three pitches.* JAY SMITH

On day 23, despite high clouds and a falling barometer, the rain ceased. While it wasn't exactly promising weather, we had only 16 days left until the plane was due to pick us up. Since the snowline usually recedes too far up the glacier for a plane to land in early August, we had agreed to meet the pilot at a makeshift site on the Kichatna River—which meant ferrying our loads of tents, portaledges, food, fuel, ropes, big-wall racks, clothes and sleeping bags over 30 miles of unknown terrain to the designated landing site. We figured it would take us at least seven days to do it. That left only nine days to complete the route. If it took only one day to get our haulbags to the end of the ropes 2,000 feet up the route, three days to finish, and one day to descend, we would have four days to spare.

L et's go!" Jay yelled, as he guzzled down a last cup of coffee. It was 7:30 a.m. by the time we left camp. Jay and I were to jug 1,600 feet and lead two more pitches while Steve and Dan hauled the six haulbags. Every inch that I now jumared up had been gained by countless hours of work. Pitch two had been my lead. Pitch three was a great roof that Dan led. He had done a good deal of back-cleaning on lead and Steve had not enjoyed cleaning the pitch. Pitch six was the crux, and it had taken Jay nine hours to aid up expanding flakes. Steve and Dan had led pitches seven and eight, which were reportedly easier. By the time we got up the fixed lines and got the rack sorted, it was early afternoon and had started to drizzle again. Jay started out up a dihedral/ledge system that in 400 feet was supposed to take us to the top of a small pillar, where we would set up the portaledges. Jay and I arrived at dinner time, but Steve, the haulbags and dinner were far below. Shortly, Dan appeared around the corner. He lit a cigarette.

"What's taking so long?" I looked down and could barely make out Steve huddled against the bags, shivering. The sun had slipped past the horizon.

"These bags are heavy—they're saturated from the rain and we can only haul two at a time."

We decided it would be faster for two people to body haul three bags at a time while one person jumared beside them to keep them from getting hung up. I was under the last set of bags when Steve jerked on the tag line to free them.

"Aaagh!" I yelled. A bag had dislodged a rock, which broke on my knee upon impact. I wasn't hurt, but I was angry and tired. At 4 a.m., 21 hours after we started, we collapsed in our portaledge.

R ise and shine, sleepyheads. It's noon already, the sun is out, and it's your turn to lead," I announced to Steve and Dan the next morning. Motivated by good weather and the realization that it was his turn at the sharp end, Steve fired up the stove to make some coffee. After a cup, a cigarette, and the sorting of the racks, Steve tied into the lead line—but Dan was still asleep.

"I hope you're ready by the next pitch, or I'll get that one, too," Steve told him.

"What?" Dan rolled over.

"I'll belay while you get ready, Dan," Jay offered.

"What's up, Dan-O?" I asked.

He was awake, trying to find his other sock.

"Well, I had to waterproof my boots again last night and then I had to work on the video recorder. . . ."

I didn't listen to the rest. Dan was just being Dan.

By now, the aid-climbing was getting easier, and within two days we fixed another five

*Kitty following 2,800 feet up, with the (unclimbed) east face of Mount Nevermore in the background.* JAY SMITH

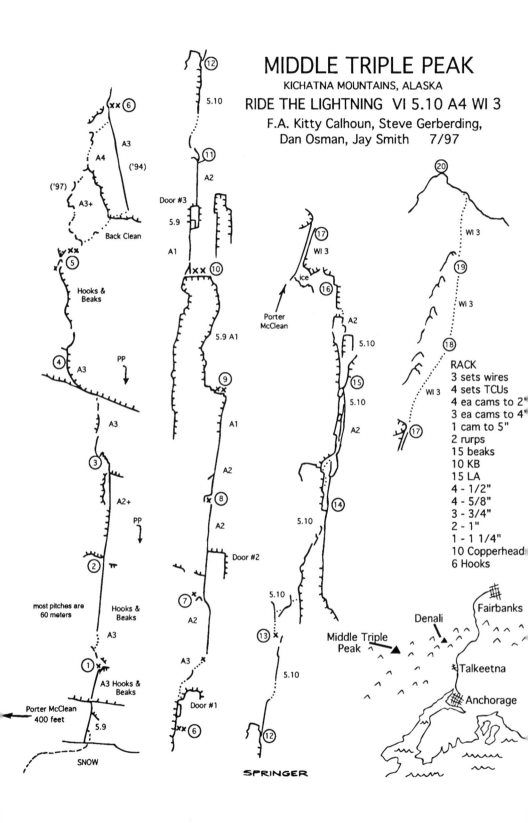

# MIDDLE TRIPLE PEAK

### KICHATNA MOUNTAINS, ALASKA

## RIDE THE LIGHTNING VI 5.10 A4 WI 3

F.A. Kitty Calhoun, Steve Gerberding,
Dan Osman, Jay Smith    7/97

RACK
3 sets wires
4 sets TCUs
4 ea cams to 2"
3 ea cams to 4"
1 cam to 5"
2 rurps
15 beaks
10 KB
15 LA
4 - 1/2"
4 - 5/8"
3 - 3/4"
2 - 1"
1 - 1 1/4"
10 Copperheads
6 Hooks

A3
A4
('94)
('97)
A3+
Back Clean
Hooks & Beaks
PP
A3
A3
A2+
PP
most pitches are 60 meters
Hooks & Beaks
A3
A3 Hooks & Beaks
Porter McClean 400 feet
5.9
SNOW

5.10
A2
Door #3
5.9
A1
5.9 A1
A1
A2
A2
Door #2
A2
A3

WI 3
ice
Porter McClean
A2
5.10
5.10
A2
5.10
5.10
5.10
Door #1

WI 3
WI 3
WI 3
WI 3

Denali
Fairbanks
Middle Triple Peak
Talkeetna
Anchorage

SPRINGER

*Dan Osman and Steve Gerberding near the end of the climbing.*
JAY SMITH

pitches. Late on the second day, it started to snow. Time was getting away and we had to do something.

Our ledges were only halfway up the route; hauling those six wet, monstrous bags up to there had been absurd, and we hadn't wanted to fix even this much of the route. It appeared that a gully above our high point might go free and lead up to the snow ridge to the summit. We agreed that as soon as the weather cleared, we would try to make it to the summit and back from our ledges in a single push.

By morning, it was raining heavily. Water had somehow seeped into the space between Dan and Steve's ledge and fly and formed a large pool. Dan bailed frantically as Steve collected their cigarettes and other items they hoped to keep dry and cradled them in his arms.

Through the mist below, I was able to spot our three tents on the glacier. The wind was gusting so hard that each of them tumbled crazily about, held down by the one or two stubborn anchors that had not yet melted out of the snow.

"Well, if the tents blow away, it'll be that much less weight that we'll have to carry out," Jay said in a half-hearted attempt to raise moral.

After two days, the wind was still gusting, and clouds raced across the sky, but the rain had stopped. At 5:30 a.m., we left the ledges for our summit push. Three of us huddled in the gully as Dan meandered up boulder-choked chimneys and across snow-covered slabs. Next, Steve led a classic mixed pitch that brought us out of the gully, finding an old piton left by his hero, Charlie Porter, along the way.

After another lead up an ice slope by Dan, I got the last two leads up to and across the summit ridge. Eight inches of wet snow barely clung to the rotten ice underneath and the entire muck threatened to avalanche. Below the summit cornice, I dug a U-shaped trough for my legs and butt, braced, and put my partners on belay.

Dan popped up through the clouds. "I've never done any climbing like those last two pitches!" he exclaimed. "This is just like in *National Geographic!*" My easy but scary lead had impressed this hard man. I smiled.

Summit day took 17 hours. On top, I shared Girl Scout cookies my sister had given me. I waited, hoping the clouds would spare us some views—when, to my horror, I noticed Dan side-stepping the 50 feet to the summit cornice.

"What are you doing?" I gasped. Every foot set off a tiny wet slide. "We're roped together with no anchors. The entire face is going to let loose if you don't be careful."

"But we have to touch the summit," Dan replied. Once he tagged it, we started down. On the descent, we left the fixed ropes in place, rappelling as quickly as we could while the afternoon sun melted the muck and large stones bounced down the gully.

As Jay and I started back up the fixed lines to retrieve the ropes the next morning, I kept reminding myself that at least our expedition had been a success. Now we struggled to clean all the fixed ropes and get our six haulbags off the wall. It was a strenuous and logistical nightmare, and we arrived back at our flopping tents on the glacier at 8 a.m. the following morning.

After a rest day, we went back to the base of the wall to retrieve the last of our gear, then packed up camp and attempted to carry and drag all of our possessions up over the pass and back down to our original landing site on the glacier. The snow had melted and was covered with deep sun cups. By the time we got to the old runway, it was 3 a.m. and raining again. Exhausted and frustrated by an endless battle to stay dry, Jay threw his sleeping bag in a water-filled sun cup and crawled inside.

We had exactly seven days left until pick-up on the Kichatna River, 30 miles away. Perhaps it was wishful thinking, but all we needed was 400 yards of firm, packed snow for the plane to land here on the glacier. Deciding we had enough snow, the four of us spent a total of 224 hours over the next week, ski-packing the mushy sun cups.

On August 4, the plane landed and took off on our runway with us in the plane. One more skeleton in the closet was gone.

SUMMARY OF STATISTICS

AREA: Kichatna Spires, Alaska

NEW ROUTE: *Ride the Lightning* (VI 5.10 A4 WI3, 4,000') on Middle Triple Peak (8,835'), June 27-August 4, 1997, Kitty Calhoun, Steve Gerberding, Dan Osman, Jay Smith

# Mascioli's Pillar

*A tribute to a climbing friend on the south buttress of Denali*

BY STEVE HOUSE

T hin evening shadows stretch out before us as we ski up the Kahiltna Glacier. The tip of Mt. Hunter glows red above and The Great One holds her usual massive presence. The night is so still that skiing feels like swimming; we leave a wake of cool air as we travel. My thoughts turn to our friend Steve Mascioli, who was killed on Mt. Hunter only a few days earlier. The peaceful moments found on journeys like this are part of what Steve loved about Alaska's mountains. The good memories of him propel me up the glacier to our camp at the head of the east fork of the Kahiltna Glacier.

M idnight is the appointed departure time for Steve Swenson and me, but the "great whiteness" has been hanging over us for two days. Dutifully, we unzip the tent: foggy. Groggily, we crawl out when, as if responding to our curses, the cloud lifts and the slender profile of the Radio Tower—what we will come to call Mascioli's Pillar— stands before us.

After a two-hour approach ski, Steve is busy stretching out the rope for six easy ice pitches. With his block complete, I hand him the pack and lead up steep blocky 5.9 rock, ending on a beautiful foot-sized perch. The next pitch gets a bit harder; grabbing the gear speeds me past an awkward exit move and we're onto the first icefield.

On our first attempt, we had worked to the left here and followed a crack system that ended with a rotten chimney and a giant roof. This time, we stay to the right edge of the icefield for two long pitches. This leads to a short snow gully below steep, polished granite. The rock is split by a six-inch ice-filled crack that bisects a small roof. Above the roof, ice clings in patches to a shallow dihedral. I tap and grunt my way up the narrow but thick ice. The roof responds to long reaches off the tools and careful crampon work on thin rock edges. The ice takes a good spectre just before it thins out.

Forty feet higher, the ice is reduced to snow crust and the rock turns mealy. A patch of snow reveals a bottoming crack and some protection. Careful climbing leads to a secure belay on a huge block.

Steve follows with wild abandon; he and the pack soon are at the belay. It's still my block and I lead another steep ice pitch that would be a proud WI6 at any ice crag. Now we cruise up snow gullies, work over short rock steps and through drifts of powder. We search for a small break in the angle where we can sit and take our bivy break. We've timed our start so that after 14 or 18 hours of climbing we are high on the pillar during the warmest part of the day. This allows us to eat, hydrate, and nap with just a down jacket. The one pack we have weighs less than 15 pounds—supplies for two for 48 hours.

We dig out a cramped spot where we can both sit under a rock overhang. We brew and try to nap, but even after a big pot of soup, Steve can't sleep, so after a three-hour break we pack up and get on our way.

Steve leads another ice-filled chimney. On the second pitch the ice tapers out and he does some spectacular stemming to a belay in a large peapod. The chimney pinches off above us, and Steve breaks out onto the face to our right. The 5.8 traverse is exposed; even a small pack gets in the way. But the steepest part of the pillar is below us and the route takes on a gentler character, meandering up ice ramps with short rock headwalls, all the time working

*Steve Swenson on pitch eight.* STEVE HOUSE

back to the center of the pillar. The headwalls provide many shorter sections of 5.10, which help ward off the chill of a clear Alaskan night.

The twentieth pitch is no different, except that I find Steve standing on moderate ground, the rack set in the snow. We untie and scramble up a bit higher. We're at nearly 16,000 feet atop the south buttress. We poke around, but it seems that there really isn't a summit here, just the end of the difficulties.

Worn through by the cold, we gingerly work back to the packs. Even our shells creak in the cold. We set the first of five rappels; keeping to the center of the pillar, we're able to locate the rotten chimney that thwarted our first attempt three weeks earlier. Now we can reuse most of our anchors, and we speed down familiar terrain. In two hours, we're over the 'schrund and at our skis—30 hours and 30 minutes after we left them.

I*t is two weeks later, and I'm standing in front of a crowded room in Bellingham, Washington. We're here to remember Steve Mascioli, and it is my turn to speak. Looking into all the faces, my strongest memory of Steve is his presence on that recent evening. The seamless snow is crossed by shadows in the alpenglow—and the mountains are stretching skyward toward infinity.*

SUMMARY OF STATISTICS

AREA: The Alaska Range, Alaska

NEW ROUTE: Mascioli's Pillar (Point 15,840' on Denali's South Buttress) (Alaska Grade 6, 3,840'), June 15-16, 1997, on Denali (20,320'), Steve House and Steve Swenson

*Mascioli's Pillar, showing A: line of ascent; B: first attempt and subsequent descent route.* STEVE HOUSE

# The Toose's Mooth

*Mixed adventures on the north face of the Moose's Tooth*

BY SETH SHAW

In the summer of 1994, Scott Simper, Kevin Sweeney and I, having climbed the relatively benign West Ridge route of the Moose's Tooth, stood on top of the West Summit and looked down the north face of the Tooth to the narrow Buckskin Glacier a dizzying 4,000 feet below. Deep in shadow, it looked cold and forbidding. Climbing it was the farthest thing from my mind.

I didn't give much thought to climbing the Moose's Tooth again until a couple of years later. Paging through some old climbing magazines, I was captivated by an aerial photo of the east and north faces. I also was familiar with the epic tale of its first ascent by Mugs Stump and Jim Bridwell in 1981. From the comfort of everyday life, the adventure sounded enticing.

In late April, 1997, Paul Roderick of Talkeetna Air Taxi eased off the throttle of his Cesna 185 and glided softly through champagne powder. Scott Simper and I hopped out.

"Here it is, boys. The Buckskin."

The two of us stood gawking at our immense surroundings. The glacier is barely half a mile wide, and surrounded by 4,000- and 5,000-foot walls on three sides. We felt small.

Scott and I had hoped to find an ice route up the 5,000-foot east face of the Moose's Tooth, but the reality of a dry winter had adorned the face with meager smears of ice separated by long stretches of kitty-litter granite. We turned our search to the expansive north face. At first sight, it looked hopelessly fortified by a broad hanging glacier. We watched frequent mega-ice bombardments as they launched completely airborne for 3,000 feet. The dust clouds filled the entire valley. We felt small.

Directly under the West Summit, a continuous ribbon of ice snaked down the mountainside. Maybe this could be our route. The next day, under light snowfall, we made our way up-glacier, giving the active hanging glacier we nicknamed The Menace as wide a berth as possible. Unfortunately, we discovered that our hoped-for route started underneath a particularly wicked section of this feature.

We discussed the possibility of sneaking along its right-hand edge—of how we probably could be out of harm's way in a matter of hours.

"Yeah, that—"

KAABOOOM.

Our recently proposed route was completely obliterated by an easy 500 tons of ice.

"Boy, that was a clear message, wasn't it?"

"Uh-huh."

"Makes ya feel kinda small, doesn't it?"

"Uh-huh."

We continued to search the face for a weakness. A thinner mixed variation, which bypassed The Menace and intersected with the obvious line a third of the way up the mountain, became apparent.

Scrape. . . catch. Crampon gouging into the weathered granite. Tick. . . tick. . . tick. Ice pick barely in the centimeter-thick ice.

*The north face of the Moose's Tooth, showing upper part of* The Toose's Mooth. BRADFORD WASHBURN #5909

"Wouldn't wanta come off here, bro."

Tick . . . tick. Scrape . . . scrape.

"Gotta tipped out number 4 in, so go easy on the jumars."

Snowflakes in the air. The face comes alive with spindrift. Time to flee.

Back to our tiny tent. We brew up and watch the hostile face—watch spindrifts big enough to wash insignificant climber specks to an icy grave. Fear creeps in. Thoughts of loved ones drive home the foolishness of alpine climbing.

Scott and I discuss the merits of spending a minimal amount of time on the face.

Four quarts of water, two days of food, butane stove, two cartridges, three-pound tent, down jackets. No sleeping bags or pads.

Dark, cold morning. Fingers freezing. Dark specter looms over us. Fear.

We walk toward the face like automatons. Boots squeak in the cold snow. We methodically ascend our four fixed ropes. Body hot, hands cold. Four a.m. Black sky turns gray. Drop the bottom two ropes.

"Time to haul ass, bro."

Scott scritches up a grainy chimney to a marginal belay. Ice smears and rock give way to a steep snowfield. We are forced to simulclimb with no protection between us. Vulnerable.

"OK, mountain, don't send anything down on us now."

Finally, I reach an ice tongue and whip in a couple of shorty ice screws. A sigh of relief.

*Seth Shaw jugging through a mixed section lower on the route.* SCOTT SIMPER

Tying our two ropes together, we can stretch 70 or 80 meters out of a pitch. Still, our progress, relative to the task, is slow. Pitch after pitch of 60° and 70° ice. A two- to eight-inch-thick ribbon of it winds through a vast granite landscape. Calves burn, but no time to slow down.

"OK, tied off."

Quickly eat, drink. Scott clips in, hands me gear.

"You're on, gone."

Landmarks we had scoped from the glacier unfold. Six pitches on the Serpent. Go right at the Headstone. Progress. At 10 p.m., we enter the fluted summit area. We've been climbing for 18 hours, and it feels it. Ice gives way to cold cohesionless snow.

"That's me," Scott yells up.

No more rope and no anchors. Frustration and exhaustion. I root around for ice under the snow. Nothing. I set our two pickets into the snow, find a feeble ice crust for screws and tie the whole mess together. Internal sirens scream, yelling back and forth. Danger. The encroaching darkness. The dizzying abyss.

We simulclimb with one good screw and the rat's nest between us. Only 100 feet to the summit, to safety. I carefully shaft each tool to the head, hands numb from the cold. Kick each foot several times, wishing for a solid placement in the sugary snow. The pitch steepens. I feel like my feet are going to shear through. Finally, a wall of ice rears in front of me and my tool

*Seth Shaw leading the beginning ice ramps to the summit cornices.* SCOTT SIMPER

bites into something solid. I sink an ice screw to the hilt. To my left, I can see a three-foot-wide snow ledge—the only bivy ledge we've seen all day. I give Scott the good news in darkness.

Inside the tent, stove hissing. The cold dry snow slowly produces cups of water. Fighting off sleep is difficult; our damp clothing sucks away precious body heat. Nod off. Wake. The task of scooping snow into the pot is not appreciated. Nod off. Wake. Shiver. Finally, hot water for food, and we eat ravenously. Sleep overpowering. Wake up stiff and shivering, gas canister empty. Our last gas canister. Huddle close to the stove. Sky turning gray.

Our theory was that the early morning sun would heat the tent and we could sleep for a few hours, thaw our gloves and boots, then deal with the final pitch over the summit cornice. Reality: The low sun angle does not heat the tent noticeably. Shiver, nod off. Wake up, shiver.

"Good vacation." Cynical smirk.

Sun leaves the face.

"I guess we should get going."

Neither of us move.

"I guess we should get going."

Fight our way into frozen boots. Fight with the frozen tent. Our perch looks scarier in the light. Cold works into cores; the traverse right is frighteningly exposed. Dig away at the cornice. High stepping on a picket, I watch it slide out. Headfirst and backward I go. Luckily the ice screw holds.

"That sucked."

The next attempt is successful. Summit and sunshine.

"You're tied off."

Scott jugs off my body weight while I counterbalance on the opposite side of the ridge. We praise the sun, its heat slowly penetrating our chilled bodies. Far below, we see climbers on the West Ridge route. Humanity. Our hearts warm. Time to descend.

We weave along the exposed ridge, careful not to let our guard down. Footprints in the distance. We are psyched that a trail down is broken. I can't believe our good fortune as I clip in and belay Scott over. Big smile: Scott sees I'm clipped into double threads and a wrap ring. Rappel anchors are in place the whole way down. Easy descent. We stop to chat with some climbers on their way up. Life is good again. Soon we are striding down gentle slopes, luxuriating in the sun and the beauty. We hike over a pass, leaving the Ruth Glacier behind. Back into shadow we go. Only 1,000 feet to descend and we will be back on the Buckskin. Complete luxury awaits us.

Slack line—punch through to deep nothingness. Almost got caught. Guard goes back up. Several rappels down a huge serac. Last chance for the mountain to kill us. Indifferently, it lets us pass.

Base camp. Huge feast. In warm sleeping bags, we drift off.

SUMMARY OF STATISTICS

AREA: The Alaska Range, Alaska

NEW ROUTE: *The Toose's Mooth* (Alaskan Grade 6) on the north face of the Moose's Tooth (10,335'), May 1, 1997, Seth Shaw and Scott Simper

J.E. SVENSON

# A New Season In Yosemite

*The Big Walls, Then And Now*

BY RYAN AND TOM FROST

*Ryan*

I never knew my father.

Now that I've grabbed you with that shameless headline, let me qualify it. My father is Tom Frost, but when I was young, that meant nothing to me. He was just Dad. I thought that everyone's parents put on slide shows, had racks of gear and piles of ropes, and covered the walls of their homes with cool climbing pictures. I wasn't ignoring his achievements. They, along with most other things, simply did not register in my small mind.

Finally, I arrived at a point in my life where I needed to clear my head and get some priorities, and what better way to do it than to drop out of college and go climbing? Moving into a Boulder apartment, I fell into a bad crowd. More precisely, I fell in with my roommate Ryan Prescott, who already was a strong climber. The rest is history. We climbed for six months straight, sometimes five or six days a week. My climbing jumped four grades. We discovered Hueco Tanks and the Valley. Feeling a desire to learn the tradition and heritage of this new passion of mine, I began to read.

That's when I found out.

My dad is not a good or famous climber, he's a legendary one. To put it another way, in all of American climbing, there is one period of time that towers above the rest in terms of adventure, innovation, audacity, and sheer excellence: the Golden Age of Yosemite. And in the 1960s, during this Golden Age, there were perhaps five or six men responsible for most of the pioneering progress. Tom Frost was one of this elite handful.

The older I got, the more I began to comprehend the significance of his accomplishments. At Tahquitz in the late 1950s, he freed the first 5.10 in California. But it was in the Valley that he came alive. At the time, Chouinard and Robbins called my Dad the best aid climber in the world. He participated in the second ascent of the *Nose* in 1960, the climb that invented the sport of big wall climbing. He helped revolutionize hauling and logistical systems to allow fast ground-up ascents of difficult climbs. In 1961, he climbed the *Salathé Wall*, since called the greatest rock climb in the world. Also during these years: first ascent of the West Face of Sentinel, and second ascents of the *Salathé Wall*, the *Dihedral Wall*, and the Northwest Face of Half Dome. In 1964, he capped off his prolific involvement in Yosemite with the *North America Wall*—ten days of difficult and terrifying A5. During the rest of the 1960s, he was chief engineer for Chouinard, designing Stoppers, Hexentrics, and RURPs, knifeblades, Lost Arrows, and angle pitons, all still in use today. He made several trips to the Himalaya and the Alps and plucked the best line in Canada—the Lotus Flower Tower. In 1970, he was invited to climb with Britain's mountaineering elite on Annapurna's South Face, and in '79, while I bumbled around in base camp, he pulled off the second ascent of one of the most photogenic mountains on the planet: Ama Dablam.

Whew! Who'd have thought that all these years my dad was actually a legendary climbing stud? So that's where all those pictures came from! I had known him all along to be a kind and loving father, but that left unanswered one important question: can he pull hard?

In 1997, it was time. We planned an extravagant climbing tour of the Western U.S. No expense was spared. Eldorado, Hueco, Indian Creek, Little Cottonwood, Zion. . . we were battered by them all. Then onward to Mecca. What a joy it was to have as my Yosemite climbing guide the legendary Tom Frost! We toured the Valley's moderate free classics, trying to get some good crack technique beaten into us. Though he is over 60, I can testify that he still pulls hard. He's right at home up to 5.9, fond of running it out, and always climbing efficiently. He has a horrible addiction to the Steck-Salathé on Sentinel, which I found to be the most strenuous and exhausting climb in the Valley. He's not afraid of a little approach hike. He is at one with nature, pausing to examine glacier polish or commune with a lizard. He adores Clif Bars.

And to make it a real Yosemite climbing trip, after 33 years without the Big Stone, Tom Frost ventured back onto El Cap. He acted as if no time had passed at all. Well, sure, a few of the cards were shuffled, but he seemed to have a story or recollection about each pitch and each bivy ledge. "That's where we ate on Camp 6, this was the crux nail-up on the *NA*, I must have put that bolt in, this is where we were snowed on. . . .." What a connection with the past!

This summer, my Dad and I climbed The Captain four times. We shivered on El Cap Tower on the *Nose,* wandered up *Lurking Fear*, zigzagged all over the West Face, and—with wild man Warren Hollinger—dangled off the *NA* for six days. Dad told stories and jokes, was cheerful and fearless, and climbed fast and hauled hard. It was a true return to style for Tom Frost, and I know him better than ever. I always suspected that he was the best dad on the planet, but now I know that he's a great person. And also, that he did a little climbing.

*Tom Frost on the the* Nose, *27 years after making the second ascent.* RYAN FROST

*Tom*

What a joy it was to have as my Yosemite climbing guide the cool Ryan Frost! It was June, 1997. We were three-quarters of the way up the *Nose* of El Capitan when I shared with Ryan my sudden realization: "This is the first time I've been on El Cap without Royal!" What comfort it brought, now with Royal absent, that his shoes should be filled by a new light and companion. I never thought I would climb El Capitan again. Thirty-seven years had passed since this route with Robbins, Pratt, and Fitschen had transformed my life. Now suddenly, as great as the adventure of 1960 had been, this new one moved once again up into the unknowns of my life. It almost seemed as though nothing had changed. My first reason to climb has always been the companionship. We climb to be inspired. I enjoy climbing only with companions that help point me toward God. Ryan and Royal do that well. It doesn't hurt that they also know how to climb.

Coming home to the Valley is sacred business. The rocks of Yosemite are so majestic and beautifully crafted that to know them is, in small measure, to know the creator of them. El Capitan, the object of our design, had not shrunk. We headed around the Valley loop and looked forward to a reunion in that Camp 4 family of which Steve Roper, in his book, had helped us catch a vision. The rock walls of Yosemite may be our gymnasium, workshop, and crucible, but Camp 4 is home. With no small amount of nervousness, we lined up at the kiosk for seven days' privilege to camp where Kauk, Bridwell, Pratt, Robbins, and Salathé had camped. We took a place in site 23 near our heroes in the SAR (Search and Rescue) camp. What change had taken place! After three decades, they don't even speak English. Heard in Camp 4 are Spanish, French, German, Japanese, British. . . .

The continuing and growing assembly of this body of climbers testifies to the historical significance of Camp 4 and Yosemite's home place in world climbing. Chouinard's 1963 prophecy is fulfilled. The "near future" has happened. In order for "Yosemite Valley. . . to be the training ground of super-alpinists who venture forth to the high mountains of the world. . . ," it is first necessary for the alpinists of the world to come to Yosemite Valley.

Several months in 1997 with these super-climbers helped me realize that our Camp 4 heritage is stronger than we imagine. Consider the following influences upon our culture. John Muir's respect for the creation established the foundation upon which every succeeding generation of Yosemite climber would build. John Salathé saw that artificial climbing and a daring, expeditionary style would open up vast, new possibilities. Like Salathé, Royal Robbins believed in commitment and invented a wall-climbing style to achieve it. Yvon Chouinard created equipment to fit our desires. Chuck Pratt and others laid a foundation of free climbing style that has kept the rest of us humble and more honest. A realization of this heritage brought wonder to every day and every night Ryan and I spent amid these trees and boulders of Camp 4.

We walked, our spirits quiet, along paths between tightly packed tents of diverse creation. We heard in our ears, if not our souls, tones of men and women who assuredly were aware of their presence in a certain type of temple of God. And these climbers no doubt were aware of being among, as our founder John Muir might say, "the rock and water spirits" of Yosemite.

So you might ask, "You returned to the Valley and El Cap after these many years. What do you find different from the early 1960s to the late 1990s?" An excellent question. First, there are so many of you (us). And second, you climb so well. Standards are soooo high. You are professional. We did not know much about training, or climbing full-time. We just enjoyed the feeling of bold, creative prospects amid a quiet Valley. Now many climbers earn a living guiding. The only loss I see in obtaining such an appealing job description is the problem of

*Ryan Frost leading out of the Black Cave on the* North America Wall. TOM FROST

losing an even more beautiful hobby. Climb to live? Or live to climb?

In the old days, we locals had a sense that routes such as the *Nose* and the *Salathé Wall* were world-classic climbs. Here in my mind is a serious change. Now they actually are. The *Nose* is the most famous and sought-after climb in the world, followed by the *Salathé*. That popular, huh? Yup. Try queuing up at the base. On early ascents, the El Cap pioneers were up there alone. Sometimes they were the only climbers—or even people—in the whole Valley. Now an entirely new social, sharing-type challenge exists. Fellow super-alpinists happily share your bivouac site with you, whether you want them to or not. And getting started on a climb doesn't mean being first—somehow, you find yourself in the way of everybody else anyway.

In June, as the time approached for Ryan and me to start up the *Nose,* we shook our heads and said, "It's a zoo." We spotted climbers on every bivouac ledge. The afternoon before our start, we hauled our gear to the base and observed four parties: 1) waiting on the ground for the opportunity to begin, 2) completely blocking the route by making a practice climb of the second pitch, 3) trying to get to Sickle Ledge, 4) already standing on Sickle Ledge.

We arrived early enough the next morning to be passed by only two superb Bulgarian climbers before we could start. Later, as we inched up the Stove-Leg Crack, they rapped by us. They had made certain logistical and route-finding errors and promised to return, which they would—completing the route in two days. In earlier times, of course, there were no ready-made, bolt rappel routes that now offer quick and less scary exit from the walls.

*Yuji and Shie Hirayama and Tom and Ryan Frost in Camp 4 in 1997.* KENJI IYAMA

In addition to the huge numbers of good climbers, the other astonishment for an old-timer like this one is the very high standard at which so many of you are able to climb. This progression in performance, I observe over these 30-plus years of time, is illustrated by two experiences.

On that September day in 1961 when I peered over the roof and tried nailing a flared crack on the lower part of the *Salathé* headwall, the exposure was so big and the piton placements so hard I thought progress nearly impossible. On a September day in 1997, I was waiting atop El Capitan for Ryan and Ryan Prescott to complete the *Salathé Wall*. Ryan was in the process of pulling over the *Salathé* roof himself when a team of Japanese photographers and cinematographers hurled their ropes into the void and rappelled past him. They were on their way down to document the next party of climbers lower on the route. Yuji Hirayama was attempting to on-sight the *Salathé*. Wow.

From the El Cap Meadow the following day, we watched Yuji at work. After taking two falls low on the first headwall pitch because of a route-finding error, Yuji rested, then led straight through without a hitch. That's performance. Yuji and I obviously are of a similar mettle. It was all I could do to aid the *Salathé* and all he could do to free it.

Also this season, we watched on as Scott Burke and his belayer implemented a strict and calculated 100-day regimen needed to climb the pitch Changing Corners. This is Lynn Hill's magically pioneered pitch 30 of the *Nose*. Scotty believes that Changing Corners is the hardest pitch on the route, now rated, I believe, 5.14a. Scotty's philosophy: "After you learn to do the hardest part, everything else is easy." He was prevented from freeing the whole *Nose* route by the onset of winter storms.

Yuji Hirayama and Scotty Burke. This is my portrait of two 1997-version world-class athletes who, but for the press entourages, are going rather quietly about their affairs.

Continuing with the subject of change, let's discuss—as Chouinard calls them—the "limited resources" of wall climbing. By what I was able to observe, these resources are holding up well, except for a few problems. Yosemite's cracks, which suffered so much during the hammer and chromoly piton days of the 1960s, do not appear in 1997, to me, to be deteriorating. Although some may be a little more slippery, their rate of destruction has relatively ceased, to the extent that cams and passive nuts are being used instead of pitons. Some aid pitches now are more difficult (for example, on the route to Sickle Ledge, certain cam-polished pockets will keep you guessing), and some now are easier (the third pitch of the *NA* is loaded with rusting, frayed bashies. All you have to do is clip and pray). I hope the future finds a way to solve messes such as pitches fixed with bashies.

Free climbing is theoretically easier than it might have been in the '60s because of the existence now of piton holes and the employment of spring-loaded cam protection. Today's footwear, chalk, and training methods also enable a higher standard for those who know how to use them. The trade routes, a name given to routes we never would have imagined would be climbed so much, now can be climbed mostly clean—despite what the guidebook says. To enjoy yourself in the odd, flared, slippery, impassable places, such as we experienced on the *North America Wall*, carry sawed-off pitons (for hand placement), Leeper cam hooks, flared Aliens, Lowe Balls, HB offsets, an interesting assortment of hooks, and a little calmness. Yuji and I agree that driving hexes into holes, which makes it harder for him to free climb and for me to aid, is the most disgusting practice in Yosemite.

On the walls, trash is a problem that needs to be re-addressed by every party that travels with too much junk or feels the heat of El Cap's pressure for survival. Come on, guys, let's stop discarding water bottles and plywood belay seats. Carry all your gear with you, and if you must toss into the void a paper sack or empty water bottle, do a big-time sweep of the base when you finish. Boom boxes and sometimes wine, beer, or marijuana characterize, in my view, a certain number of ascents of El Cap. Apparently some people go up onto this beautiful wall for reasons other than just to climb. We should go up to meet El Cap. If we go up on any other terms, or for reasons less pure, it is a loss.

A final point about limited resources would be Camp 4 itself. At this writing, Camp 4 is under attack by the National Park Service, which would build three-story concessionaire and employee dormitories and new upgraded Yosemite Lodge buildings north of Northside Drive between Camp 4 and Swan Slab. It is hoped that this plan, which currently is in process, will, in fact, not be implemented and that Camp 4 can retain its breathing room. It is hoped that Camp 4 will receive a listing in the National Register of Historic Places. Until now, the NPS has preserved Camp 4's integrity, its walk-in character, and its important first-come-first-served, non-registration status. Camp 4 is a prototype for Yosemite's future. Those dormitories would block out warm rays of sun.

How can we transmit the light of Yosemite, the beauty of what we know, to our posterity? I hope the classic routes that live on Yosemite's great walls will be cared for. The voluntary custodianship of these resources is exemplified by the likes of Chris McNamara and others of a select but growing band whose climbing style is "preservation." The style of these climbers is to give more to El Capitan than they take. Their continuing restoration of messed-up and unsafe belay anchors, and their cleaning and caring for routes, is a testimony that the heritage of Muir, Salathé, and Robbins lives. This heritage, unique in the whole world, is the power that will be the salvation of the great routes. We will find no help to preserve El Cap through government regulation and rules. The future of Yosemite—whether it be the cracks or big walls or Camp 4 itself—is in the application of its own climbing heritage by individuals who possess vision, and who know the creation.

Sometime before our Yosemite visit, Warren Hollinger, Ryan, and I had agreed to climb the *North America Wall* in the fall of 1997. On October 22, exactly 33 years after the start of the first ascent of the route, we stood together at the base. Thousands of feet of steep, gray granite and black diorite swept upward, interrupted only by overhangs. The fears and hopes and joys from a generation before flooded back in.

By a stroke of luck, I drew the third pitch—a cherished nailing memory. But this time, as I inspected placement options in the slightly more used, poorly formed crack, I was armed with modern cams, nuts, and hooks. High rpm treadwork propelled us through the several pendulums of the Borderline Traverse. We arrived at the Tenement Flats, where in 1964 hammocks had provided a bivouac and where the following morning, Royal, Chuck, Yvon, and I awakened—like laundry hung out to dry—to 1,600 feet of exposure. For Ryan, Warren, and me, it was midday. We continued on.

> *"[Ryan] led the overhang. He placed spring loaded cams up one side of it and followed a horizontal dyke of aplite around the top. Fascinated, we watched the lower part of Ryan's body move sideways 30 feet across our line of vision. Placements were difficult, and Ryan's hauling line hung far out from the wall. When all cracks stopped, he ended the pitch and belayed in slings, thus finishing the most spectacular lead in American climbing.*
>
> *I followed and was forced to leave two nuts because of awkward reaches.*
>
> *"Man, that was really a fantastic lead. What exposure! Congratulations!"*
>
> *"Thanks, Dad." (AAJ, 1965 and 1998)*

The *North America Wall* in 1997 was like returning to a familiar place but, as the poet would say, "knowing it for the first time." The overwhelming presence of the wall and the privilege of being up there with good companions felt the same as it had 33 years before.

Yet something was different. I noticed in our *North America Wall* climb, and in the Valley generally, a subtle and natural departure from Yosemite's pioneer ethic that resulted in our now-higher climbing standard. I wonder if El Capitan is being overpowered by heavier-handed tactics than necessary. For example, before we started up the *NA Wall*, Warren promised, "If we take all this stuff, I 99 percent guarantee we'll reach the top."

I was grumpy. We took the stuff. We slept comfortably each night, swallowed gourmet meals, hauled hard. And poured out gallons of water when we reached the top.

Why did it feel different? What had happened in Yosemite? Then I remembered my own climbing history and some of the way Royal thought. His desire was to keep the enterprise adventurous. By adventurous, he meant essentially uncertain. Just as in 1961, fixed ropes and overuse of bolts would ensure success but diminish joy, so also in 1997 is adventure lessened by carrying so much stuff or becoming that competent and professional. Without uncertainty, the climb is reduced to putting in the work. Why do it? Warren's climbing level is Polar Sun Spire (36 days), Nameless Tower (23 days), the *Reticent,* and the *PO* in winter with sheets of ice sailing by. Yosemite trade routes are too easy. The logical progression of the Yosemite pioneer ethic of keeping the adventure high is to employ better style, graduate to the Valley's hard, modern routes, or confront grade VII climbs in the mountains. There will always be dreamers of dreams who will find better ways to "invite nature's peace to flow into them as sunshine flows into trees," and for "the winds to blow their own freshness into them and storms their energy. . . ."

Some of the shifts and balances in ethic or style call into my mind questions about why it

*Behold the creation.* ED WEBSTER

is we climb these walls anyway. For the professional, business is business. But I believe that I and most of us recreational people still go up for the same reasons the pioneers went up. For one, because we are too afraid not to. Bart Groendycke reminded me that it is scarier looking up at El Cap from the meadow than down on the meadow from El Cap. And so we are willing to face ourselves and find out what is to be learned.

The one thing that definitely has not changed, and which is one of today's mistaken notions, is that the trade routes are easy. So and so freed it, or so and so did it in a day. Hmmm. Let us look at so and so and then look at ourselves. I'm here to testify that El Cap is just as big and scary as it ever was! Yes, cams enable faster travel. But be forewarned: The climbs are exposed and require as much hard climbing as did their first ascents.

Not knowing these things, Ryan and I continued up the *Nose*. After our friends from Bulgaria left us and we arrived at El Cap Tower an hour behind dark, rain began. We checked inside our little haul bag and confirmed that two of our three gallons of water had perished on the swing from Sickle Ledge. The night was cold. Rain continued. The next day, we observed that we had the Big Stone all to ourselves. Ryan led a treacherous Texas Flake in stiff boots and lived. The traverse toward Camp 4 was tedious, with pendulums and more wet rock. The Great Roof was not only a roof but great. To keep warm, we by day climbed. By night, shivered. Our final day, high in the huge, open dihedral that forms the top of the wall, with its planes of granite shooting outward, beams of light cut the crisp, clean air, and we ascended where pioneers before had gone.

# Yosemite's Last Stand

*The defense of the heritage*

BY JOHN MIDDENDORF

> *"Among all of the debates affecting America's national parks, the most enduring—and most intense—is where to draw the line between preservation and use."*
> —from the opening line of *Yosemite, the Embattled Wilderness*, by Alfred Runte, 1990

Yosemite is the model. It is the model for all our popular public lands. It is a model of beauty and awe. It is the model of a preserved ecosystem and an accessible wilderness. It is the model for big-wall climbing and the model for rescue techniques that, learned here, have saved lives all over the world. With resident National Park Service (NPS) and concession employees living in its midst year-round, it is the model for urbanization on the edge of wilderness. And most recently, it has become the model for an alliance between the NPS and the park concession contractor.

Ever since the passage of the Yosemite Park Act in 1864, and the subsequent establishment of Yosemite National Park in 1890 (which expanded the area to 1,512 square miles to include all watersheds), there has been an ongoing battle between preservation and use. The early battles took no prisoners: In 1905, the park was reduced to two-thirds its original size, and Hetch Hetchy Valley was dammed in 1913. Brutal battles were fought—and sometimes lost—by the conservationists of the day, including Frederick Olmsted, Joseph LeConte, and John Muir. In 1916, the National Park Service was formed to manage the natural resources in our public parks, and preservationists' hopes were lifted.

The first resource challenges addressed the park's growing pains. Roads established in 1913 opened Yosemite to automobiles. Cars could be parked in any beautiful meadow for camping. Word spread quickly. As early as 1927, Charles Michael, Yosemite's assistant postmaster, noted: "Yosemite Valley is getting to be an awful place. The air is filled with smoke, dust, and the smell of gasoline." Soon after, the NPS began restrictions on the ability to roam around in cars.

The surge of visitation resulted in increased accommodations and services within the park. Competition for the visitor's dollar among a variety of entrepreneurs created resource abuses. One concession offered a "bear show" that involved baiting bears at a certain time each night, then illuminating the feeding for tourists at 50 cents a head. Further commercialization prompted the Secretary of the Interior in 1925 to insist that the two most influential concessions, Yosemite National Park Company and the Curry Camping Company, merge into a single organization with a legally granted monopoly on accommodations, sales and services within the park, possibly on the premise that regulation would be simpler.

The newly formed Yosemite Park and Curry Company began an advertising campaign for Yosemite and built the Ahwahnee Hotel. The ads and posters highlighted amusements and diversions such as the popular firefall event at Glacier Point. As tourism increased, it became clear that a new threat to the resource was developing: overcrowding. In the years following, the NPS and the YP&CC established a relationship that maintained a balance between preservation and ever-increasing use. Some believe that too much of our public trust lands were allotted to concession infrastructure, while others say that the NPS managed the use with preservation in mind. Regardless, there existed a balance between YP&CC's dreams to build

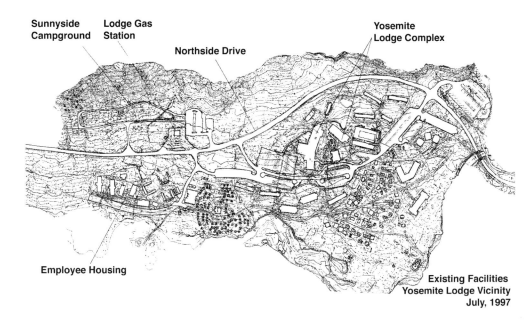

Sunnyside Campground
Lodge Gas Station
Northside Drive
Yosemite Lodge Complex
Employee Housing

**Existing Facilities
Yosemite Lodge Vicinity
July, 1997**

*The sketch above illustrates Yosemite today. The sketch below is a preliminary proposal for development put forward by the National Park Service and the park concessionaire. Where would you rather take your vacation?*

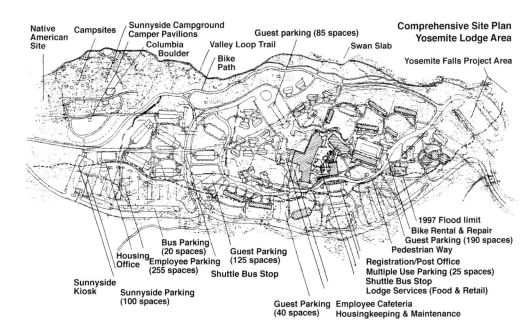

Native American Site
Campsites
Sunnyside Campground Camper Pavilions
Columbia Boulder
Valley Loop Trail
Bike Path
Guest parking (85 spaces)
Swan Slab

**Comprehensive Site Plan
Yosemite Lodge Area**

Yosemite Falls Project Area

1997 Flood limit
Bike Rental & Repair
Guest Parking (190 spaces)
Pedestrian Way
Registration/Post Office
Multiple Use Parking (25 spaces)
Shuttle Bus Stop
Lodge Services (Food & Retail)

Bus Parking (20 spaces)
Housing Office
Employee Parking (255 spaces)
Guest Parking (125 spaces)
Shuttle Bus Stop

Sunnyside Kiosk
Sunnyside Parking (100 spaces)

Guest Parking (40 spaces)
Employee Cafeteria
Housingkeeping & Maintenance

and fill hotel rooms year-round and the park's efforts to keep the user experience at a natural level. In 1980, as a result of an extensive public process, the NPS issued the Yosemite General Management Plan, which outlined the guidelines for future policies for visitor use, park operations, and development of the park.

In the early 1990s, MCA, the parent company of YP&CC, was bought by a Japanese company, Matushita. Concern was raised regarding a Japanese company running the concession in a national park. As a result, the concession was put up for auction. In December, 1992, Delaware North Companies, Inc. was awarded the concession contract in Yosemite over five other bidders, including the more environmentally conservative Yosemite Restoration Trust and the more experienced TW Services, Inc. (which operates at Yellowstone and the Grand Canyon). Delaware North's "better proposal" included, among other things, a radical increase over prior financial relationships between a concession and the NPS. While prior contracts provided 1 percent of concession gross revenues to the NPS, along with agreements between the NPS and the concession to keep prices reasonable, Delaware North's proposal included a 15 percent cut on the gross revenues (currently at $70 million) for the Park Service. Yosemite's tourism cash cow now was to be reinvested in the Park Service, with the prevailing argument that it was only fair that the concession return funds to the keeper of the land. Yosemite's current crisis, however, clearly reveals the folly of such a financial alliance.

The big floods of 1997 changed the landscape. It caused more damage to the Valley infrastructure than either of the big floods of 1937 and 1950, causing extensive damage to 50 percent of Yosemite lodging and 100 percent of the permanent concessionaire employee housing at the lodge area. It was called a disaster and Congress allocated $178 million for flood-damaged facilities. The park had a choice: restore the low -amenity tent cabins (which went for $40 per night) or upgrade to hotel rooms (at more than $100 per night). It chose to upgrade. Why? Because it is in the best bottom-line interest of both the NPS and the concession to increase revenues. The balance between the traditional objective role of the NPS as the protectors of our public lands and the concession as developers has been lost to an auction, and now the response to increased use is more exclusive infrastructure. The plans regarding the development refer to "providing a quality visitor experience," which clearly follows a trend to reduce campsites and increase exclusive hotel-style bungalows.

W hen I realized Yosemite's probable future, I finally decided to experience the "wilderness" from the comfort of a hotel room. Though I have spent more than 1,500 nights in Yosemite spread out over a 20-year climbing career, never once had I contributed to the concession's lodging profits. Seeing that high-dollar lodging was a possible future for Yosemite, I thought I should see what it was like.

After paying $100 for the priviledge of residing in Yosemite Lodge, I enclosed myself in Manzanita Room 3400. The drone of the bathroom fan and the muffled hard noises from other hotel inhabitants seemed eerie in contrast to the occasional clank of gear and cook pots and the soft murmured conversations I was used to hearing from fellow campers in the campground, only several hundred yards away. The view from the front door of the lodge was that of the post office. The wind brought the odor of chlorine from the lodge pool.

The next morning, the weather was cloudy, as it had been the night before when I went to bed. I ventured out to the lodge café, where I ran into Stephanie Davis and Warren Hollinger, who had just that morning made it down from the top of El Cap. They had finished the *South Seas* to *PO* route on the big stone and were warming up on coffee and sharing exploits with Kennan Harvey and Mike Pennings, who had come down from El Cap a few days earlier. Looking a bit weary but glowing from their experience, they told me of their efforts to top out late the day before and their subsequent descent down the East Ledges through the night in bad conditions.

"Oh," I said. "Was it storming last night?"

Suddenly, I realized the full extent of the isolation a hotel room creates. Though I myself had on many occasions battled fierce weather, slippery rock and desperate conditions on the final pitches of a big stone route, at that moment I found it hard to relate to their tales. The ferocity and savageness of the weather had eluded me in my safe, warm room. It became clear to me that the NPS should protect, preserve and encourage our ability to get close to nature, not aid and abet in an increasing isolation from its power.

The current plan for the Yosemite Lodge area is to increase the infrastructure of the hotel accommodations, expanding development into the undeveloped land around the lodge. The plan compresses Camp 4 into a smaller area hemmed in by a cultural center to the west, multi-story employee housing to the south and east and more parking for the giant tour buses. Twelve four-plex hotels are planned in the Swan Slab area. The atmosphere would further be violated by the addition of more than 300 people (employee dorms add 226 to the count, while the 48 new hotel rooms would bring in roughly 120 more) in the area north of Northside Drive. The buildings would sever the natural, peaceful connection between Camp 4 and Swan Slab. Visually, the magnificent views of Sentinel, Glacier Point, Yosemite Falls and Half Dome would be marred by the new three-story employee buildings.

Camp 4 and Swan Slab are sacred spots to climbers the world over. They offer one of the few places on the Valley floor where one can get away from the indoor life, camp with the stars and the moon, experience the morning sun, and feel the pulse of nature. Swan Slab is visited daily by climbers and is an integral part of Camp 4: without Swan Slab and the grove of trees that connect it to Camp 4, Camp 4 loses its solitude. That solitude, and the ability to remain away from buildings, is key to the experience of Yosemite's beauty and wilderness. The park's birthright was set up to preserve this elusive experience, but the new plans would disrupt the ability we currently have to roam and enjoy these areas. With every acre lost to development in our public lands, humanity's ability to connect with nature is incrementally decreased.

The NPS can and should respect their original role as the protector of our public parks. The plan to develop the area directly east of Camp 4 is both overdevelopmental and an outrage to those who love the "Sunnyside" area. Yosemite has its own unique geological and biological infrastructure. Exclusive hotels should not supercede the right to experience Yosemite naturally. The soul can not be commercialized.

# Free, Fast and Clean

*The future of Yosemite climbing*

BY CHRIS MACNAMARA

On a brisk fall night on the top of El Capitan, Eric Sloan and I sat huddled around a fire, warming our bones after a day of replacing bolts on the top of the Big Stone. Out of the darkness stepped Jim Bridwell, who had just topped out on the *Wyoming Sheep Ranch*. He sat down next to the fire, lit a cigarette and, at our prodding, eased into a tale or two from the 1960s and '70s.

Here was a man who owned a decade of climbing history—and he was still ticking off Grade Sixers. Eric and I were impressed. As the night grew long, we asked him questions and he spun out answers while the fire lit up the pine trees and kept the cold at bay. Among other things, we both wondered how his recent ascents compared with the ultra classics he had put up in his heyday.

"What do you think of wall climbing in Yosemite today?" I asked.

Jim was quick to respond.

"Yosemite is dead," Jim said. "The future of wall climbing is in the big mountains."

These were not words I wanted to hear, and I wanted him to take them back. But the godfather of big-wall climbing had spoken. Whatever disagreement I may have had was withheld as I nodded my head in agreement. The conversation continued as Jim talked about an incredible unclimbed face on Nuptse that others deemed suicidal. I was in awe of his boldness, which threaded such a fine line between vision and insanity. As the fire died down and we went to sleep, I tried to accept Jim's words about the future of Yosemite—tried to convince myself that I should spend my time in more exotic parts of the world. But in the end, I could not.

For me, Yosemite is very much alive. Granted, it may not be the same as in years past when Bridwell put up his epic ascents, but I believe Yosemite Valley today is vibrant and growing, and that its future will be an exciting one—different, of course, than it has been, but new and challenging in its own singular way.

As every serious climber knows, Yosemite is not just a beautiful place, a grand place or a special place. It is a sacred place, the place where, for decades, the world's greatest climbers have embellished upon the history of the sport. From putting up the first Grade VI climbs in the world, to making leaps in free climbing standards, to devising enormous equipment advances, Valley climbers have always explored new realms. As a result, Yosemite has been the single most influential area within the world of rock climbing. In my view, it will continue to maintain this place in climbing's future.

For nearly 40 years, the chief lure of Yosemite and the measure of its greatness was first ascents. From the landmark first ascents of Half Dome and El Capitan, Yosemite was propelled forward as the world's leader in ingenuity and boldness on rock. The extreme commitment needed for the first ascents of the *Muir* and *Salathé* walls shattered what was thought possible on the big routes. Once climbers were sure they could climb El Cap in good style, the challenge lay in finding the most difficult line. This challenge was found on routes like the *North America Wall*, which in turn paved the way for extreme aid climbs such as the *Pacific Ocean Wall* and *Sea of Dreams*. Indeed, nearly every first ascent in Yosemite seemed to make an enormous contribution to the climbing world.

Yet if we continue to gauge Yosemite's pulse by first ascents, then it is indeed in trouble. Veteran climbers have for years said that there are no new lines left in Yosemite. Still, every year, new wall routes are put up. While some recent first ascents such as *The Reticent Wall* offer brilliant nailing in well-defined features, most new routes involve lengthy sections of what appears to be blank rock. Surprisingly, these seemingly contrived lines often have remarkably low hole counts, the measuring stick for whether a line is natural or not.

So what gives? Had earlier climbers really been missing these "natural lines" for the last 20 years?

Not quite. The definition of "natural line" was simply changed to suit the situation. Some modern climbers, finding few defined features, just recalibrated. Whereas earlier climbers defined a feature as a section of rock that could be climbed without enhancement, some of today's climbers define a feature as anything that with the help of a drill and chisel can be enhanced into a copperhead or hook placement. By this theory, just about anything is a feature, as demonstrated by the first ascent of *Ring of Fire* on El Capitan in 1995.

On this route, the climbers declared that they had found a natural line and were going to prove it by not placing any bolts except at belays. They said that in lieu of bolts they had developed certain "new technologies" in order to ascend "blank corners." They declined, however, to explain these new technologies, saying it would all be in their book about the climb.

Anyone climbing on the east face of El Cap that year didn't have to wait for the book to find out what these "new technologies" were. For more than 20 days the repetitive tap-tap-tap of steel drill against rock could be heard echoing throughout the big stone.

The climbers were using tactics common on modern aid lines; they just took them to the extreme. *Ring of Fire*, however, showed just where the practice of drilling and chiseling the rock can lead. Eventually, there could be hundreds of routes on El Cap, each separated from another by only a few feet. Without some restraint, El Cap could come to look like a high-traffic sport climbing area, or a very tall gym wall with scenery. The adventure and challenge of finding natural lines and then adapting oneself to the rock would give way to using force to bring the rock down to one's level.

Still, while the prospects for first ascents in Yosemite might not be particularly bright, any lack of new route potential is made up for in other areas. In the arena of free, speed and hammerless climbing, the challenges remain wide open, begging to be tapped in Yosemite as nowhere else.

For the past several years, most cutting-edge free climbing has been done in sport climbing areas. But recently, many of the world's top free climbers have returned to Yosemite to free climb big walls. Drawn by adventure and the commitment required to climb a big wall, combined with the sheer beauty of Valley crack climbs, many climbers are finding some of the best free climbs in the world on faces that once were believed to be impossible to ascend by any means.

Free climbing big walls is nothing new; climbers have been steadily ticking off Grade V walls for the last two decades. Yet recently there has been a burst of activity. Notable climbs, like Lynn Hill's free ascent of the *Nose,* have reminded climbers that while many of the ultra classics have gone free, the list of Grade V and VI walls waiting for their first free ascents remains extensive.

While first free ascents may offer the highest rewards, repeating long routes also is becoming increasingly common. Alex Huber's free ascent of the *Salathé Wall* has set off a wave of attempts. As free climbing standards continue to escalate, ascents of routes such as the *Salathé* that once were mind-boggling will become commonplace. The *Salathé* may very well be

*Todd Skinner on pitch five, first free ascent of the Direct Northwest Face (5.13d), Half Dome.* GALEN ROWELL

*Charlie Fowler on the Triple Cracks pitch, first clean ascent of* The Shield, El Capitan. BETH WALD

*Galen Rowell en route to becoming the oldest climber to climb the* Nose *in a day in 1997.* CONRAD ANKER

Yosemite's next *Astroman*, a testpiece that prospective Valley free climbers "warm up on" before attempting the 5.14 wall routes that undoubtedly will be climbed in the future. In addition, impressive efforts like Steve Schneider's on *Excalibur* pave the way for free ascents that may contain some sections of mandatory aid but still offer thousands of feet of free climbing.

Speed climbing is another realm in which Yosemite offers immense potential. Originally, speed ascents were used by climbers to train for alpine routes in Patagonia and the Himalayas. But today, as John Middendorf points out, "The dependence on fixed gear and bolts in these fast ascents will limit their training value for climbs outside of the Valley." Instead of being reserved for alpine training, Yosemite's speed climbing today has developed into a sport of its own. It is not uncommon for two or three parties to climb the Nose in a day, while multi-day siege affairs like *Zenyatta Mondatta* and *Iron Hawk* now are falling in times just over 24 hours. Many climbers with jobs in the surrounding area now go to the Valley for the weekend, climb a Grade Sixer and are back in the office by the time a "normal" party they passed has climbed a handful of pitches.

This increased popularity of speed climbing has made the sport more competitive, as most speed climbing teams head up with the hopes of bettering the time of the fastest ascent before them. Yet while the incentive of setting a record may add a bit of fun to the game, there are too many subjective factors to keep such records from ever bearing too much weight. Fixed gear, the use of cheater sticks and whether a party has climbed a route before gives one team an advantage over the next and will keep speed climbing from ever becoming too competitive.

Clean climbing, on the other hand, is something that needs to be taken more seriously. Since Doug Robinson first wrote of it in the 1973 Chouinard catalog, clean climbing has been

*Force or finesse?* DOUGALD MACDONALD

the right thing to do. It still is; but increasingly, if climbing is to endure, it is the necessary thing to do as well.

As the sport has emerged into public view, it has caught the eye of land managers, government agencies and assorted politicians. With more and more climbers entering wilderness areas, officials now are deciding how the sport fits into the overall picture of human wilderness use. With such weighty decisions in the balance, it is more important than ever to climb as cleanly as possible.

Hammerless aid climbing is one form of clean climbing that has gained acceptance lately, but it has not gone nearly as far as it can. Despite a well-publicized first hammerless ascent of the *Shield* on El Cap, only one hammerless repeat has been made in the last five years. Hundreds of other parties have continued to nail, with clear results: RURP seams now take one-inch sawed angles and continue to widen.

Ten years ago, this might have been acceptable. Today, however, hammerless protection technology is so sophisticated that there no longer is an excuse to nail. Hammerless climbing often is faster than nailing and can be made just as safe. And while preserving the integrity of the line is the main argument for its use, hammerless climbing does more than just preserve the rock: It adds an entirely new adventure to the game.

On the first ascent of the *Shield* in 1972, Charlie Porter placed 35 RURPs in a row on the Triple Cracks Pitch. When Charlie Fowler led this pitch in 1993 on the first hammerless ascent, he hand-placed bird beaks, angles and nuts. Although the equipment was different, the sense of adventure was the same. Both parties pushed the level of boldness; Porter was trying to avoid placing bolts and Fowler was trying to avoid using a hammer. The first clean ascent of the *Shield* showed that an intricate hammerless pitch is every bit as rewarding as a hard nailing pitch—and it adds the satisfaction of knowing that you did not change the route for the next guy.

Unfortunately, when some routes have gone hammerless at hard grades, subsequent parties have been intimidated into thinking that the climbs are too dangerous for them to attempt cleanly. They shouldn't be. Instead, all climbers should be inspired to reach within themselves for the patience and resolve necessary to do the route as hammerless as they possibly can. For some, it may mean not using the hammer at all; for others, it may mean using the hammer only when the danger becomes too great. But only when every party makes the pledge to climb as cleanly as they feel possible will the true potential for clean climbing be realized.

The first ascent may always be the most glorious and rewarding climbing achievement a climber can earn. Those who only see adventure in Yosemite in first ascents will be forced up lines that are more and more contrived. But many will continue to devote time to first ascents in the big mountains as well — and rarely do these climbers go to the alpine walls without first making numerous pilgrimages to Yosemite. The world's best rock climbers and alpinists will continue to visit Yosemite, current standards will continue to evolve, and an entirely new realm of adventures for the Valley climber will be the result. I believe the potential of Yosemite is decided by what our vision lets us see. For those who are not limited by past accomplishments but are instead inspired by them, an exciting future with opportunities in speed, free and hammerless climbing is on a horizon still brimming with potential.

# Alpine-Style in the Tschang-Tang

*A long pulk through Tibet*

BY FRANK KAUPER

TRANSLATED BY CHRISTIANE LEITINGER

"*It's torture—the hands cannot be used, the map rips, and one asks oneself if one can make it alive to the next camp! The lips are swollen and split, and at the nails the skin is blistered so that the fingertips bleed! [...] One wishes oneself away, away—just away out of the Tschang-Tang!*"

Thus wrote the Swedish explorer Sven Hedin in a gripping report about his 1906 Tibet expedition. Ninety-one years later, nothing has changed. The Tschang-Tang has lost none of its hostile nature.

*Across the Tibetan plateau.* STEFAN SIMMERER

A hail- and thunderstorm unloads itself directly over our heads. Stefan Simmerer and I cower on the wide plain, 100 meters from our carts, which are placed on the ground as lightning rods. We pray that the lightning hits someplace else. We have been underway for three weeks already, walking seven to eight hours every day. We have not met another human being for more than a week. . . and we haven't even arrived in the middle of the Tschang-Tang.

*Stefan Simmerer pulling through rough wadis in the Kun Lun mountains.* FRANK KAUPER

S ven Hedin's descriptions make for fascinating reading on long winter nights in a warm room. Through his writings we first came upon the crazy idea that we could also cross the Tschang-Tang. But not on one of the many roads that now cross Tibet—rather, like 90 years ago, on a path of personal choice through the unexplored vastness. We chose the northern Tschang-Tang, an area twice the size of Germany. No roads. Practically uninhabited. Average altitude 5000 meters. We quickly found the general route on our map "The Mountains of Central Asia (1:3,000,000)." A south-north crossing appeared the most feasible.

As a treat we also wanted to try and climb the unclimbed Zangser-Kangri (6644 meters), which lies in the center of the plateau. We differed from Sven Hedin in that we could not afford a large expedition with hundreds of pack animals. We tossed around the idea of an expedition with the simplest of means—the Tschang-Tang, "alpine-style." Reinhold Messner introduced this style in the 8000-meter peaks of the Himalaya. We wanted to transfer the renunciation of everything superfluous to our expedition. In addition, we needed to be completely autonomous, independent of food drops, porters or animals. The pastures on the Tschang-Tang were too uncertain for yaks. We set up a simple calculation: for a distance of 1000 kilometers, at 20 kilometers per day, we would need 50 days. Since there was no possibility of re-stocking during the trip, we would need to take about 50 kilos of supplies with us. Including equipment, we arrived at a weight of 80-90 kilos—unthinkable to carry.

We recalled the Messner/Fuchs expedition. They had pulled 250-kilo sleds to the South Pole. There certainly was not enough snow in Tibet for such a pulka; however, if one put the whole thing on wheels…?

Many a night we tinkered over blueprints, clarifying what such a pulka on wheels should look like. The parameters were set: as little dead weight as possible, large wheels that could roll over obstacles, 30-centimeter ground clearance, not longer than two meters (so that it could be transported in an airplane), and, of course, stable enough to carry 80 kilos of food and equipment. Our pulkas were ready a week before our planned departure—far too late to test them substantially. Still, we put full faith in our construction: a two-and-a-half kilo titanium-pipe frame forms the core piece, while two "Speedtec 26" wheels with 2.5-inch-wide mountain bike tires carry the frame. We divided our 80 kilos of equipment into three watertight packbags and one backpack.

Shortly before our departure to Nepal, I could not imagine that the undertaking would be successful. There were too many uncertainties, not the least of which were questionable water sources, and the big question of whether we could even pull the pulkas across the Tschang-Tang. We had been warned about the swampy permafrost, about the deep ditches in the Yak grass steppe, and our most exact map (Scale 1:500,000) showed a number of mountain chains running northwest. I was sure we had bet too high this time, and that our preparations for such an undertaking were simply too dilettante. But we still wanted to try.

June 2. Kathmandu. Our equipment arrived safely in Nepal. Now our carts stand fully packed in front of the hotel driveway. Unbelieving stares and scornful grins of the Nepalis are everywhere. Even here, only the poorest of people would pull such a cart through the streets, and then only to earn their livelihood.

After a 200-kilometer bus ride, we reach the border with Tibet. On June 12, we arrive in Dongco, a tiny nest on the northern road from Lhasa to Ali in western Tibet. We have needed 11 days on foot and on trucks to cover the 500 kilometers to this point. Dongco is the last connection to civilization for us. From this point on, we will have to rely on ourselves. One thousand kilometers across an unexplored steppe. The next contact with people will come in perhaps seven weeks.

As we leave the road at a right angle and bear toward a chain of hills which is, according to the last GPS bearing, exactly to the north, I am overcome with a dull feeling in my stomach. It is best not to think of everything that could be awaiting us. Just walk, walk, walk. . . . There is only the monotonous "clack, clack" of our poles, and occasionally a jolt from behind when the cart rolls over a big rock. I am still everything but confident. Why should we, of all people, succeed at crossing this pathless plateau, especially in light of our laughably constructed donkey carts. . . .

But with every kilometer that we cover, my doubts become smaller. It is amazing how well we progress with our carts. We are not fast—we do, at best, three kilometers per hour; still, up to this point we have been able to overcome every hurdle. In addition, for the first week, we continue to come across evidence of truck ruts that lead north.

And in the beginning, we continue to stumble upon occasional Tibetan nomads. These meetings, with people who likely have never seen a white man before in their lives, are impressive for both sides. This must have been the way the white men were received in North America hundreds of years ago. Initially, fear prevails; women and children hide themselves in their tents at the sight of us. But curiosity about these strange people, who pull their carts themselves, is stronger in the end. The most courageous of the groups steps toward us hesitantly, and we also approach a bit, waving and trying to laugh. This is always the most effective means of establishing contact. A smile is understood everywhere, especially by the humorous Tibetans.

Once the ice is broken, we are taken in heartily. Butter tea is stamped, Tsampa is distributed. An ancient double-barreled shotgun usually stands in the corner. Nothing has changed here since Sven Hedin's day. How sad it is that we cannot communicate; how much we would have to tell one another. . . .

After about 200 kilometers in a northerly direction, the last traces finally disappear into the sand. We no longer meet even Tibetans. We are, at last, alone.

The walking becomes easier, and often is like a meditation. Our thoughts are far away—at home, with friends and girlfriends, in the past and in the future, least of all here and now. But at some point, every thought has been pondered at least once, and the past has been looked over for the nth time. What I wouldn't give for a book. . . . The landscape simply holds too few charms; every day, we walk and walk in this unending vastness. If we didn't have our GPS, we would often not believe that we were making headway.

Of course, walking is not just meditation; more often than not it is hard work. With 80 kilos, even the slightest incline (not to mention sandy or softened ground) is noticeable. It is nearly impossible to move forward in the swampy permafrost. The carts often sink to their axles in mud.

But such segments are mercifully rare. In the evenings, in the tent, while the gas stove hisses, the challenges are quickly forgotten. Generally, we treat ourselves well once the tent is up. An example of our festive menus: noodles with ratatouille and pemmikan, and for dessert, chocolate pudding and fruit brandy.

On July 3, we have reached our first stage. We stand at the edge of the overwhelming glacier of Zangser-Kangri. We have never seen such a mighty glacier in all of our lives. Even the great glaciers of the Swiss Alps seem tiny in comparison. And what seems even more incomprehensible to us: This grandiose massif, standing here only for us, has perhaps never before been seen by a human being.

We feel like aliens, like intruders in a perfect and untouched Nature. In all our amazement, however, we do not forget that we want to climb this mountain. If we are successful, we assume it will be a first ascent. We establish our base camp at 5700 meters. We leave our carts behind with the majority of our equipment. Who would ever steal them?

On the first day, we make good progress on the glacier. Maybe even a bit too good: As we reach our camp in the evening at 6200 meters, I am hit with altitude sickness. It is impossible to eat or drink, let alone get up. How sad, I think, that after five weeks of toil and only 500 meters from the summit, I can't continue. Curious: One would think that this would be the greatest disappointment of one's life. But on the contrary, I am happy to have come this far, the summit does not interest me in the least at this point. Of course, I still swallow medication in order to counter a possible pulmonary or cerebral edema, and the next day, I actually feel better.

The old ambition announces itself, and I decide to attempt the ascent. For the first time in a week, it is foggy. We see no more than ten meters in front of us. We find the southeast ridge of Zangser-Kangri only with great difficulty. I am dizzy again; I am still a bit dehydrated and have eaten little. Thirty to 45° corn snow. No vision. I walk as in a trance, very slowly, the air thinning. . . .

At some point, the ridge becomes less steep and, finally, level. We must be on the summit! Quickly, a GPS reading and a few photos. As proof of our presence on the summit, we pound a one-meter-long titanium tube, meant as a replacement part for our carts, into the ice. At base camp, we had engraved into it: Simmerer/Kauper, 7/97, Erlangen, Germany.

After half an hour, we must descend. I do not feel well. We take down our high camps after a short break; I need to get to lower levels. As a doctor, I know very well how dangerous it is to ascend in spite of having altitude sickness—yet also how easily such thoughts are repressed

*Simmerer on the Zangser Glacier.* FRANK KAUPER

when the summit is within reach.

Shortly before sunset, we reach base camp. I have never been so exhausted and drained in my life. The next day we spend simply cooking and dozing. In order to exit our base camp in the Zangser-Kangri massif, we "only" have to cross a pass at 5900 meters. Climbing a 20° snowfield with 50 kilos of equipment at this altitude is not the greatest joy, but we are slowly becoming less pretentious. At least the weather is excellent. And in some ways we feel so regenerated that we decide to make a second ascent: Directly next to our camp rises a beautiful pyramid-shaped mountain (N 34° 27, 7', E 85° 56, 7'). It is unnamed; we estimate it to be about 6400 meters in altitude. This day tour compensates us for the effort and bad weather on Zangser-Kangri. The ascent is pure pleasure. The views from the summit are breathtaking: To the west and the south we overlook the entire Zangser-Kangri massif, to the north and east to the horizon, nothing but endless rows of hills. We realize as we stand on this summit in the middle of the Tschang-Tang how tiny and meaningless we are when faced with such dimensions. A fearful but also healing insight.

July 10. The strains of the last week have marked us. With hollowed-out cheeks, furrowed faces and hands, we look ten years older. But the Tschang-Tang has not just left its traces externally. Psychologically, I also feel burnt out. Another 500 kilometers north to the Silk Road? Walking every day to exhaustion, day after day, with the uncertainty of whether we will find water tomorrow, whether we can cross the next mountain range. . . . We cannot motivate ourselves for this intense tour.

We decide on a short cut: After ten days' walking in a northeasterly direction we should, according to our map, meet up with a military road. From there we could catch trucks to the

Silk Road. Fortunately we had no idea at this point what would await us 200 kilometers to the northeast.

In the following days we take things easy: Only six hours of walking, and double meal rations. In our thoughts we are already in the next-closest city, letting ourselves be spoiled in restaurants. Our mood becomes increasingly better. The night before our expected last day I am already writing a summary in our travel log.

On July 17, the catastrophe: We find ourselves at N 35 degrees 16 minutes and E 87 degrees and 10 minutes. Precisely here, according to our map, should be a road. East of us is a giant salt lake. We came from a westerly direction. We certainly hadn't crossed a road, but just as certainly there is no road in the east. We despair. Yet still we try to see the situation rationally to avoid showing the other what we really feel: fear, plain and simple, that we will never get out of the Tschang-Tang. In spite of all our precautions in the last weeks, we have maneuvered ourselves into a dead-end. We blindly relied on the road. Through our unrestrained feasting of the past days, we find ourselves with enough supplies for only ten more days. Even worse, we have only seven liters of water left per person. The last spot we found water is two days back; going north, we will not hit the next river with running water for another 80 kilometers. Around us is nothing but salt swamps and salt lakes.

Since our scant supplies make it appear risky to go back, we decide to try and find water in a northerly direction. The mood this evening is tense. We hardly exchange a word. I think about everything I will do if I get out of this damned area. The trip has reached a new dimension at this point. Neither of us reckoned with the true risk of death.

July 18. Three liters of water left. We need to find water today. In a dry river valley, we split up: Stefan looks up-valley while I look in the other direction. After a frustrating search, I find a small puddle the size of a plate. The water is only slightly salty. I scoop out about half a cup—and the water slowly seeps back in. We are saved! We spend the whole day filling our water sacks cup by cup. In the evening, our carts are 40 kilos heavier.

Now we know that we will make it, but the following days are among our hardest. We need to overcome two more mountain ranges, the Samarsa Gya Ri and the Hoh Xil Shan. That means 11 to 12 hours of walking with only two to three short breaks. Marching strictly along the compass needle is impossible in this terrain. We continually need to cross smaller chains of hills, and we lose our way in the whirl of ridges and valleys. Nonetheless, we achieve our daily ten degrees north, which is about 20 kilometers as the crow flies. On July 22, we reach the first river. At any rate, we won't die of thirst…

Ahead of us to the north lies at least another 250 kilometers to the first road. Between us and the road rises the mighty Kun Lun range. We only have five kilos of dry food supplies per man—at best, enough for six days. The prospect of a few days of fasting is not particularly edifying; however, we probably won't starve, either.

July 24. We stand on a pass at 5500 meters, the water table between the Tschang-Tang in the south and the Taklamakan Desert in the north. This pass also forms the border between Tibet and Xinjiang. Even though Tibet now lies behind us, nothing changes. We still walk 11 hours a day, day after day. Physically, we are emaciated to our bones, we are already at an end. The only thing that keeps us going is the prospect of the road to the north.

We are hardly satisfied by our reduced rations anymore. We are constantly freezing because of our hunger. On July 29, we festively consume the last Power Bar. Now our supplies are completely gone. Is it a coincidence that at this very moment an equally hungry wolf slinks around us?

August 1. We reach the road. Three hours later, the first truck filled with women, men, children and sheep pulls up—the first people we have seen in five weeks. We all eat, sing and

*Frank Kauper and Stefan Simmerer in Quiemo after their traverse.* FRANK KAUPER COLLECTION

laugh. It is a normal day for these people, who go to market in Quiemo every week. I sit on the loading platform squeezed between two Uigurs who hand me bread and meat. I have never been so relieved in my life; I have never felt so safe as in the midst of these strangers.

One thousand kilometers lie behind us since we left Dongco, 50 days in this uninhabited, unwelcoming high-plateau, the Tschang-Tang. I would not have missed one day. It is precisely its inhospitable nature that creates a contrast to our over-satisfied and hectic life here in Central Europe. To quote Sven Hedin once more: "Everyone needs a bit of desert now and then."

SUMMARY OF STATISTICS

AREA: Tibetan Plateau

FIRST ASCENTS: The southeast ridge of Zangser-Kangri (6640 meters, N 34° 23' 29'7", E 85° 51' 18'4"), July 4-5; Peak ca. 6400 meters (N 34° 27'7", E 85° 56'7"), July 6, Frank Kauper, Stefan Simmerer

SOUTH-NORTH CROSSING: South-north crossing of the Tschang-Tang (1000 kilometers, on foot and unsupported), June 12-August 1, 1997

# Una's Tits

*Fondling the Antarctic bosom*

BY GREG LANDRETH

*Keri Pashuk descending from Wandel Peak in the Antarctic Peninsula.* GREG LANDRETH

*Northanger* in the Lamaire Channel with further potential obsessions in the background. GREG LANDRETH

It is heretical, perhaps, to begin a tale of pure mountain exploration from inside the industrial confines of a sandblasting helmet, the hideous din of compressed air carrying its own desert storm against a boat's hull, against the process that the ocean environment does best: that of rusting steel. Hours will pass like this, the roar of the sand and the skeletal ache of directing this holocaust obliterating any romantic thoughts of treading untrodden snow and sailing wild seas—and this but a tiny part of the work at hand. If I could shake my head inside this thing, I'd truly wonder whether the promise of (only) a little bit of climbing—and maybe a few dodgy telemark turns on bad snow—is truly worth all the effort. If there was ever an opposite extreme to the idea of walking through air so rarefied that the very clarity of it makes one hallucinate, on peaks that have never seen footsteps, within sight of one's own comfortable home, this is it. Yet in sailing mountaineering, one invariably involves the other: it is truly an activity of opposite extremes.

If you thought that climbing was expensive, forget it. If you thought that climbing was technical, forget it. If you ever thought, relaxing in the pub with a beer afterward, how far out there you were after a tough day on the rock, forget that, too. Ocean sailing in the high latitudes makes all these things pale by comparison; but for me, all this machinery is set in motion by the simple call of the mountain waiting to be climbed. The challenge posed by the unseen face, the conquest of the fearsome move that leads to the fulfillment of a dream, the idea that out there is a ridge that demands attention, is enough to fuel months, maybe years, of effort on the off-chance that you will be a match for the challenge on the day you arrive there. In this game, there are still huge vastnesses to explore, whole vistas of virgin peaks to wander amongst; embedded in the fierce weather of the Southern Ocean and North Atlantic are the realities that inhabit our dreams, the solid vein of gold that, much diluted by history, is the philosophical underpinning of even the lowliest plastic wall.

There is, however, one problem with all of this. Where do you start? If one were to fly over, say, Antarctica, one would see range after range of mountains stretching to the horizon, for the most part unexplored, even unnamed. Faced with such a profusion of possibility, the mind goes blank. Why climb this one when the hundreds of others around it seem just the same? Why go to the mountain tops when the valleys are just as remote? If one were silly enough to sail there in a small boat, would not the reality of just being there be sufficient reward for your trouble?

The answer is obsession. The mind knows when it sees something that is part of your future—something that you must rise to or be diminished by, something that seems like a good idea from a long way away. It is the duty of the body to transport the mind to where the gauntlet can be thrown. Such a thing was Smith Island. Such things, although not as fully matured, were Una's Tits.

Hang on, hang on, what's all this about tits and boats in a climbing journal anyway? Isn't sailing that boring sport where everyone is either rich or gets seasick? Who is Una, and what has she got to do with Antarctic vistas?

For part of the answer to this, I'll have to go back a couple of years to the Smith Island story, aptly described by Dan Mannix in last year's *Journal*. That year, our boat, *Northanger*, thundered into the Straits of Magellan, a tiny bucketful of unfinished history driven by the Southern Ocean wind and a crusader's sense that somehow man, machine and mountain must meet in perfect symmetry. The circle must be closed before we could go on to other things.

On the summit of Mount Foster in the South Shetland Islands, I felt that emotion that must be the ultimate goal—and ultimate dread—of all mountaineers: perfect satisfaction. There we were, on a sublime point in space and time, surrounded in splendid isolation by the ocean that had been the nemesis of all prior attempts, but which stood aside for us that day and allowed us to walk in Valhalla. Ten years of death and rebirth, desolation and dreaming welded together forever by a single perfect moment. After that, there was no going back to work for the bank; but what could we dream up now that could possibly compare?

The euphoria of the summit did not evaporate soon after the descent, though, perhaps because I now saw climbing as part of a much larger geographical challenge rather than an adrenaline hit on weekends. I had been afraid that climbing would lose its luster as an excuse to launch the machine; but most of all, I feared losing the simple urge to climb, unencumbered by the aura of the "expedition." It was time to get back to basics.

"We'll just go down there for a look around and see what takes our fancy," I lied to Rich Prohaska and Jia Condon as we headed south from Cape Horn. Rich and Jia had arrived in Ushuaia after Christmas, bristling with skis and other sharp appendages, the modernity of which I eyed with envy. Obviously, they had used these things a lot lately. Meanwhile, they surveyed the woeful condition of my and Keri's surviving climbing rack with evident disdain.

"You still climb with these things, huh?" seemed to be the general tenor of the verdict. I could already see the wheels turning: "Let's dump these old sailing fogies when we get there and go do something desperate." They'd come for vertical action; Antarctica had not yet penetrated their souls. And why should it? Canadians scarcely know it exists—they have their own wild frontiers to get lost in.

Unbeknown to them, we'd already gotten our next obsession on a gentle rolling boil. One cannot look upon the twin towers of the mountain that has become known as Una's Tits without lusting after its summits. Following the Smith Island excursion the year before, we'd had time for a good reconnoiter for other prospects in the Antarctic Peninsula area. Heading south down the spectacular "Kodak Crack" (Lemaire Channel) is almost a compulsory part of the experience, not only for sailors in this area, but also in days past for the ship-borne crews of the British Antarctic Survey bases at the bottom end of the Peninsula. In their own inimitable jargon, they had christened the two awe-inspiring rock towers that guard the entrance to Lemaire Channel after the least-forgettable features of probably the last female staff member they would see for several years. Today, no one remembers Una, but she still takes center stage in the south.

The year before, a strong yacht-based attempt had been made on the towers, but had been denied the prize by the combination of dirty weather and uncompromising tourist schedules. Owing to the high cost of access to this area, climbers often will choose to splice their efforts onto an existing tourist charter, thus severely limiting their windows of opportunity. This year, our plan was to roam at will, taking our opportunities where we found them and drinking beer when there were none.

As the single hump of Cape Horn diminished in the distance, though, my thoughts were drawn increasingly to the bright promise of the twin humps that awaited.

The best thing to hope for in the Drake Passage is a boring crossing, skipping through between those fabled Antarctic storms that litter the lore of the area. The crossing usually is rough, but mercifully brief, like passing through a cold twilight void on the way from one world to another.

"I'm not going to be just the boat minder this time," my wife, Keri, stated somewhere in the void. I knew what she was referring to. Stalwart sailor though she is, her passion also is lit by the lure of the inaccessible mountain, and last year she felt she'd been robbed of the action on Smith Island by having to skipper the boat. Never mind that she had made the whole thing possible, sailing back through an icy storm to retrieve us from the island; she likened this to cleaning up after a party. The dream wobbled a little. Who would do the "chores" this time? I owed her a big one, and somehow the payback had to be worked into the new obsession. Antarctica is notoriously lacking in bombproof anchorages, and this is both the joy and the bane of the sailing mountaineer. If the boat is not safe, you cannot leave it to climb—but this insecurity is part of the very reason for going there.

I started to slide references to the towers sideways into conversations.

"If the weather is too bad in the north, we could always nip down and look at Una's Tits" was a favorite. I knew darn well that Rich and Jia would rise to the bait, but for the moment they were too busy being terrified of what we'd told them the ocean could do to them. They were happy enough to count off their watches until Antarctica finally reared up out of the ocean.

One of our favorite anchorages on the Antarctic Peninsula is Port Lockroy on Wiencke Island. As bombproof as it gets, it also is backdropped by the leering walls of the Feif and Wall ranges. These are split by the Thunder Glacier, down which roars the storm wind of the northeaster when it is working. Most of the rock walls rise to about 3,200 feet and are, for the most part, rotten and over-corniced. If you look closely, though, a number of solid-looking buttresses ripple forward out of the tottering mass, and the area is a paradise for ski touring and easier climbing on postcard-perfect peaks.

We had picked out one of these buttresses in the Wall Range to firm up our sea legs, one that had all the requirements for an obsession but was too distant from the sea to recognize. Rich, Jia and I joyfully surged forward, increasing our karmic debt by leaving Keri to caretake the boat yet again. This time, though, she seemed not to mind, content with the promise of later excursions and the chance to drink in the surroundings without us.

*The object of desire: Cape Renard Tower, a.k.a. Una's Tits.* GREG LANDRETH

It was on about the eigth pitch that we realized we perhaps should not have been so joyful in our surging. We were not even halfway up and I began to be glad that I'd put two Power Bars in my pack instead of just one. The buttress was starting to rear up on us; leads were getting harder and the rock looser.

"Hope there's an easy way down the back of this," Jia said, voicing the obvious concern. The farther we climbed up, the more hideous the thought of having to rappel the route became. About mid-afternoon, we passed the point where retreat was more difficult than topping out. Solid granite alternated with ephemeral piles of choss stitched together with thin friction. At about "dark," as we cramponed fearfully beneath the rimed overhangs of the summit ridge, we could look back on 17 pitches dropping away to Thunder Glacier, the first gusts of a northeaster beginning to re-sculpt the geometry of the final pitch. Because I had on the plastic boots (deemed unnecessary at the outset), Rich solemnly handed me the waterfall tools and I began to wade through vertical sugar toward the summit.

I began to think that a sheet of plywood would have been more useful as I left Rich behind in the dark spindrift. He surely must have wondered what I was doing up there, as I termited my way through the cornice, moving heaven and Earth so that the tools might find something solid. My rare glimpses showed him cowering beneath his helmet as yet another man-made avalanche descended. "Glad I'm not going with that lot," was all the sympathy I could muster.

After an eon of fear and four-letter words, the tools found the solid ice of the windswept ridge. I collapsed onto it, wasted, but elated at the thought of running easily down the back side. We all stood there in the howling wind, laughing with conquest and relief—until I bent down to remove my crampons. I couldn't even see them, let alone a 2,000-foot descent route to the glacier, skis and boat. What really ruined the parade, though, was my discovery that overtrousers and gloves had mysteriously evaporated from my pack. "Getting sloppy—too much sailing and not enough climbing," I thought as the elation began to crumble. I quickly fashioned a pair of "breathable" overtrousers from a plastic rubbish bag as Jia ruefully ripped the Gore-tex liners from his gloves and passed them over.

We packed it in after a few hours of shuffling along the ridge, not knowing whether each footstep would find air or ice. When a handy 'schrund appeared, we jumped into its marginal shelter, hoping to outlast the storm and still find our easy descent route. None of us even wanted to imagine the alternative—that of rappelling the entire route in an Antarctic storm.

That, however, is exactly what happened. With our second Power Bar long since eaten and the sun's upswing lightening the sky, we knew we had to be gone, and fast. We were starting to lose the ability to move at all and we knew that this weather could easily last for days. For 12 hours, rappel after rappel, the last dozen or so on a rope partially severed by falling rock, my "trousers" gradually breathing harder and harder, clown hands trying to set anchors and manage ropes, we crept down the buttress. Food, glorious food awaited at the skis and then, stuporing back along the trail we'd left in the glacier 39 hours before, I had time to consider that I'd better sharpen up my act if I was going to get lucky on Una's Tits. Our "warm-up" was equal to a whole week's work in less than two days.

So *Whozuna?* was born (about 5.9 or so if you like putting numbers on mountains).

The longed-for protuberances thrust upward out of the sea, her startling white brassiere delineating the towers from the perfect blue of the sky. *Northanger*'s red hull paddled happily around the base, happy to be there, happy to be part of this kind of action once again. After *Whozuna?*, we ceased to kid ourselves. It could be years before we had another chance this good, and by then the towers would be besieged by Frenchmen in colored pants undoing her clasps with cheater sticks. This was what we had come for, and here it was, right in our faces, right now.

Of the twin ice streaks that had been tried last year, there was now no sign. In their place were two long brown streaks of rotting rock that occasionally rumbled and splashed. The west side of the towers were very steep and solid—alas, more solid than we; we decided to leave them for future portaledge-types.

*Northanger* tiptoed around to the unsounded waters of the east side and found what we needed. Enough of a rock jutting into the sea to be called a beach, a steep ice ramp to a tent-sized shelf, and, best of all, easy access to the base of the rock itself. A route up the skyline ridge looked stiff, but doable.

I know that in all things the Piper must be paid, and when he comes forward with his hand out you must have what he asks. The inflatable was being loaded when Keri, usually staunch in these situations, finally admitted what I had suspected the last day or two.

"I think I have the flu or something. I don't think I can handle the boat by myself this time."

I knew it was true; my nasty voice told me that it was finally my turn to clean up after the party. The nearest good anchorage was Hovgaard, 25 miles through the ice-strewn Lemaire Channel, and the entry to the anchorage was convoluted at best. Even for a fit crew, it would be a stretch if something went wrong. Here, 700 miles south of the place they call the end of the world, you just can't take a chance like that. If something happens to the boat, the very best you can hope for is an international incident. Pipers everywhere.

I looked at Jia and Rich, already kitted up for the move. I'd even remembered my overtrousers this time. Maybe we could have come back for it; but I knew that momentum and weather would be against us. No backup, no climb. Simple as that.

I heard myself say, "Five days, we'll be back in five days," as I threw my pack out of the inflatable and back on deck.

It was starting to get dark as I nosed the little rubber boat gingerly around the menacing shadow of a leopard seal and headed back to *Northanger,* delivery complete. Jia was already on top of the ramp, hauling skis, ropes, tent—enough stuff for a month if necessary. They were looking strong as Keri and I worked our way free of the ice at the cape and turned into Lemaire Channel. I knew they'd make it if the weather cooperated. To my surprise, I didn't even mind. I looked at the intricate dance necessary to get even this far with a half-formed obsession, and took my place in the new scheme of things, happy enough with the "assist" this time.

The weather packed it in soon after we got to Hovgaard, and we settled in to wait in warm comfort, maliciously enjoying the idea that Rich and Jia would be dogging it out in the tent, marooned beneath the tower and

*The East Buttress of Una's Tits.* Unazwhat? *follows the lefthand skyline.* GREG LANDRETH

frustrated at being so close without a chance to climb. During the next five days, there was less than one good day of fine weather, and I began to fear that maybe we would return to Cape Renard with the obsession still intact.

Snatching a weather break on the sixth day, *Northanger* nosed out of the anchorage, do-si-doed among the ice pack in Kodak Crack, and eased around to the hidden side of the towers. No sign of anyone. The bright yellow tent stood out in the white desert like an alien spaceship, but nothing stirred.

The radio squawked, "Can you see us, can you see us?"

We looked up and up, following its directions until we spotted the two tiny red spider mites against the vast gray of the rock.

"Are you on your way up or down?" we fired back.

"Down!" the radio squawked again.

The hit-list flickered and the numbers rolled upward. Una was gone, and as we watched the mites dance and dangle their way down the wall, there was plenty of time to examine our feelings. I felt strong envy, of course. I'd not be human if I didn't; but looking at the scene from far away—a tiny boat in a huge sea, two tiny figures farther out, but connected to that boat by some metaphorical umbilical cord—I realized that, regardless of one's part in it, the play is the play, and the show must go on. In the future, we'd probably have many roles, forcing many different dreams out of their easy cocoons into the harsh stuff of reality. Always interesting. Always challenging.

The summit is still the summit, though, and there we must walk, if the play allows.

*Epilogue*

Rich and Jia collapsed back onto the boat late in the evening. They'd snatched the brief weather break a few days before and fixed the first five pitches. When the weather came right on the last day, they fired up the lines and climbed the remaining ten pitches (of about 5.9 A2), topping out onto the summit ridge of the eastern tower. They had reached the aureole, but the actual nipple was about 20 feet higher, 200 meters or so away along a double-corniced line of snow mushrooms perched precariously on the knife-edged ridge. Deciding they liked the idea of living more than the urge to defile the summit, they retreated down the route, serendipitously arriving on *Northanger* just as it began to snow. We groped our way back to Port Lockroy in a dark blizzard, taking turns at spotting icebergs and growlers on the bow, only able to stand outside for 30 minutes at a time while Rich and Jia slept the sleep of the just. Cleaning up after the party.

Later, again taking advantage of the protection of Hovgaard Island, the four of us made an exploratory venture onto Booth Island, again underestimating the size of the climb. Variously pulling on scabrous rock and tiptoeing along icy ridges, the summit far out of our grasp, we began putting more obsessions into the bank. There's got to be something to hope for on the outside of a sandblasting helmet.

SUMMARY OF STATISTICS

AREA: Antarctic Peninsula

FIRST ASCENTS: *Whozuna?* (V 5.9 mixed, 18 pitches), on Pt. 1050m in the Wall Range, late January, 1997, Greg Landreth, Rich Prohaska and Jia Condon in a 40-hour push; *Unazwhat?* (V 5.9 mixed A2) via the east buttress of the Cape Renard Tower (a.k.a. Una's Tits, 747m), February 1-4, 1997, Rich Prohaska and Jia Condon (route was climbed to the east summit); attempt of Wandel Peak (c. 950m) on Booth Island via the north ridge, early February, 1997, Keri Pashuk, Greg Landreth, Rich Prohaska, Jia Condon

*Conrad Anker in Antarctica's Ellsworth Mountains.* GORDON WILTSIE

# With You in Spirit

*A solo climb with an old friend*

BY CONRAD ANKER

Interior Antarctica is a desolate place. The diversity and amount of vegetation of a normal suburban lawn far exceeds the sum of living things in the Ellsworth Mountains. The land is judged by the wind and ruled by the ice. It is lifeless. Ice, rock and atmosphere are its three components. Some might view this landscape as empty, a void of nothingness, but in the stark simplicity of this continent is an amazing beauty.

A peak between Tyree and Epperly. Alex Lowe and I look down on its northwest face from the summit of Tyree. It looks fun. I'm not sure of its history; it intrigues me because of its location. The peak becomes the focal point of what to do with my free time. Has it been climbed? I think so. Erhard Loretan has climbed out here. Where, I'm not sure. And at one time, perhaps, dinosaurs marched all about before the rock was compressed, metamorphosed and uplifted. Surely they were the first ascensionists.

I'm not able to embark on the project until the last group of Vinson climbers arrives. Flying in from Punta Arenas, Chile is conditions-dependent, and their flight is delayed for six days. While I wait, I climb Mt. Vinson's *ruta normal*. Also in the interim, Marek Kaminski arrives from the Patriot Hills base camp. He had skied to the South Pole alone in 1995. We share a few days in the weather port, exchanging notes on the various disciplines of Antarctic exploration. The beauty of the Antarctic desert is profound, yet skiing across alone seems to me akin to listening to a skipping track of your favorite CD. Even though you love the music, eventually the repetition will drive you crazy. The food. . . same sorta thing.

And also, as I wait, I sort my gear for my solo journey out onto the ice.

I had carried my sled to the pass separating the Branscombe Glacier to the upper Nimitz Glacier and left some ski tracks for the pilots. When the last group arrives, I help get them situated, explaining the importance of sunblock, then, at 11:30 p.m., I head out to the pass. I run in to Patrick and Vika, a pair of Finns who have spent the last 17 days exploring the northern part of the Ellsworth mountains. They were fortunate in climbing four virgin peaks; they also climbed Mount Gardner via the original route, running out of food along the way, only to discover the cache left in 1966 by Nick Clinch's first ascent party. In the cache, they found chocolate and pudding purchased in New Zealand—still edible, testimony to the continent's continuous cold.

It crosses my mind as we wish each other well and speak of wine upon my return that they might be the last humans I encounter. I hate these thoughts, but they hold the ring of truth. Going out alone on an unknown peak. . . . I'd be lying if I said I didn't have them.

Heading out, I have grand plans: Peak "Loretan," the south face of Epperly, and an enduro traverse over to Vinson. With the seven days I have before work calls again, good weather would allow for much of this. My physical exertion level and what that will allow are another matter.

After four hours of pulling my sled, I am at the base of the western spur of Epperly. I pitch my tent in the yellow glow of the austral summer midnight. At 82 degrees south during the summer, the sun hasn't set. It never does, orbiting above you instead on a low azimuth that brings only subtle changes in the appearance of the landscape. The changes tell you when to climb.

Eleven a.m. I awake to a very still tent with muted light. Visibility is down to 20 meters. Ground fog—a familiar weather pattern. Climbing is not an option, so back into my sack I creep.

Twenty-four hours later, the weather hasn't changed. I sleep on, amassing a total of 16 hours of shut-eye. Very quiet. I'm all alone. As time passes, it changes the grand plan. Food rationing is pretty straightforward: You set your oats aside and, if you touch them before the appointed time, well, that just don't cut it. Rationing books, on the other hand, is another matter. I have no strength; how can one stop in the middle of a page-turner? Reading *Somerset Maughn*, my imagination takes me away from the white room to the rain forests of the Amazon, the Dakota plains, the Steppes of Central Asia, the hidden spires of the Himalaya, the golden Sahara—places I've been, places I'd like to go, places in the pictures and on the maps.

On the second day, I sleep a little less, venturing out on my skis for the sake of exercise. I begin to think that if this keeps up I would rather have a few extra books than extra food.

On the third day I radio to pilot Steve King that I have encountered Sasquatch and Elvis traipsing by on their way to a climb. Sasquatch was bemoaning Elvis's bell-bottoms, calling them a hindrance to good crampon work, while Elvis thought Sasquatch couldn't really climb. (He campuses all the moves). King and the climbers on Vinson think I am a bit off.

Seven a.m., and the sun is shining on the tent. I awake to warmth and sweat on the back of my neck. It's the first clear day in 72 hours. The skis, radio antennae and sled have a rime necklace, a gift of the past three days of weather. I think back to the Inuit outfitter who helped me out five years ago up in Baffin. He described such weather eloquently: "The land," he said, "is shy."

After a few days of seclusion, the peaks cut a silhouette against the eastern horizon. Not really knowing what to do, I begin with the obvious: lots of Peet's coffee brewed full-strength and a dub compilation on my Walkman that my niece gave to me for the Ice.

*The Sentinel Range in the Ellsworth Mountains. A: Mt. Gardner, with the line soloed by Mugs Stump in 1989.*
*B: Mt. Tyree, with the line soloed by Mugs Stump in 1989. C: Peak "Loretan," with the line soloed by*
*Conrad Anker in 1997. D: Mt. Epperly, with the line soloed by Erhard Loretan in 1994. E: Mt. Shinn.*
GORDON WILTSIE

The only choice left after two Thermoses of coffee is to go up. I radio King and give him vague plans and itineraries.

"Off over there. Forty-eight hours till the next radio sked. If I don't call in at the regular times, I'm out climbing. See you soon." Can't really make any mistakes, as the rescue crew is myself and David Hahn up on Vinson.

Packed pack: Twelve energy bars, two liters of bug juice and one of high-octane extra-strength coffee. Five pitons, six small stoppers, two screws, three cordellettes and 30 meters of rope. Mittens, sun hat and a down sweater. Spare shades. Not much on paper, too much when climbing and not enough when bivying. It hardly seems as if I am heading out for a climb in Antarctica. As a reserve, I have a handful of chocolate espresso beans, more for psychological aid than anything else. Do you think 30 bits of caffeinated chocolate could turn a really dire situation around? I don't think so either; but still, they are a comfort.

So at noon on January 15, I ski off to the north. At the top of the first rise, I look over my shoulder and realize it is my decision and mine alone to continue. Alas, the draw of the mountains is strong; I keep skiing. Besides, is there anything worse than bailing off a climb and watching the weather improve as you try to justify your chicken-hearted action?

I ski three hours to the cirque formed by the southwest face of Gardner, the west face of Tyree and the northwest face of Peak Loretan. Looking up the 2000-plus-meters to the summits of these peaks I feel mighty small. Insignificant in the grand scale of things. Besides Loretan, the only other person to have ventured into this pocket of the planet was Mugs

*Antarctic vistas.* CONRAD ANKER

Stump, who soloed the faces of Gardner and Tyree eight years ago. I recall Mugs' wild eyes as he recounted his climbs to me, many degrees of latitude away, over a cup of tea. His excitement was remarkable. I was excited with and for him but didn't have much of grasp of what he had just done.

So here I am in this remote and obscure place, staring at 2100 meters of quartzite. What to do? The obvious couloir on the west face looks straightforward, each step like the last and identical to the next until it's time to turn around. The northwest face looks enticing: lots of unknown terrain. Plus I'd be climbing by the same criterion as Mugs. His spirit would be with me; I could look over and imagine him climbing similar terrain and know it would be OK. I ski over a shallow trough, a facade for a big crevasse lurking underneath. With this safe passage, I figure it's time to go forward. To the northwest face, then.

"Better get goin' now before someone tells us we're stupid," Mugs used to say. Only thing is, there's no one here to tell me if this is stupid—which is a good thing, as one comment could undermine a week's worth of motivation.

The climbing gets steeper the higher I climb. Steeper than I thought—5.8 steep in ten- to 15-meter sections. Still, solid green quartzite with a bounty of jugs keeps enticing me higher. I stop twice for fluids and a snack. Looking over the horizon halfway up, I realize I'm in deeper than I bargained for.

I think about being alone in a very empty space. Out here, nature is power. We are very much guests. In the Himal or Alaska an epic eventually will lead to a village. With a bit of craftiness, one may even live off the land. This is not an option in Antarctica.

Two-thirds of the way, it dawns on me that I am pretty committed. Bailing out, procrastinating, rappelling down or walking no longer are an option.

Overpowers the senses: big mountain, little guy.

The nature of the rock is conducive to climbing. The sun, trolling its way across the western horizon, has warmed it enough to allow me to climb without my gloves. Setting my crampons nicely onto the edges of the quartzite reminds me where I am.

I stay closer to the ridges; in the gullies, the glaciers and avalanches have smoothed out the holds. I look up to see vertical gendarmes and imagine I am playing chess with the mountain. So far, moving diagonally, I have been limited to bishop, but now I play as a knight: three horizontal moves, then up one. Yet the mountain, with all the moves and all the power, remains the queen. A solid opponent. I play my moves well, the culmination of 18 years' experience, and keep climbing.

At one gendarme, with no rock gear to set up a quick rappel, I have to downclimb ten meters to a saddle. A vein of crystals at eye level greets me at the notch. I never forcibly remove crystals from the mountains, though occasionally I take one sitting in the dust of time; but picking the first crystals I have found in the Ellsworth Mountains, I perceive things are going to be OK.

There still remain 100 meters of climbing—easy, I think, steep shady mixed terrain, the cold pulling my energy away. I see my breath in small little clouds that remind me I'm still here. The final 20 meters require tunneling through the summit cornice. Thirty centimeters of junk sugar snow overlay the solid alpine ice. With two layers of long underwear, fleece gloves and a baseball hat on, I am underdressed for the occasion. These final moves take an hour; the beep-beep of my watch marks the time. Snow has worked itself into all my folds. In this steep section, I belay at three points, leaving stoppers in small cracks. Time will tell who sees them next.

"Damn," I think, "this is critical. . ."—but then, in slow motion, I realize that it is only serious. Critical would be falling off.

Standing on the opposite side of the cornice, I put on my wind suit and swing my arms in circles to get the warm blood down to my finger tips. I'm in the sun, but the opera lady isn't singing yet. Two more rock steps to the summit. Within a few moments, I'm on the ridge close to the summit. I wander over, snap a picture, drink a sip of coffee. The very tippy top is a bit dicey, a huge cornice overhanging the east face. I don't stand there, just pass on my way. I've had enough adventure just getting here. The route was more difficult than I anticipated, and, after 11 hours of focused climbing, I am trashed.

Heading down the north ridge, it dawns on me that I am too hammered to continue on to Epperly, Tyree and Shinn. A small couloir looks like the best method for descending the peak. Before starting down, I lay down on a small patch of scree and doze off in the 3 a.m. sun. I sleep until shivering wakes me up.

One hundred meters into the descent I happen upon a single knife blade, a sign of Loretan's passage two years earlier. The descent takes the remaining juice away. The slope is hard névé covered with a tricky layer of snow. I must kick steps facing inward in the shaded gully. At the last pass, I lie out in the sun, drying my feet, trying to melt water and enjoying the dreamy consciousness of being spent. I descend to my skis and ski back to my tent.

After 30 hours of being awake and on the go, I radio Patriot Hills and let them know I'm OK. I sound "out of it"; they ask if I've been drinking. Not enough, not enough.

I sit on my sled, hardly able to muster the patience to allow the snow to melt into water. As it does, it slowly brings me back to the present. I think back to what has just transpired. In 1992, we lost a talented alpinist to the glaciers of Denali. My life changed. Mugs had been my mentor. He taught me the joy of mental toughness, the ease of hard climbing and something about a way of life. There isn't a day during which some part of Mugs's life doesn't touch me. Mugs's dream climbs were his ascents of Gardner and Tyree: climbing, with no falling allowed. It doesn't get much simpler than this. Even though I realize what I just experienced was an insignificant passage of time in a wild place, to be in the same spot as Mugs — even though a bit of distance separated us — was a very special moment.

SUMMARY OF STATISTICS

AREA: Ellsworth Mountains, Sentinel Range, Antarctica

NEW ROUTE: The Northwest Face (V 5.8, 2100 meters) of Peak "Loretan" (ca.4800m), January 15-16, 1997, Conrad Anker

# Miso Soup and M&Ms on Baffin Island

*Cross-cultural big-wall adventures*

BY MIKE J. LIBECKI

The bold Baffin Island, that wonderland of majestic granite thrones, lost in time land-scapes and hypnotisms of solitude—after a whirlwind of planning between California and Japan, Shinichi Sakamoto, Misako Koyanagi, and I had finally made it. Our expectations had been at least to study and explore the region for climbing possibilities. Now, though, we realized that a new route was within our reach.

Shinichi, a Japanese man, and Misako, a Japanese woman, had just met, but I had known both for some time. Shinichi and I had bumped into each other one sunny afternoon in 1992 while searching for climbing partners around Yosemite's Camp 4. Our similar passions for climbing and living quickly led to friendship, and our climbing partnership formed a solid team. After only a few days climbing together, we were off to Washington Column, and two days later stood on top. Throughout the next few years, we would meet in Yosemite (just before our 1997 Baffin trip, we touched up our climbing skills with a couple weeks of free climbing at Devil's Tower in Wyoming, and a quick ascent of *Never Never Land* on El Cap), and in the fall of 1995, I traveled to Japan, where, upon arrival, Shinichi welcomed me with warm sake, raw tuna and squid. My six-week stay included a solo bicycle trip across the main island, an extensive tour of steep, finger-crimping climbing areas, incredible hospitality, and an overload of unique foods. I was amazed by how honest and simple people were, and by their *motainai* (Japanese: living without waste), which I had not found in America. Japan changed my life.

Misako and I met later, in the summer of 1996, while checking out route topos in the Yosemite climbing shop. Eager to practice my newly studied Japanese, I started talking. As it turned out, we both had substantial big-wall experience, and we were both currently partnerless and eager to climb. A couple days later, we were shuttling loads to the base of El Capitan. I was slightly concerned about having no prior experience climbing with Misako, but after five days of no-hassle climbing (except for a virus I contracted, which caused six to ten bathroom stops per day for three days), we completed El Cap's *Lunar Eclipse*.

The compatibility of our climbing style fit like a glove. We did not talk much on the climb; sometimes I would say something about climbing, and Misako would reply softly, "In life we must climb." After a comment like that, I knew a climbing future awaited us. When we topped out, we talked about when we would climb together next.

"Have you heard of Baffin Island?" I asked.

Like every other big-wall climber, Misako had read and heard about Baffin Island's granite monoliths. So had Shinichi, and individually we had all pondered putting together an expedition to the northern Arctic to climb a new route on an unclimbed wall. Because my partners lived on the other side of the planet, and summer was getting closer, I wondered if our thoughts were merely a fantasy. A random fax to both revealed that their thoughts corresponded to mine. Unclimbed big-wall fantasies started occupying my mind. Not surprisingly, the same thing was happening to my friends in Japan. Intense planning and research began.

Several months passed. Shinichi and Misako met one another via a high-tech introduction,

*The Weeping Wall, site of the team's route*, Stoneagin. Mike Libecki

and our communication and planning became a little easier. Misako and I concluded that time and money would allow us to plan an expedition only in late summer. Shinichi was having difficulties with his schedule and could not commit to our plans. As this would be the first time any of us had gone to such a remote area, the ideal plan was a three-person team: It would give us a better chance to handle an emergency should one arise, reduce the physical strain on each partner, and unite our climbing and mountaineering experiences for a safe and successful expedition. As research continued, we hoped that some kind of universal power would allow Shinichi to join us.

Finally, Shinichi confirmed that he could make it. A mental smile did not leave my mind for the next few weeks.

After much confusing faxing, gear planning, disagreement, and frustration, we decided to meet in Montreal for three days of clearer communication. We arrived within a couple days of each other with huge smiles, emanating optimism. Shinichi and Misako met face-to-face for the first time. We checked into a cozy little motel with a tasty Vietnamese restaurant (the best fried bananas I ever had) just a few minutes away. With only a couple of opposing opinions about our menu for the expedition, it was time to head for the island.

A bit of ostrich and cake for lunch, some relaxing liqueurs, and a couple of planes later, we arrived in Pangnirtung, a small town on the southern end of the island, and settled down in a comfy campsite on the outskirts of town that also was just outside the boundaries of our destination: Auyuittuq National Park Preserve. The people of Pangnirtung were comforting, greeting us with full-teeth smiles and immediate conversation. One local man insisted on giving us and all of our gear a free ride to our campsite, provided us with pertinent information about where to find food and the local government offices, and turned down our offered tip again and again. The local children, who spied on us from behind boulders just outside of our camp, provided first-class entertainment. Their curiosity proved to be strong, and soon they were drinking our hot chocolate, dancing and singing around us, and reminding us with their carefree nature to have fun and not to take ourselves too seriously.

We had a few days on our hands and used them to plan the food, fuel, and gear for our excursion. We had enough supplies to last for about 35 days, half of which would be spent on foot, shuttling gear 15 to 30 miles or more as we searched for an unclimbed wall in Auyuittuq. As luck (or possibly fate) would have it, that same day, while registering at the local government office, we got word of a team of geologists studying in the area who happened to be traveling via helicopter. Off we went to the only lodge in town in hopes of finding the pilot. After a small negotiation and the proper paperwork, we had an airlift scheduled for the next morning.

With mostly clear skies, low wind speed, and a thumbs-up from the pilot, the helicopter lifted, then swung and swayed like a drunken bumble bee from the weight of our eight haul bags clipped below as it slowly made its way up the glacier-carved Weasel Valley. Massive rock formations entwined by serpentine glaciers surrounded us. We studied our maps and wiped drool from our chins, passing by Mt. Turnweather, Mt. Thor, the Asgard twins, and Tyr Peak. Thanks to our pilot, Jim, who flew the helicopter like a child playing with a Christmas toy, we got an in-depth tour of the Auyuittuq area. What we saw was a mountaineer's dreamland—hundreds of climbing possibilities, from alpine routes to free routes to aid routes, and spectacular trekking galore. Our hearts raced with excitement; at last we were getting a chance to see what we had visualized for so long.

Mesmerized as we were by our visions, we realized we needed to choose a wall—an unclimbed one, of course, but something feasible, given our team's experience together, our amount of supplies and time, and how far we would have to walk back to civilization. It was

*Shinichi Sakamoto and Misako Koyanagi about to start pitch five.*
MIKE LIBECKI

like trying to choose only one piece of candy from a favorite candy shop. As the agreed-upon one-hour flight neared its end, deciding on a landing point became necessary. Just a few miles east of Summit Lake, on the Weeping Glacier, past Breidiblik Peak, stood a prominent 600-meter white granite wall with red and black streaks, like a warrior's painted face. Directly in the center of the wall loomed an enormous roof that looked like a huge closed eye. Though there were no prominent corners, cracks, or features, the three of us spoke at once. An immediate agreement was made. We had found the wall we would attempt to climb. The helicopter unclipped the burden of our gear and landed us on the glacier.

As the helicopter drifted out of sight, we digested the interesting reality of our new glacial home. We had no means of communication; a rescue was not a possibility. Our thoughts were lost to views of our new world as a chilling breeze eased us into a meditative silence. Marvelous granite towers capped thick with ice and snow could be seen in every direction. A black raven flew by screaming a cold welcome; it was the only kind of animal we would see until we left.

We spent the next couple of days studying rock and icefall patterns, shuttling gear to the base of the wall, and scoping for a possible crack system. There seemed to be consistent snow and icefall over all of the wall. The wall itself looked quite blank, but there was one system of cracks and features that departed from a beautiful 100-meter-plus pinnacle attached to the wall. Although it had some noticeably featureless sections, it looked possible for a route— and, fortunately, it seemed to receive the lowest amount of snow and icefall of any sections of the wall. After a *totemo oishii* (Japanese: delicious) meal of white rice, wakame soup, green tea and M&Ms, we drifted into dreams crowded with visions of the climbing ahead.

Our first day of climbing proved to be *sugoi* (Japanese: great); a thin A1 splitter took us

60 meters up to a small ledge, from which we climbed an easy 5.8, 40-meter chimney/gully to the top of "Stonehenge Pinnacle," named for its resemblance to the ancient carving. After lunch, we hauled, shuttled, and organized our extensive gear, getting a taste of the intense work that awaited us. As the day ended, I was anxious to get back to base camp for Misako's bag of Japanese treats. With any luck, she would pull out another surprise—perhaps some kind of sweet-bean candy bar, dried squid, or some crispy rice crackers.

Our thoughts danced merrily that night; blue skies had graced our progress and the climb was under way. As we talked about the unexpectedly perfect weather, Misako noticed her barometer reading dropping, a sign the nice weather was definitely too good to last. I fell asleep that night with difficulty, thinking with contained excitement about the climbing to come.

A new test awaited us the next morning as we awoke to heavy snow and strong wind. We had to make the transition from climbing in comfortable weather to climbing in cold, wet, miserable conditions. I vigorously rammed my ascenders up the ice-dressed ropes to the top of the pinnacle. Misako followed. Even as the wind howled and the snow whipped our faces, Misako moved slowly and gracefully. She spoke softly, her facial expression peaceful, as though she was sleeping. I felt quite safe with her, for I could tell she was always aware of the current situation and took it seriously, whether it was sewing up a line of copperheads or preparing breakfast.

Our bodies were soaking wet by the time we reached the anchors. We got out the hammers and cracked our gear out of its ice cocoon, and I started leading. After a couple of hours, the snow still fell consistently. Looking back at my last solid piece of gear 12 meters below, already several hook moves out, with too big of a rack, my rope and gear soaked, and plastic boots on, I started to feel heavy. I looked down at my crooked Fish hook on a small flake; now was not the time to think about the flake's inner strength. A thin crack started only a couple meters above. Feeling like a ballet dancer, I carefully slid my boot into the top step of the etri- er, then searched for a small Alien and immediately attached it to my daisy chain. With my longest reach, I stretched for solid crack and inserted the piece.

A split second later, before I could even weight it—crack!—the flake I was on broke. Misako let out a shriek. A one-meter daisy-chain fall and a hundred heartbeats later, the Alien held. A few freezing hours and 50 meters after that, I fixed a few pins and sucked on my fin- gers to get the blood flowing again. We quickly rappelled down to ground, where Shinichi welcomed us with hot green tea and oatmeal.

Shinichi and Misako were up early the next morning and off into the snowy winds at an attempt for more upward progress. After words of encouragement, I nestled into my bag and sipped coffee, trying to watch them through the heavy flakes of snow. As the snow fell hard- er and harder, they could barely be seen from the ground. Hours later, they returned, report- ing ten meters of copperheads higher up.

During the next few days, we made little progress as the heavy storms continued. Though slightly frustrated because we were almost completely confined to our tent, we knew we were finding out how to climb in this weather. There was little room for three people in the tent and the body odors were becoming quite noticeable, but everyone seemed *shiawase* (happy) and *kokochioi* (comfortable). Eventually, we awoke to sun—quite a pleasure, as we could dry out and have breakfast outside for the first time in several days.

Due to our cultural differences and sharing of the same space, compromise and respect for our different ways of living were often necessary. Sitting at our breakfast table carved from snow one morning, I spit, necessarily and noisily, away from our eating area. Misako went quiet. Shinichi sternly informed me such a thing was quite rude to him. I stubbornly debated my feelings; such an act was normal to me. Still, it seemed like a good time to get more water for breakfast.

Since we were on the northeast side of the wall, a good weather day offered us about five hours of sunlight. An anchor at our route's high point now was necessary. It was time to commit to the vertical world. Another day drifted by, lost to opposing opinions and disagreement about our hauling system, supplies we would need on the wall, and where our first wall camp would be. Finally, we tried to move our supplies in a single haul only to find out that, due to weight, a double haul was necessary.

The sun shone once again the following morning, and a no-hassle double haul to our high point was made with just a little more than 16 days' worth of food and fuel. We now occupied the vertical quarters we had hoped for. A couple of roomy expedition portaledges and plenty of luxuries, including reading and writing material, a radio, lots of chocolates, and other soothing remedies, made our portaledge camp quite comfortable. Gazing out the rainfly door, I could not find words to describe the beauty; it would have been like attempting to describe an example of eternity, magnificence, or a place where fairy tales and magic were real. For all I knew, a dinosaur could have walked around the corner at any time.

Unsurprisingly, strong winds and heavy snow returned our first morning on the wall. The following four days were spent in our 'ledges trying to keep warm and occupied. We drew food topos of our favorite pizza or sushi (I spent an hour drawing my favorite beer), brushed up on each other's languages, and had a few debates about Japanese and American culture. It occupied storm-time nicely, and before we knew it, the winds had died down. Though it was still snowing, climbing was feasible again. After contemplating our route's direction, more upward progress began.

Shinichi called a warning about loose rocks from above as he hammered small knifeblades into a loose, rotten corner. Misako belayed, shivering, while her head and shoulders grew layered with snow. It was a rest day for me; I read my book of meditation and sipped green tea. I kept hearing loose rock warnings from outside my cozy expedition rainfly. Fortunately, I had a pad of paper, a jacket, and my book resting on my lap, for they absorbed the impact of the football-sized rock that barged in straight through the top of my rainfly directly onto me — as though it were being served for dinner!

After patching the hole in the rainfly with sheets of ripstop-nylon and duct tape, we decided to take an alternate (and safer) route than the one above our portaledges. It was, at times, difficult and somewhat frustrating agreeing on decisions about the climb. There was a small language barrier as well; fortunately, Shinichi's English was excellent, Misako's English understandable, and my Japanese improving. We learned that our seriousness on all decisions, whether agreed upon or not, was a sort of positive soil in which communication was planted. By listening to each other's ideas, understanding sprouted and grew into an incredibly deep connection with one another. The communication between us bloomed into new levels of appreciation, trust, and respect as the climb progressed.

Moving to the left of our wall camp proved not only safer, but offered up some great crack systems as well. Two more long pitches brought us about 80 meters up and 40 meters left of our original wall camp, underneath the enormous sheltering roof we had seen from the helicopter. A relaxing sensation came over us as we settled into our new portaledge camp underneath it. Nothing but the roof itself could fall and hit us now.

New thoughts concerned us. There were five to ten pitches to go and about six scheduled days left on the wall, leaving us seven days to walk back to our contact 18 miles away and catch our plane. With a questionable (if any) crack system above the roof, we needed every day to offer good climbing weather. We completed two pitches the next day. Misako led an

*Misako Koyanagi, with Asgard in the background.* MIKE LIBECKI

impressive hook and free pitch over the roof to a series of scary expanding flakes. My heart beat like a drum while I watched flakes crumble beneath her feet as I belayed. Shinichi continued up a splitter expanding corner/flake to what looked like a blank section of the wall. It was my lead. As I started off on the crackless, almost featureless section, my rack of hooks, copperheads, and the bolt kit were readily accessible. Shinichi nervously belayed as I eased out on interesting hooks and copperheads. As I placed another malleable, I heard strange hisses of doubt from Shinichi.

"What?" I asked.

"Mike, that one look very bad," Shinichi whispered reluctantly. I appreciated his communication but needed his confidence. A little frustrated, I tested the dicey hook piece and tiptoed on to more hooks that eventually lead to a cruiser Lost Arrow nailing frenzy.

Fabulous weather smiled upon us. Gazing down at the glacial pool that grew smaller as we gained elevation, we knew we were getting closer to the top. We were blessed with clear, albeit freezing, weather, but even the cold was almost a comfortable one, offering a real feeling of being alive.

One more loose and funky pitch presented us with a clean, solid corner system that looked as though it would lead straight to the top. We waltzed through a couple more sweet A1 and easy free pitches to the top of the wall. A last 100-meter-plus snow and ice pitch brought us to huge, teetering boulders, loose rock, and ice that seemed to stare evily at us. We stood at the top of the wall wondering if it was really over, staring down at our melted base camp and the once-huge, now-tiny glacial pool below. Our feelings were calm and content; we were ready to go down.

A cantaloupe-sized rock bounced off my knee pad, underscoring the danger still lurking before us. After quick handshakes of victory and a few photos, we descended back to our portaledges seven pitches below. We had one more scheduled day on the wall, so we decided to stay a last night in the vertical world. We celebrated our ascent with an all-we-could-eat feast of freeze-dried stew, salami, cheesecake, chocolate, hot milk and sugar, and whatever else was hidden in the bottom of our food barrel. The last days on the wall, when we had needed good weather, had not only been amazingly gorgeous, but substantially warmer. I felt as though some kind of universal power had let things fall into place.

Still, the journey remained very much alive and dangerous, and a new goal of a safe descent and walk out to civilization occupied our attention. After watching our haul bags make a one-minute descent, we carefully rappelled the rest of the route. Surprisingly, even with 100-meter rappels, our ropes never got completely stuck or damaged, and we eventually stood on mostly solid ground again after 15 days of living on the wall. Though it was quite a pleasure to feel my weight over my feet, I immediately missed the harmony and challenge of living in the vertical world with my Japanese friends.

On our jaunt back to our boat-contact, we came across the tent of Japanese climber Go Abe, a friend of Misako's, and an acquaintance of mine from Yosemite. It looked like it had been abandoned. Misako told us something was wrong with his tent like that; she felt he was in trouble.

We continued on our walk for the next few days. After arriving back in Pangnirtung, we reported the situation to the local government office, where we found out that a Spanish team, Juan Espany and Cristobal Diaz, who had been climbing on Mt. Thor, saw Go Abe climbing only to suddenly lose sight of him. By the time we left Baffin we found out that Go Abe, a soft-spoken hardman, had died soloing a new route on Mt. Thor. Our trip ended with an array of feelings.

But it also taught us new communication skills, safety techniques, and ideas. A magical

*Mike Libecki on thin aid, pitch seven.* SHINICHI SAKAMOTO

relationship was forged between Shinichi, Misako, and me, and new doorways to adventure were discovered. One part of the journey that grew within me remains with me now: Responsibility for impact on any place on Earth is just as important as any other aspect of an adventure into the outdoors. Our arrival in a hidden glacial valley and spectacular climbing area in the northern Arctic drove home the amount of environmental impact just a few people can have in a little time. We left as little evidence as possible of our passage. Adventuring in the best style possible and using proper etiquette is our responsibility not only to practice, but to communicate to fellow and future adventurers throughout the world.

SUMMARY OF STATISTICS

AREA: Auyuittuq National Park Preserve, Baffin Island, Northwest Territories, Canada

FIRST ASCENT: *Stoneagin* (VI 5.9 A3+, 550 meters) on the Weeping Wall on the Weeping Glacier, July 30 to August 19, 1997, Shinichi Sakamoto, Misako Koyanagi, Mike J. Libecki

# Waiting for the Sun

*A year's worth of climbing on Escudo's east face*

BY JEAN-DANIEL NICOLET
TRANSLATED BY MARINA HEUSCH

*The southeast face of Escudo.* JEAN-FRANÇOIS ROBERT

Patagonia remains an unconquered country, an oasis of solitude, an ideal place for discovery and adventure. It is battered by winds and endures the violent assaults of capricious weather. The lay of this land offers no obstacle to the winds; it is an empire of the sky. The gusts sweep through everything, beating down vegetation and humans alike in their way. The Torres del Paine region is carved by mountainous relief, the horizon opening up to abruptly severed cliffs that seem smooth and inaccessible. They are the most beautiful granite walls on this planet, and they taunt and intrigue.

The commitment must be total, the adventure, seductive. Our dream is to open up a big-wall route. Plotting a path through these formidable granite shields constitutes a challenge that is somewhat crazy. The meteorological conditions are unfavorable, the immensity of these faces less than engaging. Driven by a passion for the mountains, we attempt (twice) an ascent on the fantastic wall of Escudo, the Shield. The scene is set; the actors are left to play.

Veni, vidi. . . but not vici.

As for veni: Nine friends from Neuchatel, Switzerland (Thierry Bionda, Denis Burdet, Régis Dubois, Christian Meillard, Jean-Daniel Nicolet, Jean-François Robert, Pierre Robert, Yann Smith, Jean-Michel Zweiacker) spent the months of January and February, 1997, in the Torres del Paine National Park in Chilean Patagonia, with two objectives: the Torre Sur and the El Escudo.

As for vidi: a majestic landscape, impressive faces, a wild and somewhat hostile nature.

And as for vici—alas, it's more complicated. In spite of elaborate battle plans and attack strategies, when the mountain (and, above all, the weather) says "no," it's no. The Patagonian wind did not fail to live up to its reputation. The rain and the snow seemed to appraise us; as for the sun, we didn't see it for more than 48 hours during the month and a half we spent at the foot of the faces. Under such circumstances, the fight becomes unequal, and our morale had difficulty moving beyond zero. Christian's bad fall didn't help the situation either. In other words, the conditions were difficult. And to hear the locals, who hadn't seen a summer that rotten in nine years, one could only tell oneself that the die were cast. We left a little disappointed, but not discouraged. The experience was still beautiful. Defeat is part of the game, even if it sometimes hurts one's ego.

Back in Switzerland, we dressed our wounds. Most of the injuries were to our morale, for Christian and Thierry (broken tibia and ankle, torn fingers), to their physique. We would be back. For my part, I was sure of it, as was Jean-Michel. As if to keep us from changing our mind, we had left materials and freeze-fried food at Werner and Cecilia's, our hosts and the owners of a guest house in Puerto Natales. But when?

In the end, the project quickly took shape and we decided to return to finish the route I had started with Yann, Regis, and Pierre on the southeast face of the Escudo. We decided to take up this climb again because it is more of a wall climb than the south face—and also because we had already climbed 500 meters (about half the face) on our last expedition. Little Louis (Jean-François) was immediately interested; he would accompany us as photographer for part of the trip.

On November 30, 1997, after some time in the United States (including Yosemite, where we climbed *Zenyatta Mondatta* on El Capitan), Jean-Michel and I arrive in Puerto Natales. We are soon joined by Little Louis, who comes directly from Switzerland. That leaves us two days to get everything ready. This time, we had decided to come earlier in the season. Would the month of December be preferable? Our first day in Puerto Natales leaves us dreaming. The sky is black, and it rains all day. Come on! No panic—the weather here in Puerto Natales is not the same as in the Torres, and, besides, in those mountains, the conditions change very quickly and are different from one valley to the next. So . . . patience.

We meet up with Lionel Daudet. He is back in Puerto Natales after having spent a couple of days in the park. He intends to repeat *The Dream*, Brad Jarrett, Chris Breemer, and Christian Santelices' mythical route, established in 1995 up the middle of Escudo. We will be "neighbors" on the wall. Unfortunately, Lionel has had to come back to town to take care of a bladder infection.

Little Louis finally arrives. Time begins to feel like it is dragging here. Even though it is a small city of some 13,000 inhabitants, we feel oppressed and are impatient to leave Puerto Natales behind to find ourselves face-to-face with our objective.

On December 3, we finish gathering together all of our food and the following day take a bus toward the park with our 250 kilos of gear. While Jean-Michel busies himself dealing with the administrative problems, we dispatch Little Louis to the lodge at the foot of the mountain with our equipment. We rent four horses; thanks to inflation, they cost more than the last time around, and furthermore, they will not go all the way up to the Torres base camp, but only to the Chilean camp, which means an extra day of carrying for us. Within five days, we have moved all of our equipment to the base of the wall at the rate of three to four trips per person.

Here we are at the foot of our goal. We set up our camp on the glacier split by crevasses and covered with piles of rocks and dirt. We prepare as good a

*Traversing across the snow bench.* JEAN-FRANÇOIS ROBERT

platform as possible for our tent, and, despite the hope that we won't spend more than a day or two at the foot of the wall (the climate has been relatively mild until now), we build walls to protect us from the wind and bad conditions. You never know.

The space is sobering; we are surrounded by gigantic cliff walls. The face of Escudo is 1200 meters high and blocks our view and any access to other slopes. The proportions are completely distorted; because we are used to distances in the Alps, we are unable to measure our insignificance in this Goliath-like landscape.

The first part of the route is made up of 50 to 60° slabs that come together at a snow bench. We estimate at first that three pitches will get us to the névé. Actually, it takes seven.

We are on the attack, ready and confident. One can't be jinxed twice in a row. Upon waking the next day, however, I have a feeling of déja-vu. No, it can't be—not this again. It has snowed 20 centimeters during the night—truly difficult on morale, but we try to make the best of a lousy situation regardless. In the end, a day of rest is welcome after five days of hauling supplies. We brew coffee (the real stuff, with our Italian coffee pot; for caffeine addicts such as us, it's more a necessity than a luxury), shuffle the cards, divide up for a game of two

*Jean-Daniel Nicolet rappeling pitch 17. In the background is the north face of Torre Sur.*
JEAN-FRANÇOIS ROBERT

against three. Time passes slowly.

The wind blows throughout the next night, bringing us a wonderful surprise. In the morning, the sky has cleared, the snow has melted, and the slabs are, for the most part, dry. In one day, with Jean-Michel, we free-climb the first seven pitches, slabs that took a month's effort to aid the first time around when they were covered with snow. We fix 350 meters of rope in a sort of umbilical cord that connects the base of the wall to the snow bench. From there, the wall soars into an overhang. The following day again is branded with bad weather. Despite the poor conditions, we haul up equipment—long, tiresome work, especially on the slabs.

October 12 is the big departure, and we flake out the ropes. Belayed by Little Louis, I repeat two pitches above the snow bench. Jean-Michel pulls up the rest of the equipment and retrieves the fixed ropes. While I'm fighting my way up the first tough aid pitch, I hear Jean-Michel calling me. He tells me that Lionel, who started up *The Dream* that morning, is giving up on his solo attempt. He is still weak from the antibiotics and not 100 percent up for such an undertaking. Instead, he would like to join us. Excluding the issue of food, whether we continue with three or four people doesn't change anything for us, and we're happy to take on this unexpected passenger.

Two of us move upward while the other two rest in the ledges. The next day, I continue the ascent with Lionel. Three pitches remain before we reach our high point from the year before—three pitches up familiar terrain before the big question mark. What will happen next? Will the route be obvious? The hours we spent scrutinizing the wall allowed us to plot out a logical course via a crack some 100 meters long; but in order to reach it, we will have to traverse a seemingly blank area without any noticeable weaknesses. We fear we will have to rely on rivets. Furthermore, there still remains the infamous double crack formed by questionable flakes. It has intrigued us since day one.

Lionel repeats two traverse pitches out of three and agrees with the A3+ grade we had given them. In four days, we repeat the 12 pitches opened up in January and February. The weather has been mild. It certainly isn't warm, but if the conditions remain the same, we have high hopes of success.

It is Jean-Michel and Little Louis's turn to lead the next section. From the portaledge, I watch them fix the ropes. Ah—what luck to stay "in bed" while our friends work. For Lionel and myself, it's a day of rest. Not completely, however; we have to melt snow, preparing the approximately 80 liters of water necessary for the rest of the ascent. We have already fixed 150 meters of rope since the snow bench, and we estimate that 200 meters higher, it will become too difficult and too long to jug the lines each morning. We will have to move the snow camp 200 meters higher in the middle of the wall. No more snow benches—no more benches, period. We will be suspended in open air.

I watch Jean-Michel, who has reached the flake system, a double crack 15 meters high. The middle flake, sandwiched between the wall and the outer flake, makes one think of a sheet of paper. About ten centimeters thick at its base and two at its tip, it is not welded to its surroundings, existing instead in a precarious equilibrium, balanced by the winds. It is only when one reaches the top of the flake that one becomes aware of its fragility. Upon Jean-Michel's return, I ask him how the crack was.

"Expanding!" he responds—when aid-climbing, a word to fear.

After the flake, Jean-Michel protects another half pitch along a soft, sandy slat with rivets. We are right in the middle of the question mark zone and hope the climbing higher up will be better.

It snows the next night. When we wake, everything is covered with ice. It looks like a day of rest. Lionel, who had just finished taking his prescription of antibiotics, has a relapse. The

*Jean-Daniel Nicolet resorting to rivets.*
JEAN-MICHEL ZWEIACKER

fever sets in again, and despite the numerous drinks prepared by Little Louis, he is delirious throughout the night.

The sun makes an appearance in the middle of the day, and I no longer can stay put. I gear up, and Jean-Michel takes over for Lionel. I complete the pitch begun the preceding day. Our fears were justified. There is no other way to proceed than right up the middle with a line of rivets—14 in all. What a nightmare.

Lionel is again on antibiotics and in a critical state. He must go back down. Little Louis will accompany him. Jean-Michel and I find ourselves back to our original plans. What follows passes as if in a dream: We move the camp from the snow bank to the 15th belay beneath a roof, just under the black dike. This is Escudo's "vein," which cuts diagonally through the face and reminds one of a large scar. It takes us all day to haul our gear and set up our second camp.

Now we are in open space. I am not very far from the corner of a big dihedral, but it is impossible to see what it looks like. I am impatient to find out more . . . perhaps a bit too impatient: The hook I am on pops, and I fall 15 meters. I scream out, cursing; even if it doesn't change much, it at least serves to calm me down. The only thing I can do is climb back up and repeat the traverse on hooks. This time, I concentrate a little more, and finally reach the dihedral. The surface of the rock is sandy, but the crack is perfect, climbing up 20 vertical meters to end underneath a roof. I belay from there. I cannot see the continuation of the route and will have to be patient.

I spend nine hours hanging at this belay—nine hours during which Jean-Michel likewise will experience fear and the occasional adrenaline rush. He also tastes the "pleasures" of flight. I watch him place a green cam in an offwidth. Two seconds later, he is no longer five meters above the anchor, but five meters below me. He starts again from scratch, but this time he makes it through the offwidth and disappears from view, hidden by the roof. By leaning backward, I can see him, and call up, "Everything okay?" An unsettled grunt explains that the crack continues another 15 meters, but that it is quite precarious. And as for the next move. . . another big question mark.

We had positioned ourselves to get to a crack that began a little to the left. From where he is, Jean-Michel can see only smooth rock. Thirteen rivets later, he has climbed diagonally up to the left and arrived exactly upon the start of the line we wanted. It is more than we had hoped for. The crack, where two absolutely compact and overhanging walls meet, goes up more than 100 meters. We had doubted its true existence; whether it was the play of shadows and light or the different color of the seam, doubt had set in. But there it is. Magnificent. Fifty meters above us, it disappears, but by some divine providence, another crack begins some three meters to the left and continues uninterrupted to a series of roofs that we reach within three pitches. An unsullied line, the only weakness in this overhanging section of the wall, where the overhang increases the beauty of the climb, adding another dimension to our happiness, to our being the first climbers to move through here. It is magical. It is like a dream.

Well, not quite. When you dream, you sleep. For us, the hours of sleep are rare. For three days, the weather remains mild: little wind with the occasional ray of sun, but neither rain nor snow. The temperature remains wintry, however. In these conditions, we don't have the right to dawdle, even if fatigue sets in. Our hands are cracked by the cold, and handling all of our iron makes us suffer enormously. The chapstick no longer helps. It is equally impossible to climb with gloves on. The up and down on the fixed ropes exhausts us.

We have moved beyond the roofs to reach a highly structured area. From the glacier, we had guessed that the face would kick back at this exact point. In reality, that is not the case, and the wall remains at an incline, hanging over us. Furthermore, there's no obvious line. Several ways are possible. But which one do we follow to reach the shoulder? We know we are not far from the summit, but it is difficult to orient oneself on these huge walls. We curse ourselves for not having brought along a photograph of the wall. We left the glacier ten days ago, and the weather has remained relatively mild. We know it won't last; the barometer is spinning. Tomorrow, we absolutely must finish the route.

When we wake up, the sky is still clear, and the sun is still in view, but we haven't finished retrieving the ropes when the wind picks up. Funny—we had almost forgotten it. It blows in with Patagonian force, swinging us along in huge pendulums.

Jean-Michel attacks what we believe is the last pitch. For seven hours, he fights to move forward. The wind is joined by snow. The temperature dips significantly; everything freezes instantaneously. A resurgence of water in the middle of the wall transforms itself into icicles at an incredible rate. We had expected an easy pitch, but instead the wall is still overhanging and the placements remain difficult to get. And amidst the uncertainty of the route, the gusts of wind, and the snow, there comes the crushing pressures of time. The situation becomes more and more critical. Our progress becomes difficult and very slow. The gusts of wind are so violently strong that we are immobilized occasionally. In a word, it's hell. Finally, after 55 meters of effort, pulling out all the stops on a perfect A4 climb, Jean-Michel reaches a ledge. He is at the end of the steep wall, just beneath the shoulder. He climbed up exactly where he needed to. This time, I'm positive it wasn't just coincidence. He really does have a sense of the route.

I clean the pitch, stripping five- to ten-millimeter sheets of ice from the rope in order to jumar. When I join Jean-Michel on the ledge, it is 4 p.m. Before us lies a 5.8 crack. The rock flattens, and the shoulder is just 60 meters away.

What should we do? Go on to bivy wherever we can? In these conditions it would be suicide. Downclimb to a protected spot and leave all of the pieces in place with a fixed rope in order to finish the pitch tomorrow? If the ropes freeze, there will be no way to climb back up. Downclimb and retrieve everything along the way? For now, that seems to be the best solution.

In retrospect, we still believe we made the right decision. The weather the following days did not improve. We had already mildly frostbitten several fingers; another bivouac would have been dramatic. We had made it through all of the cruxes and to the end of the steep wall.

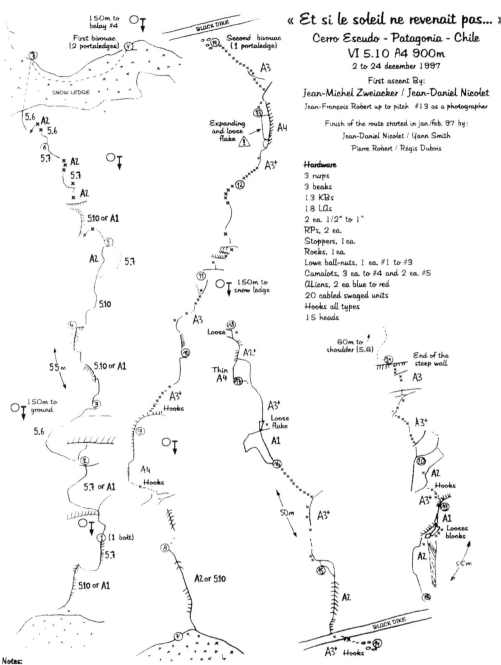

### « Et si le soleil ne revenait pas... »
### Cerro Escudo - Patagonia - Chile
### VI 5.10 A4 900m
2 to 24 december 1997

First ascent By:
Jean-Michel Zweiacker / Jean-Daniel Nicolet
Jean-François Robert up to pitch #13 as a photographer

Finish of the route started in jan/feb. 97 by:
Jean-Daniel Nicolet / Yann Smith
Pierre Robert / Régis Dubois

**Hardware**
3 rurps
3 beaks
13 KBs
18 LAs
2 ea. 1/2" to 1"
RPs, 2 ea.
Stoppers, 1 ea.
Rocks, 1 ea.
Lowe ball-nuts, 1 ea. #1 to #3
Camalots, 3 ea. to #4 and 2 ea. #5
Aliens, 2 ea. blue to red
20 cabled swaged units
Hooks all types
15 heads

**Notes:**
All belays equiped for rappels (two 8mm bolts with a sling and a carabiner). From belay #13 you need to leave a fixe line to rappel because the overhanging face. All rivets in place but be careful they look like bolts but they aren't! We used 80m lead ropes and 300m fixe ropes.
Our route is located on the right side of the Escudo (right to the german route «via del invalidos»). The 7 first pitches are slabs. From the snow ledge, the face becomes steeper and from pitch #11 the face is overhanging to belay #21. We didn't climb the last section to reach the shoulder because of the bad weather conditions. We estimate that the last section is about 60m length, 5.8 rating on slabs.
"And if the sun didn't come back..." It is the question we were asking us the first time we came in january-february 97 because in 2 month we had only 48 hours nice weather.

Our lives are worth more than one 5.8 pitch. At least we have the satisfaction of leaving a clean route without any fixed ropes.

We fold up the portaledge, close the bag, and begin the descent. In these conditions, it will not be easy. The first rappel goes all right. On the second, we can neither see from one belay station to the next nor understand one another. The ropes fly in all directions. We finally meet up at one belay station with a bag, one fixed rope, and three 60-meter ropes. According to the laws of gravity, a rope should fall down when we throw it; instead, it remains completely taut, held up vertically by the wind. We spend an hour untangling everything and working out a technique. The answer: fold each strand of rope. Don't let anything fly loose. It is a gigantic task, but it works.

At 11 p.m., we reach the portaledge, having retrieved everything except the last belay anchor (which, of course, is stuck). We will look into that tomorrow. For now, we're well on our way. The following day, Jean-Michel loosens the ropes while I take down the camp. We embark upon the last 15 rappels. Our practiced technique this next day is perfect, and we arrive at the tent at 8 p.m. We treat ourselves to a day of rest and within three days, we carry down all of our gear in two trips. We arrive in Puerto Natales the evening of the 24th. We've been working like animals some 22 days. We are wrecked—but we are happy.

SUMMARY OF STATISTICS

AREA: Torres del Paine National Park, Chilean Patagonia

ATTEMPT: *Et Si Le Soleil Ne Revenait Pas. . . .* (VI 5.10 A4, 900m) on the east face of El Escudo, December 2-24, 1997, Jean-Michel Zweiacker, Jean-Daniel Nicolet, Jean-François Robert as photographer (up to the 12th pitch), the continuation of a route begun in January/February 1997 by Jean-Daniel Nicolet, Yann Smith, Pierre Robert, and Régis Dubois

# The Riddle of the Cordillera Blanca

*Who Names a Mountain?*

BY ANTONIO GÓMEZ BOHÓRQUEZ
TRANSLATED BY BEAN BOWERS

In July of 1985, Onofre P. García and I did a wall route in Peru's Cordillera Blanca on a peak we knew as "La Esfinge" (The Sphinx), but which other climbers called the Torre de Parón. A French climber, Philippe Beaud, wrote about the climb three years later in his book *Les Cordilleras du Perou*: "An important route in the evolution of rock climbing in the Peruvian Andes. . . the first [on] . . . 100% rock—excellent granite. It is a fantastic free climb. . . ." Problematically, the photo that illustrates this glorious and impromptu text does not correspond to "The Sphinx" that we had climbed.

Since then, various notes about ascents of this mountain have appeared in well-known magazines, accumulating a series of errors that would confuse anyone trying to research route specifics, such as who did it, when it was done, and the many names associated with the climb. The notes I present here are an attempt to clear up the mystery about this mountain.

*The Sphinx? A Story of Men And Names*

In the early 1980s, a 5325-meter peak in one of the most impressive glacial cirques of Cordillera Blanca in Peru called the attention of climbers. These climbers were not drawn by the usual peaks of snow and ice typical in the Blanca, but by huge cathedral-like rock walls. This was a new paradise for rock climbers who would find large alpine crags and big walls in an exotic land that began at an altitude where the walls of Europe and North America top out.

In 1982, two andinistas, Francisco Aguado (Spain) and Américo Tordoya (Peru), decided to climb the 5325-meter peak via the large arête between its two most spectacular walls: the east and south-southeast. It all ended without a summit, and understandably so, because the andinistas, who had come in the first place to climb snow and ice peaks, had tried to implement traditional Blanca tactics to the rock walls. They were defeated by a mountain that clearly would require a new approach.

*Seven Names for One Mountain?*

There appeared a point on a map of the Cordillera Blanca made by the German Alpine Society in 1932 that had no notation other than an altitude of 5325 meters. This point was situated west of a mountain known as Aguja Nevada, and located above a large depression called the Quebrada de Parón (Parón Gorge).

Six years later, the same point appeared with the name Cerro Qollga (Colca) on a monograph depicting the province of Huaylas, in the north of the Cordillera Blanca. This monograph was drawn by the Provincial Association of Primary Teachers of the Huaylas province and published in Volume 7 of its magazine, *Antena*. It is very possible that this educational group did not climb the mountain, through which it would have established the right to give such an arbitrarily curious name.

*The southeast and east faces of La Esfinge from Nevado Pisco.* ANTONIO BOHÓRQUEZ

On June 9, 1955, an early pioneering expedition of the Peruvian Andes entered the Quebrada de Parón. It was composed of the German alpinists Hermann Huber, Alfred Koch, Helmut Schmidt, and Heinz Gradl, and accompanied by porters Pedro Méndez and Guillermo Morales, who knew the country well. Throughout their march in, the expedition marveled at how Point 5325m (Cerro Colca) protruded from behind the north face of the Quebrada de Parón. They therefore labeled it as "the guardian of granite that dominates the gorge." The high, cold, vertical beauty of the granite rampart kindled the fires of their desire to reach its summit. For all the equipment with them, however, they lacked the gear necessary for climbing the 300- to 800-meter rock walls.

The expedition arrived at the Laguna de Parón. The following day, they embarked across the lake in old inflatable rubber rafts with smaller vessels in tow, and crossed the three-and-a-half kilometers that divided them from the other bank. The wind gave them problems cross-

*Onofre Garcia leading the first pitch on the 1988 ascent of the southeast face*. ANTONIO BOHÓRQUEZ

ing the cold, green waters, but did not impede their travel too much and, in two days, they were fully installed in their final base camp in the most beautiful glacial cirque in the area. Huber later would write: "The next morning, we started the first attempts of the climb. Due to poor acclimatization and the heavy weight of our packs, the group suffered from 'el soroche' (altitude sickness), and Gradl had to quit immediately."

Fifteen days later, they returned to the other side of the lake. They had reached summits where no one had been before, from which they had seen that the "Guardian of Granite" seemed to offer a realistic flank by which the summit could be reached. On June 26 at 6 a.m., they left in the direction of "the peak of rock yet to be explored." They arrived at a snow col via a steep scree slope. Next, they climbed the north prow,

". . . and after a not-so-easy ascent, we reached the summit at 5:30 p.m. We began our descent in the darkening night without moonlight. We traversed steep moraines, and worked our way through the cliffbands. After 19 uninterrupted hours of work, we arrived happily at the tents to be warmly welcomed by the porters who had stayed behind."

This excerpt corresponds to the route information that Huber wrote in a series of climbing publications, in which the "Guardian of Granite" received the name "Cerro Parón."

Nine years after the 1955 climb, Evelio Echevarría, a Chilean climber residing in Colorado, and a great student of andinismo, wrote to Huber asking him for information. This is what Huber answered from Grenoble, France: "June 26, 1955, Cerro Parón, 5325 meters (the farthest west of the high spires), Koch, Schmidt, and Huber; we believe [ours was] the second ascent." But, in that letter, Huber did not reveal what led him to believe that theirs was the second ascent. (Only later was it revealed that the reason they figured they were the second ascent was a cairn of two rocks 100 meters below the summit. If these were placed by a previous party, it begs the question of who they were. These rocks could just as easily have been there naturally, which is common in the Cordillera Blanca.) The Germans were not aware of the peak's name as Cerro Colca; after climbing it, they called it Cerro Parón. Little did they realize that, 30 years later, this peak would be the jumping-off point for a new approach to climbing in the Cordillera Blanca.

In 1977, a book entitled *Yuraq Janka* came out, written by a climber-geologist named John F. Ricker. In his text on page 72, Ricker recognizes the German ascent as the first. There also appears the reference to "Cerro Kqolca"(Qollga), a.k.a. Colca, that according to Ricker is in the Quechuan language, "the space below the eaves of the tiled roof."

According to Echevarría, "colca" means "grain silo" in the Quechuan. Thus, the peak probably could take on the form of a Quechuan grain silo. The name Cerro Parón probably was intended to be Cerro Marrón (Marrón, Castillian for maroon, being easily misinterpreted by the Germans as Parrón, and substituting the double "rr" of the Castillian language with the single "r," as in German there is little distinction between the two).*

In 1982, Francisco Aguado and Américo Tordoya (known as Penike to his friends) gave the peak yet another name after their attempt of the east ridge. (Sadly, Penike later disappeared in the Chilean Andes.) They called it the Aguja Nevada (Snowy Needle), and the neighboring peaks from then on were known as Nevados Aguja. Some months later, in the Spanish magazine *Desnivel,* reports of their attempt on the mountain gave it the name of Torre Aguja.

---

*Evelio Echevarría writes: "[In the] Parón vs. Parrón [debate,]. . .Parón is correct. The Austrian-German map of 1932 listed the valley as Parrón (Spanish: *grapevine*). But [*AAJ* Editor 1960-1995] Ad Carter, who traveled a lot in the Cordillera Blanca, introduced the corrected word as it is accepted today: Parón (from the local Quechua, *paru*, meaning maroon)."

At the beginning of August 1982, I arrived in Huaraz, the jumping-off point for trips into the Blanca. In Huaraz, Aguado and Penike told me of their recent attempt on a mountain they believed to be called Aguja Nevada. At that point, my objective was to climb some peaks, and for that I went to the Parón Gorge.

For many kilometers prior to entering the gorge, I could not take my eyes off a certain rock obelisk to the right of the pass we were traveling. As we crested the pass, my eyes peered through the dust to quite a scene: There was yet another mountain of even larger dimensions that jutted out from behind the left wall, seemingly piercing the clouds like the point of an arrow. At that moment, I became aware that to climb the steep wall in front of me, I would have to adopt the mentality of a pure rock climber, a concept different from traditional tactics in the Blanca. From views I got while on surrounding peaks, I was able to get an idea of how to climb that enormous rock. When I came home to Spain, I promised myself I would return to climb it.

The following year, I traveled back to Peru with Jesús Gálvez, one of the best Spanish rock climbers at the time, but our objective was the northeast face of Nevado Huandoy. From its base, we could see, seemingly at our fingertips, the far-away "needle of granite" that was reminiscent of an Egyptian sphinx. My partner drew it in his notebook and noted its name as "La Esfinge" (The Sphinx), and we began to refer to it as such to differentiate it from the neighboring Nevados Aguja peaks, which were far too similar to Aguja Nevada and Agujas Nevadas. We said we would return to climb it the following year; but due to a spinal injury to myself and a frostbite injury Jesús received in the French Alps, we did not return.

In 1985, I prepared to return to The Sphinx with Onofre García, a regular climbing partner of mine. It seemed smarter to us to climb the east face because it offered quicker possibilities and less time in the shade. Rigoberto Angeles from Huaraz helped us transport our gear to a base camp about an hour from the wall. Next, we prepared ourselves for an ascent, not to return to the ground until after we reached the summit.

Differing from all other previous climbs in the Blanca, we used only rock gear, employed pure rock technique, and did not carry heavy boots for snow or ice (a decision we regretted on the ninth and final night on the climb because of a snow and ice storm).

The following morning, on July 8, at 10:45 a.m., we reached the snow-covered summit. As we descended the next day, we could see the southeast face, taller and colder than the wall we had just climbed; we decided at that point that we were in for another adventure on that aspect the next year. On returning to Laguna de Parón, we asked our porter what name the locals gave to the mountain we had climbed, and he said they only knew it as La Roca (The Rock). In Huaraz, a few climbers who questioned us about the Sphinx referred to it as La Torre de Parón, perhaps without even knowing that others had been referring to it as such as it is the obvious granite obelisk in the center of the gorge.*

The following year I could not return to the Blanca due to a hurt shoulder and second-degree frostbite to my feet.

Four Madrid climbers—Eduardo de la Cal, Chema Polanco, Alejandro Madrid, and Manuel Olivera—climbed the Sphinx in 1987. They divided into two rope teams; one party would climb ahead while the others jugged lines and hauled food and water. During the first ten days, they climbed during the day and returned to the base to sleep at night. When they

---

*According to Bohórquez, the Sphinx is completely different from the true Torre de Parón, a photo of which appears on page 171. Because both peaks have the same shape and are located in the same massif, the mistake is a reasonable one, but everything in this article refers to the Sphinx, not the Torre. Dr. Echevarría adds that the true Torre de Parón, located on the southern side of the Quebrada (valley) de Parón, is perhaps also called Cerro Torohuacra (4805 m).

THE
SPHINX

5325 M.

1996

1985

SPRINGER

1988    1987

SPHINX   AGUJA NEVADO
5325

LAKE PARÓN

CARAS

PARÓN RIVER

HUANDOY

TORRE
DE PARÓN

5 km.

N

*1988: Bohóroquez-St. Vincente (VI 5.10a A4, 950m); 1987: De La Cal-Madrid-Olivera-Polanco (VI 5.10a A3, 900m); 1985: Bohóroquez-García (VI 5.10a A1, 750m); 1996: Ortuño-Salvadó (VI 5.9 A2, 650m).*

*The true (and still unclimbed?) Torre de Parón.* ANTONIO BOHÓRQUEZ

reached the large ledges on the wall, they decided to go for it without descending to the base, but due to the horrendous weather they had to abandon their attempt. Fourteen days later, three of them returned to the mountain to continue their climb, and on August 18, they reached the summit via the same route that Aguado and Penike had tried five years earlier. The four climbers referred to the formation afterward as the Sphinx or the Torre de Parón.

In June, 1988, the southeast face remained unclimbed, and my injuries had almost completely healed. To see if my feet would handle the cold nature of that wall, where the sun seems never to shine, and to see if my shoulder could resist the continual force of the vertical world, I left for Peru.

I completed climbs of four peaks in the Blanca with two Basque friends who, upon arriving in Peru, introduced me to a few climbers of their homeland. One of the men I met, Iñaki San Vicente, was at the time a strong climber who was doing many rapid solo ascents and was looking to do some climbing before going to the rock towers of Argentine Patagonia three months later.

Onofre García arrived at the beginning of June, and as we had planned in Spain, the two of us departed for the wall that we had promised ourselves three years earlier we would climb. After climbing the first 60 meters and returning to the ground to continue climbing the following day, García accidentally slipped and took a tumble down a snow and ice slope, and after gathering himself up figured it was time to give up on that mountain range.

A few days after that, while in Huaraz, I ran into Iñake who took me up on my invitation to go finish the route I had just begun. During the first four days, we climbed during the day, then descended to sleep at our camp below the east buttress. Next, we hauled a portaledge to our high point, along with all the other accoutrements we would need for ten days, with the objective of not descending until after reaching the summit. But, after climbing and sleeping three consecutive nights on the wall, we had to descend to Huaraz. We returned a week later, better stocked and better prepared. After getting back on the wall, we spent 12 consecutive nights until finally, on August 14, at 10:50 a.m., we reached the top of this peak with several names that represents a new kind of climbing in the Cordillera Blanca: pure rock.

La Esfinge? La Roca? La Torre del Parón? Torre Aguja? La Aguja Nevada? El Cerro de Parón? El Cerro Colca? Above all, we need to now give this mountain a name that will stick and put an end to confusion. What needs defining here is, who names a mountain? Until that is answered, there remains the riddle of the Cordillera Blanca.

*Editor's note: Based on Bohórquez's research and a studied nod from Dr. Echevarría,* The American Alpine Journal *will herein refer to Pt. 5325m as La Esfinge, a.k.a. The Sphinx. We will also agree to the suggestions by the two scholars that the unclimbed pillar in the same massif be referred to as La Torre de Parón. Our best to those who next enjoy the Blanca's finest granite.*

# Mountain Medicine

*A review of the eye at altitude*

BY GEOFFREY C. TABIN, M.D.

In 1988, on the southwest face of Mt. Everest, two climbers died above 8000 meters; their last radio message was that they were both totally blind. In 1996, near Everest's summit, a (highly publicized) case of blindness that was blamed on a popular surgical procedure done to correct refractive errors almost caused a climber's death from exposure. These and other less dramatic episodes prompted this year's review of mountain medicine to concentrate on the human visual system.

The eye is like a camera. First, lenses focus the light. The image is formed on a delicate and sensitive nerve layer called the retina, which is analogous to the film in the camera. The patterns that the eye observes are then transferred along a nerve to the brain. This optic nerve can be thought of as the messenger taking the film to the store to be developed. Finally, the film processing takes place in the visual cortex of the brain. The nerve impulses are interpreted into our visual world. Sight is dependent on the lenses, retina, optic nerve, and brain all functioning properly. All of these structures can be affected by high altitude.

The eye has two lenses that focus our visual world on the retina. Two-thirds of the power of the eye comes from the cornea, the clear window in the front of the eye. One-third of the power comes from the crystalline lens. It is important to note that the outer corneal surface and its interaction with the lubricating tear film is the most important refractive surface. If the cornea is too wet or too dry, vision will blur. In addition, the cornea has one of the highest densities of sensory nerve fibers in the body, making it exquisitely sensitive to pain.

The colored ring visible through the cornea is the iris, which serves as an aperture does in a camera. The iris will expand or contract to change the amount of light entering the eye. Immediately behind it is the lens that can be "focused" to see close objects ("near vision"). Everyone slowly loses their accommodating ("focusing") power in this lens, which is why younger people with perfect distance vision require reading glasses after age 50. People who are "far-sighted" can use this focusing power in the lens to see well at a distance when they are young, but require glasses to see both near and far as they age and lose their accommodating power. "Near-sighted" people are unable to see at a distance without glasses, but can always see near objects as light is brought to a point in front of the retina when accommodation is totally relaxed.

The most common ocular problem in mountaineering is minor damage to the surface of the cornea. The top layer of cells, called the epithelium, can be damaged by a scratch, drying of the surface, or UV light causing a sunburn. Corneal scratches can occur in any climbing activity; they are painful and lead to a flooding of tears that blur the vision. "Snowblindness" from the intense direct and reflected UV light from the sun can quickly disable a mountaineer, even on a cloudy day. Dehydration, cold and wind can also damage the corneal surface. Fortunately, these injuries heal quickly, though antibiotics are needed to guard against corneal infections. Because blinking rubs the eyelids over a raw surface and exacerbates the pain, people with snow blindness are more comfortable with the eyes patched shut.

Virtually all cases of snow blindness, corneal freezing, and superficial abrasion heal completely, with restoration of normal vision occurring within 48 hours. During the acute period, however, a climber can be rendered totally disabled by blindness. Thus, the best treatment is prevention. Dark glasses, with side shields, must be worn at altitude, particularly when climbing snow and ice. Clouds do not block UV light energy, so it is imperative that glasses or goggles with UV blocking capability are worn on overcast days. Several cases of snow blindness have occurred when climbers' glasses fogged because of condensation and they removed the lenses. This is a problem that is often worsened by the use of supplemental oxygen, when warm gas may leak around the mask. A good anti-fog preparation applied to the glass, prescription "no fog" ski goggles and being certain the oxygen mask fits well with no leakage of warm air are preventative measures that can preserve vision.

The retina is the second most common visual structure to be damaged when climbers venture to high altitude. The delicate nerve cells of this layer connect directly with the brain and share a similar physiology. Both the brain and the retina require an enormous and steady supply of oxygen. A specialized network of blood vessels feed the retinal cells. In order to allow clear focusing of light, a barrier prevents blood or fluid from escaping into the retinal spaces. Either decreased oxygen to the retinal cells or leakage of fluid or blood into the retina causes loss of vision.

At high altitude the pressure in the atmosphere decreases, leading to less oxygen diffusing into the bloodstream. Because the retina and brain require a constant amount of oxygen, one of the responses to a lower saturation of oxygen in the blood is an increase in the flow of blood to these vital structures. Elsewhere in the body, arteries have muscular coats to deal with flow increases, but the retinal vessels are designed to remain clear and not obstruct the light signals with big beefy muscles. Instead, they have delicate support cells called pericytes that surround the vessels. These pericytes are sensitive to damage from lack of oxygen and can also rupture in high-flow situations. The result is a leaking of blood into the retina known as retinal hemorrhaging.

High altitude retinal hemorrhages (HARH) occur in a majority of people who have summited 8000-meter peaks, but they have also been reported in visitors to ski areas in Colorado. Most high altitude retinal hemorrhages do not affect vision. However, leakage into the area of nerve cells that carry signals of central vision, called the macula, can cause a profound loss of vision. Upon return to lower elevation the hemorrhages resorb completely, but they can lead to a disorganization of fine neural connections and leave the climber with a permanent decrease in vision in the affected eye.

As noted above, the brain and the retina have similar physiologies. It therefore makes sense that similar events happen in the retina and brain. High altitude cerebral edema has been well described. A similar swelling of the retina without the frank bleeding of high altitude retinal hemorrhages may occur, accounting for the blurred vision that is often reported by people with high altitude cerebral edema. In addition, some scientists believe that tiny hemorrhages similar to those in the retina occur in the brain. This thought has led some to advise climbers with HARH to descend, but since HARH are so common this advice is largely ignored. Persons with a macular hemorrhage probably should descend in case the bleed spreads.

The worst retinal problem climbers encounter is damage to the retinal cells from lack of oxygen. This is similar to a stroke, and the visual loss can be extensive and permanent. The central retinal vasculature is particularly susceptible to occlusion when the blood becomes more viscous from the combined effect of increased red blood cells and dehydration. The retinal cells that are responsive to dim light are called rods and are especially sensitive to lack of oxygen. The result is a sharp decrease in night vision even as low as 2000 meters.

The next structure essential to vision is the optic nerve. This vital connection links the eye to the brain. Increased pressure in the brain from swelling of the nerve cells, increased blood volume and edema is transmitted to the optic nerve. This leads to papilledema, a swelling of both optic nerves that causes transient blackouts of vision. Blockage of the blood flow to part of the optic nerve can cause a permanent visual loss.

Climbers who have glaucoma must be careful when ascending to high altitude. Glaucoma is damage to the optic nerve associated with increased pressure within the eye. The decrease in oxygen at altitude makes the optic nerve much more vulnerable to glaucomatous damage. Diamox is often taken to help the kidneys correct the problem of respiratory alkalosis caused by rapid breathing at altitude. Diamox is also a potent drug for glaucoma that decreases the amount of aqueous fluid in the eye. Glaucoma patients should take all of their current medications and also consider taking Diamox when climbing high.

An increasing number of climbers are describing brief blurring or, rarely, complete blindness at altitude, sometimes no higher than 4500 meters. The symptoms disappear promptly with descent. A similar condition called amaurosis is rare at sea level. The blurring is sometimes accompanied by flashes of light (scintillating scotomata). Because such events have been described in migraine victims, with or without headache, this temporary blindness may be due to a migraine equivalent triggered by hypoxia.

Finally, the brain can be damaged by the lack of oxygen either with cerebral edema or strokes. Unlike retinal or optic nerve problems that affect one eye only, brain injuries always affect both eyes. The visual cortex is the area of the brain where sight is interpreted. With prolonged lack of oxygen or an acute blockage of blood flow, "cortical" blindness can develop, ending all vision in both eyes.

Fortunately, blindness from the retina, optic nerve and brain are relatively uncommon. The most common ocular problem (on flat land as well as in the mountains) is a refractive error that requires glasses. Perfect vision requires that the image be focused on the retinal surface. In myopic (near-sighted) people, the combined power of the cornea and lens brings light to a point in front of the retina. Without corrective lenses, the image spreads out and is blurred on the retina. Far-sighted people, on the other hand, focus behind the retina. Far-sighted people can bring light into focus by using the accommodating power of their lens. With age the amount of extra lens power to overcome far-sightedness declines.

Eyeglasses are the first option for correcting refractive errors. Anti-fog treatments, prescription glacier glasses or goggles can improve their adaptation for mountaineering. However, in misty conditions and rain, glasses can be a real handicap. Contact lenses provide better vision in inclement weather. New extended-wear disposable soft contact lenses can give added comfort and convenience on multi-day climbs where care and cleaning of the lenses is difficult. However, on extended climbs when the contact lenses are worn too long, they can predispose the climber to corneal infections. Moreover, any contact lens will decrease the flow of oxygen to the cornea, thereby compromising the corneal health. And at high altitude, contact lenses can lead to considerable eye discomfort. Thus, climbers have eagerly embraced new developments in refractive surgery to eliminate the need for eyeglasses.

The first refractive procedure to decrease near-sightedness was radial keratotomy (RK). In this technique, radial incisions are made in a spoke-like fashion around the cornea, allowing the corneal curvature to relax and decreasing the amount of focusing power of the cornea and thus decreasing the near-sightedness. This procedure, which was wildly popular for several years, has many disadvantages for climbers. First and foremost, the radial incisions permanently weaken the cornea. A normal eye that receives blunt trauma will retain its integrity as the structures behind the globe give way prior to rupturing of the eye. When one has had a radial keratotomy, the 90 percent thickness cuts of the surgery become the weakest component of the eye, and even relatively minor trauma can result in a vision-ending rupture of the globe. This is a concern for climbers when you consider the risk of ice- or rock-fall or how frequently an ice axe bounces out of the ice and strikes the eye.

A second problem of the radial keratotomy is an irregular astigmatism that can cause a slight distortion of vision if the cuts are not made perfectly. And, even when the cuts are made perfectly, the scars can still affect vision when the pupil is widely dilated as occurs in both dim light and with maximal adrenalin (climbers). These scars near the visual axis will produce halos, ghost images and blurring.

A final concern of radial keratotomy is fluctuating refractions, particularly at high altitude. Recent research has suggested that the lack of oxygen on the outer corneal surface causes a transient swelling around the incisions, resulting in even more flattening of the cornea. This leads to a shift of the refraction, making the radial keratotomy patient more far-sighted at high altitude. A young climber with radial keratotomy may notice no ill effects as the accommodative power of the lens can easily overcome the change. Thus, many climbers who have had RK have spent considerable periods of time above 8000 meters noting no problems with their vision. However, in older climbers who have lost their accommodative faculties, the change toward far-sightedness causes blurry vision at altitude.

In the last few years, great improvements have occurred in the realm of refractive surgery with the development of the excimer laser. The excimer laser is a very short wave length laser that is able to carve the prescription into the cornea without damaging other structures. This is much more accurate than the radial keratotomy, does not weaken the structure of the eye and is stable at high altitude. The first excimer laser procedure to be developed was photo refractive keratectomy (PRK), whereby a laser carves the prescription into the cornea from the top surface. This results in a total abrasion of the top surface of the cornea that is painful for several days. It also takes several days to heal. Finally, PRK is only able to treat a moderate amount of myopia.

In order to expand the range of PRK, a new procedure, known as Lasik (laser assisted in situ keratomileusis), has been developed. In Lasik, a small flap is cut into the top corneal surface beneath the layer where scarring cells are located. This flap is lifted up and the prescription is carved into the bed underneath. This allows correction of larger degrees of short-sightedness with great accuracy. It also causes minimal discomfort and quicker visual rehabilitation. Like PRK, the post-surgical refraction will not shift with altitude.

The one disadvantage of the Lasik procedure is that Lasik is a surgical procedure: Complications can occur in both cutting the flap and repositioning the flap after the laser procedure. These complications are extremely rare but can result in a decrease in best-corrected visual acuity. My current recommendation is that people with small amounts of myopia have the relatively less-risky PRK and people with larger amounts of myopia have Lasik. In 1998 no climber should still be getting radial keratotomy.

A second question is what refraction to aim for. The laser can leave any refractive error that is desired in the eye. It is worth remembering that a climber with no refractive error will start to need reading glasses when they are around 50. This can mean difficulty in seeing well at arms' length—that is, in seeing a distance useful in slotting protection. If the laser leaves a small amount of residual myopia, vision will remain adequate at a distance and allow clear focus at near distances for a longer period of time. Thus, if one aims for a refractive error of approximately -0.50, a climber will be able to see his or her footholds until a very advanced age.

# The Mountain Environment

*The year in garbage*

BY BRENT BISHOP AND CHRIS NAUMANN

Each year, climbers push the limit of what previously was thought possible in the mountains. Eight thousand-meter peaks, once considered the domain of only a handful of elite mountaineers, now are visited by scores of expeditions each season. This natural progression represents the core of climbing. As human limits evolve, however, and the popularity of climbing increases, the pressure that climbers place on the environment increases as well. Unfortunately, this leaves the environment hanging in a delicate balance. Visit any popular destination point around the world, be it a local crag or the Himalayas, and witness the negative impact that climbers have had. Trash, erosion, graffiti, and human waste all are telltale signs that climbers have not treaded lightly in their playground.

Historically, expeditions have judged their success by two criteria: whether members reach the summit and whether anyone was injured or killed in the process. Today, with a growing awareness of the environment's importance to climbing, it is imperative that we add a third component to the equation of a successful climb. Climbers now must include the environmental impact of a team as part of their criteria. In this day and age, an expedition can hardly consider itself successful if it contributes to the degradation of an area. At the very least, "minimum impact" must be the goal of any team. Adopting such an environmental approach should not prove too difficult, as part of the challenge of climbing is grounded in problem-solving. As responsible climbers, we need to be the vanguards of all the outdoor users on the environmental front and generate solutions for the dilemmas we face. We don't have to sacrifice our climbing goals to achieve this aim. Instead, concerted effort and awareness will make a significant, visible difference. The result will no doubt be impressive.

The Mountain Environment section in *The American Alpine Journal* is a result of this new orientation. Environmental issues should not be scattered throughout the pages of the journal, but consolidated and treated as a component with the same importance as expedition and climbing news. Mountain Environment will focus on the problems we face as climbers and, more importantly, the solutions we bring forth.

## Mt. Everest

On Mount Everest, for the fourth consecutive year, progress was made to reclaim the "world's highest junkyard." Since its inception, a unique incentive-based program has resulted in the removal of 17,500 pounds of garbage from the base and flanks of Mount Everest. This "cash for trash" plan was instituted by the 1994 Sagarmatha Environmental Expedition (SEE '94). Many teams and individuals have contributed to the reclamation efforts on Everest thus far, including: the late Scott Fischer and Mountain Madness; the late Rob Hall and Adventure Consultants; Todd Burleson and Alpine Ascents International; Wally Berg, Brent Bishop and Nike-ACG.

The incentive program involves paying the Sherpa staff in addition to their salaries to collect and transport garbage to base camp. Base camp staff collect tin, plastics, glass and batteries from the mountain's lower reaches, while the high-altitude Sherpas focus on Everest's upper camps. Having carried loads up the mountain to stock the logistical pyramid of camps, Sherpas fill their then-empty packs with trash and discarded oxygen bottles for the return trip

*Collecting trash at Mt. Everest base camp.* BRENT BISHOP

to base camp. The incentive rates for base camp trash are 100Rs (approximately US$2) for every ten kilos. The payment for an oxygen bottle, for example, carried from Camp IV at the South Col to base camp would be 250Rs to 450Rs (US$5 to US$9) depending on weight (the antiquated bottles from the 1960s and 1970s can weigh as much as 12 pounds, while the modern Poisk kevlar-wrapped bottles weigh less than five pounds).

The incentive program on Everest exemplifies expeditions that accomplish climbing objectives while contributing to the reclamation of a mountain's environmental health.

SUCCESS, 1994-97
1994:  5,050 lbs
1995:  3,600
1996:  5,650
1997:  3,200
———————
Total: 17,500 lbs

*Mt. Vinson, Antarctica*

Despite its remoteness, Mt. Vinson receives more climbing traffic each year. The pristine arctic environment is impacted by climbers quite easily and takes decades to recover because of the extreme cold and exceptionally arid conditions that dominate the continent. Increased traffic, coupled with an extremely fragile environment, would most certainly show the strains of human impact.

The environmental integrity of Mt. Vinson is not, however, currently threatened. This is in large part due to the efforts of Adventure Network International (ANI). ANI provides flight service to the Antarctic continent and Mt. Vinson, and staffs the base camp with a full time manager. Dave Hahn managed base camp for the winter 1997-98 season and was responsible for overseeing climbers on the mountain. A primary service provided by the base camp manager is to ensure that climbers have no lasting impact on the mountain. Teams on the mountain are required to haul all trash and fecal material back to base camp, where it is flown off the Antarctic continent for disposal. The consensus is that expeditions to Vinson are following these guidelines set forth by ANI, rather than adhering to the old practice of discarding trash and fecal material in crevasses.

The accepted environmental practice on Vinson illustrates that behavior can change with a little education and effort. Despite the extreme conditions that dominate the mountain, climbers now are removing all traces of their endeavors.

*Orizaba, Ecuador*

Although much work has been concentrated in Nepal, and particularly on Mount Everest, the other mountainous regions of the world are in need of environmental attention as well. Similar problems due to increasing adventure travel persist throughout the popular climbing areas of Mexico and South America.

Environmental Mountaineering International organized a ten-day expedition to Orizaba in March, 1997. The group included the three founders of EMI (Erik Mueller, Matthew Shupe, and Matthew Walker) and three other team members (Aaron Beitler, Matthew MacKinnon, and Matthew Novak). The expedition involved cleaning the main climbing routes and camps at 14,000 and 16,000 feet.

The area around Piedra Grande, Orizaba's 14,000-foot base camp, was in dire need of attention. At base camp, on the route above and along the road below, the group collected about 300 pounds of trash in large durable bags. The garbage was transported down the mountain in conjunction with the Reyes family, which runs a climber's support business out of the mountain village of Tlachichuca. Along with the cleaning, multi-lingual literature was posted at camp Piedra Grande and the Reyes' hostel. The literature reminds people to stay mindful of their actions and their impact on the surrounding environment. This work on Orizaba was a significant improvement, but continued work is needed to maintain and further improve the mountain's environment.

*The Baltoro, Pakistan*

At the center of the Karakoram, more than sixty peaks above 7000 meters form the apex of India, China and Pakistan. This 100-mile radius area contains the greatest consolidation of high peaks on the planet. The pinnacle of the Karakoram range is K2 (28,611'), the world's second-highest mountain. For more than a century, the Baltoro has attracted explorers, mountaineers and, more recently, adventure trekkers. Since the opening of the Karakoram Highway, the influx of alpine enthusiasts has altered the socioeconomic and environmental stability of the entire region dramatically.

In 1993, Greg Mortenson traveled to the Karakoram on an expedition to climb K2. For Mortenson, the local Balti people proved more inspiring than the mountains. Mortenson returned the following year and built a school in the village of Korphe to combat the 5 percent literacy rate—the first of many projects he would coordinate in the upper reaches of the Karakoram.

To organize and complete his projects better, Mortenson founded the Central Asia Institute (CAI) in 1996, the mission statement of which reads: "supporting mountain villagers of the

Central Asia region through locally initiated education projects, and promoting literacy, women's vocational skills and increased awareness of public health and environmental issues." In contrast to the hundreds of foreign organizations working in Nepal, Tibet and India, Mortenson's CAI is the only foreign entity working in Baltistan on a full-time basis.

In 1997, Mortenson teamed up with Brent Bishop and Nike-ACG to begin working with the Baltis on a porter training program and several clean-up initiatives. The program emphasized issues related to working with trekkers and expeditions, general mountain travel, and environmental topics. Specific sessions included: reviewing government regulations pertaining to expeditions and their porters; conducting clinics in first aid, high-altitude sickness and crevasse rescue; and discussing sanitation, hygiene, water-sup-

*Porter training seminar (left), and (below)*
*crevasse rescue training on the Baltoro.*
BRENT BISHOP

ply issues and the handling of expedition garbage. Bishop and Mortenson stressed how all of this information could be assimilated in the local villages, and how it also would benefit entire communities in public health and resource management.

In addition to these training sessions, the Balti porters participated in the clean-up of several camp locations en route to K2 base camp. In all, the group collected more than 2,400 pounds of garbage, including 1,770 pounds of tin, 60 pounds of batteries and 660 pounds of paper and plastic.

This successful porter training program and clean-up was conducted in each of the major valleys around K2, including the Hushe, the Braldu, the Shegar and the Skardu valleys. A total of 251 porters attended the training seminars. As with all of their projects in Nepal and Pakistan, Mortenson and Bishop focused on incorporating the local people of the region. Noted Mortenson: "In the long run, it is their input and initiative that will be paramount to long-term conservation of this pristine region."

The work of Mortenson and the CAI includes construction of five schools in remote villages and a high-altitude water transportation and filter model in Korphe, establishment of two women's vocational training programs, and work with Everest summiter Geoff Tabin, M.D., to develop a comprehensive eye-care program for northern Pakistan. When asked about his motivation, Mortenson replied, "The Baltis inspire me. Despite the adversity in their daily, life their spirits soar. Working with them to help preserve their mountain home and centuries-old traditions is much more satisfying than standing on the summit of a Himalayan peak."

In 1998, Bishop and Mortenson plan to train 500 porters in the training institute. CAI also is working in conjunction with the Environmental Mountaineering Network (EMN) to develop a porter training manual. The manual will outline and detail the curriculum of the porter training courses. It is being prepared in English and Urdu and, in consideration of a literacy rate in the area of less than 5 percent, for use by illiterate porters.

*Island Peak, Nepal*

In the fall of 1996, Frank Gibney led an Explorer's Network (TEN) expedition to Island Peak in Nepal. This was the 18th TEN expedition to various mountainous regions throughout the world. TEN usually concentrates on various medical aspects of human physiology and high altitudes. The Island Peak trip had three main objectives: 1) Climb Island Peak; 2) conduct medical research on P.R.K. (cataract) surgery patients at altitude; and 3) undertake a clean-up project of Island Peak base camp and Lobuche.

The clean-up efforts were organized by Greg Glade in conjunction with EMN. The group collected more than 75 pounds of glass, tin and burnables. The garbage was transported down valley via yaks to the Sagarmatha Pollution Control Committee (SPCC) headquarters in Namche Bazar. In all, the clean-up project cost less than US$50. This effort exemplifies a small, motivated group conducting a successful clean-up project in conjunction with other objectives.

*Huascaran, Peru*

The Mountain Institute (TMI), headquartered in West Virginia, recently opened an office in Huaraz, focusing on natural-resource management, community-based conservation, eco-tourism planning and management in and around Huascaran National Park. A year ago, Bob McConnell met with TMI representative Miriam Torres, and volunteers Adam Kolff and Dr. Kees Kolff, to begin planning the collaborative effort to document a traverse of the

Cordillera Blanca in Huascaran National Park, Peru, from Olleros to Chavin. McConnell, Ann Rockhold and Carlos Buhler were joined by an impressive group of participants including: the Technical Designer of Huascaran National Park; representatives of The Mountain Institute; an archaeologist from the National Institute of Culture; the Director of Tourism and Culture for the City of Huaraz; two councilmen from Olleros; and two photojournalists.

The group spent four days testing and filming minimum impact techniques discussed in *Gentle Expeditions: A Guide to Ethical Mountain Adventure*, recently published by the AAC. McConnell and Buhler presented a slide show the night before the group departed, combining McConnell's experience with minimum-impact techniques in the Himalaya and Buhler's extensive guiding experience in the Huascaran National Park area. The traverse coincided with the 14th Annual Celebration of Mountain Activities hosted by the Region of Chavin.

A "Traveler's Code of Ethics," developed by TMI in conjunction with and endorsed by many local and regional organizations, also was endorsed by the AAC Conservation Committee. The Code is an attempt to get people, be they tourists, guides, park or city officials, to think about how to minimize the adverse impact of tourism that has become so important to the economic development of this area.

Blessed with beautiful weather, good companionship, and the rugged beauty of the Cordillera Blanca, the trip was an outstanding success. Several hours of film footage, funded by a grant to TMI from the American Alpine Club, were taken during the expedition. This will be condensed into a half-hour documentary. The documentary might be made available to tour operators, guides, and cultural groups in the Huascaran area. Perhaps more importantly, it may be made available to the tour-bus operators who transport about 90 percent of the tourists who come to Huascaran National Park. Rockhold, McConnell, and Buhler were able to participate in this project, thanks to generous grants from the American Alpine Club, the Everest Environmental Project, and Cascade Designs.

JOHN SVENSON '97

# Climbs and Expeditions, 1997

A ccounts from the various climbs and expeditions of the world are listed geographically from north to south and from west to east within the noted countries. We start with the Contiguous United States and then cover Alaska in order for the climbs in the Alaskan Wrangell-St. Elias Mountains to segue into St. Elias climbs in Canada.

With this volume we include unreported 1996-97 accounts in addition to full reports from the 1997-98 season. Climbers returning from the southern hemisphere can help us in future volumes by submitting accounts as soon as they return home. We encourage climbers to submit accounts of other notable activity from the various Greater Ranges to help us maintain complete records.

Appendices at the back of the book list addresses for expedition permits and regulations, conversions of meters to feet, and comparisons and explanations of the various ratings systems.

## NORTH AMERICA

### Contiguous United States
### Washington

#### Cascades

*Mt. Rainier, Fickle Finger of Success.* From July 21 through July 25, Alex Van Steen and Richard Alpert led a Rainier Mountaineering party of four (David Branton, Mark Kelly, Steve Northern, and Pete Laird) to a summit camp via the westernmost couloir of the Success Glacier Headwall. There is mention in Jeff Smoot's *Adventure Guide to Mount Rainier* (1991 edition) of a descent in 1946, but there are no recorded ascents. From Van Trump Park, traverse beneath the lower Kautz Glacier Icefall at 7,500 feet to the Success/Pyramid Divide at 8,400 feet, then ascend to an unobvious "balcony" camp at 9,800 feet (i.e., the base of the Success Glacier Headwall). This camp is somewhat protected from possible rock fall by the bergschrunds that separate the glacier from the snow couloirs above. We ascended the westernmost (left) couloir of the three parallel couloirs that lead up from the head of the Success Glacier. From ca.10,000 feet (at the bergschrund) to the confluence with the standard Success Cleaver Route at 11,700 feet (where Success Cleaver traverses east toward the Kautz Cleaver), the couloir remained consistently moderate (40°). Owing to the heavy snow year, the rock bands on the upper mountain, which normally are exposed at this time of the year, simply presented steep snow climbing (no steeper than 50°). Camp was made on the summit, and we descended via the standard Disappointment Cleaver Route.

ALEX VAN STEEN, *Raineer Mountaineering*

*Double Peak, East Face.* On June 29, Mark Ronca and I made the first ascent of this sheer face on the northeast summit of Double Peak (6,199') in Mt. Rainier National Park. The six-pitch climb followed an obvious crack system on the left side of the face, then finished on an exposed knife-edged ridge to the summit. The first pitch was the crux, consisting of a fun hand crack followed by a hard 5.10 roof. The second pitch started with a 5.9 fist crack followed by a 5.8 squeeze chimney. Two more pitches of mid-5th class and two pitches of easy 4th class climbing led to the summit. The quality of the rock was surprisingly excellent considering that all the other peaks in the area have extremely poor rock. Some cleaning of moss and vegetation was required on lead, though.

JOSEPH PURYEAR

## OREGON

*Second Spire, First Ascent.* On August 3, Rob Morgan and I made the first ascent of Second Spire in four pitches (5.7 R A1) from a base camp at Jefferson Lake in the Mount Jefferson Wilderness, Oregon. This is the second of several striking spires southeast of Jefferson Lake and is readily apparent from the trail. We ascended the east face, which involved 300 feet or so of technical climbing on sometimes loose volcanic rock. We followed a prominent gully from tree line, and then the line of least resistance and best rock. The approach is about six miles on the Jefferson Lake Trail, which starts near Camp Sherman. The first of these spires would be an excellent objective for those who enjoy airy, insecure aid climbing. Routes on the north or west faces of these spires would be considerably longer—probably more than 500 feet.

JEFF MCCARTHY, *Canada*

## CALIFORNIA

### YOSEMITE VALLEY

*The American Safe Climbing Association, Formation and Activity.* It's been a busy first six months for the American Safe Climbing Association. We have replaced about 500 old, unsafe bolts in Yosemite, half of the goal for this season. We've picked up support from a strong group of climbers ranging from John Middendorf to Jon Krakauer. We also are getting a boost from commercial sources such as Metolius, Patagonia and The North Face.

Though it now appears obvious that the ASCA's mission is something that needs to be accomplished, we were far from clear about it when the idea first presented itself. In late July, 1997, Jason Smith and I set out to clean up *Zenyatta Mondatta*, removing superfluous bolts, rivets and fixed copper heads. Our intention was to restore the route to a more natural state. In the end, however, we spent most of our time making the anchors bomber for subsequent ascents by removing rusting quarter-inchers and placing new stainless steel 3/8" bolts. After the climb, we decided that although returning routes to their natural condition sounded good in theory, it was a far greater (and more practical) service to the climbing community to focus energy on making the anchors safer.

With this as our goal, Jason, Erik Sloan and I continued to replace anchors for the rest of the summer on El Cap as well as on several free climbs. Although we were able to replace more than 200 bolts in three months, we had just scratched the surface of what needed to be replaced in Yosemite. Clearly more help was needed. With the goal of getting more climbers involved, and the legal assistance of Armando Menocal, founder of The Access Fund, I moved to found the American Safe Climbing Association, a California non-profit organization. Our mission is simple: The ASCA wants to make America's rock climbs safer by educating climbers about how to maintain safe fixed anchors, as well as to advance wilderness causes generally. To date, the ASCA has replaced over 500 bolts in Yosemite Valley, Indian Creek and Zion National Park. For more information about which routes have been replaced as well as how you can help, check out the ASCA website at www.safeclimbing.org.

CHRIS MCNAMARA, American Safe Climbing Association

*Yosemite Valley, Various Ascents.* For the third year in a row, action on the *Salathé Wall* led the headlines. This time, it was Yuji Hirayama (Japan) who stole the show with attempts to onsight the entire route. Training for weeks in Yosemite, Hirayama onsighted, among other serious crack leads, *Love Supreme*, a 5.13a crack in Tuolumne. His onsight hopes for the *Salathé* were dashed, however, on pitch 24, where he fell on the Skinner variation. He then pulled his rope and sent the Huber (5.13a) variation first try. After a bivy on the Block, Hirayama then flashed to the headwall. He fell on both headwall pitches, but, amazingly, after working the moves, did both pitches (5.13b) on his second try. Accompanied by Hans Florine and Hidetaka Suzuki, Hirayama finished the climb a mere 38 hours after starting. Previously, the *Salathé* had been climbed free only after months of effort. When asked how he felt about the climb, Hirayama replied "Yeah, I'm pretty happy." This was the fourth free ascent of the *Salathé*.

Many hard El Cap routes saw repeats this year. *The Reticent Wall* (VI 5.9 A5), known as possibly the hardest route on El Cap, saw four repeats. Chris Kalous, Mark Synnott, and Kevin Thaw made the second ascent over seven days in May, finding the climbing sustained and consistent. They also reported that the A2 climbing seemed harder than anything on *Zenyatta Mondatta*. The third ascent came at the hands of two Spaniards, Sylvia Vidal and Pep Masip (see Vidal's account below). In early October, Chris McNamara and Eric Sloan made the fourth ascent, with McNamara leading every pitch. The fifth ascent went to Warren Hollinger and Russel Mitrovitch later that season.

Eric Kohl's routes on El Capitan all saw repeats this year. *The Surgeon General* (VI 5.9 A5) was repeated, except for the last two pitches, by Brad Bond and John Rzeczycki, who drilled five rivets past the "Crystal Chandelier," which had fallen off several years before. The pair bailed onto Zodiac two pitches from the top. *Get Whacked* (VI 5.10 A5) saw a second ascent by Gabor Berecz (Hungary) and Thomas Tivadar (Germany). The pair also established *Cool Pool* (VI 5.8 A5), a 14-pitch route on Glacier Point Apron's 9 O'Clock Wall. Hungarians Oskar Nadasdi and Enci Szentirmai made the second ascent of *High Plains Dripper* (VI 5.11 A5). Lastly, Chris Kalous and Kevin Thaw made the second ascent of *Plastic Surgery Disaster* (VI 5.8 A5). Thaw was especially entertained on the "Trust Your Mechanic" pitch, which sports a loose flake that must be hooked for progress. All four routes were established by Eric Kohl, two with partners, and two by himself.

*The Gulf Stream* (VI 5.10 A4), known for its extensive hooking sections, saw four repeats this year. Conrad Anker and Thomas Huber made the fourth ascent, with Brendon Thau and partner making the sixth. The route then received two solos, first from Wally Barker, and then from Chris Kalous.

Other notable repeats were the fifth ascent of *Kaos* (VI 5.10 A4) by Erik Erikson, Bill Leventhal, and Kevin Thaw. Nate Beckwith and partner also made a fifth ascent, this time on *Jolly Roger* (VI 5.10 A5). Another fifth ascent, on *Shortest Straw* (VI 5.10 A4), came solo at the hands of Cameron Lawson. Scorched Earth had a solo by Southern Californian "Eric."

Reportedly, he avoided the 5.11 offwidth with a new variation.

The season's only new route was *Continental Drift* (VI 5.10 A4), which was established by Anker, Gerberding, and Thaw. They spent 12 days on the wall, four of them storm-bound. Of its 15 long pitches, just two and a half were shared by other routes. The route takes a line near *New Jersey Turnpike* and *Heartland*.

Two El Cap routes received their first clean ascents. *Mescalito* (VI 5.9 A4) was climbed without hammer by Dave Dyess and A.C. Robertson, and the *North America Wall* (VI 5.8 A3) was climbed clean by Dougald MacDonald and Chris McNamara.

On Half Dome, Chris McNamara finished a new five-pitch line to the left of the Regular Northwest Face. The second pitch took "Mac" 15 hours to lead over two days, and at one point sports a string of 22 beaks in a row.

Elsewhere in the Valley, Kohl, partnered with Brian Law, made the first ascent of *Clusterfuck 2000* (VI 5.10 A3+) on the Yosemite Falls Wall. Eric Rasmussen and Mike Zawaski established *A Sad State of Affairs* (VI 5.? A3+) on Glacier Point's Firefall Wall. The route is mostly overhanging and finishes at the snack bar. [Rasmussen also climbed *Ashes to Ashes* (VI A4) on the Firefall Wall with the late Chris Purnell in 1995, *40 Ounces of Freedom* (VI 5.10 A3) on Mount Broderick, and *Ecstasy of Gold* (VI 5.10 A3+) in the Ribbon Falls Amphitheater.]

As usual, several Valley speed records were broken. *Lost in America* (VI 5.10 A5) was climbed on sight in 24:47 by McNamara, Synnott, and Thaw. Synnott broke his ankle partway up, but still kept leading! Peter Coward, Hans Florine, and Steve Schneider flew up *Eagle's Way* in 14:27. Willie Benegas, Cameron Lawson, and Jared Ogden sailed the *Atlantic Ocean Wall* (VI 5.10 A5) in 50 hours. Dave Bengston, Steve Gerberding, and Scott Stowe drove *New Jersey Turnpike* (VI 5.10 A4+) in 24:48. Coward, Florine, and Schneider stayed dry on the *Waterfall Route* (VI 5.10 A4), turning in a time of 18:12, amidst a frenetic week for Florine and Schneider. The pair climbed seven walls (Grade V or more) in seven days. Day one was the West Face of Sentinel in five hours; day two was the *Waterfall Route*; day three was the Direct North Buttress in four hours; day four was *Skull Queen* in 5:21 (record, and also clean); day five was the *Rostrum;* day six was Half Dome for Florine and Abby Watkins, while Schneider did Leaning Tower with Greg Murphy; and day seven was the *Prow* for Florine and Murphy, and *Astroman* for Schneider and Sue McDevitt. McDevitt teamed up with Nancy Feagin for the fastest female ascent of the *Salathé,* turning in a time of just over 30 hours. Fatigued near the top, the women slept a few hours before continuing.

STEVE SCHNEIDER

*The Porcelain Wall, Sarganata.* From August 22 to 27, Pep Masip and I put up a new route on the Porcelain Wall. We took six days, with five bivouacs (no pre-fixing), to do 12 60-meter pitches. Initially, we wanted to repeat Pete Takeda and Erik Kohl's *When Hell Was In Session* (A5) which, along with Warren Harding's *Porcelain Wall*, were the only two routes on the wall. While hauling loads, we saw a line of cracks, more to the right of the two aforementioned routes. It was very obvious and logical, and we decided to climb it. *Sarganata* means lizard, as we waited for the sun like the lizards do.

The first six pitches are simple aid with a bit of free climbing. If it were repeated, it would result in more of a free route, because the crack had a lot of shrubbery. The last six pitches are very vertical and technical. I'd like to point out that there are no bolts on any pitch, nor in the six first belays. There are nine bolts in the last six belays.

Later, with Pep Masip, we did a third ascent of the *Reticent Wall* on El Cap. We were on

*Sylvia Vidal on pitch eight,* Sargantana, *first ascent.*
PEP MESIP

for 11 days (no pre-fixed ropes), including one day of bad weather. It is a very beautiful route, but it was very difficult to get information about it, because few people actually gave us any. In the end, we had to go with the topo from the poster of El Cap. It was a very laborious route on every pitch, without exception.

SYLVIA VIDAL, *Spain*

*Half Dome, Blue Shift.* On June 1, Karl McConachie and I completed a new route on Half Dome. *Blue Shift* (VI 5.11c A4) follows crack systems that lie between *Arcturas* and *Same As It Never Was*, a route that Karl, Randal Grandstaff and I put up in 1985. It then follows Arcturas for a pitch and a half before cutting out left on new ground again. The last few feet join the Regular Northwest Face route to the summit. We spent four nights on the wall after fixing and drilled a total of 46 holes, of which 20 were for belays. Seven of those were used to pass a stack of loose blocks on pitch 11. *Blue Shift* is a modern aid route up thin and expanding flake systems characterized by some difficult free climbing and exciting direct aid. This route is sure to become as popular as *Same As It Never Was*, which I doubt has seen a second ascent. Bring plenty of beaks, hooks, RURPs and a 60-meter rope.

JAY SMITH, *unaffiliated*

*El Capitan, The Nose.* Single-day ascents of this 3,000-foot vertical granite wall have become rights of passage for top rock climbers in their prime. On September 23, Galen Rowell became the oldest climber to do so. Starting by headlamp with no fixed ropes at 4 a.m., the 57-year-old Rowell and Conrad Anker shared leads to reach the summit just before eight in the evening. They brought only a single rope, a two-quart water bottle each, plus enough PowerGel and chocolate-covered espresso beans to pass other teams from France, England, Norway, and the United States during the first half of the climb.

Thirty-one years earlier, in 1966, Rowell had made the fifth ascent of the *Nose* in five days. The 1958 first ascent led by Warren Harding required 18 months of siege climbing and a final 12-day push, which seems to prove that climbing advances much faster than aging.

GALEN ROWELL

SIERRA NEVADA

*Bubbs Creek Wall, Samurai Warrior.* Over three days in September, Dave Nettle and I established a new route on Bubbs Creek Wall in Kings Canyon. *Samurai Warriors* (V 5.11 A1) follows the first pitch and a half of *Crystal Bonzai* before taking an independent line to the right. All but two of the 14 pitches are 5.10 or harder, and a 60-meter rope is required. One short pendulum and 50 feet of bathooks are the extent of the aid. The first half of the route follows corners up to a prominent right-leaning straight-in crack. The route then goes through the brown headwall via a finger crack to a scenic hanging bivy. The rest of the climb is mostly bolt-protected face climbing with knobs, mantles and friction. It is a beautiful, varied, user-friendly backcountry route.

BRANDON THAU

*Moro Rock, El Niño.* Grant Gardner, Jody Pennycook and I completed a new route on the east face of Moro Rock in Sequoia National Park during an extended Veteran's Day weekend. Three and a half days were spent on *El Niño* (V 5.10 A3+). This nine-pitch climb starts up a crack system that connects near the top of and ends at the first pitch of *Full Metal Jacket.* Then it follows the ramp of *FMJ* for 30 feet and goes up a gray half-moon section to a shallow straight-in crack. The pitch ascends a hidden 5.6 chimney and belays at the base of the prominent headwall crack. Follow this crack up to a 70-foot straight-in micro-birdbeak crack. Belay under the roof. Traverse around the roof and follow right-slanting cracks to the summit. Aside from bolted anchors, only one rivet was used on the ascent. A full wall rack is required, with heads and extra birdbeaks. The highlight of the climb was when the first of the El Niño storms of 1998 hit us on the sixth pitch. The three of us shivered inside a double portaledge while 18 inches of snow fell. We abandoned all our gear in the morning for a dash to the summit during a break in the storm. This difficult, overlooked line has gorgeous views of Castle Rock Spire and Angel Wings.

BRANDON THAU

*Thor Peak, South Face, Lucifer's Hammer.* In September, Bruce Bindner, Em Holland and I climbed *Lucifer's Hammer* (III, 5.10a) which starts from *Odin's Wrath*, a route we climbed the previous year (*AAJ* 1997, p. 142). From the flake ledge on top of the first pitch above the Pink Perch, *Odin's Wrath* goes up and left. *Lucifer's Hammer* goes straight up for six more pitches. There are six bolts, three at belays and three for protection.

PAT BRENNAN, *unaffiliated*

*Nameless Pyramid, East Face, Direct Finish.* The East Face of Nameless Pyramid (5.8) is a popular backcountry route, often done car-to-car in a long day. In July, Eric Tipton and I climbed the route, doing two new final pitches. From the notch on the ridge where the regular route eases in difficulty, we moved out left and climbed up via mostly left-facing ramps and corners. Our variation, the *Direct Finish* (III, 5.10a), ended at the base of the final summit pinnacle.

PAT BRENNAN, *unaffiliated*

*Mt. Hoffman, North Face, Meteor Shower.* The north face of Mt. Hoffman is a wide face with many potential lines. In August, Sarah Schneider and I established what we believe to be the fourth technical route on the face, the farthest left one done to date. It follows the second continuous crack system from the left edge of the face (there are two lesser faces left of the "main" north face. Both of these have potential lines, but I don't believe any routes have been done here yet). A prominent overhanging offwidth was passed via a traverse right about 150 feet up. The climbing then went up and left on flakes to regain the crack above the offwidth. In general, the route, *Meteor Shower* (III, 5.10a), slants slightly right for much of its length. The route involved four pitches, with the crux—a fist crack through a small roof—on the last one. Poor rock, continuous climbing and dicey protection and anchors seemed to be the norm on this potentially dangerous route.

ALAN BARTLETT, *unaffiliated*

*Balch Camp Flake, Flicker of Time Arête and The Passionate Life.* On February 23, David Cotter and I climbed the east (right-hand) arête of the huge Balch Camp Flake, naming it the *Flicker of Time Arête* (5.9 AO). We started on the bolt ladder of the original 1954 route, then free climbed up the arête to the top. A day later, Jay Anderson and Ann Yeagle climbed the left-hand of the two very impressive and obvious wide cracks on the south side of Balch Camp Flake. This offwidth and squeeze chimney, which they named *The Passionate Life* (5.11c), had been attempted before, but never completed.

RICHARD LEVERSEE

*The Fin, North Arête Chimney.* In June, Dave Nettle, Kevin Daniels and I climbed an obvious crack system directly up the north face of The Fin starting on the spine of the ridge that joins the base of the north face. Based on the old rusty quarter-inch bolt and sling we found about halfway up the first pitch, we think the route, the *North Arête Chimney* (III 5.10+, five pitches) had been started a long time ago.

RICHARD LEVERSEE

*Tehipite Dome, Too Hip.* In July, 1996, Ron Felton and I climbed a crack and face line, *Too Hip* (III 5.11, six pitches with 60-meter ropes) starting about 400 feet left and up from the point where the Kroger and Beckey routes intersect on the huge bush-covered "Halfway Ledge" high on the southwest face of the dome.

RICHARD LEVERSEE

*Tehipite Dome, Southwest Face, In the Niche of Time.* In October, spending 14 days out from the trailhead and six days climbing, Ron Felton, Guy 'Zelly' Zielsky and I succeeded in establishing the first completely independent and first big new route to be climbed on this immense wall in 27 years, *In the Niche of Time* (VI 5.10 A3+, 21 pitches with 60-meter ropes).

In October, 1991, John Vargas and I hiked the 20 miles to Tehipite Valley only to be overwhelmed by heavy backpacks and debilitating heat. In October, 1995, Ron Felton and I returned again and made the approach but retreated before beginning. In the autumn of 1997, we returned again, this time recruiting Guy Zielski to assist in the project. Ron and I led while Guy graciously helped with the moving of freight.

We spent a day and a half hiking in and, during the next two and a half days of welcome, cooling rain, we moved loads toward the base of the wall. After periodically hiding from the

rain in talus caves, we scrambled 500 feet to the start of our route just left of the 1970 Kroger Route and at the left side of a prominent pyramid formation.

We went left up some wet and slimy shelves to a small tree ledge to keep us out of the path of potential rockfall. On the second lead, Ron nailed up and right on a thin ramp in order to cross the prominent arête (which marked our line of ascent) to attain a crack that headed up to a huge pillar above. Ron led into the night, using all 12 of our beak pitons in the process. Upon arriving at the belay, I found him almost unresponsive and hypothermic. After warming him up and giving him a shell garment, we squeezed out a bivy back at the tree ledge. The next morning, I led a steep crack on aid to a difficult and partially loose wide section to get us to some mausoleum-like ledges behind the pillar. The climbing to the top of the pillar proved extremely difficult; Ron mixed free and aid, then traversed left to the arête, nailing a long, impressive horizontal roof.

I found spectacular climbing up steep thin cracks on the arête above, reminiscent of the headwall passage on the *Shield* of El Capitan. The illusions of steepness were confirmed each time Guy launched into space to ascend the rope to the belay. This was Guy's first wall. I was impressed by his 'go for it' attitude, especially since he had never used ascenders prior to this climb!

On the next lead, the features we had hoped were cracks turned out to be mere ripples in the sea of granite above. Ron boldly bat-hooked, riveted and beaked to just short of a good crack system. A mixed pitch followed, including some welcome hand cracks, nailing and nutting, ending in a scary mantle onto the belay stance.

Ron nailed a short section above, then climbed down and right to a diagonal ramp and a ledge at the base of a huge corner. In three long difficult free pitches, we made it to a ledge that divides the lower wall from the upper dome. That night, we split less than a quart of water and the food that remained between the three of us. The morning of our sixth day and tenth day out from the trailhead, we decided to escape, and worked our way across the ledge to water and our lives back home.

By mid-October Ron, Guy and I were able to return. Traversing back to our high point, we continued the route on the upper dome. Starting up the line of the corner which got us to the ledge from the lower wall, we moved left out onto an arête. Ron cruised up a classic, difficult steep face pitch to a blocky ledge below a steep headwall. Following straight thin cracks up through two major horizontal crack/bands allowed me to tension-traverse left to a diagonal ramp ending at a belay just below a prominent right-facing corner/chimney. Ron led up an awkward step left and then right, climbing some difficult moves up the chimney to a belay at the intersection of a wide crack from above and left. Following this crack system gave us a more direct line to the summit. Above this wide section, intricate free and aid moves headed up to a ledge just left of another, but a much easier wide crack. Belaying only about 80 feet out, we then headed right a few moves to an enjoyable left-facing corner.

In the autumn darkness, climbing toward a seemingly unreachable horizon, four more long pitches of easy but runout face climbing brought us to an unroping spot at blocky ledges well below the true summit.

E.C. JOE, *Southern Sierra Climber's Association*

*Mt. Hoffman, Southeast Face Central.* This route, the Southeast Face Central (5.8-5.9, three and a half pitches) in the Wishon Reservoir Area of the Sierra National Forest, starts to the right of the obvious 200-foot tower/buttress on the southeast face. In July, Mark Leffler and I climbed the obvious diagonal crack up and right for one and a half pitches to a good ledge

*Tehipite Dome, showing A:* In the Niche of Time, *and B: Beckey-Kroger Route. E.C. Joe*

*Peter Croft on the first traverse of the Evolution Peaks.* GALEN ROWELL

below a long right-facing corner/arch that heads toward the top. We followed this corner, then moved right to an obvious crack and belay. The last pitch followed this crack to the top. We walked off for the descent. The approach is made via the dirt road and trail cross-country from the Wishon Reservoir.

RICHARD LEVERSEE

*Finger Rock, Boldfinger.* A long time ago (1970s?), Fred Beckey and crew climbed a route on the south side of Finger Rock, which is a short drive/hike from the Wishon Reservoir. On the east face of Finger Rock are a couple distinct features. There is an obvious diagonal line of weakness going up from the lower left to upper right. This ends below an ominous, rust-colored overhanging headwall chock-full of wild huecos, chickenheads and plate flakes in the center of the east face. This featured section is directly above several gigantic boulders on the slope below the east face. Climb up the diagonal ramp for two pitches until directly below the wild central headwall above a short (30') chimney. Belay at a flake covered in bird droppings. The next pitch is steep and wild, heading up and right through the incredible featured headwall. It ends on a huge ledge 50 feet below the top. Descent is third class off the back (north) side. Mark Leffler and I did the route in July, calling it *Boldfinger* (5.10+, three pitches).

RICHARD LEVERSEE

*Evolution Peaks, Grand Traverse.* The Evolution Peaks were judged to be the scenic culmination of the High Sierra by the 19th century scrambler Theodore Solomons, who named them after the great evolutionary scientists and thinkers of the time. Located far from roadheads at the middle of the John Muir Trail, they have had very little technical rock climbing. Peter Croft and I followed this tradition by not using ropes or hardware on the first traverse of the Evolution range in mid-July.

At 4:30 a.m., we started by headlamp from our camp at 10,800 feet on Evolution Lake, climbing a 4th class route on Mount Mendel to reach the summit ridge at dawn. From there, a mile of knife-edged ridge (4th and 5th-class climbing) brought us to the summit pinnacle of Mount Darwin (13,831"). As we continued south, we came to the crux of the day, which involved exposed, unroped 5.9 climbing with some loose rock along a series of pinnacles just below Darwin.

We continued traversing several more 13,000-foot peaks with spots of 5.8 until we reached the easier classic Northwest Arête of Mount Haeckel. Having completed all the peaks on the main crest, and with hands that could barely touch the rock, I decided to descend. Peter continued alone, veering off the main crest to traverse over mounts Wallace, Fiske, Warlow, and Huxley to complete the entire arc of Evolution Peaks. He returned to camp at about 7 p.m., having traversed 35,000 feet of horizontal rock climbing with close to 10,000 feet of vertical gain, which he considered to be more than the equivalent of a one-day Grade VI wall climb.

GALEN ROWELL

*Mount Darwin, Southwest Arête.* While camped at Evolution Lake in July, I noticed a surprisingly clean and well-defined granite arête on the 13,831-foot Mt. Darwin's jumbled and broken southern wall. The arête rises continuously apart from the main wall for more than 2,000 feet from a bench above the inlet of the lake. I set out alone one morning with a 9mm rope and a few cams to self-belay if necessary. Third-class scrambling brought me to a steep buttress of white granite laced with 5.8 cracks, which I managed to solo with a tail line to haul my pack with water and a camera. From there, an exposed, easy ridge angled higher to another headwall with more 5.8 climbing just below a prominent pinnacle a few hundred feet from the top. Getting past the 100-foot-deep notch separating the pinnacle from the mountain proved to be the highly exposed crux of the climb on perfect rock. (III 5.8)

GALEN ROWELL

*Mount Huxley, North Buttress, Left and Right Sides.* As seen from Evolution Lake, the north buttress of Mount Huxley (13,086') rises into a classic horn split by a deep cirque. In July, Dick Duane and I climbed a series of perfect finger cracks on the left side up to a long, fractured ridge of giant blocks that leads to the summit. A 5.9 pitch ascending a one-inch crack splitting perfect alpine granite offered some of the best rock climbing in the entire High Sierra, Tuolumne Meadows included. The rock looks as if it were quarried yesterday. While Dick and I were climbing this route (III 5.10a) on the left side of the north buttress, Hans Florine and Jerry Dodrill made a very similar new route (III 5.10a) up long clean dihedrals on the right side of the cirque. We met on the summit and descended south to Sapphire Lake.

On the same trip, Hans and I noticed a surprisingly featureless 250-foot cliff above Sapphire Lake. Late one afternoon, we headed up the only obvious cracks on the right side of the cliff. They begin beside a large block, traverse left on a ramp, then go up and left on a vertical wall to the top. The 5.11a face climbing crux came on the third and final pitch, where Hans traversed right onto the open face and back left again 30 feet higher to avoid an overhanging seam that we both had backed off from leading.

GALEN ROWELL

## UTAH

### ZION NATIONAL PARK

*Zion, Various Ascents.* During late winter, Dan Stih and I made the first ascent of the Altar of Sacrifice, as well as the remaining four Towers of the Virgin in Zion National Park. Over three days in early March, we climbed and fixed the grotesquely loose gully (on the southeast side of the formation just across from the Quinn route) that leads to a large plateau. Much credit needs to be given to Dan for leading the worst of the rotten chimneys, often totally unprotected and in excess of 5.10. Steve Burgess of Switzerland also helped out for the first two days on the lower section of the route.

Once on the plateau, we jumared food, water and a full aid rack, as well as winter gear, to the hanging valley at the base of the towers. On March 8, we climbed three long pitches (5.10+ Al) of chimneys on the south side of the Altar that led to the summit. The second of these pitches was choked with thick ice and Dan was forced to use his piton hammer and a long angle piton as ice tools for about ten meters. Three holes were drilled for belays and six protecting chimneys above the plateau were drilled below the plateau. On top we built a five-foot high cairn on the edge of the east face, commemorating my late friend Chris Clark, who was killed in November, 1995, climbing in the Sierra. A summit register is at the base of the cairn, which can be seen through the spotting scope at the visitors center.

The rest of the towers are approached from the plateau. The Rotten Tooth (4th class) and the Broken Tooth (5.10, four pitches) were climbed in one day. These are the two smaller towers left of the Altar, and are the names given by the rangers. The Witch Head (5.10, five pitches) was climbed via the west face. This is the huge formation just right of the Sundial.

The Sundial (5.10+, seven pitches) was the last of the towers we climbed. Originally traversing across the east face, we attempted a route on the south face. After two death pitches on the horrid Whitecap sandstone, we retreated and climbed a route on the northwest face to the summit, thus having made the first ascents of all of Towers of the Virgin. We believe that water possibly exists in two pools year-round, the first beneath the south face of the Altar Of Sacrifice, and the other (and more likely) in a deep slot beneath the north face of the Sundial in a previously unexplored valley.

RON RAIMONDE

*West Temple, Gettin' Western.* On April 30, Andrew Nichols and I made the third ascent of *Gettin' Western* on the east face of the West Temple, one of the biggest walls in Zion.

In 1990, Brad Quinn and Darren Cope made the first ascent of this proud line. Several efforts over eight days eventually brought them to the summit. (Darren's uncle made the first ascent of the West Temple in the 1930s.) In 1993, Doug Hall and Doug Byerly made the second and first free ascent, an outstanding effort that included a crux pitch of 5.11 thin hands crack with minimal protection behind a hollow flake. Doug and Doug spent two days ascending and descending the route.

Andrew and I set off at midnight. Slightly lost, we climbed three pitches through a rock band to gain the lower flanks of the east face. We arrived at the base of the wall at about 4 a.m. and started climbing. The first 1,500 feet offers hard climbing on steep cracks (many 5.10 pitches with the occasional point of aid). By 2 p.m., we were eating lunch under a huge pine tree that sits on a ledge at about mid-height. Climbing the upper half of the route was somewhat like gardening, for the steep walls were covered with various types of plants, grasses and trees. They all offer good handholds. By 8 p.m. we pulled onto the top of the route.

We spent the night on the shoulder of the West Temple. In the morning, we set off for the main summit. The descent proved to be devious and very dangerous. Many loose blocks abound on the upper flanks of this proud sandstone mountain.

JONNY ALLEN, *unaffiliated*

*Right Twin, Paca-Lolo Dreams.* From October 15-October 20, Brad Bond, Bryan Smith and I climbed a new route, *Paca-Lolo Dreams* (V 5.9 A3-, seven pitches) about 350 feet right of *Peyote Dreams.* The climb begins in a 5.9 hand crack that had been climbed previously. Another pitch of free climbing and a pitch of aid gain the base of a major corner with a hand crack. This corner pitch is shared with *Lost in Transit*, a route that begins to the right of *Paca-Lolo Dreams.* After the major corner, three quality sustained aid pitches climb some splitter thin cracks. We placed six anchor bolts and six aid bolts in addition to drilling two incomplete holes for aid. I would encourage subsequent parties to complete the drilling of the two holes on pitch 5 and fill them with half-inch angles. No bolts were placed at belays shared with other routes (i.e., the first pitch and the corner of *Lost in Transit*).

BOULOS AYAD, *unaffiliated*

*Temple of Sinawava, Soul Craft.* On December 12, Karen Hilton and I completed the first ascent of *Soul Craft* (VI 5.11 A4+) on the steep wall left of the *Monkeyfinger* route. In

*Paul Turecki on* Soul Craft, *Temple of Sinawava.* KAREN HILTON

ca.1,100 feet, only the first pitch and last 35 feet went free; the remainder of the route yielded to moderate and difficult aid. We gave the "+" rating for the potential ledge fall on pitch 5. In typical Zion fashion, the climbing was quality and fairly sustained. It was possibly the last wall to be done before the initiation of the park's backcountry permit fee. For the descent, we rappelled the *Monkeyfinger* route. Two anchors were added at the second and fourth (counting from top to bottom) *Monkeyfinger* stations on the way down.

PAUL TURECKI

*Streaked Wall, Latitudes, Second Ascent.* It was reported that in early November, John Varco and Bryan Gilmore made the second ascent of *Latitudes* (VI 5.9 A4+) on the Streaked Wall. Varco first teamed up with Greg Grasso to climb, fix and haul to Rubicon ledge. He then spent nine days with Gilmore on the upper eight pitches finishing the route. *(Climbing* 176)

*Twin Brothers, Levels of Doom, and Isaac, Middle Earth.* It was reported that Amanda Tarr and Eric Rasmussen put up a new 14-pitch line, *Levels of Doom* (VI 5.9 A3+), to the right of *Peyote Dreams* on the Twin Brothers, in late September. In late November, Rasmussen and Luke Miller climbed *Middle Earth* (VI 5.11c A4), a 19-pitch bottom-to-top crack climb to the right of *Tricks of the Tramp* on Isaac. *(Climbing* 174)

*Zion, Road Kill.* It was reported that, while filming a video about big wall climbing, Jeff Lowe and his "student," Scott Thompson, put up the route *Road Kill* (V 5.11 A4), a nine-pitch route on an 1,100-foot wall near the park's west entrance. *(Rock and Ice* 83)

SAN RAFAEL SWELL

*San Rafael Swell, La Piñata.* On November 9, Franziska Garrett and I were surprised to find the big hulk of a desert tower adjacent (west-northwest) to Mexican Mountain still unclimbed. After driving the Mexican Mountain Road and parking at its terminus, we waded across a shallow section of the San Rafael River. We then weaved our way up the northern flank of Mexican Mountain before traversing westward to the tower. Unsettled weather steered us toward the eastern side, where we climbed a short pitch (5.10 A0) to a prominent ledge on the south ridge. Then, a 60-meter pitch led over 5.8 slabs to a short, steep A1 bolt-hole-bolt section and some nailing and free climbing to the top (5.9 A1). We rappelled the route, *La Piñata* (II 5.10 A2), after savoring wide-angle views of the Swell.

JAMES GARRETT

FISHER TOWERS

*Fisher Towers, Various Ascents.* It was reported that Crusher Bartlett and Dave Levine climbed *Beaking in Tongues*, a seven-pitch route on the west face of the Oracle that was rated "somewhere between A2+ and A4" and used no bolts. On the south face of the Oracle, Kevin Chase and an Englishman known as Heavy Duty climbed *Nightmare on Onion Creek* (5.3 A4). Heavy Duty and Keith Reynolds put up a new route on the north side of the Citadel that used very few bolts. Tim Wagner made the second ascent of the Jim Beyer route *Deadman's Party* and soloed Beyer's *Intifada*. *(Rock and Ice* 80)

*King Fisher, The Hazing.* It was reported that Eric Kohl, Bryan Law (joined by Pete Takeda on the final push) climbed *The Hazing* (5.8 A3) on the west face of the King Fisher. Also, Stevie Haston (U.K.) reportedly freed *Phantom Spirit* on the Echo Tower at 5.11-5.12. (*Rock and Ice* 81)

*The Titan, The Wasteland.* It was reported that Walt Shipley and Bill Lee nailed "what may be the Titan's last natural line," *The Wasteland* (A3+ 5.8), an 1,100-foot nine-pitch route that required roughly 35 bolts. It lies on the tower's west face, in the obvious chimney left of Scherezade, and generally follows the gargoyle arête beside the Finger of Fate. (*Climbing* 176)

*Doric Column, The Big Nasty.* It was reported that Bill Lee and Walt Shipley put up a new 600-foot route via the "obvious" line on the Doric Column's southeast face. *The Big Nasty* (A4 5.9R) was climbed over three days in November; ten holes were drilled for progress. (*Climbing* 176)

*Fisher Towers, Various Ascents.* In 1997, I climbed four small, "new" towers in the Fisher Towers with various partners. In April, Jon Butler and I made the first ascents of two towers, Large Marge and The Projects, below the Titan Trail. In December, Jesse Harvey, Mike Baker and I climbed two "new" towers, Putterman's Pile and Rocky Top, which lie between Dock Rock and the King Fisher. Putterman's Pile lies 300 feet south of The Great Googly Moogley, which saw its first ascent in November, by Walt Shipley, solo. Shipley and Keith Reynolds later free climbed *The Great Googly Moogley* at 5.10+. The Great Googly Moogley lies just east of Dock Rock, and is obvious from the parking lot.

In May, Mike Baker and I made the first ascent of the western prow of River Tower via a four-pitch route called *The Flow* (III 5.8 A2). The 450-foot route climbs the tallest portion of River Tower and had been previously attempted by an unknown party.

CAMERON M. BURNS

*The River Towers.* CAMERON BURNS

CAPITOL REEF NATIONAL PARK

*Factory Butte, Clarification.* I was a interpretive park ranger at Capitol Reef National Park from June, 1992, through October, 1994. During my time there, I set my sights on a prominent monolith called Factory Butte.

Rumors among the locals were that it had not been climbed, which I doubted because of its prominence and because of the famous climbers who got their start in the Torrey area. The approach and the base of Factory Butte are made of the clay/silt mudstone of the Mancos rock type, which erodes into sharp rills, deep gullies and badland-type rock (fine-grained clay/mud). Mancos rock makes up 70 percentof the monolith. The crown of the Butte is Mesa Verde sandstone, which erodes into sheer vertical cliffs. The Butte is long and thin; the long sides faces east and west, while the thin faces run north and south. On the west and north side, the erosion is at its worst. The east and south sides also are extremely steep, with angles increasing from 35 to 50° in the Mancos to vertical in the Mesa Verde. The Butte itself rises about 2,000 feet above its base; at the contact point between the Mancos and the Mesa Verde rock types, the Butte goes vertical for 200 to 350 feet.

I made four to five planning trips to the area from 1992 through 1994, first to find a route through the Mancos rills and gullies. To stabilize myself on the steep siltstone, I began using my old McKinley wood ice axe and my old crampons. I found one potential route in 1992 on the east face near a huge slab of fallen Mesa Verde rock that can be seen from a distance. The gully directly in front of the slab was passable and probably the easiest gully on the east side. Two small ledges allowed me to zig-zag up the Mesa Verde face into a crack, which led to within 50 to 75 feet of the tabletop summit. I was unable to finish the route due to time, heat (it was the middle of July) and lack of aid gear.

On my next trip, I totally circumnavigated the Butte at the base of the Mesa Verde (again using ice axe and crampons, the only way to approach the steepest areas of the Mancos safely), working my way across the large arm that extends west from the south Butte area. After crossing the arm, I moved over a series of gullies, beyond an area of sheer Mancos in the southwestern corner, to the next series of gullies. I then climbed the Mancos to the base of the Mesa Verde. At the corner area, a series of angled, tilted ledges on the Mesa Verde allowed me to work my way up to a rock-filled gully, which took me south to the corner's interior. From there, I entered the crux area, an extended overhang, about 15 feet wide, with fun exposure. I topped the overhang by moving directly across the nose with some good hand holds and friction, but with little for my legs or feet. At the south side of the crux, I entered another rock-filled gully that led directly to the south tabletop area. At this point, there are many cracks that can be chimneyed to the summit on the southernmost point of the Butte.

This route was done solo and free of any aid except the ice tool and crampons. I climbed it twice (winter, 1993, and November, 1994). I found an arrow from one of the 1950 movies filmed in the area, plus a small cairn on the south summit. I placed a small note to my parents, who both had died just before this climb, underneath this cairn.

I later would show my route to a person whom I thought was my friend. This person would share my route information and the ice axe-crampon technique with a third party, who later would make a claim of a first ascent of Factory Butte almost a month after my last climb. This individual can claim a possible new route, but not a first ascent. Nor can I; but I will name my route *Flo and Al's*.

JOHN FLEMING

## ARIZONA

### OAK CREEK CANYON

*Fear and Loathing.* In early September, Dan Stih, Paul Reinshagen and I climbed a new 400-meter route in Oak Creek Canyon, just north of Sedona, Arizona. The wall is located just behind Christopher's Tower, high in Counterfeiter Canyon. The line, *Fear and Loathing* (V 5.10 A2+), runs for ten pitches, following a right-facing thin dihedral on excellent rock for the first five. The last two pitches consist of a slightly overhanging three-inch splitter crack that runs for nearly 60 meters. All belays are equipped with good bolts and/or fixed pins. With four ropes fixed, we spent one night on the wall on a huge heavily foliated ledge at the top of pitch 8. The bottom half of the route is almost all aid, requiring much thin nailing; it consumed the better part of two days. We feel the grade (V) is a conservative rating, and the aid is of a high standard.

RON RAIMONDE

## COLORADO

### BLACK CANYON OF THE GUNNISON

*Hallucinogen Wall, Solo Ascent.* It was reported that Amanda Tarr soloed the Hallucinogen Wall in the Black Canyon of the Gunnison over five days in June. This was the first female solo of the route. (*Climbing* 171)

*North Chasm View Wall, Link-up of Stoned Oven and Air Voyage.* It was reported that Jeff Hollenbaugh and Mike Pennings linked up *Stoned Oven* (5.11c) and *Air Voyage* (5.12a), both on North Chasm View Wall, in a day, freeing everything apart from the 5.12a offwidth on *Air Voyage.* The pair managed the 3,000 feet of climbing by beginning an hour before light and finishing an hour after dark. (*Climbing* 170)

### GORE RANGE

*Peak C, New Route.* On August 9, Benny Bach and I climbed an eight-pitch, 5.7+ route on the north face of Peak C in the Gore Range. The incessant rain of the summer of 1997, supposedly a side-effect of the El Niño weather phenomenon, left the face extremely wet. We know little of the history of this impressive face but suspect our route was mostly new.

CAMERON M. BURNS

### ROCKY MOUNTAIN NATIONAL PARK

*Long's Peak, The Diamond, Smash the State.* Between May 15-20, Ken Sauls and I made the second ascent of *Smash the State* (VI- 5.8 A5) on the Diamond of Long's Peak. Jim Beyer made the first ascent of this route in April of 1988, solo. Doug Hall and Ken had discussed doing the route, but Doug was killed in an avalanche in January, 1997. When Ken invited me to join him, it appealed to me as a memorial ascent for Mr. Hall, whose great spirit I will never forget.

We started hiking close to noon on Thursday, May 15. We carried all of our gear in one (large) load. We arrived at Chasm View at about 9 p.m., set up the ledge on a boulder and crawled in for a very windy night. At about 10 a.m., we made our way to the rappels for the descent to Broadway. We roped up for three pitches across Broadway to the base of the route, fixing lines and then ferrying our loads across.

The first pitch went quickly. We hauled up our bags, then Ken set off on the second pitch, leading about one-third of it, then rapping back to help set up the ledge. A good night's rest and Ken finished up the second pitch through steep roofs and corners. The difficulty (A3) is demanding due to the quality of the stone. In the afternoon, I set off on the third pitch (A4); some A1 gear led to a hook move, then I placed five heads to another hook, which led to some circuitous flakes (somewhat dubious), and to the S-shaped roof. After this lead we discussed style; it became clear to me that it is better to use pitons if possible, as they make cleaning easier and therefore have less impact.

Ken led the fourth pitch (A5a). A sharp edge stands out from the lip of the S-roof. By using duct tape, Ken was able to lessen the sharpness of the edge. Up and away he went, a brilliant lead on hooks, nuts, copperheads, beaks, etc. Ken found an A1 stopper at about 40 feet height, calling into question the A5 rating. This pitch just ends in blankness and it is necessary to pendulum to the right to join the *King of Swords* route.

Late in the day, I headed up pitches familiar from a 1993 ascent, using a mix of free and aid on the 5.12/A1 climbing to make it to Table Ledge, where we camped. On day 5, two more pitches of 5.10/A1 brought us to the top. Wild place.

JONNY ALLEN, *unaffiliated*

*The Ship's Prow, Bologna Pony.* It was reported that Jim Redo and Pat Adams put up a new 500-foot line on The Ship's Prow that follows the obvious overhanging arête on the formation. *The Bologna Pony* (5.12b/c) features thin crack climbing on the first pitch and face climbing above. Protection is a mix of bolts and traditional. All belays are bolted, but the top rappel requires back clipping to avoid hanging in space. (*Climbing* 173)

# WYOMING

*Fred Beckey on the first ascent of* Bomber Lake Arête. CAMERON BURNS

## WIND RIVER RANGE

*Goat Flat, Bomber Lake Arête.* On September 5, Fred Beckey and I climbed a long, low-angled ridge south of Bomber Lake in the northern Wind River Range. The ridge leads to Goat Flat, an enormous, flat plateau south of the Bomber Creek drainage. The majority of the 1,500-foot ridge was 4th-class climbing with short sections of lower 5th class. We climbed unroped for all but the final 120 feet of the ridge, which Fred led via 5.6 slabs right on the very crest of the arête (II 5.6). In his mid-70s, Fred looked pretty old while walking along the trail. When he climbed, however, he had the grace and style of a 20-year old.

CAMERON M. BURNS

*Watch Tower, South Buttress, First Free Ascent.* Last August, John Merriam and I did the first free ascent of the South Buttress (IV 5.11b R) of the Watch Tower in the Wind River Range.

JONATHON COPP

GRAND TETON NATIONAL PARK

*Middle Teton, No Cumbre, No Ruta.* On July 14, Alex Lowe and I climbed *No Cumbre, No Ruta* (WI5 M7 A0, 240 m) on the north face of the Middle Teton. From the Lower Saddle, approach the north face as you would for the Goodrich Chimney and/or the Jackson-Woodmency Dihedral. The route is the obvious chimney to the right of the Goodrich route. The route was named in response and protest to bogus debates circling the climbing community that new routes must top out on true summits of a claimed peak or they do not and should not exist. Hence, we did not go to the summit of the Middle. One hell of a good route, though.

TRAVIS SPITZER

MONTANA

*Crazy Peak, North Face.* On June 13, Paul Richer and I hiked into Big Timber Canyon to climb the north face of Crazy Peak. Access is through Half Moon campground (24 miles northeast of Big Timber). Two and a quarter miles of easy hiking brings one to a second bridge. Do not cross the bridge; instead, head left into the trees and uphill to the right. Eventually, the north face of Crazy Peak will come into view above treeline.

Our north face route takes a direct line up the face, slightly left of a main wide chute and a rockband at mid-height. Below the rockband the snow angle is 40 to 45°. The second third of the route involves low angle snow (less than 50°) and 5th-class rock through chimneys and slabs (5.6). Up to that point the climbing was enjoyable and fun. The last third of the face was the crux: loose and unconsolidated 65° snow.

The route tops out on a knife-edged ridge (4th to 5th class rock). Downclimbing is necessary to reach the final chute, which leads to the summit of Crazy Peak (11,214'). The Richer-Gallagher route (a.k.a. *Stoker-Goo*, 5.6 AI4) was about 2,500 feet long and technically committing. Gear was sparse in the upper third of the route. Fall/winter would produce excellent snow conditions and better protection. I would highly recommend this range for further possibilities.

JOHN GALLAGHER

*Glacier National Park, Various Ascents.* Beginning in the winter of 1995-96, new ice routes have been discovered and climbed in Glacier National Park. The first area to be explored was the southwest face on Mt. Cannon. Kirby Spangler and Marc Venery climbed *Cannon Fodder*, which featured 2,000 feet of moderate ice and steep snow, ending in two pitches of WI4. January, 1997, brought good weather and stable snow, allowing the insatiable Spangler and Venery to climb *Looking Up a Loaded Barrel* (WI4, 800') and *Lost in a Crowd* (WI4, 1,200'), both on Cannon. Spangler also soloed *Goat Chaser* (IV WI3, 500') on the south shoulder of Cannon in March.

The Snyder Lakes Basin also was found to have excellent potential for new routes. *Brain Stem* (WI5, 200') on the south slopes of Mt. Brown is the farthest climb left in a series of three

*The north face of Mt. Edwards.* RYAN HOKANSON

lines. The middle line, *Controlled Burn* (WI4, 200'), was first climbed by Lane Johnson and John Runge sometime in the early '90s. The right line (WI3+, 200') also was climbed; very old slings were found at the top. On the north face of Edwards, Lane Johnson and John Runge climbed *A Six Pack and Nothing To Do* (WI3) in the massive 1,400-foot gully that splits the face. Soon after, Jim Earl and Chris Trimble climbed *Baby Semmler* (WI4+, 450'), just left of the main gully. Then in March, Johnson and Spangler climbed two difficult lines, producing *Spinal Tap* (5.7 WI5, 800') and *The Missing Tooth* (WI5 A2+, 450').

RYAN HOKANSON, *unaffiliated*

*Glacier National Park, Various Ascents*. El Niño gave northwest Montana the unusual mix of cold weather and little snow in November and December. As a result, most of the park roads were kept open, giving climbers easier access to several remote basins. The new route action began in the Avalanche Lake area. On November 15, I soloed a route called *Claire De Lune* (IV WI3, 300'). This climb is situated to the right of *The Pig*, and is approached via a tight ice-filled cleft which in itself sports about 300 feet of WI2-3. Soon afterward, Missoula climbers Jim Earl, Chris Trimble, and Rafael Graña climbed a route on the spectacular headwall to the left of *The Pig* and *Claire De Lune*: *Slog and Flog* (IV WI5, 150') is approached by the same ice-filled cleft. Trimble then teamed up with Kelly Cordes, also of Missoula, to produce another classic, *Staggering Corps* (IV WI5, 300'). This line is just left of *Slog and Flog*. The headwall that contains these two routes was named "Bubba's Moonshine Wall."

Still psyched for early season ice, Cordes and Graña returned to Avalanche Lake for another round. Setting their sights on one of the massive gullies on the west face of Bearhat Mountain, the two climbed about 1,000 feet of steep snow with intermittent ice. Their excit-

*Ryan Hokanson skiing out after the first ascent of* Brain Stem *(farthest left) on Mt. Brown.* MARK VENERY

ing finale included intermittent avalanches produced by a sudden storm that nearly ripped Graña off the last pitch while Cordes belayed from the shelter of some trees. *Wanda's Wicked Sister* (IV WI4, 1,000') is a steep slot with no obvious exits for its entire length. It fills with snow as the season progresses, and is not recommended.

MARK VENERY, *unaffiliated*

ALASKA

BROOKS RANGE

*Arrigetch Peaks, Parabola Peak, Northeast Buttress.* On August 4, Lara Karena Bitenieks and I flew into Circle Lake to commence a three-week rock climbing trip in the Arrigetch peaks of the Brooks Range. After a two-day approach, we established a base camp at the head of the south fork of Arrigetch Creek at the foot of the Maidens. We chose a line on Parabola Peak (one mile due west of Point 6320' on Survey Pass (B3) Quadrangle), as it was consistently drier than the shaded north-facing Maidens. Over the next 12 days, we had just one climbing day, due to incessant fog and drizzle. Tent time was interrupted by wanderings, during which we explored the magical valleys and rock formations around us and discovered many beautiful boulder problems. Finally, on August 18, it was clear and cold. We departed camp either to finish our route or just retrieve our gear. Hiking around the backside up to our high point (the Arrigetch are characteristically steep on one side and low angle on the other, which is nice for descents) to find our pack full of a "gear popsicle." The sun thawed us out as we climbed ten beautiful pitches (5.10 A0) to a sub-summit, where we beheld an amazing sunset and sunrise, before climbing the final 500 feet to the true summit.

On August 20, we hiked our loads out to Circle Lake, leaving nothing. We then spent the next four days canoeing the Alatna River, reveling at the abundance of wildlife in the Alaskan wilderness.

JOE RIECHERT

*Arrigetch Peaks, Various Ascents.* On June 15, I flew to Fairbanks, Alaska, where I met up with Fred Beckey, Dave Medara and Canadians Rick Clements and Kai Hirvonnen. Fred was the trip organizer; Dave had invited me to join him. From Fairbanks, we flew Frontier Airlines in a small plane to the town of Bettles, located centrally and on the southern side of the Brooks Range. On June 18, we flew from Koyukok River and landed on Takahula Lake. We hiked one day to reach the site where supplies had been air-dropped to help ease our approach. On the third day, Fred, concerned for his health, decided he would turn back. At 75 years old, Fred is a living legend and, with his ability to carry heavy packs and hike all day, an inspiration. He still does trips with the same fervor as ever. With his departure, our party then consisted of only the four youths. On June 21, we had a camp established high in the Aiyugomahalla Creek Valley (a.k.a. Creek 4662).

On June 23 and 24, Dave Medara and I climbed a new route on the northwest face of the Shot Tower. We began climbing at about 6 p.m. on the 23rd; by 5 p.m. on the 24th, we sat on the summit admiring the majestic view of the surrounding peaks. We descended in about five hours down the west ridge, Dave Robert's first ascent route. We named the route the *Alaskan Magnum Wall* (V 5.10 A3) after the brand name of pepper spray we carried for protection from bears. We climbed the route in 11 roped pitches; the wall is about 1,800 feet high.

While we climbed the Shot Tower, our friends Rick and Kai climbed a new route up the north face of the Pyramid, one of the sweetest looking lines in the region. It ascends a prominent ridge that divides two symmetrical faces on the Pyramid. They climbed 15 roped pitches, then rappelled their route, climbing and rappelling for about 30 hours during their 48-hour assault.

After a little rest, Dave and I decided to climb another mountain, the Badille, via the 700-foot southeast buttress. The route went all free in five pitches at 5.10+. It took us about nine hours round-trip from our camp.

As we did this route, Rick and Kai headed up the Shot Tower, where they climbed the West Ridge, calling it "a great alpine rock climb in a fantastical setting." After our forays, we were all slightly tired out and decided we would climb the more moderate east face of the West Maiden. From camp we climbed the steep talus slopes to the base of the West Maiden, where four roped pitches up good 5.9 cracks brought us to the summit. Looking down, we could see the proud 2,000 foot north face of the West Maiden, which all goes at 5.9. From here, we rappelled down the east ridge, and a moderate 4th-class scramble brought us to the summit of the East Maiden.

On July 1, we all shouldered huge backpacks and arrived back at Takahula Lake on July 2.

JONNY ALLEN, *unaffiliated*

*The Western British Mountains, Traverse.* The winter in the Brooks Range lasted right up to

the last day in May. On the first day of June, the final winter storm ended and the white carpet of snow gave way to the gray carpet of spring tundra. Six of us landed on the aufeis sheets
of the lower Kongakut near Pagilak Creek. Our hope was to cross the western British
Mountains from the Kongakut River in Alaska to the Firth River in the Yukon Territory. We
succeeded in this endeavor. Deep snow limited our movements for the first days but, by June
7, we had ascended Pagilak Creek and crossed the pass into the upper Malcolm River at the
international border. As if to accommodate our political imaginations, the Brooks Range
changes in character abruptly at this place, showing a heavy glacial history to the west and
appearing almost entirely unglaciated to the east. On a tributary of the Malcolm leading to
Sheep Creek, we found an anomalous expression of white spruce, the northernmost spruce on
the American Continent. Grizzly and wolverine also were present. Three minor climbs were
made at the passes, along with ascents of limestone walls and pinnacles (5.4). Our members
included Victor Bradford, Mary Weidler, Jerry Weidler, Fred Smith and the prominent Swiss
ornithologist Peter Balwin.

DENNIS SCHMIDTT

*Ascent and Descent of the Echooka River.* In early July, a successful attempt was made to
reach the headwaters of the Echooka and descend the entire drainage to its confluence with
the Sagavanigiktok. Crossing a high pass in relays from the Ivishak, we found a fabulous
world of limestone pillars, promontories, canyons and waterfalls. But the main drainage was
without water. The headwater summit (marked 7240 a mile west of the actual peak) is aproned
with two trunk glaciers that constitute the main source of the river. An ascent of this peak
directly up the north ridge was made in rain and snow. The corniced ice walls of the north face
give way to a rock summit. The descent of the river was arduous, beginning with relays of
equipment 12 miles to a small promontory that I hoped would prove an aquifer. The river did
rematerialize at the base of this promontory. Four days' travel through shallow strands, aufeis
sheets and deep wide channels brought us to the Sagavanigiktok. The Echooka was one of the
Arctic's last unexplored rivers.

DENNIS SCHMIDTT

*Endicott Mountains.* Peak 6800 is one of the most astonishing limestone walls in the Brooks
Range. It stands above a beautiful canyon on the upper western fork of the Itkillik River,
immediately east of the Cocked Hat Glacier. Approaching from Anaktuvuk Pass, we were
exploring the various terraced headwalls and canyons of the eastern Endicotts. We crossed
Nanushuk Glacier to a pass into the upper Itkillik. Exploring the glaciers, shelves and lakes
along the way, we eventually set up camp eight miles below that pass. Peak 6800 was
approached initially from the celebrated canyon under the north face. We ascended at a point
where this canyon turns south into the glacier. Crossing this glacier, we reached the pass under
the south face of 6800. We were to find the summit by this face. Continuing east through the
southern canyon, we made a complete circumnavigation of the massif. Members included
Nicholas Stielau, Charles Stielau, Martha Davis, Ronald Fried, Howard Kamentsky and the
customary leaders, Dr. Ruthmary Deuel and me.

DENNIS SCHMITT

*Mt. Prindle, McCloud.* Around July 4, Ian McRae and I climbed a five-pitch (200-foot rope)
route to the right of *The Fleecing of America.* The route, *McCloud* (5.9 A2), was a combina-

tion of mixed and free. The climb was typical of the rock at Mt. Prindle—it's either A4 or runout 5.9. We named the route after the weather, the terrain, and a bad joke about a sheep.

JEFF APPLE BENOWITZ

*Franklin Icefields, Traverse and Ascents.* Craig Deutche and I established a new and fascinating route across the Franklin Icefields in late July. From a small shelf on the Sadlerochit River, we proceeded up Whistler Creek and over the pass that leads to the canyon of the Franklin Ramp. Crossing Franklin Creek, we continued up the adjacent drainage to the base of Peak 8270 (Igluvuk or Mansion Mountain). This very prominent peak is built of steep walls surmounted by an undulating ice-capped roof. This roof was reached from the northwest ridge. The summit, falling away to the Triumvirate Glacier system, affords one of the most remarkable alpine views in the Brooks Range. The glacier under the south face of 8270 leads to an icecap and trunk glacier at the western source of the Canning River. Peak 7200 at the top of the West Triumvirate Glacier was climbed late in the day and in variable weather, and camp was made on the Canning Glacier below. From the upper Canning, we were able to cross the southernmost divides of the Chamberlin Spur to reach a western tributary of the Hulahula, which we descended to the Patuk Region.

DENNIS SCHMIDTT

DENALI NATIONAL PARK

*Denali National Park, Mountaineering Summary.* The 1997 climbing season for Mount McKinley and most of the Alaska Range started with mountaineers making unsuccessful summit bids in the chilly month of December and concluded in mid-July. Thirty-seven different countries were represented as 1,110 mountaineers attempted routes to the top of North America's highest peak. More than half of the mountaineers (51 percent) reached the summit, right in keeping with the historical average.

Mount Foraker, the second highest peak in the Alaska Range at 17,400 feet, saw 27 mountaineers attempting routes to its summit. Nine of those (30 percent) mountaineers were successful in their summit bid. Lower in altitude, but still technically demanding, Mount Hunter (14,573') saw approximately 43 mountaineers attempting routes to its summit. (Because registration for Mount Hunter in not mandatory, summit statistics are not available.)

The number of serious accidents in the Alaska Range continued its three-year downward trend with a total of ten major rescues. Mountaineering accidents this year claimed the lives of two mountaineers: an American on Mount Hunter and a British mountaineer on Mount McKinley. In addition, a Russian climber drowned while crossing the McKinley River in the park's backcountry after completing his Denali climb.

In 1997, the Alaska Range experienced a lower-than-average snowfall for the second year in a row, which led to an early breakup of the glaciers and affected route conditions for the mountaineering season. During the month of May, weather patterns were very unstable. Mountaineers battled strong winds that proved relentless for days at a time. A sudden storm caught climbers, including a guided group, near the summit, stranding them overnight. The effects of this storm were one British fatality in an independent expedition and four guided clients requiring rescue for severe frostbite, which resulted in significant tissue loss including that of fingers and toes.

Fantastic weather in June was a significant factor in the greater-than-normal number of mountaineers standing on the summit. Unfortunately, the mild weather did not hold over through early July, when many mountaineers found themselves stranded on the mountain due to high snowfall and rain at lower elevations. After receiving assistance from the 14,200-foot camp in the form of food and fuel, the stranded expeditions flew off the mountain, some as much as seven days late.

Weather is one of the most critical factors for Denali's mountaineering expeditions. It's not only the present weather conditions that affect an expedition's progress, but also the weather pattern for several months prior to the season that sets the hazards for the route. In 1998, a new weather-monitoring station will be installed at the 14,200-foot ranger camp to provide mountaineers with the most accurate and timely weather information available.

DENALI NATIONAL PARK

*Mt. Foraker, North Face, and Circumnavigation.* Historically, getting to the north side of Mt. Foraker has been a serious endeavor. The conditions of the terrain during the climbing season tend to be horrible; there is usually poor-quality snow, raging rivers, aggressive alders, and swampy tundra that needs to be dealt with, while blood-thirsty mosquitoes attack continually. With horse-packing and airplane landings not permitted within Denali National Park, all but a few expeditions have approached from just outside the park's western boundary. The other three groups experienced a 75-mile journey from Wonder Lake, the first two using horses prior to the park restrictions and the third beginning its epic with a nightmare approach. By the time many of the climbers reached the base of their routes, they found themselves behind schedule, poorly acclimatized, and pushing to make up lost time. With this increased commitment level, the end results have been few successful climbs and a higher percentage of

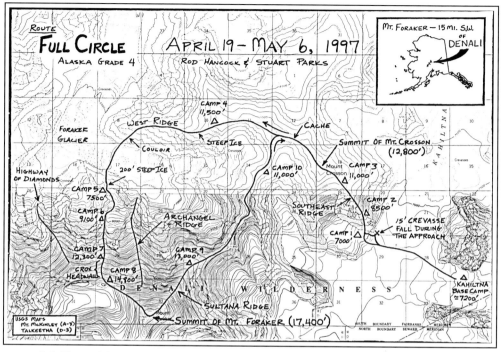

*Left: The north face of Mt. Foraker, showing the approach, line of ascent and descent of* Full Circle. BRADFORD WASHBURN #4404. *Above:* Full Circle. STUART PARKS

expeditions requiring emergency assistance (i.e., food drops and rescues).

The thought of climbing in this area was especially appealing to us. All three existing routes (the Northwest Ridge, the *Archangel Ridge*, and the *Highway of Diamonds*) offered a true remote Alaskan climbing experience without the crowds seen on the neighboring peak, Denali. Additionally, the north face had fewer objective hazards than many areas in the Alaska Range. The ridges mysteriously lacked cornices, and the north side did not have a reputation for avalanches. Finally, an obvious line existed up the central spur of the north face, probably unclimbed only because of the hellish approach.

Limited by time, Rod Hancock and I considered approaching from a more accessible area, the Kahiltna Base Camp (7,200'). This would require traversing Mt. Crosson (12,800') to reach the north side of Mt. Foraker. We believed that this could be done in a week while providing the needed acclimatization for a quick ascent of Mt. Foraker. If problems occurred during the approach, we could redirect our energies to Mt. Foraker's *Sultana* (Northeast) *Ridge* or easily retreat back down to the airstrip. On the afternoon of April 19, we flew into the "Kahiltna International." Load carrying and unsettled weather started our adventure off slowly; it took us eight days to climb the southeast ridge of Mt. Crosson to its summit. During the ninth day, we left a cache of extra food and gear at the junction of the *Sultana Ridge*. After overloading our huge packs, we began to explore new territory in alpine style.

We headed west over a couple of sub-peaks to a camp at 11,500 feet on the West Ridge of Mt. Crosson. The descent of this ridge involved moderate, albeit interesting, climbing. We downclimbed short, airy sections of ice and weaved around crevasses to reach a couloir that dropped southwest off the ridge crest. Descending the 1,200-foot couloir put us at 6,000 feet on the Foraker Glacier. The temperature was sweltering as we crossed the glacier, but it quickly cooled off as we went into the shadows of the 11,000-foot north face. Taking advantage of the continued clear weather, we began climbing up a steep snow couloir to a 200-foot ice headwall. I belayed Rod up this 65°, consolidated ice-cube wall and then followed. Exhausted from a long day with dusk beginning to steal our light, we found a place to dig out a camp at 7,500 feet.

The next morning, we awoke in a snowstorm with six inches of new snow. With ominously steep slopes above us, we were easily persuaded to move out of avalanche terrain. We climbed to the top of a small sub-peak and onto a large glaciated area below the central spur. Circumnavigating left around large crevasses, we reached the beginning of the spur at 9,000 feet. The weather began to improve as we continued up a couple hundred feet to a fairly flat, but crevassed, tent platform. The following morning, we left this camp in excellent weather and ascended a beautiful knife-edged ridge. As the ridge blended into a steep, crevassed snowfield, we continued upward until we reached the base of the crux rock buttress (12,300'). Challenged by our overloaded packs on another day of beautiful weather, we climbed up excellent alpine ice along the left edge of the clean, white granite. As the angle let up, we traversed onto the rock and scrambled to the top of the central spur and our final camp on the north face (14,800'). Once again, blue skies and the frigid morning air greeted us with excellent views of Denali. Concerned about the weather taking a turn for the worse, we decided to forego a planned acclimitization day and head for the summit. We broke camp, shouldered our heavy loads, and began the long, slow trudge to the top.

A cold breeze quickly drove us off the summit and forced us to begin the knee-jolting descent of the Sultana Ridge. Exhausted from a long summit day, we slept at 13,000 feet. The following day, we continued the descent into a whiteout at 11,000 feet, where we were forced into our tent for another day. As the weather cleared, we were able to reach our cache, thus completing a circular path mentally and physically. Practicing a minimal-impact philosophy, we loaded everything into our packs and, with shaking legs, headed for the Kahiltna Glacier. We descended Mt. Crosson cautiously as the intense solar radiation deteriorated the snow conditions. Dealing with horrendous snow balling on our crampons and a close call with rockfall, we finally reached the glacier. After an evening ski across the glacier, we were back in base camp enjoying a beer with friends. We named our route *Full Circle* (Alaska Grade 4).

STUART PARKS

*Mt. Hunter, Moonflower Buttress, Ascents, Attempt and Tragedy.* The *Moonflower Buttress* on Mt. Hunter saw two ascents this year and one tragic attempt. Steve Larson and Charlie Townsend began up around May 22; a day later, Joe Terrevecchia and Carl Tobin followed, catching up to them on the first ice field. The two teams continued to operate independantly, though they covered the same ground each day, until the top of the buttress, where all four men made camp in close proximity of each other. After three days of poor weather, they continued to the top together in blustery unsettled conditions, then recovered the ground on the descent. Terrevecchia and Tobin rapped through the night, while Larson and Townsend stopped at a ledge they had chopped at the second ice field, where they used a lightweight awning pulled over their tent to deflect the spindrift. They rappelled the rest of the route the next day.

On June 6, Steve Mascioli and Alan Kearney were attempting the *Moonflower Buttress*. On their fifth day on the wall, and after Kearney had just led pitch 17 (a rock pitch leading up to the shaft), a 30-foot-wide and 12-foot-thick dense snow cornice beneath a rock overhand gave way. It missed Kearney and dropped 100 feet onto Mascioli, killing him instantly. Kearney then spent two and a half days rappelling the wall with one rope, reaching the glacier on June 8.

*Mt. Hunter, South Face, Variation.* On June 11, Jack Tackle and I flew into the Thunder Glacier (6,800') below the south face of Mt. Hunter. Our objective was a face at the end of the cirque, but due to the steady stream of serac fall scraping our intended route, we decided to put our efforts elsewhere. We saw a line up the south face that would intersect the Southwest Ridge (Kearney, 1979) and decided to try this instead. For the next six nights we waited for freezing temperatures to make travel safer and faster. On the early morning of the June 17, we started up. Unbeknownst to us, a part of the route we were attempting had been climbed in 1989 by Preston and Ruddle and named *Eroica*.

The route started up-glacier at an obvious ice couloir below some relatively stable seracs. Jack and I simulclimbed the ice for a few thousand feet up to where we intersected the 1989 route. We then continued up the long snow ramp system of *Eroica* that put us at the upper rock band on the face (11,500'). We chose a more direct line than the one done in 1989. We had enjoyable, moderately hard mixed climbing for eight pitches. At the end of these technical difficulties, we intersected the Southwest Ridge, where we set up the tent (12,150').

The next day, we attempted to reach the summit via Kearney's route. Unfortunately, we were in a whiteout for most of the upper section, but did manage to climb to within 200 feet of the summit. We waited for quite some time for a small clearing to occur so we could see where we were, but when this failed to happen, we retreated.

On the 19th, we descended the Southwest Ridge. This ended up being quite complex and tedious. We did not have freezing conditions and found ourselves doing many more rappels than anticipated. We didn't research the descent route much and wrongly assumed that it would be a cruise. It took us 28 rappels and all day to get back down to the glacier. The Southwest Couloir was just a constant stream of wet avalanches, which made us all the more thankful to get out of there. We named our variation *Sound of Freedom* after all the sonic booms we heard from the flyboys while we were climbing.

DOUG CHABOT

*Mt. Hunter, Southeast Spur, Third Ascent.* Jeff apple Benowitz and I started up the initial couloir of the Southeast Spur on May 24. Once on the ridge proper, a few pitches of snow and mixed climbing brought us to the base of a 350-foot headwall. The first pure aid moves looked down an impressive and airy 2,000-foot drop. Jeff dangled from an A1 overhang, then swam up a corner gushing with water. We found a small ledge and called it home. Our first night on the route had us almost spooning because one quarter of the Bibler was hanging over the great beyond. After more A1 with occasional free moves and easy mixed climbing, the second day brought us to the top of the headwall. Jeff snapped the hammer off his ice tool. I accidentally trundled a rock that chopped 65 feet off our rope. The remaining 135 feet had many mushy spots of questionable strength. Commitment was not a big problem from there; bailing would have been as difficult as continuing.

A section called "The Court of the Lords" traversed horizontally with steep snow walls and small rock outcroppings. While we had much better conditions than the previous parties, we encountered everything from plastic ice to unconsolidated corn snow. We reverted to a night schedule because the snow was even worse during the day. Using a Fairbanks belay (the rope threaded between protrusions on the ridge), we weaved across the sharp and often

*Rick Studley on the start of Mt. Hunter's South Ridge.* JEFF APPLE BENOWITZ

heinously corniced ridge. Pickets or deadman-type devices proved mostly worthless in the unconsolidated fluff that graced a lot of the ridgetop; they were, however, far superior to ice tools when mining up steep, shitty snow, and we used them the same way we would use the shaft of an ice tool.

We groveled up to stand on the South Ridge. Officially, we had completed the Southeast Spur, but it only marked a middle point in the climb. The South Ridge lay ahead. Waterman had done the first ascent of the South Ridge, too. It resembled a troupe of cone-hatted gnomes who had been tortured, strung on a line, and frozen in hell. There was no respite in sight for us.

The famed "Happy Cowboys Pinnacle" was only a few difficult rope lengths away from our initial camp on the South Ridge. Snaking, fluttering blades of snow and rock radiated out in all directions along this stretch of ridge. Small portions of the pinnacle needed to be scooted across cowboy-style; Jeff led a foot-wide piece of snow with vertical sides by straddling it and spurring his way forward. As it is theoretically safe for the second person, I walked the tight rope upright. An enormous adrenaline buzz fueled me as we polished off the next section of ridge and made camp within sight of the end.

On the ninth day of the trip, we tackled the final obstacle, the "Changabang Arête," a 900-foot arête composed of all the alpine mediums. There were rock moves, some sloppy ridge, and several hundred feet of orgasmic ice. The order of the day was traversing up and left over castle-like fortifications of snow and ice that steepened to near vertical, with one section of overhanging styrofoam snow. Eventually, it was Jeff's lead again. I begged it from him. The rest of the route consisted of moderate, solid blue ice.

I belayed Jeff over the abrupt lip that separated the South Ridge from the 13,000-foot summit plateau. We shared a bagel and a hug. It was a quick transition from the steep ice of the arête to the horizontal expanse of the plateau. We could only begin to ponder how it had felt to John after nearly three months of solo climbing. On a day when the rest of the universe huddled in clouds, we waltzed to the top sans shirts for some hero photos. It took us seven more days to reach base camp via the north summit. We descended the West Ridge to the Northwest Basin route and back to base camp, where Base Camp Annie greeted us warmly. She was happy to see us.

RICK STUDLEY*, *unaffiliated*

*Recipient of an American Alpine Club Mountaineering Fellowship Grant

*Denali, New Route.* The northeast side of Mt. McKinley attracted our attention even before literature about the region became accessible to us. After reading Jon Waterman's book *High Alaska*, it became clear that our route would closely follow the *Traleika Spur* route, which was climbed for the only time in 1973. The members of our team were Fedor Lounev (Leader, 40), Otto Chkhetiani (35), Iliya Mikhalev (35) and Dimitry Oborotov (33), all from Moscow; all had experience in high-altitude ascents and long glacier expeditions in the Pamir and Tien Shan mountains.

We started from Wonder Lake on June 20. After fording the McKinley River and shuttling loads, we established base camp on McGonagall Pass on June 25. To acclimatize and view an ascent route from the side, we went into the upper Brooks Glacier to Silverthrone Col. We began to move at night. In this mode, we made it up to 11,000 feet. We made an easy ascent of Mt. Silverthrone on June 30. Before us, excellent views of the east side of McKinley and the nearest Alaskan Range peaks opened up. (On the pass, we found an old cache, presumably from World War II times). We descended to the main fork of the Traleika Glacier on the

*The north and south peaks of Denali, with the Traleika Spur in the foreground, from Mt. Silverthrone.*
OTTO CHKHETIANI

western side of the pass (ice up to 35-45°). To ascend the ridge that divides the west and east forks of the Traleika Glacier we decided on a new, straightforward route that brought us to a steep 3,200-foot ice slope with a small icefall below, then rising directly up to a col at 11,500 feet (Camp III in 1973).

The beginning part of the 1973 route was, in our opinion, quite avalanche prone. We left camp at 8,300 feet on Traleika Glacier on July 5. The angle of the slope varied from 35 to 45°, with sections up to 50° (on which we used ice screws). The narrowest part of the icefall, in the bottom of the gorge, required fast passage for safety. An intermediate (and safe) camp was placed on the right side at 10,400 feet. At the top of the icefall we found areas of windslab. After a two-day snow storm we continued our advance on the ridge, where we encountered big cornices and ice climbing up to 50°. We rested for a day on July 10, then continued up from the saddle at 11,500 feet to the base of the upper icefall. The next snowfall made a detour of the icefall on the northern slopes of the East Buttress extremely dangerous, so we rose directly up the icefall into Thayer Basin. Movement through the icefall was extremely tiresome because of the deep snow; in addition, we experienced strong winds.

On July 14, after a day of dense fog, we climbed a 35 to 40° slope of hard water ice on the northeast ridge. In the previous days, the mountain was wrapped in clouds that would open up for only a few hours at night. On July 16, the elevations below 16,000 feet were in dense clouds. McKinley was completely open. After six hours of climbing we were on top, with excellent views of Foraker and Huntington. The next front of clouds bore in on us from the west. Before we made it back to camp we were hit by strong winds. We made our descent via Karstens Ridge; the only difficulties were in "swimming" up to our waists in the deep snow on the Muldrow Glacier between 8,000 and 7,000 feet. We made it back to McGonagall Pass on the night of July 19-20.

Fedor and Dimitry had decided previously to return via a known "shortcut" to Wonder Lake. Iliya and I preferred the original plan, an 80-kilometer route east to the Trans-Alaskan highway through Anderson Pass and on the West Fork River Valley, which we made in four days. It was not simple; we had to ford separate streams of the West Fork River and climb rocks and forested slopes. (We flew the last 11 kilometers in a helicopter we met at random).

For Fedor, the journey to Wonder Lake was his last. Three kilometers from the park road, while fording the McKinley River for the fourth time on the trip, he was tragically lost. Dimitry and the rescuers could not resuscitate him.

OTTO CHKHETIANI, *Russia*

*Denali, Attempt, and Ascent of Browne Tower; Mt. Koven, Second Ascent; and Mt. Tatum, North Rib.* Our goal was an ascent of Browne Tower and the subsequent rocky ridge line to the summit of Mt. McKinley. The upper portion of this ridge (above the mound at 17,425') previously has been climbed during various ascents of the East Buttress and Traleika Spur. Browne Tower itself and the ridge line to 17,425 feet remained unclimbed. From April 29 to May 20, Stephen Leary, Peter Way, Paul Weber and I, all from New Zealand and Australia, established a camp at the base of the tower following an approach via the Muldrow Glacier and Karstens Ridge. Before attempting the tower, we ascended the Harper Glacier by the standard route, acclimatized at a camp at 16,500 feet, and placed a food cache at 17,200 feet on the upper ridge before returning to camp at Browne Tower. On May 16, we climbed the Tower via a direct line up from the crest of the upper Coxcomb. After initial scrambling on mixed ground, we encountered three pitches of mixed rock and ice-filled cracks (5.7) followed by more mixed scrambling to the top of the tower. The rock was of excellent quality, beautiful orange granite blocks that continued to stud the ridge for almost a mile beyond the tower. Progress along this ridge was free and fast with spectacular views of the east face and steeply down to the West Fork Traleika icefalls. Unfortunately, strong afternoon winds forced us to abandon the ridge at 15,800 feet via a couloir onto the Harper Glacier. The storm that followed kept us tent-bound for four days and prevented completion of the route.

We made camp for the ascent of Mt. Koven's Northwest Face at 10,000 feet on the Muldrow Glacier. On the morning of May 22, it was snowing lightly and we left camp at 11:30 a.m., intending to reconnoiter the route. Access onto the face proved to be straightforward. A large bergschrund wall at about 10,400 feet was negotiated via an ice pitch up a convenient serac and an airy step across to the iceslopes above. At 11,200 feet, another 'schrund cut across the entire face but still was bridged in places by the season's snowfall. At this point, we broke through the morning cloud layer into a gloriously calm and sunny afternoon. The ice before us swept to the summit ridge at about 60° and tempted more than a reconnoiter.

A broken rib protruded from the face just left of center. Our line followed hard ice up to the right of this rib, then onto the blocks of the rib itself at about 12,000 feet. Negotiating the seracs and crevasses of the upper rib, we arrived at a beautiful summit icecap at about 6 p.m. With breathtaking views of Karsten's Ridge, Browne Tower and the summit of Denali less than five miles away across the Harper icefall, it is remarkable that this peak has received so few visitors. Descending by the same route with several rappels, we were back at camp on the Muldrow by 11:30 p.m., content to enjoy a most memorable cheesecake prepared by Paul for his 26th birthday.

A prominent ice rib protrudes from the jumbled crevasse fields and icefalls of the north face of Mt. Tatum (11,140'). The rib has a north-northwest aspect and leads directly to the summit. On May 25, we left our base camp at 6,300 feet on the Muldrow Glacier and ascended firm snow on the lower rib. Progress was fast and the terrain interesting with seracs and gaping crevasses on both sides. At about 9,600 feet the rib runs straight into a 45-meter ice cliff with crevasses and fragments from the wall peeling off either side. Just below this, we placed a high camp and spent a beautiful evening exploring the wall.

The 26th dawned clear and we set about finding a way through the blocks above. We followed the snow-bridged bottom of the long crevasse bordering the right side of the ice cliff. The crevasse curved right, the wall relentlessly overhanging above us on the left. Eventually, the wall laid back, allowing a single 90° ice pitch up and out of the crevasse onto a small plateau at 9,800 feet. This whole section of the rib could have been traversed widely either to the right or left. The remaining slopes were straightforward except for another crevasse head-wall immediately below the summit, which we were able to bridge at the right end. After an early evening summit, we descended via the same route and a magnificent 45-meter rappel off the lower icecliff, still bathed in the orange glow of an Alaskan midnight summer sunset.

NED NORTON, *unaffiliated*

*Denali, Butte Direct.* On April 18, Jim Blow and I took Hudson Air to Kantishna and traveled 40 miles to the base of our climb at the end of the West Fork of the Tralieka Glacier. Earlier in the year we had Will Foresberg dogsled most of our heavy gear into the lower ice fall on the Muldrow Glacier. After three days we arrived at our cache and spent a day preparing our gear for the trip up the Tralieka Glacier to its West Fork. Two days later, on April 23, we arrived at the base of the climb and began up a snow talus slope near the center of the base of the face. We climbed the snow talus for three pitches leading up to a tight gully, then headed right for one pitch on mixed rock and ice to a belay point. From the belay point we went right up a rock band (5.5) then left onto another steep snow field. At the top of the snow field we were able to drop our loads and dig out a tent platform. From the tent platform we headed up and right for one pitch on mixed terrain to the base of a sloped horizontal snow slope. From here we headed one pitch to the left to a gully directly above the tent platform and belayed at its base. The gully was steep rock and ice (WI4) for one full pitch that leads to another snow-field. We followed the snowfield for two pitches to an alcove below a large 180-foot rock band. From the alcove over the rock band we climbed 5.8 rock to a steep snow slope, then traversed two pitches to the base of a steep overhanging face. Here we spent considerable time digging a safe tent platform under the overhang, which protected us from rockfall. From the tent platform we headed down and right to an obvious corner which marks the center of the entire face. From this point we climbed good rock (5.9-5.10) for three pitches. After the second pitch the rock was defoliated granite, eliminating the ability of hauling our packs safely behind us. We left our ice gear behind and continued up the obvious chimneys for another three pitches, encountering a move of A2 and a final move out onto a ledge system of 5.10+. From the ledge system we traversed right for several pitches, then headed left and up.

The next pitch was up a gully which during dry conditions would have been 5.5 or 5.6; because of constant snowfall these pitches turned out to be the most difficult. The next five pitches led up and right to a snow and ice field facing southeast. Unable to continue without our ice gear and running out of food (we had been on the face for five days), we decided to rappel down and back to the Muldrow to replenish our food supply, then head up the Muldrow to Karstens Ridge, climb Karstens Ridge to 12,000 feet, and descend the long arm at the top of the route, rappel down the face to our high point and climb the 1,200 feet of ice to its top.

The trip around the Tralieka and Muldrow glaciers was 30 miles with heavy loads. On May 9, we descended down the face in marginal weather. We spent half the day rappeling the face in a snow storm. Descending down a face that you weren't sure you could climb out of was one of the most intimidating events of the trip. After ten or 12 rappels in a blinding snow storm we finally stopped; Jim Blow recognized our previous high point up and left. We headed back up. The approximately ten pitches to the top of the route followed an obvious gully of mixed rock and ice ranging from 5.5 to 5.8 rock climbing and WI2-3. The final pitch of ice leading to the safety of the ridge above was WI4. The climb back to the camp at 12,000 feet was approximately one mile.

We spent the next six days moving up Karstens Ridge, then onto the lower Harper ice fall at approximately 16,500 feet. On May 16 we were hit by a storm that pinned us down for ten days. The wind blew at more than 100 mph and we encountered the worst temperatures of the trip. During the storm we began rationing our food to a meal a day between us. On May 25 (day 38 on the mountain) the storm broke and we headed for Denali Pass. By nightfall, we had made the pass, but were too weak to continue down to the 17,000-foot camp. The next day we ate our final meal and spent the better part of the day hydrating. We heard on our small radio that the weather was going to be good for several days so we discussed our options for the summit. We knew that the summit was a six-hour round trip; even though we knew we had no business trying to do it, we decided to give it a go.

On May 26 we made the summit, returned to Denali Pass and crawled into frozen sleeping bags and no food. The next three days we made our way down the West Buttress, receiving food from many climbers. After 43 days on the mountain and with each of us 40 pounds lighter, we returned home to Montana. We named the route *Butte Direct* for the people of Butte, Montana.

JIM WILSON, *unaffiliated*

*Denali, Winter Ascents.* Two winter ascents were made in the winter of 1997-'98, both of which merit considerable note. On January 16, 1998—when Denali receives five hours, 41 minutes of sunlight per day—Russians Artur Testov, 32, and Vladimir Ananich, 40, topped out on the West Buttress route to become the first to stand on the top of McKinley in "the dead of winter." (Their partner, Alexandr Nikiforov, 29, remained in a snowcave at 14,200 feet.) A first try at a mid-winter climb the year before by Testov and another man failed at around 12,000 feet. Over four weeks in February and March, Masatoshi Kuriaki, 25, of Japan, made the first solo of Denali in winter in nine years.

*Denali, Wickersham Wall, Continuous Ski Descent.* Adrian Nature made a continuous and complete ski descent of the Wickersham Wall, adding 7,000 vertical feet of new terrain on his descent. Ice cliffs prevented him from skiing the Harvard route as he had intended, forcing a one-mile traverse to the Canadian route.) He had climbed the mountain via the West Buttress, then skied the Wickersham solo in seven hours, an accomplishment that included a bad fall at the top and a subsequent jettisoning of his backpack, which he then skied roughly a mile down the face to retrieve. From the Peters Glacier at the base of the face, he then hiked 25 miles to the road. His was the first solo traverse of the mountain.

*Denali, West Rib, Variation.* Jason McHam and I climbed the West Rib route on Denali, summitting on June 26. We believe we made two variations to the standard route. The first variation, from 11,000 to 12,800 feet, is a section of Alaska Grade 4 rock and ice (5.7 to 5.9). The route is high angle with rockfall. It starts at a large diamond-faced rock and travels up the ridge west of the initial couloir.

The second variation, from 17,600 to 19,000 feet, lies between the Orient Express and the traditional West Rib upper couloir section. The route is straight up a rock and ice section of the buttress to the 19,000-foot plateau by the Kahiltna Horn exit. The travel is Alaska grade 4+ (5.9, poor if any anchors). A two-man team from New Zealand and the U.K. followed our route two days later because they did not like the postholing in the névé/slop snow. Brad Washburn and Roger Robinson believe these were new variations to the West Rib route.

MICHAEL S. SMITH

*Denali, Mascioli's Pillar, New Route.* On June 15-16, Steve House and Steve Swenson made the first ascent of what formerly was known as the Radio Tower on the South Buttress of Denali, renaming it Mascioli's Pillar in honor of their friend, Steve Mascioli, who had been killed on Mount Hunter's *Moonflower Buttress* shortly before (see above). The pair first attempted the climb in early June, climbing 15 pitches to a prominent chimney system high on the left side of the pillar. Instead of the ice they had hoped to find, the chimney contained only poor dirty rock. They retreated to the base of the pillar, then to base camp. On their next try they followed a large corner system up the right edge of the pillar Their nearly 4,000-foot route involved both hard rock and mixed climbing, and was climbed in a 30-hour push with short stop. It was House's third difficult new route on the mountain in the last three years. A full account of their climb appears earlier in this journal.

*Mt. Silverthrone, West Face.* In late March, Mark Westman and I ventured up the Traleika Valley, east of Denali, to try the massive 5,600-foot unclimbed west face of Mt. Silverthrone (13,220'). We skied in 40 miles from Kantishna and set up base camp in the wild eastern fork of this raw glacier. On March 31, we made an attempt to climb a narrow couloir on the right side but were weathered off nine pitches up. On April 2, we climbed a left-side couloir that consisted of 40 to 70° unconsolidated snow and hard ice that led to an icy headwall. In unsettled weather, we continued to the knife-edged ridge leading to the summit. We descended a more moderate couloir off the west ridge back to camp. The climb took 15 days round-trip to complete.

JOSEPH PURYEAR

*Approaching the west face of Mt. Silverthrone.*
JOSEPH PURYEAR

*The north face of Mt. Deception.* The Abortion Blues Arête is the sharp snow ridge in the center.
JEFF APPLE BENOWITZ

*Deception, North Face, and Mt. Brooks, Northwest Ridge.* In late July, Rick Studley and I scampered into the Muldrow via Glacier Creek. We climbed a low angle arête on the north face of Deception Peak and descended the east ridge back to base camp in nine hours. We named the climb *The Abortion Blues Arête.* After Deception and some rain, I soloed the northwest ridge of Mt. Brooks in 17 hours. It was the second ascent of the route. An electrical storm, complete whiteout, blowing snow and two pitches of 5.6 rock made for an interesting outing. After Brooks, we hiked out via McGongal Pass and swam while crossing the McKinley Bar.

JEFF APPLE BENOWITZ

*Thunder Mountain (Peak 10,920'), South Face, Peak 11,200', South Face, and The Moose's Tooth, Southwest Face, Attempt.* Jim Hall, Paul Ramsden and I flew into our base camp on the Tokositna Glacier below the south face of Thunder Mountain on May 5. We made five attempts on a line up the impressive Central *(Lightning)* Spur on the south face, climbing 1,000 feet of steep mixed and aid before the repeated bad weather forced us to look elsewhere. We turned our attention to the south face of the striking Peak 11,200' to the east of Thunder Mountain which we suspected was unclimbed. Carrying only day sacks, we crossed the bergschrund at 9 p.m. on May 18 and moved together most of the way up the face on moderate ice and mixed ground. We reached the alarmingly corniced summit at 6 a.m. on the 19th in a storm before rappelling and down-climbing straight down the south face. We made it back to our skis 18 hours after leaving them. At the time of writing, the virgin status of this peak remains unconfirmed despite discussions with the Denali park rangers. It has been suggested that the late John Waterman may have climbed the peak from its eastern col while en route for his first ascent of the South Ridge of Hunter. If this is not the case, then we have chosen to name the peak Mount

Providence on account of a lucky escape with a stuck rope while rappelling.

After the ascent of Peak 11,200', we decided that the Central Couloir to the left of the Lightning Spur on Thunder's south face might fall to another light-and-fast approach. With only a liter of drink and a handful of energy bars each, we left camp at 10 p.m. on May 24 and moved together up the initial snow slopes, turning the first serac in the huge gully on the left. Above, two large icicles hung for 50 feet from an overhang, forming a half pipe between them with the right-hand icicle ending six feet above the base of the couloir. The half pipe finally was surmounted by chimneying between the two icicles and finally swinging out onto the right-hand icicle and climbing it directly up above the overhang. We continued up in magnificent surroundings with huge blank granite walls towering on both sides of the narrow gully, belaying only for several steep Scottish-style sections. At 10 a.m. on the 25th, the sun began to touch the couloir and it was time to find somewhere to sit out the hottest part of the day. We cut a small ledge under a rock band and drank and dozed uncomfortably while the sun slowly traversed the sky. At 4 p.m., we continued up the crux top section of the couloir, which involved three steep and sustained ice and mixed pitches. The summit ridge was reached at 6 a.m. on May 26. The highest point was a section of cornice situated between two pinnacles on the summit ridge. Because none of us was keen to tread that particular point, we chose the west summit pinnacle which was nearest us. We descended the west ridge and rappelled a couloir on the side of the south face, finding good belays for the majority of the descent. The skis were reached 42 hours after leaving them. It had been a long "day" out. The route was christened *Dream Sacrifice* (Alaskan Grade 5, ED2, Scottish 6).

On June 4, Lewis and Ramsden attempted to repeat the new Donini-Crouch route of the previous week on the south face of the Moose's Tooth. At 2 a.m., halfway up the icefall and with clear skies above, the temperature was still 7°C and running water poured down the granite walls all around. We turned back to camp to wait for it to get colder. It never did, and on June 5, feeling a bit jaded after 32 days on the ice, we called Paul Roderick and flew back to Talkeetna to start the trip home.

NICK LEWIS, *unaffiliated*

*Mt. Barille, East Face, Attempt.* Silvo Karo (Slovenia) and Jerry Gore (U.K.) attempted a new line on Mt. Barille's east face. They landed below the face on June 2, but bad weather prevented them from climbing until June 11. They fixed some ropes on the lower part of the route. The lower pitches provided hard aid climbing with hooks, bird beaks and copperheads. They graded it A4; Karo reported it as the most demanding aid climbing he had ever done in the real mountains. On June 18, while fixing the last two ropes, a rock/ice/snow avalanche swept down the face, injuring Gore. He was unable to climb farther and the pair retreated. During the descent, another avalanche damaged their ropes. They left the mountains by plane on June 19.

MIHA PETERNEL, *Planinska zveza Slovenije*

*The Wisdom Tooth, South Face, New Route.* It was reported that Graham Fontella, Bill Gambel, Mark Davis and Kevin Daniels put up a new route, *Novocain* (VI 5.10 A2), on the south face of the Wisdom Tooth in the Ruth Gorge over a five-day spell of good weather in May. The route follows a prominent red dihedral for 16 pitches with what was described as mostly moderate free and aid climbing on good rock. (*Climbing* 172)

*The Moose's Tooth, The Toose's Mooth, New Route.* In May, Seth Shaw and Scott Simper climbed a new route on the north face of the Moose's Tooth in one continuous 36-hour push. Their Alaskan Grade 6 route is included in a full article earlier in this journal.

*The Moose's Tooth, South Face, Shaken, Not Stirred.* Jim Donini and I did a new route on the south face of the Moose's Tooth at the end of May, an ice route that heads directly to Englishman's Col. *50 Classic Climbs of North America* has a good photo of this face on the lead page for the article on the Moose's Tooth West Ridge. We climbed the prominent couloir that drops straight down from the first saddle (Englishman's Col) from the left. Jon Krakauer did *Ham and Eggs* in the '70s up the couloir that leads to the immediate left of the main summit, and Bocarde, Charlie Porter, et al did *The Moose Antler* up one of the rock buttresses on the south side. I can't believe that such an obvious route had not been climbed, but that seems to be the case. I found no mention in the *AAJ* and no evidence during our climb.

   We left camp at 1:30 a.m. and made a four-hour glacier approach to the base of the couloir. After a final cup of coffee we set off up the couloir hoping to encounter moderate alpine terrain. One hundred meters up the route I got an unpleasant surprise: a 50-meter lead on rotten vertical and near-vertical ice with very poor protection. (The granite up this route is remarkably monolithic with few cracks.) Next Jim led a tedious mixed section that gave us access to the hoped-for moderate mid-section of the route. Two hundred to 250 meters of simulclimbing on perfect névé brought us to what we expected to be the crux of the route, a rock wall that appeared to have no ice from below. Instead we found a deep, hidden cleft full of thick ice that was seldom more than two shoulder-widths wide. Jim led the first, and most difficult, pitch of this section, which went on for 200 meters like a Scottish gully in the high mountains. Fabulous.

   When the gully finally widened a little and the angle lessened we expected the easier 45-

*The south face of the Moose's Tooth (with unidentified peak obscuring lower half).* Shaken, Not Stirred *follows the prominent ice couloir splitting the face. Greg Crouch*

50° névé slopes to take us all the way to Englishman's Col, safety, and a brew of tea (we were utterly parched). They did not.

The couloir turned a corner and above us loomed a chockstone wedged across the gully with a curtain of rotten ice dripping past the overhang created by the chockstone. This was the sting in the tail. A drip of real ice about a foot wide and three inches thick coming down from under the left side of the chockstone, and desperate stemming, thin axe-picking, a solid #1 Camalot, and good sticks above the overhang, made the pitch possible.

The last few hundred meters of the route were not as easy as we would have liked (especially considering our screaming calf-muscles), but eventually we made it to the Englishman's Col, *Shaken, Not Stirred* (the route name, in keeping with our booze tradition), for a much-needed rest and brew of tea. We lacked the courage to brave the corniced ridges to the main summit of the Moose's Tooth, but instead did one more hard pitch (sugar snow over a steep slab) above the Col and plodded the rest of the way to the West Summit of the Tooth. We descended the West Ridge overnight.

GREG CROUCH

### KICHATNA SPIRES

*Middle Triple, Ride the Lightning.* From June 27 to August 4, Jay Smith, Kitty Calhoun, Steve Gerberding and Dan Osman climbed a new route, *Ride the Lightning* (VI 5.10 A4 WI3, 4,000 feet) on the west face of Middle Triple Peak in the Kichatnas. A full account of their climb appears earlier in this journal.

### CHUGACH RANGE

*Mount Zeke, Northwest Arête.* In early April, local Natanuska Glacier pilot Billy Stevenson and I flew an aerial recon for Nova Adventure Company, scoping mountain and glacier routes for guiding. After looking at peaks in five major drainages, we flew over Monument Glacier, which is surrounded by some of the most rugged peaks in the range. As we passed over the glacier, I noticed the largest (unnamed) mountain on the southeast corner of the glacier. It had a spectacular 400-meter-plus ice face high on its north face. I had Billy leave me on the glacier five minutes later with my survival gear. Karen Hilton flew in later that afternoon with the rest of our gear. After several days of unstable weather, we got a break long enough to make a one-day attempt of the face.

After moving camp to above a small icefall below the northwest ridge proper, we bivied for a couple of hours. Early the next morning we ascended a 350-meter couloir that averaged 50-55° and led directly to the ridge. Traversing the 500 meters along the ridge to where it joined the face involved chest-deep sugar snow. Upon joining the face, the ridge and deep snow quickly faded out, becoming a steep S-shaped ice arête leading directly to the summit 500 meters above us. Soon we were frontpointing leads up the densest, hardest, most brittle 55-75° ice I had ever encountered. Six full 60-meter pitches on the face, which was so smooth as to not have a foot hold to rest on anywhere, found us on a small rock outcrop with calves flaming. Time was not with us at this point. We had three hours of good light and still had to get down the mountain. I set our time limit at an hour and a half and took off on lead. The ice steepened, and after two more pitches I had more than used up my allotment. I set the first rap anchor about a rope length from the summit ridge. I could see we were high above adjoining peak "Moe" and were very close to the summit. The sky to the west was black with incoming weather and the sun was gone. We rapped as quickly as possible and ran down the unstable snow of the ridge and couloir. After a couple days of storm, we skied off the glacier into Monument Creek with avalanches pouring down all around us. After two and a half days of Class V bushwhacking with heavy packs and skis, we crossed the Matanuska River on the last good ice bridge and hiked up to the Glenn Highway. We had crossed some ski tracks in the drainage; as it turned out, Willi Peabody and Mike Wood had been in a week earlier and made an ascent of Mt. Awesome (the major peak on the west side of the lower glacier) via a couloir on the south side with horrible snow conditions.

The peak we climbed (ca.8500') was unnamed. Sizing up a rare opportunity, I named it after my five-year-old son, who is growing up in this region of the world.

PAUL TURECKI

WRANGELL-ST. ELIAS MOUNTAINS

*Mt. Drum, Southwest Ridge.* On June 10, Paul Claus of Ultima Thule Outfitters flew Anchorage climbers Judith Terpstra and me from Glennallen to a 6,200-foot glacier at the base of the 12,008-foot Mt. Drum's southwest ridge (Alaska Grade II+). We established camps on the southwest ridge at 8,000 feet and 10,000 feet. We were turned back from our summit attempt due to poor weather at 11,200 feet. We descended the route to base camp and were picked up by Claus on June 14. Anchorage climbers Paul Barry and Dave Lucey succeeded on this climb, summitting in marginal weather on June 14 and flying out two days later.

DAVID HART, *Mountaineering Club of Alaska*

*Hanagita Peak, Possible First Ascent.* On September 1, Gary Green of McCarthy Air flew me into the Bremner mine airstrip some 30 miles southwest of McCarthy. That day and the next I hiked west over two passes to reach a camp at around 4,000 feet just northeast of Hanagita Peak. On the 3rd, I got a late start, so I decided to reconnoiter only the glacier that lies south of the main summit and flows east. The glacier was bare of snow to about 6,000 feet, then a light layer of snow covered the ice; the crevasses were still full of snow. At 6,700 feet I decided to keep on going and crossed the bergschrund to reach the broken rock. I climbed a pitch or so of 5th-class rock before scrambling the last few hundred vertical feet over scree and loose 4th-class rock to reach a col at 7,300 feet. I crossed over the col to the southwest side of the mountain, then crossed the bergschrund and headed up an ice face of up to 45°. The ice was covered with an inch or so of new snow and ran for about 1,000 feet before it brought me to easier snow slopes just below the summit. There were scattered clouds, but otherwise the panoramic views from the summit were rewarding, especially the 4,500 feet down toward camp to the northeast and on to the Klu River drainage. This may have been the first ascent of the peak.

DANNY W. KOST

*Wrangell Mountains, Various Ascents.* On April 3, Paul Claus of Ultima Thule Outfitters flew Anchorage climbers Paul Barry, Kirk Towner and me from Chitina to "Bona Basin" at 10,500 feet on the upper Klutlan Glacier.

From this base camp we were able to summit three peaks during the next week. We made the third ascent of Mt. Tressider (13,315') up its northern slopes (Alaska Grade I). (The 1969 *AAJ* details the first and second ascents.) We also completed the first ascent of Peak 12,610', approaching the col below its west ridge from the north (Alaska Grade II). Interestingly, its summit contours are depicted accurately but mislabeled on the USGS topographic map; we confirmed that its true elevation is 500 feet lower than its name indicates. We unofficially named it Mount Pandora, in tribute to the people and history associated with an abandoned mining claim in the nearby upper Kotsina River valley. Finally, we made a one-day ski ascent of Mt. Churchill (15,783') up its southeastern slopes (Alaska Grade I), enduring -70°F wind chill.

On April 9, we loaded up our sleds and spent two days skiing 25 miles down the Klutlan Glacier toward our final objective, Mt. Riggs (11,738'). Riggs is located one mile west of the Alaska/Yukon border, and, until our ascent, was the highest unclimbed named summit in Alaska. We established our base camp just off the Klutlan Glacier at 6,700 feet on the southern slopes of Mt. Natazhat. A fourth friend, Harry Hunt, flew in and met us for this second week of our trip.

On April 11, Harry, Paul and I set out toward Mt. Riggs with four days of food and fuel, while Kirk remained in camp due to a foot infection. Our intended route up Mt. Riggs was the south-southeast ridge, still five miles distant. That evening we placed our camp at 7,200 feet in a beautiful valley due west of the south ridge. Riggs' impressive south face loomed overhead. An encroaching low pressure system convinced us to try for the summit from this camp the following morning. By noon we had reached 9,500 feet and could finally view the 2,300-foot crux leading to the summit. We roped up and began climbing the narrow and slightly corniced ridge using pickets and ice screws as running belays. The exposure was impressive, with 3,000-foot drops looming on either side of the ridge. Two short ice bands at 10,500 feet and 11,000 feet defined the technical cruxes of the route. (We would later rappel each of these barriers on our descent.) A final 300-foot, 50° snow face prolonged the uncertainty of our success until the very last moment. Finally, at 5 p.m. on April 12, we could climb no higher. We had succeeded in making the first ascent of Mt. Riggs via the striking south-southeast ridge (Alaska Grade 4-). We returned to our valley camp at 9:30 p.m., just after dark. Six days later, Claus returned for the four of us and brought our 16-day Klutlan Glacier adventure to a close.

DAVID HART, *Mountaineering Club of Alaska*

*Wrangell-Saint Elias, Various Activity.* Climbing and skiing in the Wrangell-Saint Elias mountains yielded a wide variety of adventures for 1997. I started with a relaxing family trip to a side valley east of the Barnard Glacier, one valley south of Mt. Bear. Shawn and Michele O'Fallon, Carlos Buhler, Siri Moss and I spent a week ski touring and exploring side valleys near the north face of Mt. Donna. Maintaining our strict, self-imposed rule of no movement before 1 p.m., Shawn, Carlos and I left camp at 1:30 on April 23 to attempt the first ascent of an 11,300-foot peak just north of camp. Climbing sans rope and with a single ice tool per person, we ascended more than 5,000 vertical feet up the southeastern slopes and stood atop the summit at 7 p.m. While not technically demanding, the exposed summit ridge and elevation gain blew the carbon out of our systems. We named it Mt. Benkin, after Carlos's climbing partner who died while descending from the summit of K2 in 1996.

After Paul Claus picked us up, we helped entertain a North Face marketing team by leading the pack up a splendid 450-foot waterfall on the south side of the Chitina River. A highlight was Siri leading a rope team that included Paul's eight-year-old son, Jay Claus, who gave ice-climbing beta to The North Face crew.

Carlos and I then turned our attention to the season's big project, the unexplored 8,500-foot east face of University Peak. We successfully completed the new route on May 4, then traversed the peak and downclimbed the north ridge. (A full account of this climb appears earlier in this journal).

Along with the customary climbs of Sanford, Blackburn, Bona, Saint Elias and Logan, Paul Claus and Ultima Thule Outfitters helped a number of people with their adventures. The most notable achievements included (besides other climbs listed in these pages) the first one-day ski ascent of Mt. Wrangell, by Auden Endestad and Andy Embick in early May, and the first guided ascent of Mt. Saint Elias via the south ridge (by guide Bill McKenna with clients Paul Sharwell and Larry Krutko) in mid-June.

CHARLIE SASSARA

*University Peak, North Ridge.* University Peak (14,470') is a relatively unknown pyramid-shaped mountain lying within the University Range of the St. Elias mountains; its south, west and east faces rise more than 8,000 feet above the glaciers. If University were in a more popular or accessible region, it would be highly prized and often attempted. The mountain was first climbed in 1955 after a failed attempt the year before. The first ascent party scaled the peak via the Hawkins glacier and intimidating upper icefall to reach a basin northwest of the peak at 10,000 feet. The party then ascended the north ridge. This group also made the second ascent of Mt. Bona (16,421') by a new route on the south ridge, and the first ascent of P.12,980'. University Peak and Range were named for the University of Alaska Fairbanks by Terris Moore.

Having grown up with the mountain at his back door, Paul Claus had wanted to climb University Peak for most of his life. He had always dreamed of climbing the awesome south face, but this year finally decided it was more realistic to climb the north ridge. We made tentative plans revolving around Paul's schedule for early April. On April 6, Paul picked me up in Chitina and we flew in to his lodge near Bear Island. Later that day Dave Staeheli, Ruedi Homberger, Paul and I flew to "Beaver Basin" at 10,500 feet just northwest of the peak. On April 7, we all skied up to the col between University and P.12,980' at around 11,500 feet. We traversed the col and ascended about 500 feet of the north ridge to reconnoiter before stashing some gear and returning to camp. On April 8 we got an early start in clear weather with some hanging clouds and light winds. The temperature was around -10°F. We retraced our route of the previous day, then ascended the north ridge proper. The ridge is not technical, but requires a lot of route-finding to surpass the many crevasses and seracs. We climbed most of the route unroped (at times traversing either face, climbing the ridge crest, or descending and ascending inside crevasses or through seracs) until Dave fell some 20 feet into a crevasse while leading at around 13,000 feet. We had light snow and some wind, but the cold temperatures allowed for steady progress. The snow was deep powder or sugar. At around 14,000 feet we left some gear to lighten our packs, and proceeded to the summit. By mid-afternoon we had all reached a summit that for each of us had significant meaning.

Our ascent of the mountain was the second, and would be followed by the third, by Charlie Sassara and Carlos Buhler, a few weeks later.

DANNY W. KOST

*P.10,000+' and P.8580', Centennial Range, St. Elias Mountains.* On April 25, Paul Claus flew Mimi McDougall and myself into the Centennial Range of the St. Elias mountains, landing at 7,200 feet on an unnamed glacier only two miles from the Canadian border. We were between the Walsh and Chitina glaciers just south of Mt. George. On April 26, we ascended the boundary peak to our immediate northeast which I believe is 10,000+ feet. We ascended the steep glacier flowing to the south from the western end of the peak, beginning at around 7,500 feet to reach a small basin at about 9000 feet. From here we went up a 40 to 45° slope above the bergschrund to reach the ridge, which we followed to the north. The main summit ridge runs west to east, and at around 9,800 feet we meandered to the east toward the main summit. The summit ridge is corniced to the north, and we finally sneaked up to the main summit in the thickening clouds and light snow late in the afternoon. The snow conditions were varied, with some sections having deep sugar snow.

April 27 was spent in the tent due to snow, wind and whiteout conditions. On April 28 we ascended the glacier and icefall leading up to P.8580' to our south, staying on our skis up to the ridge crest to avoid the deep sugar snow. We were hoping to follow the ridge to the west and climb P.9874', but the deep sugar snow was too frustrating and we decided to enjoy the day and not push it. Our high point was P.8984' between P.8580' and P.9874'.

We spent April 29 skiing in bright sunshine up the glacier to check out the higher peaks of the Centennial Range to our east, stopping at around 8,500 feet or so. Later that day Paul flew in just as a snow storm was descending on the glacier, and we got off just as the weather closed in behind us. I believe both climbs were first ascents of the peaks.

DANNY W. KOST

*Peak 3596, East Face.* It was reported that in June, Eddie Fay, Dan Krueger and Jay Rowe made the first ascent of the 3,000-foot east face of Peak 3596 in Prince William Sound. The trio climbed 14 rock pitches up to 5.10+ C2, followed by 1,000 feet of 30° snow during a period of good weather. Further details are lacking. (*Rock and Ice* 83)

*Mt. Fairweather From the Sea.* Last April our team of five left Port Townsend, Washington on an odyssey to sail to and climb Mt. Fairweather (15,320') without any assistance. We all worked for the Pacific Crest Outward Bound School (which helped us with an expedition grant) and all had experience on boats and in the mountains. Our challenge was to put all our skills and resources together to get ourselves to the summit and back home.

We sailed out the strait of Juan de Fuca on April 21 aboard my 40-foot racing sloop *Highland Fling* with enough gear and supplies for almost two months. After a relatively uneventful sail up the outside of Vancouver Island, through Hecate Strait and up the coast of Southeast Alaska, we managed (barely) to land our gear through the surf just north of Cape Fairweather on May 2. The Fairweather Slough is much larger than past accounts had reported and the snout of the Fairweather Glacier is now approximately three miles inland. It took us nearly a week to re-anchor the boat safely at Lituya Bay, consolidate our gear and penetrate the coastal vegetation. We then had to cross a swift stream and climb 50° ice seracs to gain the moraine rubble on the surface of the glacier. We made good progress weaving up the dry glacier and skirting ice falls by climbing snow and lateral moraines first north, then south of the Glacier. We saw no evidence of prior expeditions at the usual 5,000-foot base camp at the foot of the south (Carpe) ridge. We chose the southeast ridge because the access looked more feasible and it proved to only require a couple of belays on 50° ice to gain easy snow fields to about 7,800 feet where we camped. The next section required exposed climbing on a beautiful knife-edged ridge and steep snow and loose rock. As food was short and the route was looking difficult, two of us descended to the 5,000-foot base camp. Scott Dinham and Dan Evans summited the next day after negotiating continued steep slopes, cornices and the infamous "ice nose" in perfect weather on May 19. We had the only sustained clear weather right when we needed it.

The 30-mile descent/retreat had its interesting moments with snow bridges melting out, a

*Mt. Fairweather.* STUART LOCHNER

150-foot free rappel off the glacier, and crossing the slough with a raft which had been shredded by a grizzly bear. *Highland Fling* sailed back in to Port Townsend on June 8 after battling headwinds much of the way south.

STUART LOCHNER, *unaffiliated*

*Kayak Ski Mountaineering in Glacier Bay.* I left the Salmon River at Gustavus in a single kayak on May 12 with a full load of food, fuel, water, and ski mountaineering gear. My skis and ski poles were mounted on deck in a homemade waterproof bag. The light head winds and counterweight placed deep in the kayak produced a comfortable level of stability. I paddled mostly with the tide for 26 nautical miles to a small beach near Geikie Inlet. The next day I paddled the remaining 25.5 miles to Reid Inlet. On day four, the slow advance up Reid Glacier began. A mostly sedentary winter spent in Gustavus had shrunk my leg muscles, and progress hauling three weeks of food and gear was slow. On the sixth day a long hard pull under an unexpectedly hot sun brought me to the 2,600-foot plateau three miles east of the northeast spur of Mt. Bertha. On day eight I moved camp to 3,200 feet beneath a spur leading to what I perceived to be the Washburn route. Any attempt on that route was blocked by mushy snow and large moats. A few days of ski laps gave my legs a familiar resilience and I began to wonder what opportunities the Bertha-Crillion col might provide.

On day 12, I followed a low angle route, throwing an avalanche probe out front with each step. A route up toward the col at 6,500 feet looked feasible. I left at 5 a.m., taking food for one day, a liter of water, a stove and fuel, several layers of warm clothing, ice axe, alpine axe, crampons, skis and climbing skins. I progressed northwest up a heavily crevassed slope toward the Bertha-Crillion col and picked up the first couloir to the right. The climbing was easy and quick to approximately 7,500 feet, where the slot topped out on a southeast-facing slope. A turn to the left over loose snow softened by the already high sun brought me to 8,000 feet on the southwest ridge above the B-C col.

Before too long I was on the plateau at 9,700 feet adjacent to the Washburn route. Nearly a mile of dead reckoning was needed to reach the hidden summit knob. Eleven hours of climbing, a switch back to crampons and a quick 600-foot gain brought me to the 10,204-foot summit. After a quick lunch and switch to skis I began skiing down, then switched back to crampons, then skied across the plateau and carved slow survival turns down portions of the headwalls adjacent to the southwest ridge. I got off course and bivied only a few hundred feet above my tent for a few hours until cooler temperatures and brighter skies allowed for a safe descent.

The skies cleared once again the following day and July Fourth Peak proved to be a beautiful ski tour. The descent back to the head of Reid Inlet was uneventful, though travel and navigation was more difficult due to considerably less snow cover. The nearly three weeks my kayak spent resting on the snow near the beach was not kind to it. It had apparently attracted much attention, as evidenced by muddy bear tracks in the snow and a crack resembling a tooth bite on the hull. A quick duct tape repair and I was headed for Gustavus with a stop at Margerie Glacier to check out future routes in the Fairweather Range.

MIKE DZIOBAK, *unaffiliated*

# CANADA
Kluane National Park Reserve

*Mountaineering Summary and Statistics, 1997.* Last year year saw 38 expeditions comprising 137 people within the icefields of Kluane, a slight drop in numbers from the last few years. (The maximum number of climbers in a single season was 186 in 1992.)

There were 22 expeditions and 74 people on Mount Logan this year, representing 54 percent of the people in the icefields. The *King Trench* route, on the west side of the mountain, saw 12 expeditions and 49 people; the East Ridge had eight expeditions and 22 people. Two groups and three people attempted routes adjacent to the *Hummingbird Ridge*. Of interest to climbers this year was the appearance of a large crevasse bisecting the *King Trench* route at 5100 meters. This obstacle, not evident during the 1996 season, slowed the progress of each expedition. A very thin bridge early in the season was gone by late season, forcing later groups to explore alternative routes that detoured widely from the preferred ascent route. It will be interesting to see what effect this crevasse has on climbers in 1998.

Other mountains that were attempted included Mount Kennedy, Mount Hubbard, Pinnacle Peak, Mount Slaggard, Mount St. Elias, Mount Steele and Mount Walsh. In commemoration of the 100-year anniversary of the first ascent of Mount St. Elias, several attempts were made on the Canadian side. Poor conditions turned all back.

Ffew groups managed to reach the summits they were aiming for. On average, 60 percent of expeditions successfully get at least part of their team on the summit. In 1997, only 30 percentof all groups in the icefields seemed to have succeeded.

There were no serious accidents in 1997 and no search-and-rescue operations were required.

Anyone interested in climbing within Kluane should contact: Mountaineering Warden, Kluane National Park Reserve, Box 5495, Haines Junction, Yukon, Canada YOB lL0 and ask for a registration package.

ANDREW LAWRENCE, *Park Warden*

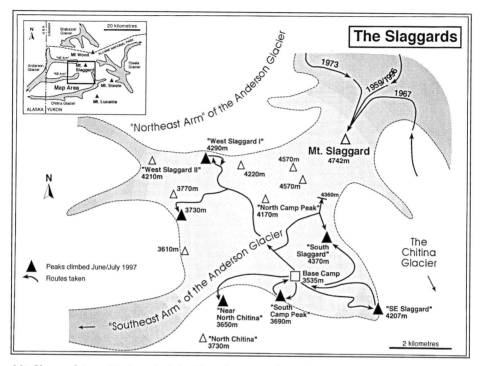

*Mt. Slaggard Area, Various Activity.* Ten of us spent June 28 to July 14 at a base camp five kilometers south-southwest of Mt. Slaggard on the uppermost eastern basin of the southeastern arm of the Anderson Glacier at an elevation of 3535 meters. There is an excellent ski plane landing site at this location, with two kilometers by half a kilometer of gently rising glacier, without any crevasses, and with suitable "bumps" for take off and landing of ski planes. Paul Claus of Ultima Thule first used his Supercub to pack down a landing strip, then brought people and gear in by Beaver in a 40-minute round trip from Ultima Thule lodge in the Chitina.

During our stay, we made the following ascents: South Slaggard (4370m), the highest unclimbed peak in Canada at the time of our ascent, a fine mountain with at least five excellent snow/ice/granite ridges. Martin LeRoux and Norm Greene made the first ascent via the east face on July 1. Paul Geddes, Willa Harasym, Mark McDermott, Joe Piccininni made the second, also by the east face, on July 10. The third ascent was made via the north ridge. The route was climbed in its entirety from the Mt. Slaggard/"South Slaggard" col by Bill McKenzie, Roger Wallis, Dave Britnell, and Tony Marshall, on July 10.

"West Slaggard 1" (4290m), the second-highest unclimbed peak in Canada at the time of our ascent, is a fine independent mountain, with a large rock face on the south side and 800-meter ice slopes on the north side rising directly out of the northeast arm of the Anderson Glacier. The first ascent was made via the east face on July 6, by the entire party of ten, in three ropes: Paul Geddes, Martin Le Roux, and Mark McDermott; Norm Greene, Dave Britnell, and Tony Marshall; Roger Wallis, Willa Harasym, Joe Piccininni, and Bill McKenzie. (Our first attempt on July 4 was abandoned at the serac barrier due to zero visibility, heavy snow and much too warm temperatures.)

"Southeast Slaggard" (4207m) is an isolated, independent mountain at the far east end of our basin. On July 2, Paul Geddes, Willa Harasym, Mark McDermott, Roger Wallis, Dave Britnell, Tony Marshall, and Bill McKenzie ascended via the northwest face and descended via the north ridge, all on skis (except crossing the bergschrund). "Southeast Slaggard" was the sixth highest unclimbed mountain in Canada at the time of our ascent. It has been attempted twice before, in 1967 and 1983 from the Chitina Glacier.

An attempt was made on Mt. Slaggard (4742m), which has had four previous ascents: 1959, from the northeast Anderson Glacier, northeast face and north-northeast ridge; 1967, from the Chitina Glacier and east ridge/north-northeast ridge; 1973, from the northeast Anderson Glacier and west ridge/north-northeast ridge; and 1996, as per the 1959 ascent. It had, however, never been climbed from the south. Martin LeRoux and Norm Greene left camp at 10 p.m. on July 9, ascending the south ridge from the Mt. Slaggard/"South Slaggard" col, carrying skis to a height of 4300 meters, 150 meters below the plateau from which it seems possible to ski to the summit cone and southwest ridge of Mt. Slaggard. The climb was abandoned at 4 a.m. on July 10 when the dawn sunlight hit the two feet of new snow lying very precariously on old crystalline, wind slab. Ominous settling sounds indicated that it was time to leave.

Some "microbumps" surrounding camp were also ascended as route finding viewpoints and/or entertainment: P.3690m, by a party of eight, to celebrate Canada Day (July 1); P.3650m, by a party of four, on July 11, on yet another snow day; P.3730m, by a party of four on July 3, as a "video experience" but really as a "wanding" trip, to scout a route to "West Slaggard II" (4210m), a large, very attractive snow mountain that remains unclimbed. But with four feet of new snow, the "trench warfare tactics" that would have been necessary to climb it were less attractive than enjoying gourmet meals in camp.

ROGER WALLIS

*Mt. Walsh, Northwest Ridge, Spring Peak, Jekden Mountain.* On May 27, Janez Ales and I flew to the Upper Donjek Glacier, just west of Mt. Walsh (4507m). We set up base camp at 3000 meters. The next day we climbed the standard West Ridge route on Mt. Walsh, a fairly straightforward snow and ice ridge. The most difficult section was around 4000 meters where the ridge narrowed to a steep ice-crest for a few hundred meters. In our very unacclimatized state the climb took 18 hours return. On the descent we left wands marking our route, as we planned to descend the west ridge if we were successful climbing the northwest ridge.

After our "warm-up" climb, we both needed a rest day. The following day, after we had recovered, we skied up "Jekden," the 3756-meter snow peak west of camp. We had hoped for great views from this peak, but were unfortunately engulfed in clouds on the summit.

On the 31st we skied through Walsh Col and descended to the Spring Glacier. Here we nearly had a disastrous setback. Janez, who was skiing ahead, broke through a thinly bridged crevasse. He was able to stop his fall without weighting the rope; however, one of his skis continued down the crevasse. Fortunately he was able to downclimb and retrieve it. We continued to a camp on the first major eastern tributary of the Spring Glacier.

From this camp we climbed "Spring 1," the 3976-meter peak east-northeast of Mt. Walsh, on June 2. We skied to the west side of the peak at about 3100 meters. We then ascended a steep ice couloir through a rock band to the southwest ridge, which we followed to the summit. The climb took 15 hours return from camp.

On June 4 we moved camp to the base of the 1800-meter northwest ridge of Mt. Walsh. We waited there several days, hoping for a break in the weather, which had now turned snowy. Finally on June 7 we set off just before sunset under promising skies.

The lower section of the northwest ridge is a broad snow slope, beginning at 25° and steepening to 45° near the top. Fortunately most of the new snow had avalanched off this section so we had fast cramponing on ice. The next section of the ridge is a narrow 1.5-km knife edge of snow and ice, a very enjoyable piece of climbing in a spectacular position. The sun rose on us as we front pointed along this section.

At 4000 meters the northwest ridge meets the north ridge. The remainder of the route followed the broad, snowy north ridge, over the north peak and finally to the main summit. This section of the route is very straightforward, but we found difficult traveling because of the deep drifts of semi-consolidated new snow. We reached the summit on June 8, 18 hours after leaving camp. The view was less spectacular than we might have hoped, as only Mt. Walsh and a few of the other higher summits projected above a layer of clouds.

The descent down the west ridge was also plagued by great deposits of new snow. We interrupted our descent with a few hours of attempted sleep, bivying in a partially filled crevasse. Early the next morning we continued down. Rather than descend the entire west ridge, we chose to downclimb the northern spur of the ridge, which led more directly back to our camp below the northwest ridge. Thirty-eight hours after setting out we arrived back in camp. On June 11 we flew out to Kluane Lake.

MARKUS KELLERHALS, *Alpine Club of Canada*

*St. Elias Range, Various Ascents.* On August 2, Tiffany Scrymgeour, Rafael Grana, Jon Webb, Chris Brick, Steve Sheriff, Kim Beatty, Brendan Beatty, Gray Thompson, Eloise Thompson, and I put on to the Tatshenshini River at Dalton Post, Yukon Territories. Our goal was to explore the glaciers and peaks of the St. Elias Range surrounding the Tatshenshini and lower Alsek Rivers.

Two days and 35 miles downstream, we cached our rafts and gear at the confluence of Sediments Creek and the "Tat," where a popular side hike leads above timberline to "Goat Mountain" (a misnomer: it is actually the buttress between Sediments Creek and the next drainage to the north). From here we had an excellent view of Peak 2549 (or 8345'), the high point of this part of the Alsek Ranges. We dropped 1,500 feet onto the toe of "Little Alsek Glacier" in the drainage immediately to our north, which led directly to this peak. The next day we climbed it and christened it "Deak Peak." The only difficulties were a section of broken glacier and some very loose 4th class rock scrambling on the ridge near the summit. The following day we returned to the river.

Two more days on the river found us another 50 miles downstream at Walker Glacier, a prominent glacier that reaches nearly to the river's edge five miles south of the U.S.-Canadian border. We festered in classic Southeast Alaskan weather (rain with fog and wind) for four days. The river rose about ten vertical feet to 250,000 cubic feet per second, an 18-year high, probably due in part to a glacial dam breaking upstream and releasing the lake behind it.

When the weather cleared, we hiked four miles up the Walker Glacier, and the following day broke into groups: Rafael and Jon climbed the north glacier and west ridge of the 6,350-foot "Mt. Eloise" (IV 5.7, 55° ice). Tiffany and I climbed to the plateau southeast of "Serratus Peak" (II 70° ice), then looped south of it to reach its 6,440-foot summit. Gray, Steve, and Chris climbed the west glacier of "Brickette Needle" (5,600'+). Mt. Eloise (referred to by river guides as "Third Peak") and Serratus Peak are prominent landmarks from the river on the south side of the Walker Glacier. Brickette Needle is immediately across the Walker Glacier from Mt. Eloise.

Back on the river, we floated past and missed the upper Brabazon Range. Instead, we floated down-river to Alsek Lake, a five-mile by three-mile lake with the toes of three glaciers calving into it and icebergs floating on its surface. We scouted access to some peaks via

the glaciers in this area, but the broken glaciers, long approaches, and several more days of poor weather discouraged us from attempting any others. I did manage, however, to race to the top of a nunatak (elev. 2,200'+) two miles from the snout of Alsek Glacier at the lake.

We floated to Dry Bay, the exit of the river, and were flown out on August 24 by Gulf Air.

JIM EARL, *unaffiliated*

*Mt. Newton, Ski Descent, and Mt. St. Elias, Attempt.* The Abruzzi Ridge of 18,008-foot Mt. St. Elias, the second-highest peak in the United States, was first ascended in 1897, but by 1997 it has become nearly impossible to approach safely. The Newton Glacier route to Russel Col has been the sight of fatal accidents; it is heavily crevassed and constantly swept by ice-fall avalanches off the 9,000-foot northeast face. Instead, Jim Hopkins, Julie Faure and I attempted to reach the elusive, but perhaps skiable, Abruzzi via 13,811-foot Mt. Newton to the north.

We were landed by expert Yakutat pilot Kurt Gloyer at 6,800 feet on a spur of the mighty Seward Glacier in Canada's Yukon Territory on May 12. Four days of storms, sled hauling, and route finding got us established at 10,000 feet below the spectacular north arête of Newton. Negotiating a bergschrund there, we slogged up the knife edge, building a 'schrund camp at 12,000 feet and another on the summit. We skied between camps to ferry 15 days of food and fuel to the apex of Mt. Newton. The snow was wind-affected, but avalanche stable, and we managed linked turns on all portions of the 25 to 50° ridge using telemark and ran-donnée gear.

Next we attempted the increasingly exposed, undulating coxcomb toward Russel Col (12,000'). Two south-facing steps offered enjoyable ice climbing with decent screw protection. The first crux was a 600-foot rotten ice cliff (70 at the top and 45° at the base). We fixed the upper half. We were turned back, however, as several other parties have been, by the double-corniced, wickedly exposed final 1,500 horizontal feet to the col. The snow was like sugar cubes, providing no solid pro whatsoever, and our boot steps washed out on the near-vertical flutations.

Given the excellent weather pattern and preparedness of our team (we had ten days of food and fuel remaining), backing off was a painful decision. The Japanese team that succeeded on this traverse in July, 1964, found blue ice that accepted "ice pitons." However, by July the upper Abruzzi would likely become uncarveable ice. Hence, we must someday return to ski the world's highest maritime peak, the loftiest unskied summit in the Americas, from another side.

TYSON BRADLEY

STIKINE ICE CAP

*Noel Peak, West Face and Mt. Ratz, West Face.* Fred Beckey, Dave Creeden, and I arrived in Petersburg May 24 at the tail end of a rare month-long streak of excellent weather, hoping to access a group of three 10,000-foot peaks approximately 50 miles northeast of Petersburg just east of the Alaska border. Fred was the only person in our party to have climbed in the Stikine, having completed the first ascent of the striking Devil's Thumb in 1947 as well as the first ascent of Mt. Ratz (one of our objectives) in the early 1970s. Climbing accounts and/or photographs of the area proved to be practically non-existent, so our intended route(s) were limited to analyzing the topographic maps and depended a lot on what we saw on the helicopter flight in.

We flew up the Baird Glacier, eventually arriving on the Icecap at the head of the Dawes

*The Abruzzi Ridge on Mt. St. Elias is the prominent feature in the background. Mt. Newton sits just in front.*
TYSON BRADLEY

*Above: Mt. Noel. Below: Mt. Ratz, with the first ascensionist.* Wes Bunch

Glacier. We made base camp on a sheltered rocky knoll at approximately 6,000 feet. It snowed several inches that night; given the poor visibility the following day, we were surprised by the sound of the chopper arriving with Wesley Bunch and Judd Stewart. After guiding them through the fog with the radio, it took almost an hour to de-ice the rotors so the pilot could lift off. The next five days of snow and sleet kept us close to camp. Day six dawned clear so Stewart, Bunch, Creeden and I set out for an attempt of Mt. Noel's west face. Fred, leery of the weather as he monitored the barometer, opted to remain in camp. An easy hike up on firm snow on the lower northwest ridge brought us even with the head of the glacier, from where we traversed out to the approximate center of the west face. After roping up and negotiating the bergschrund, we moved up steadily, using running belays. The route provided wonderful, 45 to 50° alpine snow and ice climbing for 1,800 feet. Three separate ice gullies were used to ascend the face. A short, strenuous pitch of loose 5th class climbing was required to exit the face and join the northwest ridge a few hundred feet from the top. We found a short piece of cord tied to a rock on top as an temporary testimony to the first ascent, pioneered on the southeast side of the mountain by a Canadian team. We carefully descended the route with a combination of rappels and belayed down-climbing as the sun began to overheat us. By 7 p.m. we rejoined Fred in camp, anxious to relate the day's adventure.

Two days later, the pilot arrived to retrieve Dave, Fred and I. Wes and Judd had another week to use so they waved goodbye and set about planning the next project.

*(The following is reported by Judd Stewart:)* While on the summit of Noel, Wes and I scoped a promising line on Mt. Ratz. The northeast face is a shining 2,000-foot sheet of 60 to 70° ice, approached via a broken glacier and a 1,500-foot couloir. The day after our friends left, we loaded our packs and skied the six or seven miles to the base of Ratz's precipitous north face. Once again the weather was awful. For six days we struggled to remain sane in the cramped Bibler tent. With only two days left until our scheduled pick-up, the weather cleared and we set off for the climb. Even though there were many crevasses, the snow was firm as we easily marched over frozen bridges, enjoying perfect visibility. The couloir above the glacier went quickly and we soon found ourselves under the face, challenged by a large bergschrund. Leaning across the maw at a narrow spot I could touch the overhanging snow on the uphill side, but it was soft and wouldn't hold a tool. I finally struggled over the problem by doing a few insecure snow picket aid moves—a first in my experience.

On the face, we were presented with perfect ice. We simul-climbed for 2,000 feet, switching leads as we used up the screws. At last we reached the summit ridge, from where we could look down the complex of gullies on the south side of the mountain. Beckey's first ascent route had worked up through that maze. A few pitches of exposed ridge traversing took us to the summit, the last pitch consisting of nasty, rotten snow studded with loose rock. At the summit I fashioned a hanging belay on a rock horn protruding from the snow a few feet from the top. Wes came up and we took turns crouching on the tiny summit, too concerned with the descent to celebrate. We rappelled the route using v-threads. The descent of the glacier was harrowing, with very poor visibility and soft snow. We postholed down in the murk and fell repeatedly into the small crevasses, fortunately never going deeper than our bellies. The climb and descent required 26 hours of continuous movement.

Upon returning to Petersburg, we enjoyed the hospitality of resident climber Dieter Klose, the self-appointed mountaineering historian for the Stikine region. While perusing his journals we discovered there had been several previous attempts on Noel's west side, but the ever-present coastal weather had prevented success.

SAM GRUBENHOFF *and* JUDD STEWART, *unaffiliated*

BRITISH COLUMBIA

COAST MOUNTAINS

*Cambria Icefield Traverse*. The Cambria Icefield lies east of Stewart, B.C., in the Boundary Ranges of the Coast Mountains. It is a large expanse of ice, punctuated by numerous peaks of 6,000 to 9,000 feet. From the south end of the Cambria Icefield, more glaciated terrain stretches south to the Nass River.

Between May 5-18, our group of four (Joe Fillipone, Matthias Jakob, Dave Williams, and I) traversed the Cambria Icefield on skis. We traveled from north to south, starting where the Bear Glacier descends to the Stewart Highway and finishing at a logging camp located near Kwinamuck Lake in the Nass Valley. We climbed several peaks en route: an 8,000-foot peak one mile north of Otter Peak, an 8,000-foot peak three-and-a-half miles northeast of Otter Peak, an 8,200-foot peak 14.5 miles east of Stewart, Lavender Peak, Tchitin Peak, and several minor summits between Lavender and Tchitin Peaks. We found cairns on Lavender Peak and one of the 8,000-foot peaks. All the peaks were straightforward climbs on steep snow and easy rock. Lavender Peak was a particularly pleasant ascent as it offers an uninterrupted 4,000-foot ski run on the descent.

MARKUS KELLERHALS, *Alpine Club of Canada*

*Mount Asperity, South Ridge*. Dave Hesleden and I flew in by helicopter to the Tiedemann Glacier on August 3. The weather was unsettled when we arrived, so we kicked off with a two-day ascent of the Southeast Chimneys route on Mount Waddington. We then turned our attention to the unclimbed south ridge of Mount Asperity on the 1500-meter Combatant-Tiedemann-Asperity wall. The south ridge is made up of a series of towers divided by deep notches. We started on August 8 and reached the summit on the morning of the third day after some tricky route-finding and 65 pitches of varied climbing on good granite and mixed ground (VI 5.9 A1 WI3). The weather was superb, so rather than risk a descent down the dangerous southeast couloir, we decided to traverse the Serra Peaks to reach the Upper Tellot Glacier. The traverse began with the free-standing tower of Serra V (ca.3600m), reputed to be the hardest summit in the range. We climbed a new variation on the north face (III 5.9 WI4) and made the fourth ascent of the peak. Our route then followed the line of the 1985 traverse of the major peaks of the range (Waddington-Combatant-Tiedemann-Asperity-Serras V to I, Don Serl, Peter Croft and Greg Foweraker, 1985). As expected, the abseils down the overhanging loose diorite on the east face of the Serra V into the IV-V notch were the technical crux of the traverse. We bivouacked that night below the summit block of Serra IV, continued along the complex mixed ridge to Serra III the next morning, and descended the icy Serra II-III couloir to reach the Upper Tellot glacier by mid-afternoon. We reached the Plummer Hut early in the evening and were back down on the Tiedemann Glacier that night. Concerned that the weather was about to break, we flew out the next day.

SIMON RICHARDSON, *Alpine Climbing Group*

*Waddington Range, Various Activity*. The wettest spring on record drifted into a pretty scruffy summer, but four noteworthy new routes, including Dave Hesleden and Simon Richardson's; (see below) and one significant "completion" got done in breaks when the weather settled down a bit. In late July, Greg Foweraker and Sigg Isaac spent a week or so getting chased around the Upper Tellot Glacier by clouds while looking for "big rock." They got stormed off

*Mounts Tiedeman and Asperity, Serra V, Serra IV and Serra III from Tiedeman Glacier. To give a sense of scale, the buttress on Serra V is taken by the 17-pitch route* Thunderbird *(V 5.10 A1).* SIMON RICHARDSON

the northwest side of Stiletto Peak (3397m) only two or three pitches from the top, but did manage to put up a very powerful new line on the east face of McCormick Needle (ca. 2960m). *Highland Fling* (IV 5.11+/12, seven pitches) follows crack systems about 50 meters left of the prominent *Last Tango on the Tellot* dihedral toward a huge detached block. This was bypassed via hand and finger cracks on the left, the continuations of which were followed to the top. Three roofs were overcome, one of which provided the crux, which was enlivened by a bit of doggin'.

Sean Easton and Dave Edgar tackled the rocks of the true crest of the right-hand rib on the northeast face of Waddington later in August. They climbed about a dozen pitches before reaching the lower-angled upper crest. The bottom two-thirds was on great rock (at 5.7 to 5.8, with one short A1 section), but the rock deteriorated for the final two or three leads. The crux was a 5.9 pitch on poor rock. The earlier Michael Down-Bruce Kay Northeast Spur line (which angled in from the right) was joined on the snowcrest, and (as previously) a variety of seracs (ice to 90°) and crevasses on the upper glacier were overcome or out-foxed to gain the base of the summit tower. Unfortunately, bad weather forestalled any summit attempt, and the pair bailed via the Bravo Glacier (IV 5.9 A1 AI4, 1200m).

One final new route capped a fine Indian Summer spell in September. Michael Down and Mike White choppered into the Upper Tellot Glacier and spent a day fixing a rappel descent and traverse (difficult) from the top col on the glacier down into the north (Radiant Glacier) face of Serra Three before returning to camp. The following morning they repeat-ed their unusual approach to climb *The Hose* (III WI3, 350m), the beautiful ice-line on the upper north face of Serra Three. There were six pitches in the couloir, the last three of them being a continuous three-meter wide runnel of perfect 70-75° Grade III waterfall ice in a corridor of beautiful granite. Three further rope lengths led to the summit, where the pair bivied. All that remained was to rap off in the morning, throw camp into the returned heli-copter, and fly home.

A final climb is worthy of note. David Hughes led a large B.C. Mountaineering Club party into the Radiant Glacier in late July, and six of them (including David and his son, Eric) com-pleted the North Ridge of Tiedemann (3848m) by linking a previously climbed east-side couloir to a completion up the old 1961 Harvard route on the middle and upper ridges. Given the difficulty of passage through the Radiant Glacier icefall and the seeming-impassability of the original Harvard west-side approach, this plainly is the logical way of tackling this huge (1400m) feature, which is one of the outstanding moderate mountaineering features of the range, and unjustifiably ignored.

Don Serl

Bugaboos

*Snowpatch Spire, Sweet Sylvia.* In the Bugaboos during the last week of July, Craig Luebben, Will Hair, Brad Jackson and Kennan Harvey teamed up to establish *Sweet Sylvia* (V 5.12b) on the right end of the east face of Snowpatch Spire.

Will and I arrived a day before the others. After losing several inches in height from beastly loads and the hellacious uphill hike to Applebee Camp, we walked across the most-ly flat approach to the base of the *Tom Egan Memorial Route*, an aid route from the late '70s. *Power of Lard*, established over several stormy and wet weeks last summer by Germans Tony Lamprecht and Gunter Dengler, climbs a pitch and a half of the *Tom Egan* before head-ing right toward a left-facing dihedral and a spectacular headwall crack. I had noticed a 400-

*The east face of Snowpatch Spire, showing* Sweet Sylvia. Kennan Harvey

*Brad Jackson on pitch five (5.11+), Sweet Sylvia.* KENNAN HARVEY

foot offwidth to the left of *Tom Egan* and had spoken with Tony and Gunter about the start of their route. I liked the juxtaposition of hard face climbing and offwidthing: two different racks and techniques in one route. And the golden granite. . . such temptation!

Will won the toss for the second pitch, given 5.13a by the Germans. He worked through the moves barechested, sweating and sunburned in unusually warm conditions. This superb pitch diagonals up below a small overlap on TCUs and nuts, then steps around the overlap with bolt protection to sinker steep jams. I followed on top rope to warm up and then led it, feeling way too solid, to a spacious ledge. I felt it to be 5.12b after we found a hands-off knee-bar in the middle of the crux. Will cranked the sporty third pitch (5.11c), and we rapped off, noticing that the *Tom Egan* got to the same belay on natural gear (5.8). My hope was to add no bolts, so we climbed the 5.8 when we returned. We passed a few bolts left by people retreating high off the *Tom Egan*, but other than the second pitch, the route is all crack.

Craig and Brad showed up early the next day and we entered the 350-foot right-facing sister corner to *Power of Lard*. Although a bit wet, grassy and loose, we climbed pitches of long 5.10 and overhanging 5.11 to the top of a huge detached flake with a perfectly flat top. I have never had a more perfect belay. Ahead lay perfect granite and the route's best pitch: 160 feet, 92°, hands to 4.5 Camalot, slowly widening—a real tricky bitch. Brad almost hyperventilated from anticipation as he left the ledge, but calmed a bit and dashed to the belay and another perfect ledge.

As we walked to the route that morning, we heard one lone wail that chilled us all. We waited, then walked on, disturbed and wondering. As I jugged up the lines, I saw some commotion below Bugaboo Spire's east face and heard shouts. Craig, still on the ground, went over to investigate. Within a half-hour, a chopper arrived and took away the body of Sylvia Florence, who had broken a snow bridge at the base of *Herr2* and been crushed by a rock that followed her down. We had met her at the trailhead; everyone was stunned by the suddenness and the pointlessness of her death. We knew there was an accident, but never considered death because of the supposedly mellow terrain. We felt selfish for our great day when we returned to Craig, who was worked over from several hours of CPR.

The weather stayed bad for several days, allowing a needed break. We used the time to reflect, read and hike down to my Chinook camper for beers. Applebee Camp had great camaraderie after the tragedy and we stayed pumped for the rest of the adventure.

We jugged to our high point as a group in the early morning of a splitter day. Craig led a 5.11a rope stretcher of fists and hands to join with the *Tom Egan* again. I squirmed through 100 feet of weirdness into the "Bugaboo Corner Chasm," a deep cleft three pitches long that splits the shoulder of Snowpatch and traverses behind several routes on its way to the summit. I tried to work around a thin intimidating seam but ran out of run-it-out gumption, down climbed 50 feet and cranked to the end of the rope on tips with slab-dish footwork, in full demand of mind and body.

On aid, I cleaned grass and wetness from a ten-foot overhanging corner to a stance, then retreated to a hands-off rest, pulled the rope and (barely) climbed another pitch at 5.11c. Craig did one more 195-foot pitch to the ridge, which tops out with the *Sunshine Route*, a fixed descent to the northwest. Will and Brad joined us directly, and we all marveled at views of the snowy Howser Towers.

Steep, east-facing routes are a good choice during periods of unsettled weather. Several parties retreated off the west face of Snowpatch during days we climbed dry and warm. For a competent small team, this route offers the nugget of a one-day onsight ascent, which is one reason second ascents in the alpine world provide some of the most fun a team can have. All the work and wonderment is done—time to have fun.

KENNAN HARVEY, *unaffiliated*

*North Howser Tower, West Face, New Route.* On August 8-10, Cameron Tague, 29, and Eric Greene, 32, both from Boulder, Colorado, took advantage of three days of cloudless skies to establish a new route on the 2,800-foot west face of the North Howser Tower in Bugaboo Provincial Park. *Spicy Red Beans and Rice* (V 5.12a A1) shares the first two pitches of *Seventh Rifle*, then trends left through chimneys and left again onto a lichen-covered face where a continuous wide crack leads to a bivy ledge midway up the route. The brilliant free climbing on the upper headwall follows various splitter cracks, incipient seams, and massive dihedrals possibly overlapping previous aid pitches on *Warrior*. The last pitch, which contains the only aid, was full of heavy black lichen and would probably go free after a bit of cleaning. Unfortunately, neither of us had the energy to deal with it. The headwall terminates on the northwest ridge with another thousand feet of 4th and easy 5th-class climbing leading to the true summit. We reached the summit at 4 a.m. on the 9th after simul-climbing for what seemed an eternity. Fortunately, the discomforts of the long summit push were tempered by a glorious show of northern lights gradually fading into the dawn.

CAMERON TAGUE, *unaffiliated*

PURCELL MOUNTAINS

*Block Tower, Trout Fishing in America.* Guy Edwards and I spent seven days in early September in the remote and practically untouched Leaning Tower group, west of the town of Kimberly and south of the popular Bugaboos. Our first day was spent reconnoitering the

*Block Tower, showing* Trout Fishing in America *(V 5.10+ A3).* SEAN ISAAC

impressive east face of Block and Wall towers and climbing the South Ridge (Enagonio-Mank, 1988) of Block Tower via a direct line through the overhanging headwall instead of traversing around the difficulties as the original route does. Our *South Ridge Direct* (III 5.10d) was the third ascent of the spire. The next two days were spent fixing the first three pitches on the unclimbed east face of Block Tower. We found a discontinuous crack system that yielded to thin nailing, beaking and hooking with the odd rivet move producing challenging aid; both Guy and I took short yet powerful falls. After a rest day (during which Guy soloed the northwest ridge of Wall Tower, a IV 5.7) we jugged our fixed ropes, committed to completing the route. Three more deceptively difficult aid pitches deposited us at the base of the final rope length as the darkening clouds released their contents just in time for Guy to lead the 5.10+ crack (the only free pitch on the route). Two wet and tired climbers popped out onto the summit of Block Tower in near darkness for the second time that week. We named our mini-alpine big wall *Trout Fishing in America* (V 5.10+ A3) after the bizarre yet entertaining Richard Brautigan book we had with us. Our route was the first ascent of the east face of Block Tower.

SEAN ISAAC*, *unaffiliated*

*The members were recipients of The Canadian Himalayan Foundation Grant

# NORTHWEST TERRITORIES

*Bustle Tower, Club International.* Andreas Taylor and I (Canada) spent the month of July in the Cirque of the Unclimbables doing a bit of climbing and a lot of vegging. After a nauseating air drop of the majority of our gear into Fairy Meadows, bush pilot extraordinaire Warren LaFave dropped us off at Glacier Lake, where Andreas and an airsick version of my former self were left to our own resources. We ferried our gear and scoped our intended object, the unclimbed east face of Mt. Flattop, but quickly changed our minds as the face turned out to be lower angle and more broken up than our blurry photos indicated (not to mention that the entire face was soaked with melt water from the summit snow cap). The beautiful southeast face (1,800') of Bustle Tower, one formation down valley from Mt. Flattop, resembled a large version of Washington Column and immediately intrigued our imaginations. After tracing a line of virgin face cracks and dihedrals up the vertical to overhanging face, we fixed the first three pitches

during unsettled weather. After only two days of wet weather, our hoped-for high pressure arrived and we committed to the face for three days of splitter cracks, featured face and huge roofs armed with a portaledge, haulbag and enormous aid rack. Ironically, aid was limited to about 200 feet, and used only because of wetness and moss-choked cracks; an all-free ascent at around 5.11+ would be probable in dry conditions. Fourteen hand drilled 3/8" bolts were used for belays so the route can be rapped; only five pins were placed on the whole route. We named our new 12-pitch route *Club International* (V 5.10+ A2) after the multicultural base camp and, more so, after our quality reading material.

Our final two weeks were spent glutonizing and hibernating in the shelter of our cave as typical northern weather (read: rain, rain, rain) hammered the walls. Numerous false starts

*Andreas Taylor, pitch four,* Club International. SEAN ISAAC

ended in soaked failure as we attempted the classic Lotus Flower Tower during brief lulls in the deluge, which became blue sky and dry on our pick-up day.

SEAN ISAAC*, *unaffiliated*


*The climbers were recipients of The Mugs Stump Award and supported by The Canadian Himalayan Foundation


CANADIAN ROCKIES


*Canadian Rockies, Various Activity.* The 1997-98 season ended up a below-average year for ice formation, but new route activity, with the major emphasis now switched to mixed rock and ice, continued at a fevered pace, making this winter one of the most interesting in the history of local "ice" climbing.

Two of the longest routes of the season were plucked in October by Grant Statham and partners a mere half hour from Canmore. His *Cabrio* (WI5 R, 400m) with Larry Stanier climbs four pitches of thin ice to easier terrain. A hundred meters left is *Centaur* (5.9 WI4, 350m) climbed with Joe Buszowski.

El Niño did its magic early, as temperatures remained mild and kept any significant snow-falls at bay until January. Early season routes included *Burning Man* (III 5.11 WI4, 150m) by Keith Haberl and Ken Wylie, while Raphael Slawinski made the first free ascent of the classic *Auto de Feu* (5.10 WI5). Wylie and Steve DeMaio squeezed a "sport ice" route between two classics of other genres. *Hovering Half Breed* (M8, 40m), with small patches of ice and 14 fixed bolts and pitons, lies between the classic pure ice of Whiteman Falls and the truly mixed Red Man Soars.

Sean Isaac found a rarely iced up corner farther down the valley, which produced a brilliant unnamed 5.10 turf route. Steve House later soloed this route along with *Whiteman Falls* (WI5+) and *Red Man Soars* (5.10 WI4).

Thomson and Issac started the season with a direct rock pitch to the 200-meter-plus ice route *Suffer Machine* to give *Teddy Bear's Picnic* (V M8 X WI5+, 200m). The pair also added independent routes on either side of Suffer Machine. To the right is *Uniform Queen* (WI 4+ M7-, 180m), which is probably the best pure mixed route on the Headwall. To the left is *Fiasco* (M7+ WI5+, 180m), which offers a 5.12- variation with your hands or M7+ drytool-ing over a large roof to reach an elegant three-and-a-half pitch ice line. Just around the corner, Slawinski and Chris Geisler found *Blind Eye* (V 5.10 mixed WI5, 170m), a quality four-pitch route immediately right of Nemesis. Thomson and Issac also finished a route started last season to the left of *The French Reality* (WI 6+). Their *French Toast* (M7 WI5, 150m) climbs two rock overhangs interspersed with steep and thin ice. Immediately after Fiasco, the pair went to work on a variation to anther Headwall route, *The Day After Les Vacances de Monsieur Hulot.* After numerous efforts to clean, bolt and finally lead the first M9 pitch (a combination of bolts and natural gear), the ice on the second pitch (out of four) had melted away, leaving the route for next year. (Unreported from last year was Slawinski's on-sight first free ascent of *The Day After Les Vacances de Monsieur Hulot* with the two overhanging aid pitches going at 5.10+ mixed climbing.)

After cleaning up on the Stanley Headwall, Thomson took his drill elsewhere to produce a series of spectacular routes that climb large sections of overhanging rock to reach large icicles that rarely or never form completely. The first and probably hardest route was *Mixed*

*The southeast face of Bustle Tower, showing* Club International. SEAN ISAAC

*Monster* (III M8, 120m) on Mt. Wilson. After a short ice pitch, two short rock pitches (25m, 15m) were climbed to reach a six-meter overhang that was drytooled to reach a 45-meter section of ice. Because of sloping holds on the third pitch, Thomson used rock shoes and ice tools.

Also on Mt. Wilson, Thomson, Kefira Allen and Eric Dumerac added the beautiful *Stairway to Heaven* (M7+, 100m) above the classic ice route *Midnight Rambler*. Down the road from the popular area of Field, Thomson and Allen climbed an often-looked-at problem on Mt. Hunter described in the guidebook as a route that would be "an exciting exercise in classic Rockies frigging around." At the time, of course, this meant aid climbing with pitons and shaky gear. Nowadays, it means cleaning and drilling. Their *Sure, Why Not?* (V M7 WI5, 410m) follows several classic ice pitches, using two pitches of difficult and overhanging rock to link them.

Thomson and Allen also made the long walk up to the compelling line *Sky Pilot* near Banff. This Grade 6 pillar formed early in the season for only the second time ever. It is unknown if anyone managed to climb the fragile column before it fell off, but in March, Thomson added bolts up to a dynamic icicle that hung down from the main broken-off curtain. Thomson declared *Dog Fight* (M7 WI6 X, 80m) his best mixed route all season, because in one full 50-meter pitch one is faced with difficult drytooling and a significant amount of challenging ice.

The only other route of the season to compare to these is *Unicorn*, next to the popular *Kitty Hawk*. Eyed for years, it was finally attempted by Eric Dumerac, who climbed the first (M7-) pitch with widely spaced but good natural gear. Realizing he needed bolts for the upper free-hanging dagger, Dumerac recruited Thomson and his drill. Re-leading the first pitch, the pair then drilled a number of bolts to reach the ice to create a second spectacular M7 pitch. With its difficulty and quality quickly confirmed by Tim Pochay and Statham, Unicorn may prove to be the best mixed route in the range, although it doesn't always come in enough for an ascent.

A significant factor for all of these climbs is their size and their significant distance from the roadside. Unlike the short 20 to 30-meter mixed routes in Vail and other areas, these climbs are generally started from the bottom and combine long stretches of strenuous rock climbing and drytooling as well as significant portions of ice.

JOE JOSEPHSON

*Mt. Andromeda, Andromeda Strain, First Free Ascent.* In September, John Culberson and I made the first free ascent of *Andromeda Strain* on Mt. Andromeda in the Canadian Rockies. This 2,300-foot route is alpine climbing from the car at its best. I freed the former A1 crack in crampons at 5.10d. Other attractions on the climb included an icy 5.9 pitch, a pitch skirting an ice blob rated M5, and an ice pitch of WI5.

DAVID A. TURNER

## BAFFIN ISLAND

*Mount Thor, Ascent and Tragedy.* A team of Parks Canada rescue specialists were in Auyuittuq late last August in response to a climbing accident on Mt. Thor. A solo climber named Go Abe from Japan was overdue on his second attempt on a central line on the face. It turned out he had been killed in a fall in which he landed on the ledge at two-thirds height. I believe the fall happened as he was approaching his previous year's high point, one rope length above the ledge. It appeared he had tried to follow his own line as much as possible on the lower face, but it must have paralleled the first ascent line closely. His main aim was obviously to take a direct line through from the ledge to the top, a point where the other parties had jogged several hundred feet to the left to pick up a natural line.

The first report of concern about Go Abe came in from the two Cristobal Diaz and Juan Espany, who had just completed a new route also on Thor's face. Their line is about halfway from the central route to the right-hand side of the wall, also a very direct line. They named their route *L'Arome de Montserat*. It took about a month on the wall.

Go Abe's body was found and evacuated from the prominent ledge at two-thirds height on the Thor face.

TIM AUGER, *Banff National Park*

*Weasel Valley, Various Ascents.* Louis-Philippe Blanchette and I spent six weeks in the Arctic from June 1 to July 11. We did more than 260 kilometers of load carrying in the Valley to move our camp. We took advantage of the dry weather of spring and opened a new 800-meter route on the West face of Mount Overlord. Our route, *Traversee Pyramidale* (IV 5.10), takes the right side of a pyramid on the left side of the main face. Most pitches are in the 5.7-5.8 range with excellent cracks, clean rock and good protection. The starting point is right behind the Overlord emergency shelter. We descended the north face of the pyramid after 12 hours of continuous climbing.

We climbed the South Ridge-East Face of Thor in 19 hours (IV 5.8). Most of the route is 4th class and only the last 300 meters are technical and require belays and protections. We found many slings and pitons along the route.

We also repeated the classic 1200-meter Scott-Henneck route on the northeast pillar of Asgard (2013m) in a 45-hour marathon. The difficulties are sustained (V 5.10 A1), and the crux chimney is an intimidating pitch! The last third of the ascent was done under whiteout conditions and sub-zero temperatures. We were too high to even consider retreat; the safest way was to keep climbing and switch to the "bulldozer" mode. We descended the south face before reaching the usual Swiss route and avoided the hanging glacier by doing six long 60-meter rappels to the right side of it. The only dangerous crevasses we saw were on top of the King's Parade Glacier.

JEAN-PHILIPPE VILLEMAIRE

*The Weeping Wall, Stoneagin.* From July 30 to August 19, Shinichi Sakamoto, Misako Koyanagi and Mike Libecki made the first ascent of The Weeping Wall via *Stoneagin* (VI 5.9 A3+, 550 meters. The Weeping Wall is on the Weeping Glacier close to Breidiblik Peak. An account of their climb appears earlier in this journal.

*Tirokwa, West Face.* It was reported that a group of Italians from the Bregaglia area—Adriano Carnati, Luca Cattaneo, Danilo Galbaiati, Massimo Mazzucco and Pietro Piccinelli—climbed a new 500-meter line (VII+ A0) on Tirokwa above Windy Lake in Auyuittuq National Park. The climb was completed over three days; during their 20-day stay, only four days were good. (*High Mountain Sports* 178)

*Great Cross Pillar, Tunuk.* It was reported that Lou Bartell and Russ Mitrovich climbed a new line on Great Cross Pillar left of *Crossfire* (Synnott/Hollinger/Gore, 1995). The pair fixed lines for four days over a week of storm, then committed to the wall. Over 14 days they climbed 20 pitches on the route, enjoying substantial free climbing in the unusually warm weather, including a 600-foot El Cap Tower-like formation with splitter 5.11 hand and finger cracks and a full pitch of offwidth. The route, which they named *Tunuk,* also sported 1,000 feet of "sick" aid. *(Rock and Ice* 81)

QUEBEC
TORNGAT MOUNTAINS

*Mt. d'Iberville/Mt. Caubvick, Ascent.* On August 14, Tom Bennett, Hope Bennett, Tony Daffern and I made an ascent of the Koroc Ridge (south ridge) of Mt. d'Iberville from a small unnamed lake at the foot of the ridge. This is possibly a new route, as the mountain is usually climbed from the north. Mt. d'Iberville is the highest point in Quebec, with the summit of Mt. Caubvick, the highest point in Newfoundland, only a few meters north. The Koroc Ridge, although somewhat precarious, required only one roped pitch and one rappel down the north face of a pinnacle in a notch of the ridge. With this climb, it is believed that Jack Bennett became the first person to climb the Highpoints of Canada (the highest point of each Canadian Province and Territory). The entire project took five years and 115 days to complete. As of April 1, 1999, the Highpoints of Canada will again be unclimbed, when Canada christens the new Inuit Territory of Nunavut. Its high point is Barbeau Peak on the icecap of Ellesmere Island—at 2216 meters, the highest point in eastern North America.

JACK BENNETT

# GREENLAND
SCHWEIZERLAND

*Champs Elysees Glacier, Various Ascents.* It was reported that in late July, on the Champs Elysees Glacier, a five-member British all-women's group (Lisa Holliday, Pippa Manson, Lizzy Popham, Catrin Thomas and Clare Waddington) made an extended tour through the Kristian Glacier region, making the first ascent of the north face of a 2400-meter peak two kilometers north of the Champs Elysees watershed. Later, they moved camp to the southeast of the Tangent base camp, making second ascents of many of the peaks climbed by Gregson et al *(see below).* On the day that group climbed Hidden Peak, the women made the second ascent of P2200m. The two groups were able to shout at each other from their respective summits. The women also made the first ascent of Little Tryfan (ca. 2350m), a beautiful rock peak overlooking Pourquoi Pas Glacier. *(High Mountain Sports* 181)

*Champs Elysees Glacier, Various Ascents.* The British Tangent East Greenland Expedition comprising Paul Walker, Rod Pashley, Jim McLuckie, John Starbuck, Phil Lightfoot, Glenn Morris, Peter Baillie, Peter Watson, Sandy Gregson and Jim Gregson arrived in Kulusuk on July 18. Our intention had been to fly on by Twin Otter to the Kronprins Frederik Bjerge, but a 12-day spell of rain, fog and low cloud pinned us at the coast. On July 30, by switching to a helicopter with more limited range and payload, we made a scary, turbulent flight to a drop-off point on the lower reaches of the Champs Elysees Glacier.

After another day's delay in very wet conditions, we were able to ski and pulk east to make a base at N 66° 45' W 35° 52' (elev. ca. 1900 m). Another night and day of storm dumped more snow before the sun came out again on August 3 (good weather remained for the rest of the trip). We then went on a spree of ski ascents and roped climbs, making a series of first ascents on peaks bordering the Kristian, Champs Elysees and Pourquoi-Pas glaciers. Mountains

*The view from atop Tangent Peak, with the high peaks of the Pourquoi-Pas Glacier on the skyline.*
JAMES GREGSON

climbed included The Sphinx (two summits, 2050m and 2080m); Tangent Peak (2420m) by the south ridge; several summits of Coxcomb Peak (2180m), including the highest, a jutting prow of rock over a big rockface; Parrotspitze (2400m) by the Parrot's Beak Arête (West Ridge); Two Peters Peak (ca. 2370m); Hidden Peak (2270m) by its northeast flank; and Well-Hidden Peak (2240m). A number of other repeat ascents were also made by team members, along with several additional attempts given up in the face of unsafe snow or loose rock. Many other fine objectives remain to be accomplished in this area.

Two other British groups also operated in adjacent areas, making a number of ascents before a final rendezvous at the Tangent base camp from where everyone was flown out by Twin Otter on August 11.

JAMES GREGSON, *Alpine Club*

Mont Forel Area, Various Activity. It was reported that a CAF expedition with the goal of making the 50th anniversary of the Expeditions Polaires Francaises to Mont Forel flew to the Femstjernen Glacier via the Bell 212 helicopter provided by Tangent Expeditions. They made base camp two kilometers southeast of the Bjornepas (ca. 2100m), were pinned down by bad weather, then, on August 5, ascended Mont Forel (3360m) via the normal Southeast Ridge route, summitting at 1 p.m. They returned to base camp by 5 p.m. and took two days to ski back to a rendezvous with the helicopter. A decision was made to make only one flight out, which forced the "highly controversial decision" to abandon a load of equipment on the Femstjernen Glacier, very much in contrast to efforts of all other visitors to maintain the pristine character of the Arctic environment.

A Norwegian group led by Eirik Tryti landed on the Fenrisgletscher near the end of July and, on August 4, made an ascent of Nordposten. They then made three possible first ascents, all around ca. 3050 meters high, in the Bredekuppel area in the vicinity of N66° 54' W36° 53'. Afterward, they climbed two peaks further to the south before moving to the northeast of Forel. On August 7, they climbed the northeast flank to gain the col, from which they climbed the standard Southeast Ridge, reaching the summit after five hours of climbing. The same day, Jorn Hauge made the first known solo of the mountain when he followed the team's footprints, catching up to them on the last pitch. All climbers were able to follow the tracks of the French group, which had climbed the mountain two days before.

On August 8, five members of the group climbed Sydbjerg via the north ridge from the north col, finding two pitches of mixed climbing and easy scrambling. The next day, the team made a straightforward ascent of Perfektnunatak. (*High Mountain Sports* 181)

CAPE FAREWELL

*Icecap Crossing and Various Ascents.* It was reported that in July and August, Douglas Campbell and Malcolm Thorburn crossed the icecap from Narssarssuaq to the western/central icecap, making several ascents of peaks up to 2000 meters at a grade of AD- along the way. (*High Mountain Sports* 181)

*Torssuqatoq Spires, Various Ascents.* It was reported that Andy and Pete Benson, Kenton Cool and Al Powell (U.K.) visited the Torssuqatoq Spires, a short distance southeast of Tasermiut Fjord, making some 18 new routes up to 800 meters in length. They established base camp on July 29, then split into pairs. On August 1, Cool and Powell made the second ascent of Magic Line via a new line up the north ridge (D- V+, 300m). The Bensons climbed the 400-meter southwest face of Blizzard Ridge. Cool and Powell climbed the south face of Maujit Qaqarssuasia via the route *Rampart* (TD/TD+ VII, 800m), stopping shy of the summit while on the west ridge in the face of a storm. They descended the ridge and then the north face. On the Prow, Cool and Powell climbed *Portion Control* (VII, 375m), a seven-pitch line on excellent gneiss. On August 9, the Bensons climbed the south couloir and ridge to the main summit of Maujit Qaqarssuasia in 11 hours (D-). Cool and Powell climbed the 14-pitch *Colour of Magic* (ED2 VII A1, 750m) on the 1550-meter northeast-facing granite wall of Navianarpoq in 15 hours, bivouacking on the summit and descending the north flank the next day. The Bensons, meanwhile, climbed The Totem, a finger of rock on the ridge north of Magic Arrow, employing aid (A1) to make the ascent. On August 13-14, they climbed the right-hand tower of Navianarpoq (a.k.a. the Wall of Early Morning Light) via *Steel Drum* (ED2, 600m) in 14 hours. Cool and Powell climbed *Totty* (ED2 VII+, 750m) on Maujit Qaqarssuasia, then the south flank of Agdlerussakasit (1763m) at AD+. Two more routes on the Prow were climbed as well: *Deathflake 2000* (E4, 5c) by Cool and Powell, and *Skirmish* (D HVS, 400m) by Benson and Benson. The team reported much scope for new routes in the area, but stressed that minimum-impact style is to be employed on any new activity. (*High Mountain Sports* 186)

*Gunnbjornsfjeld, Ascents.* I took a group of (mostly) senior citizens to climb Gunnbjornsfjeld, the highest peak on Greenland, and in the Arctic. This was my third guided ascent of the peak. We flew out of Iceland and landed on the ice of Greenland on May 3, and on May 4 established our base camp on the glacier below the peak at 7,500 feet. After a couple of days of acclimatization outings, we established Camp I at 9,500 feet on May 7 and returned to base. The next day we skied up to occupy Camp I, and were shocked to see tracks of a single canid, presumably an Arctic wolf, intersecting our track, following it quite a ways up, then angling up and over a broad glacial pass above 10,000 feet, continuing out of sight toward very rugged and remote terrain. Its tracks showed that it screeched to a halt as it came upon our tracks, being just as surprised as we were with the encounter. This is a high, sterile region, with nothing to eat or drink, but the wolf nonetheless avoided our exposed supplies at Camp I.

On May 9, after five hours of climbing, we reached the summit of Gunnbjornsfjeld. On the summit team were Bob Gries, at 67 the oldest person ever to reach this summit, Jon and Ginny Lindseth, both 62 (Ginny being the oldest woman to summit), George Shaw, 50, assistant leader Mark Tucker, and I. Remaining in Camp I in support was Ron Bell, 65. On May 11, we flew back to Iceland.

SKIP HORNER

# SOUTH AMERICA

## MEXICO

*El Gran Trono Blanco, Giraffe, Second Ascent.* In February, Lionel and Damien Daudet made the (possible) second ascent of the *Giraffe Route* (6c+ A3, 500m) on El Gran Trono Blanco.
JEAN-MARC CLERC, *France*

## PERU

CORDILLERA CENTRAL

*Cerro Yana de Colac, Cerro Ventanilla and Cerro Yana Pucara, First Ascents.* In 1997, I visited the two more accessible districts of the Cordillera Central, located inland from Lima. I first traveled to the Cordillera de la Viuda. After traversing four high passes while vainly searching for some elusive ice peaks shown on the official maps, I made the first ascent of Cerro Yana de Colac (5028m, easy rock) on May 30. It is located eight kilometers west of the village of Shanglar. A week later, I visited the second district, Cordillera de Cascacocha. On June 10 and 12 respectively I made the first ascents of Cerro Ventanilla and Cerro Yana Pucara, both 5000 meters high and both located at the head of the Ventanilla stream. After a failed attempt on the rocky tower of Cerro Ajutanca (5050m), I returned to Lima.
EVELIO ECHEVARRÍA

*Nevado Padrecaca, Quepala, Llongote, and Ticlla, Ascents.* While Peru is a popular destination, the Cordillera Central is not. Pamela Caswell, Stuart Gallagher, Peter Holden, Ken Mosley, Christopher Woodall, David Wynne-Jones, Ken Findlay and I arrived July 22 and stayed until August 28. According to the journals at the Royal Geographical Society in

London, a large 1963 Spanish expedition was the last one to visit the area; the interest our generated by our arrival in Mireflores indicated the lack of visitors that the village gets. Base camp, chosen by Christopher, was just a four-hour mule trek from Mireflores. From base camp, the summit of Ticlla (5897m) could be seen to the north, and Llongote (5780m), also in view, lay a short distance away to the south. Our early exploration of the area, indicated on the Peruvian map (Yauyos 1:100,000 25-1 1969/reprint 1994) as being quite heavily glaciated, was, in fact, rather bare. The glaciers had receded quite a lot and now lay mainly on the high summits or on the southern aspects of the mountains. The covering was about only 50 percent of the area shown on the maps.

We all climbed Nevado Padrecaca (5362m) by its south-southwest face as a training peak. We think this was its first ascent. It was no longer joined to Ticlla by glaciation. All except Ken and I followed a route on the extreme left of the face, using the ridge. Our route varied at the bottom as we ventured into the center of the face to visit an ice cave but then were forced to traverse across to the left as there was no continuous snow/ice route above us.

Peter and Christopher climbed Ticlla by the southwest ridge; Pamela and David followed their route some days later. Peter and Christopher had found the bottom section straightforward, but finding the route through the seracs and crevasses near the top took some time. They completed the mountain in one day with a continuous push from advanced base camp. The other teams preferred to bivy.

Ken and I climbed Quepala via an easy and long ridge that ran north from the summit. The once-glaciated area was now just bare rock and provided easy walking. The only difficulty was in surmounting the final rock summit which, devoid of snow and ice, was composed of loose blocks of various sizes and areas of shattered rock, where extreme care was required.

Stuart, Ken and I started up Ticlla, but after a bivy due to the weather, Stuart opted to return to base. Ken and I continued, reaching the previous day's high point below the rock and ice cliff, then traversing right under threatening icicles and loose rock bands. After an hour I passed a break in the cliff. One hundred feet farther on, I traversed upward. Slowly we made progress to the base of the main slope. Ken crossed a bergschrund on a soft snow bridge, then surmounted a snow wall and climbed higher up the slope before belaying me up. I worked my way left to a gap where the rock gave way to a continuous snow slope. We made good progress by climbing together, placing protection near the end of each rope length to provide a running belay. Though we did not know it, we were being watched by Peter and Christopher from their route on Llongote. Just as they decided to call it a day on a narrowing rock ridge that quivered as they moved up it, we broke through to the upper half of the slope. The 65° slope had been quite mixed since the first rock band.

We struggled on and were pleased to find the footprints of our friends all around the top. We looked forward to an easy descent by following the footprints, but soon they disappeared in shadow. After a short time of fruitless searching, we decided to continue on, but after an hour, we gave up and bivied. We made it back to advanced camp the next morning. Ken had sustained frostbite on the big toe of his right foot, and five days later rode back down to Mireflores on a horse.

PAUL HUDSON, *United Kingdom*

CORDILLERA BLANCA

*Torre del Parón and La Esfinge.* The granite formations of the Parón Valley offer the best granite climbing of the Cordillera Blanca but have suffered from misinformation in the past. An article earlier in this journal gives an overview of their history and details the routes done to date on La Esfinge. The Torre del Parón, meanwhile, still awaits a reported first ascent.

*Yanapacha, West Face.* It was reported that the three-man team of Caffarena/Kleinberg/Mauriz climbed a possible new route on the west face of Yanapacha (5460m) in the Llanganuco Valley. The route had sections of 80° and a rock pitch V+ that was avoidable; they climbed it on July 24, 1996. It is unclear how this route relates to the 1959 American route on the left side of the face. (*High Mountain Sports* 177)

*Pucaraju, Ascents.* It was reported that, in 1995, Cordier and Maynet climbed *La Princesse au Petit Pois* (TD) on the 300-meter south face of Pucaraju (5090m) on a gully line immediately to the right of the 1995 route *Hot Line*. In 1996, Abramowski and Carrard repeated *La Princesse* on May 27. The next day, they climbed *Adam and Eve* (TD-) to the left, establishing anchors on the route. On June 11, a Swiss party repeated *Hot Line* and made a descent of *Adam and Eve*. On July 12, Kike Ortuno and Gilbert Salvador climbed the remaining (leftmost) gully on the face, naming their route *Mururoa* (TD+ 85°, with a rock section of V+). They descended via the *Adam and Eve* rappels. (*High Mountain Sports* 177)

*Pucaraju, Hot Line.* In May and June, Nahuel Campitelli and Marcos Frischknecht from Bariloche, Argentina, made a (possible) third ascent (with some new pitches) of *Hot Line*, a couloir/gully with decomposing rock and little ice on Pucaraju (5400m). They descended the east ridge.

FACUNDO JOSE, *CLUB ANDINO BARILOCHE*

*Chopicalqui, North Ridge.* It was reported that a 12-man Italian team made the first integral ascent of the north ridge of Chopicalqui (6345m). Tarcisco Bello and Giuseppe Tararan reached the main summit on August 1, 1996. The team began seiging the lower section of the north ridge to the northerly foresummit on July 21. Ropes were fixed and three camps established starting from the col at 5050 meters. The climbing involved friable rock down low (5.4-5.5) and a problematic serac above Camp II (30m of 85-90° ice, once section 95°). The two climbers left Camp III (5970m) on July 30, making two more camps before reaching the summit. They descended the 1932 Southwest Ridge route. (*High Mountain Sports* 177)

*Huandoy, South Face, Demaison Route, Second Ascent, and Other French Activity.* In June, Y. Graziani and J. Blanc Gras made the second ascent of the Demaison route on the South Face of Huandoy, taking 11 days. Further details are lacking, but this route is one of the most technical in the Cordillera Blanca and a second ascent has long been anticipated. In May, the following ascents were also made by French climbers. Gael Boucquet made two solo ascents on Point 5300m on the south face of Nevado de Copa: *Goulloumme Labouthe* (6a, 400m) and *Au Pays des Twins* (6a+, 400m). On the same point, G. Boucquet and G. Gindler climbed a new route, *Top 93* (TD, 600m). On Point 5900m, G. Boucquet and S. Goriatcheff climbed the mixed route *La Marguerite* (90° ice ED, 1300m).

JEAN-MARC CLERC, *France*

*Caraz III and Santa Cruz Norte.* On July 15, Brett Wolf, Kris Erickson and Patrick Knoll completed a new route on the south face of Caraz III (5720m) in the Parón Valley. The route, *The Usual Suspects* (ED mixed V 85°, 600m), followed a line linking two couloirs up the central portion of the face. Several pitches of snow gave way to increasingly steeper ice and mixed climbing. The south face had been attempted in 1987, but the summit was not reached by several rope lengths, due to the lethal knife-edge ridge. Our line met the ridge only two or three meters below the atmospheric summit mushroom.

*Caraz III, showing* The Usual Suspects. KRIS ERICKSON

Several weeks later, Erickson joined me for another project in the Yuracohcha Valley. On July 29, in a 21-hour push, we climbed the southwest face of Santa Cruz Norte (5829m) via *Caveat Emptor* (ED, mixed 90°, ice to 95°, 750m). We were stopped short of the summit (which was about 100 meters higher) due to deep unstable snow on the double corniced ridge. I had attempted this line in late May with David Sharman, but I fell ill and was forced to retreat.

BRETT WOLF, *unaffiliated*

*Palcaraju Sur, New Route.* Palcaraju Sur (6100m) is at the end of the Cojup range in the Cordillera Blanca. Pedro Gonzales Bris and I established base camp at 4300 meters on July 3 in the ruins of the site Electroperu once used to modify runoffs into the lake that retains the water from the glaciers. After acclimating by going up Jacomontepunku (5400m) on July 4 and resting the next day in base camp, we started our ascent on the 6th. We slept in an ice cave on the glacier so we could begin the climb at five in the morning on July 7. We started the climb on the right of a rocky pillar, which gave a more protected and safer line, then traveled to the left to get to the most direct line that comes down from the south summit. The first third of the route was done over ice with a moderate incline of 65-70°, then we found a mixed area that was steeper and with poorer ice conditions (80°) which made the ascent slower and more precarious. After this section we were benighted and had to bivouac in an ice cave below a meringue-like cornice formed typically in this area. The next morning, after a short section of rock (V+ AO) and an upward traverse on vertical ice, we arrived at the summit of Palcaraju Sur. Our intent had been to follow the summit arête until the joining of the main and southern summit points and then to descend from the main summit. But due to the instability of the arête, which was formed by meringues of rotten powder snow, we decided to descend on the

*Santa Cruz Norte, showing* Caveat Emptor *to its high point.* KRIS ERICKSON

opposite side from where we had done the ascent. After eight rappels of 60 meters each we arrived at the glacier where we bivied again in an ice cave. The next day we crossed the ridge between Pucarranra and Palcaraju and descended to base camp. We named our route *Un Rayo de Sol* (ED- 90° A0, 800m).

JOSE MARIA POLANCO, *Spain*

*Cordillera Blanca, Slovenian Activity.* Meta Boncelj made a ski descent from the summit of Pisco (5752m) on July 14. She then made a ski descent of Chopicalci (6350m) via the normal route from 6200 meters on July 22. This was the highest Slovenian female ski descent to date. On the east face of Cayesh (5721m), Grega Lačen and Peter Mežnar made a variation to the 1983 American route, calling it *Tretji Svet* (ice VI, rock F5c, 950m), on July 17-18. The ascent was done in alpine style and they rappelled down the route. They reported hard and dangerous mixed climbing with bad protection. The new route strays right from the American route, joins it in the middle of the face, follows it for four pitches, and then continues directly toward the summit. Prior to the ascent, they also attempted a completely independent line to the left, but were stopped by an overhanging rock barrier without natural cracks. The rock was so hard that even bolting was almost impossible.

MIHA PETERNEL, *Planinska zveza Slovenije*

*A topo of* Tretji Svet *shows that, although it began to the right of the 1983 route, it shares the same ground from 5200 meters to the top. This was confirmed with Mark Richey, one of the 1983 ascensionists.-Ed.*

*Ranrapalca, North Face, Variation.* It was reported that Patrick Knoll and Peruvians Guillermo Mejia-Ordóñez and Eduardo Angulo-Zambrano did a new start to the north face (TD+ 5.9 A2, 3,000 feet) of Ranrapalca (6162m) in the first week of August. The variation follows a single crack in the buttress at the base of the face for 500 feet and is mostly protected from rockfall.

Americans Brad Johnson and Blues Voisard also were active in the Cordillera Blanca, climbing nine peaks in two months, including the rarely climbed 2,000-foot east face of Artesonraju, which involves 60-80° mixed climbing. (*Climbing* 173)

CORDILLERA OCCIDENTAL

*Cordillera Occidental, High Altitude Archaeology and Various Ascents.* High altitude archaeology was again the focus of several expeditions on the volcanoes near Arequipa during the last three months of 1997. Team leaders Jose Antonio Chavez (Universidad Catolica) and Johan Reinhard (The Mountain Institute, Explorer in Residence at the National Geographic Society) were supported by Jim Underwood (The Mountain Institute's Sacred Mountain Program), Peruvian archaeology students Jimmy Bouroncle and Orlando Jaen, and a climbing/excavation team of seven. Most of the team have been working together for several years.

Volcan Pichu Pichu (18,600') was climbed in October from the east for two weeks of excavation just below the summit from a high camp of 18,300 feet. Most of the work was an extension of the excavation that took place in late 1996 (and some preliminary work in 1989 and 1981) which produced extensive artifacts and remains (filmed by the Discovery Channel, broadcast in January, 1998). This year we worked the site to bedrock, found nothing more, and then performed backfill and recovery. Most noteworthy is that the entire main summit seems to have been a ceremonial platform, much of which collapsed long ago. The expedition was generously supported by Bell Sygma of Canada with extensive power supply and communications gear; a team of six engineers, managers, and family led by Doug Tipple and John Lochow came along for a week to get the gear working and climb the peak. As a result, the expedition was updated on the Web daily from the mountain by Yancy Hall of *National Geographic*. Pictures and details can be found at www.nationalgeographic.com or www.reinhard.sympatico.ca.

Volcan Ubinas (c.18,602') was climbed in one day in late October during the return from Pichu Pichu for the purpose of briefly searching for archaeological sites (and just for fun). This peak is one of the sacred group listed in early documents of the sixteenth century, but no archaeological remains were found (there is a history of volcanic activity here, and current venting).

Huarancante (a.k.a. Chucura, c.17,800'), the site of significant finds of Inca figurines and a bronze club-head in 1981 and 1989, was climbed next and was found to have been heavily looted many years ago. Ampato (20,700'), site of the Ice Maiden find several years ago, was the last climb of this season. Two other mummies had been found in October, 1996, and another was found in December at 19,300 feet. The team spent 19 days on Ampato this year.

Climbs made in 1996 in addition to Ampato, but not reported previously in *The American Alpine Journal*, were on Sara Sara (18,061') (detailed on the website pbs.org/nova/peru) and Hualca Hualca (c.20,000').

None of the climbs are particularly difficult from a modern mountaineering perspective. Our real challenges lie in the logistics of being able to do careful work in frozen earth at altitude over long periods and to maintain electronic, communications, and energy systems. The Inca were doing heavy work at these sites five centuries ago with much less supportive climbing and camping gear. Hualca Hualca is particularly significant in light of the challenging steep rock sections that the Inca ascended by hauling logs up for aid. Wild grass (ichu) was used to help as climbing footholds.

All expedition finds remain the property of Peru in the possession of Universidad Catolica and its museum, established for this purpose.

JIM UNDERWOOD

# BOLIVIA

*Bolivia, Various Activity.* In June, a U.S. climber died of a heart attack on the normal route on Huayna Potosi. In August, a guided French climber died on Sajama from pulmonary edema at Camp I after descending from high camp. A Japanese woman died of edema while attempting the Payachatas, two 6000-meter-plus peaks on the Bolivia-Chile border. These were the only reported climbing deaths in Bolivia in 1997.

The Austrian guide in charge of the June, 1994, disaster on Illimani, Wilfrid Studer, was back in Bolivia, climbing on Sajama despite the loss of both feet to frostbite in 1994. That year, Studer climbed the normal route on Illimani in a storm with two clients and was forced to make an unplanned bivouac at more than 6000 meters. Continued bad weather prevented descent the next day, so the three snowholed again. During the night, one went mad, attacked his partners, then later walked out of the snowhole saying he was going to a restaurant. He was never seen again. The weather improved on the third day and Studer, together with the surviving client, started descending, but the client dropped dead from exhaustion. Studer continued down the southeast side of the mountain and back to La Paz, a hospital, and Austria, in quick succession.

The year saw the first signs of the development of weekend climbing in Bolivia. The late Stanley Shepard, a U.S. citizen living in La Paz, wrote in the 1981 *AAJ*, "At the moment, La Paz has one weekend climber: me. I solo a lot." Little has changed, even though there are no practical reasons why someone living in La Paz at 3660 meters should not make weekend forays to the surrounding mountains. A jeep to the base of Huayna Potosi (6088m) takes one and a half hours from the center of the city; to Illimani (6439m) takes two and half hours and the Condoriri group can be reached in two hours. But the small number of climbers who own jeeps—and the fact that those who do tend to work Saturday mornings—means that virtually no weekend climbing takes place.

La Paz resident geologists Brock Bolin (U.S.) and Rod Feldtmann (Australia) climbed Cabeza del Condor (a.k.a. Condoriri, Gran Condoriri, 5648m) over one weekend in August via the route of first ascent (done solo in April, 1941, by Wilfrid Kuehn from Germany). The route (AD+ 55°, 400m) is a classic alpine ridge and is without doubt one of the best routes in Bolivia. The pair returned later the same month to climb the imposing south face (60° D-, 600m) of Ala Izquierda (a.k.a. Ala Norte, Condoriri West Peak, 5532m). Jean Steege (U.S.) and I did the French Route (AD+ 55°, 300m) on Huayna Potosi from the bergschrund in a straight push from the Zongo Pass (4770m). We were up and down in 26 hours (August 23-24). We encountered deep snow between the Campamento Argentino high camp and the base of the route and spent a rather long time getting back to the normal route to descend. Another feat no non-resident climber should attempt was the climbing of Illimani (6439m) in less than 24 hours by resident engineer Robert Riesinger (Austria) and partner Carlos Cancino (Chile) on September 14. The pair left La Paz at 11 p.m. and drove to the first camp, Puente Roto (4400m), via an unused mining track. They set off at 2 a.m. and reached the Nido de Condores high camp at 5400 meters at 6 a.m., where they stopped for breakfast. They left high camp at 7 a.m., summited at 1:15 p.m., descended, and got back to the jeep at 5:30 p.m., arriving in La Paz at 8:30 p.m.

Also this year, French-born guide Alain Mesili was released from jail.

YOSSI BRAIN, *United Kingdom*

*Apolobamba Area, Various Ascents.* The first team out during the 1997 season was the Walsall expedition of Dean Wiggin, Eamonn Flood and Yossi Brain (U.K.), who climbed in the Katantica group north of the Pelechuco Valley. The torture of the 18-hour bus journey to Pelechuco was alleviated by the liberal use of Valium. On May 24, we climbed the southeast ridge of P.5550m and continued along the northwest ridge to Katantica Oeste (5630m)—a new route (PD). We camped just below the col between P.5550m and Katantica Central, and the next day climbed a new route on the west ridge of Katantica Central (5610m) via a beautiful line (75°+ AD+, max. 65°). The cornice switched from right to left; on the right-hand (south) side, we found bottomless powder. It was also the first British ascent of the mountain. We then dropped down the east-southeast face to camp below the col between Katanticas Central and Este. (The east-southeast face was used by the Germans Karl Gross and Dieter Hain for the first ascent on May 27, 1968.) On May 26, we went through the pass between Katanticas Central and Este and headed up the north face (AD 65°, 300m) in three hours (a new route), then followed the ridge up for 15 minutes to the summit of P.5560, a first British and second-ever ascent of the mountain. We continued for 30 minutes along the impressive ridge southeast to the base of Katantica Este's summit pyramid. We climbed a beautiful 50-meter pitch (70° AD) up the southwest face to join the mushy northeast face, which we followed to the summit (5592m). It was the first British and possibly the second-ever ascent of the mountain. We descended to a dry spot between two lakes surrounded by a glacier due south of Katantica Este.

On May 27, we climbed up to a col on the northeast ridge of Katantica Sur, then headed northeast to reach P.5200 (PD), a probable first ascent. We crossed the glacial basin and followed the southeast ridge to Katantica Sur (5300m), finishing up on loose rock (AD-, 45°). It was a new route, the first British ascent, and (probable) second ascent of the mountain. We descended the German route (north face), returned to camp, and crossed the extremely broken glacier to get back to first camp. The next day was spent descending to the road, and the following day we squeezed onto a bus going down to Pelechuco. The team then had to wait in Pelechuco for four days while the presidential elections took place (there is only one bus a week out of Pelechuco and all transport is suspended while elections take place). The three of us then attempted the traverse of Illimani but bailed because of strong winds on day three, having climbed 3000 meters of vertical to reach the base of Pico Layca Khollu, the first peak of the five-peak traverse. Morale had not been helped by the discovery the previous day of the remains of a Spanish climber, José Ignacio Zuazubiscar Eguidazu, reported missing in September, 1994. He appeared to have soloed the normal route, got lost on the summit and descended in the wrong direction, falling 300-400 meters to his death.

Andy MacNae (U.K.) and Kevin Dougherty (Kenya) put in a couple of productive weeks in the Apolobamba, climbing A Glaciar on August 11 and then, on August 14, climbing *Radioaficion* (second ascent) from the northwest (AD+) to reach a ridge. They then continued traversing Bures, Apollo and Presidente. On August 16, they climbed the south ridge of Montserrat South and continued along the ridge to ten meters below Montserrat North, where they were stopped by an overhanging section. This was farther than the 1969 Spanish expedition got and included a new route up the south ridge of A Suches. They descended via a snow gully between A Suches and Montserrat North. The next day, they climbed the impressive south ridge of Soral Oeste and continued to traverse Sulka, Manresa, Quire and Montserrat North before heading back to a pass west of Manresa and dropping back down to a camp on rock above the Collado Ingles. MacNae went on to make an attempt on a new route on Pico Norte of Illimani with Pete Grosset and me but was beaten back by bad weather. Dougherty failed to make an attempt due to the attractions of La Paz nightlife and a combination of giardia and alcohol poisoning.

YOSSI BRAIN, *United Kingdom*

*Condoriri East Peak, Illampu West Face, and Climbs in the Apolobamba.* The 1997 University of Edinburgh Apolobamba Expedition comprised Tom Bridgeland, Sam Chinnery, Rob Goodier, Jane McKay, Heather Smith and me. We spent July and August climbing in Bolivia's Cordillera Real and the Apolobamba Range. We first went to the Condoriri area and climbed Pequeño Alpamayo (5370m) and the main summit of Condoriri (5648m) by the normal routes. Condoriri's East Peak (Ala Derecha, 5330m) has four prominent couloirs visible from base camp. The right-hand couloir is the most obvious and was climbed by Mesili in 1976, but now appears to be badly melted out. On July 16, Sam and I climbed the narrow left-most couloir (Scottish VI/6, 450m) of the four (possible second ascent). This was an excellent line, reminiscent of classic Scottish gully routes. There were three sections of vertical ice and a hard mixed section where the ice was discontinuous. We think this is probably the *Couloir Colibri* climbed by Gabbarou and Astier in 1989 (who reportedly found it hard). On the same day Rob and Tom climbed the second couloir (Scottish III/4, 450m) from the left (sans ropes), which was mostly névé with sections of steeper ice. It was probably a first ascent.

On July 19, Jane and Heather climbed Huayna Potosi (6088m) by the normal route on the east side, while Rob, Tom, Sam and I climbed the West Face (1000m of 55° névé). Jane and Heather then climbed Illimani (6438m) by the standard route. After this Sam and I traveled to the Illampu region, and on the east side of the range we climbed, together with Jenz Richter, the Austrian Route on Pico del Norte (6045m). This was an excellent 1000-meter ice face, beginning with 55-60° névé and leading to an upper rock band where a right-hand exit was taken, resulting in several hundred meters of water ice up to 70°.

On August 19, Sam and I did the probable second ascent of the French Direct Route on the West Face of Illampu (6438m). This 1000-meter line was first climbed by Gabbarou and Villerroel in 1990. The bottom half of the original ice ramp was badly melted out, so we opted for a thin ice ribbon cutting through the first major rock band well to the left of the French Route. This involved a short overhanging section (Scottish technical 6) to enter the narrow couloir, then several pitches of good ice to eventually join the French Route. The upper ramp was mostly 65° ice with very little snow or névé. The weather deteriorated in the afternoon and we had to climb through blizzards and whiteout. We reached the summit in a storm at midnight, and were forced to bivouac with no food or bivy gear. We descended the normal route the next day.

While Sam and I were in the Illampu area, the others traveled to the Sorel Oeste region of the Apolobamba range. On August 6 the foursome did the first ascent of the beautiful Southwest Face of Sorel Oeste (5471m). They approached the face by ascending the west side of the glacier on the south side of Sorel Oeste. The lower section of the face was 300 meters of 50° snow/névé, while the upper section was an icy runnel to the summit, with about 200 meters of 60° ice. Finally, from August 10 to 14, Rob and Tom did a four-day traverse of the Palomani group.

PAUL SCHWEIZER, *University of Edinburgh Mountaineering Club*

CORDILLERA REAL

*Illampu, West Face, New Route.* It was reported that a French pair climbed a new route, *Entourloup* (TD, 800m+) on the west face of Illampu (6368m) in September, 1996. Further details are lacking. (*High Mountain Sports* 176)

*Cordillera Real, Overview.* In the Cordillera Real, snow consolidated on the normal routes to give perfect conditions for most of the season. The normal route on Huayna Potosi was regularly climbed by guided parties in four hours from high camp and the Illimani normal route in five hours from high camp. A bad weather period during one week in August was blamed on the El Niño phenomenon, as are most things at present. There was a major theft problem from tents at Camp I (Puente Roto) on Illimani in July, but decisive police action appeared to put an end to that. However, climbers should make sure everything is inside the tent (not the vestibule); tying packs together seems to work.

YOSSI BRAIN, *United Kingdom*

*The Jallawaya/Nigruni-Mountains, Various Ascents.* The Jallawaya/Nigruni-Mountains, part of the Cordillera Real, have a lot of small glaciers. The highest peak is Jallawaya (5660m). A small rough road accesses the range, but if there is a lot of rain and snow, the "road" is impassable (there are a lot of river crossings, with no bridges and stoneslides and landslides).

For the approach, you need a four-wheel-drive vehicle. Theft can be a problem, so we made our base camp near a shepherd's hut at 4600 meters. During the last few years, the glaciers and steep ice faces have receded very quickly. On the steep faces, you now have more rock, but its quality is bad, with a lot of rotten rock and loose blocks. You can also have problems with rockfall.

We climbed in February, when there is more snow and ice on the steep faces. This meant that the conditions for mixed climbs were acceptable. In the main season (June-September), most of the faces will be pure rotten rock faces. But in February, we had a lot of bad weather! A big landslide destroyed the rough road to base camp on February 16, making the road impassable. We walked 30 kilometers back to civilization.

On February 2, we climbed *Pan Durro* (IV 65/70°, 450m), a new mixed route on the southwest face of Cerro Culin Thojo South (5350m). We left three pitons and found rotten rock. On February 12, we climbed *Andalé* (IV-, 55-65°, 380m), a new mixed route on the small north couloir of the peak P.5350m west of "Cerro Ventanani." We left one piton and found rotten rock and rockfall. On February 14, we climbed *Caramba* (IV+ 65-70°, 350m), a new mixed climb on the east face of a subsidiary peak (P.5400m) near Cerro Wila Lloje. This was a first ascent. We left two pitons and one sling and found rotten rock and loose blocks. We removed all other pitons and slings from the new routes. We removed our rubbish at Base Camp and took it back to La Paz for recycling. To protect this part of nature is important. We even tried not to leave footsteps.

EDUARD BIRNBACHER, *Germany*

CORDILLERA QUIMZA CRUZ

*Cordillera Quimza Cruz, Various Ascents.* In early August, Thomas Miyagawa, Andrew MacAllister and I set up a base camp around abandoned miners' housing in the Ataroma valley. On August 10 we climbed the two lower peaks of the Garciela group, P.5620m and P.5580m. The third and higher peak of this group we had climbed two years earlier from the adjoining Malla Chuma Valley. These two summits were reached by following the southwest ridge of the group and then ascending the west face of P.5620m and then the south face of P.5580m. On August 12 we made a direct ascent of the southeast face of P.5520 (5510m) with the final headwall reaching 65° on styrofoam-quality snow.

Andrew MacAllister and I then climbed Mt. Ataroma (a.k.a. P.5540m), the most prominent peak in the valley, by a direct route on the southwest face leading directly to the summit on August 15. This face also reached an angle of 65°, but had much poorer-quality snow than the previous climb, mixed with hard ice and a one-and-a-half meter bergschrund five meters below the summit. The lower glacier climbing involved swimming through steep waist-deep snow and an inordinate amount of postholing for this late time in the Bolivian mountaineering season.

DAKIN COOK

*Nevado Satelite, New Route.* Matež Kramer and Miha Valič climbed a new route on Nevado Satelite, *Ražikža smer* (V+, 270m) in the northern part of the Cordillera Quimsa Cruz on September 17. They reported good granite. The route, which took them three hours to climb, was to the right of *Que Pasa Condor* put up by E. Martinez, M. Sivila, T. Caballero and R. Solis.

MIHA PETERNEL, *Planinska zveza Slovenije*

*Nevado de las Virgenes is the snowy massif on left. Chiara Janco Cuno is the rocky point on right.*
JAVIER SANCHEZ

*Nevado de las Virgenes, First Ascent, and Other Activity in La Choco Cota.* Although pre-viously reported as ascended, Nevado de las Virgenes, so christened by Theodor Herzog in 1911, remained unclimbed until June, when our Spanish expedition (Adolfo Díaz, Isidro Gónzalez, Miguel A. Yagüe and I) arrived. We established base camp near Choca Cota Lake. The Bolivian Juan Alaña accompanied us to the summit of our third peak. From the head of the Choco Cota valley we first climbed P.5500m on June 28, southernmost within the basin. We named it Jaya Cuno (Aimara: "Distant Peak"). Two days later we made the first actual ascent of Nevado de las Virgenes (5500m) by its west face, which averages 50-55° (Dakin Cook believed he had climbed Nevado de las Virgenes some years before, but now says that his was an ascent of Corichuma). On July 2, we climbed P.5450m, south of the former. We christened it Chiara Janco Cuno (Aimara: "Black and White Peak"). After these three first ascents we moved to the southern Cordillera Real, where we ascended Tarija, Fabulosa and Huayna Potosi.

JAVIER SANCHEZ, *Spain*

*Sajama, Scientific Expedition.* A scientific expedition to Sajama (6542m) saw a team of sci-entists drill two 120-meter by four-inch core samples in the summit to check out weather pat-terns during the last 30,000 years. The initial idea was to float the samples off by hot air bal-loon. [Anyone who has been to the mountain or read up on it knows that it suffers from relent-less and strong winds; during the second (undisputed) successful ascent of Sajama in 1946, T. Polhemus (U.S.) got separated from his three companions on the summit plateau in high winds, which whipped up fresh snow and reduced visibility to 45 meters. He was never seen again, and aerial and land searches failed to find any trace of him.] The balloon, apparently in the shape of a giant penguin, never took off and so the samples, in 28-kilo loads, were carried off by porters, one of whom registered 27 summit ascents in under six weeks.

YOSSI BRAIN, *United Kingdom*

*Condoriri Group, Various Activity.* Slovenes David Podgorelec and Aleš Kovač from the

Kozjak Maribor Mountaineering Club spent a week at Condoriri in 1997. On June 28, they attempted Aguja Negra (5280m) and got to the breche on the eastern arête, within 100 meters of the summit, before backing off due to bad rock and lack of acclimatization. On June 29, the two climbed Pequeño Alpamayo (5370m) via the southwest face direct (D+, 55/70° with the final three meters at 95°, 150m). Descent was made via the normal route. On July 1 they climbed Ala Derecha (5482m) via the southeast face (D 70°, 700m), a possible new route. The pair started directly over seracs because the snow in the couloir was awful and headed up to better snow. The route starts to the right of Ala Derecha and to the left of Huallomen (Wyoming). On July 3, they climbed Piramide Blanca (5230m) via a possible new route on the west face (D+ 75°, 250m). They followed the snowy diagonal from right to left and then a 50-meter couloir to the arête left of the summit. Snow conditions were not good, with the last section being soft cornices.

Italians Marcello Sanguineti and Alessandro Bianchi put up a hard new route on Wyoming (a.k.a. Huallomen) on Condoriri on August 19 that they named *Sognando un 8000 (Dreaming an 8000er)* (TD+ 90°, 350m). The pair approached via the normal route to Pequeño Alpamayo until they were below the southwest face of Wyoming. They crossed the bergschrund and went up the snow slope (60°, then 65°, then 70°) to reach, after 150 meters, a narrow rock band which was crossed with difficulty (80°). Another 80 meters of snow at 60-65° brought them to the base of the obvious couloir. The first part went with sections of 75 to 90°. This brought them to the base of a narrower goulotte that ended in a snow and ice cornice. They therefore went left up through mixed ground and a chimney at IV+ that brought them to the top. They descended off the back to the col on the normal approach to Pequeño Alpamayo.

Pico Schulze (5943m) stands northwest of Illampu across the high camp above Aguas Calientes and was first climbed in 1928 by Erwin Hein (Germany), Alfred Horeschowski, Hugo Hoertnagel, and Hans Pfann (Austria) via the Northwest Face route. The mountain has been climbed from three sides, with the south face having the hardest routes. Anyone climbing Illampu can see Pico Schulze, but due to its sub-6,000 meter height, it tends to be ignored in favor of its higher neighbor. An Anglo-Belgian pair of John Walmsley and Jean-Marc Dunstheimer traversed (AD+ 55°, 343m) the peak on September 3. From base camp, they climbed up onto the south ridge, meeting it at the point marked 5765m on the DAV map Cordillera Real Nord Illampu. They passed the rock section and followed the knife-edged ridge to the summit. From the summit, they descended north to reach a flatter area and then rappelled one or two ropelengths rightward down one of the rocky couloirs to reach the lower snow slopes. They then followed a ramp back down to the base camp glacier.

Yossi Brain, *United Kingdom*

# Argentina

*Aconcagua, South Face.* We arrived at Plaza de Mulaz on December 26. We made our first attempt on the normal route up to c.6500 meters on December 31, but returned because of storms and deteriorating weather. On January 3, 1997, we summited via the normal route. On January 5, we arrived at Plaza de Francia. From January 8-14, we climbed the south face by the French route and Messner variations. We began climbing at the bottom of the face/buttress on January 8 at approximately 3 p.m. There were very dry conditions in the rocky sections of the route, with almost no snow between 4000 and 5700 meters, so that most of the climbing was on very bad rotten rock. From the big serac zone (5700m to 5900m) we climbed on mostly good snow and ice, particularly on the 30 meters of vertical ice at the serac up to the exit of the upper Messner variation. We found no danger of avalanches. We made six bivouacs, the last one just 50 meters below the saddle between the two summits of Aconcagua. We finished the climb and descended to Plaza de Mulas via the normal route on January 14.

The weather between December 26 and January 16 was fine and very warm except on December 31 and January 7. The team members for the South Face were Germans Walter Hadersdorfer, Hans Lochner, Wolfgang Schulz and Norwegian Petter Georg Stole; and for the Normal Route, Miss Ines Pappert, Ulrich Pfiffner and all members of the South Face team.

WALTER HADERSDORFER, *Germany*


*Aconcagua's Centennial, Aconcagua Mummy Disagreement and the Gendarmeria Nacional Rescue Team.* Aconcagua was first ascended by Mathias Zurbriggen on January 14, 1897. On the centennial of the first ascent, many climbers from throughout the world visited the mountain. Between late December and February, 2,666 people entered the Provincial Park to climb the mountain; another 660 went trekking. The success rate was around 30 percent. There were two casualties, a Swiss and an Argentinian. Twenty were evacuated due to different problems, particularly edema.

A controversy began when Governor of Mendoza Arturo Lafalla (who was among the season's summitters) made a commemorative statement in Plaza de Mulas. He declared that the lack of rainfall and water in Mendoza was due to the taking of the Inca Mummy, found some years ago, from its ancient tomb. He also declared to the 500 people gathered that he wanted it replaced. Dr. Juan Schobinger, one of Argentina's more respected archaeologists and chief of the expedition who brought down the Incan child, disagreed with Lafalla, saying such things were superstitions with no scientific base at all. In reality, 1997 experienced some of the greatest snowfall of the century.

The Gendarmeria Nacional (the border police) now has a very professional rescue team directed by the Second Commandant Balada. Its base is the Escuadrón Punta de Vacas near Aconcagua. They have very good equipment that includes a Hagglunds amphibian and snow vehicle.

MARCELO SCANU, *Buenos Aires, Argentina.*


*Aconcagua, Attempt by Blind Climber.* In December, Erik Weihenmayer, a blind climber, made an attempt of Aconcagua by the normal route, reaching 1,500 feet shy of the summit with guides and a film crew. We went for the summit on our 17th day on the mountain, reaching Independencia at 21,000 feet. We went down from there due to high winds. The mountain is a slag heap. It's strictly a roll of the die as to whether the weather lets you summit or not.

HANS FLORINE, *unaffiliated*


*Clarifications and Corrections.* On pages 240-41 of the 1997 AAJ, Bonete Chico and Famatina were incorrectly placed in the Chilean section. They lie entirely in Argentina. On page 233 ("Ampato, Discovery of Mummies") it was erroneously stated that a mummy was found on Incahuasi. The Incahuasi finding was composed only of statuettes representing human beings, but not actually the corpse of a human. Ampato, not Incahuasi, has the highest tomb on earth. Incahuasi (6638m, not 6610m as listed) has the second highest ruins, which lie on its summit. Only Llullaillaco (6739m) has higher ruins.

MARCELO SCANU, *Buenos Aires, Argentina*

NORTHERN ANDES

*Volcán Llullaillaco, New Route.* Llullaillaco, a volcano on the Argentine-Chilean border, was a sacred peak for the Incas who built on its summit the world's highest buildings. In March, a caving expedition went to Volcán Llullaillaco; Gustavo Lisi and Rafael Monti, both from Salta, were part of the expedition. They were transported by the expedition's vehicles from base camp on the southeast face to the south face. They were left at 5000 meters in the moraine, and continued on terrain formed by basalt rock up to 5200 meters. From there they climbed a gradual couloir then put up camp at 5600 meters behind a knoll that protected them from avalanches. It snowed heavily but the next day, March 29, they left at 9 a.m. toward the summit. It was very cold. They attempted the central couloir and then took another route (60°) to the left. From the couloir, it was another 300 meters to the top over steep, mixed terrain. The last 50 meters were rock. At 4:15 p.m. they reached the summit. They descended to the camp and the next day reached base camp, where the rest of the expedition waited.

It should be noted that on the Chilean side of Llullaillaco, as well as on other parts of the border, there are land mines placed by the Chilean Army in the pre-war events of 1977 and 1978. An American climber disappeared there some years ago under mysterious conditions; some say that he was a victim of the mines. Fortunately, due to improved relations with Argentina, the Republic of Chile has said it intends to abide by the Ottawa agreement and will clear the zone of mines.

MARCELO SCANU, *Buenos Aires, Argentina*

*Cerro Ojos del Salado, Possible New Route, and Other Activity.* Among the many teams active in the region, two Brazilian teams made climbing attempts; one was unsuccessful on Ojos del Salado and Pissis, while the other party claimed a new route, the Brazilian route, on Ojos del Salado.

MARCELO SCANU, *Buenos Aires, Argentina*

CENTRAL ANDES

*Valle Encantado, Various Ascents.* Since April, 1995, some new ascents have been made in this attractive and off-the-beaten-track area near Bariloche. Eduardo Lopez, Pablo Muller, Walter Rossini, Sebastian Mazzaro and Pablo Pontoriero did the second ascent of Torre Gebauer, the biggest tower of the valley, via a new route, *Sol de Otorno* (5+ A1, 250m, eight pitches). Recently, Alfredo Aliaga, Peti Olivieri and Facundo Jose did the third ascent of the tower by a new route, *Horizontes Semiconquistados* (6a+, 300m). It is interesting to note that the first ascent was done in 1974.

FACUNDO JOSE, CLUB ANDINO BARILOCHE

*Monte Pissis, Attempt, and Possible First Ascent.* In April, I made a solo attempt on Pissis (6759m) via the route first pioneered by Greg Horne and Fritz Radun (documented by Horne in the 1996 *AAJ*). Later, an attractive alternative summit—the western peak of the Pissis summits—presented itself to the south-southwest. This was ascended. No cairns or other markers were found on this summit. I estimate its height at 21,650 to 21,850 feet. I believe this to be a possible first ascent of this peak and also the first solo ascent.

BOB VILLARREAL

*The east face of La Hoja*. Bohemian Rhapsody *takes the central dihedral*. CHRISTIAN OBERLI

CHILEAN PATAGONIA

*With both Chilean and Argentine Patagonia reports, we rely heavily on climbers to contact us as soon as they return in order to include their accounts in appropriate volumes of the* Journal. *This means we sometimes miss first-hand accounts. When possible, we include them in the following volume. We include here some first-hand accounts from the 1996-97 season that we included as notes in last year's* Journal.

*Cerro Timonel, First Ascent.* Our expedition was composed of Nicolas Boetsch, Alberto Gana, Giancarlo Guglielmetti, Felipe Howard, Pablo Osses and me, the leader. On our second try, a Chilean patrol vessel disgorged us at the very southern end of Hielo Patagonico Sur, an ice tongue in the Fiordo de las Montanas flanked by the Cordillera Riesco and Cordillera Sarmiento. Wind and constant rain were great obstacles during our 20-day (December, 1995) expedition. We managed to make the first ascent of an ice peak, P.1330m, which we christened Cerro Timonel ("The Helmsman"). Stormy weather forced us to cancel all other projects and we retreated painfully to Istmo Resi, then marched along the seashore to arrive in Puerto Natales.

CRISTIAN BURACCHIO, *Santiago*

*La Hoja, Bohemian Rhapsody, and Expeditions to the Pingo Valley, Clarification.* Between January 5 and February 6, 1996, Sven Bruchfeld (24) and Christian Oberli (24), both Chileans, made the first ascent of the east face of La Hoja in Pingo Valley, Torres del Paine National Park.

The route (5.10 A2, 650m,14 pitches) was completed in nine climbing days over almost three weeks. Four hundred sixty meters of rope were fixed in seven climbing days and the summit was reached on the second attempt on February 2 in a 25-hour push. Regular to bad rock quality was found between pitches ten and 12. All the gear was taken off the wall (and out of the park), including fixed ropes. Only the gear necessary for rappelling safely down was left at the belays (belays remain well protected with bolts, rivets, pitons and/or nuts). La Hoja's east face is very well protected against the strong stormy Patagonian west winds, making climbing possible even during bad weather, which is why we named the route *Bohemian Rhapsody* after Queen's famous song, because "Any way the wind blows, doesn't really matter. . . to me." On the other hand, the route is in a shady corner of the wall because of a southeast facing pillar to the north of the route.

Our expedition was the second one to visit the Pingo Valley. One year earlier, a British team (Louise Thomas, Mike Turner, Martin Doyle and Ollie Sanders) made the first ascent to the east face of Cuerno Norte (*Fist Full of Dollars*, A3+, 800m). The third expedition to climb in the Pingo Valley (not the second, as stated in the 1997 *AAJ*, pp. 264-5) was that of Michael Pennings and Cameron Tague, who climbed *Vuelo del Condor* (IV 5.11 A1), a new route on Cuerno Oriental, and *Anduril* (IV 5.11 A1), on the east face of La Hoja, the second new route on the face.

Climbers who take this wonderful lifestyle-sport seriously are invited to contact me by email at coberli@ing.puc.cl with any further questions.

CHRISTIAN OBERLI, *Club Aleman Andino*

*Peineta, Duraznos para Don Quijote, and First Canadian Ascent.* In early January, 1997, Guy Edwards and I (Canada) traveled to the Paine region of Chile for two months of some southern summer. On January 17, the skies cleared for long enough to lure us onto Peineta for a probable new route on its southwest buttress that we dubbed *Duraznos para Don Quijote* (IV 5.10+ C1). The ten-pitch route was established in one day with no fixed rope or bolts and only three points of clean aid. After another week of the most hideous weather I've ever witnessed, the barometer began to rise, so we escaped our fetid tent and climbed the *Monzino* route (IV 5.10) on the North Tower of Paine for the first Canadian ascent of the mountain.

Another three weeks passed with no climbing at all. Guy, deciding that he'd rather check out the beaches of Chile and their abundant wildlife than spend quality time with me at base camp, left all his gear to Steve Normandin, a friend from Canmore who was trekking. Steve and I immediately took advantage of some mediocre weather and began fixing on a new line we scoped out on the west face of the north summit of the North Tower. With five pitches fixed and only about four remaining to the summit, we received a perfect day after a week of gnarly storms only to find most of our rope shredded by the wind. With no gear or time remaining, we called it quits and descended to town for a long-awaited fiesta.

SEAN ISAAC, *unaffiliated*

*The climbers were recipients of the John Lauchlan Award

*Patagonia, Traverse.* Carsten Birckhahn (Germany) and partners made a traverse from the Pacific to the Atlantic oceans across Patagonia in the spring of 1998. They started at the Pacific Ocean in Fiordo Calvo, then crossed the Hielo Continental Patagonico carrying their kayaks. They then traveled over the Perito Moreno Glacier, then crossed Lago Argentino in their kayaks. In April, they finished the traverse on the Argentine side in the Atlantic Ocean via the Santa Cruz River, having crossed all of Patagonia from west to east.

FACUNDO JOSE, *Club Andino Bariloche*

*North Tower, Spirito Libero.* On February 2, 1998, the team of Fabio Leoni and Elio Orlandi from Trento, Italy, put up a new route on the north spur of the North Tower of Paine. The route, *Spirito Libero* (V 5.11a, 500m), was put up in alpine style. They climbed the 12-pitch route in 18 hours, leaving their bivouac at 7 a.m., summiting at 8 p.m. and returning to their bivouac at 1 a.m. Fabio and Elio took advantage of the only day of good weather in one month at base camp. El Niño conditioned the expedition of the two Trento climbers as it did the majority of the teams in the Towers of Paine National Park. The wave of bad weather, with torrential rain, was particularly bad in the middle of February.

MARIO MAICA, *Italy*

*Torres del Diablo and The Bader Valley, Various Ascents.* On January 18, John Merriam, Dylan Taylor, Darrel Gschwendtner and I teamed up with Mark Slovak and Robert Bodrogi to visit the Torres del Diablo (a.k.a. Grupo La Paz). Five hours south of Puerto Natales by fishing boat, steep metamorphosed towers rise from glaciated terrain. Amazing couloirs separate one tower from another. Donini and Chouinard climbed one of the three in the late '80s via a north face route. Our attention was drawn by the soaring south faces. Unfortunately the weather and wind battered us for 13 days, at which point we had run out of food, sustained broken tent poles, ripped flys, and had headed down to the shore line with hopes for a boat. Mussels and seaweed nourished us for a few days until a friend arrived, late, with a fisherman, a boat, and, most importantly, bread, coffee and sugar.

In early February, after refueling in Puerto Natales, Dylan, Darrel, John and I hauled

*Peinata, showing* Duranzos para Don Quixote. SEAN ISAAC

climbing gear and 20 days' worth of food into the Bader Valley of the Torres del Paine. On February 9, John and I completed the second ascent of *Vuelo Del Condor* on Cuerno Este, finding perfect golden granite. The good weather had begun, and the Bader's east faces are sheltered from the furious westerly winds. On the eleventh day we ascended a golden pillar on Cuerno Norte, lying about 1,000 feet to the north of *Fist Full of Dollars*. We call it *Little Debbie's Golden Pillar* (IV 5.11 A1). The route involves some steep, loose, wet rock as well as immaculate golden splitters. We topped out on the pillar in early evening. To climb to the shale from there would have meant a few rotten vertical and overhanging pitches—not impossible, but the wind was ripping above us at nearly 100 mph, knocking rocks off the summit that soared past both us and the sheltered face. The rain that had been pestering us all day had returned and the glacier below was creaking and groaning. The land, amazingly alive, overloaded the senses.

Looking to the north as we began the 1,700-foot descent, a perfect line up Cerro Mascara (a.k.a. the Mummer) showed itself. It topped out with what appeared to be a 600 to 800-foot golden dihedral. Three days later we were there.

On February 19, with no fixed lines or use of a hammer, John and I made the first one-day ascent of Cerro Mascara. Beginning in the Bader Valley, five pitches with much simulclimbing brought us to the notch between Cuerno Norte and Mascara. From there the cold south face lent us passage, flawless hand and finger cracks and a soaring corner system. *Duncan's Dihedral* (a fantastic IV 5.11 A1), as we later named it, engendered the beauty of the surrounding land. The 2,300-foot descent was the most fearsome part.

After refueling once more in Puerto Natales and stopping by Amerindia, a great local bar and café, John and I headed up to Japanese camp for an attempt at one of the Torres. El Niño returned with heavy rain and snow. The 100-year flood soon followed. At 2:30 a.m. on February 28, Steve Schneider, John Merriam and I woke in waterbeds. The Rio Paine had broken its banks and forced our camp under a foot and a half of rushing muddy water. Some food and gear was lost, along with optimism for another climb. The next few days were spent in a plastic shack that a few Spanish climbers had built. The three of us played chess and harmonicas and reminisced about the glorious sun. Little did we know the park had been evacuated by helicopter and boat. Bridges had been destroyed and trails were under water. We were alone. Patagonia had expressed its wild character; El Niño accentuated it. We left with love, in awe, in a boat.

JONATHON COPP

*La Mascara, Cuerno Principal, Cuerno Este, and Cuerno Norte, Various Activity*. In mid-January, 1998, Darrell Gschwendtner, John Merriam, Jonathan Copp, and I traveled to Chilean Patagonia with hopes of climbing new routes. Following an aborted attempt (*see above*) at climbing some remote metamorphic towers, we focused our attention on route possibilities in the Bader Valley of Torres Del Paine National Park. The Bader Valley is virtually untouched, and only a few routes exist on the wind-sheltered east-facing walls. In early February, we were blessed with a rare spell of sunny weather lasting for almost three weeks.

Darrell and I spent some time scanning the east face of La Mascara (a.k.a. the Mummer), finding several route possibilities. We chose a wandering line that ran directly up the east buttress. It required awkward nailing on expanding flakes (A2+?) with only a small amount of free climbing (up to 5.10). Disappointed that our line was so time-consuming and lacking in the free climbing that we hoped to find, we abandoned our efforts after only a few pitches. Simultaneously, on the other side of the valley, our friend Fletcher Yaw, fresh off of

*La Mascara, a.k.a. The Mummer, from the Pingos Valley.* Duncan's Dihedral *takes the shining arête.*
JONATHON COPP

Aconcagua, soloed what is probably a new route up the west face of El Almirante Nieto. The route follows a snow couloir for a couple thousand feet until it turns to a small ice runnel that winds through the final headwall.

We then focused our attention on climbing a new and hopefully easy route up the low angle northeast face of Cuerno Principal. We hoped to climb the granite quickly and easily so that we would have time to complete the last hundred feet of hideously rotten slate that makes up the summit. Our bad luck returned early on the day before our scheduled climb when a large rockfall wiped out our proposed route. Plan B was another "easy" looking line 100 meters to the right. High winds blew rocks down on us as we simulclimbed approximately 300 meters of easy terrain with occasional moves of 5.9. Later, as we began to belay individual pitches, I pulled a suitcase-sized flake off, which missed Darrell by inches and caused him to slide off the belay ledge. The flake landed on our rope, cutting it in several places. Again, we were forced to retreat.

Our luck finally improved as we climbed stellar crack systems terminating at the rotten metamorphic layer on the east face of Cuerno Este. The route roughly follows Penning and Tague's *Vuelo del Condor* (III 5.11 A1), but unfortunately did not allow for a summit. Knowing our weather window could end any day, we pushed our timetable up, traded our shredded ropes for a packhorse, and headed up the Rio Ascencio Valley to the ever-popular Japanese camp occupied by a large Spanish team, a Brazilian team, and the lone American, Steve Schneider. Steve gave us a topo for an all free route up the west face of Torre Norte called *Taller del Sol* (V 5. 10+). The next day Darrell and I climbed the spectacular 500-meter dihedral system in 24 hours, base camp to base camp. The experience was special not only because of the high quality of the route, but also because it was the only summit that Darrell and I would stand on in Patagonia. The feeling was bittersweet, though: Only seven hours after Darrell and I descended the couloir below the North Tower, a huge rockfall from the summit of the Central Tower fell 1000 meters, killing two members of the Spanish team in an avalanche of rock and snow in the adjacent couloir (*see below*).

DYLAN TAYLOR

*The Mummer, Cuerno Oriental, and the Sharksfin, Various Activity.* During March and April of 1998, Tom Bauman, Alan Kearney and Jack Lewis climbed in Patagonia and performed clean-up work with the help of a grant from Polartec. On March 24, Bauman was hit in the arm and ribs by rockfall on the yet unclimbed East Face of the Mummer in the Pingos Valley (Chileans have indiscriminately renamed the valley the Bader Valley, which is very confusing as most maps and books refer to it as the Pingos Valley). The party bailed off the Mummer after climbing only two pitches and then changed objectives. On March 29, Lewis was blown 15 feet through the air by a gust of wind while hiking. He tumbled down talus another 20 feet, sustaining cuts and bruises. On April 7, all three climbed a nine-pitch route up the granitic East Face of Cuerno Oriental (sometimes referred to as Cuerno Este) (5.11 A2) and did not go to the summit, a half mile to the northwest and up rotten black rock. On April 14, Kearney soloed the South Ridge of the Sharksfin (a.k.a. Aleta del Tiburon) in the Frances Valley, Grade III or IV 5.9 (a route put up by the French in 1982). This was during a spell of four days of good weather, the longest during their stay. The party carried trash out of the Japanese and Torre Camps in the Rio Ascencio Valley and from the British and Italian Camps in the Frances Valley. They also spoke with Paine Park officials about the problems of overuse in the park. They found the climber's camps actually cleaner than those camps used only by trekkers.

ALAN KEARNEY

*Recipient of a Polartec grant

*Torres Del Paine, Various Ascents.* Andy McAuley of Australia and Carsten Birckhahn of Germany climbed in a climbing area called Grupo la Paz, four spectacular towers without names or topos, four hours from Puerto Natales by boat on the shore of Canal Santa Maria. They made a first ascent on the east tower. (*The Grupo La Paz, a.k.a. the Torres del Diablo, lies in the Canal Santa Maria. A parallel fjord, the Canal Las Montanas, holds the Cordillera Sarmiento, an article about which can be found in* AAJ *1993, pp. 109-113. The two fjords are about an hour apart by boat.*)

Alexandre Portela and Sergio Tartari from Brazil climbed the Bonington route on February 15, reaching the summit at 4:30 p.m. The route took them 20 hours from bivouac to bivouac.

From February 8 to 17, Andres Stambuck and Jose Pedro Montt of Chile climbed the central summit of Paine Grande (3050 meters) and Punta Bariloche. Janus Golab, Jan Muskai Ryszard Pawlowski and Adam Potoczek of Poland climbed the North Tower via the Piola/Sprungli route on March 13, and went on to climb the Central Tower via the Bonington/Whillans route.

Claudio Retamal and Andres Labarca of Chile climbed a new route on the southwest face of Cuerno Principal. *Junto a Vasquez* (5.10d A2+, eight pitches) was climbed in one 17-hour push on March 18. They reported excellent rock quality. Their advanced camp was one hour from the wall and three hours from the Italian camp.

Erich Mueller and I from Chile climbed to the col between Mascara and Cuerno Norte via the west face (5.9+, 16 pitches to high point) in one 19-hour push from base camp in Valle del Frances on March 15. This is the beginning to an excellent climb on La Mascara or Cuerno Norte; for such a climb, be prepared for a night on the wall and a good rack of aid climbing gear. From here, the views of the Valle Bader and Frances are amazing. We also tried, on February 15, a new route on La Mascara's west face, but after eight hard pitches the night arrived and our sleeping bags were so far away that we rappelled in a beautiful and clear night to cook spaghetti. The route is a nice project for speed climbers and looks like it would go at 5.10d A2 in 15 pitches, with excellent quality granite. The base camp is one and a half hours from the wall, with water, some boulders problem, no tents necessary and a beautiful view of the walls.

Number of days with good weather (in terms of climbing conditions) in Paine during the 1997-98 season: October: 5; November: 6; December: 4; January: 3; February: 20; March: 5.

HERNAN JOFRE, *Amerindia Concept*

*El Escudo, Et Si Le Soleil Ne Revenait Pas. . . .* On December 18, 1997, Swiss climbers Jean-Daniel Nicolet and Jean-Michel Zweiacker climbed a new wall route on the east face of Escudo. *Et Si Le Soleil Ne Revenait Pas. . . .* (VI 5.10 A4) takes a line to the right of the German route on the far right side of the face and is 900 meters long. The pair spent nine nights on the face in mostly bad weather. The route had been attempted the previous season by a Swiss team that included Jean-Daniel Nicolet. This is the third route to be established on the wall. A complete story on the climb appears earlier in this journal.

*Torres Del Paine, Various Activity.* On December 12, I arrived in Patagonia for what was to be a three-month stay. The weather had been bad for the last month with no recorded climbing activity. Amidst the usual foul weather patterns were occasional windows of nice weather. December 16 and 17 found decent climbing conditions, as did December 29-January 2 and February 1-3. During February 9-23, a two-week spell of mostly perfect weather settled in on the Towers. But along with warm temperatures came melting couloirs and vastly increased

*Andreas Zegers on pitch three, the Italian route, Central Tower of Paine.* STEVE SCHNEIDER

rockfall that made approaching the normal routes of Torre Norte and Torre Central a suicidal proposition. Afterward, a 30-year flood hit the park, which was closed to all trekking activity. Climbers were left scrambling to save their tents from rapidly rising floodwaters, and the hut in Camp Japanese had a high water mark of six inches inside the structure.

On El Escudo, Chileans Rodrigo Fica and Dario Arancibia were unsuccessful in pioneering a new route up the south ridge. Based in a snowcave during the bad weather of January, the pair only managed two pitches.

Americans were especially active in the Paine. Steve "Shipoopi" Schneider climbed the 500-meter west face of Torre Norte three times. *Via Giorgio Giannicci* (V 5.10 A2) with Peter Mayfield, on December 17, was especially entertaining as their ropes became hopelessly wedged in a fissure on their second rappel, and they were forced to descend with just two 50-foot ropes for the remaining 1,300 feet in gradually deteriorating weather. *Taller del Sol* (V 5.10+) fell to Schneider and his wife, Heather Baer, on February 10. This route, established two years ago by Americans Paul Butler and Eli Helmuth, is a great all-free route up the west face, as well as being the best descent route down the west face with good anchors every 45 or 50 meters. Both of these climbs were second ascents. *Ultima Esperanza* (V 5.10 A1) received its fourth ascent from Schneider, Chilean Andreas "Chili Dog" Zegers, and American Sean Plunkett on February 23.

On nearby Peineta, on February 14, Heather Baer and Schneider made the first free ascent (second overall) of *Duraznos para Don Quijote*, finding the crux section to be mid-5.11.

On the west face of the Central Tower, Schneider, again partnered by Andreas Zegers, made the second ascent of the Italian (Defrancesco-Manica-Stedile) route in 22 hours, 45 minutes, summiting at 1 p.m. on February 19. The route (VI 5.11 A3) features more than 400 feet of wide cracks from four to ten inches. Schneider, lacking a number six friend, made a mandatory 25-foot runout on a 5.11 offwidth section of pitch 5, and was "glad for every inch of offwidth I'd ever done." It was the first on-sight push of a Central Tower route besides the normal route. Near the top, the pair was bombarded, without injury, by a huge rockfall that swept the entire approach couloir to the North and Central towers. Tragically, Basque climbers Antxon Alonso and Gaizka Razkin, who were beginning to descend the couloir, were swept 3,000 feet to their deaths. Alonso and Razkin were attempting to repeat a line just established by their countrymen Gerardo Tellechea, Andoni Areizaga, Josetxo Rodriguez, and Martin Zabaleta. Their new route, *Anton eta Gaizka* (VI 5.10d A2) is a 12-pitch direct to the Bonington-Willans. The foursome summited on February 18, and placed two bolts with fixed carabiners at every anchor, probably making this the easiest descent from the Central Tower's summit.

STEVE "SHIPOOPI" SCHNEIDER

*Chilean Patagonia, Various Ascents.* On Monday, December 29, I crawled out of my cave at 5 a.m. I didn't think the weather was terrific, so I went back to sleep. I woke up and started to the gear stash cave at 9 a.m. I organized things and at noon decided I might head up the couloir and see how things would go, figuring I would just stash my rope and gear for better weather later. At 4:30 p.m. I arrived at the notch between the Central and North towers. I began up the *Monzino* route on the North Tower, combining the first three pitches in one 70-meter rope length—climbed, rapped, and jugged it in maybe 35 minutes. I soloed over some 4th class for about 150 feet, then stashed my pack and much of my gear rack, figuring I would go for it. I soloed to the top from there with the rope on my back for retreating. I topped out one hour and 31 minutes after starting at the notch (it was 6:21 p.m.). I knew it was light enough to see until 10 or so. I made it back to the notch in exactly one hour and 30 minutes, rapping the whole way except maybe 20 to 100 feet of downclimbing here and there on 3rd-class terrain. I stashed my rope and gear at the top of the couloir and headed to my cave camp, which I reached by 11:15 p.m.

The next day, December 30, Steve "Lucky" Smith and I left the cave at about 6 a.m. We made it to the top of the coulior by 11 a.m. or so and started the Bonington route on the Central Tower at about 1 p.m. I lead the first two pitches and Lucky the next three, then we simul-climbed to one pitch from the top, switching leads once. We topped out at about 7 p.m., having done the whole route from the notch in six hours, 15 minutes. We made it back to the notch in about three hours and were back to the cave at about midnight.

Two days later, on January 1, Lucky and I started up the British/Strappo unfinished route (see *AAJ* 1997, pp. 260-1) on the Central Tower at about 11 a.m. We swung a few leads each. When we were about 100 meters short of the Brit's high point (where the booty bag is), snow was building up on my arms and protection. We decided to retreat, and did, without much trouble, other than messes of torn rope confusing us at times all down the route.

On January 12, Lucky and I started up the *Cave Man* route in the French Valley. It was about noon when we started the first pitch. There was snow covering the slabs leading up to the route and we had to belay four times before getting to the base of the route proper. We made it up six pitches; it was 7 p.m. We hadn't really intended on getting this far when we left camp, so we didn't have full bivy gear, or enough food. We opted to retreat. On the last technical rappel, we wrapped tattered rope around a thread and backed it up. Lucky went first; it held. Then I went, and, while "bumping" the knot around to avoid a snag, the thread of rock broke. I slid 30 feet, rolled onto the talus, and came out of it with a broken thumb and a bad road rash on each hip.

HANS FLORINE, *unaffiliated*

## ARGENTINE PATAGONIA

*Cerro Piergiorgio, Esperando La Cumbre, and Other Activity.* Maurizio Giordani and I made the first ascent of the northwest spur of Piergiorgio (east summit) via *Esperando La Cumbre* (VI+ A1, 850m), which included couloir ice up to 75° (WI4) and mixed climbing using only pitons, with belays equipped on the ridge. We climbed it in alpine style on December 3, 1996. We approached the mountain and bivouacked in an igloo beneath the northwest face (the location of our 1995 attempt, *Gringos Locos*, which we intended to complete). We verified that the fixed ropes left on the wall the year before had been destroyed by wind, and changed our itinerary.

On December 4, we departed across the glacier between Piergiorgio and Cerro Pollone. We began to climb a glacier and mixed couloir that brought us to the snowy col between Pollone and Piergiorgio (VI- A1 WI4, four pitches). We bivouacked at the col after having climbed the eastern foresummit of Cerro Pollone (easy).

On December 5, we began the northern spur of Piergiorgio, where we found traces of previous attempts (Cesarino Fava and Augusto Mengelle, 1963). The first part was on rock and couloir ice (VI A1 WI3, five pitches), then easy snow (passing the point where *Pepe Rajo* on the north face ends), then up three pitches of rock (VI+) to the summit crest of Piergiorgio (East Summit). We descended the route to the col, then began the long traverse beneath the east slope of Piergiorgio toward Fitz Roy. We followed all the ice of the Pollone Glacier, reaching the Cuadrado Pass at around 1 a.m., a little beneath which we bivouacked. The next

*Cerro Piergiorgio, showing* Esperando la Cumbre *(Cerro Pollone is to the right).* GIANLUCA MASPES

day we descended to the Piedra del Fraile.

On December 8, I made the third solo ascent of Aguja Guillaumet's entire northwest spur (following the 1990 Giordani variation plus the 1965 Argentine route) (VII- AO, 1000m) in five hours, self-belaying on only the most difficult pitch.

GIANLUCA MASPES, *Italy*

*Cerro Marconi Norte.* It was reported that Maurizio Giordani climbed a new route (5.5, 500m), solo, on on the north flank of Cerro Marconi Norte, on December 9, 1996. (*High Mountain Sports* 176)

*Effects Of El Niño On Patagonia's 1997-'98 Climbing Season.* Briefly explained, El Niño is a sporadic warm water current that flows clockwise from west to east along the equator and then south along South America's west coast against the normal polar current. In an "El Niño year," water temperature on the South American coast rises about 3°C, increasing rainfall significantly. Peru usually is the most severely affected country and influences in Chile decrease with higher southern latitudes.

According to locals, the winter of 1997 was mild and warmer than usual, and spring was rainy, also with temperatures above average. But then, after a still rainy January, almost three continuous weeks of good weather followed in February! El Niño revealed itself not only as a long period of good weather, but also with higher temperatures during 1997. The snow line on the Southern Patagonian Icefield was much higher this year than usual. Crossing the Icefield became a painful adventure. In February, Soames Flowerree (Chile), José Vélez (Ecuador), Derek Churchil (Chile) and Ralph Rynning (Norway), who crossed the Southern Patagonian Icefield from Jorge Montt Glacier to Paso del Viento, had to work very hard under lots of rain in January on Jorge Montt to make any advance over an awful crevasse labyrinth until they reached the plateau. Then, in February, good weather returned, and the sun soon melted what little snow was left, turning the usually flat icefield into an irregular suncup and crevasse-covered surface. Sometimes, they advanced as little as one kilometer in three hours.

The explanation for the good weather was a strong high-pressure system that positioned itself over the Southern Pacific Ocean in Patagonian latitudes, obstructing bad-weather fronts on their way from west to east toward Patagonia. The origin of this high-pressure area might be very related to El Niño. Weather in central Chile is mainly regulated by a high pressure area over the Southern Pacific Ocean in front of the Chilean coast. It moves north in winter and south in summer. This year, probably due to the influences of the higher temperatures brought by El Niño, the high-pressure area moved farther south than usual, bringing good weather to Patagonia.

The climbing season in Fitz Roy and Cerro Torre areas also was different than usual. Although good weather was by itself a blessing for climbers, approaching the peaks was unusually difficult because of the low amount of snow on the glaciers, as well as the lack of ice holding together rotten rock sections on the approaches to some walls.

Torres del Paine, on the other hand, was not as affected by the conditions, as it is at a lower altitude than the Fitz Roy area. There was good weather during the first three weeks of February, too, but the most important influence of El Niño occurred during the last week of the month. Unprecedented rain and thunder flooded the park, forcing local authorities to evacuate people and close the park entrance.

CHRISTIAN OBERLI, *Club Alemán Andino, Chile*

*Cerro Gorra Blanca, Ascent.* Well-known Argentine climbers Jose Luis Fonrouge and Alfredo Rosasco ascended Cerro Gorra Blanca (2907m). The ascent was an ice climb that ended with a summit mushroom. Other details are lacking.

MARCELO SCANU, *Buenos Aires, Argentina*

*Argentine Patagonia, Various Activities.* The 1997-98 climbing season in Patagonia began in typical fashion, with frustrated climbers sitting in huts for most of November, December, and January. However, an unprecedented three-week weather window in February enabled many teams to climb impressive routes in the Fitz Roy regions.

Argentinians David Albert and Gatito Dura climbed the 1974 British route (5.10+, 13 pitches) on Rafael Jaurez in late January. Gatito followed this up with a rapid rope-solo ascent of Aguja de la S. He then teamed up with Albert for an ascent of Poincenot's Whillian's route. On the summit, the team met up with Gatito's brother Marco Dura, and a Spaniard who had just made the third ascent of the lengthy Carrington-Rouse Route (5.10). Finally, on February 18, David Albert and Marco and Gatito Dura climbed the Kearney-Harrington route (5.10+) on the north face of St. Exupery, in 26 hours round-trip from the Polish Camp.

MARK SYNNOTT

*Argentine Patagonia, Various Ascents.* On December 31, 1997, thanks to a three-day spell of good weather, Spanish climbers Manel de la Matta and Hugo Biarge climbed Cerro Torre via the Maesti route. They started from a snow cave in the glacier at the base of Cerro Torre and Torre Egger at 2 a.m on the 30th. That same day they bivouacked at the ice towers, and the next day they completed the climb, reaching the summit at 4 p.m. on the 31st. They didn't climb the final ice mushroom because of approaching bad weather.

Also on December 30, following the steps of Manel and Hugo, two parties (Nacho Orviz, Francisco Blanco and Mikel Berasaluce from Spain, and Italians Giovanni Ongaro and Lorenzo Lanfranchione) reached the Col of Patience. They fixed some 100 meters of rope that evening. On the 31st, running before the storm, they managed to reach the summit a little before midnight. Caught by the storm on the descent, they bivouacked for two days at the Col of Patience before finally reaching base camp.

The very fine route *Claro de Luna* on Saint Exupéry was climbed by the Italians Giovanni Ongaro and Lorenzo Lanfranchione in early season. This pair also climbed El Mocho via the Piola-Anker route.

Another good summit, Aguja Bífida, was climbed on January 31 to February 1 by Agustín Rodríguez from Spain and Andorran-based Belgian Fran Van Herreweghe. Van Herreweghe also climbed Cerro Tore via the Maestri route with Spanish big waller Cristóbal Díaz in mid-December.

MANEL DE LA MATTA, *Spain*

*Argentine Patagonia, Slovenian Activity.* On Aguja Guillaumet, Damjan Kočar and Peter Subic climbed the left couloir (V+ 65°, 300m) on February 12. Klemen Mali and Monika Kambič (female) climbed it on February 17. Mali and Kambič then added a new start to the Swiss route on the East Arête (VII- A2, 230 m) on February 19-20; their high point rejoined the Swiss route. On Aguja della S, Klemen Mali and Monika Kambič climbed the Austrian route with a variation (VI+ 55°, 450m) in five hours on March 1. On Poincenot, Janez Skok and his wife Ines Bozic attempted the second ascent of Piola's route *Patagonicos Desperados* (6c A3+, 600m) on February 17-18. They bivouacked after the seventh pitch. The next day, they climbed the major difficulties, but then retreated because of ice-choked cracks and lack of time. On Cerro Torre, Grega Lačen and Dani Vezovnik wanted to climb a new route in the central part of the east face. They arrived at base camp at the beginning of December, but because of an injury Vezovnik returned home around Christmas. Lačen joined forces with Carlos Suarez (Spain), but by the end of February, they had climbed only 250 meters to the icefield in the lower part of the wall.

MIHA PETERNEL, *Planinska zveza Slovenije*

*Aguja Saint Exupery, Buscaini Route, Variation.* The early part of March, 1997, witnessed a spell of ten days of good weather. Diego Magaldi and Jorge Kozulj climbed Aguja Saint Exupery during this window, following for the most part the Buscaini route on the east face and putting up a four-pitch variation to it (6a+ A2).

FACUNDO JOSE, *Club Andino Bariloche*

*Aguja Saint Exupery, Chiaro de Luna, Techada Negro, Attempt, and Shady Wilson Spire, House of Cards.* Chad Garner and I made an ascent of *Chiaro de Luna* (5.11, 25 pitches) on Aguja Saint Exupery. The route takes a line near an indistinct prow on the west face. We climbed the route in 15 hours and 35 minutes from base to summit and took about three hours to approach via an easy ramp and a wide snow couloir. Due to cold temperatures in the morning and no training because of months of rain and holiday gluttony back in North Carolina, we found the crux third pitch too troublesome to free; we did, however, free the rest of the route at 5.11b. The route included the usual stunning Patagonian features, splitter cracks systems, corners and an especially nice finger crack and layback flake near an arête high on the route. We summitted at sunset and rappelled leisurely in the light of the full moon to a wide rocky ledge at half-height, where we rested and shivered till sun-up. We reached the Polish Camp 36 hours after departure, having contended with a few stuck ropes.

Earlier in our trip, we attempted to climb Techada Negro from the Bridwell Camp only to find a grim band of chossy slate barring access to the easy snowfields leading to the summit. Unwilling to risk our lives for that particular chosspile, we opted to traverse east into a cirque ringed by a number of spires and cliffs. We chose a prominent spire in the middle and, armed with four stoppers and three tricams, charged the west ridge. Helmetless in double boots, we climbed two pitches of the most fractured and loose basalt imaginable. On pitch two, I dislodged a 60-pound block which actually shook the summit pinnacle. We opted to downclimb the route, as most every feature was about as trustworthy as a career politician. We dubbed our climb of "Shady Wilson Spire" the *House of Cards* (5.8, not recommended). The south face is much steeper and less blocky and may yeild some more difficult, and possibly more solid, routes in the future.

FRANK CARUS

*Aguja Saint Exupery, Condorito.* Kurt Albert, Bernd Arnold and Edbert Dozenkaff did the first ascent of *Condorito* (5.12d A2, 400m + 300m via the Buscaini route) on the southeast face of Aguja Saint Exupery. Jens Richter and Rainer Treppter did the second ascent of the route on February 18.

FACUNDO JOSE, *Club Andino Bariloche*

*Fitz Roy, West Face Attempt, and Supercanaleta, Ascent.* On December 6, 1997, Jack Tackle and I arrived in Chaltén to attempt a new variation to the unrepeated Czech Route on the 6,000-foot west face of Fitz Roy. The next four days were spent carrying gear to Campo Bridwell and to an advanced base at the so-called Polish Camp below Poincenot in the Torre Valley. On December 11, we carried a load up the 3,000-foot ramp on the southwest side of the Hombre Sentado (Sitting Man Ridge). This consists of snow and ice up to 55° with 300 feet of moderate mixed climbing at the top. On December 14, we climbed the ramp again and continued farther up the Hombre Sentado (two 5th class pitches) and cached our ropes and hardware near where the ridges run into the west face. On descent, we fixed 300 feet of rope in the final goulotte on the northwest end of Hombre Sentado, which allowed us to bypass the tiring ramp via the easier northeast side and mostly avoid the seracs at the end of the Torre Valley.

Perfect weather arrived on the 15th, which we needed to rest and dry out. Early on the 16th, we left Polish Camp and ascended the fixed line, walked under the *Supercanaleta* and continued to our high point on the ridge. The rest of the day was spent following the Czech Route to a good bivy at the top of the prominent 450-foot corner some 5,000 feet up the face. The Czechs had reported that they removed their fixed lines. But it appears they cleaned only a few pitches, as the route was littered throughout with tattered rope. The next day, despite a malfunctioning stove, we left the Czech Route and headed straight up, aiming for the prominent 1,500-foot corner that leads to the ridge. After two new pitches, we retreated due to slow climbing, surprisingly crumbly rock and an overwhelming abundance of wide cracks. We decided to attempt the regular Czech Route and climbed several more pitches of that. Continued hard climbing and deteriorating weather sent us back to our previous bivouac. On the 18th, in increasing wind and clouds, we made 18 rappels, climbed five sideways pitches and left two chopped ropes behind to arrive back at the Glaciar Fitz Roy Norte and then Polish

Camp. We then switched our energy to the 1965 *Supercanaleta* route, which we climbed from December 30-January 1, arriving back at Campo Rio Blanco at midnight.

Most parties have approached *Supercanaleta* from Piedra del Fraile on the Rio Eléctrico and arrived at the Glaciar Polone via Paso del Cuadrado. Unless you are already based in the Torre Valley for other ascents, it is our opinion that this traditional approach would remain the best option for parties attempting any route on the northwest side of Fitz Roy. As for the descent, you remain on your own to figure it out.

JOE JOSEPHSON, *Calgary Mountain Club*

*Fitz Roy Area, Various Ascents.* On February 11, 1998, Rainer Treppter and two partners (all from Germany) summited Fitz Roy via the *Royal Flush* route (second ascent). On February 12, German Jens Richter and Jack Tigle (Scotland) climbed the Franco-Argentine route after five attempts. On February 14, three parties summited Fitz Roy: Slovene Klemen Mali and Argentine Monika Kambic, Sandi Kelneric and Bostjan Sterbal from Slovenia via the Franco-Argentine route. Two Spanish Basques climbed the *Supercanaleta* route.

There also were several repeats of the Willans route on Poincenot, and two parties did Carrington-Rouse route on the same peak.

FACUNDO JOSE, *Club Andino Bariloche*

*Torre Egger and Cerro Standhart, Attempts.* Hugo Biarge, Pere Vilarasau and I tried an alpine-style ascent of *Badlands* on Torre Egger on December 15-16. We were unsuccessful. January was awful: there wasn't a single day of good weather; our ice cave got buried by snow with all the gear in it and it took us several tries to find it. During our last try on February 1 (five days before the plane was leaving), the weather improved a little so Hugo, Santiago Palacios and I went for it. We wanted to link *Tomahawk* and *Exocet,* so we started to climb at 9 o'clock at night. The route was in very bad condition but we kept going anyway. At sunrise, we reached the snow slopes on the middle section of the wall. The day was gorgeous and we were super-motivated to go on, but as soon as we climbed the first pitch on the upper goulotte of *Exocet,* the day got warmer and huge blocks of ice started to fall everywhere off the wall. The couloir was one of the most dangerous places to be because all the falling ice was funneled down it. We were only seven pitches below the summit. We went down and suffered an epic descent, rappeling off shitty gear while being hit by chunks of ice all over. It took us the whole day to reach the ground, but when we got back to the ice cave we were the happiest men on earth just because we were alive.

We still think alpine style is the right way to climb mountains, even if you have to push the limits, even if you have to fail like we did.

SIMON ELIAS, *Spain*

*Cerro Torre, Ferrari Route, and Cerro Standhart, Tomahawk and Exocet Routes, First Link-Up.* Laurence Monnoyeur and I have been to Patagonia two times, once in 1996 and the second time last year. In 1996, we climbed El Mocho via the Goulotte Grassi (IV 4+, 250m), Cerro Polone via *Mastica e Sputa* (V 5+, 650m), a route established four weeks before by Luigi Crispa and Lorenzo Nadali, and made two attempts on Fitz Roy, via the *Supercanaleta* and Franco-Argentine routes. In 1997, we arrived with good weather at Chaltén with the goal of climbing the west face of Cerro Torre. We decided to climb *A La Recherce du Temps Perdu,* which finishes at the Col of Hope (VI 5, 800m), to get on the Ferrari route. We climbed it in

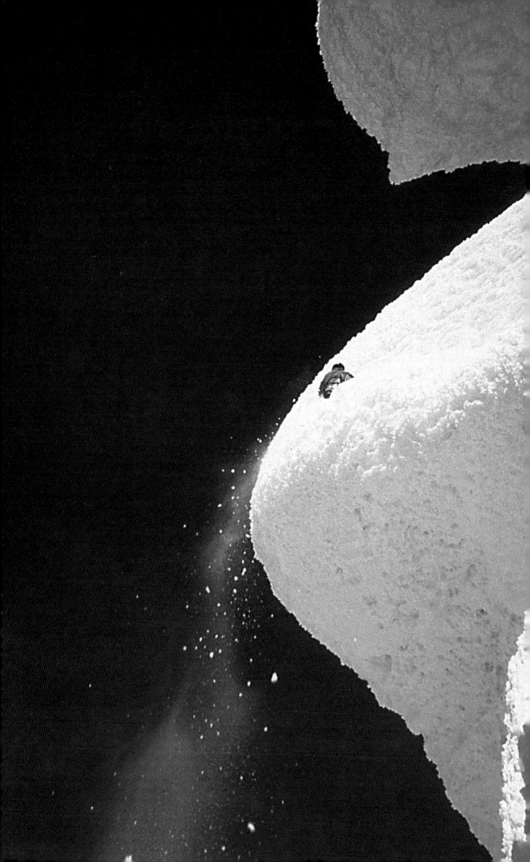

eight hours, then bivied at the Col, but the weather changed, so we returned to Chaltén via the Wind Col in two days. During this trip, we used snow shoes for the approach and the return on the Hielo Continental (October 14-18). On the return, we traveled for three days via the Passo Marconi with skis and pulka to the Circo de los Altaves. From there, we approached the Ferrari route in a half day with a bivy 450 meters beneath the Col of Hope. From this bivy, from October 27-28, we free climbed (no aid, no jumaring) the Ferrari route (VI 6+, 800m) until 40 meters from the top (the rime was too bad for climbing; also, I had fallen 15 meters while on The Helmet, one of the hardest pitches of the route). We rappelled the same day via the same route to our bivy.

On November 15 and 16, we climbed *Tomahawk* (IV 6 A1) and *Exocet* (V 6). We started climbing *Tomahawk* at 12:30 a.m. and bivied at the bottom of *Exocet*. The day after we climbed *Exocet* to the top of Stanhardt and rappelled to base camp (Norwegian Camp) the same day. We free climbed both routes except for five meters at the bottom of *Tomahawk*. During the 80 days we spent in the region in 1996 and 1997, we had 20 days of good weather.

BRUNO SOURZAC, *France*

*Cerro Torre, Compressor Route, and Fitz Roy, West Face, Attempt.* On February 11, British legal alien Kevin Thaw and I climbed the *Compressor* route from the Norwegian Camp, making the trip in 27 hours. Earlier, we had attempted a new route on the west face of Fitz Roy, following approximately the same line as Joe Josephson and Jack Tackle. (The west face has one route, a 57-pitch 5.10 free climb put up over two seasons by a Czech team in 1985-86.) We climbed approximately two-thirds of the wall, in two days, before being turned back by a storm. Several teams now have attempted to climb this huge face alpine style, with no success.

MARK SYNNOTT

# ANTARCTICA

## ANTARCTIC PENINSULA

*Lamaire Channel, Various Ascents.* Greg Landreth and Keri Pashuk, with their boat Northanger, were active again in the Antarctic Peninsula, making ascents of a number of peaks with their climbing guests Rich Prohaska and Jia Condon. In late January, Landreth, Prohaska and Condon climbed *Whozuna?* (V 5.9, 18 pitches) in a 40-hour push on P.1050m in the Wall Range. Rich Prohaska and Jia Condon then climbed *Unazwhat?* (V 5.9 mixed A2) via the east buttress to the east summit of the Cape Renard Tower (a.k.a. Una's Tits, 747m) from February 1-4. An attempt of Wandel Peak (c.950m) on Booth Island was made via the north ridge in early February by all members of the group. A full account of their climbs appears earlier in this journal.

## QUEEN MAUD LAND

*Queen Maud Land, Various Ascents.* In the 1996-97 season, I was involved with the following ascents. Gordon Wiltsie, Michael Graber, Rick Ridgeway, John Krakauer, Alex Lowe and I made the first ascent of Rakekniven via the *Snow Petrel Wall* (VI 5.10 A3) on January 5. Krakauer, Lowe and I made the first ascent of Trollslottet via *The Three Sons* (IV 5.11 AO).

*Bruno Sourzac on the ice mushroom of the Ferrari route, Cerro Torre.* LAURENCE MONNOYEUR

*Conrad Anker and Jon Krakauer beneath Rakekniven.* The Snow Petrel Wall *ascends the right skyline. Below: on Media Peak, with Trollsloppett in the background.* GORDON WILTSIE

On Media Peak, directly across from the Trollsloppet, Graber, Ridgeway, and Wiltsie climbed a snow route that involved a pitch of 5.8 rock climbing. It was the first ascent of the peak. Both peaks were climbed on January 11. On Kyrkjeskipit, Graber, Ridgeway and Lowe climbed an alpine route, which Lowe then skied. It was possibly the first non-helicopter ascent. On Kubus, Wiltsie, Krakauer and I climbed an alpine route. A ski descent was made by all members of the group.

CONRAD ANKER

ELLSWORTH MOUNTAINS

*Antarctica, Various Ascents.* From December 3, 1997 to January 19, 1998, I was in Antarctica, providing light service and ground support for scientific and recreational expeditions for Adventure Network International (ANI). During that time, I was involved with the following ascents: Minaret, a marble tower located 20 kilometers from Patriot Hills Base Camp. Alex Lowe, Steve Pinfield (camp manager, Patriot Hills) and I made the first ascent (IV 5.10 A0) on December 8. The climb involved loose rock, but generally was moderate with one 5.10 X (serious) pitch led by Alex. On December 14, Alex, Dave Hahn and I climbed Pyramid Peak (a.k.a. Peak Gyska after the first ascensionist who died in a glacier fall), a quartzite peak located on the northern end of the Patton Glacier. The climb was moderate scrambling for 1300 meters to a snow summit. A French military expedition had made the first ascent of this peak two weeks earlier. On December 16, on Mt. Tyree, the second highest peak in Antarctica, Alex Lowe and I climbed the *Grand Couloir* on the east face. The route was first climbed by a French Military team three weeks prior. Mt. Tyree's first ascent was in 1966; the second was made by Mugs Stump in November, 1989; the third, by the French; and the fourth by Alex and I. I made a repeat of the Grand Coliour, established by a French Military team three weeks prior. The climb involved 2400 meters of snow, ice and some rock scrambling. On Mt. Vinson, I did the standard route with a client (December 30), then climbed Mt. Shinn on New Year's Eve in -35°C+ wind-chill temperatures in two hours, 15 minutes. Anselme Baud (France) and I made a ski descent of the south ice stream on the west face (45-55°, 1900m) of a sub-peak of Mt. Vinson on January 2. (This sub-peak first was ascended by Jay Smith and Jo Bentley in the 1993-'94 season.) I then made a speed ascent (January 7) of the normal route on Vinson in nine hours 11 minutes round trip from Vinson Base Camp on the Branscomb Glacier in less than ideal weather. It's basically an intermediate ski run. On January, 15-16, I soloed Peak Loretan (5.8 80°) between Tyree and Epperly—2100 meters of alpine climbing on solid quartzite. (*A complete account of this climb appears earlier in this journal.*)

CONRAD ANKER

*Antarctica, Various Ascents.* The Norwegian pair of Patrick and Vika Gustaffson spent 17 days exploring the northern part of the Ellsworth mountains. They climbed four virgin peaks; they also climbed Mount Gardner via the original route, running out of food along the way only to discover the cache, left in 1966 by Nick Clinch's first ascent party. In the cache they found chocolate and pudding purchased in New Zealand—still edible, testimony to the continent's continuous cold.

CONRAD ANKER

*Mt. Vinson Area, Various Ascents.* On January 3, Viki Groselj, Stane Klemenc, Rafko Vodisek (Slovenia) and Stipe Bozic, Josko Bojic (Croatia) arrived in the Patriot Hills Base Camp. On

*The west face of Mt. Vinson, showing the 1993 Smith-Bentley line.* VICKI GROSELJ

the same day, we took a one-hour flight to Base Camp at the foot of Mount Vinson (4897m). On January 4, Bozic, Klemenc, Vodisek and I started up the 2000-meter west face of Mount Vinson at 3 p.m. On January 5, at 3 a.m., after a 12-hour ascent, we climbed to the edge of the face. Seven hours later, at 10 a.m., we reached the summit. The climb (45-55°, 2500m) took us 19 hours. (*This route was climbed by Jay Smith and Joe Bentley in 1993.-Ed.*)

Mount Vinson is the last of the seven summits to be conquered by Slovenes, by Croats, and by Bozic and myself. My ski descent from the summit to Base Camp took four hours. The relief was 2900 meters, at an angle of 30-40°; one third of the slope was 45-50°. Bozic, Klemenc and Vodisek completed their descent in eight hours.

On January 7, Bozic and I took three hours to make first ascents of two unnamed, ca.2850-meter summits above Base Camp; we descended from both on skis to Base Camp and named them Slovenia and Croatia.

On January 8, Bozic, Klemenc, Vodisek and I made an ascent of a ca.2650-meter summit above Base Camp and named it Matija. (*This peak is referred to as Ski Hill by the local guides and pilots and has been ascended previously.-Ed.*) After traversing the mountain, the party descended on skis. We then continued, crossing the glacier a few kilometers southward. The four of us climbed another unconquered and unnamed 2250-meter summit. Bozic and I descended on skis. Bozic returned to Base Camp while Klemenc, Vodisek and I proceeded to climb a third unnamed mountain, making a traverse of the mountain and a ski descent from the summit.

On January 9-10, we had unfavorable weather conditions. The next day Klemenc and I made a first ascent of another unnamed summit above Base Camp in three hours and a ski descent from this ca.2900-meter summit back to Base Camp. Another span of bad weather hit us from January 12-14. On the 15th, we flew from Base Camp at the foot of Mount Vinson to Patriot Hills Base Camp. Bozic, Klemenc, Vodisek and I crossed the 400-meter south face (50-55°) by three different routes and climbed to the east summit of the Patriot Mountain

Chain, which is 1210 meters high, then followed a ski descent to Base Camp on the east slope (40°). On January 16, Bozic, Klemenc and I climbed the 1200-meter west summit of the Patriot Mountain Chain, crossing its south face (50-55°). I made another ski descent along the ridge between the south face and the east face (45-50°). On January 18, we flew from Patriot Hills Base Camp to Punta Arenas.

VIKI GROSELJ, *Slovenian Alpine Club*

*Peak Shear, First Ascent, Mt. Tyree, Northeast Couloir, and Mt. Vinson, Tragedy.* The French High Mountaineering Military Group (GMHM) was in Antarctica this season. It established several new routes from a base camp on the Patton Glacier. P. De Choudens and B. Virelaude made the first ascent of Pic Shear (4050m) (D, 1500m). De Choudens and J.M. Gryska made the first ascent of the 2300-meter northeast couloir on Mt. Tyree (4852 m). J.M. Gryska and B. Virelaude took a spectacular fall on Mt. Vinson; Gryska died. A. De Choudens (27) succeeded this year on the north ridge of Everest without oxygen as well.

JEAN-MARC CLERC, *France*

# AFRICA

## KENYA

*Benny Back on the* Ice Window Route, *Mt. Kenya.* CAMERON BURNS

*Mt. Kenya, Various Ascents.* In late February, Benny Bach and I spent a month on Mt. Kenya, making ascents of several of the bigger summits (Batian, Nelion, Point John, Point Lenana) by their standard routes, then climbing several obscure but excellent routes, including the *Point John Couloir* and the *Point John Minor Original* route, which we thoroughly recommend. In getting to the major peaks, we followed various routes, but the most interesting was the Burguret Route. A rough bushwhack, the Burguret Route closely follows the route taken by Felice Benuzzi and his companions during World War II. Benuzzi's story is documented in the book *No Picnic on Mt. Kenya.*

While on the mountain, we were involved in the rescue of an African schoolteacher, who came down with altitude sickness at the Austrian Hut. We helped carry her from the Austrian Hut down to MacKinder's Camp. She recovered shortly thereafter.

CAMERON M. BURNS

## TANZANIA

*Killimanjaro, First Descent, and New Route.* On February 10, we left the Impala Hotel for the *Umbway* route, a drive of a few hours. The Umbway route is known to the local porters and guides as the *Whiskey* route because it is steeper and more technical than the normal route (the "*Coca-Cola*" route). Our plan was to make the first snowboard or ski descent of the mountain and to document it on video (Scott) and with photographs (Wade). As far as we could find out, Kilimanjaro had not had a true descent. Rumor had it that someone carried skis up the *Coca-Cola* route and put them on near the summit on the glacier for a few photos, took them off and walked down their route of ascent.

Once we got permits and porters, we began our ascent of Kilimanjaro. The snowboards were brought in under cover of darkness as "no pleasure devices" were now allowed on the flanks of Kilimanjaro. We hiked through dense jungle for about six hours before we made our

*Mt. Killimanjaro. The Heim Glacier is the large snowfield to the right.* Sick Day *takes one of the ephemeral ice lines on its left.* CAMERON BURNS

first camp at 9,650 feet. The next day, on the 11th, we hiked through moss-covered trees and, soon after, were treated to the sight of the giant groundcell trees, multi-headed trees found only at these elevations in Africa. We arrived at the Borranco Hut camp (12,800') then continued up to make a gear drop at an elevation of 14,800 feet. This would be our last camp with porters. Our mandatory "guide" had never been on the snows of Kilimanjaro. We would be going alpine style from there.

On the morning of the 13th, Jason woke early and told us he was sick and wouldn't be able to go up. We went down to Borranco camp, hoping the descent of 2,000 feet would be sufficient for him to recover. It was not, and on the morning of the 14th, Jason was escorted by our guide and a porter down to the Impala Hotel in Arusha, where he would try to recover and meet up with us when he was able.

That same day, Wade, Scott and I went back up to our camp at 14,800 feet, planning to begin the technical climbing up the Heim Glacier the next morning, going alpine style from there. After a couple hundred feet of ice climbing, Wade decided to go down and around the mountain on a more moderate route. Scott and I lowered Wade off the ice, then continued up. The route was much steeper and icier than it looked from the guide book; it had receded much over the years, and, in doing so, steepened. The climbing involved one grade V ice pitch. Scott and I made rapid progress to 17,800 feet, where we put up our small two-man tent. It snowed for about an hour soon after we got the tent up. I thought the snow might enable me to descend the icy slopes. The following morning, Scott and I set out for the top of Africa at about 6:30 a.m. and summitted at 8:30 a.m. Soon after we arrived on top, we saw Wade nearing the summit. He had been going for 28 hours with a two-hour nap via the *Arrow* route. We took a nap at the top before heading toward the Kersten Glacier (where I left my snowboard, not wanting to get our guide or porters in trouble for having a pleasure device).

Scott and I climbed the ice serac near the top for fun while Wade shot photos. The clouds were rolling through at high speed: beautiful and sunny one moment and no visibility the next.

I made the change from mountaineer to snowboarder by exchanging my crampons for a snowboard. I still was not convinced I would be able to hold an edge on the icy slopes below, but with ice axes in hand, I had to try. I made one turn and then continued down. Scott shot video as we went. Wade took a couple of photos at the top and descended the way he had come up.

Scott and I made it to our high camp after a couple of hours. The following morning, we packed up all our gear and continued the descent, this time with a full pack and cold, sore muscles. After a couple of scary turns, I finally got my rhythm and continued down. The crux of the descent was too steep and icy to hold an edge, so I took my back foot out of my board and put on one crampon. I then downclimbed for about 30 feet of 70° ice until the angle mellowed and I could snowboard again.

Back in camp, Scott and I planned on climbing an ice line that snaked its way down from the Heim Glacier. In the morning, Scott was sick and I set off alone. The route was fantastic. I belayed one pitch near the top and soloed the rest. I called it *Sick Day* (VI, 700m).

STEPHEN KOCH

*Kilimanjaro, Various Activity.* In January, my wife Ann Robertson and I made three complete traverses of Kilimanjaro, taking in six trekking/approach routes and three summit routes on Kibo in the process. They included the *Marangu, Machame, Mweka, Umbwe, Shira Plateau, Rongai, Western Breach, Barafu* and *Normal* routes. While we were on the mountain, a forest fire burned an estimated 150,000 acres on the southeast side of the mountain. When interviewed, Kilimanjaro National Park officials said they believed the fire was set by poachers.

CAMERON M BURNS

# EUROPE

## NORWAY

*Hemsedal and Laerdal Valleys, Various Ascents.* On March 13, Mark Wilford and I flew to Oslo for an ice climbing adventure. We climbed approximately 4,000 feet of ice over a seven-day period. Our first major climb was in the Hemsedal Valley. *The Hydnefossen* is a 600-foot (WI6) monster consisting of mostly vertical and overhanging ice. Ice chimneys and over-hangs, along with -10° wind chills, provided some very interesting climbing. This climb took us eight hours to complete, with Wilford leading the way. The descent time was three hours with miserable postholing most of the way down. After climbing some shorter routes we drove to the Laerdal Valley, where we were amazed at the number of long routes in the area. We started on the south side of the valley with a long route called *Seltunfossen* (III WI5, 1,300'). This straightforward route is located just off the highway. We soloed past the first 300 feet of mostly low angle climbing. We then used the full length of a 100-meter rope to climb the main flow in three long pitches of 80 to 90° ice. The two final pitches are of lower angle ice and not really worth the effort. We were interested in covering a lot of ground, so we drove farther north to the town of Otta, where we noticed a large flow just off the highway (name unknown). This climb had a fully mature pine tree growing right in the middle of the climb. This was another long route of easier climbing (WI5) for 1,000 feet. Most of the climb was moderate with one interesting pillar section accessed from a small cave. This climb gets sun all day. We then decided to drive to Sweden in search of more ice. Based on what little infor-mation we had, the town of Ostersund seemed to be the most practical option. The local climbing shop employees directed us to the Offerdal crags. This area is not impressive com-pared to the other areas. Most of the climbs are straightforward and short by Scandinavian standards, although we did manage to find a few interesting mixed lines. Mark then led the first ascent of what we named the *Betterhoser* (M5, 100'). With sore shoulders, we decided to be tourists for the last few days.

JAKE LATENDRESSE, *unaffiliated*

*Troll Wall, the Russian Route and Baltica.* During the last quarter century, the most difficult routes on the Troll Wall have been the 1965 *Norwegian Route* (VI 5.10 A3), the 1967 French *Diretissima* (VI 5.10 A4) and the 1972 *Arch Wall* (VI 5.11- A4+). Strikingly, no new route has been put up since then, even though there is quite enough space and relief on the wall. These and other considerations, such as easy access and financially affordable travel, convinced us to choose the Troll Wall as a climbing objective for the debut of a small Russian team and the beginning of a larger project: to establish a series of Russian routes on the world's most famous big walls outside the Former Soviet Union.

The initiator and leader of the project (called the "Russian Way: World Big Walls") was Alexander Odintsov from St. Petersburg. Team members included Igor Potanikin from St. Petersburg, Alexander Ruchkin from Omsk, Ivan Samoilenko from St. Petersburg, Ludmila Krestina of St. Petersburg, and Yurii Koshelenko from Rostov-on-Don. The team reconnoi-tered possible routes on the wall and, after several consultations with Norwegian moun-taineers, decided on two first ascents. On July 14, two pairs, Odintsov and Potanikin and Koshelenko and Ruchkin, started on the wall. Odintsov and Potanikin envisioned a diagonal route from left to right, beginning with an obvious 600-meter buttress and continued on the main wall, crossing the *Norwegian* and *Arch Wall* routes. The second pair's route stayed completely on the main wall between the *French* and *Arch Wall* routes, crossing them at some point, then going to the summit right of the *French Route*. After the first pitons were hammered, the two pairs worked absolutely autonomously.

Ruchkin and Koshelenko spent the first two days fixing several ropes and filming. Then, after two days of rest, they went up on July 17 and finished on July 25 at 8 p.m., getting ahead of the St. Petersburg pair. The route, called the *Russian Route* (VI 5.10 A4, 1100 m) took eight and a half days. At the same time, Potanikin and Odintsov worked on the quite difficult overhanging buttress before reaching the main wall. Loose rock caused several leader falls. In total, they took seven days to complete nine pitches on the buttress.

When the *Russian Route* was completed, Odintsov and Potanikin were about to start, but a rainy week stopped them. They finally started on August 1, getting through the nine fixed pitches and leading three more the same day. They completed the climb, *Baltica* (VI 5.11-A3+, 1300m), in seven and a half days, finishing on August 8, a day of glory for the common success of the Russian teams.

Both pairs used the same tactics: the leader went ahead on a double rope, the portaledge was transported in a backpack by the second climber, haulbags were pulled up by the leader and the two slept at the end of the last completed pitch. The leaders changed every day. Both groups took about 30-35 liters of water. The major technical difficulties were loose overhanging terrain and cracks that were overgrown with grass and moss. For instance, on the *Russian Route*, tens of kilograms of turf were removed from some cracks.

These two new routes are comparable and somewhat superior to the hardest existing ones on the wall. They are the first contribution of Russian mountaineers to big-wall ascents abroad, outside the boundaries of the Former Soviet Union. Both climbs were announced for participation in the Russian Mountaineering Championships.

YURII KOSHELENKO, *Russia*

*The Shield, Attempt.* My Norwegian climbing trip this summer was a surprise and a disappointment. First I flew to Oslow and spent three days gathering a team that consisted of me and two Swedish climbers, Ludde Hagberg and a friend of his named Marco. I had climbed several routes on El Capitan with Ludde two summers ago; Marco was a climbing partner of his.

We made contact with what were said to be most of the experts on Kjerag climbing. They were all in agreement: "The Shield in Kjerag is the greatest unclimbed feature in Norway." They reported the route as being 1000 meters tall, severely overhanging at its top and having some of the highest quality rock in Norway. Most of my own big-wall climbing has been in Yosemite, so I began dreaming of El Cap-like walls. When we arrived at the base of the cliff, I was shaken to discover a completely different reality. The wall was technically more than 3,000 feet tall, but the bottom 2,000 feet were not only low angle but were covered in grass and trees! Even worse, the upper 1,000 feet, although steep and impressive, appeared blank. Despite our letdown, no one said anything. This was "the prize" of big-wall climbing in Norway and we couldn't expect to find anything better.

The route had already been attempted by the late Aischan Rupp and a partner, but for reasons unknown, the pair had bailed after reaching the steep section. We set out and, after spending three days leading 5.10 jungle pitches in 30 minutes and then spending four hours hauling them, we arrived at the base of the steep section. There, we discovered why the pair had bailed. They must have hoped—as we had—that linkable features would appear. But

*Ludde Hagberg jugging up the initial (heavily vegetated) pitches on the Shield.* CHRIS MACNAMARA

after climbing only 50 feet and having to drill more and more frequently, it became clear they wouldn't.

First we wondered if we had enough drilling equipment to get through The Shield. But a more important consideration was whether it was worth drilling that many holes in a country that historically embraces as clean a passage as possible. We bailed.

Aischan reportedly called The Shield the "hardest big wall in the world," implying that it was possible not to drill but instead to hook, beak and head a passage through the featureless rock. Maybe this will be the case someday—though at current levels of equipment and sanity, it will be some time in the future.

CHRIS MCNAMARA, *unaffiliated*

## SLOVAKIA

*High Tatras, Ridge Traverse.* In January, Vlado Plulik made a solo traverse of the main ridge of the High Tatras in Slovakia. He had tried to climb the ridge in winter for the first time in 1992. His idea was to climb this problem non-stop very quickly with minimal gear. Many attempts with partners left him more and more experienced. The final problem was weather. Finally, in January, a stable weather system arrived in the High Tatras. Plulik started the climb on Thursday, January 16 at 2:30 p.m., alone, without support, from the Kopske Col (the starting point for the main ridge for an east-to-west traverse. He reached the first crux of the main ridge Ostry Peak at 1 a.m., climbing it in climbing shoes. By dusk, he had climbed the very dangerous ridge of Batizovsky Peak and reached Popradsky Ladovy Peak in the middle of the main ridge. The batteries to his headlamp were dead and he had to climb the next crux, Zlobiv·and Rumanov peaks, by the slight light of the moon. By midnight, he was tired and waited for dawn in the Rumanove Col. The next morning, he decided to omit the difficult Ganek. His progress was very good and he quickly climbed through Vysok· and Rysy to the next rock crux, Zabi kon (Frogg's Horse), climbing it in light shoes. By dusk, he had overcome the final problem, the Mengusovsky Peaks, and reached Cubrina. He was unfamiliar with the last part of the main ridge from Cubrina to Laliove Col and thought it would be easy. But after many hours of hard climbing, his hands were bloody. By midnight, at the very end of the main ridge, close to Svinica, he had to wait until dawn because of exhaustion and dis-

orientation. Finally, on Sunday, he reached Laliove Col in one hour's time.

The main ridge of the High Tatras is 26 kilometers long with much hard climbing, an altitude difference of about 7000 meters and comprising 90 main peaks. Plulik's solo achievement was accomplished in only 50 hours of actual climbing. It is without a doubt one of the best achievements in the history of High Tatras mountaineering.

VLADO LINEK, *Jamesak*

# ASIA

## BURMA

*Hkakbo Razi, First Ascent.* It was reported that Nyama Gyaltsen from Burma and Takashai Ozaki from Japan made the successful first ascent of Hkakbo Razi (5881m), the previously unclimbed highest summit of Burma and the mountain marking the easternmost point of the Himalayan chain, in 1996. The ascent was the culmination of four years of work by Ozaki, who had begun negotiations for permission to climb the mountain in 1993, then spent 30 days walking in to the north side of the mountain in the winter of 1994-'95 with his ten-year-old son and a major from the Myanmar (Burma) Hiking and Mountaineering Federation. That attempt ended a day from base camp when bad weather and avalanche danger prevented them from even seeing the mountain.

In the summer of 1995, Ozaki returned with his French wife, his son and daughter, six Burmese team members and a Japanese film crew. They followed their approach of the year before, using machetes to reach the north side of the peak in early August. An Advanced Base Camp was established on the moraine at 3900 meters. Rope was fixed to Camp I (4300m) and then to Camp II (5100m). The climbing featured poor granite, avalanche danger and difficult route-finding; Ozaki and Gyaltsen made it 100 meters above CII before abandoning their attempt.

In July, 1996, they returned, using the same 30-day approach to arrive at BC on August 20. The two re-achieved their high point, then were forced to climb a dangerous hanging glacier to reach the summit ridge, which had many rock sections with climbing up to V+/VI. Camp III was established at 5400 meters and, on September 4, the pair reached a snow dome on the ridge. It had been snowing every day and continued to do so. A faulty stove forced them to return to base camp, and a porter was sent the 60 kilometers to the last village to retrieve their spare high-altitude stove. Gyaltsen and Ozaki returned to CII on September 12, were confined to CIII by heavy weather on the 13th and 14th, and set out for the summit on the 15th. The final 250 meters of climbing presented them with eight pitches of up to V+/VI. A final 50-55° snow slope brought them to the highest point. They made it back to base in time to pack up and leave on September 17. (*High Mountain Sports* 178)

## INDIA

*Environmental Security Deposit and Environmental Fees for Expeditions.* Col. J. P. Bhagatjee, Director of the Indian Mountaineering Foundation, states that the IMF does not take require environmental security deposits from visiting expeditions. However, non-refundable environmental "levies" of US$400 are being charged for expeditions with a maximum number of 16 members.

## GARHWAL - KUMAON

*Srikanta, All-Women's Ascent.* A 12-members all-women's expedition from Uttarkashi, India, led by Chandra Prabha Aitwal, approached Srikanta (6133m) in September, establishing base camp at 4000 meters ahead of Jangla in the Dudu Bamak. After setting up three camps, the summit was reached via the north ridge on September 27. The summitters were Suman Kutiyal, Lata Joshi, Nari Dhami, Radha Rana and Kavita Budhathoki. The second attempt was foiled by bad weather. This climb was the first of the peak since 1984.

HARISH KAPADIA, *Honorary Editor, The Himalayan Journal*

*Shivling, Attempt.* Satyendra Rana led a five-member Himalayan Alpine Adventure Club from Delhi to Shivling (6543m). Continuous rockfall on the summit ridge compelled the expedition to be called off on July 5.

HARISH KAPADIA, *Honorary Editor, The Himalayan Journal*

*Changabang, North Face, Ascent and Tragedy.* In May and June, a six-member British team climbing in pairs attempted the north face of Changabang (6864m). Andy Cave and Brendan Murphy summitted, while Mick Fowler and Steve Sustad reached the summit ridge only to suffer a fall down the south face that left them unable to continue to the top. The two pairs joined forces for the descent. Brendan Murphy was killed when an avalanche swept him off the face. A full account of the climb appears earlier in this journal.

*Thalay Sagar, North Face, Ascent.* Athol Whimp and Andrew Lindblade (Australia) made the first integral ascent of the north face (VII 5.9 WI5, 4,950') of Thalay Sagar (22,650') from September 13-20, climbing through the shale bands at the top that had repulsed all attempts in the past. A full account of this climb appears earlier in this journal.

*Suitilla, Attempt.* A five-member Sahyagiri Trekkers expedition from Mumbai, led by Makarand Pendse, attempted Suitilla (6373m), an unclimbed peak in the eastern Kumaon that rises from the Yangchar Glacier (near the Kalabaland Glacier and Ralam Pass). The five-day approach march from Munsiary took almost two weeks due to landslides, bad weather and porter desertion. Base camp was set up (ahead of the village of Ralam) on the Yangchar glacier on September 14. They decided to attempt the peak from the southwest. An advance base camp was set up below the southern icefall on September 18. For the next six days, they opened the route through the 610-meter icefall to the base of the southwest rib in heavy snowfall. The high point (5800m), which was the proposed site of Camp II, was reached on September 27, but the attempt was abandoned due to another long spell of bad weather.

HARISH KAPADIA, *Honorary Editor, The Himalayan Journal*

## LAHAUL-SPITI

*Fluted Peak, Ascent.* K. P. Mitra led a ten-member expedition from Bengal, India, to Fluted Peak (6122 m), climbing it on July 12. This is a well-known peak on the Losar nala, Spiti. The summitters were: Uttam Das, Ajit Biswas, Ashok Adhikari, Narendra Nath Dutta and

Tashi Chhopel.

HARISH KAPADIA, *Honorary Editor, The Himalayan Journal*

*Peak 6100m, Ascent.* A seven-member expedition from Bengal, India, led by Himadri Shekhar Bose, climbed an unnamed peak of 6100 meters near Kali nala, Losar area. The peak was climbed on August 31 by Soumen Deoghoria, Bijan Dey and Chhering Palden Bodh. Their attempt on nearby Peak 6163m failed.

HARISH KAPADIA, *Honorary Editor, The Himalayan Journal*

*Traverse of the Himalaya.* Bachendri Pal (the first Indian woman to climb Everest and a member of the Indian Mountaineering Foundation) led the Indian Women's First Trans-Himalayan Journey, which made a successful traverse of the entire Himalayan chain from the Arunachal Pradesh to the East Karakoram. Team members Chawla Jagirdar, Chetna Sahu, Vineeta Muni, Sumita Roy, Nanda Patel, Malika Virdi and M. Kokila Sudha went across Bhutan, Sikkim, Nepal, Kumaon, Garhwal, Kinnaur, Spiti and the Ladakh Himalaya to finish their trek by reaching the Indira Col at the head of the Siachen glacier on September 2. This traverse was organized in accordance with India's 50th year of freedom celebration.

Three members of the group, Vineeta Muni, Sumita Roy and Malika Virdi, went separately from Kumaon and completed their trek under a separate name and banner. They completed their traverse by reaching the Karakoram Pass on August 20.

HARISH KAPADIA, *Honorary Editor, The Himalayan Journal*

*Winter Traverse of the Indian Himalaya.* From January 27 to February 21, Susie Patterson and Ned Gillette went from Leh to Zanskar to Manali, covering about 225 miles and crossing three mountain ranges: Zanskar, Great Himalaya and Pir Panjal. It was a very cold winter with less snow than any local could remember. This was lucky and worked to our advantage; the rivers were nicely frozen, yet the walking usually did not demand major trail breaking.

We hired a 4WD taxi and drove from Leh to Nimmu west along the Indus River, then 15 miles south up the Zanskar River to the village of Chiling. There was no snow on the ground. With three Zankari porters who we'd hired in Leh, we walked for six days up the sometimes more, sometimes less frozen Zanskar River to Padam. It was fascinating to learn to read the ice on the big, swift river and decide what was safe. We all got our feet wet at times but nobody fell in. We slept in caves. Night-time temperatures were -20° to -30°F. There is no permanent trail through most of this spectacular gorge and it is only walkable in winter. For centuries, this route has been the only way in or out of Zanskar during winter months. Although we saw several groups of Zanskaris traveling on the frozen river, we saw no other Westerners during this or any other part of the trip.

From Padam, we veered southeast up the Tsarap Lingti River, then south up the increasingly small Kargyak (Kurgiakh) River to Kargyak, the last village, at 4000 meters. All along this part, we were welcomed into houses, where we slept and ate. The great thing about being here at this time of the year was that we had the place and the people all to ourselves. It was a magical journey. Our porters turned back from Kargyak, saying, "Ahead OK in summer; never in winter." We waited out bad weather, then the two of us continued on our own. The weather deteriorated and we had a very difficult time guessing which canyon led up toward the Shingu La (5100m). Suddenly, the snow was deep and hid all traces of the summer trail. For the first time, we strapped on our lightweight MSR snowshoes over our Sorel shoepacks.

"Crampon" teeth on the bottom of the snowshoes allowed us to climb up icy cascades. We lucked out and, at dark, stumbled upon a rock-walled shepherd's hut that the locals had told us about. At least we knew we were going right. The storm pinned us down for two nights. We wondered if we'd get skunked this close to getting over the key pass.

On February 11, it was very cold and windy but clear. We raced through the narrow throat at the bottom of the pass, which was clogged by the debris of a huge slab avalanche that had let loose the day before. A gradual climb on windslab led us to the top of the Shingu La. We dropped down the south side and out of the wind. We figured it'd be a cake walk from here, but the snow was deep and it was hard going even downhill, with many detours to minimize the constant threat of avalanches. Temperatures now were warmer. I made a dumb mistake and fell through rotten ice into the river; Susie hauled me out. After four days, we came to Rarig, the first village, where people were wide-eyed to see us coming from the north. At Darcha, we joined the snow-covered Leh to Manali highway and followed it for several days, finishing up by crossing the Rohtang Pass at 3978 meters and descending into Manali, which looked and felt like the tropics. It was a wonderful trip for a husband and wife to do together.

NED GILETTE

# NEPAL

*Newly Opened Peaks in the Nepal Himalaya.* The Ministry of Tourism has opened 19 of the less popular Expeditions Peaks to mark the celebration of Visit Nepal Year 1998. These peaks are free of charge in 1998 and 1999, though a Sirdar and permission from the Nepal Mountaineering Association still are required.

1.  Changla (6563m)
2.  Nala Kankar (6062m)
3.  Jethi Bahurani (6850m)
4.  Tripura Hiunchuli (6563m)
5.  Hongde (6556m)
6.  Jagdula Peak (5764m)
7.  Shey Shikhar (6139m)
8.  Kande Hiunchuli (6627m)
9.  Kanjiroba (6883m)
10.  Nampa (6755m)
11.  Sisne (5849m)
12.  Fimkof West (6645m)
13.  Nampa South (6580m)
14.  Raksha Urai (6593m)
15.  Saipal East (6882m)
16.  Surma Sarovar (6523m)
17.  Tso Karpo (6518m)
18.  Kagmara (5960m)
19.  Api West (7100m)

The following peaks are free from peak fees and the need for a Liason Officer in 1999, though permission from the Ministry of Tourism still is required.

| | |
|---|---|
| Naya Kanga* (5863m) | Rasua District |
| Yala Peak (5732m) | Rasua District |
| Chhukungri (5550m) | Solukhumbu District |
| Gokyo Ri (5450m) | Solukhumbu District |
| Rambrong (4499m) | Lamjung District |
| Dama (6855m) | Taplejung District |
| Ramchaur (4500m) | Taplejung District |
| Ramtang (6601m) | Taplejung District |
| Tengkoma (6215m) | Taplejung District |
| Kangtokla (6294m) | Dolpo District |

*As we go to press, Naya Kanga has been deleted from the list. We are not sure of its status at this time. Please check with the Ministry of Tourism before making any arrangements.*

*Union Internationale Des Associations D'Alpinisme (UIAA) Recommended Code of Practice for High Altitude Guided Commercial Expeditions.* The UIAA has adopted the following recommendations for high altitude guided expeditions:

1. Definition. This code applies specifically to commercial operators attempting 8000-meter or other comparable peaks that offer to guide or accompany climbers above base camp and to operators who offer more limited facilities. It also may concern operators who supply transport, etc. to base camp, and that also may supply base camp services and High Altitude Porters.

2. Rationale. A variety of organizations offer to take clients on 8000-meter peaks. They vary from those that provide a full service to the summit or nearly to the summit, to those that offer minimal support for clients above base camp. At the present moment, however, it is difficult for clients to deduce from brochures exactly what is offered in terms of guiding and support, and whether it corresponds to their needs. This code supplies clients with pointers to assist them in making an informed choice.

3. High Altitude Warning. Mountaineers climbing at very high altitude, especially above 8000 meters, are at the limit of their mental and physical powers and may not be capable of assisting others as has always been traditional in mountaineering. This fact is of particular importance to mountaineers of limited experience who rely on professional guides to bring them safely up and down 8000-meter peaks. They should be made aware that the risks involved in climbing 8000-meter peaks are such that a high degree of self-reliance is always necessary.

The Code

1. The leader or chief guide and as many as possible of the guides should have high-altitude experience appropriate to the altitude of the peak to be climbed. There is no qualification appropriate to high-altitude guiding, so the term "guide" does not imply that the person holds a professional qualification. Clients can judge only from the previous experience of the guides, who may be Westerners, Sherpas or other local mountaineers.

2. The guiding and portering staff on the mountain and the material supplied must be adequate for the aims of the party and stated level of service offered.

3. A doctor in the party is very desirable, but at the very least, advance arrangements must be made for medical help. Advance arrangements also must be made for evacuation assistance in case of emergency.

4. The minimum safety equipment available must be walkie-talkie radios and recommended medical supplies.

5. Advertising must give a true picture of all the difficulties and dangers involved and avoid promising the impossible. Biographical information about the guiding team should be included.

6. The client must truthfully reveal his experience, medical history, etc., to the organizer so that the organizer can make an informed choice about the potential client.

7. Information supplied in advance should include a clear statement of the guiding, porterage and equipment which will be supplied by the organizer, together with details of the clothing and equipment to be supplied by the client.

8. Operators and clients must take account of the UIAA Environmental Objectives and Guidelines and follow the UIAA Expeditions Code of Ethics.

THE UIAA EXPEDITIONS COMMITTEE

*Nemjung*. It was reported that a nine-man French team led by Jean Paul Bouquier reached 6410 meters on the west ridge of Nemjung (7140m) via the north flank before poor weather called a halt to their expedition. (*High Mountain Sports* 179)

*Raksha Urai Massif, First Attempt*. In far western Nepal, a team of 14 Austrians had some difficulty getting through a very deep gorge to their virgin massif of Raksha Urai, which is east of two better-known mountains, Api and Nampa, and west-northwest of the more distant Saipal. No climbers are known to ever have attempted Raksha Urai, which has six summits between about 6500 and 6600 meters high. The Austrians, led by Guenther Mussnig, were told at the Dhula village police checkpost nearest to their mountain that they were the first foreigners ever seen at the post.

The Austrians reported that four of Raksha Urai's peaks are entirely composed of unstable rock, while the other two are snow domes with an ice face or ice ridge below. This expedition was unable to make much climbing progress because of unstable snow on the lower slopes and avalanches "everywhere" from frequent new snowfall while they were there in the first half of October. Their attempts to climb two of the peaks got no higher than 5100 and 5200 meters.

ELIZABETH HAWLEY

*Annapurna, Attempt and Tragedy*. On December 2, Anatoli Boukreev and I, accompanied by the alpinist and videographer Dimitri Sobolev, flew by helicopter from the last lodge to a base camp at 4095 meters. A long glacier separated us from the beginning of Annapurna's south face and the traditional Base Camp, where, due to the abundant snow in which the helicopter would have "sunk," it had not been possible to land. We were forced to break trail along the glacier to get to the base of the face, an exhausting task compounded by much new and abundant snows.

Our stay on the mountain continued to be christened by snowfall that accumulated to four meters. This forced us to change our climbing itinerary (though we kept the summit of Annapurna I as our final objective). The new line of ascent we picked wound its way up the steep east face of Annapurna Fang (7847m) to the line of notches situated between this summit and that of Annapurna II. Once we reached this col we would be able to make a long traverse along the ridge that would bring us to the summit of Annapurna Fang (which is avoidable) and then on to that of Annapurna I. A new itinerary, possibly more difficult, surely longer than an ascent via the Bonington route but, in our minds, much safer given the conditions.

We grew accustomed to proceeding with snow up to our bellies and with packs weighing as much as 34 kilos. On December 25, we began a constant advance in piolet traction on fine mixed terrain to reach the ridge. As we had agreed, I led and equipped the most technically demanding pitches. Thus, after an hour's climb, Anatoli made a small stance for himself on the slope to deal with the unspooling and joining of the rope coils as I slowly dragged them toward the ridge.

After a couple of hours, I was about 50 to 70 meters from the exit onto the ridge at 6300 meters, but a yell from Anatoli announced the end of the last coil of rope. He suggested I set up an anchor to fix the long umbilical cord that connected us. I carried out the task and, given the high difficulty of the last section remaining to be climbed, I decided to wait for him, who now had been joined by Dimitri.

I spent the first few minutes filming and photographing my two friends, then concerned myself with putting the video camera away in my pack so I could get my gloves back on. In the time it took to think of doing this, but before I actually could begin, I realized the moment of my death was silently approaching.

Blocks of ice and rock in a cloud of snow were falling down on me. In a state of animated "peaceful resignation," I thought only of yelling out the danger to Anatoli and Dimitri. I remember seeing them make a rapid lateral move in an attempt to get out of the way of the avalanche while I crouched and leaned against the wall, gripping with my bare hands the rope that had just been fixed.

I wasn't able to resist the fury of this mass for even a second, and I fell rapidly, grasping the rope between my hands as it burned and lacerated my fingers almost through to the bone. The series of flights, slides and ricochets seemed like they would never end. All I could do was go along with the movement of the avalanche, often tumbling at break-neck speed and losing orientation.

It was 12:37 when I stopped, half-buried in the snow, at 5500 meters. I could not see out of one eye, my hands were stripped to the bone, my clothes were in shreds, and I had lost all my equipment except for my crampons. I immediately called Anatoli and Dimitri many times but no one answered. I staggered about in the avalanche for about 15 minutes without seeing or hearing anything from them.

I was alive, but unsure of my survival given the conditions and the 1500 meters of wall yet to descend before getting to Base Camp. There, I would be able to organize the rescue that I knew would arrive within a few days' wait.

Good fortune willed that only 50 meters from the avalanche stood our Camp I tent, inside which I had a supply of clothing. After exhaustingly redressing, I started the long, dramatic descent without use of my hands and able to see out of only one eye. After six hours, I arrived exhausted at the 4095-meter Base Camp where my Nepalese cook attended to me, ignorant of what had just happened. Thanks to his nocturnal walk of more than ten hours to a village, and the subsequent radio contact with a friend, Nima, from Cho Oyu, who was trekking in Kathmandu, I was able to take advantage of the help of a helicopter that came and got me on

December 26 at Base Camp.

Three days later, I was once again in a helicopter trying to fly over the avalanche and possibly see my friends still alive. Unfortunately, there still is no trace of them today, apart from what remains of Anatoli in the pages of the history of alpinism.

SIMONE MORO, *Italy*

*Dhaulagiri VII, North-Northeast Face. (This first-hand account supplements the notes written on page 304 by Elizabeth Hawley in last year's* Journal.) The Singapore Dhaulagiri VII Expedition, which I led, took place from September 26-October 27, 1996. We made the approach via Dunai, trekking east through Tarakot and along the Barbung Khola river. Heavy snow on the trek delayed progress as the team began moving south and up along the flanks of the Kaya Khola. Base camp (4500m) was reached six days later. Dhaulagiri VII, also known as Putha Hiunchuli, has seen few attempts by the north-northeast face since its first ascent by the route in 1954, and none since 1978.

The route began with a long march over moraines and some dry glaciated stretches. It steepened as a broad shoulder was climbed from Camp I. There were vertical rock and ice bands on both sides of this shoulder, so the route on the northeast face was rather obvious. The shoulder linked the lower snow slopes to the upper terrace. Camp II at 5900 meters was placed just beyond the skyline. After that, broad, featureless, gentle slopes lead to a short summit ridge, which runs from left to right (as seen while on the northeast face) to the summit, a small snow dome. We used no fixed rope and all climbing was done unroped. Camps were placed at 5300, 5900, and 6300 meters over the period of October 7-13. The only other party on the rarely climbed route was a French party comprising about six professional guides and an equal number of Sherpas. The initial advance party of Y. J. Mok, R. Goh, M. B. Tamang and Mingma Sherpa were poised for a summit attempt on the 13th, but strong windstorms on the nights of October 14-16 and an extended period at 6300 meters made them fall back to BC. The support team of S.C. Khoo and I moved up from the 5900-meter camp to the 6300-meter camp on the 15th.

The two Sherpas rejoined us and we went for the top on the 16th. Despite the successful French ascent days earlier, there were no traces of a trail owing to the week's windstorms. We reached the summit at about 12:45 p.m. after six hours of climbing on mainly soft, crusted snow. Ours was the fourth ascent of the peak by this route.

On October 18-19, after all the camps had been taken down, R. Goh and M. B. Tamang climbed from Base Camp to the summit and back in a round trip of about 36 hours. Dhaulagiri VII is the first 7000er climbed by a team from Singapore and, at the time of writing, the highest peak to be climbed by climbers from the tropical island. The team comprised: D. Lim, S. C. Khoo, R. Goh, Y. J. Mok, S. Yogenthiran, M. Sherpa and M. B. Tamang.

DAVE LIM, *Singapore*

*Tukuche, Ascent and Attempts.* It was reported that three teams attempted Tukuche (6920m) in the pre-monsoon. Bart Vos (NL) made the first ascent when he climbed the northwest ridge from the French Pass on April 10. Dutch climber Aad Buijtendijk and partner relied heavily on Sherpa support later in the season but were able to reach only 6300 meters by May 1. A ten-member Australian team attempting the same line reached the south summit on May 3 but were unable to progress farther. (*High Mountain Sports* 179)

*Nepal, Various Winter Ascents.* In the winter of 1996-97, only four expeditions came to Nepal, one each on Ama Dablam, Annapurna I, Makalu and Pumori. One Korean expedition, led by Park Young-Seok, reported success on Ama Dablam by its standard Southwest Ridge route; another, led by Um Hong-Gil, reached 6850 meters on the Dutch North Rib of Annapurna I; and a Manuel Gonzalez-led Spanish expedition reached 7200 meters on Makalu's northwest ridge. But the more interesting ascent of the season was accomplished by a six-man French team led by Christophe Profit on 7161-meter Pumori. First, Profit and a colleague scaled the mountain by its normal Southeast Face route. Then they went around to Pumori's south pillar, which had not been climbed since its first ascent in 1972. Profit and three teammates followed this pillar much of the way but then moved over to the right up an ice gully. It was a difficult climb with several steps of vertical rock, but they accomplished their ascent without fixed camps, fixed ropes or Sherpas. (They went down by the normal route since they had fixed no rope for a descent by the pillar.) Altogether, it was "a very nice adventure," Profit said with quiet satisfaction.

ELIZABETH HAWLEY

*Manaslu, Ascents and Tragedies.* Peter Sperka, an experienced mountaineer and ski alpinist from the High Tatras, organized the Slovak expedition to Manaslu (8163m). They had bad weather and conditions. In spite of this, they pitched Camp III at 7400 meters, where mountaineers from Spain and Japan were also camped. Three Slovakian climbers (Peter Sperka, Miroslav Rybansky and Juraj Kardhordo) waited there for better conditions, which had been promised by the Sherpas. In the morning of October 8, the weather cleared up and all climbers set off for the summit. The Slovak climbers were last. Juraj Kardhordo, who three months earlier had summitted GI and GII, was slowest. During the expedition, he suffered from slight stomach problems. The Spanish climbers reached the summit first at 2 p.m., then the Japanese climbers, using oxygen. Just before 5 p.m., Peter Sperka, together with one Spaniard, reached the summit of Manaslu, half an hour after Miro Rybansky from Spisska Nova Ves. During the descent, they met Juraj Kardhordo. Sperka tried to persuade Juraj not to continue to the summit because of the late hour. But Juraj felt OK and continued. Rybansky met him 150 meters from the summit at the beginning of fixed ropes leading to the sharp ridge. He was the last to see him alive. Juraj did not return to the last camp, and the next day, the Japanese found his ski pole and his bag at the beginning of the fixed ropes. Sperka is convinced that Juraj made it to the top of Manaslu, and probably fell from the sharp ridge because of very strong winds in an area where there were no fixed ropes.

The descent from Camp III in deep snow was very dangerous. Both of our mountaineers suffered frostbite, but walked together with the Spanish and Japanese climbers nonetheless. But the tragedy of our expedition was not finished yet. Miro Rybansky died suddenly at the fixed ropes. It was probably a sudden heart attack or a collapse from total exhaustion after a long stay at high altitude. This is a cruel price for the summit of Manaslu.

VLADIMIR LINEK, *Jamesak*

*Manaslu, First American Ascent, and Last 8000er to be Climbed by an American.* On September 11, on Manaslu's standard Northeast Face route, Dr. Alan McPherson Jr. (British) and I placed Camp I at 5800 meters above the rock band south of the Naike Col. We spent our first night at Camp II (6850m) on September 20. Because of the ice-fall danger, we limited our forays between Camps I and II, deciding to spend more time acclimating down low before pushing high. Camp II was placed in a sheltered spot below a serac wall, just under the exposed North Col. Camp III was placed at 7500 meters, amongst some rocks on the edge of the sum-

*Manaslu.* CHARLEY MACE

mit "plateau" on September 26. The next day, 18 days after arriving in base camp, we left the tent at 6:30 a.m., summitted at 12:30, spent two hours on the summit, descended to Camp III in one hour, spent an hour packing up the tent, and another hour descending to Camp II. The next day, we collected all of our remaining equipment and returned to base camp (5160m).

While we are both very happy with the ascent, we are most proud of the style in which we climbed. The trip came together very quickly with about a month's total planning. Ours was a small team of only two climbers and one base camp cook. We traveled light and fast, with a minimum of impact. We used no radios, oxygen or Sherpas. We used mostly locally purchased foods, the exceptions being two stuff sacks of PowerBars and Power Gel, and one bottle of duty free. We removed all of our garbage from the hill, including spent fuel cartridges.

CHARLEY MACE

*Kwangde Shar, Northeast Spur, Attempt.* It was reported that a British team led by Phil Wicken had hoped to make an ascent of Kwangde Nup (6035m), but unstable weather forced them to change their objective to the northeast spur of Kwangde Shar. They reported very fine rock climbing around gendarmes on the crest of their route, but bad weather stopped their attempt. (*High Mountain Sports* 179)

*Ama Dablam, West Ridge.* Second place in the High Altitude Class of the Russian Climbing Competitions went to the team consisting of B. Ceducov (leader), E. Vinogradskie, N. Zakapov, V. Kapataev, A. Karlov, V. Lebedev, V. Pershin, and G. Tortladze for an ascent of Ama Dablam. The climbers traveled from Kathmandu to Lukla by helicopter, then by caravan through Namche Bazaar, Tyangboche and Pangboche to base camp at 4500 meters beneath the west face of Ama Dablam. On the ridge were numerous cornices and snowy mushrooms. The danger of the crumbling cornices took away the climbers' physical and mental strength. One participant was blown by the wind like a spruce tree, characteristic of the Himalaya's steep, snowy landscape. The team also included Vladimer Laratayev from Divnogarsk, who had a few amputated fingers and toes.

VLADIMIR SHATAEV, *Russian Mountaineering Federation*

*Nepalese Himalaya, Various Activity in the Post-Monsoon Season.* On Ama Dablam, 72 climbers from all but one of 12 teams summitted via the same narrow southwest ridge; there were so many people on the ridge that they had to pitch their tents at odd spots up and down the route or skip some camps altogether.

Several expeditions this autumn came in for criticism for poor leadership or organization. A disastrous attempt by four Czechs and three Slovakians on Pumori ended in the fatal fall (*see below*) by three only moderately skilled Slovakians. They had been climbing without Sherpas and during the absence of their sick Czech leader, Michael Brunner, who was not a professional guide in any case. A Spaniard at a nearby base camp praised the Slovenians and Mexican for an astonishingly fast climb to rescue the man who survived; they are credited with saving his life.

ELIZABETH HAWLEY

*Pumori, Attempt and Tragedy.* Along with the Czech trekkers, the Czech Trekking Expedition CK Montana consisted of four Slovaks: Dusan Myslivec and Peter Lenco from the town of Nitra, and Pavol Dzurman and Frantisek Miscak from Presov. The goal for the Slovak mountaineers was to make the first ascent of the southeast face of Pumori (7161m). They worked with Slovenian climbers Janez Jeglič and Tomaž Humar, who planned to make a new route, and who wanted to link up with our mountaineers on the upper part of the wall. For acclimatization, the four Slovak climbers wanted to approach the col by the Normal Route and leave a tent there for the descent after finishing the new route. Dusan Myslivec came down with health problems; the best member of the Czech trekking group, Milos Kijonka, then joined the team. In October, after reaching the col at 6500 meters, they decided to climb to the top of Pumori. All four climbers were on the same rope. About 150 meters above the col on the ice wall, one of them probably fell and the rest were pulled with him. They stopped on a broad col (they did not fall into Tibet as reported). Peter Lenco, Pavol Dzurman and Frantisek Miscak died. Only Milos Kijonka survived. It is very hard to say what happened. Such a fall could occur in the Alps or in the High Tatras as well. Climbing four on a rope on moderate terrain was not a good idea. In such circumstances it probably is better to climb alone or to protect oneself more. Regardless, our young mountaineers are still dead.

VLADIMIR LINEK, *Jamesak*

*Everest in the Pre-Monsoon.* On Everest this spring there fortunately was no such dramatic disaster as the fatal storm of May 1996, although the Internet and other communications media led the public to believe there was. Sadly, a total of eight people did die while climbing with the 12 expeditions on Nepal's side and 16 teams and splinter groups in Tibet. But the Internet reported five Kazakhs had died in a storm when actually three Russians had died on one day (though not because of the weather; one fell and two were victims of the altitude). A New Zealand radio station even broadcast an item saying that it was seven New Zealanders who had died together; actually there were not seven New Zealanders among all the climbers on all the expeditions on the mountain, and not one of those who were there had any kind of accident.

By now, following all the publication of misinformation last spring and this, it is clear that instant reporting about Everest developments is quite unreliable and sometimes irresponsible. The radio station apologized later for its mistake, which had understandably caused great distress to the families of the New Zealanders who were on Everest.

The total number of people who have stood at the highest point on earth now has passed the 700-mark. This spring a total of 86 men and women reached the 8848-meter summit. They brought to 726 the total number of people who have now summited Everest since 1953, and to 932 the total number of ascents that these climbers have made.

Thirty-six of this spring's summitters had been there at least once before. All except one of these repeaters, a Mexican surgeon, were professional climbers: five were foreign guides with commercial expeditions, and 25 were Nepalese Sherpas.

Of course, Mount Everest attracts some not-so-highly-skilled amateur climbers as well. Among this spring's summitters who do not climb professionally was the first grandson of any summiter, Tashi Tenzing from Australia, whose grandfather, Tenzing Norgay Sherpa, made the mountain's first ascent with Edmund Hillary on May 29, 1953. Tashi Tenzing was a member of one of this spring's several commercial expeditions, and he summitted on May 23. (Fittingly, on May 10, 1990, Hillary's son Peter had become the first son of a summiter to get to the top.)

Everest summitters this spring also included the first Indonesian men, Misirin and Asmujiono, who also were the first men from southeast Asia; after them came the first Malaysians, Magendran Munisamy and Mohandas Nagappan; the first three Icelanders, Hallgrimur Magnusson, Bjorn Olafsson and Einar Stefansson; the first Australian woman, Brigitte Muir; and the first Kazakh woman, Lyudmila Savina.

Last year's tragic deaths focused the attention of a wide public on the ongoing debate about the merits of commercial expeditions, and the controversy has not disappeared. The first woman ever to summit Everest, Junko Tabei of Japan, speaking in Kathmandu early this year, was reported to have agreed that such teams have their favorable aspect since they enable people to climb Himalayan peaks who do not have the time or perhaps the organizing ability to put an expedition together themselves.

But she touched on their unfavorable side as well when she said she felt the world's highest mountain should be off-limits to commercially organized teams so as to preserve the grandeur of an Everest success: "Lots of people now feel you can climb Everest if you have the money. An Everest conquest doesn't enjoy the kind of accolade it once did." But Nepal's government has not indicated any intention to prohibit commercial teams or anyone else from climbing Everest or any other peak if they obey the regulations and pay the royalties for permits. Last year, mountaineering fees for all Nepalese peaks earned $1.8 million for the government of this impoverished country.

There actually are several types of businesses that organize commercial expeditions. Some are highly reputable and provide excellent services with experienced guides, plenty of Sherpa helpers, first-class equipment and all the bottles of oxygen their clients would want. But others do not fit this description. Amongst the latter is a German company called International Mountain Climbing (IMC), managed by Hans Eitel, who accepted payments from 30 or 40 people to join expeditions to Everest, Cho Oyu or Shishapangma (or even all three mountains), this season, but who failed to forward any payment to the Kathmandu agent for transport costs to reach base camp, for staffs to help the clients make their ascents or at least to prepare their food, for the purchase of foodstuffs and other necessary items, and so on. When the climbers arrived in Kathmandu, they learned from the agent that he could not provide any services unless they paid him directly, and that IMC already was so deeply indebted to him from past years (by about $200,000) that he no longer could extend credit to IMC's clients. Some of them turned around and went back to Europe to try to get their money refunded, while others paid a second time and stayed on; from one team of 14 Germans with plans to attempt all three mountains, only eight now could afford to make a second payment, and they were able to pay for just one peak, Cho Oyu.

There also are various types of guided climbs. Groups sometimes are made up of people who are strangers to each other and who are placed together in rather haphazard fashion. One such group this spring consisted of six very dissatisfied clients of a Polish guide who arranged for them to be on a permit to scale Everest in Tibet but did not actually climb with them because he was hired by another expedition and went with that group instead, leaving his first party to its own devices, without leadership or guidance on the mountain. Only one person in this "cocktail expedition," as they called themselves, reached as high as 8100 meters, and most of them did not get above 8000 meters. It is quite possible that the one who climbed the highest, Joao Garcia from Portugal, might have made it all the way to the summit under different circumstances.

On Everest, two of the climbers who perished during the pre-monsoon season were western Europeans. One was a Scotsman, Malcolm Duff, who was leading a commercial team to the Nepalese side of Everest, and who was found dead in his tent at base camp one morning when a Sherpa went to give him a cup of tea. He had fallen over onto his side but still clasped an open book in his hands; it was speculated that perhaps his heart had failed him.

The other western European was a German mountaineer on the Tibetan side, Peter Kowalzik. He was ascending alone on May 8 when he was met by two Frenchmen coming down from the summit. The three chatted briefly at the bottom of the Second Step at about 8570 meters, exchanged "good luck" and "congratulations," then continued on their different ways. It was 1 p.m., and the French estimated that if Kowalzik had gotten to the top, it would have been at about 4 p.m. By then at that altitude he would have been experiencing strong winds and poor visibility from cloud cover. He was never seen again.

Altogether, five people died on the Tibetan side of Everest (Kowalzik, the three Russians, and a Nepali, Mingma Tamang, with Koreans), and three on the Nepalese side (Duff plus two Sherpas, Nima Rinzi and Tenzing Nuru, on Malaysian and American teams). Duff's body was escorted home by his widow, but the others remain on the mountain. At the same time, one from last year was removed: the body of the Japanese woman, Yasuo Namba, who perished in the terrible storm of last May, now was brought down from the edge of the South Col, where she had died, to base camp and to a Sherpa village below, and cremated. And the body of Bruce Herrod, a Briton who had climbed with a South African team last spring, was released from its ties to fixed ropes at the bottom of the Hillary Step above the south summit and dropped into a southwest face crevasse.

ELIZABETH HAWLEY

*Nepal, Various Activity in the Pre-Monsoon.* Britain's Alan Hinkes arrived in Kathmandu at the end of March with a film crew and publicity material describing him as "the most successful high-altitude mountaineer in Britain," and quite rightly pointing out that no one has ever successfully climbed as many as six 8000ers in a single year, which was the goal he was now setting out to reach. This spring, he was to scale three in Nepal, first Lhotse, then Makalu and finally Kangchenjunga; in the summer, he would move on to Pakistan and climb Nanga Parbat; and in the autumn, he would finish up back in Nepal on Dhaulagiri I and Annapurna I. Moreover, he said, he would do his spring ascents alone as much as possible; he would climb without companions or the use of any artificial oxygen, and much of his climbing would be in alpine style with only one fixed camp (or perhaps none) on each mountain and no Sherpas helpers.

But that is not how things actually worked out. Weather conditions were terrible for several weeks this spring with the winds a special problem. When Hinkes went to Lhotse, he was on a commercial team's permit, and it was not as a soloist but as a member of this group that he finally managed to be the first person this spring to gain the summit of Lhotse—and the only one to get to the top on his summit day—after having made good use of the group's camps, equipment, food, Sherpas and bottled oxygen. He summited Lhotse on May 23. A helicopter picked him up from the Lhotse-Everest base camp area as he had originally planned. But he had planned this to be on about May 10 or so and not on the 28th, as it actually was. The aircraft dropped him near an advance base camp which had already been established for him by another Briton, an American and a small Nepalese camp staff for his Makalu attempt.

The two teammates who were with him on his own Makalu permit had also already pitched two higher camps and stocked them with food and gear for his quick push for the summit. But Hinkes and the American colleague, Fabrizio Zangrilli, who went for the summit bid with him on May 30, got no higher than 7200 meters on this giant mountain when at midday they turned back; Zangrilli had been hit on the side of his head by a piece of falling ice and made ill by this, and both were fearful of more hits by rockfall during the hot part of the day. Hinkes could see that the winds up high were very strong, and on June 2 he decided to give up. Kangchenjunga was not even visited. He said he hoped to return to Makalu and go to Kangchenjunga next spring after having carried on with his attempts on this year's three other 8000-meter objectives.

Hinkes was not the only climber this season to be trying to close in on his goal of summiting all 14 of the world's 8000ers. On Kangchenjunga was the Italian mountaineer, Fausto De Stefani, who already had 12 to his credit and lacked only Kangchenjunga and Lhotse. He went to Kangchenjunga with a Spanish team, but he didn't like their route. The leader of an American-British expedition said De Stefani asked to join their effort but they preferred to climb without him, so he finally teamed up with some South Koreans, but was unsuccessful nonetheless.

ELIZABETH HAWLEY

*Mount Everest Group, Attempted Traverse.* A program similar to Reinhard Patscheider's (*see Tibet*) was Anatoli Boukreev's more elaborate idea for a traverse from Lhotse's summit (8516m) over to the top of Everest, and then, "if I feel like it," a traverse of Everest down the normal Tibetan route. He said he was on three permits: a British-organized commercial team's Nepalese permit for Everest from the south, the Kazakhs' Everest permit for the north side, and a Russian expedition's Lhotse permit.

Boukreev first went to the top of Everest from the Nepalese side rather early in the season, on April 26, as one of three Russians employed by an Indonesian army expedition (who called them their "mercenaries"), and he then came all the way down to Kathmandu with the victorious Asians. After spending nearly a week at this much lower altitude, he returned to the Everest-Lhotse base camp on May 18 to join an Italian climber, Simone Moro, who was already climbing with a big Italian Lhotse team and was on the same Nepalese Everest permit as Boukreev.

Boukreev and Moro now climbed together up Lhotse's normal route on the west face to the summit on May 26. (It was Boukreev's second ascent of this peak.) But they made no move to go over to Everest. The weather was becoming unsettled that afternoon, and, more importantly, the normally very strong Boukreev was not now in good health: He suspected he had picked up a lung infection in Kathmandu, and his April ascent of Everest and descent to Kathmandu doubtless did not help. Moro had no interest in trying to go to Everest alone, so both men turned down and reached base camp the next day.

ELIZABETH HAWLEY

*Lhotse, First American Female Ascent.* It was reported that on May 26, Christine Feld Boskoff became the first American woman—and second woman ever—to climb Lhotse. She had climbed to Camp IV (7805m) by her husband, Keith Boskoff. After waiting out a day of storms, Keith was not up to the ascent, so Christine continued alone to the summit, which she reached at 12:30 p.m. (*Climbing* 171)

*Lhotse Intermediate, Attempt and Tragedy.* Vladimir Bashkirov, a Russian climber who summited Everest with his Indonesian employers this season had, amongst his many accomplishments, led the successful first attempt to climb the very steep south ridge of a peak known as Annapurna South (7219m) in 1994. While he was engaged with guiding an Indonesian team via the north ridge on Everest, some of his Russian teammates had been fixing rope and pitching camps up Lhotse's West Face route while others had attempted to prepare a possible descent route for him and several colleagues, who would traverse from Lhotse to make the first ascent of the middle summit of the massif. This exit route was to be on the south ridge of a peak named Shanti Shikhar (or Shartse II) next to the massif's eastern summit, Lhotse Shar. Although his friends had not reached the top of Shanti Shikar, Bashkirov said in Kathmandu after his descent from Everest and before going to Lhotse, that he still believed it could provide a good descent route from the east from Lhotse Shar.

No one had ever tried to reach this middle peak, known as Lhotse Intermediate (8410m), which is the world's highest unclimbed peak and is guarded on each side by a very difficult ridge at great altitude connecting it with Lhotse's main summit and with Lhotse Shar. On May 4 Bashkirov came down to Kathmandu, then flew back to the mountains with Anatoli Boukreev on about the 10th, and arrived at base camp in apparent good health a week after that, ready to make the first traverse across the great Lhotse massif.

Bashkirov, who already had six other 8000-meter summits to his credit, got to the top of Lhotse on May 26. He was among the last of his summit party of eight Russians to arrive there; he told a teammate that he had a slight fever, and he explained to a member of another team climbing the mountain at the same time that he was waiting for the last of his party to come up. When the last of them, including Bashkirov, got to the top, it was late in the day, nearly 4 p.m. The weather was very cold, visibility was poor, and Bashkirov was not well.

Neither he nor any of the others tried to make the traverse to Lhotse Intermediate. Instead, they all turned down toward the shelter of their camp at 7700 meters. But Bashkirov never got there. He managed to descend to 8000 meters unaided, then collapsed and was pulled down the snow slope to 7900 meters, where he was found to have no pulse or any other signs of life. He had died of exhaustion and perhaps the same infection that Boukreev had gotten. His teammates buried his body on the mountain in snow inside a sleeping bag.

Is the traverse from Lhotse to the middle summit to Lhotse Shar possible? His deputy leader, Vladimir Savkov, who did not climb above base camp, answered "it is very, very, very difficult" along the sharp, steep ridge. Said one of the men who did summit that fatal day, Gleb Sokolov, "maybe" it is possible, but he would like to try traversing from Lhotse Shar to the middle peak only; the section of the ridge from that eastern end, he thought, is not so sharp nor so steep as the climb between Lhotse Intermediate and the main summit, and the descent would not be so difficult.

ELIZABETH HAWLEY

*Lobuche East, Pumori, and Nuptse, Ascents and Tragedy.* Tomaž Humar, Janez Jeglič, Marjan Kovac, Berčič Cene, and Kokalj Franc from Slovenia, along with Carlos Carsolio from Mexico, were active in the Nepal Himalaya during the post-monsoon. From September 29 - October 1, Humar, Jeglič and Carsolio climbed *Talking About Tsampa* (V-VI 85°, 900m) on the northeast face of Lobuche East (6119m). From October 9-11, Humar, Jeglič, Carsolio, and Marjan Kovac climbed 800 meters of an independent line on the southeast face of Pumori (7165m) leading to the French South Pillar route, reaching 6300 meters before being called down to aid in a rescue of four climbers who had been attempting Pumori's east ridge and fallen down the north face. (*Czech Milos Kijonka was the only one to survive. See above.*) After the rescue, Humar, Jeglič, Bercic Cene, Marjan Kovac, and Kokalj Franc ascended Pumori by its normal route for acclimatization. On October 26, Humar, Jeglič and Kovac approached the base of Nuptse's west face; Carsolio considered the face to be too dangerous given the unfavorable weather of the last few weeks and opted not to climb. Kovac bowed out the next morning due to illness, leaving Humar and Jeglič to solo the 2500-meter wall in five days (belaying, according to Humar, would have made the climb too slow). The pair moved over rock and ice that averaged 50°-60° and was occasionally 80°, reaching Nuptse's north-west summit (7742m) on October 31. Tragically, Jeglič was blown off balance by the wind and fell down the 2500-meter south face, leaving Humar to descend the west face solo, which he did in two and a half days, frostbiting four toes and sustaining injuries to his face and head in the process (the men climbed without helmets to save weight). A full account of this bold but tragic ascent appears earlier in this journal.

*Nuptse, Southwest Ridge, Attempt.* Hans Kammerlander (Italy) and his only other teammate, Maurizio Lutzenberger, attempted to be the first people ever to reach Nuptse's slightly higher east summit (7804m). But they could manage to go no higher along the southwest ridge that leads to this summit than 6600 meters on October 18 because of deep powder snow already on the mountain and more snow falling. "It's a very nice route for an alpine-style climb," Kammerlander said, adding that he believes the 400-meter rocky summit face he had planned to ascend probably is not difficult, "but nobody knows."

ELIZABETH HAWLEY

*Nepalese Himalaya, Peak Bagging and Other Activity in the Post-Monsoon.* This autumn's weather seemed unremittingly bad for climbing, without the normal break of a couple of weeks of fine days and nights between the end of the monsoon rains/snowfall in late September and the onset of fierce westerly winds in mid-October.

This autumn, success came to some of the men going for all of the 8000ers. A Spanish Basque, Juanito Oyarzabal, summitted Manaslu in early October and thereby knocked off his twelfth 8000er; he says he may finish off all of them by 1999. It also came to a South Korean, Park Young-Seok, who reported that he reached two 8000-meter summits this autumn, Cho Oyu in September and Lhotse in October. Since April, Park now claimed an unprecedented total of five 8000-meter summits in only six months (adding these to two others, including Everest, which he had climbed previously), and he is getting ready to go to Manaslu in December. Before Park, Carlos Carsolio was the only person to have summitted as many as four 8000ers in one calendar year (1995).

A new pair of peak-baggers suddenly appeared on the scene this autumn with ambitious plans for the fast track. They are two Spanish brothers, Jesus and Jose Antonio Martinez, who set for themselves the goal of summitting all the 8000ers without Sherpa helpers or bottled oxygen within a year from the date of their first success. That first was achieved on Dhaulagiri I, which both of them scaled on September 24. They then went to nearby Annapurna I but stopped that climb at 6400 meters on October 15 when a huge avalanche roared down the mountainside. Next they crossed the Nepalese border illegally, and Jesus summitted Cho Oyu from the Tibetan side on a Nepalese permit on November 6. In mid-November, they left Kathmandu for Shishapangma in Tibet before going home for Christmas.

Two prominent Italians, Sergio Martini and Fausto De Stefani, have been much slower in scaling their 8000ers, having begun together with K2 in August 1983, and they are not in their 20s like the Martinez Brothers or in their 30s like Park, but are 48 and 55 years old. Now close to completing the job with 12 successes already, Martini still had Everest to climb, De Stefani had not yet summited Kangchenjunga, and neither of them had climbed Lhotse yet.

This season, they came as a two-man team to climb Lhotse by its normal West Face route without artificial oxygen or help from Nepalese Sherpas. They had a one-month struggle to go for the top under unhappy conditions ("much wind, much snow, no satisfaction," as Martini described it). But at last, on October 15, they reported, they had gained the summit. Or to be more precise, they elaborated, they had been so very near the top that they considered they could rightfully claim a successful ascent. They were unable to say exactly how near they had gotten because wind was blowing snow in their faces and they were in mist at the time, but they decided they were as close as they could possibly get to the summit without being blown away by the fierce wind.

"For me and my friend, we feel that we reached very, very near the summit," Martini said when they came back to Kathmandu. "We are convinced that with the bad weather and with-

*Lobuche, showing the Humar-Jeglič-Carsolio line.* TOMAZ HUMAR

out fixed rope we could not have gone higher. In this condition, for us this is the summit. We know we were not at the very last point, but for us this is the summit."

But the South Korean climber Park Young-Seok, who followed their footprints in the crusted snow three days later in clearer weather, does not consider that they actually gained the summit. While Martini and De Stefani indicate they were perhaps only a few meters below the top, Park claims that their footprints stopped about 30 meters below a small foresummit and 150 vertical meters below the highest summit, which, he says, was slightly to the right and behind the lower point; he asserts he himself did get to the very top.

The well-known Frenchwoman, Miss Chantal Mauduit, the only woman currently engaged in the contest to climb all of the 8000ers, has claimed success already on six of them, including Gasherbrum II in July, and this autumn had hope of summitting two more, Dhaulagiri I and Annapurna I, without bottled oxygen but with one Sherpa climbing with her. However, she reported failure on the first, and she never actually went to the second one. Dhaulagiri I had been successfully summitted by the Martinez Brothers and one Bulgarian in late September, but when Mauduit started her climb of the mountain at the very end of the month, she managed to reach no higher than 7500 meters, where she arrived on October 18, because of heavy new snowfall and very low temperatures. She had considerable difficulty even getting away from her base camp through very deep snow in the passes and had to leave all her climbing gear behind, so she was unable to attempt Annapurna I and had to return to Kathmandu instead.

A Briton who should have come to Nepal to add several summits to the nine 8000-meter "conquests" he claims, Alan Hinkes, failed to turn up at all. He had been disappointed in the spring by having been able to get to the top of only one of the three he planned to summit that season. His program for the rest of the year included one during the summer in the Karakoram, Nanga Parbat, and two in Nepal in the autumn. But his hopes of quickly becoming the first Briton to top all the 8000ers were thwarted by a sneezing fit. He had gone to Nanga Parbat in July to knock that one off when the flour covering the chapati he was eating got up his nose, and he sneezed so violently that did some sort of injury to his back. He was unable to move and was in great pain; he had to be removed from the mountain by helicopter and hospitalized in Britain. He told his agent in Kathmandu that he would definitely come to Nepal in the autumn, but he never showed up, and finally his British sponsor informed the agent that Hinkes would not be coming.

ELIZABETH HAWLEY

*Makalu, West Face, Ascent and Tragedy.* A team of climbers from Ekaterinburg, Russia, led by Sergei Efimov, made an ascent of Makalu's west face in the pre-monsoon season. Their ascent followed the right-hand ice faces to the great headwall, then joined the French West Pillar route by climbing a rock buttress. Two team members perished on the ascent. A full account appears earlier in this journal.

*Jannu, North Face, Attempt.* In the fall, our team went to attempt the north face of Jannu (7710m) in Nepal. We fixed ropes to 6000 meters but were turned back by weather and a dwindling team effort. The face remains unclimbed on the right side. It is an outstanding feature and will make for an amazing climb. Team members were Jared Ogden, Stephen Sustad, Guillermo and Damian Benegas, Travis Spitzer, Cameron Lawson, Vera Wong, Fernandito Grahales, and Todd Gilmore.

JARED OGDEN

*Gimmegela, Third Ascent.* It was reported that a 14-man British Services expedition made the third ascent of Gimmegela (7350m) via the southwest ridge. The team (Pat Parsons, leader, Rob Magowan, Tug Wilson, Huan Davies, Nigel Lane Neil Peacock, Bob Ewen, Larry Foden, Marty Hallet, Callum Weeks, Dave Sheridan, Andy Gibson, Paul Hart, Ted Atkins) set up base camp at Pangpema, the traditional base-camp site for Kangchenjunga ascents on the north side, and set up ABC six kilometers to the northeast at the foot of Gimmegela's southwest ridge. The climbing from CI (5580m) to CII (6400m) proved difficult, involving 800 meters of hard mixed climbing (HS/Scottish 3) up shattered blocks and loose slate. Inobvious route-finding higher up led to a number of dead-ends before an ice gully (Scottish IV) was climbed to where the ridge eased off in angle. From there the team followed the ridge crest, finding good climbing and increasing winds, a gust of which blew Hart completely off the crest (he was held by his partner). After two more camps, the summit was reached on May 10 by Lane and Peacock. On the 12th, Aktins, Foden, Magowan and Wilson followed. The team stripped all ropes and departed base camp on May 18. (*High Mountain Sports* 179)

*Kangchenjunga, North Face.* Kangchenjunga, located in remote eastern Nepal, lies on the border with India's autonomous state of Sikkim and is the world's third highest peak at 8586 meters, after Everest and K2. On Kangchenjunga, six expeditions, representing Great Britain, our mixed international team, Korea, the Slovak republic, Spain, and Switzerland attempted to reach the summit by various routes. But only our team was able to attain the top, on May 24, placing Scott McKee from Montana on the summit after 51 days. Scott thus was able to make the first ascent of the north face of Kangchenjunga by an American. One of our main goals was to place the first woman on the summit, and Heidi Howkins (Oregon) very nearly reached the top on May 14. Our expedition was conducted in lightweight style with no high altitude Sherpas and no bottled oxygen.

DANIEL MAZUR

*Kangchenjunga, Attempt.* The main goal of an 11-member Slovak expedition was to climb Kangchenjunga by the 1981 Czechoslovak Route. The leader of this expedition was Jaryk Stejskal, who in the 1980s summitted Lhotse Shar, Dhaulaghiri and Cho Oyu. The weather was very poor the entire time. The first attempt was made by three climbers: Juraj Kardhordo (Cho Oyu, 1995), and two novices to the Himalayas, Vladimir Plulik and Jaroslav Vondercik. On May 5, they reached 7700 meters, where they decided to retreat because of deep snow and strong winds. The second attempt was made from the Camp III (6800m) by the next three climbers: Jindro Martis (45), Martin Gablik (43) and Stanislav Glejdura (39). By 11 a.m. on May 8, they were at 8300 meters. There was a lot of new, waist-deep snow, and their progress was very slow, forcing them to descend. The third attempt was made by Kardhordo and Vondercik. On May 13, at 5 p.m., they reached 8500 meters, very near the summit. They climbed the whole day in a very strong wind, continually thinking about retreat options. Kardhordo and Vondercik climbed 40 meters above the col, where a very strong wind was blowing. They realized that they would be not able to reach the summit until dusk, and that they had no chance to bivy there. They decided to descend because they did not want to take such a high risk. The Slovak Expedition came very close to the summit of Kangchenjunga, missing its goal by a lack of good fortune.

VLADIMIR LINEK, *Jamesak*

# PAKISTAN

## HINDU KUSH

*Karambar Region, Various Ascents.* The Montecchio Maggiore section of the Club Alpino Italiano spent from July 22 to August 27 in the Karambar Valley north of Chitral. They found no indication in their documents of any preceding alpine activity in the area, and found no traces of previous passage during their climbs. During their stay, they made ascents of the following: Aorat Zon (4960m), the summit of which was reached on July 27 by nine alpinists and on August 8 by another five; Ana Sar (5630m), the summit of which was reached via the white ridge that rises from the north out of the eastern branch of the Zhoe Sar Glacier. Claudio Meggiolaro, Augusto Pagliarusco, Alberto Urbani and Riccardo Zanini used Camp "A" to make the ascent, which was long and difficult, involving ice and mixed climbing (60-65°). The ascent took 24 hours of non-stop climbing.

Sub Vicum Sar (5640m) was climbed on August 8 by Alession Gualdo and Mirco Scarsa. Chota Pahad Sar (5660m), the highest peak in the Karambar area, was climbed by Alberto Urbani, Riccardo Zanini, Giampaolo Visona with Ruggero and Almuth Zanini on August 7. The team also made ascents of Lupsuk Sar (5645m); Dosti Sar (5480m); Chota Sar (5150m); Scaphoydes Sar (5425m); Young Climbers Sar (5415m); Pachas Sal Sar (5380m); and Karambar Tso Sar (5520m).

## WESTERN KARAKORAM

*Rakaposhi, First Iranian Ascent.* With only a few previous expeditions from Iran, and as our first experience to the Himalayan mountains, we chose Rakaposhi (7788m), a mountain of moderate height and difficulty. After three days' march we started climbing from base camp (4400m) on July 13 via the first ascent route of the southwest spur. The same day we placed Camp I at 5200 meters and fixed 150 meters of rope. On July 19, we placed Camp II at 5750 meters with 350 meters of fixed rope. Bypassing a gendarme and fixing 250 meters of rope, Camp III was established on July 25 at 5750 meters. The Monk's Head could be reached by a 600-meter 50-60° ice slope that we fixed completely, and thereby reached Camp IV at 6400 meters on July 10, the end of the technical climbing. The first assault team reached Camp V at 7010 meters on August 6, but was too exhausted to go for the summit the next morning, so they came back to Camp IV to rest. I had planned to bring everything we needed to set up Camp VI at 7350 meters (as the first expedition had done in 1958, and the Belgian in 1983), but the first summit attempt from Camp V reduced our allotment of time and the team's energy. We had had four days of continuous good weather; another two days to reach Camp V and then the top would leave little room for the second assault team to reach the summit in the same period of good weather. There were also only snow slopes without technical difficulties remaining to the top, so there was no risk of delay in a move. Therefore all six members who were at Camp IV went to Camp V, and on August 9 at 2:30 a.m., we left for the summit. The first climbers reached the top at 10 a.m. and the last person at noon. The next six days were spent cleaning up the mountain. On August 15, we left base camp for home. Team members were Mansoor Afsharian, Daryoush Babazadeh, Jalal Cheshmeh Ghasabani (summitter), Farshad Khalili Khoshemehr (summitter), Hosein Khoshcheshm (summitter), Ramin Shojaei Baghini (summitter), Esmaeil Motehayerpasand, Reza Zarei (summitter), Mohamad Jodeiri, Alireza Amzajerdian, and Mohamad Oraz (summitter).

RAMIN SHOJAEI BAGHINI, *Iran*

*Spantik, Ascents*. Frenchman Daniel Petraud climbed Spantik (7027m) twice, the first time on August 15 with three other climbers. He then went on to scale the peak another time, following the ridge all the way from base camp to top and back on August 18-19 in 16 hours. "We first went up the Normal Route (southwest) behind the ridge. Later I went up alone, starting on August 18 at 8 p.m. It took me ten hours to reach the top and the next day at noon I was back at Base Camp. The entire time involved was 16 hours. The ridge is much safer than the Normal Route." The expedition took 11 days in all from Base Camp to top and back. All the climbers except the leader were visiting Pakistan for the first time. The summiters were: Daniel Petraud (leader), Dr. Annie Delale (expedition doctor), Laurent Vivier and Patrick Variot. The expedition made Base Camp at 4380 metres, Camp I at 4830 meters, Camp II at 5550 meters, Camp III at 6300 meters. The expedition used 330 meters of fixed ropes.

ASEM MUSTAFA AWAN, *The Nation, Pakistan*

*Bolocho I, Bolocho V, and Bolocho VI, First Ascents*. The British team of Stuart Muir and Dave Wilkinson were reported to have made ascents of three virgin peaks south of the Hispar Glacier during July and August. They began with a 5240-meter peak they called Bolocho V, climbing it by its east ridge and encountering one pitch of Scottish III/4 (the rest was easy snow). They then started out for Bolocho I, a peak Wilkinson had seen in 1995 while climbing Haramosh II. They made it to a col (5300m) at the base of the north ridge, but a stretch of bad weather forced them back to base camp for five more days. When the weather cleared, they made it back to the col and proceeded up the 55° ridge (which was covered in up to a foot of fresh snow). They continued along the heavily corniced summit ridge, achieving the summit at 9 a.m. via a steep gully (Scottish IV/5) and easier ground to the top. They descended during the morning and evening, spent a day at high camp, and reached base camp on August 9.

On the 14th, the pair was joined by teammates Andy Forsyth and their base camp assistant, Fidali, on a climb of Bolocho VI (5200m) via snow and a 35° icy slope. (*High Mountain Sports* 183)

*Ruwiduri Sar, Zarsanic I, First Ascents*. It was reported that Annabelle Barker, Pru Cartwright, Margaret Clennett, Sally MacIntyre and Sue Williscroft visited the Shimshal Pass area in July, making ascents of Ruwiduri Sar (5500m) via the northeast ridge and Zarsanic I (5900m) via the southwest ridge, both from the same bivouac site at 5000 meters. They also attempted Mingli Sar but were turned back by a day of bad weather. All ascents were non-technical. (*High Mountain Sports* 183)

*Malubiting West, Ascent*. On July 29, Matthias Dischinger (28) from Lorrach, Germany, Roland Brandli (35) from Zurich, Switzerland, Ruedi Karrer (38) from Zurich, Switzerland, and Dieter Funfschilling (25) as expedition leader, started the walk-in from Tisar together with 26 porters with the goal of climbing Malubiting West (7454m). On August 2 we reached base camp at 4300 meters along the Chogolungma Glacier. Malubiting and Spantik base camp are the same. On August 4 we established CI (ca.4800m) halfway between base camp and Polan La (5800m). On August 7, we reached CII at ca.5300 meters, just at the foot of Malubiting North. The heat was the biggest problem, turning the Chogolungma glacier into a labyrinth of lateral crevasses. The next day we tackled Polan La. After 9 a.m., the 350-meter "wall" below Polan La became dangerous.

On August 11, we started our summit attempt from base camp and, on August 15, slept at Polan La (CIII) for the first time. Over the next two days we fixed ca.230 meters of rope on

*Malubiting East and Central from Camp I on Malubiting West.* DIETER FUNFSCHILLING

the mixed ridge above Polan La. From CIII to the summit we climbed alpine style. CIV (6300m) is just one terrace above the Austrian camp. We used our one-meter skis for the first time to reach the beginning of the large plateau (CV, 6650m).

On August 19, we crossed the plateau and rested at 7100 meters, just below the pass between Malubiting West and Central. Matthias and Roland went for the summit on foot via the northeast ridge, while Ruedi and I returned within one hour to CV because of headaches and exhaustion. We basically followed the first ascent route of Horst Schindelbacher et al. From base camp to summit to base camp we enjoyed perfect weather

DIETER FUNFSCHILLING, *The Mostly Harmless Climbers' Club*

NANGA PARBAT RANGE

*Laila Peak, First Ascent.* Our German team of five made the first ascent of Laila Peak (5971m) in the Rupal Valley. (This peak should not be confused with the famous Laila Peak in Hushe Valley.) The peak is situated at the right end of the Rupal Valley and can be seen from Nanga Parbat Latoba base camp as a rounded white dome. But Laila Peak is more like a long wall rising up from a big but hardly accessible glacier plateau. The unseen south face is a very steep rock wall, while the north face is covered with ice. The icy north face looks very attractive but finding a good route to access the big plateau would seem to be the hardest part. The Rupal people told us about one former serious attempt to climb the peak.

We established base camp below Mazeno Camp at 3950 meters on July 2. First we tried to find a way through the crevasses directly to the smaller plateau which, we hoped, would allow access to the big plateau. We failed. Next we climbed up a beautiful ice ridge directly

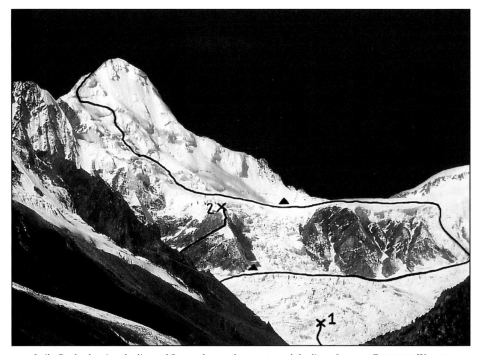

*Laila Peak, showing the lines of first and second attempts and the line of ascent.* CHRISTIAN WALTER

to the big plateau but could not manage to enter the plateau itself because of a big crevasse between the end of the ridge and the plateau. So we went down again. On July 6 we explored an access route to the lower plateau using a moderate debris gully, putting up one tent (Camp I) here (4600m). Two days later we all moved to that camp. From there we had to climb a big slope to reach the only point from which we could cross the bergschrund to the 40° ice wall leading to upper plateau (5100m). Bad weather stopped us there for one day. On July 11, we went up. Miss Henrike Suess and Thomas Berthold gave up at 5500 meters, while Miss Anne Riedel, Christian Walter and Thomas Niederlein reached the summit at 4:30 p.m. after crossing a lot of bergschrunds, steep snowfields and crevasses. The average steepness of the route does not exceed 40°, but we had to climb some tricky pitches that were up to 60° or partial vertically. Abseiling and climbing down took us another six hours.

Some days later Walter and Riedel climbed Rupal Peak (5642m). On the ascent they climbed a new route via the steep northwest ice col; they took the normal east route for the descent. Suess and Berthold used the east route to summit.

The area is a nice playground for lightweight expeditions like ours. The approach is easy: you can reach the base camp within only two days' drive and two days' walk from Islamabad. And all summits except for Nanga Parbat itself are a little bit lower than 6000 meters, which means you don't need a permit, Liason Officer, etc., so an expedition can be made very cheaply. The valley is frequently visited by trekkers, but only one to two parties a year attempt peaks other than Nanga Parbat, and nearly all of them attempt Rupal Peak via the normal route. Incomprehensible, because there are lots of virgin peaks and faces.

CHRISTIAN WALTER, *Germany*

*Nanga Parbat, First American Ascent.* Carlos Buhler became the first native-born American to climb Nanga Parbat when he ascended the mountain with a Russian team in July. It was also the first Russian ascent of the mountain. Further details are lacking.

*Nanga Parbat, Various Ascents.* It was reported that a number of teams made successful ascents of Nanga Parbat in 1997. A China-Pakistan expedition that fixed rope up to 7400 meters on the Diamir Face put eight climbers on top June 15. Two Japanese teams climbed the Kinshofer route in July, all placing climbers on the summit. Two Korean teams were successful on the route as well. A six-man Catalan expedition put five members on top, but one of them, Joan Collet, fell and died while descending to Camp III. (*High Mountain Sports* 183)

CENTRAL KARAKORAM

*Choktoi Glacier Area, Various Ascents.* It was reported that a British expedition of Alex Franklin, Will Garrett, Fiona Hatchell, Colin Spark and Guy Willett operated in the Choktoi Glacier area in late June and some of July. They attempted Hanipispur South (6047m) via the east face and north ridge, reaching 6000 meters before being turned back by windslab danger. Two members attempted P.6166m, finding climbing up to Scottish VI and A2 before the line they were attempting blanked out. They also tried two rock spurs on the flanks of Latok III, getting one-third of the way up (HVS A1/A2) before realizing the route was bigger than they thought. They did climb P.5400m via a loose ridge (AD).

   Another British team (Richard Garnett, Dean Grindell, Mark Harris and Oliver Howard) also was in the area during July and part of August, climbing the smallest of the Biacherahi Towers (c.5900m) via an easy snow couloir on the north side. They also climbed an arête on one of the rock buttresses of Latok III over two days, finding climbing up to E2 5c on good granite. (*High Mountain Sports* 183)

*Baintha Brakk, Attempts.* It was reported that Germans Jan Mersch and Jochen Hasse attempted the South Pillar on Baintha Brakk (a.k.a. the Ogre, 7285m), reaching 6250 meters. (*High Mountain Sports* 183)

*HAR Pinnacle, First Ascent, and Latok I, Attempt.* Our expedition consisted of John Bouchard, Barry Rugo, Tom Nonis, and me. We had two permits, one for the often-attempted north ridge of Latok I (7145m) and one for the south pillar of the Ogre (Biantha Brakk, 7388m). In August, Bouchard and I made three attempts on Latok I. The final attempt was with Nonis and Rugo, moving alpine style. We reached a point on the pillar just below the halfway point. The climbing was superb. Unfortunately, extreme heat was causing considerable melting and rockfall from high on the face. Despite the stable weather, we felt conditions too unsafe to continue. Due to the very dry conditions, we followed the rock pillar from the very bottom of the route. Rock climbing was on solid granite up to 5.10 in difficulty.

   Nonis and Rugo's attempt on the Ogre was stopped at the base of the main rock pillar due to dangerous avalanche conditions and bad weather.

   In between our second and third attempts on Latok I, Bouchard and I made the first ascent of a previously unclimbed/unnamed spire directly behind our base camp at the head of the Choctoi Glacier. We estimate its altitude at 5700 meters. We climbed the spire in one long day from our base camp following moderate 3rd-class mixed gullies for 1,000 feet, then 11 pitches of rock climbing up to 5.10b on the south face. The actual summit is a spectacular perch, flat and about the size of a large table. In the absence of any official or local name for this lovely peak, we named it HAR Pinnacle after the names of our three base camp staff, Hassan, Abdul, and Rassool.

MARK RICHEY

*Latok II, West Face and Northwest Ridge, Ascents, and Other Activity.* A mostly German expedition of Alex and Thomas Huber, Toni Gutsch, Franz Fendt, and Christian Schlesener, plus American Conrad Anker, succeeded in making the second and third ascents of Latok II (7108m; see clarification below on the naming and altitudes of the Latok group). The team arrived on the Uzum Brakk Glacier in the middle of June. The Huber brothers, Gutsch and Anker began fixing rope up the central couloir to access the 1000-meter-plus face that begins at more than 6000 meters. Their route, *Tsering Mosong* (VII 5.10c A3), involved 26 pitches and was climbed over 11 days. A full account of the west face climb appears earlier in this journal.

Christian Schlesener and Franz Fendt made the third ascent of the mountain via the west face's central ice couloir to the northwest ridge. They placed their advanced base camp at 6000 meters in the couloir. From there, they followed the central couloir to the crest of the ridge at 6600 meters, then started up the remaining 500 meters of the ridge. Thirty hours of climbing put them near the summit, but they were unable to see it and began to doubt their chances of success; fortunately, a radio message from base camp, from where the climbers could be seen, confirmed that they were close. They reached the summit after a 36-hour push. On the descent, the pair rappeled for 14 hours down the horizontal wall; Fendt narrowly escaped an ice avalanche before they arrived back in advanced base 50 hours after leaving. They got three hours' rest at ABC, then continued down, using up all their climbing gear for rappel anchors. After having placed their last ice screw, they tied their ropes together and rappelled one last time, then downclimbed the last 300 meters. They had been moving nearly non-stop for 70 hours. They named their route *Nomadu* (VI 5.10a WI5 A2, 1100m).

Thomas Huber and Gutsch also made the second ascent of Spalding via the 900-meter Northeast Pillar (V 5.12b), climbed for the first time in 1995 by Volker Benz, Alex Huber, Karl Sptizof and Ruta Florschutz. Alex and Thomas, together with Gutsch, also climbed Bravo Brakk (ca. 5999m) via a snow/ice couloir up to 70° on the southwest flank in seven hours from base camp.

*The Latok Group, Clarification.* The 1997 ascents of Latok II have allowed us to clarify the naming of the three peaks of the Latok group. Below, we list the altitudes given to the peaks by three different sources: the *Ortograficzna Mapa Szkicowa Karacorum*, elaborated by Jerzy Wala in 1971; the triangulation results from the 1977 Italian expedition led by Professor Arturo Bergamaschi that made the first ascent of Latok II; and the map *Karakoram*, published in 1990 by the Swiss Foundation for Alpine Research.

|  | Latok I | Latok II | Latok III |
|---|---|---|---|
| Wala (1971) | 7145 m | 7108 m | 6956 m |
| Bergamaschi (1977) | 7086 m | 7151 m | 6860 m |
| Karakoram map (1990) | 7145 m | 7108 m | 6949 m |

# The Latok Group

Panmah Muztagh, Central Karakoram

Pakistan

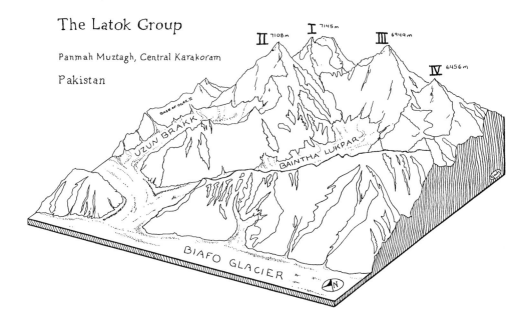

The heights given correspond as follows: Latok I is the central peak of the group; Latok II, the western peak; and Latok III, the eastern peak. (See above sketch.) The triangulation results from Professor Bergamaschi's expedition, which surveyed the peaks with Galileo and Salmoiraghi instruments, indicated the peak accepted as Latok II as the highest at 7151 meters. Based on these findings, Bergamaschi proposed that the designations for Latok I and Latok II be switched. He therefore called his the first ascent of "Latok I," but the peak has continued to be called Latok II in most publications. *The American Alpine Journal,* while acknowledging Professor Bergamaschi's work, will continue to refer to the Latok group by its designation in the 1990 *Swiss Foundation for Alpine Research Karakoram* map. The 1997 ascents of Latok II were thus the second and third ascents of the mountain.

We are indebted to Professor Bergamaschi, who has been kind enough to supply us with both a map that clarifies the results of their triangulations and a photo that shows his team's original route.

*Shipton Spire, Ship of Fools.* Mark Synnott and Jared Ogden established a new route on the east face of Shipton Spire (5852m) called *Ship of Fools* (VII 5.11 A2+ WI6), spending 20 nights on the wall and summitting on August 6. A full account of Synnott and Ogden's climb appears earlier in this journal.

*Hainablak, Ascent.* Hainablak is the prominent granite aiguille named by Ardito Desio in 1929 during his exploratory reconnaissance up the Baltoro Glacier. The tower, which can be seen in in this journal on page 25 and in *AAJ* 1997 on page 322 behind the climber (mis-captioned as Chuck Boyd; it is actually Greg Foweraker) as he ascends fixed lines on Shipton Spire, is west of Uli Biaho and hides Shipton Spire from most viewpoints. It was reported that Hungarians Gabor Berecz and Oskar Nadasdi and German Thomas Tivader visited the

Shipton Spire area a bit earlier than Synnott and Ogden. According to various reports, including that from a Liaison Officer at Trango Base Camp who had talked with the climbers as they were walking out, the trio had spent three weeks climbing 21 pitches on the splendid granite of the slightly lower "East Tower" but had not reached the summit. Seven copperheads and 17 bolts were placed with the maximum difficulties rated at 5.10 and A4. (*High Mountain Sports* 183)

*Great Trango Tower, New Route.* It was reported that the Korean team of Kim Hyung-Jin, Lee Sang-Co, Choi Seoung-Chul and Shin Yun-Jeong climbed the Great Trango Tower on its east face, adding a five-pitch variation to an established route. Further details are lacking.

*Nameless Tower, Yugoslav Route.* The Scandinavian Trango Expedition (Jan Stenstrom, leader; Magnus Nilsson, Jon Haukassveen, Torbjorn Ohlén, Fredrik Schlyter, Bo Strand, videofilm, and Anders Schmidt, doctor) climbed the 1987 Yugoslav route on the south face of the Nameless Tower. Stenstrom and Ohlén made a recon trip in the summer of 1996, scrambling up to 5200 meters where the actual climbing starts. This year's expedition arrived in Islamadad on June 7. The administration process went smoothly and the team continued to

Skardu on June 11. Sixty-five porters and five jeeps were hired. The road to Askole was in good condition. The cable crossing at the Jolla bridge, however, was swept away. The expedition crossed the Domondo river five kilometers upstream on another cable. Base camp was placed on Trango Glacier at a small lake.

Four strong porters stayed in base camp and carried loads up to Advanced Base Camp I (behind the big boulder on the left side of the gully; we found room for three tents) at 4900 meters. The porters took some of the loads further to Advanced Base Camp II (a small ledge on the right side of the gully, with room for one tent) at 5100 meters.

After three climbing days, we established CI at the

*Jan Strenstrom jugging to CII on the Nameless Tower.*
JON KAUKASSVEEN

shoulder (5600m) on July 4. Supplies for two weeks were hauled to CI (we fixed ropes to the ground). The team stayed in advanced base camp during a five-day storm that delivered 50 centimeters of snow. Three climbing days took the team to CII (a big snowpatch) at 5900 meters. A storm forced a retreat from CII on July 10. Ropes were left fixed to CII.

The team split into two groups. Two climbers, Ohlén and Schlyter, stayed in CI, while Stenstrom, Nilsson and Haukassveen went down to base camp for a rest. The storm ended on July 11, and nice weather appeared again. Ohlén and Schlyter jumared rapidly to CII and reached CIII (a big snowpatch) at 6100 meters late in the evening. On July 12, they continued and climbed icy rock to the summit, which they reached at 3 p.m. Back in base camp, the doctor examined them, finding symptoms of pulmonary edema in one.

On July 13, at 4 a.m., Stenstrom and Nilsson started from base camp for a second summit bid. They reached CI in the afternoon the same day. They stayed for a few hours' rest. At 3 a.m. on July 14, they jumared, reaching CIII at 8 a.m. They reclimbed the four final pitches and reached the summit at 3 p.m.

After cleaning the mountain, all climbers returned safely to base camp on July 17. The expedition returned to Denmark on July 26.

JAN STENSTROM, *Denmark*

*Nameless Tower, North Face, New Route.* Our ten-week expedition to Pakistan was successful in establishing a new big-wall route on the north face of Nameless Tower, *Wall Fiction* (a.k.a. *Choss Up Another One*, VI A4 5.10 WI3). The route was somewhere between 3,500 and 4,000 feet and, except for the top, was steep to overhanging, which was fortunate for us, as the face was subject to significant amounts of falling ice, which occurred daily when the sun hit the upper wall late in the day. One point worth noting: our expedition approached the north face from the south (Trango Glacier side) and avoided the extreme objective hazards faced by less trick parties approaching from the north (Dungee Glacier) side. The route followed an improbable line up very thin features a few hundred yards to the right of *Book of Shadows*. John Rzeczycki, Bard Jarred, Warren Hollinger and I summitted during the second week in August after 21 days on the route. The weather was quite cooperative. With regards to difficulty, the route is on par with the more difficult modern El Cap routes. Except for infighting among expeditions members, the ascent went without incident. On the descent, however, Hollinger was injured by rock fall that easily could have resulted in death. The accident occurred in the dark at the bottom of the last rappel while pulling ropes and was indirectly caused by poor communication among quibbling expedition members.

Our expedition was sponsored by The North Face and assisted by the very fine people of Nazir Sabir Expeditions in Islamabad; our expedition doctor, Janet Sweetman; and our Liaison Officer, Captain Farouq, who was extremely helpful during every aspect of our trip and a pleasure to spend time with. Special thanks to the American Alpine Club, which made special arrangements with the U.S. Embassy to post the $5,000 helicopter rescue bond required by the Pakistani Government. It is important to note that our L.O., Captain Farouq, was particular perplexed by the recent, very disparaging article in *Climbing* magazine, "L.O. from Hell," about one expedition's bad experience with what was depicted as a very unpleasant Liaison Officer. The implication was that this kind of experience was rather standard. Our experience could not have been more different: L.O. Captain Farouq was highly educated, articulate, interesting, and very tolerant of our offbeat, strange and often off-color Western ways.

WALLY BARKER, *unaffiliated*

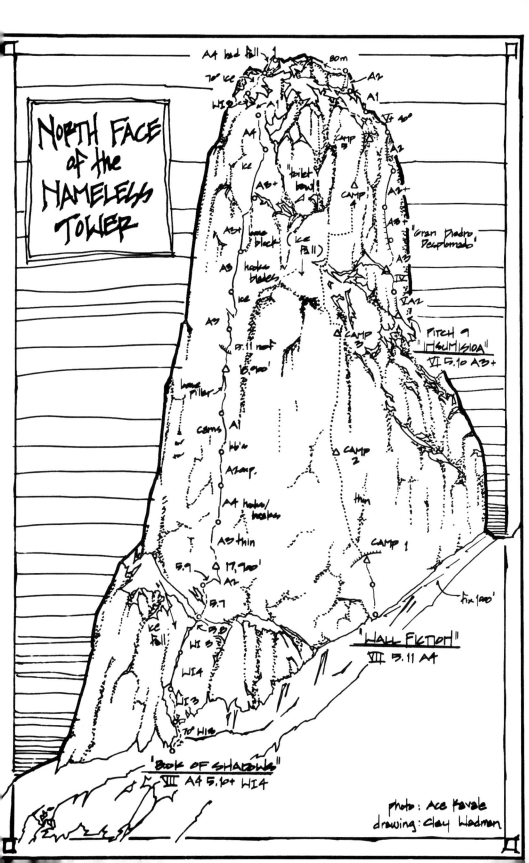

*Skilbrum, Ascent and Tragedy.* A 17-member Japanese expedition made the second ascent of Skilbrum (7360m) via either the original Southwest Face route or the South Face (it is unclear which) on August 17. Eight climbers made it back to base camp on the Savoia Glacier, but on the 20th, an avalanche roared off nearby Angel Peak. The blast was great enough to destroy base camp, blowing climbers across the moraine. Six of the 17 were killed, including the leader, Hiroshima Mitsuo. (*High Mountain Sports* 183)

*K2, West Face, Variation.* In 1994, the Tokai Branch of the Japanese Alpine Club started its exploration of new routes to the summit of K2. After a long exploration, we came to the conclusion that, taking the West Ridge route of the 1981 Waseda University team up to 7800 meters, then climbing up to the left, we would move onto the west face at the altitude of 8000 meters. We expected the greatest difficulty at this point moving on to the west face. We calculated that, once we got on to the upper part of the west face, we would be able to reach the North Ridge, just beneath the summit, by climbing one snow wall, and then another above it. The new route was estimated to be about 800 meters long from the 7800-meter point to the summit.

On May 5, ten days before our departure from Japan, Kazuo Tokushima, who had been preparing for the expedition as our leader, was killed in an avalanche while walking along the Karasawa Valley of Mt. Hotaka in the Japan Alps. It was then decided that Osamu Tanabe should take his place and become leader.

On May 16, our party left Japan as scheduled, and on June 4, our caravan started from Tongal. On our way, in Paiju, we stopped to help the Himalayan Green Club members with their reforestation activities. On June 10, we set up our base camp at 5150 meters, whereas base camp usually is set up to climb K2 by its normal route. It had been our plan to make the 5500-meter point on Savoia Glacier our base camp site, but the change was compelled by troubles with our porters.

On June 14, we set up advanced base camp and began a reconnaissance to find a route to move up the mountain. We soon were forced to halt our reconnaissance, however, when we received a call for help from the Shizuoka Broad Peak Expedition team, which had been hit by an avalanche on June 16. We aided them in their search for those in distress, and were able to recover two bodies on June 18.

On June 20, we resumed our climbing, but were unable to advance very far due to inclement weather. With the beginning of July, however, the bad weather changed and the Baltoro area was blessed with what many felt to be the finest weather in 20 years. Taking advantage of this, we were able to advance at a faster pace. We proceeded up to the 7800-meter point, taking the Waseda University West Ridge route except for the rock wall around 6900 meters. There we chose to take a right-hand course since we thought it would be easier to transport our gear via this new way. On July 16, we managed to climb through a tunnel-like gully less than 50 centimeters wide. From there we climbed along an unknown route. Referring to Mr. Saburo Hiroshima's aerial photographs, we stretched our route toward the left, and found an ideal Camp V site on the shoulder of the West Ridge pinnacle area at a height of 8000 meters. From the shoulder, it was possible to descend onto the snow-covered west face in two pitches.

On July 18, the first advance party, Tanabe, Suzuki, and Nakagawa, set up Camp V, and on July 19, started for the summit. Climbing left from one unstable wall to the next on the west face, we reached a col on the northwest ridge at about 8000 meters. Fear of avalanches would have made this area the most dangerous leg of our climb if we had had bad weather, as

*The west face of K2, showing the route taken by the 1997 Tokai branch of the Japanese Alpine Club.*
OSAMU TANABE

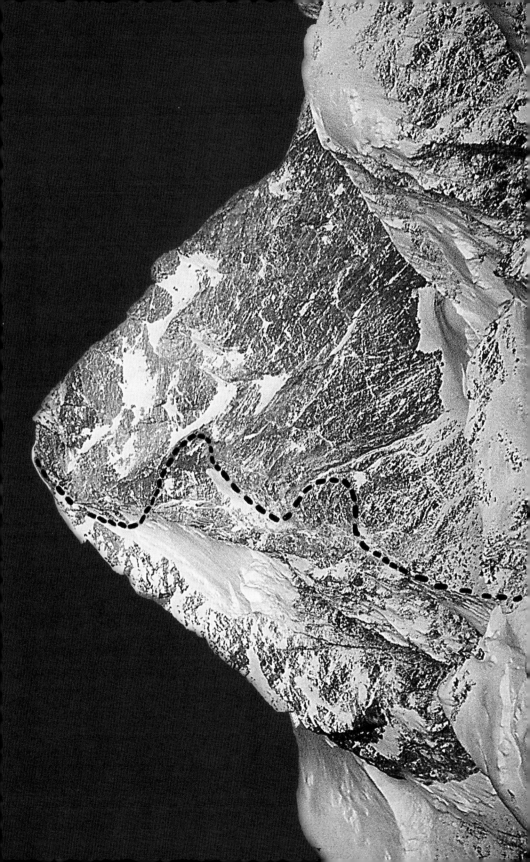

is often the case in this region. From the col up to the uppermost point on the north ridge, we climbed about 200 meters across a slope that was covered with unstable, loose rocks. One more careful traverse pitch brought us to the round snow dome, and then to the summit. There, we were able to lay to rest the ashes of two mountaineers who had been most eager to stand on this summit: the late Tokushima, who was to have been our leader, and the late Yamazaki, who was an earnest climber of our club and who passed away on Ultar II in 1996 after reaching the summit.

After 20 consecutive days of fine weather, bad weather arrived on July 21. This prevented the second advance party from reaching the summit. On July 28, however, eight members (Takine, Nakajima, Yamada, Kobayashi, Dawatasi, Gyarbu, Mimma, and Pembadolge) stood on the top. Thus, our expedition ended successfully. Team members were: Noboru Onoe (54, general leader); Osamu Tanabe (36, leader); Hiroaki Kanada (49, base camp manager); Masamiki Takine (46), Akira Nakajima (35), Ryoji Yamada (34), Masami Kobayashi (32), Manabu Miyosi (31), Mikio Suzuki (30), Kunihito Nakagawa (28), Shouichi Yamabe (34), Asahi Shimbun (news reporter), and ten high-altitude porters from Nepal.

OSAMU TANABE, *Tokai Branch of the Japanese Alpine Club*

*K2, South-Southeast Spur, Attempt.* A seven-member Basque team led by Ramon Agirre (38) reached 7000 meters on the south-southeast spur but were turned back by too much snow and avalanches that came down from the Shoulder (8000 meters). While establishing Camp II (7000m), members of the team were hit by an avalanche. They survived, but were then forced to wait for two days without food and water while conditions stabilized. The team made Base Camp at 5000 meters, Camp I at 6400 meters and Camp II at 7000 meters. Team members were Juan Vallejo (26), Alberto Zerain (35), Mikel Saez De Urabain (29), Peio Angulo (31), Txingu Arrieta and Patxi Ibarbia (32).

ASEM MUSTAFA AWAN, *The Nation, Pakistan*

*Broad Peak, South-Southeast Ridge, Attempts.* It was reported that two teams attempted Broad Peak by its south-southeast ridge this year. Spanish brothers Alex and Félix Iñurrategi made it as far as ca.7200 meters to the start of a difficult rocky section before they realized the undertaking was too great to be accomplished alpine style as they had hoped. They then climbed the mountain from base camp to summit to base camp in a day and a half via the normal route on July 12-13.

Rick Allen (U.K.) and Andrew Lock (Australia) attempted the same line, reaching roughly the same point before coming to the same conclusion. After the retreat, Allen was forced to return home, but Lock reached the main summit via the normal route on August 7. (*High Mountain Sports* 183)

*Broad Peak, Attempts and Tragedy.* A number of climbers were reported to have reached Broad Peak's foresummit this year, including Anatoli Boukreev, in 36 hours return from base camp, Ed Viesturs, Vekka Gustafsson (Finland), and an unspecified number of Japanese climbers. One of the Japanese groups on the mountain experienced tragedy when Jeffrey Bubb (U.S.) and Fukuzo Yokotagawa (Japan) were struck by an avalanche and killed while descending from CIII (6900m) to CII (6400m). (*High Mountain Sports* 183)

*Gasherbrum I, Gasherbrum II, and Broad Peak, Ascents.* A strong 20-member Japanese Gunma Mountaineering Association team and an equally strong team of 12 Nepalese Sherpas scaled the three Pakistani 8000ers, Gasherbrum I and II and Broad Peak, one after the other in different groups and on different dates. The expedition put five Japanese and two Nepalese on Gasherbrum I (8068m), 11 Japanese and four Nepalese on Gasherbrum II (8035m) and eight Japanese and three Nepalese on Broad Peak (8045m). The three teams attempted the peaks via the normal routes and used fixed ropes on their climbs. The teams were as follows. Team 1 (Gasherbrum I and II): Nazuka Hideji (leader), Miyazaki Tsutomu, Baba Yasuo, Iwazaki Sakae, Ezuka Shinsuke. The Nepalese members were Ang Galzen Sherpa and Ang Chhiri Sherpa. Pemba Norbu Sherpa stayed at Base Camp. Team 2 (Gasherbrum II and Broad Peak): Sato Mitsuyoshi (leader), Yoshida Hideki and his wife Yoshida Fumie, Yanase Saichi, Iwazaki Hiroshi, Nakajima Koji, Fukumoto Masashi. The Nepalese climbers were Dawa Chiri Sherpa and Arjun Tamang. Team 3 (Broad Peak and Gasherbrum I): Goto Fumiaki (leader), Ogata Yoshio, Nozawai Ayumi, Hoshino Ryushi, Terada Tsutomu, Watanuki Takeshi, Tajima Takayuki. The Nepalese climbers were Danawang Dorje Sherpa and Norbu Sherpa.

ASEM MUSTAFA AWAN, *The Nation, Pakistan*

*Gasherbrum II, First Iranian Ascent.* Gasherbrum II was the first 8000-meter peak organized and climbed independently by Iranians. The ascent was via the normal route from the south in Pakistan. We set up four camps on the ascent: Base Camp (5200m), CI (5950m), CII (6500m), CIII (6800m), and CIV (7400m). The expedition reached Base Camp on June 26, and 14 days later reached the summit. They started the last attempt at 2 a.m. and in ten hours, at 12:06 p.m., three members (Rasool Naghavi, Hammid Olanj, leader, and Hassan Najarian) stood on the summit. The second group (Dr. Bayatani, leader, Bahmman Rostami, and Ibrahim Shekhi) started at 1 a.m.; at 5 a.m. they reached 7700 meters, but because of bad weather and heavy snow, and following the orders of the expedition leader, they returned to camp IV. The other members of the expedition were Sadegh Aghajani (leader); Dr. Shahbazi (physician); Mohssen Noori, Mohammad Noori, and Hassan Nejatian. We also are preparing for Everest in spring, 1998.

SADEGH AGHAJANI, *I.R.I.M.F/President*

*Gasherbrum IV, Northwest Ridge, Attempt.* It was reported that the Basques Jon Lazkhano, Kiki de Pablo, José Carlos Tamayo and Paco Txabarri attempted to make the second ascent of the Northwest Ridge, reaching an altitude of ca.7300 meters before unstable weather thwarted their attempts. Additional information may be found in the story on the ascent of GIV's west face that appears earlier in this journal. (*High Mountain Sports* 183)

*Gasherbrum IV, West Face.* Sung Dae Cho, who had led an attempt on the 2500-meter west face of Gasherbrum IV (7925m) in 1995, returned in 1997 with an 11-man team that succeeded in making the third ascent of this mountain via the western rib from May 23-July 18. A full account of the climb and its place within the framework of Korean climbing appears earlier in this journal.

*Beatrice, Southeast Face, New Routes.* It was reported that from the end of August to mid-September, a British team put up two separate new routes on Beatrice (ca.5800m) by its 750-meter-plus southeast face on the north side of the Charakusa Valley in Hushe. Mike "Twid" Turner, Steve Myers and Grant Farquar, and Louise Thomas, Kath Pyke and Glenda Huxter operated as two separate teams on the face, with the men putting up the 20-pitch *The Excellent Adventure* (VI E3 6a A3+) and the women establishing an unnamed line to the right of roughly the same grade. The two teams shared a base camp, then worked on a common approach to a snow terrace 100 meters above the glacier where they established different portaledge camps some distance apart. The men fixed 300 meters of line through a large bulge over four days before the good weather broke, forcing them back to base camp for ten days. One aborted start later, they jugged to their high point, fixed their remaining rope, retreated to the portaledge bivy, then reascended the fixed lines and freed the rest of the route in one push at HVS to E2. They opted not to continue on to the summit, which they estimated at some two days' climbing away, and stripped all their ropes on the descent. They placed 20 bolts on the route, all of them at belays.

The women moved out from the snow terrace portaledge some 200 meters right of the men's line, free climbing five or six pitches at up to E3 6a before they were forced to aid their way up the next four pitches (A3+). They then continued up a series of cracks and corners (E2-E3). They returned to their portaledges, then reascended the fixed lines one day after the men had topped out and completed their route in bad weather, reaching the top of the wall after another few free pitches. They stripped their route of lines in bad weather as well. (*High Mountain Sports* 183)

# COMMONWEALTH OF INDEPENDENT STATES
# RUSSIA
CAUCASUS

*Mt. Shkelda, New Route in Winter.* Shkelda is a well-known mountain in the Caucasus. Its "Majesty Fence" consists of five main peaks. From west to southeast, they are the First, Second and Third Western peaks, Central Peak and Eastern Peak, plus a few gendarmes. In the 1970s, a full traverse of Shkelda was considered a very serious ascent. Though the rock walls and ice faces of this beautiful mountain have been very well-mastered by climbers of several generations, an inquisitive eye will always find new routes. This happened with our team from Rostov-on-Don in the winter of 1995, when we put up a new route on the Central Peak of Shkelda by the left buttress of the North Wall (VI 5.10 A3).

From February 24 to March 1, 1997, our team (Yuriy Koshelenko, leader; Vitaliy Polohov, Michael Astahov, Victor Nikitenko, Alexey Kniajev, Anataliy Popov) ascended another new route on the same massif, this time to the Western peak (4310m) from the Svanetia (Georgian Republic) side on the south-southwestern wall. We needed to cross two passes through the snow and blizzard to get to the route. We spent 54 hours total on the route (VI 5.10 A4); the entire endeavor took us 12 days. The total height of the wall is 450 meters; the average angle of the wall is 73°.

The beginning of the route was relatively uncomplicated, involving mostly free climbing (IV-VI) with some spots of aid (A0), then climbing up a steep overhanging section with several roofs. The main reference point is a black water streak, the beginning of which is the start of the key sections. From here, we progressed with very little free climbing and a lot of aid (A2 to A4, with most of it A3) to the roof. The climbing here was either monolithic with blank closed cracks or loose parts, sometimes in the overhanging rock of the roofs. It was risky to hammer a piton because the rock could be destroyed, so we used mostly stoppers, cams and sky hooks. There were a lot of traverses and pendulums on the route. We used 12mm bolts for belay stations.

We climbed capsule-style, using seven 50-meter ropes. Two people—the coach of the team, Alexander Pogorelov, and the doctor, Gariy Karbishev—remained at the Sredniy

KUSNETZOV
Rout,
1969

DROBOT
Rout, 1977

NEW
Route
1997

Ahtiurski
Rout

ShCELDA 2 WEST

▲ CAMP

*The Western Peak of Mt. Shkhelda. Yuriy Koshelenko*

("Middle") Pass during the climb, acting as a liaison for the rescue team.

YURIY KOSHELENKO, *Russia*

*Kiukiurtliu, Lukashbili Route.* Climbers from Dagistan chose Kiukiurtliu, a mountain located on the southeastern spur of Mt. Elbrus (4.5 kilometers from the west summit), for their entry in the high altitude class of the Russian Climbing Championships. They made the fifth ascent of the T. Lukashbili route, climbing it in 54 hours from August 4-8. The route is probably the most difficult route in the Caucuses for the technical class and very rarely attempted. The main difficulties come in the remoteness of the mountain, the large frozen area around the cold wall, and the fact that the route starts at 4000 meters. The sun hits the wall at 2 p.m. Due to its steepness (there is snow only on one section on the middle part of the route), there are problems with water. The region is known for its harsh weather; usually it clouds over and snows in the afternoon. This complicates the ascent and creates psychological tension. The wall is composed of volcanic rock. On the ascent, the pro barely held; half of the stoppers protruded out from the surface. The approach beneath the wall via the headwall ice was 45°. On their bivouac, the climbers used pipes to make a "greenhouse" one meter wide and two and a half meters long. It made it possible to put their bivouac bags inside, and although it gathered condensation, it was relatively comfortable.

VLADIMIR SHATAEV, *Russian Mountaineering Federation*

*Suganbashi, East Face.* Sixth place in the Russian Climbing Championships was the team from North Osetin (S. Egorini, leader, I. Afanacev, V. Ivanov) which climbed the right side of the east face of Suganbashi (6A) in the Suran range of the Caucuses. It's interesting to note that the team found descent slings from the K. Khamitsayev team, which was awarded sixth place in the competitions for a route in the winter of 1996. This made it appear that the K. Khamitsayev team did not complete the route.

VLADIMIR SHATAEV, *Russian Mountaineering Federation*

# TADJIKISTAN

*Muzcol Area, Various Ascents.* It was reported that the British-based company, EWP, led two trips into the Muzcol, a group of high summits in the southeastern corner of the Pamir. The first took place in 1996, when a team made ascents of five unclimbed summits. In August, 1997, a second EWP expedition of seven U.K. climbers, together with seven Russian guides, climbers and staff, visited the area, making a number of other ascents. The activities began on August 12, when, from a bivy at ca.4650 meters, Peter Bournell, Mark Dancy, Chris Mockett, Dominic and Suzanne Reid, Colin Sprang and Andrew Wielochowski climbed easy snow and ice slopes (2A) to the 5660-meter summit of Salters Peak. On August 15, Boursnell, Dancey, Wielochowski, Domenic Reid, Andrej Paschin and Sergei Semiletkin climbed Muzkolski (5895m) via the northeast ridge (3A). Meanwhile, Sasha Bolotov, Igor Gavrilov and Valera Morozov walked up the Zartoshkol Valley to the north, bivying at ca.5100 meters. From there, Gavrilov climbed North Muzkol (6129m) via the center of the southeast-facing snow slopes, which was repeated the next day by an easier line (3A) closer to the east ridge by Bolotov.

On August 18, Sprang and Paschin climbed Panorama (5929m) from the west (3A). Bolotov, Gavrilov, Semiletkin and Wielochowski climbed Fay's Peak (6115m) via an easy glacier to the west face to the northwest ridge in four hours, giving the route a grade of 5A. On August 21, Edward Kapitsa climbed Odinakaya (5687m) via easy snow slopes on the west. (*High Mountain Sports* 182)

# KYRGYZSTAN

PAMIR-ALAI

Lailak Region

*Rocky Ak-Su, North Face, Various Ascents.* Out of the six teams that entered the Technical Class of the Russian Mountaineering Championships, four decided to climb the north face of Rocky Ak-Su (5217m) in the Lailak region of the Pamir Alai. The champion team was the Cverdlov Sports Club (A. Klenov, leader, A. Vedenchuk, M. Dzvi, I. Nefedov, S. Starov, S. Tarasov). They climbed the route in ten days from Aug. 5-14; the ascent involved 104 hours of climbing. They attempted to move as close to the central wall as possible and to improve on the achievement of previous climbers. They used natural pro on their ascent of the Nose near the north cornice and the overhanging section, which they free climbed, using as little aid as possible. To climb the smooth "mirrors" in the middle of the ascent, the team used skyhooks. After all the cracks filled with ice, it was necessary for them to clear for anchors constantly. The route was constantly in shadow and this played on the psyche; only the Nose

*The 5,000-foot north face of Rocky Ak-Su.* CARLOS BUHLER

became bright late in the evening. Because of this, on the icy sections of the descent, it was very difficult for the climbers.

The Competition prize went to Perm's Sports team (A. Shabpovich, leader, U. Zhizhin, A. Mochalov, V. Puchnin, S. Smirnov, N. Rilov), which climbed the Shabalin route by way of the Nose from August 7-16 in 93 hours. It was the second ascent of the route's upper section. Before the ascent, the team waited three days for the snow to stop. All the nights out were organized under cornices or on overhanging walls on portaledges. A safety loop went through the inside of the tent and their helmets were not removed. They worked on the route from day-break (7 a.m.) to sunset (9 p.m.).

The Bronze medal was given to the Kirov team (A. Antonov, leader, I. Tukhvatylin, P. Shabalin), which climbed a new variant on the upper part of the ascent that they called the *Cold Corner* (6A). They made their ascent from July 29-August 5 in 65 hours. Not once dur-ing the time of the ascent did the sun illuminate the route. This was the character of the *Cold Corner* and created problems as far as movement and the setting up of anchors.

The 5th place team from Krasnayarsk (N. Kuzhetsov, leader, V. Alexandrov, N. Zakharov, A. Savinich, U. Stepanov, S. Surobegni) climbed the L. Troshinenko route from August 19-22 in 39 hours to the summit of Rocky Ak-Su.

VLADIMIR SHATAEV, *Russian Mountaineering Federation*

*The Peaks of the Lailak Ak-Su Valley.* While there has been a recent surge in publicity about the Karavshin Ak-Su Valley, fewer American climbers are aware of the alpine rock walls of the Lailak Ak-Su Valley. We here print a number of photos of the Lailak Ak-Su Valley and encourage climbers to consider this area for future climbing trips as well. As with the Karavshin region, the Lailak Ak-Su region has seen considerable development by local climbers, but adventures will undoubtedly still be discovered by the industrious. Further read-ing may be found on pages 26-36 of the 1992 *AAJ* in an article that encompasses peaks in both the Lailak and Karavshin areas.

*Left: Peak Alexander Blok (5229m) and surrounding peaks. Above: Iskander (5163m).* FILIP SIHAN

*The 900-meter Admiral Peak in the Lailak Ak-Su Valley.* FILIP SILHAN

*The upper 1,000 feet of Asan Peak's west face in the Karavshin Kara-Su Valley.* DOUG BYERLY

Karavshin Region

*Kara-Su and Ak-Su Valleys, Various Ascents. (The following account is a combination of three individual notes by Doug Byerly, Stephanie Davis\*, and Patience Gribble\*.)* Jimmy Surette and I arrived at the Kara-Su fork of the Karavshin Valley in the Pamir Alai range in Kyrghyzstan on August 10. We had come to central Asia with hopes of applying Yosemite speed climbing tactics to the higher rock peaks of the world. We were part of a six-person team, but logistical problems conspired to prevent all of us from meeting in Tashkent, Uzbekistan. Jimmy and I had only a 72-hour transit visa, so we forged on alone, without the aid of the interpreter, who would wait for the others. The trek was very hot and physically demanding, especially with a stomach illness and diarrhea. The horsemen, with whom we communicated via gesticulation, were surly with discontent upon arrival in the Kara-Su. They had not eaten enough on the trek and demanded $320 for their services, for which they had already been paid by our host. We spent a tense night deliberating before giving in to their threats of violence. We parted ways in the morning, ending a shaky alliance based in equal parts on trust and betrayal, money and greed, and poor communication. Everyone was a victim as well as an antagonist.

At last it was time to climb! After a few rest days we set out to do the first one-day ascent of the beautiful west face of Asan peak. We chose the 1988 British route, which is predominantly freeclimbing. On August 14, we climbed the 850-meter route in 11 and a half hours, finding excellent crack climbing on sound granite. We suffered through a long bivouac at 4000 meters before descending the scary east face, which had been the scene of a huge rockfall the previous night. Back at base camp we met our interpreter, who informed us that the others were in the fantastic Ak-Su valley to the east, so we packed up and joined them. Then, on August 18, Jimmy and I set out for the first one-day ascent of *Perestoika Crack* on the Russian Tower (a.k.a. Peak Slesova). Eight sessions of diarrhea on the two-hour approach left me exhausted, but we carried on. We completed the 850-meter route in 13 hours, finding fabulous crack climbing up to 5.12. It was hard to imagine a better alpine rock climb anywhere. On August 23, we climbed Peak 4810 via the south face, finding tricky route finding and runout climbing up to 5.10+. The 750-meter route took us seven hours to complete. We both freeclimbed this route rather than having the second jumar as we did on the first two routes, which were technically more difficult. This was a very special climb for me, for I was able to spread my friend Doug Hall's ashes about the summit.

After our only period of poor weather, we climbed the 1300-meter northeast buttress of Peak 4520, simul-climbing the entire route in seven and a half hours, likely the first one-day ascent of the mountain. We stopped to exchange gear only five times on the 4,500-foot climb. Although Jimmy and I were in the mountains for only two weeks, we climbed over two and half miles of granite in 39 hours. Perfect weather and relaxing rest days were a key to our success. The rock climbing in the Pamir Alai is undoubtedly the least stressful and most userfriendly we had ever done. It was a refreshing change from spending months in a tent in Alaska and Patagonia. (*Doug Byerly*)

Kennan Harvey, Topher Donahue, Patience Gribble and I hiked into the mountains from the village of Katran with seven horsemen, a week behind Jimmy and Doug. When our horsemen heard about Doug and Jimmy and how they paid double for their horses, they promptly went on strike and demanded more money. We had a translator, but dealing with the horsemen kept us in a high state of excitement throughout the rest of the approach.

We got to base camp at last, sent our cook/translator off to find Doug and Jimmy, and settled down to climb the beautiful granite peaks around us. Sunny, cloudless days and the complete lack of snow or ice around the peaks made us feel as if we were in a free climbers' paradise. Kennan and I freed a 15-pitch French aid route on Peak 3850, placing two bolts on the 5.12a crux pitch. We spent much of the descent dodging rockfall and creeping down a loose gully.

We also climbed two short six-pitch routes on small peaks on each side of the valley, took a trip up to the glacier to check out the Bird, and then went over to the Kara-Su to climb the Diagonal route on the Yellow Wall. We then returned to do the *Perestroika Crack* on the Russian Tower, one of the best routes I've climbed.

I finished the trip by soloing the French route on Peak 4520 (a.k.a. Peak 1000 Years of

*Jimmy Surette on top of Slesova. Peak 4810 in the background.* DOUG BYERLY

Russian Christianity), which was 30 pitches of beautiful granite. I spent one cold night on the route and was glad I hadn't decided to climb any later. August offered much better free climbing temperatures than early September, and our base camp was now getting only six hours of sun each day.

Overall, we found that there are many aid routes with free climbing potential, but few completely new lines to do unless one is interested in placing a lot of bolts. (*Steph Davis*)

Topher and I warmed up on the French route on 1000 years of Russian Christianity. We both carried backpacks, ascended the 4,000-foot face over two days and spent one full day on the descent. The climb averaged 5.8, with a crux of 5.10, and made its way up many low angle dihedrals on the right side of the peak. The second peak that we climbed, The Middle Pyramid, was the most beautiful climb of all. Toph and I fixed the first four pitches and finally went for the summit. The route, *The Totem*, had been climbed by a French team; our goal was to do the first free ascent. We did the climb in big-wall style, hauling while the second jugged. For me, it was incredible because we were able to swap leads almost the whole way, with Topher leading the hardest pitches, and I pushing myself to the limit as well. We completed the first free ascent after 24 rope-stretching pitches (60-meter rope highly suggested). This climb basically followed crack systems up the middle of the face. The last climb we did was the famous *Perestroika Crack*, on the Russian Tower. Magnificent climbing as well! For this climb, I had the luck to lead the first eight pitches, which meant the four pitches of splitter hands to offwidth granite crack visible from the ground. Topher led the last eight pitches, and when we summited, we knew that would be the last of our Kyrgyzstan climbing. We were saddened but joyous to have had the trip of a lifetime. (It was also reported that Harvey and Donahue climbed a 500-meter new route up the right side of the west face of the Middle Pyramid, *Black Magic*, 5.12a.)

DOUG BYERLY, STEPH DAVIS* AND PATIENCE GRIBBLE*

*Recipients of AAC Mountaineering Fellowship Grants

*Karavshin Region, Various Ascents*. It was reported that the British team of Paul Pritchard, Dave Green, Johnny Dawes and Noel Craine visited the Ak-Su valley in September, making some notable ascents. They began by repeating the Donahue/Harvey route *Black Magic* on the Middle Pyramid. Green and Pritchard then climbed a new route on the rock formation to the right of Pik Slesova, fixing six pitches over five days on the west face before committing to the route. The first six pitches were the crux, and also treated the men to a broken thumb (Green) incurred while drilling a hook placement, 5.11 climbing with a hook for protection (Pritchard), and a 5.12 traverse (Pritchard). From the top of their fixed lines they climbed another 700 meters up easier ground (5.7) to the top. They called their 1200-meter line *The Great Game* (5.12b), and called the wall it was on the Wall of Dykes. (*High Mountain Sports* 182)

*Slesova Peak, Moroz Route*, Ascent. In the Russian Mountaineering Championships, third place was taken by the Moscow team "Treksport" (S. Pugachev, leader, T. Akhmegkhanov, A. Guceva, S. Kovalev, A. Lastochkiy, and I. Pekhtepov) who climbed the Moroz route (6B) on the central north face of Peak Slesova. The ascent, which took place from July 18-20, involved 34 hours of climbing. This was the first time that a place in the championships was awarded to a team that included a woman (A. Guceva). Fifth place in the championships went to Alpclub "Barc" from St. Petersburg (V. Lebedev, leader, A. Pashin, S. Semiletkin), who climbed a 6A route on the north face of Slesova in 69 hours over six days.

VLADIMIR SHATAEV, *Russian Mountaineering Federation*

KYRGYZSKY ALATAU

ALA ARCHA NATIONAL PARK

*Peak Free Korea, Variation.* Two summits caught Bernard's and my attention: Mt. Korona (4860m) and Mt. Svobodnaya Korea (4740m). The first one is a granite tower surrounded by a vast glacier. Many difficult lines remain untouched, while various rock routes of 20 to 30 pitches in length have already been climbed. Mt. Svobodnaya Korea (a.k.a. Free Korea Peak) has a very impressive north face with an overhanging wall. As we had no information on the area, we decided to explore the northeast spur of Mt. Svobodnaya Korea. The north face has a magnificent spur that rises to the west summit of the mountain. An 1100-meter couloir, the Lowe Route, which has never been skied before, runs parallel to this spur. The lower part of the spur has many steep ice or mixed possibilities that finish high on the spur. After one night spent in a bivouac that reminded us of the golden age of Soviet alpinism, we started to move early in the morning of July 7, 1996. That night we approached via the Ak-Sai glacier to the bottom of the face on foot. After crossing a bergschrund, we went up the first slopes without any troubles. To be as light as possible, we brought a nine-millimeter rope, four screws and three pitons. The climb rapidly became engaging in the vertical ice pitch. I joined the spur after ten hours of intense climbing. We stopped for a while in the sun, then continued on easier terrain on the spur. Unfortunately, our enthusiasm was dampened by huge quantities of new snow that reached my belly, making progress impossible and dangerous. We decided to descend by the Lowe route. Hours later we finally arrived on the glacier. The northeast slopes were avalanching all day long, and Andrei, who had watched our progress from the hut, took us in his arms and gave us tchai, the local sausage, upon our arrival.

The north face of Mt. Svobodnaya Korea can be easily compared to Les Droites in the Argentiere basin in the Alps. I can now better imagine what went on in the heads of the first climbers in the Alps.

ALAN DELIZEE, *France*

*Box Peak, New Route.* In July, Misha Michailava, Andrei Molatov, Dmitry Jumakov, Valerie Fedem and Alexandar Chernov ascended a new route (5B) on the west face of Box Peak in the Ak Sai region. At 11 rope lengths, it is not the longest route in the area, but one of many possible new routes. Most climbers have chosen to climb only the traditional routes in the area, or if determined to put up a new route, choose the longer lines. This climb is an example of the many shorter unclimbed routes still to be done.

The entire climb took a total of four days. The first day was spent ascending two pitches to a cornice, which was overcome by drilling a small hole in the face, then standing on a sky hook (the crux of the climb). On the second day four more pitches were climbed, including another aid pitch to overcome a small cornice; a 30-meter slightly overhanging section was also aided cleanly. Four more pitches were climbed on the third day. The final day involved two more difficult pitches, followed by a few rope lengths of low angle dirt and ice. The descent was completed on the same day. There were comfortable belay and bivy ledges for the entire route. Many other routes remain unclimbed in the Ak Sai Valley. For 1998 the same climbers hope to ascend Peak Free Korea, which still has unclimbed routes of up to 20 rope lengths left.

GARTH WILLIS, *The Bishkek Bohemians*

WEST KOKSHAAL-TAU

*Dankova Group, Various Ascents.* It was reported that a 1996 expedition to the eastern end of the West Kokshaal-Tau resulted in the first non-C.I.S. climbers to enter the range, which is the southernmost range of the Tien Shan mountains and lies on the border with China. Michail Lebedev (Russia) had visited the eastern end in 1993, and made the first ascent of the northeast face (6A) of Peak Alpinist (5492m) a striking limestone pyramid somewhat overshadowed by the higher and equally striking pyramids of peaks Dankova (5982m, the highest in the range), Koroleva (5819m) and Chon-Tura-Su (5982m, still unclimbed). The German Kai Würster arranged with Lebedev to return to the range in 1996, and the expedition grew to include Frenchmen Alexis Deschamps, Francois Onimus and Oliver Renault, Germans Juergen Christ and Gesa Weyhen-Meyer, plus 20 Russian climbers. Upon arrival at base camp (ca. 3300m), Weyhen-Meyer, who has a heart pacemaker, quickly developed pulmonary edema and had to be evacuated by helicopter. The team remained behind, and on August 24, Christ, Deschamps and Onimus climbed the north ridge of Alpinist in two days, finding good limestone down low and horrible rock higher up. They attempted to descend the east ridge, which Lebedev et al had used to descend the mountain on its first ascent, but lost the way. By the time they regained their bearings it was night. They continued by moonlight, meeting up with Russians Valeri Boiko, Roman Saliy and Vladimir Vishniakov, who were preparing to ascend the east ridge the next day. After eating and resting with the Russians, the trio continued down, reaching advanced base camp at noon the next day after 55 hours on the go.

Meanwhile, Renault, soloed the west ridge of Peak Zhenit (ca. 5150m), making a possible second ascent up a 2B snow and ice climb.

All four Europeans then made the first ascent of Peak de l'Entre Aide (5030m), a snow pyramid in front of Peak Zhenit, via the north face (50° max) in six hours from ABC, descending south to the col between it and Zhenit. The Russian climbers, meanwhile, had made a reconnaissance circumnavigation of Peak Koroleva to assess the possibility of a new route on the east face. During the same period Starostin and friends had attempted Kibalchichi but had lost some gear and been forced to descend. A team composed of Lebedev, Shimohin, and

unnamed others had attempted Chon-Tura-Su via a pillar on the north face, where a very cor-
niced summit ridge prevented them from reaching the top. Romanov, Shimohin, Smirnov and
Stgarostin made the first ascent of Peak Trapez (5240m) via a 5B route on the southeast face.
Team members also climbed the previously ascended Maron (4900m).

In 1997, a 15-member guided expedition headed up by Pat Littlejohn (U.K.) traveled to
the area in the second week of September. They started their activity with a warm-up on a
4785-meter peak southwest of base camp, which they named Sabaday, finding two and half
pitches of 45-50° hard ice on the northeast ridge. Peak Zhenit was climbed by the east ridge
(55°, AD+). Peak de l'Entre Aide was ascended by a new route up the east ridge (AD), which
gave eight pitches of hard ice overlaid with slabby snow. A third group made the possible first
ascent of a 4910-meter peak immediately north of Peak de l'Entre Aide via a snow/ice couloir
on the southwest flank followed by an exposed narrow ridge of poor rock to the summit. It
was named Peak Serpentine, and descent was made by climbing directly down the south
flank. (*High Mountain Sports* 182)

*West Kokshaal-Tau, Various Ascents.* I traveled to Kyrgyzstan in August, beginning my trip
once again in Ala Archa National Park outside Bishkek, the capital. The area offers a perfect
chance to shake off jet lag and get one's mountain boots banged around a bit, which I managed
to do in the company of Lindsay Griffin (Britain), Matthias Engelien (Germany) and Garth
Willis, an American ex-pat living in Bishkek. After 12 days of climbing we returned to
Bishkek, where, on August 31, we were joined by Nick Green and Brian Davison (Britain). We
left for the West Kokshaal-Tau on September 3, arriving September 6 to begin our exploration.
All research indicated that we were the first climbers to visit our area, which is one valley to
the right of Peak Kizil-Asker (5842m) at the confluence of the three prongs of the Komorova
Glacier (the mountains around which we called the Moonshadow Mountain group). We also
believe we were the first climbers to enter through the western end of the range since Kazbek

*The Dankova group, West Kokshaal-Tau. From left to right: Peak Zhenit, Peak Molodyozhny, Peak Alpinist,
Peak Dankova, Peak Dzhalda. The glacier is the Essledovateley Glacier.* RUSSIAN MOUNTAINEERING FEDERATION

*The Moonshadow Mountain group. Peak Jerry Garcia (ca. 5083m) is the nipple left of center; Peak Unmarked Soldier (ca. 5335m) is the pointed peak center right.* CHRISTIAN BECKWITH

Valiev in 1985, and the first non-C.I.S. climbers to climb in the western end at all.

Lindsay and Brian had both contracted viral illnesses, and spent the first days acclimating up some easy walk-ups. Lindsay netted the first mountain of the trip via the easy north slopes of Peak Lyev (ca. 4600m). Meanwhile, Matthias, Nick and I made the first ascent of Peak 52 Years of American Duct Tape (ca. 5225m) via the western slopes and north ridge before reaching the summit via the west face of the summit gendarme (5.9 AI3). We descended that night only to find that Brian had contracted pulmonary edema and been evacuated by helicopter.

The remaining four of us established ABC at the head of the West Komorova Glacier on September 14, from where we all climbed to the summit of Peak Jerry Garcia (ca. 5083m) via its 40° western ice slopes. We had hoped to continue on up the west ridge of a beautiful pyramidal peak just to the southeast but did not due to indecision in the group. We returned to ABC, then, the next day, with Lindsay again down due to illness, Nick, Matthias and I made the first ascent of Peak Unmarked Soldier via the northeast couloir (ca. 5335m), roping five pitches of ice (65°) then soloing the remaining 500 feet up the eastern summit slopes (40°) in a storm that wreaked havoc on ABC. We stopped short of standing on the summit a meter away, as it was a precarious cornice. We downclimbed and rappelled the way we had come and made it back by dark after a 17-hour day.

After another day's rest in Base Camp, Nick, Matthias and I returned to our ABC to attempt the pyramidal peak one last time. This time we soloed the 500-meter west face ice slopes (55°) and north ridge of Peak Jerry Garcia, but by the time we reached the summit ridge a storm had consumed our objective. We called off our attempt and returned to Base Camp the same day, then departed the West Kokshaal-Tau on September 23.

CHRISTIAN BECKWITH, *The Wayward Mountaineers*

# KAZAKHSTAN

## TIEN SHAN

*Peak Pobeda, Zhuravleva Route.* First place in the High Altitude Class of the Russian Climbing Competitions was taken by the team "Sever" from Severod (S. Penzov, leader, M. Ishytin, M. Strelkov) who climbed on Peak Pobeda (7439m) by the 1990 Zhuravleva route on the northeastern buttress. It was the second ascent of the route. The snow was very deep and unconsolidated. They worked one section of the route for 14 hours. The remains of a short letter from the V. Bezzubkin group (1981) were found on the summit. The climbers ascended the route from August 19-21 in 34 hours.

VLADIMIR SHATAEV, *Russian Mountaineering Federation*

*Peak Pobeda, Ski Descent, Attempt.* "Mt. Victory" (pronounced po-byeh-da in Russian) was the last major peak in the Soviet Union to be scaled, and despite the popularity of skiing in the adjacent Pamirs, it still remains unskied in its entirety. Dave Braun, Julie Faure, Pete Keane and I attempted to ski it in August, but were repulsed by a common but frustrating cause in Asian mountaineering: Our stoves became terminally clogged by the "benzene" we were burning. We were forced to turn back despite reasonable weather and a healthy cache of food and "fuel," leaving the upper 700 meters of the mountain still to be carved.

We acclimatized on the incomparably majestic marble and ice pyramid of Khan Tengri (6995m), "the Lord of the Spirits." After a pleasant recovery at Inylchek Base Camp, where sauna and fresh food are provided by ITMC-Tien Shan Mountain Service, we flew to the base of the 10,500-foot Abalakov Ridge. The line of first ascent in 1956, this series of prows and snow faces leads directly to the broad summit, which is also the Chinese frontier. Due to avalanche danger below 18,000 feet, however, the route is now rarely ascended. Most parties today climb Pobeda via its west ridge (the Dikey Pass Route).

We found melt-freeze and powder snow surfaces on the lower ridge, which made for smooth climbing and skiing. However, at the sight of the 1960 avalanche disaster that caught 29 climbers and killed ten, we found that a series of huge avalanches had recently fallen. Fracture lines up to four feet high and 500 feet wide loomed above shimmering bed surfaces. Wide crevasses were choked with debris. Despite the intimidating presence of the fractures, we took it as a good sign that the stress had been released from the slope. Until the next storm we'd be relatively safe scaling the bed surfaces. These provided challenging skiing, especially where they fall away at 45-50°. Dave and I hop-turned, leaving no trace, and brought up additional supplies while Julie and Pete negotiated a nasty crevasse field on the snow plateau.

The next day we all carried to 19,000 feet and cached below a 60° crest, the gateway to a 1,000-foot section of low-angle, protruding ridgeline. Pete declined to posthole any farther in the rotten snowpack, and Julie descended with him to try the Dikey Pass Route. After skiing from 19,000, Braun and I climbed past our cache, enjoying honeycombed ice, and established high camp at 20,000 feet. Dropping back for our cache the next day we skied the 60° step on a snowy ramp.

Dave and I cramponed up to 22,000 feet on August 20, and I linked turns on wildly variable saastrugi/alpine ice while Dave downclimbed with mild AMS. We intended to hydrate and rest for a summit push the following day, but the stove rendered only a pitiful candlepower flame. Survival without a way to melt snow is, we realized, impossible, so we descended on skis, proud at least to have gotten away with free-heel carving on 8,000 feet of the northernmost 7000er in the world. Meanwhile, Julie and Pete reached a similar height on the west ridge before their stove *simultaneously* failed.

TYSON BRADLEY

*Above: On the mass first ascent of Peak Nazarbaev. Below: Peak Nazarbaev on the left.* STEVE BAIN

*Peak Nazarbaev, Mass Ascent.* On July 6, our party of about 300 made the first ascent of Peak Nazarbaev (4376m) in the Zailiysky Alatau range above the city of Almaty. Peak Nazarbaev had not been climbed because it had not existed prior to July 6, when it was renamed after Kazakhstani President Nursultan Nazarbaev on the occasion of his birthday. The previous name had been Peak Komsomola (Peak of the Communist Youth League).

The Kazakhstani Army Sports Club provided excellent support for the climb. The chair-lift began before dawn to carry everyone up to 3100 meters. It was just as well that only about 300 of the expected 1,500 climbers appeared, because it took the single-chair chairlift a while to get everyone up. Five minutes up the trail from the top of the chairlift, doctors had set up a M.A.S.H.-like medical tent and several tables to check each participant's pulse and blood pressure. After getting medical clearance, everyone set off up the glacier.

For the first few miles, a hundred helmeted soldiers from the Kazakhstani Army led the way. The route was hard to miss because men in bright orange coveralls were posted every 200 feet to offer assistance. For the last 150 meters below the summit, members of the recent-ly returned Kazakhstani Everest expedition had fixed two sets of ropes to allow for travel in each direction. Except for a bottleneck at the bottom of the ropes, the system worked well and nearly everyone reached the top. Given the right conditions, both meteorological and politi-cal, many other first ascent possibilities (perhaps Peaks Lenin and Communism) in the for-mer Soviet Union await.

STEVE BAIN

# SIBERIA
## ALTAI MOUNTAINS

### NORTHERN CHUISKY RANGE

*Maashey, Northwest Wall, Bydonov Route.* The Rubtsov Mountain Club (D. Sergcev, leader, E. Vinnikov, A. Drakie) made an ascent of Maashey (4173m) via the P. Bydonov route on the northwest wall from July 31-August 1 in 24 hours of climbing. The ascent earned them sixth place in the Russian Mountaineering Championships.

VLADIMIR SHATAEV, *Russian Mountaineering Federation*

*Maashey Valley, Various Ascents.* The Altai mountains straddle the border area of Russia, Kazakhstan, Mongolia and China. Much of the mountaineering interest in the range lies with-in Russia—broadly speaking, in southwest Siberia, or more precisely in the Altai Republic. The Siberian Altai is probably best known for the Katun Range, and in particular the Ak-Kem wall of Bielukha (4506m). This area has been visited by a number of British parties (includ-ing the author's in 1990); it was also, for a number of years, the site of one of the established base camps characteristic of the Russian mountaineering scene.

Some 80 kilometers east-northeast of Bielukha lies the Northern Chuisky Range. This range, like the Katun Kange, had a Russian camp for many years in the Ak-Tru valley. The Ak-Tru camp has easier access than the Ak-Kem, and perhaps for this reason remains very popular with local climbers. Despite this, it has still received little attention from foreign par-ties. Curiously, it lies somewhat east of the highest part of the range and, characteristically, other areas have received much less attention from mountaineers despite being well fre-quented by trekking parties.

The only significant foreign climbing team was a British school party organized by Leslie Fox, then of Trent College, in 1990. From a base in the Shavla valley, at the western end of the range, ascents were made of a number of peaks, of which Krasavitsa (3700m) was probably the most impressive.

The Maashey Valley is central to the Northern Chuisky Range, and at its head lie the highest and most glaciated peaks of the range. The main peaks were climbed in the 1960s-70s, but generally only by their easiest routes. Prior to our trip there had been virtually no new route activity since. Visits by non-Russians had been few, and of these the only climbing teams were one from Poland in 1994 and one from Hungary in 1996. The highest peak both in this valley and in either of the Chuisky massifs is Maashey (4177m). This has an extensive north face; the only existing recorded route on it is the Northwest Face ( Russian 5B, ~TD+). Reports of considerable new route potential on this extensive face were instrumental in the choice of location for this expedition.

Immediately east of peak Maashey lies the smaller, but arguably more photogenic, Karagem (3972m). Its north face is broken by a series of five rock ribs (although later in the trip these became almost completely snowed over). Identifying the existing routes on this face proved problematic. The rock on Karagem, as elsewhere, is a dark brown sedimentary rock. This and other problems such as the discontinuities in the ribs and the threat of seracs in the gullies may make the routes both harder and more objectively dangerous than they appear. In addition, the easiest descent (given the impassable state in which we found the Tamma Pass) appears to be the north face of Peak Bars, which calls for reasonable snow/ice conditions.

During our stay we met a number of Russian trekkers who came to see the glacier, to visit the two mountain lakes above it to the west, and sometimes to cross to the Shavla valley. There was also a German party, guided by Sergei Kurgin and his team, that spent several days in our base camp area. The only climbers were Andrei Kolesnikov and Kostya Vinnikov from Barnaul, who completed a traverse from Kurkurek round to Maashey. This traverse had been achieved before, by Valery Karpenko in May 1997, and is a logical expedition given that the main ridge is generally easy and safe in comparison to the ascents on the north wall.

When Justin Canny (U.S.), Michael Doyle (U.K.). Bili Fischelis (U.S.), and I visited the Maashey Valley from July 16-August 1, we were the first British or American climbing teams to do so. Despite boasting the most impressive north wall in the Altai outside of the Bielukha region, the valley remains known to relatively few climbers even inside Russia. Success came early with two new routes on the north side of Maashey (4177m), the highest peak in the Chuisky massifs, though both produced 23-hour epics due to their length and difficulty of access. The next trip out was curtailed by a prolonged storm that blew avalanche-prone snow onto many slopes, but achieved ascents of peaks Tamma (3800m) and Burevestnik (3700m). Finally, ascents of Ak-Tru (4044m) and Kurkurek (3982m) confirmed that the snow conditions still precluded routes on the north face of Karagem (3972m), a major remaining objective.

PAUL KNOTT, *United Kingdom*

# TIBET

*Self-Sufficient Crossing of the Tibetan Plateau, and Ascents of Zangser-Kangri and Peak ca.6400m.* From June 12-August 1, Frank Kauper and Stefan Simmerer made a south-north crossing of the Tschang-Tang (1000 kilometers, on foot and unsupported), making two first ascents en route: Zangser-Kangri (6640 meters, N 34° 23' 29'7", E 85° 51' 18'4")via the southeast ridge, July 4-5, and Peak ca. 6400 meters (N 34° 27'7", E 85° 56'7") on July 6. A full account of the odyssey appears earlier in this journal.

*Loinbo Kangri, Ascent, and Qungmo Kangri, Ascent.* It was reported that a joint Chinese-Korean expedition managed to make the first ascent of Qungmo Kangri (7048m) in the Trans Himalaya north of the Manaslu-Annapurna region of Nepal. On October 7, Wang Yon-Feng, Jung in-Kyu, Cha Jin-Chol, Moon Young-Soung and You Seok-Jae climbed the mountain, followed by Lee Shoong-Jik and Cha-Yo-Han on the 8th. The team then turned its efforts to the first ascent of Loinbo Kangri (7095m). On October 23, Cha Jin-Chol (China), You Seok-Jae and Bang Jung-il (Korea) summitted via the northeast ridge. (*High Mountain Sports* 175)

*Jumo Ganker, Attempt.* It was reported that Huw Davies and John Town (U.K.) attempted Jomo Ganker (7048m) in the Western Nyanchen Tangla Range in Central Tibet in late July and August. They were hoping to make the first western ascent of the mountain by following the line of the other two ascents up the south face. They reached 5900 meters; the weather was unsettled throughout their climb. (*High Mountain Sports* 186)

*Sepu Kangri, Attempt.* There is a range of mountains in Tibet comparable in length to the entire Swiss Alps that remains almost unknown. The eastern section of the Nyangla-Qen-Tangla Shan lies barely 300 kilometers north of the Himalayan frontier crest, stretching across a remote area of central Tibet. This land is sparsely populated yet fertile, a tract of forested valleys coursing through the Tibetan plateau. Its peaks range from gentle hills of around 5000 to 5500 meters in the north to a range of dramatic, steep, and difficult ice peaks in the central and southern sectors. There is a pattern of inhospitable weather throughout most of the warmer summer months, with much fresh snowfall. Sepu Kangri (6690m), at 30.9°N 93.8°E, is the highest summit.

This mountain region northeast of Lhasa, loosely called the Sino-Himalayan axis by explorers earlier this century or sometimes referred to simply as the Tang-La, is the source of three great rivers of Asia, the Yangtse, the Mekong and the Salween I. We reconnoitered the northern side of Sepu Kangri in the summer of 1996, finding a route south from Diru into the valleys leading to the glaciers of its north face. In a separate journey, we also visited the southern side of the range.

For the local people, the principal summits of the Sepu Kangri massif are Sepu-Kung-Lha-Karpo, The White Sky God, the highest, and its immediate neighbor to the east, Bon-Che-Dadhul, Sepu's Son. Yu-Yi-Metok, The Turquoise Flower, or Sepu's Daughter, is a stark 6800-meter pyramid west of the main peak. There are six other summits with Tibetan names. These peaks are sacred; the Samda monastery, an 800-year-old Bonpo fortress shrine presently housing 40 monks, is a day's journey below them. Our view from base camp was hard to reconcile with a comment from one of our own elders at the Alpine Club before we left: "Really, there are no mountains of any interest in that area of Tibet."

For our hosts on this expedition, the China Tibet Mountaineering Association (whose cooperation could not have been better), this area also remains a relative blank on the map. Like much of the Himalayan crest, good maps doubtless exist, but are still restricted for military use only. The whole region remains firmly closed to foreigners. Our own journeys were the product of lengthy negotiation. The file of correspondence, commencing with a photo taken from a Chengdu-Lhasa flight one early morning in March, 1982, tells a story of despair, hope, disappointment, giving way to encouragement, commitment and, finally, travel, to this remarkable area.

We reached base camp on April 30. On our recce in August the year before, I had identified the northeast ridge of Seamo as the most feasible route up the mountain, but we wanted to have another look before committing ourselves. That afternoon, John Porter, Charlie Clarke, and Jim Lowther climbed a 5600-meter hill to the north of base camp, while Jim Fotheringham and I visited the hermit who had lived for four years at the foot of the valley leading up to the northwestern end of the main peak of Sepu Kangri. After talking with him and receiving a blessing, we walked on over a frozen lake and up a snow-covered moraine to catch a glimpse of a possible route up to a col immediately north of Seamo Uylmitok. Jim thought there might be a route from this col onto the much easier angled west face of the mountain.

A couple of days later we made a recce in force, camping on the glacier on the night of May 4 and the following morning carrying heavy sacks with camping equipment and a couple of days' food.

Even in the cold of the early morning, we broke through the crust that covered the deep soft snow. It was an exhausting process, with Fotheringham trail-breaking all the way up to the col 700 meters above. The weather was windy with flurries of snow, a pattern with which we were to become all too familiar in the coming weeks.

Early that afternoon we reached the col, only to find it was a knife-edged, gendarmed ridge with a startling drop on the south side to a glacier far below. The view along the ridge wasn't encouraging, for it seemed to run into the northwest ridge of Seamo Uylmitok, with a steep drop onto the glacier to the south and a ferocious icefall to climb behind the peak. The following day we returned to base and decided to focus on what we named the Frendo Spur, the ridge leading to the summit of Seamo Uylmitok, but with the prospect of taking the easier ground on the face itself, which was glaciated.

We established Camp I on some rocks on the glacier below a large snow bowl leading up to a diagonal gully-cum-gangway that seemed to give a safe route up to the foot of the

*The Sepu Kangri massif, with Sepu Kangri on left, in a photo taken from the 1996 reconnaisance.*
SIR CHRISTIAN BONINGTON

Frendo Spur. We made our first foray on May 10, when Fotheringham led a desperate pitch on steep mixed ground in a bottleneck that barred the way at the bottom of the gully. Beyond this the angle dropped off, but the following morning we very nearly turned back when Porter was engulfed in a spindrift avalanche generated by high winds and flurries of snow on the face higher up.

This was to be the weather pattern in the days to come. It was usually cloudy and windy first thing in the morning, clear for a short time in the middle of the day and then deteriorating into cloud and snow in the afternoon. It didn't give much time for climbing.

It took us two days to push the route up to the crest and this provided a perfect site for Camp II with a snow hole and room for a tent. Fotheringham and Porter moved up on May 14 and started pushing the route out, initially on the crest of the spur, but as it steepened they cut out through a corridor between serac walls to get onto the main face, reaching a height of 5850 meters. Lowther and I moved up to the camp on the 15th and continued working on the route on the 16th. There was undoubtedly an element of danger in going up the face, as there was a huge quantity of snow and the ever-present risk of avalanche. We felt that the unsettled weather combined with this threat justified the use of fixed rope. The weather was still far from perfect, starting the day with snow squalls but clearing up around midday. It took us about three hours to reach the high point, and we then shared the lead up a series of snow fields, pulling over bergschrunds and only occasionally getting ice screw belays.

As we gained height we could see there was a ramp leading out to the left end of the col, but I, leading the final pitch that day, cut back to the right to get an anchor in what seemed a stable serac wall immediately beneath the Frendo Spur, thus making it relatively free of avalanche danger. We decided this would make a good site for a third camp and, at 6050

*The Sepu Kangri massif. Sepu Kunglha is the highpoint of the massif. The pointy peak on right is Seamo Uylmitok.* SIR CHRISTIAN BONINGTON

meters, a jumping-off point for an alpine-style push for the summit.

That night we were full of optimism, but the following day, the weather seemed unsettled once again. We decided to return to base camp for a couple of days' rest while we waited for the weather to settle and then make our bid for the summit.

It wasn't to be. On the night of May 19, half a meter of snow fell at base camp. Much more must have fallen on the face. It snowed off and on for the next ten days with the mountain almost continually hidden in cloud. We were prepared to extend the expedition but there was no sign of an improvement in the weather and in the end we were very lucky to have a single clear day to rescue the equipment we had left at Camp II. We started our descent from base camp in a violent blizzard the following day.

Although the continuous bad weather had been frustrating, the area is so beautiful, our neighbors, whom we got to know well, so kind, and the team itself such a well-balanced one, none of us felt depressed as we walked back down to the road head. We were already planning our return in 1998.

SIR CHRISTIAN BONINGTON, *Alpine Climbing Group*

*Shishapangma, Attempt.* The main goal of the Slovenian Shishapangma 1997 autumn expedition was to climb the British route on the Shishapangma's southwest face. Besides that, we planned an alpine style ascent and a ski descent from the top across the British route. After two nice weeks when we put up the first and the second high camps on the British route, a period of bad weather forced us to give up on an alpine-style climb. The highest point, at about 7200 meters, was achieved by Blač Navranik, Mira Zori and Sandi Vaupoti. They were just about to put up the third high camp when the sudden snowstorm forced them to descend to the lower camps. In the following days, when there was no end to bad weather, we finished the expedition, and the last members left base camp on October 15.

FRANCI SAVENC, *Planinska zveza Slovenije*

*Shishapangma.* It was reported that Goran Kropp (Sweden) led a 12-member expedition to Shishapangma on which Renata Chlumksa became the first Swedish woman to climb above 8000 meters and Cyril Destremau managed to make the first snowboard descent from the Central Summit all the way to base camp. (*High Mountain Sports* 180)

*Gaurishankar, Northeast Ridge, Attempt.* Gaurishankar (7134m) lies on Nepal's northern border with Tibet; it is visible from Kathmandu on the northeastern horizon, and it was once thought to be the world's highest mountain until the British Survey of India made more careful measurements. All climbing attempts until this autumn on this rugged mountain were made with permits from the Nepalese government, for the Tibetan/Chinese authorities did not open it to mountaineers until a few years ago. A British attempt led by Don Whillans in the autumn of 1964 did go around from Nepal's southwestern side to the northwest in Tibet and reached 6700 meters before avalanching turned them back. Since then no one had repeated this approach; in fact, the mountain is seldom climbed from any side.

In September, two well-known Japanese mountaineers, Yasushi Yamanoi and his wife Taeko (who was known by her maiden name, Taeko Nagao, until she married Yamanoi recently), went onto the northeast ridge but were quickly turned back at 6300 meters, where the ridge became very narrow and steep and numerous mushrooms blocked the way. It was not possible to escape from the ridge because of extreme danger on the north face from many falling seracs, so they abandoned their attempt on September 23. They thought the climb might be possible in colder weather in mid-October, but they do not recommend attempting the mountain from Tibet at all: the local people demanded a lot of extra money, and they were informed that the road leading to it is frozen after the end of October.

ELIZABETH HAWLEY

*Dranang Ri, North Ridge, Attempt.* It was reported that an eight-man Japanese team led by Susumu Kobayashi attempted the unclimbed snow/ice crest of the north ridge of Dranang Ri (6801m) in 1996, reaching ca. 6000 meters before being turned back by difficulty. (*High Mountain Sports* 175)

*Cho Oyu, New Route.* It was reported that during an Out There Trekking Expedition in the pre-monsoon season, Russian guide George Kotov and American client Bill Pierson managed to find 1000 meters of new climbing on the north side of Cho Oyu. From the normal Advanced Base Camp, the two set up Camp I on the Palung La (6500m) below the north-northeast ridge climbed last year by Sebastian Rucksteiner and Oscar Cardiach. Camp II was established at 6600 meters on the prominent rib to the left of the ridge and forming the left edge of the triangular facet. After a rest at ABC, the two began climbing on May 18, reaching the 6600-meter camp the same day. On the 19th they climbed farther up the rib, camped, and continued on the next day to the top of the rib, reporting angles of up to 40° on new snow over blue ice, with the last day involving a section of waist-deep snow. From the top of the rib they traversed across to the top camp of the standard route (7600m) and made it to the summit on the 21st. (*High Mountain Sports* 181)

*Mt. Everest, North Face, Variation.* A Russian expedition led by Kazbek Khamitasayev ascended what they said was an unclimbed rib on the north face to an altitude of perhaps 7500 meters before abandoning that line and traversing left to the standard route up the north ridge to put two of their 19 climbing members, Alexandre Zelinski and Sergei Sokolov, on the summit.

ELIZABETH HAWLEY

*Mount Everest Group, Attempted Traverses.* There were two ambitious plans for very light-weight traverses via the highest point on earth (*see Nepal for that of Anatoli Boukreev*). An Italian, Reinhard Patscheider, who was an independent climber on the north side, reportedly wanted to descend the south side, but he unfortunately developed some unexplained stomach illness and after two attempts to climb the mountain was forced to go home without having gotten any higher than 7100 meters. He had climbed from the north on a permit arranged by a Polish mountaineer who actually did most of his own climbing with an Indonesian team.

Patscheider's intention had been to go down the southeast ridge, which forms part of the international border, to the South Col, the very high saddle between Everest and Lhotse, and from there descend the standard Nepalese route. He was enrolled on the Lhotse permit of a British-led commercial expedition, and the leader of that team left for him at the South Col, as requested by Patscheider, a tent, sleeping bag and mat, stove, fuel and food. These items still await his arrival.

Although Patscheider had put his name on two permits, one from the Tibetan authorities and the other from the Nepalese, such a trans-border traverse would have been illegal, and he could have gotten into trouble if he had actually carried out his intention and been discovered. All permits require climbers to go down the same routes they go up. Furthermore, there is no agreement between the two countries for such border crossings, and the Nepalese penalty for this can be banishment from climbing in Nepal for five years.

ELIZABETH HAWLEY

*Everest, Various Activity on the North Side, and Cho Oyu, Various Activity.* Ten commercial expeditions on the Tibetan side and two in Nepal (several of them commercial as well) made attempts on Everest, but not a soul got to the top. This was the first autumn season since 1987 in which no one summitted Everest. (Ten years ago, all four teams on the north side and all three from the south failed.) Fierce winds and new snowfall were the villains this autumn.

A highly experienced Nepalese Sherpa, Apa, and the Swiss mountaineer Jean Troillet, who himself has seven 8000ers to his credit, including Everest already in a remarkably swift ascent of the mountain in 1986, reached together the highest point on the vast mountain that anyone achieved this season, 8700 meters or only 150 vertical meters below the top, on the north side. Troillet had intended to descend from the summit by snowboard; he went down on one from 8700 meters.

Everest claimed one life this autumn. A South Korean expedition sent a party to the North Col very early in the season, on September 8, to deposit gear there. One of them, the expedition's climbing leader, Choi Byung-Soo, was buried without trace by a big avalanche just below the Col.

Commercially organized efforts on Cho Oyu fared much better. On Cho Oyu's normal route on the northwest side, 17 out of 22 teams managed to put a total of 75 people on its summit. A 19-member Italian team led by Giacomo Scaccabarozzi was faulted by others on Cho Oyu for leaving the mountain and deserting one of their teammates, Claudio Mastronicola, who was still there struggling to climb it and soon afterward had to be rescued and taken care of by other expeditions when he became seriously disoriented and frostbitten. One member of his group explained in Kathmandu that this had been a north Italian expedition with most members sympathetic to the movement favoring the north's secession from Italy, while the man they had left behind was a southerner.

ELIZABETH HAWLEY

*Kula Kangri, Third Ascent.* It was reported that a Spanish expedition made the third ascent of Kula Kangri (7554m) in May. Base camp was established on May 4; by May 15, a route that roughly followed the west ridge had been established to Camp II at 6450 meters, and on the 18th, with a break in the weather, the team reached the summit. They also reported ascending two unclimbed subsidiary summits to the east, one (Kula Kangri II?) at 7430 meters, and the other (Kula Kangri III?) at 7150 meters. (*High Mountain Sports* 186)

# CHINA

*Geladaintong, Northeast Face.* I was invited by Geographic Expeditions to guide two American clients, William Rom, M.D. and Dan Luchtel, Ph.D., on a peak called Geladaintong (one of a few spellings), which is 6621 meters high and located at what the Chinese like to call the source of the Yangtze River. Technically speaking, there is a source located farther south and west that is a half mile or so farther from the mouth of the river, but it's an unspectacular mud flat at a lower elevation than the glacial source at the foot of Geladaintong. To geographers, tourists and travel agents alike, Geladaintong makes a more attractive source for the mighty river that China is damming to create the largest hydro-power plant in the world.

Geladaintong is located in Qinghai Province, just north of Tibet, approximately 60 kilometers northwest of the Tangula Pass. The main road from Tibet to China, which goes from Lhasa to Golmud and on to Xining, traverses the Tangula Shan mountains via the Tangula Pass.

We arrived in Tibet on August 27 and spent several days touring cultural sights and accli-

*Geladaintong. Mark Newcomb's solo ascent took the snow face up to the central couloir. The north ridge follows the right skyline to the summit.* MARK NEWCOMB

matizing. Then we spent three days driving to the base camp, two along the highway to Golmud, Qinghai Province, and one traversing 90 kilometers overland on a track that disappears entirely several kilometers before base camp. We spent September 3 and 4 doing reconnaissance and acclimating. The mountain had been climbed first by Japanese in 1984 and second by a team from Beijing University in 1994. We found garbage from the '94 expedition at base camp and Camp I, along with deep ruts from the large truck they drove over delicate tundra vegetation in order to place their base camp two kilometers farther up the valley than where we placed ours.

Bill and Dan rested on September 5, but in order to keep our momentum up and carry out more recon, I carried a load of gear to CI on my own. After dropping the load, I crossed the glacier on the flank of the northeast face and proceeded to climb a steep snow line up the northeast face that I had carefully scrutinized two days before. Presumably it was a first ascent, as neither the Japanese nor the Chinese had mentioned anything about climbing any route other than the north ridge. The line started at the lowest point on the face (5800m), crossed a small bergschrund, traversed up and slightly right past a small serac, entering a 50° couloir at around 6300 meters, and topped out within five meters of the knife edge summit. The crux of the climb was a section of 55-60° ice about four meters long. The rest of the climb was entirely on snow, varying between ankle and knee deep. I downclimbed the standard route on the north ridge. The round trip took just over nine hours from base camp.

The next day Dan, Bill and I started up together, stopping for the night at CI (5600m) on the east edge of the glacier that aprons the northeast flank of the peak. We spent a second night at 6100 meters in a col at the base of the north ridge. The glacier that spawns the Yangtze river is several hundred meters below the west side of this col. The following morning (September 8), we set out at dawn along the gradually steepening north ridge toward the summit. The climb is non-technical, though it's worth carrying two or three ice screws and/or some snow protection in order to protect a couple of short, 45-50° bulges. We encountered weak, sugary snow on two of these bulges, triggering a small slab avalanche (about 15cm deep) on one of them.

The ridge leads to a plateau a couple of hundred meters long at around 6550 meters. Geladaintong's sharp summit rises from the southeast end of this plateau with one short pitch of steep snow leading to the peak. We summitted around 1 p.m., and returned to CII around 4:30 in the afternoon, descending all the way back to base camp the following day.

MARK NEWCOMB, *unaffiliated*

## SICHUAN PROVINCE
### DAXUE SHAN

*Daxue Shan Range, Various Ascents.* During the month of October, 1996, Fred Beckey led an expedition to the Daxue Shan range of central Sichuan Province in the People's Republic of China. The marketing people at Ross Labs agreed to support the trip financially as Fred offered his services as spokesman for their nutritional drink Ensure. The climbing team included John Chilton, Jia Condon, and Rich Prohaska, all from Whistler, B.C., Mark Carter from New Zealand and Steve Must from Seattle. Three mountains were summited for the first time in an area north-northeast of Gongga Shan known as the Lamo-she range. The three peaks extend north from the mountain known as Lamo-she (the Goddess Peak, 6070m), which was first climbed in 1993 by Grey Thompson and Jon Turk (see *AAJ* 1994, pp. 269-70). The compact range of mountains all hover around 6000.

Fred had extensively reconnoitered the surrounding terrain during the 1993 trip. This eased most of our logistical problems. With the assistance of our Chinese liaison Shao and Jing Jing, a few Tibetan horsemen and their team of horses, we established an initial base camp at 13,500 feet in a valley below two of our objectives and only a day's hike from the nearest village. We arrived at a high camp around 16,000 feet, and woke to a few inches of snow. This gave us another day to acclimatize and it turned out to be the only inclement weather we were to encounter up high. Although the valleys were consistently lost in a lake of clouds and damp drizzling rain or snow, the skies were clear and sunny above 14,000 or 15,000 feet. Fred had problems with the altitude and returned to base camp after two sleepless nights. The rest of us set off to explore the glacier and continued on to the top of the smaller peak. Carter and I went up the corniced north ridge as the clouds climbed out of the east to meet us. A few steep sections made the rest of the deep stepping interesting. We reached the summit and found the three Whistler climbers waiting patiently and getting cold. They had opted to climb a steep face that led to the gentle west ridge. We all descended the north ridge. The local name for this mountain is Snake Lake Peak (5760m).

The next day, the Whistler trio were eager to launch an assault on the towering and unnamed summit, just to the left, or north, of Snake Lake Peak. Carter and I were feeling the altitude and exhaustion from the previous day's work and retreated early. The others continued on and reached a rock band that required 5th-class climbing. They fixed a few ropes and returned to high camp. Meanwhile, Carter and I had returned to base camp. Rich, John and Jia completed the climb the next day via the northwest ridge during a technical and strenuous 14 hours and called the peak Wu Shan, "Misty Mountain" (5987m).

Our support team congratulated us all with ample supplies of *py jiu* (Pabst Blue Ribbon), *bai jiu* (rice whiskey) and fresh yak meat. While most of us struggled to recover from the poisonous beverages the next day, our smiling Tibetan horse team efficiently saddled the horses and we moved camp to the next valley to our north. I learned their secret as they passed

*Steve Must bouldering at CII in the Daxue Shan.* JIA CONDON

around another bottle of whiskey during the trek. It seemed to aid them in verbally directing the horses as we heard their hoots and howls resonant through the mists.

Our second base camp beheld an excellent view of our next objective, San Ping Fong (6010m). From here we carried everything up to two higher camps in one push. The high camp, also around 16,000 feet, included a spectacular tent sight on an enormous boulder with an amazingly flat surface perched high above the rubble and talus. From here, while Fred remained at high camp, the five of us climbed the north ridge by gaining the glacier, maneuvering crevasses, negotiating the steep ice at the col and tramping our way across a broad summit plateau. We were calling it Slog Ping Fong by the end of the climb. San Ping Fong means "Peak Number Three" in Mandarin. There are two peaks to the north, which were named Yi Ping Fong ("Peak One") and Er Ping Fong ("Peak Two"); Wu Shan, just south, was designated Sze Ping Fong ("Peak Four"). These uninspired names were given by the assiduous German explorer Edward Imhof, who surveyed these mountains in the 1930s. I found an excellent map of the region at the (Seattle) Mountaineers library. I believe that it is from Imhof's work, although its source and date of origin are unknown. It is labeled Minyag Gangkar, which could be German for Minya Konka (Gongga Shan). From this survey, the elevation of San Ping Fong and Sze Ping Fong are listed at 6010 meters and 5987 meters respectively.

Fred was bent on accomplishing as much as possible after working so hard to get to the Daxue Shan range. Much to his chagrin, we left peaks One and Two unclimbed. Before we could call together the horses and leave the cold, damp mists of She He Dz valley, he tried to get a consensus from the group to remain in the area and explore another elusive unclimbed mountain in the vicinity of Kangding. After over-riding his veto, we were all soon soaking in hot springs at the village, crashing a Tibetan wedding, and boarding a bus the next day bound for Chengdu. Meanwhile, Fred remained in Kangding with Jing Jing, determined to find a viable approach to the peak. We eventually met up in Chengdu and gradually retraced our journey home.

The support from the Zhang brothers, who operate Sichuan Adventure Travel in Chengdu and with whom Fred had worked in the past, was excellent.

STEVE MUST

## SICHUAN
### CHOLA SHAN

*Chola Shan I and Chola Shan II, Ascents, and Gurla Mandhata, Attempt.* It was reported that in late summer and early fall, Charlie Fowler visited China and Tibet, making a solo second ascent of Chola Shan I (6168m) and a first ascent, also solo, of Chola Shan II (6119m) via its southeast ridge. Later, he turned his efforts to Gurla Mandhata (7728m) near the Nepalese-Indian border, where he set out to guide Soren Peters and Quinn Simons, two young climbers from Santa Fe. The trio began with first ascents of two 6900-meter peaks in the area. Thus acclimitized, they began up Gurla Mandhata, reaching a bivouac one pitch below the west ridge on their third day on the mountain. Peters and Simons had led much of the climbing to this point, but Simons seemed exhausted, forcing the team to take a rest day. A storm blew up, pinning them down another day, then collapsing their tent. Simons frostbit his hands while helping to dig it out, then developed signs of pulmonary edema. On day six, they began down. They were roped up and glissading a 50° slope when one person slipped. With his frostbitten hands, Simons was unable to self-arrest, precipitating a 1,500-foot fall that took the party over a 50-foot cliff and landed them, miraculously, in deep, soft snow. Fowler had a badly sprained his leg, but the others had suffered no injuries. It took a day to get to the glacier, where Peters and Simons went to base camp for help. The camp cook, Kwang Tamang, returned for Fowler 24 hours later. Fowler lost the tips of four toes, Simons lost portions of both hands and feet, and Peters likely will lose fingers and toes. (*Climbing* 176)

*UIAA International Camp, Various Ascents.* On September 7, all 23 members of the Third UIAA International Mountaineering Camp from ten different countries arrived in Chengdu in the province of Sichuan in China after a long journey via Beijing, Hong Kong, Shanghai or Bangkok. The staff, international as well, consisted of: UIAGM Mountain Guide Robbie Fenlon from Ireland, Co-leader and UIAGM Mountain Guide Jorg Wilz from Germany and Dutch Leader and UIAGM Mountain Guide Edward Bekker, who lives in Chamonix and is a member of the UIAA Expeditions Commission. Wilz and Bekker also guided and organized the highly succesful camp to Hushe Valley in Pakistan in 1993. The expedition doctor was Dr. Eckart von Delft from South Africa. After spending one day in Chengdu to buy food for base camp and general organizing, we left Chengdu and traveled for four days by bus to Maniganggo near the Tibetan border. Traveling with us were the Chinese officials from the Sichuan Mountaineering Association, which is affiliated with the Chinese Mountaineering Association. There were, amongst others, Mr. Jiang Yi, Executive General Secretary and Mr. Luo, our interpreter and Vice General Secretary. The liaison officer was Mr. Mong. Also travelling along were the cooks Mr. Dzu and Mr. Ten. The organization of hotels and food was immaculate. Also to be mentioned was our bus driver, who drove us safely over very rough roads.

On September 13 and 14, we established Base Camp in pouring rain at about 4000 meters on the southwest side of the holy Xinluhai (Lhamcoka) Lake in a lovely spot with small trees and a nearby river. The campsite was surrounded by many rocky peaks on one side and green hills on the other.

Camp I was established on the 15th at 4650 meters. From the 15th to the 27th, small teams were formed and, despite the generally bad weather, quite a few mountains were climbed, some by fine new alpine routes. The highest altitude reached was between 5800 and 5900 meters. It is a pity that Chola Shan, the highest summit of the area at 6168 meters, could not be climbed, solely because of too much avalanche risk. In 1988, Chola Shan was climbed for the first time by Chinese and Japanese, and two small Japanese groups climbed on Chola Shan in 1995 and 1996.

We found September to be a little too late in the season with a lot of new snow. July is reported to be rather wet. August could be the best time for climbing in this remote area.

The most important climbs (*some of which are listed below in greater detail*) were as follows. September 16 and other days: Slab climbing near camp. *Amsterdam-Tel Aviv Diretissima* (III-VI+, 200m), Jochai Lelior (Israel), Mark Heine and Leopold Roessingh (Netherlands). September 16-18: A large team set up CI and CII and tried Chola Shan. They set off two big slab avalanches one to each side, and turned around at 5850 meters. The group included Christof Friemel, Lukas Knechtle (Switzerland), Robbie Fenlon (Ireland), Bram van de Kam, Miriam Knepper, Martijn Schell, Chris v.d. Berg (Netherlands), and Megan Beaumont (South Africa). All went down in bad weather on the 19th.

On September 17-19, Mark Heine, Leopold Roessingh, Edward Bekker, Jochai Lelior, Jorg Wilz, Eckart von Delft, Keun Lee Soo and Sang Jin Kim (South Korea) all went to CI. Bekker, von Delft, Kim and Lee went to CII, but the weather was too bad for Chola Shan.

French Manu Pellissier and Fréderique Salle focused on the "Chinese Droites," but were unable to try it because of weather and a stolen rope from the depot at 4600 meters!

British Liam Reinhardt and Belgian Mario Deroo teamed up for rock climbing and did two pitches on *Son of a Yak* (IV-V), finding bad rock but a nice bivy.

September 20 was nice weather that produced three new routes on "Hero Shan" (5700m) from CI. Lelior and Wilz climbed a 450-meter ice route, the *Jo-Jo Couloir*, from the 'schrund up to 85°. Heine and Roessingh climbed *Voie Kurai*, a 450-meter mixed route (EDinf 90°), possibly the most difficult route of the Ccamp. Bekker and von Delft tried the possibly unclimbed Pyramid opposite Chola Shan, near Chola Shan II, but turned around at 5850 meters because of avalanche-prone slopes.

Another rocky ridge and peak called "Groenlo Shan" was climbed by Knepper, v.d. Kam and Beaumont on September 23. Pellissier, Salle and Fenlon sat out a few stormy days in French CII, but conditions were never right.

Beyond the climbing, a lot of exploring was done in other valleys. The area has a lot of scope for both rock and mixed, but one needs a lot of time and good nerves to wait for the right moment. Even though the weather was not very good, the expedition was a great success and all members enjoyed it a lot. The team spirit was really good, as was the cooperation with the Chinese. We did not see even one other tourist and the exploring of an unknown area was especially highly appreciated.

EDWARD BEKKER

*Chola Shan, Slovenian Activity.* During the UIAA International Training Camp, we climbed

*The north face of The Needle, showing* The Sichuan Adventure, *with "Hero Shan" (5700m) to the right.*
EDWARD BEKKER

three new routes on four new peaks between 5000 and 6000 meters. On the north face of Slovenian Peak (5500m), Miha Manence, Matej Brjnik, and I climbed the new route *Cleopatra* (ED-85°, 800m) in seven hours on September 9, then descended the south face, thereby making the first traverse of the mountain. From base camp we made the four-hour approach on the Geimian glacier and from there one to two hours to the wall. The lower part of the route was technically not difficult. In the middle, it is about 70° in the couloir, but at the top it was 85°. Fifty meters below the summit we reached the col and went left to the top of the mountain. The conditions were ideal in the narrow couloir (85°), but below the 60° section there was a lot of new snow. (The weather on all 14 days was like in Patagonia). We soloed the route because the rock was so monlithic we couldn't protect. It is quite comparable technically to *The Shroud* on the Grande Jorasses, but the lower part is easy, the altitude is higher and the descent is more difficult. The climb was very good; the only problems were spindrift and thin ice (3-5cm) We descended the south face in eight rappels, then exited via the Nanmian Glacier to base camp (11 hours of descent).

On the north face of the Needle (5650 m), Miha Marence and I climbed *The Sichuan Adventure* (ED V+ 70°, 750 m) in ten hours on September 20. The approach was made as for Slovenian Peak, but more to the west. The mountain is very beautiful and daring. The first half of the climb, which we soloed, was snow and ice (60-85°). The first 200 meters, with the risk of stone- and icefall and thin ice, was very dangerous climbing. The upper part was mixed climbing (V+ 70-90°). The conditions were ideal—like in the French Alps, but protection was minimal because the rock was very compact (no cracks. . . .). After ten hours of climbing, we reached the top and abseiled immediately. Bad weather was coming.

We made five abseils, the fifth on a bolt because we couldn't find any cracks. We bivouacked in only a bivouac sac. During the night it stormed, which made the descent the next morning risky because of new snow and bad weather.

On the southeast face of Son Peak (5710m), M. Manence, M. Brajnik and I soloed *The Memories* (III D+ 80°, 250 m) in three hours on October 23, finding snow and ice climbing with only the upper 60 meters mixed (IV+ 60°). From the summit of Son Peak we abseiled once on the col and then climbed another peak we called Father Peak (5700m). The route and peaks are dedicated to Matej's father, who died in the Slovenian Alps during an exercise for the Slovenian Mountain Rescue.

ANDREJ MARKOVIČ, *SLOVENIAN ALPINE CLUB*

CATCHING THE VIEW —

D.E. SVENSON

# Corrections

In the Preface to the 1997 *AAJ*, it was incorrectly stated that the November 1995 ascent of Cerro Torre by Paul Moores, Max Berger, Mark Wilford and Adrian Burgess via the Maestri route stopped at the top of the rock pitches but beneath the summit mushroom. In fact, Paul Moores and Max Berger successfully summitted the ice mushroom by circling clockwise around the back, where they reported a relatively easy three-pitch climb to the top. The following pair, Adrian Burgess and Mark Wilford, reached the top of the headwall (i.e., the end of the rock pitches) in the first stages of deteriorating weather. While Burgess belayed, Wilford continued a full pitch up the 30-40° ice slope leading to the summit mushroom until he could look over the west side of the Continental Ice Cap, but then reversed the route as the weather grew worse. Moores is British; this was the first time the peak had been summitted by British climbers. It additionally was the first time the peak had been climbed in its entirety since 1991.

In the opening color photos of last year's journal, the photo of Sergei Penzov and Carlos Buhler in their tent at Camp V after summitting K2 by its north ridge was taken by Andrei Mariev, not Carlos Buhler as stated. The photo on page 221 labeled as "Schweizerland, Greenland," is actually of the Apostle's Thumb in Greenland. On Page 244, the Aconcagua account signed "Author Unknown" was penned by Hank Midgeley. The route line on page 321 indicating the high point of the 1996 ascent of Shipton Spire stops short of the actual high point, which was approximately 30 feet below the top. On page 322, the man in the photo captioned "Chuck Boyd, jugging with a view on Shipton Spire" is Greg Foweraker.

For all the above mistakes, and any others we may have missed, we offer our sincere apologies, as we do for the incorrect route line drawn for *Spindrift Couloir* on the north face of Big Four Mountain. The correct line is as follows:

# Reviews

EDITED BY DAVID STEVENSON

*Into Thin Air*. Jon Krakauer. Villard: New York, 1997. 293 pages. Black-and-white photos, woodcut illustrations. $24.95.

I approached *Into Thin Air* warily. I think it was all the hype, all the people insisting, "you must read it," all the talk of million-dollar advances. What, I wondered, is so special about this book? The answer, of course, is the uniquely compelling human drama of its subject matter. It requires a skilled writer to do justice to that material, and *Into Thin Air* has been praised as great "literature," but to my mind this is not so much literature as a highly competent piece of journalism.

Even the best journalism runs the risk of oversimplification. Krakauer's slickly sketched pen portraits do not always quite convince and the shorthand historical summaries sometimes trample on subtlety. The 1953 expedition, for instance, is dismissed as "a large British team organized with the righteous zeal and overpowering resources of a military campaign." It was, in fact, a very modest, understated affair in comparison to the type of expeditions surrounding Krakauer in 1996. South African climber Cathy O'Dowd, who reached the summit two weeks after Krakauer, is described as having virtually no mountaineering experience. This simply is not true. Why dismiss her so perfunctorily, while bending over backwards, in the early pages at least, to find something tactful to say about the appalling Ms. Pittman?

Perhaps I am being pedantic, but I think one should be suspicious of a book that claims to be "the definitive account" of the 1996 tragedy. The more one looks into such complex events, the more obvious it becomes that there are any number of different versions of the same story—and there is no such thing as a definitive account. Despite these reservations, however, I was enthralled by the book. For the first time, I was able to get a coherent view of what really happened in 1996. Krakauer handles complex events and a huge cast of diverse characters with great skill. And, even if there are moments of glib oversimplification, the historical background is grafted seamlessly into the narrative, giving the layman a clear, compelling view of the Everest tradition. All the little details familiar to a seasoned Himalayan climber, like the chortens at base camp, or the symptoms of pulmonary edema, are introduced gradually, enticing the lay reader into a world that we already know for ourselves. The approach is deliberately popular, but unlike, say, James Ramsay Ullman, Krakauer actually is there himself, with all the experience of a seasoned mountaineer, at the center of events, fully, emotionally involved. So, as well as being investigative journalism, *Into Thin Air* is a deeply moving personal account.

One of the many non-climbing friends who exhorted me to read the book said that it left her with the impression of "one really screwed up guy." Right from the dramatic opening pages, as storm clouds gather on the summit, there is a sense of doom and guilt. Krakauer is engagingly honest about his feelings and agonizes about what he sees as a failure to help others in distress. I think he is unnecessarily hard on himself, but he is right to explain his mistake over Andy Harris's disappearance. I remember well, that week in 1996, sitting at my desk, trying to make sense of garbled reports for my own newspaper article, reiterating the news that Andy Harris had been seen disappearing over the edge of the South Col. Only months later did Krakauer discover that he had not seen Harris at all—that Harris actually had been up near the South Summit, trying heroically to help Doug Hansen and Rob Hall. In the book, this incident of mistaken identity takes on a chilling, ghostly quality, suffused with remorse, that epitomizes the whole horror of that terrible night on Everest.

As a climber with little experience of large-scale commercial and nationalistic expeditions, I was fascinated by Krakauer's description of the bizarre drama that Everest has become. What struck me most was the amount of suffering that goes on. I know that it can be tough at high altitude, but do people really feel that ill, even at base camp? What happened to all the fun and joy and laughter that I remember? I was intrigued and amazed to read about people carrying emergency syringes full of dexamethazone, incredulous that Lopsang Jangbu Sherpa should have to exhaust himself lugging Pittman's 30 pounds of telephone equipment all the way to the South Col, appalled yet fascinated by the prevailing mood of brash arrogance. I also was amazed at the sheer quantity of fixed rope employed by modern commercial expeditions, even above the South Col, where, ten years ago, there was just one short piece on the Hillary Step. It seems that the jumar has replaced the ice axe as the basic item of mountaineering equipment.

As the drama builds on summit day, Krakauer reveals how far this game has diverged from real mountaineering, where "the emphasis on self-reliance, on making critical decisions and dealing with the consequences, on personal responsibility" are paramount. As a guinea-pig client, he had to learn passivity and "felt at times as if I wasn't really climbing the mountain— that surrogates were doing it for me." He had to bite his lip and resist commenting about the obvious contradictions and inconsistencies that became ever more apparent as the assembled masses crawled inexorably toward disaster. Only afterward, in his articles and his book, could he speak his mind—and by so doing angered a lot of people.

Was the anger justified? Was Krakauer unduly critical about the various expedition leaders and guides? Probably not. His analysis of events seems to me to ring true. There are, however, points of emphasis some people are bound to question. Read Colin Monteath's excellent overview in his book *Hall and Ball*, and you will detect significant differences. I think Krakauer is unduly harsh on Anatoli Boukreev, failing to give credit to Boukreev's extraordinary strength and courage, struggling repeatedly into the storm to bring in the survivors on the South Col. I also sympathize with those who were angry at Krakauer's reporting of Rob Hall's achingly poignant last conversation with Jan Arnold. Of course it is deeply, deeply moving, but was Krakauer right, even in the dirty world of journalism, to ignore pleas for privacy?

One of the refreshing things about the book is the absence of glossy color photographs. The publishers settled instead for Randy Rackliff's stark woodcuts, two pages of informative black and white photographs, the author's excellently selected chapter-heading quotations and attractive typography. Cynics might suggest that Villard was just trying to maximize its mega-dollar profits by keeping down printing costs. I, on the other hand, suspect that the publisher realized that in this image-obsessed age, the words should be left, for once, to speak for themselves; for this is a powerful piece of writing. It does not describe mountaineering as I know it or as Krakauer knew it before he went to Everest, but that is not the point. This is an evocation of human tragedy that goes beyond everyday climbing. The mountain is merely a focal point for the universal elements of fate, risk, pride, greed, weakness, muddle, confusion—and rare moments of supreme heroism—that amount to an irresistibly compelling story.

STEPHEN VENABLES

*The Climb: Tragic Ambitions on Everest.* Anatoli Boukreev and G. Weston DeWalt. St. Martin's Press: New York, 1997. 256 pages. $24.95

After all that has been written about the 1996 Everest tragedy, why should we care to read yet another account? The media avalanched us with an unprecedented depth of raw facts, yet left us with the escalating controversy that drew head guide Anatoli Boukreev of Kazakhstan to publish his side of the story with a co-writer, G. Weston DeWalt. In *The Climb*, Boukreev describes how he single-handedly performed one of the most amazing rescues in Himalayan history a few hours after climbing Everest without oxygen.

Depending on your source, Boukreev was either the villain or the hero of the unfortunate events on Everest. Just a month after *The Climb* was published in November 1997, he died in an avalanche on a winter ascent of the South Face of Annapurna. When DeWalt was called for a national news quote, he learned that they planned to say Boukreev would be best remembered as the villain of Jon Krakauer's best seller, *Into Thin Air*. DeWalt cautioned that the American Alpine Club had just given Boukreev a major award for heroism and would be remembered by his peers as one of the greatest Himalayan mountaineers of all time.

When Boukreev disappeared on Annapurna, his newly published book and AAC award were fanning the flames of controversy to new heights. *The New York Times* included the following in a report of Boukreev's death: "Krakauer accuses Boukreev . . . of compromising his client's safety to achieve his own ambitions . . . and endangered them by making the exhausting climb without the aid of bottled oxygen.... However, Krakauer credits Boukreev with bravely saving the lives of two [sic] climbers." Here is the controversy reduced to a sound byte.

*The Climb* presents a much-needed breath of fresh air, written from a guide's point of view, that dissipates some of the intriguing thin air surrounding the media-created search for blame. We learn, for example, that every one of Boukreev's clients survived the tragedy without major injuries, while those who did die or incurred major injuries were members of Krakauer's party. The leaders of both teams, Scott Fischer and Rob Hall, also did not live to tell their story.

The question of why these two competing leaders stayed so high so long, pushing clients toward the summit beyond a reasonable turn-around time, is never directly answered. Between the lines, however, the spotlight shines on those who have asked for it most forcefully. The extreme pressure Fischer and Hall felt to get the most positive free ink in *Outside* that would lure more high-dollar clients comes across as clearly as if the words were penned in blood. The reader senses that the presence of an *Outside* journalist as a client on the most fatal commercial Everest venture was no coincidence.

Far from trying "to achieve his own ambitions" that day, Boukreev fixed the Hillary Step for clients after Sherpas failed to do so, foresaw problems with clients nearing camp too late, noted five other guides on the peak, and descended to the South Col to be rested and hydrated enough to respond to an emergency. Boukreev now had climbed Everest three times without oxygen. His high-altitude performance, often alone and in extreme conditions, was unparalleled. He had climbed Manaslu in winter, Dhaulagiri in 17 hours, Makalu in 46 hours, and had traversed all four 8000-meter summits of Kanchenjunga in a single push, to select just a few here. When he learned that climbers were lost in a blizzard in the dark, he made several solo forays late into the night to rescue three people near death. No other client, guide, or Sherpa could muster the necessary strength and courage to accompany Boukreev as he went from tent to tent, asking for help.

Late the next day, Boukreev climbed alone back up to 8350 meters on the slim chance he could save Scott Fischer, last seen by Sherpas lying comatose in the snow. Meanwhile, *Time* magazine was preparing a sensational three-page story about the tragedy, based on satellite phone and fax reports from the mountain, that failed even to mention Boukreev's name.

On May 16, after just two days' rest in the Western Cwm, as helicopters, Sherpas, and other expeditions helped evacuate the survivors, Boukreev set off to solo Lhotse in the record time of 21 hours, climbing on a permit Fischer had obtained to guide the peak after Everest. Had Fischer survived unscathed, he almost certainly would have passed on Lhotse and accompanied his clients back to Kathmandu.

In *The Climb,* Boukreev reveals his thoughts as a professional guide, but holds the iron curtain over his own persona. With classic Russian reticence, he doesn't brag, mention his degree in physics, or apologize for actions on the mountain that others judged to be self-centered and uncaring. He counters a strong rebuke from Scott Fischer by saying that it had not been made clear to him that "chatting and keeping the clients pleased by focusing on their personal happiness" was equally important to focusing on the details that would bring safety and success. Unlike Krakauer, he is afraid to admit human failings that could help endear him to his audience and his climbing companions. He lets down his armor only far enough to admit to sometimes being a difficult person.

Even with DeWalt's impassioned prose and editing of Boukreev's transcribed interviews, *The Climb* fails to sustain the superb narrative quality that brought *Into Thin Air* to the pinnacle of literary success atop the *New York Times* best seller list. But while it lacks the carefully choreographed structure and characterizations that make *Into Thin Air* impossible to put down, it forces the reader to think, rather than to accept armchair answers passively.

Boukreev avoids Krakauer's penchant for focusing on the idiosyncrasies of his companions by simply accepting fellow climbers at face value for who they are on the mountain. He succeeds without more complete characterizations because most readers already are very familiar with the players and the basic setting from *Into Thin Air* and a plethora of media stories.

Writing about a person invariably honors them or devalues them. Both Boukreev and DeWalt err on the side of honoring those attempting Everest, while Krakauer draws his reader toward tabloid-style assumptions that erase heroism from the Himalaya as surely as modern journalism erases greatness from the presidency.

A vastly experienced guide told me over dinner that he loved *Into Thin Air* and felt somewhat chagrined never to have paused to question its conclusions until he read Boukreev speaking his own language, thinking his own thoughts. He strongly related to the behind-the-scenes guide talk and the dilemma of being a nice guy attending to a client's every need versus nursing that person up into the Death Zone, where their survival would be dependent on their ability to keep going under their own power. DeWalt includes an especially fascinating three-page, first-person account of client Lou Kasischke's inner thoughts as he made an agonizing personal decision to turn around on the summit day.

The media circus surrounding the Everest tragedy appears to be a post-modern American phenomena. Single tragedies have claimed the lives of more climbers in the Himalaya many times before, but not Americans, not clients paying up to $65,000 each, not with daily reports on the Internet, not with a journalist climbing on assignment, and not with a broadcast phone call from a dying man to his wife. Thus the regrettable deaths of five climbers on Everest on May 10 degenerated from a real-life tragedy involving heroism and compassion into a veritable O.J. trial in which no participant is left unscathed. With *Outside* indirectly pulling media strings (as live television influenced Judge Ito's court), it is little wonder that justice and dignity took a back seat to the entertainment value of the sufferings of well-intentioned climbers. To much of the public, high-altitude mountaineering itself has been on trial. It is to this end that *The Climb* may have its most lasting significance.

Motivations are all important. If, as Krakauer suggests, the people who now climb Everest (graciously including himself) do it for questionable reasons, then our avocation is indeed in trouble. As Eric Shipton wrote in 1938 after several attempts on the mountain, "The ascent of Everest, like any other human endeavor, is only to be judged by the spirit in which it is attempted. . . . Let us climb peaks . . . not because others have failed, nor because the summits stand 28,000 feet above the sea, nor in patriotic fervor for the honor of the nation, nor for cheap publicity. . . . Let us not attack them with an army, announcing on the wireless to a sensation-loving world the news of our departure and the progress of our subsequent advance."

The mass appeal of the 1996 Everest story relates to the clear violation of every one of Shipton's tenets of more than a half-century ago in a new era in which blame is God.

GALEN ROWELL

*Everest: The History of the Himalayan Giant.* Roberto Mantovani. Introduction by Kurt Diemberger. Mountaineers Books: Seattle, 1997. 143 pages. Hardback, large format, with numerous historical images and color photographs. $35.00

If you enjoyed Walt Unsworth's *Everest*, but were left craving for sumptuous color photos of Chomolungma and her various climbs, this is your book. The quality and prodigious numbers of these Italian-printed pictures (some in sepia, others hand-colored, many not seen before) are of impeccably high quality. And for once, a sensitive, skillfully written text matches the awe-inspiring imagery. Roberto Mantovani obviously has done his homework, and leads us capably through the stages of Everest's development. From the India surveys of the mid-19th century to Mallory and Irvine in 1924, Hillary and Tenzing in '53, Hornbein and Unsoeld in '63, Messner and Habeler in '78, and Loretan and Troillet in '86, the whole colorful cast of characters is here, driven upward by ego, fame, and desire, and struck down callously by high-altitude edema, capricious storms, and disastrous fate. To these many tales, Kurt Diemberger adds a cautionary and typically heartfelt introduction.

This stylish book is a joy to read and browse. It also will inspire dreams of treading the cold, snowy heights, especially while sitting in a warm, cozy armchair. The book's only noticeable shortcoming is in the otherwise useful expedition-by-expedition compendium, "All the Ascents," where, regrettably, several photo captions don't match the photos. (Other captions and photos are switched on pages 81, 88, 89, and 139.) On page 29, the upper portion of the Messner Route is marked wrong. On pages 30 and 31, our 1988 Kangshung Pace route is marked incorrectly and an accompanying photo and caption is switched. Furthermore, our climb was an International expedition, not a British-led effort, it does end on the South Col (not near it), and Stephen Venables had three companions on his ascent, not two, an unfortunate mistake Diemberger also perpetuates.

Additionally, the famous ice axe was Irvine's (a little known, yet verified fact), and the book concludes with "The Chaos of the Last Seasons," a chapter chronicling the tangled web of recent "guided expeditions" and the 1996 tragedy.

ED WEBSTER

*Everest, Mountain Without Mercy.* Broughton Coburn. Introduction by Tim Cahill, afterword by David Breashears. National Geographic Society, 1997. Color photographs. 256 pages. $35.00.

Everest, *Mountain without Mercy* is the story of the 1996 International IMAX Expedition to Mount Everest whose goal it was to carry an IMAX camera to the summit of the world. From the beginning of the project in 1994, expedition leader and head camera man David Breashears had his hands full. After experimenting with the normal 85-pound IMAX camera on Mt. Washington in winter, he realized that enormous modifications had to be made to adapt it to the harsh high altitude and arctic environment of Everest. The IMAX format is three times larger than 70-mm film and uses film at the rate of 5.6 feet per second. A 500-foot roll of film weighing 51 pounds would last a mere 90 seconds.

Breashears, working with the IMAX Corporation's engineering department, built a new camera for Everest. Its weight could not exceed 261 pounds and it had to function reliably in temperatures of -40°F. Large control knobs would allow the oxygen-deprived operator to run the camera with the simplest of technique.

When he was satisfied with the new camera, Breashears began the major task of organizing the 1996 International IMAX Expedition. This expedition, funded by MacGillivray-Freeman Films and the National Science Foundation, included as team members: Robert Schauer, assistant camera man; Ed Viesturs, America's strongest high-altitude climber, who had already summitted Mt. Everest four times; Araceli Segara of Catalonia, Spain; Jamling Norgay, son of the famous Sherpa of Everest, Tenzing Norgay; and Sumiyo Tsuzuki of Japan. The team was truly an international team with young climbers on their first trip to Everest and older Everest veterans to lead the way. Sherpas, led by Sirdar Wongchu Sherpa, also would add to the success. Without Sherpa power, a filming project of this magnitude would not get out of base camp.

The Everest IMAX Expedition's story would be a great book by itself, but expeditions are no longer on the mountain alone. Everest is not a wilderness experience and must be shared, like it or not. In the spring of 1996, the Everest IMAX team shared the base camp with 13 other expeditions. This caused the base-camp population to swell to more than 300 climbers and Sherpa staff.

In addition to the traditional expeditions from various countries, there was a new breed of expedition, the "commercial, for-profit expeditions." Leaders like Scott Fischer, Rob Hall, Todd Burlesen, Pete Athens and Henry Todd arrived with clientele paying up to $65,000 each for the opportunity to climb Mt. Everest with these experienced Everest veterans. There surely was an edge of competition amongst them, especially between the two largest expeditions led by Scott Fischer and Rob Hall. Success was extremely important to these climbers' businesses. Clients, paying $65,000 each, expect success.

As has been well-documented elsewhere, things went very wrong on Everest on May 10. A blizzard claimed the lives of eight climbers, including Scott Fischer and Rob Hall.

The IMAX team was in Camp II and responded in the rescue effort, saving and rescuing survivors of a terrific night out. This book gives the reader an on-the-scene account of Mt. Everest's most tragic event.

After the events of the May 10 tragedy, most of the expeditions on the mountain packed it up and went home. The Everest IMAX Team regrouped and faced the challenge of placing the IMAX camera on the roof of the world. Filming Everest with IMAX photography has created the most spectacular mountain movie ever filmed. *Everest, Mountain Without Mercy* is their story.

This is not a cheap, quickly put together book. Its 256 pages are of the highest quality paper to allow for not only "can't put down reading," but also to enhance the reproduction of the excellent color photography. Team members' photos and IMAX camera images make this a wonderful combination of coffee table book with a story to go with it. This book was awarded Literary Achievement of the Year by the American Alpine Club for 1997. The afterword by David Breashears is the frosting on the cake, making *Everest, Mountain Without Mercy*, in my opinion, the finest book about Mt. Everest ever published.

RICK WILCOX

*Dark Shadows Falling*. Joe Simpson. The Mountaineers: Seattle, 1997. 27 color photos. 207 pages. $24.95.

Joe Simpson's *Dark Shadows Falling* is his third non-fiction work since his mega classic *Touching the Void*. This latest book probes what Simpson sees as increased immorality amongst Everest climbers. Simpson recounts events surrounding the 1996 Everest disaster and buttresses these by additional unsavory episodes from other expeditions. All of the above can be found in Krakauer's *Into Thin Air*. Some examples of this high-altitude moral failure include the following: a Dutch expedition headed by Ronald Naar that decides not to render help to a dying climber only a few feet from their tent because they didn't want to jeopardize their chances for a summit attempt the next day; a Japanese summit team that instead of helping a dying climber simply steps around him on their way up; and the infamous Ian Woodall, who won't even lend the use of a radio desperately needed by climbers trying to call for help. In the immortal words of Eisuke Shigekawa, one of the Japanese team members, "Above 8000 meters is not a place where people can afford morality."

Simpson is rightly outraged by these actions and words. As moral philosophers have done since the time of Aristotle, he wants to find the source of such loathsome behavior. Simpson believes some of the blame may be laid at the door of exorbitant peak fees and the concomitant excesses (fixed ropes, climbing Sherpas and oxygen) of national teams and commercial guiding that those fees necessitate.

The problem with this seemingly simple solution is that Simpson has confused the ethics of access with the ethics of high-altitude rescue. The British philosopher Gilbert Ryle once called this a "category mistake." When talking about the ethics of high-altitude climbing and the ethics of turning your back on a fellow climber in mortal danger, it seems like we are talking about ethics in general. But we aren't. Both issues involve the word "ethics," so they seem related. In actuality, one issue is a matter of access and style, where access is limited to those who have money but not necessarily skill, so they must climb Everest in a different style. The other issue is a matter of compassion and respect for human life. It's like trying to compare the ethics of rap bolting to the ethics of animal rights or genetic engineering—it's too far a stretch.

While my complaint may seem a petty technicality, it has, in fact, some very practical ramifications. Even if the Nepalese government could be persuaded to cut off its financial nose by banning the use of Sherpas, ropes and oxygen, I don't see how it would make people like Ian Woodall become more compassionate, caring, selfless people. The fact of the matter is some people are just going to be assholes no matter what altitude they happen to be at, and nothing short of genetic engineering and removal of the asshole gene is going to change that. Everest is simply a microcosm of the world at large, albeit a higher, more beautiful—and, at times, a far more cruel one.

Exacerbating Simpson's confusion of style with morality is the fact that he is idealistic. This is never more apparent than when he states: "We know intuitively which is the correct way to behave. In our hearts we know what works best for everyone. To 'love thy neighbor as thyself' is a precept that everyone understands. . . ." This is coming from a guy who should know better, who in his last book, *Storms of Silence,* wrote about such disparate evils as the brutal Chinese oppression of Tibet and Nazi death camps. It seems pretty obvious that some people just don't give a damn about the "correct way to behave" or loving one another; they just want to get to the top, no matter what the cost. Wistful appeals to their 'intuition' and 'hearts' just don't cut it.

Because Simpson believes that everyone really does know in their heart the difference between right and wrong, and because their judgment is simply being clouded by all the money involved, his book reads like a check list or a concatenation of all the things that went wrong on Everest. Ultimately, all this recounting makes Simpson violate Krakauer's most fundamental caveat, a caveat that applies not just to Everest, but all of climbing and beyond:

> But to believe that dissecting the tragic events of 1996 in minute detail will actually reduce the future death rate in any meaningful way is wishful thinking. The urge to catalog the myriad blunders in order to 'learn from the mistakes' is for the most part an exercise in denial and self deception. [To] convince yourself that Rob Hall died because he made a string of stupid errors that you are too clever to repeat... is injudicious. *(Into Thin Air*, p. 274)

But this is how *Dark Shadows Falling* sometimes reads: as a categorization of mostly stylistic mistakes that Simpson hopes might lead us to some higher moral ground. Logically, this just isn't a sustainable or convincing argument (nor is it "judicious").

On another level, however, I can deeply admire what Simpson is trying to do. For what we do learn from the 1996 Everest disaster and other climbing disasters of lore, including Simpson's own, is that the human spirit can be a truly remarkable thing. While some will always choose to "cut and run," and others will choose to simply step over the dying on their way to the summit, still others will choose to stay behind and fight it out to save another despite all odds.

It is this kind of sacrifice and selflessness to which Simpson himself alludes when pushing a bold new route on Pumori. Within striking distance of the summit, and with most of the technical difficulties behind, Simpson chooses to turn back when he detects signs of illness in his partner. As for putting his partner at risk by trying to coerce him on farther, or perhaps bolting for the summit with lame promises to return, Simpson simply states that as far as his friend's life was concerned, "there was no way I was going to take the risk." Granted, Simpson is hardly the most sentimental writer, but his disappointment is palpable. Selflessness and sacrifice have always been fundamental to heroism.

Simpson has made explicit what often is implicit: that moral dilemmas have always been intertwined with the great dramas of alpinism. And this is the claim that they all make upon us: after the "string of stupid errors" have been made, then what do we do? Cut the rope as Simpson's own partner did on Siula Grande? Give up your own life trying to save your client's life, as Rob Hall did on Everest? Try and stop Maurice Herzog from going insane, or follow him up to the top of Annapurna, the first 8000-meter peak ever to be climbed, only to be horribly frostbitten? It may be 'injudicious' to think that we are too clever to repeat those "stupid mistakes," but when misfortune occurs, what happens next? Do we declare morality to be an unaffordable luxury at some predetermined altitude?

While I may disagree with some of *Dark Shadows Falling*, and I am definitely not a fan of Simpson's digression upon digression whatever-comes-to-mind writing style ("solipsistic exegesis," John Thackray called it in last year's *AAJ*), I nevertheless am always thankful when someone tries to make a thoughtful examination of this sometimes sublime and sometimes stupid sport that we pursue.

DAVID HALE

*A Deathful Ridge: A Novel of Everest.* J.A. Wainwright. Mosaic Press: Ontario, Canada and Buffalo, New York, 1997. Hardback. 138 pages. $24.95

I f you are the least bit intrigued by the 1924 disappearance of George Leigh Mallory and Andrew "Sandy" Irvine on the upper reaches of Everest's Northeast Ridge, you will savor every word and be utterly astonished by this superbly researched, brilliant first novel by Canadian poet and author J.A. Wainwright. This book (a novel of fiction, lest you forget) is impressively detailed in its outrageous yet believable story line that is intimately and passionately told. You may never again think of mountaineering's most famous unsolved mystery quite the same. Did Odell really see Mallory and Irvine going "strong for the top" above the Second Step on June 8, 1924? And how did the famous ice axe (identified as Irvine's by its three short parallel nicks carved into the wooden shaft; I've seen it) come to rest near the First Step? And most entrancing of all: did Mallory actually reach the summit? The novel's only-at-first incredulous premise demands that I don't tell you more. Secrecy is absolute, "till death do we part," and a gentlemen's honourable pact. In this year of Everest and the Titanic, even the great ship gets a couple of pages! (Quite logically, I might add.) Read this book and delight in reconsidering the myriad riddles of the intertwined mythology of George Mallory and Mt. Everest. This profound investigation of the mountaineering psyche, of the climber's life, blinding ambition, and high-altitude death—succinctly rationalized by Mallory's infamous quote "because it's there"—will leave you reeling.

ED WEBSTER

*In the Zone: Epic Survival Stories From the Mountaineering World.* Peter Potterfield. The Mountaineers: Seattle, 1996. Photographs. 270 pages. $22.95.

T wo of the three tales from *In the Zone* are of a most compelling kind—the sagas of those victims of catastrophic events in the mountains who, against great odds, live to tell their stories. What makes this kind of story especially rare is the balance of circumstances that allow it even to exist and yet not be common. These are solitary ordeals where if the protagonist were more hurt or in a more remote setting there would be no one to tell the tale. Conversely, if they were less hurt in a less exotic situation, their story may not be so interesting.

Author Peter Potterfield relates these two tales along with a third story that falls into a different and more familiar category of mountaineering story: epic endurance, survival, and heroism in a hostile environment, but ultimately under more voluntary circumstances. The fact that one of the three stories is Potterfield's own helps to overcome the loss of visceral punch that might be expected when someone tells someone else's story. There is a certain credibility that comes through in Potterfield's words at times—particularly when he's describing pain—that would be very difficult to conjure straight out of imagination.

The first story takes place in June of 1992, when Colby Coombs, Ritt Kellogg, and Tom Walter begin climbing up a hard route on Mt. Foraker. Nine days later, Colby Coombs returns alone. His is a moving story with haunting images that are hard to shake. I finished this story with a great respect for Coombs. His survival is a testament to a combination of fine mountain skills and a self-knowledge that allowed him to escape a situation that might well have killed the rest of us.

The second epic, Potterfield's own, takes place on remote Chimney Rock in the North Cascades. What should have been a short roped fall becomes a 150-foot body-shattering tumble leaving Potterfield marooned on a small ledge with terrible injuries. His partner (luckily a marathon runner) goes for help as Potterfield does what he can to keep the life force from leaving his body until he is rescued 30 hours later. The clock was ticking very fast for Potterfield and the rescue itself was a monumental effort.

Potterfield's rendering of his story, as well as of Coombs', which was based on extensive interviews, both are clean effective narratives. The power in these types of stories ultimately resides in the events that actually transpire, and it's easy to overwrite and overwhelm them. When I read Joe Simpson's *Touching the Void*, which has become a de facto touchstone for mountaineering epic survival stories, I found myself burning out on his super-descriptive style in the second half of the book. Additionally, as his book wore on, Simpson, as I perceived it, began more and more to recreate the finer details of his ordeal in lieu of actual recollections, essentially writing a novel based on a true story. Some authenticity was lost and, to a large degree, I lost interest in whether Simpson survived or not. Coombs' and Potterfield's own story, told more simply and truthfully, rang deeper chords in me, and I was intensely invested in their survival.

Irony suffuses the third story. Set on the slopes of K2 in 1992, climbers fight their way up, then down the mountain. Now, both the protagonist and one of the survivors of this story—friends and professional rivals who became fellow victims in the events of May 1996, mountaineering's most infamous episode in the public eye—lie dead on Mt. Everest.

The story ostensibly belongs to Scott Fischer (it's told from his point of view), but, with the exception of one element, belongs equally to his partner, Ed Viesturs. Fischer and Viesturs buy spots on an ad-hoc-style Russian/American expedition to K2's Abruzzi Ridge. Early on, Fischer dislocates his shoulder, yet stubbornly stays on in the nearly vain hope that his shoulder will heal enough to climb K2. In time, he mends sufficiently to give it a go—twice—and not only eventually succeeds with Viesturs, but in the process, the two of them, at no small risk and sacrifice of their own energy reserves, rescue other climbers seemingly left and right, including Rob Hall and his desperately ill partner, Gary Ball.

The telling of this story is fairly unique because Potterfield is neither a participant in the story nor an insider in the world of professional high-altitude mountaineering. He is, however, a climber who understands and appreciates what climbing is all about. The standard first-person expedition narrative that we've read so many times generally is not a particularly guileless document. The authors endlessly make a case for themselves—one eye cocked toward posterity—regardless of whether there is anything they need to make a case about or not. It's a type of insecurity.

I really liked the K2 story because not only is it exciting, it's straight. Even though Potterfield obviously is an admirer of Scott Fischer and sometimes expresses some quaint notions about the world of "big league mountaineering," the story is mercifully free of the bending and skewing found in nearly all expedition narratives and provides a refreshingly clear view into the world of climbing big mountains.

The pithy subject of Everest and the connection with this book—a book about people surviving—can't be ignored. What struck me most about the events in May 1996 on Everest was the clear dividing line between those who survived and those who succumbed. Anyone who was a seasoned climber, Sherpas and Westerners alike, survived that storm rather handily (the exceptions, of course, being Scott Fischer and Rob Hall who, in my opinion, were artificially crippled that day in both their decision-making and, ultimately, in their efforts to save themselves by the extraordinary circumstances and concerns which were, sadly or ironically, of their own contrivance). Those who died or nearly died were the under-experienced ones.

Guiding and clients dying while being guided is as old as climbing itself—it's no use even to discuss what things guides should or shouldn't attempt to take their clients up; how the clients could be screened better beforehand, or whatever. You read about people on Everest that year giving themselves up for dead well before the gig was up and then you read about Colby Coombs on Foraker, Potterfield on his ledge, Fischer and Viesturs on K2, all of them never giving up. Maybe this book would be a good read for those people who want to be guided up the big peaks. They could read it and then ask themselves, "Have I 'been there and done that' enough to survive like this if I had to? And if so, why am I hiring a guide?"

MICHAEL BEARZI

*K2: Challenging the Sky.* Roberto Mantovani and Kurt Diemberger. The Mountaineers: Seattle, 1997. 144 pages. $35.00.

Second only to Everest in height, K2 also has been subordinated in the attention it has received from writers and photographers. That may be changing, although it's doubtful it will catch up. For a wide group of climbers, K2 may be the peak of choice, but the highest mountain in the world undoubtedly will always maintain its lead.

With the publication three years ago of Jim Curran's *K2: The Story of the Savage Mountain*, the mountain received its long overdue climbing history, a stellar effort necessarily concentrated on the narrative with photographic coverage limited to a few selected shots. *K2: Challenging the Sky*, published the same year—but not previously reviewed in this journal until its republication by the Mountaineers Books—fills that gap nicely. With its large oversized format, K2's rugged grandeur can be fully displayed for the first time without the constraints of standard book size.

I thought I had seen all the photographs from our 1978 expedition, which succeeded in making the mountain's third ascent. Now I realize that John Roskelley must have tucked away a few shots that didn't find their way into the issue of *National Geographic* that chronicled the climb or *The Last Step*, Rick Ridgeway's absorbing account of the expedition. Best of all is Roskelley's stunning photograph, which appears on the dust-jacket cover. The foreground is mundane but instructive. Ridgeway is seen ploughing his way up thigh-deep snow we had to contend with each time a major storm blew through. But beyond the struggling human figure is the ferocious, knife-edged crest of the northeast ridge, and soaring above everything the colossal summit pyramid of K2. It looks close, but it took weeks of effort by our 14-member team to get anywhere near the top.

I wish I could be a bit more salutary about the book's text. The few brief sections Kurt Diemberger contributes are up to his usual high standard, but, overall, the historical treatment that accompanies the photography is decidedly inferior to Curran's well-written book. Not being able to read Italian, it may be that Roberto Mantovani's original narrative fares better than in this translated version. There are the usual number of niggling errors. For instance, it's hard to see how careful editing could not have caught misspelling—Lou Reichardt's name is spelled as "Lou Richard" on one page, after getting it correct the page before. That would have to be particularly galling to John Roskelley—a careful writer himself—in whose contribution on our summit climb the error appears. Both Reichardt and Roskelley deserve better.

This book's value, however, is primarily in its photographic coverage of K2 and its climbing history. For that reason alone, it definitely belongs on the shelf of every K2 aficionado, myself among them.

JIM WICKWIRE

*Mont Blanc: Discovery and Conquest of the Giant of the Alps.* Stefano Ardito. The Mountaineers: Seattle, 1997. Profuse color photographs. $48.00.

Twenty years ago, when I first visited Chamonix, I was amazed to discover that the book many alpinists had adopted as the definitive guidebook to the area was Gaston Rebuffat's *The Mont Blanc Massif: The 100 Finest Routes*. Amazed because the book was an expensive, hardcover, coffee-table volume filled with glossy color photographs—a far cry from the typical pocket climbing guide. True, the route list was selective, the topos were crude, and the French text in most local copies was incomprehensible, but those marvelous pictures—orange granite pillars and glistening blue couloirs in such sharp detail—they made toting that brick of a book around the Alps worth every ounce.

Now there's an oversized collection of superb Mont Blanc photography guaranteed to break the backs of a new generation. Measuring a whopping ten by 14 inches—a third again the size of Rebuffat's classic—Stefano Ardito's *Mont Blanc: Discovery and Conquest of the Giant of the Alps* has taken the "picture is worth a thousand words" concept to the extreme. Many of the finest photographs ever made on and around this important mountain have been assembled here and reproduced with rich detail and in near poster-sized dimensions. One chapter alone boasts 26 plates showing the classic Mont Blanc perspectives (Brenva, Frêney, Jorasses, etc.) with important routes clearly marked. And fortunately, the book is far more comprehensive than its title implies, for as anyone who has ever visited or studied this area understands, Mont Blanc is much more than just the highest summit in Western Europe; its satellite peaks and formations, like the Dru, the Verte, and the toothy "aiguille" above Chamonix, all are part of the great collective that makes up the Mont Blanc massif—and all are included in this book.

Ardito's text has been translated almost flawlessly from the original Italian (although the icefield on the north face of the Grandes Jorasses that most English-speaking mountaineers know as the Shroud is referred to as the Linceul) and is primarily a chronological history. Beginning in the mid-eighteenth century when the first mountain "tourists" arrived in Chamonix, he traces the birth and the evolution of mountaineering—all within the microcosm of the Mont Blanc massif—right through to the super enchaînements and audacious solo climbs of the present era. This discourse, though cursory (the entire book can probably be read in just a few hours), does an excellent job of bringing together many familiar names, routes, tragedies and triumphs and putting them all into an historic, "big picture" perspective that, until now, probably has eluded all but the most well-read mountaineers.

In fact, the only important bit of Mont Blanc history missing from these pages is the building of the téléphériques, the amazing cable-car network that revolutionized access and climbing throughout the range. The author has compensated, however, by including a unique and delightful chapter focusing purely on the diverse and extensive hut system that has similarly helped to make these mountains so accessible to the masses.

Regardless of what he is writing about, though, Ardito is at a distinct disadvantage. By opening *Mont Blanc* to any page, it is clear that this is primarily a "picture" book—and even Hemingway's pen would have a hard time competing with Mont Blanc's visual elements. The design team of Patrizia Balocco Lovisetti and Anna Galliani have given the book a dynamic but appealing layout through which the text ebbs and flows—and often disappears, with very little consequence. The earlier historical chapters are lavishly illustrated with colorful engravings and prints, as well as fascinating artifacts, such as the elaborate certificates of accomplishment the local mountain guides fashioned for their elite clientele. As the chronology progresses, historic black-and-white photos by the likes of Whymper, Mummery, and Sella precede the color negatives of the post-war generation, which, in turn, give way to stunning aerial and telephoto images of the modern tigers in action. Throughout the book, overlapping, cut-out and drop-shadowed design elements, artistic color treatments, and sidebar-length captions combine to create a stylish presentation that looks, feels, and reads more like a high-quality magazine or catalog.

It is ironic then, that *Mont Blanc's* only conspicuous flaw concerns one of the most time-tested graphic elements: maps. Visualizing just how the myriad peaks and valleys that make up the Mont Blanc massif fit together is perhaps a visiting climber's greatest challenge. It is disappointing then that this book, which clearly aspires to be the definitive printed resource for the Mont Blanc area, contains only a very few old or simplistic maps. One less two-page photo spread would not have been missed, but one more very detailed, up-to-date map could have strengthened the overall presentation greatly. It also is curious that the oblique overview illustration of the range—precisely the sort of thing that can really help a reader or visitor put everything into perspective—is a winter representation, as the vast majority of the climbing done here and documented in this book has been accomplished during summer conditions.

These are, however, minor chinks in an otherwise magnificent creation. With all due respect to the memory of Gaston Rebuffat, his must now be considered the penultimate book on Mont Blanc; for anyone with an interest in this important mountain and its history, Ardito's *Mont Blanc* is the book to own. Whether it will ever find its way into the rucksacks of climbers visiting this area remains to be seen (although opened slightly and stood on edge, it could provide an effective A-frame bivouac shelter), but there is no doubt that *Mont Blanc: Discovery and Conquest of the Giant of the Alps* is destined to become the essential reference for scheming and dreaming between trips.

DAVID PAGEL

*Escape Routes.* David Roberts. The Mountaineers: Seattle, 1997. 267 pages. $22.95.

It is hard to imagine a regular reader of this journal who is not familiar with at least some of the climbs of Dave Roberts. And it is almost as hard to imagine someone who has read an article or book by Roberts and has not been inspired to seek adventure where he found it.

*Escape Routes* is a collection of 20 articles written during the past decade—or, to give it a certain perspective, since *Moments of Doubt*, a previous collection of articles, was published. Where has Roberts been in that time? Moving roughly east from his home in Boston: Iceland, Mali, Fontainebleau, Provence, Grindelwald, Kitzbühel, Cortina, Ethiopia, Beijing, the Brooks Range, The Wind Rivers, Moab, New Mexico, Patagonia, and the Gunks. What has he been doing? Climbing, caving, bicycling, bouldering, golfing, river running, llama herding, elbow bending and writing, writing, writing. Whom has he seen? Jeff Lowe, Roman Dial, Ed Viesturs, Richard Bangs, and his long-time tramping buddies, Jon Krakauer and Matt Hale, among others.

I could end this review right here by saying there is not a trip that he describes that does not stimulate the green worm of envy (those wriggling words again). How come he gets to have all the fun? But that would be too superficial a response. While some of the pieces belong to the been there/done that genre (e.g. "Storming Iceland," "Wandergolf in the Tirol," "Quiet Days in the Brooks Range"), others raise issues that increasingly thrust themselves upon the (post?)modern adventurer.

"First Down the Tekeze" describes an 18-day first descent of the Tekeze River in Ethiopia. What made this trip special as far as the general public was concerned was the reunion of five river rats who several decades before had punched a number of first descents down rivers in exotic lands in the face of genuine danger and who subsequently formed an adventure travel company, Sobec. But what made it known to the public was a film crew of eight and five additional scribes, photogs, and computer jockeys who, with four tons of gear and a satellite link direct to Redmond, Washington, brought it to the whole wide world via the Web site Mungo Park. And if danger should bite, well, one could perhaps use the phone to call in the helicopter.

Techno-tripping has ineluctably brought changes in two directions. It clearly changes the nature of the adventure itself, usually in the direction of reducing or removing adventure, but it also changes the vision/version of the adventure projected to the world. This is not completely new. For those of us who suckled on Annapurna, the recent revelations of Herzog's tyrannical control of the expedition and the resulting book in the face of Lachanal's diaries and misgivings have left a sour taste. As Roberts admits, if the public wants thrills, then it is up to the film crew to give it the most smashing, thrashing white water that low camera angles can provide, even though most of the trip is Class II and much more time is spent setting up cameras than running rapids. And in his piece about Ed Viesturs, Roberts describes Viesturs as being so far ahead on his push to the summit of Everest that Dave Breashears had to make do with filming the Sherpas topping out. There are no close-ups of the soloist. Nor was there any footage of Viesturs coming upon the body of his friend Scott Fischer and then, a while later, the body of his friend Rob Hall. It is left for Roberts, who wasn't there, to tell us about it in uncluttered, understated, and therefore moving, prose.

In "The Moab Treehouse," Roberts muses over the changes in Edward Abbey's backyard. What is the wilderness for? What is a town for? And for whom are either of these places in the age of the carbon-fiber frame, the oil-damped fork, and the ellipsoid granny ring? Similar questions arise in "Roman Dial and the Alaska Crazies" and "The Race Diabolique," the latter an account of the 1995 Raid Gauloises held in Patagonia (the Eco-Challenge, an offshoot of the Raid, was held earlier in that year near Moab), and they arise in a more tangential way in a number of the other articles.

Krakauer, in his foreword, says that "Dave's best writing has always been characterized by a ruthless even brutal candor," and in this collection there is ample evidence for that claim. Still, Roberts' candor is revealed primarily in his description. When it comes to taking a position about the issues raised in his accounts, he often is ambivalent. Ordinarily, this could be taken as something to be condemned, but not here. What makes it interesting is that Roberts, like all of us, approaches his experiences with values intact. Like a well-oiled six-shooter, his responses are loosely holstered. But the actual situation, as opposed to a vision of it, keeps catching him up short. He also encounters others with values different from his own (one suspects he actively seeks them out). The result is a certain tempering, a movement to a position more tentatively held and vaguely defined—a good position, I would think, for thinking through the issue anew. And this is what Roberts invites the reader to do, not by laying out the strands of opposing arguments, but by vividly portraying the kinds of experiences and desires different individuals have in the face of something like an adventure. This rethinking also is invited by his accounts of those very different from ourselves: the Amhara and Agow on the Tekeze, the Dogon and their predecessors the Tellem in Mali, and the Anasazi in the Four Corners region.

Finally, as an echo to Krakauer, I would say that Dave's best writing has always been characterized by good writing. He helps us to see things not only vividly but freshly. Faced with the end of an idle in the Winds, he writes, "Back home, responsibilities lurked like tax collectors." Ambivalence again, akin, I suspect, to that felt upon arriving at the end of this book.

JOE FITSCHEN

*Wild Snow: A Historical Guide to North American Ski Mountaineering.* Louis W. Dawson. The Mountaineers: Seattle, 1997. 214 black-and-white photographs, ten maps. 292 pages. $40.00.

Lou Dawson values nothing more than a stimulating ski descent from a hard-earned summit. Knowledge of his forefathers in the growing sport of ski mountaineering is one of his intellectual passions. The combination makes the Coloradan the perfect author for a *Historical Guide to North American Skiing.* His enthusiasm for the routes, the turning, and the stories he relates are infectious. I found it difficult to finish a chapter without my mind wandering to plans of how and when I could orchestrate a visit to the runs he outlines.

The 250-page hardback covers nine regions of North America, separated in terms of off-piste skiing. The author offers a sampling of "classics" in California, Colorado, Utah, Alaska, Wyoming, the Northeast, the Northwest, British Columbia and the Canadian Rockies. Naturally, his picks are controversial. Every skier has his own list of favorites within his or her region. Yet Dawson has chosen a representative handful of lines in the backcountry skiing hotbeds of this continent, and they are destined to compose a "hit list" for "piste off" skiers.

Above and beyond being a guidebook, however, *Wild Snow* serves its readers with fastidiously researched historical background. The tradition and styles of "Glisse Alpinism" have evolved for 7,000 years, as Dawson informs us. Important characters and their influence on the sport add depth to the volume as well as humor. Austrian pioneer Mathias Zdarsky's best quote can't be fully appreciated without seeing his photo, but the self-proclaimed expert of the late 1800s included discussions of attire in his ski wisdom. For example, he wrote that "calling attention to the upper parts of the female body distracts the men from skiing." (A prophetic and profound truth, indeed.)

Other historical anecdotes focus on the legacy of classic ski mountains. Included here are Bill Briggs' first descent of the Grand Teton, Fritz Stammberger's stunning ski of Maroon Bell near Aspen, and more recent envelope pushing, such as 1990s descents of Mt. Robson's North Face and Denali's Wickersham Wall. This latter "State of the Art" section compiles information previously recorded only in scattered magazine articles. Inclusion of this recent history helps make this volume an unofficial "encyclopedia" of ski mountaineering.

Lou Dawson has climbed and skied all 54 14,000-foot peaks in Colorado, an unequaled feat that exhibits his unswerving dedication to skiing wild snow. Only a ski mountaineer of such stature could write as convincingly as he does. Dawson's vast personal experience lends credibility and accuracy to his route ratings and descriptions. He takes on the unenviable task of judging and ranking the backcountry skiing feats of heroes past, both famous and unsung. But his background enables him to do so remarkably well. The writing is like the man: honest, clear and decisive.

With its excellent, original descriptions of access and routes on classic glisse peaks, Dawson's guide is a must for avid ski mountaineers, past and present. Yet its easy readability, wide-ranging topics, and abundance of intriguing photographs also will appeal to aspiring backcountry skiers, mountaineers, and historians of all types.

TYSON BRADLEY

*Rock Stars: the World's Best Free Climbers.* Heinz Zak. Bergverlag Rudolf Rother: Munich, 1997. Distributed in the U.S. by John Barstow's Photography. Profuse color photography. 216 pages. $59.95.

W OW! The only thing more impressive than the resumes of the climbers featured in *Rock Stars* is Heinz Zak's accomplishment of getting 78 of the top climbers on film at climbing areas all over the world. At first, I was skeptical as to whether I would like this book because I was afraid there might be too much sport climbing. But there isn't. This book represents traditional rock climbing (Arnold, Bachar, Dawes), long routes, sport climbing, competitions, soloing (Croft, Robert), and bouldering (Gill, Godoffe, Nicole) equally well.

Some of my favorite climbing partners over the years are featured in the book (which I hope doesn't hurt its success). And there seems to be quite a few top climbers missing, which means Zak has plenty of material left to produce a second book. Coverage of French climbers is predominant, but there are plenty of climbers from the U.S., Britain, and Germany covered as well. I like the inclusion of Yuri Hirajama, and climbers from Slovenia, the Czech Republic, and the former Soviet Union, as it gives the reader a better perspective of world climbing accomplishments.

Highlights include: a selection of quotes about soloing, competitions, route manipulation, and the joys of climbing. This collection highlight the experiences, passion and focus that climbers have from throughout the world. For instance, it is clear that route manipulation is not okay. It also is clear that both competitions and soloing require great concentration and that neither is right for everyone.

I enjoyed the pieces on Bernd Arnold because his home in Dresden is my favorite and its serious nature as a climbing area is well captured here. The Antoine Le Menestrel piece with photos of a performance of *The Flying Carousel*, and Alain Robert's extreme solos and skyscraper climbs offer perspectives of climbs in another realm. The longer routes, such as Hill on the *Nose*, Huber on the *Salathé*, and Mariacher and Kammerlander in the Alps, show everyone how the explosion of free climbing during the last 20 years has left virtually no discipline or place on earth untouched.

I would be remiss in not mentioning the photography, as this is what the book is really about. The photos are fantastic. Too often today we see the close-up of the big pump. The photos Zak has collected here range from the scenic, to the home gyms, parties with friends, and depict a range of moods: serious, funny, beautiful, and inspiring. These images, coupled with a short bio introducing each climber, make a beautiful book (as well as great historic reference) for any serious library or coffee table.

HENRY C. BARBER

*A Most Hostile Mountain: Re-creating the Duke of Abruzzi's Historic Expedition on Alaska's Mount St. Elias.* Jonathan Waterman. Henry Holt and Company: New York, 1997. 30 photos, two maps. 253 pages. $25.00.

B eing in the party that achieved the first American ascent of 18,008-foot Mount St. Elias in July, 1946, this reviewer had more than passing interest in the account of the two-man mini-expedition to the mountain a half century later. And the story is enriched by alternating parallel coverage of the century-ago 1897 first ascent of the peak by the famed Italian explorer Luigi Amedeo di Savoia, Duke of the Abruzzi.

Included in the coverage of the Italians' journey is that of an American party led by Henry Bryant, which started for the mountain two weeks ahead of the Duke. Although Bryant's party turned back only halfway toward the mountain, they and the Italians enjoyed amicable relations.

Waterman obviously has done considerable research on the Duke's trip, perusing books and archive libraries of major universities and mountaineering organizations throughout the U.S., England and Italy. His access to the diaries of expedition members also brings out information missing from the Duke's own *The Ascent of Mount St. Elias*. Of special interest are accounts of the sometimes sad and turbulent life and times of the Duke, before and following the historic ascent.

The author's minimally financed and equipped (virtually "alpine-style ) mini-expedition is in sharp contrast to that of the well-supported Italian party. Besides ten American packers hired in Seattle and four Tlingit native porters, the original party comprised seven climbers and four professional guides, including scientists and famed alpine photographer Vittorio Sella. Enhancing Waterman's text is the liberal use of quotes from the diaries of the Italians and of the Americans, and from the old classics of Whymper and Mummery.

Waterman's own journey begins in Seattle with the father-and-son team of Gary and Jeff Hollenbaugh, and in a small sailboat they motor and sail north up the Inside Passage to Yakutat and into Icy Bay. From there, Jon and Jeff leave the father in charge of the boat, and they hike and haul a bare minimum of gear and food to the base of the south face below 10,000-foot Haydon Col. They contend with mosquitoes, up-and-down morainal debris, and the heavily crevassed Malaspina and Libby Glaciers, then slug their way up the face to the col, living with storms, heavy snowfall, and in constant dread of massive avalanches down the face.

But the summit attempt on this elusive and "most hostile mountain" seemed doomed from the start: The author left his mittens on the boat; the party of two travels crevassed glaciers and steep slopes of avalanching snow—with no radio contact and a minimum of time, food and equipment. Heavy snowfall and continuous avalanches experienced in the ascent discourage any attempt to return to a food cache left far below the col. With food and time running out they are forced to abandon hopes for the summit some 8000 feet above, and they descend to the peak's base via the crumbling South Ridge ("Shale Ridge"–the route of our 1946 ascent).

The book's appeal includes the author's spirit of self-discovery while seeking the unknown in the uninhabited, heavily glacierized terrain of southeastern Alaska. In his forties and just through the aftermath of a divorce, Waterman has turned his attention to Mount St. Elias, which had fascinated him with its history of few successes and many failures. Before "settling down to a wife and kids," the author responds to the need for personally experiencing this "most difficult of North America's major mountains."

The book will appeal to all with a taste for boating and climbing adventures in Alaska, and expeditioners will empathize with Waterman's sensitive observations and philosophical musings: "The true alpinist is the man who attempts new ascents. . . Since the beginning of alpinism, one climber's 'justifiable risks' have always been perceived as another's death trap. . . . Dreams are perhaps the best recreation when you're stormed in. Aside from their entertainment value, they put you in touch with your desires and vulnerabilities. . . . Mountain expeditions used to seem like powerful metaphors. They are replete with challenge, strained communications, dead ends, uncertainty, leadership stalemates, and the overwhelming bewilderment you always feel beneath the big mountain itself. If you could pull through this gauntlet . . . you could have the tools to cope with the rest of life. But in practice . . . life in the 'real world' had none of the same grandeur."

There are only a few negatives: a couple misspellings, and most photos occupy less than a half page, with one of St. Elias printed backward. To this map buff, the two maps are oversimplified and suggest the lack of appreciation for one of the world's most spectacular coastlines, bordered by some of the highest peaks and largest glaciers in North America.

DEE MOLENAAR

*Cook & Peary: The Polar Controversy Resolved.* Robert M. Bryce. Stackpole: Mechanicsburg, PA 1997. 1133 pages. $50.

The literature of polar exploration, unlike that of climbing, is known for its historical tomes. Yet Robert M. Bryce's *Cook & Peary: the Polar Controversy Resolved* is the lengthiest and perhaps, the most painstakingly researched of all the voluminous polar exploration titles, including Pierre Berton's *Arctic Grail*, Roland Huntford's *Scott and Amundsen*, and *Shackleton*. Bryce's behemoth (the first 998 pages is followed by 135 pages of Bibliography and Source Notes) is about two explorers who both claimed to first tag the North Pole.

Frederick Cook and Robert Pyres' dealings with the North Pole should be of no small interest to the readers of the *AAJ*. Cook was one of the founders of the American Alpine Club, and conquering the Pole was all the rage with explorers and alpinists alike at the turn of the last century. And it is in the nuances of Cook's life, more so than Pyres', that the book comes alive. The details of Cook's marriages, frauds, and legitimate explorations are unveiled through a litany of footnoted events, congressional investigations, newspaper stories, lawsuits, tedious correspondence, and telling anecdotes.

I was initially compelled by the story, then several hundred pages later, somewhat inundated, unlike in *Arctic Grail* or *Scott and Amundsen*. Bryce was clearly aiming for an Arctic version of Huntford's dualistic Antarctic biography. Yet unlike those other two books of human tragedy and crafted profiles, Bryce dismisses Peary to the extent that we don't get to know him, and Cook is revealed only by sifting through Bryce's considerable research tailing piles. A skillful editing (even those other voluminous polar histories are half the page length of this) would have made Cook more accessible.

By the time we learn all about Cook's 14-year jail sentence for mail fraud, halfway through the book, an odd portrait of the man emerges. If he were alive today, it would not be hard to like the man, described by a contemporary as "a child and a foolish, head-strong one when it came to dealing with worldly realities. His enemies made him a victim of his own naive honesty." Cook's personality, in a word, was irresistible.

Initially, the author seems to be an objective biographer, and we are made aware of a plethora of minutiae about Cook. We feel his sorrow after his first wife dies. Then we wonder how Marie, the second wife, hangs on through all of Cook's lengthy departures and fraudulent dealings. After digging long enough, we read one of her letters about how she was "hypnotized" by him. And we merely learn that she divorced him after finding him naked in a room with another woman. End of story there.

His cell mates in Leavenworth, of course, revered him (it took the paroled Cook an hour to exit the prison yard through the throng of well wishers). *The New York Times* wrote about the same release (and explained his fraudulent claims on Denali, the North Pole, and his bilking of thousands of similarly charmed people through mail fraud): "It was only when left to his own devices and fancy that his moral principles took a queer twist, his imagination led him astray, and he fell."

Cook is indeed a fascinating study and it is to Bryce's credit that he tracked his subject's life so assiduously. Bryce shares one of Cook's notes for a planned posthumous book that would clear his name: "After this [posthumous] document appears in print it should be followed promptly by a book an elaboration of same with the appeal of a bleeding heart all thou for a little understanding for a life intended as a service to humanity." This is one precious lodestone in which the biographer actually holds up the mirror to Cook's face.

But Bryce's investigation of the Denali climb of 1906, like Cook's own claim, made me question the book's credibility. The author spends a lot of time on an aging gardener's theory about how Cook really did make the climb. The author also elevates men like Walt Gonnason, one of the few Denali climbers who actually believes that Cook made the summit. Gonnason summited once on a well-traveled Denali route, then, sponsored by the Frederick Cook Society in 1956, failed on Cook's supposed East Buttress route—and still maintained that Cook did the climb.

The vastly more experienced pioneer, Bradford Washburn, is given short shrift in the text. We learn in the Source Notes that Washburn probably spurned Bryce because of his absurd pro-Cook theories. Bryce similarly dismisses most of the respected sources in Denali history in order to keep Cook's claim afloat. He proposes that the Sourdoughs could have faked their climb in 1910, and that Belmore Browne's memory and motives are suspect. Bryce, in fact, systematically deflates all the most credible pioneers of Denali: Washburn, Browne, and Hudson Stuck (alleging pedophilic tendencies) and others. He then infers that they, like Peary, all came from the same sort of political or societal fabric that would defrock Cook. Bryce reveals more negativities about the nay-sayers of Cook in the Source Notes than he does about Cook in the text.

The author's endless postulations might make fine filler for a historical novel, but not for a historical biography. The sad thing is that to Denali amateurs, and to Bryce himself, his theories might seem logical. To any alpinist who is a student of the mountain and its history, Cook was an audacious pioneer for his 1903 circumnavigation, and then, in 1906, a bald liar. Cook's claim to have climbed up the wildly corniced East Buttress and to the summit, all in eight days without crampons (Bryce refers to them as "ice creepers"), was not possible for the luminary alpinists of the day, let alone an amateur climber like Cook. The East Buttress route that Cook attempted was not finally climbed until 63 years later. And traversing over to Karstens Ridge from the East Buttress (which Bryce claims was Cook's probable route) has never been done, let alone attempted. Certainly Cook, for all of his brash optimism as an explorer, didn't even get high enough on the mountain to try this unappealing and difficult traverse.

I believe that Bryce, for all of his careful research, was drawn in by the inexorable charm of the long-dead Frederick A. Cook. In the Preface, Bryce refers to feeling the "spell" from one of Cook's books, as the writing "whispered" aloud to him. This is *Cook & Peary*'s power: through its comprehensive treatment of Cook (if you had never set out on an uncrowded flank of Denali or dragged a sledge on broken sea ice) you too would be swayed up out of your basket. This is how Cook worked his eerie magic. Like thousands of other Cook supporters, Robert M. Bryce, for all of his erudition, cannot help himself from buying, then selling, Cook's snake oil.

By page 802, my suspicions had been sufficiently aroused to turn to the Acknowledgments, pages 977-978. Sure enough, the first person acknowledged is a staff person of the Frederick Cook Society (dedicated to restoring honor to that family's besmirched name). And in the entire last paragraph of this section, thanks are given "to the many stout supporters of Dr. Cook," ending on a note of apology that they might be disappointed by the book.

It seems there are other omissions or short treatments in this otherwise lengthy treatment of the high latitudes, such as Cook's theft of the Fuegian language dictionary, or his purported Eskimo mistresses and children (Bryce mentions Pyres' Eskimo children, but only in brief; Bryce seems leery of sexual scandals throughout). Finally, Bryce comes to the same conclusions of most arctic historians: Cook did not make the pole; Peary might have made it. This is, as the book's subtitle claims, The Polar Controversy, Resolved?

We are given a scholarly treatment of Cook's extraordinary achievements outside of his frauds, such as his year adrift in the Antarctic, his remarkable sledging journeys in the Arctic, and his ethnographic accounts of the Eskimo. The book could be retitled: *An In-depth Study of the Movements of Doctor Cook*, which from my perspective is the best reason to read it. Yet the wealth of this Cook and Peary material, in the hands of a Roland Huntford (or a good editor), could have made a classic book.

Meanwhile, the Cook saga lives on. Washburn was invited to a debate in Fairbanks two years ago about the Denali climb, but the Cook Society's representative canceled at the last minute. In 1994, some experienced Denali climbers again were financed by the Society to climb Cook's route. They failed, and none of them had the heart publicly to admit that Cook also failed, or that he executed the greatest lie in Denali history. It's a tribute to his charm, 58 years after his death, that flowers, condolences and donations are still being accepted.

JONATHON WATERMAN

*The Climb of My Life: A Miraculous Journey from the Edge of Death to the Victory of a Lifetime*. Laura Evans. Harper: San Francisco, 1996. 268 pages. $22.00.

The Climb of My Life is a truly inspirational book, not just for women but for anyone who is faced with what may seem to be insurmountable odds. The book is interwoven with Evans' reflections on her mountaineering experiences, its influence on her psyche and the almost-overwhelming impact of breast cancer. Unlike many mountaineering accounts, wherein the reader is gripped by the adventure of predictable danger, the attitude of this story is summarized eloquently with the passage, "The Mountain before me is one I did not choose to climb. I woke up instead at its base, looking up at its towering peaks, anticipating the unknown hardships that lay ahead."

Evans' story begins with her diagnosis of breast cancer, then switches back and forth between her diagnosis and incidents that apparently flashed through her mind during her initial discovery of a lump and her diagnosis. The transitions between the two are abrupt, making it difficult to follow, and I sometimes had to reread to determine where we were. This pattern of shifting from thought to thought without connection continues throughout the book until she begins her description of the actual climb of Aconcagua. Here her focus is much clearer.

The book has some very good ideas regarding mental attitude and motivation. My favorite was an exercise she did with the self-help group she started, in which everyone makes a list of the things that make them smile. When they examined the lists, they found that most of these things were easily obtainable. (I actually did this with my disgruntled teenage students–and it works.)

There are other feelings and thoughts the significance of which might be more obscure to those who have never been there. But I have been there, and I think I understood the significance of her story about Buster only because I had a similar experience. I prayed that I might have several years at the end of my chemotherapy to enjoy life and, a few days later, a dear friend who had become one of my guardian angels during my treatment was killed. I felt he had somehow taken my place in death.

*The Climb of My Life* is by no means a captivating, "can't-put-it-down-until-I'm-finished" mountaineering account, like a *Touching the Void*. Evans' story is better appreciated as a motivational novel. The conversational passages I found somewhat dry and the jumps from one train of thought to another annoying at times. But her story of fighting back against the odds of survival to climb the highest peak in the Western Hemisphere to raise money for Breast Cancer Research is truly inspirational. When you are told you have breast cancer, for which there is no known cure, it's like a death sentence. When your body is scarred from surgery, wasted from the effects of chemotherapy and your odds are less than 50/50 for the next five to ten years, it's sometimes hard to not give up. Laura Evans didn't give up; instead, she continued reaching higher goals. In my opinion, the best part of the book was the conclusion in which she sums up her emotions on her journey by likening herself to the cartoon dog, Lucky. Despite the difficulties and the long lasting effects of the cancer and treatment, she feels lucky not only to be alive but to be able to climb for all those who can't.

MARGINA RHYNE

*G2: A Climbing Journal.* Produced and directed by Thom Pollard. TRT: 53 minutes. Shot on Beta SP and Hi Band 8 video tape. $30.00.

G2: *A Climbing Journal* is a story about an attempt by Americans to climb Gasherbrum II. The story is told in the past tense, using a combination of expedition footage and talking-head interviews shot long after the trip. The action drags in a few sections (the 12 minutes to reach base camp seem to take forever) and the voice-over narration suffers due to the inherent problems of retelling events months after they happened. But overall, *G2* is a very honest account of the mountain experience. It is shot extremely well, and edited professionally. It should do well on the mountain film-festival circuit where knowledgeable audiences will appreciate the effort that went into producing it.

"My documentaries are always produced for the love of it," writes filmmaker Thom Pollard. This passion is evident throughout *G2.* The opening sequence, a beautifully photographed image of a lone figure on a training run during a New England snow storm, sets a high standard for everything that follows, and the quality of the visuals rarely disappoints. The talking-head interviews, which easily could have become dreadful, are interesting and attractive. Pollard attempts to draw out real feelings from his climbers but aside from a few isolated sound bytes, most of this reveals little insight into their personalities. I didn't feel that I knew the climbers any better after listening to them for nearly an hour than I did before.

There's not much in the way of drama here—no body bags, no knife fights over the last packet of oatmeal, no angst-ridden psycho-dramas about how to find happiness in the hills post-Everest disaster. In a way, it's rather refreshing. Pollard, fortunately, escaped the pressures of broadcast television by producing this with love and his own resources. It's tempting to discount *G2* because it didn't have a big budget where everyone was getting paid or at least getting a free trip. But look closely and you'll see the real thing in scenes such as the one in which the team is descending through fresh, waist-deep powder lying precariously on a steep wind slab. As the camera pans up, you see what appears to be miles of the same deadly stuff, ready to rip off in a massive avalanche. It's a grim situation and, for a moment, you feel their resignation: they know they are riding a psychotic horse into a burning barn but after weighing all the options, only this one was reasonable. So there you have it: incredibly small dots on a giant 8000-meter peak. They slog downward knowing it's better to be lucky than good, but hoping they might be both for just another day. Good stuff.

The video's production value is solid, even at its $30 price tag. But the best reason to buy a copy is to encourage Thom Pollard to make more films. He has talent and I'll look forward to seeing more from him in the future.

MICHAEL GRABER

*The Duke of the Abruzzi: An Explorer's Life*. Mirella Tenderini and Michael Shandrick. The Mountaineers: Seattle, 1997. 216 pages. $24.95.

Climbers of any age or experience level will treasure the biography of explorer and alpinist Luigi Amedeo di Savoia, *The Duke of the Abruzzi: An Explorer's Life*. Authors Mirella Tenderini and Michael Shandrick have crafted an excellent book that lends insight into an extraordinary man and member of the Italian royal family. Famous among the climbing set for his ascent of Mount Saint Elias and attempt on K2, the Duke was not only a mountaineer but also a polar explorer, war hero and ambassador of good will.

First impressions might lead one to believe that the Duke was a golden child with spoils to travel the world. Tenderini and Shandrick provide us with information to the contrary. A victim of family jealousy and political infighting, the Duke spent much of his life avoiding scrutiny of the press. The story of his failed relationship with a wealthy American heiress is included because it was the source of much worldwide media attention. Much more than a dry expedition account, this biography sheds light on the personal life of a guarded and enigmatic man.

Walter Bonatti pays tribute to the Duke in a heartfelt foreword. The body is organized chronologically into chapters about each of the major periods of the Duke's life. It is clear that an exhaustive amount of research has gone into this book. At times, facts such as names and dates are overwhelming, but this only adds to the book's value as a reference tool. Much attention is given to the Duke's expedition companions, such as famed photographer Vittorio Sella, dedicated assistant and scribe Filippo De Filippi, and many loyal guides who helped him realize his goals. Many black-and-white photographs, some by Sella, are included, which give a face to the legend.

In his foreword, Bonatti writes: "I have but one regret with regard to the Duke of the Abruzzi: to have not lived in his time." After the last page of this book has been turned and the cover closed, readers also will dream of joining the Duke on a foray to an unexplored range or following in his steps to a virgin summit. This book deserves a place in your library.

LEN ZANNI

*Against the Wall*. Simon Yates. Jonathan Cape: London, 1997. Distributed in the U.S. by Trafalgar Square, North Pomfret, Vermont. Color photographs. 176 pages. $35.00.

Okay, let's get this over with: Simon Yates is the guy who cut the rope on Joe Simpson in the Andes. He doesn't mention it until the last chapter of this book, but his publisher, who is also Simpson's, spreads it all over the dust jacket. The back flap even includes a blurb for Simpson's *Touching the Void*, which is ten years old. It may be true, as a prominent bookseller says in his catalogue, that "Yates will be forever known as the man who cut the rope." Few recall Ralph Branca's rookie year, when he won 21 games and started the World Series for the Dodgers, but almost everybody remembers that one bad pitch to Bobby Thomson. Yates's critics should reread *Touching the Void*. They might ask themselves what they would have done in Yates's place, and consider whether either Yates or Simpson would have been better off had the rope remained intact.

Now to *Against the Wall*. It describes a fine new route on the 4,000-foot vertical granite of the Central Tower of Paine. The four-man team faced major technical difficulties, as well as Patagonia's notorious wind and storm. Much aid was used (though few bolts), and some 3,000 feet of line were fixed. Many of the ropes were jumared repeatedly, because the weather forced numerous retreats. Several leaders fell when their protection popped, though they were stopped unhurt.

Yates is very good at describing the airy feel of the climb, as well as the messy details of cooking and portaledging—and the moves: "The handholds were enormous, but having got used to aid climbing, relying completely on my own body seemed strangely unfamiliar. The weight of equipment made me feel cumbersome and strength quickly drained from my arms. Realising that I could not hang on for long, I lunged to the left, and in a series of rapid ape-like movements, swung across the flake. . . ."

Yates prefaces his account with an apology for perhaps being too frank and critical. He need not have worried. Except for a little irritability and forgetfulness, the climbers are portrayed as remarkably polite and thoughtful under the stressful circumstances. His own moments of frustration and rage seem pretty mild. I'm not asking for personality clashes, enlivening though they can be, but for more vivid characterization.

Even so challenging a route as this one is not ordinarily worth an entire book. No high peaks here, no first ascents, no accidents or rescues. Another participant described the whole thing with clarity and wit in a few pages of the 1993 *AAJ*. But Yates's Introduction promises more than fixed ropes and spectacular granite: "For me, the Patagonian expedition was a turning point, marking a very sudden shift in my attitudes to many things and the start of a new phase of my life." This phase is treated only in a brief epilogue (and mentioned on the dust jacket). Yates, it seems, after years of hard climbing (including a winter attempt at Nanga Parbat), has settled down. The transition is anticipated by a number of introspective passages in the last third of the book. He realizes that "I did care not only for myself, but also for those around me. Drifting along in a world of my own was no longer enough. I needed to try harder to do things better, for myself as well as for others." This perfectly believable declaration sounds like a pallid New Year's resolution or an excerpt from a pop psychology text. It is not grounded in enough personal detail to carry weight. Only in his acknowledgments does he mention a woman who helped him "through a difficult patch in [his] life." How did she help? What patch was this? The Simpson episode? The few pages about it here do little more than assert that: "My decision [to cut the rope] had been right." It is hard to write a revealing account while remaining as reticent as Yates is in this book.

Although *Against the Wall* misses its largest ambitions, it is an engrossing account of a major climb. Its eight pages of color photos make the reader wish for more (the best of all is on the cover). It surely will persuade a lot of climbers to hurry down to Patagonia.

STEVEN JERVIS

*The Measure of a Mountain: Beauty and Terror on Mount Rainier.* Bruce Barcott. Sasquatch Books: Seattle, 1997. 278 pages. $23.95.

During the past decade, I have read and reviewed many inferior books about mountaineering. I have been bored with 8000-meter-peak quests and grown contemptuous of padded, egocentric autobiographies. I have scorned an attempt by an amateur to delve into the "personal insights" of climbers. A recent encyclopedia was, in my view, not worth the trees sacrificed. My half-dozen negative reviews in this journal since 1989 have burdened me with angst and despair (shared, I hope, by six cringing authors). Someone must review such books, but why me? Am I to be a hatchet man forever?

Reading Bruce Barcott's book on Mount Rainier, I felt a surge of pleasure and optimism, as if gazing upon a fine new cliff for the first time. Barcott is not only a master of the language but a man who has done his homework: this is not a book spewed out in a few months. And, as a pleasant sidelight, it has been copy edited and designed by true professionals, and I applaud Sasquatch. How gratifying to have, along with Mountaineers Books, a second competent mountain publisher as the millennium turns.

Barcott, Seattle raised, has been mesmerized by Rainier since his teens. He isn't a climber, or a botanist, or a glaciologist, but he quickly realized that the mountain is more than a summit, a wildflower paradise, or a mound of earth containing 25 icefields. A grand eminence like Rainier is the sum of all these things and much, much more. Barcott went to the mountain, waited, listened, and learned.

The book is composed of a series of essays bound by an admittedly thin thread: Barcott the non-climber realizes he must attempt to reach the apex of the monster volcano some day. But this is a commitment he'd better think about for a while, absorbing everything he can about the peak before he clicks crampons to boots. So he hikes, fleeing during deluges; he observes marmots and tourists; he talks with climbers, guides, rangers, naturalists, volcanologists, historians. What a unique way to approach a peak! What a contrast to those who race up the 50 state high points!

Had Barcott been a mediocre writer, short on curiosity, this would have been a dull book. For instance, an entire chapter about the controversy of renaming the mountain Tacoma, in the early part of the century, might not make for compelling reading. But Barcott eloquently manages to convey the boosterism of the city of Tacoma, the economic issues involved, and the craziness of congressional wranglings. It's amusing and instructive to learn of this strange, archaic tale.

Other chapters deal with the meaning of Scott Fischer's life and death, the secret lives of marmots, climbing accidents then and now, modern climbing writing, and the airplane crash of December 1946, when, during the next summer, mountaineers Dee Molenaar and Bruce Meyer, along with many others, worked for days to excavate corpses from the ice—only to entomb all 32 later into the glacier at 12,000 feet. An even more sobering chapter describes the potential for a mudflow disaster when the volcano next rumbles, an event undoubtedly to happen during the next 100 years.

Barcott's honesty and perceptiveness are refreshing. In one of my favorite passages, he writes:

> I'd begun my Rainier explorations with a passing interest in the summit. Now I found myself caught between a curiosity urging me to explore the upper mountain and a conscience deeply opposed to the macho ethos of climbing. Having read through thousands of pages of mountain carnage and witnessed the grief brought on by Fischer's death, climbing a mountain could no longer be written off as an innocent lark. Too many questionable motives underlay the whole culture of mountain climbing. Too many people died pursuing goals that were unworthy of their deaths. I didn't want to become one of them.

(I should point out that the hideous dangling modifier in the third sentence is one of the very few grammatical mistakes in this otherwise well-edited book.)

While some readers of this journal may consider the above excerpt a cowardly view of our fabulous, risky sport, I find it provocative and worthy of discussion. Let us hope Barcott will write another mountain book, though I have a hunch he will move in another direction. Our loss, if this is true.

STEVE ROPER

*Big Wall Climbing: Breakthroughs on the Free-Climbing Frontier.* Paul Piana. Sierra Club Books: San Francisco, 1997. Hard cover, profuse color photography. 190 pages. $35.

In large part, the history of modern world rock climbing is a response to the history of modern American rock climbing. Prior to about 1940, Americans had taken the Europeans' lead in how to climb. At that time, the vast majority of rock gear was imported from Germany and France, and the means of using it was oftentimes passed on by ex-pat Europeans who had taken their love of climbing to their adopted homeland and enlisted Americans to follow them up their peak. The Euros had long since worked out the basics: how to secure the rope to the cliff by way of anchors; how to protect the leader via pitons and belay; how to free climb and how to aid climb (though the line between the two were oftentimes blurred). All of these techniques were readily espoused by the Americans.

The Americans more or less followed the European model right up to the day Chuck Wilts took a crack at free climbing the previously aided *Piton Pooper*. Chuck succeeded, and the idea of a first free ascent became fact. Slowly, American climbers followed his lead. While there were exceptions, the vast majority of leading American climbers put a high premium on free climbing; first free ascents and the creation of new free routes that would previously have been aid climbed became the norm. The thinking was: If I can free climb it, I will. Otherwise, I'll aid it.

American and world rock climbing entered another phase when people set to work on the great walls in Yosemite. While the Yosemite pioneers valued free climbing, the big walls were so intimidating that simply getting up them remained the first ambition.

By 1968, modern big-wall techniques were established and their utility proven on what then were the greatest pure rock climbs in the world—routes such as the *Nose, Salathé,* and *North America Walls* on El Cap, the South Face of Mt. Watkins, The Northwest Face and Direct Routes on Half Dome, and many more.

About half a dozen years earlier, the second coming of Chuck Wilts arrived in the person of Frank Sacherer, widely considered the Father of American free climbing. Starting on a small scale, Sacherer set out to free climb the existing aid routes. Finding immediate success, Sacherer spread his wings, and by the time he'd left the Valley in 1968, he'd made spectacular free ascents of such climbs as the East Face and Direct North Buttress of Middle Cathedral, the *Lost Arrow Chimney*, the Southwest Face of Half Dome, and many others. Sacherer did not introduce a new level of difficulty—Chuck Pratt, Royal Robbins, Bob Kamps and several others were also free climbing at a very high level. What Sacherer introduced was the revolutionary concept that scale was not a limiting factor. To Frank Sacherer, the bigger, the better. It was a philosophy readily embraced by the next generation of free climbers who arrived in the Valley around 1971.

The next quantum jump in free climbing came in 1975 with the first free ascent of Washington Column's East Face (*Astroman*) and the Chouinard/Herbert route on Sentinel's North Face. These ascents bred the belief that anything short of a blank wall could be free climbed.

By 1980, another generation of free-climbers, their techniques enhanced by the demands of modern sport climbing, set to expand the horizons first broached by Chuck Wilts, 40 years earlier, expanded by Frank Sacherer in the 1960s, and pushed to new heights by the leading free climbers of the 1970s. Two of the most talented of this new wave were Todd Skinner and Paul Piana, whose partnership pushed free climbing difficulty to a scale no less grand than that attained by the Yosemite pioneers.

*Big Walls: Breakthroughs on the Free-Climbing Frontier*, penned by Piana, is a celebration of his and Skinner's free ascents of four spectacular big walls: El Cap's *Salathé Wall*, the Southwest Face of Proboscis in the Northwest Territories, the North Face of Mt. Hooker in the Wind River Range and the Direct North Face of Half Dome. Ironically, all four walls were originally pioneered by Royal Robbins in the 1960s, and were then seminal climbs at the top of the scale of both difficulty and beauty. Piana's opinion that the freeing of these four routes make them the most important wall climbs in North America is a claim supported neither by history nor by the climbs themselves. Free climbing big walls had been established for more than a decade when the duo made its dramatic first free ascent of the *Salathé,* which is questionably the finest free-wall climb in the world, but historically represents raising the ante of an already established phenomenon rather than inventing a new mode.

But the gargantuan claims aside, *Big Walls* is a thrilling effort—a lavish coffee-table book bursting with shocking color photos and spirited writing. It is a must-read for anyone interested in the outer envelope of what free climbers have yet accomplished, and to those who aspire to reach similar heights someday.

JOHN LONG

*A History Of Mountain Climbing.* Roger Frison-Roche and Sylvain Jouty. Flammarion: Paris and New York, 1996. Hardback, large format, numerous color plates and photographs. 236 pages. $65.

A history of mountaineering, lavishly illustrated, in a coffee-table format. No mean feat! The book gets off to a good start: the initial chapters are superb and justify the high-altitude price tag. Alpinism was born in the Alps, primarily in the Chamonix/Zermatt environs, so the French authors speak with considerable artistry on the highly contested first ascents of Mont Blanc and the Matterhorn. But following their nationalistic chronicling of European alpinism (including British, German, Austrian, but most enthusiastically, French) in the book's first half, they should have stopped while ahead. Once they launch into the book's second half and "Other Mountain Ranges," factual mistakes multiply like mushrooms after a rain. Ascents in the American "lower 48," the Canadian Rockies, and Alaska are conveniently described alongside exploits in the Caucasus, Andes, Africa, and New Zealand.

Chapter titles like "The French to the Fore" make it obvious this book was written for the French market. Yes, climbers are naturally competitive—with the mountains and each other—but as an historical constant, the theme of nationalism is stated ad nauseam. There is, however, excellent historical trivia: the precursor of the ice axe, a small hatchet, was called a pioulette, hence the term piolet. Grand Jorasse was the nickname of a chamois hunter and early guide on Mont Blanc named Lombard. Jacque Balmat's sick baby actually died the same day that he and Dr. Paccard reached the Mont Blanc summit (August 8, 1786), and Balmat hurriedly descended to be with his wife.

Numerous misspellings and factual errors interrupted my reading. Samples: Miriam (NOT Myriam) Underhill. Mick (NOT Mike) Burke. Hans C Christian Doseth (NOT Donseth) and Finn Daehli (NOT Doehli); and NOT ALL four Norwegians died on the descent after the first ascent of Great Trango (only the two with misspelled names died!). Likewise, Rand Herron was killed in a fall down the Second Pyramid at Giza, NOT down the Great Pyramid. Plus Heinrich Harrer "subsequently spent the next seven extraordinary years climbing in Tibet." No kidding? And Todd Skinner did have a partner on the first free ascent of the *Salathé Wall*: his name is Paul Piana.

The photos illustrating American climbing are generally weak. The start of the North America section—surprise!—offers photos of 1950s French alpinists logically juxtaposed with engravings of John Fremont and Major Powell. None of the '30s-era American rock climbers, K2 veterans, or Yosemite Golden Age-ers (except Harding) are seen. There is one photo of Skinner and Piana, and two of Lynn Hill. But the effect is slapdash. One paragraph describes the FA of Yosemite's Sentinel by Salathé and Steck in 1950; the next, the FA of Popocatepetl in Mexico in 1519 by the Conquistadors! The Cassin Ridge: two sentences. The FA of Hidden Peak by Andy Kauffman and Pete Schoening: two sentences. You get the picture. . . .

The history of the Alps (superbly illustrated and engagingly written) clearly came at the expense of an abbreviated world climbing history. Four sentences on Mt. Kenya; minimal descriptions of the 1938 and 1939 American K2 expeditions, with incorrect facts on the latter. Fritz Wiessner and Pasang Lama's descent was not caused "when Wolfe and two Sherpas were killed"—and actually, three Sherpas later died. There are multiple Everest errors. The benefits of breathing bottled oxygen while sleeping at high altitude was "discovered" on the 1922 Everest expedition by George Finch, Geoffrey Bruce, and the Gurka, Tejbir. To suggest it was "a French technique" first championed on Makalu is absurd! On the 1921 Everest expedition, Mallory and Bullock DID NOT immediately perform "a key task by climbing up to the North Col." Rather, they couldn't find the approach to the Col until after weeks of recon! It is Irvine's ice axe that was found by the First Step in 1933, NOT Mallory's and Hornbein and Unsoeld DID NOT meet another American team on Everest's summit in 1963; they met Jerstad and Bishop later, while descending the Southeast Ridge.

In the positive, women's alpine and Himalayan climbing achievements, from Annie Peck on Huascaran to Catherine Destivelle soloing the Matterhorn are given equal mention (as they should be), plus are well-illustrated. Artistically, numerous paintings of mountain scenery and climbing history, enchanting archival photographs of guides and gear, plus climbing-movie posters of K2, Tirich Mir and others add visual splendor to the book. Two useful appendices, "50 Great Names in Mountaineering" and "100 Key Dates," round out the story. Mountaineering is indeed "the pointless if wonderful struggle between humans and peaks," but someone on this team should have fact-checked with considerably greater diligence.

EDWARD WEBSTER

*Deep Play, A Climbers Odyssey from Llanberis to the Big Walls.* Paul Pritchard. Seattle: The Mountaineers, 1997. 16-page color insert. 192 pages. $22.95.

*Stories of a Young Climber: An Autobiography.* Pat Ament. Two Lights: Boulder, 1996. 262 pages. $15.95.

*D*eep Play, winner of the prestigious Boardman Tasker Award for mountaineering literature in 1997, is a collection of essays, mostly short non-fiction accounts of "cutting edge" climbs by Paul Pritchard. The book is distinguished by two qualities: the nature of the climbs he describes and the impressionistic style in which he describes them. Of these two features, it is the nature of the climbs that leaves the strongest impression on the reader. In fact, one wonders if the award was made more in appreciation of the climbing Pritchard does and the sacrifices he has made to it rather than the quality of the writing.

The climbing is traditional in the best sense of the word: ground-up, alpine-style, minimal bolting, a penchant for new lines in exotic locales—Meru in the Himalaya, Mt. Asgard on Baffin Island, the Central Tower of Paine in Patagonia. The organization of the text is chronological: we follow Pritchard from his childhood ("I was born on top of a quarry") to the scene of his recovery from a fall (four crushed vertebrae, a broken sternum, and a fractured skull). This latter, one gathers, is of lesser seriousness than the accident recalled in an earlier essay, "A Game One Climber Played," which recounts a groundfall (no, that's wrong, it's a fall to the *water*) from which he has to be resuscitated.

When I say "one gathers," I mean it literally—it's hard sometimes to tell exactly what happens. Pritchard quite consistently abandons the literal for the figurative, imaginative, impressionistic. The reader can't always tell exactly what happens, but nonetheless has arrived (if he's patient) at a sense of what has happened that's somehow larger than the literal. In fact, my accounting of his injuries from a "Healing Lesson from Andy Parkin" comes not from the essay itself, but from the very useful "Notes About the Essays" that conclude (and clarify) the text.

The book opens with "Firestarter," a short piece about his childhood among the industrial dereliction of an abandoned mine. Climbers often feel compelled to start the story of their climbing lives at the beginning, and it's often dull stuff. In Pritchard's case, however, "Firestarter" is illuminating, rich, and evocative. "My old man didn't like me going to school," he tells us, and the only school-related tale in the whole book is of his jumping four stories down a stairwell, an event from which he "woke up in hospital," the first of many such awakenings. Off hand, I can't think of another climber writing about his childhood in a way that made me care, or in a way that made me want to read it on its own merits as opposed to because it was attached to someone who later became a climber of interest.

There are numerous memorable moments throughout, often descriptions of falls, fears, or friends. This one from "Just Passing Through" gives a general sense of Pritchard's level of both observation and lyricism:

> . . . new rock was the essence of climbing for us. Throwing loose holds over the shoulder, feeling the exposed grains crush like sugar on footholds, no chalk ahead to show the way and no idea, apart from a contract the eye has with the body of whether you are capable of getting up a thing or not . . . . I felt then that Frey was another special place. A place where climbers lived who cared for it, and knew it well enough to say that the yellow rock was more brittle than the red, or that there are hidden holds inside that crack, or that the number of condors is on the up, that the boulder in the next valley gives good shelter, or at what time exactly does the sun shine on that face of the mountain. Simple shared knowledge. That which we have of our home rocks.

I have always admired climbers who explore the limits of the endeavor, that is, whose personal limits are at the very edge of what's humanly possible at the moment. But one wonders if Pritchard does not rather define this line a little too loosely. In his introduction, Pritchard admits to wishing to emulate the writing of Joe Tasker and Menlove Edwards, but one worries that he may also unwittingly follow them to an early death. Even as his climbing career begins, he exhibits an attitude about risk entirely foreign to my view: "The falls you could take off the hard slate were legendary and I wanted to take one." He continues: "I didn't have to wait long"—falling 80 feet, ripping out nine nuts, and stopping four feet off the ground. So when he takes even longer, more serious falls, or when his friends die (three of them recounted in the book), or when I hear that he's recently been in another serious life-threatening climbing accident, I am deeply saddened but hardly surprised. In fact, I worry that in praising the work, I encourage him to climb on in a manner I myself would not: Are we not then complicitous in his next accident?

Is this the best of mountaineering literature published in 1997, as the Boardman Tasker

Award would have it? The judges' criteria were: "Which of the books went closest to the heart of the nature of modern mountaineering? Which were concerned to describe, explore, respond to what mountaineering has become?" I understand their rationale, although I may not necessarily have voted their way. A couple prospective reviewers declined to review it, citing that they thought it poorly written. For me, the strengths of the prose far outweigh its flaws, which others may perceive as too impressionistic, too sloppy (verb-tense changes for example, a conspicuous disinterest in the concept of "complete sentences") and a general sacrifice of spatial and temporal specificity for an interior view.

Apparently some American readers have complained about his being on the "dole," our equivalent of unemployment compensation, to support his climbing. The dole was a pittance by any measure and Pritchard's standard of living seemed to border on subsistence level. The man lived to climb. There's a glossary of climbing terms—hardly needed as it's doubtful the book will reach many non-climbing readers. There's also a "chapter-by-chapter glossary of British colloquialisms" for which, though far from complete, I will be eternally grateful for the etymology of "knacker". The colloquialisms and their lyrical flow are very much the charm of Pritchard's writing style.

At Sron Ulladale in the Outer Hebrides, he and Johnny Dawes—amid a trip on which they eat little else but cabbage and "glutinous gruel," and on which they endure a non-stop midge attack—wave at two fisherman out on the Loch, their only human contact of the week. "On our return to our dining cave," he tells us, "we were warmed by the sight of two trout lying there." Pritchard, I believe, returns this gesture in *Deep Play*, a gift that surprises, warms, and nourishes.

•

In Pat Ament and Tom Higgins' well known co-authored piece "Nerve Wrack Point," Higgins says, "Ament and his traveling medicine show. Riding freights. Cutting records. Walking a tightwire over some canyon in Colorado. Running from the law. Having three affairs at once!" Higgins' description may not quite be literally true (then, in '73, or now), but Ament's life story does have that feel: it's a wild and varied show, tempered in the years since Higgins described him with the sort of self-examination that Socrates claimed makes life worth living.

To paraphrase Stephen Venables opening to his review of *Into Thin Air*: I approached Pat Ament's autobiography, *Stories of a Young Climber*, warily. In a letter to the editor of *Rock & Ice*, Tom Frost complained rather vehemently of Ament's treatment in a review. Indeed, Frost and Royal Robbins speak enthusiastically for the book on its back cover. Conversely, others declined to review it because they believed anything bad they might say would be dismissed as a product of envy, rivalry, or some long-standing dispute of which I am happily unaware. In order to avoid assigning the review to the wrong person, I decided to do it myself.

I was greatly relieved to find much to praise here. And while I can't place myself in one of Frost's extreme camps (he says you'll either love the book or hate it), if I had to choose, I'd say that the kind of life he's led, the sort of climbing he has done, represent the very best aspects of our endeavor.

Ament's gift as a writer is his ability to evoke a mood, to describe the feeling of what it was to be there, whether it be on the Diamond, the *Nose,* or England's *Cenotaph Corner*. But most often and most specifically, there refers to the crags around Boulder where Ament was raised in the 1950s and early '60s, and where he continues to live. Ament exemplifies, as well as anyone can, that "simple shared knowledge" of "our home rocks" of which Pritchard speaks. In passing, he mentions that he's done perhaps 100 ascents of the Bastille's West

Buttress. By 1969 (when he was in his early 20s), he tallied ninety-five 5.10 routes and 253 5.9s. (If you think it's bragging or compulsive to keep count, you would do well to remember that this list was compiled for an application to the AAC!)

Ament does sometimes come off as egotistical, a charge that seems to puzzle him. But in my view that sense of egotism is almost never in descriptions of climbing but more in service of his other interests: martial arts, chess, music, poetry. His listing of awards, favorable reviews, and particularly the comments of well-known persons on his writing all come across to me not so much as signs of a large ego, but of a fragile, needy one. There are far more occasions in the book on which he comes off as genuinely modest. In fact, his list of material possessions—the things of the world that matter to him—is touchingly modest and best of all, it shows a life committed to matters of the spirit, instead of telling us of such a commitment.

Showing is the far superior narrative mode, for it allows the reader to make up his own mind. For example, the early chapters on childhood and adolescence evoke a Wordsworthian sense of innocence and wonder in nature. For me, this is somewhat undercut in a later chapter when Wordsworth is literally invoked several times. Likewise, the repeated references to what this or that person said of him come off as testimonials and seem to me more likely to produce in the reader the very opposite of their intended effect. Let the work speak for itself. These are really my only criticisms of the book, and in my opinion, could be addressed by a good editor.

Ament is clearly an intuitive spiritual soul and, once in a while, he garners meaning from a coincidence or a glance or a moment that he asks us to take on faith. Sometimes this comes across as new-agey or incommunicable. But more often, and repeatedly, I found myself thinking, "Exactly—he's hit it exactly right here."

And for a person of such strong religious beliefs, I think Ament has a light touch—he tells us of a journal of spiritual experiences too private to share. Good move, I think.

I was thinking about this book in relation to *Deep Play*—one an international award winner and one not even short-listed. And yet, the books seem somewhat similar to me, both in their intents and their strengths: evocative, lyrical, and heartfelt. Though the writers' commitments to climbing are similar, their approaches are not. In *How to be a Master Climber in Six Easy Lessons* (a quirky and wise little volume that reminds us that safety and adventure need not be mutually exclusive. Also available from Two Lights, $10.95), Ament begins by stating that "the truly best climbers had to be, by definition, also the safest and . . . one does not have to sacrifice safety to push standards." This seems inherently true to me, but apparently not to Pritchard or by extension, to last year's judges of the Boardman Tasker Award.

While Frost's judgment that this is the finest work to emerge from American climbing writing is perhaps colored by years of friendship, I can see why he makes the claim, and I think it's a claim well worth considering. When reading *Master of Rock* or *Spirit of the Age* (his bios of Gill and Robbins, respectively) one must admit that Ament has terrific subjects. But when the gaze is directed back at the self—then what? If anything, Ament is more interesting than Gill or Robbins, simply because he's essentially more mysterious, more troubled, more unknowable, perhaps even to himself. His suffering is a palpable thing and we watch him struggle with the world, well-meaning and misunderstood.

In a year of mountain books dominated by sensational tragedies and gorgeously slick coffee table tomes, Pat Ament's book is beautiful reminder that a climber's life might be a modest and holy thing. It's a reminder we need.

DAVID STEVENSON

# Club Activities, 1997

EDITED BY FREDERICK O. JOHNSON

T*he American Alpine Club 95th Annual Meeting, Bellevue, Washington, December 5-7, 1997.* The energetic and diversified nature of world mountaineering was evident at the 95th Annual Meeting as the roughly 400 in attendance at the December weekend in Bellevue, Washington, were treated to a variety of illustrated programs on climbs and expeditions ranging from remote low-altitude peaks to daring adventures on the highest in the Himalaya. The first evening's dinner was followed by Ed Viesturs' rendition, "Endeavor 8000," which portrayed his pursuit of the highest summits without the use of supplemental oxygen. His accomplishments are truly remarkable.

The Saturday schedule, which included a general membership and board meeting, ranged from lectures on mountain safety, the history of ski mountaineering in America, a glance at Smith Rock climbing, and a perspective by Piotr Pustelnik about Polish climbing achievements. The Yosemite master plan was discussed; in addition, there was a panel on the future of our public lands. The accomplishments of women rock climbers were framed in a video by Lee Goss, and Naoe Sakashita described his major climbs, including the Japanese ascents of K2 and Jannu. The Southern Hemisphere was not forgotten: an Emmy-award winning film by Dan Mannix showed sailing to, then climbing on, Mt. Foster in the South Shetland Islands. Gordon Wiltsie's camera captured almost unknown peaks and a multi-day first ascent in Antarctica. The dinner program was brought into motion by an auction enlivened by Mike Clifford before the awards presentations began. Introductions and presentations underscoring the great worthiness of these special awards played out to applause from an appreciative audience. Awards were:

The Angelo Heilprin citation for honorable club service was given to George Ross Sainsbury, the Literary Award to Broughton Coburn, the Robert and Miriam Underhill Award to Steven J. Swenson, the David Brower Conservation Award to Louis French Reichardt, the Robert Bates Award to Stephanie Davis and Jeff Hollenbaugh, and the David Sowles Memorial Award to Anatoli Boukreev, Pete Athans and Todd Burleson.

After, when both audience and recipients had returned to their seats, renowned Polish alpinist Krzysztof Wielicki kept us spellbound with his epic accomplishments on the highest Himalayan summits in all seasons, reminding us with his slides of the risks, skill, endurance, and suffering encountered on such quests.

On the final day, a panel discussed climbing and the media. Greg Mortensen explained his efforts to build schools and provide public-health programs in Pakistan's Baltoro region. Siri Moss overviewed ski mountaineering and alpinism in the Wrangell and St. Elias Mountains, then Charles Sassara illustrated the range's potential with a slide show of his difficult new route with Carlos Buhler on University Peak. Mark Synnott portrayed a new multi-day climb on Shipton Spire in the Karakoram. Don Serl and Fred Beckey pictorialized Mt. Waddington and the glacierized British Columbia Coast Mountains, a region destined for an impetus in mountaineering.

FRED BECKEY

*AAC, Oregon Section.* In February, Tom Bennett and I organized the premier Mazama Denali Conference, which featured 26 speakers from all over Alaska and the lower 48 states and included Bradford and Barbara Washburn as our special guests. Jack Grauer, past president of the Mazamas, commented, "Never will there be such an incredible gathering of Alaskan alpinists. It was like living 60 years of Alaskan history in four days."

During the year, the development proposed for the Rim Rock Destination Resort loomed over Smith Rock State Park. The Mazamas, Tom Thrall, Gary Rall of the Portland Rock Gym and others wrote letters to representatives and senators to stop the Smith Rock Climbing Destination Resort from happening. There were 36 newspaper articles in the Oregonian about this controversial resort. Domestic conservation chair Gail Billings assisted with her talents to keep Smith Rock from being commercialized. The Portland Rock Gym also pitched in with a letter-writing campaign.

Gary Rall, Laura Potter, Candy Morgan and Andy Fritz served on the Washington State Advisory Board for Beacon Rock and Horse Thief Buttes. Beacon Rock Ranger Steve Johnson wants to open the east face to sport climbing. Gary Rall of the Portland Rock Gym negotiated the use of epoxy on Beacon for loose holds. There are three different proposals monitoring birds on the rock. Wildlife biologists want the trails around Beacon defined through the talus fields to protect rare plants and the Larch Mountain Salamander.

Currently, the best sport climbing area around Portland is closed. The Madrone Wall, which boasts 150 sport and traditional routes, may be turned into a gravel quarry. Previously, District Attorney/climber Darryl Nakahira kept the area open.

Blake Hankins, Tom Thrall and I worked at Smith Rock in preparation for the Spring Thing, during which all climbing is stopped and 200 climbers and hikers work on Smith Rock's trail system every spring.

Oregon member Jeff Alzner and partner and AAC member Fred Ziel climbed above 25,000 feet in high winds on Cho Oyu, summiting with Canadian friends. The pair had previously climbed on Broad Peak. This was their fourth Himalayan expedition.

Jim Petroske, whose son, John, has been on expeditions to K2, Manaslu, and Everest, worked with his other son, Bill, and J.P. Books to set up an excellent display of modern and historical climbing books for sale at the AAC annual meeting. Jim has mailed out his catalog of mountaineering books for eight years.

Oregon Section member Bob Lockerby this year self-published a monumental 100-year index of the Mazama annual that incorporated the work of Vera Defoes, a Parker Cup winner, along with other members.

Members Peter Green and John Youngerman and AAC Oregon Section student member Robert Johnson took Explorer scouts on an expedition to New Zealand from December 18, 1996, until January 7, 1997. The three adults and seven students climbed seven peaks. In August, the same group completed four new routes and four first ascents on peaks near the Thaikazan Glacier in the Mt. Waddington area. They dubbed one of the peaks Mt. Becker, after Terry Becker, a Mazama president who gave his life in an attempt to rescue fellow climbers. We're waiting to see if the Canadian Board of geographical names approves. Peter Green and the Explorer scouts also organized a climbing presentation by writer/climber Joe Simpson. It was Simpson's largest audience ever with 1,100 people.

Oregon section members Neil Cramer, Jeff Sheets and others ran the month of climbing weekends at Silcox Hut on Mt. Hood. The renovated W.P.A. Hut is an excellent warming hut for the south side ascentionist. Neil has done an excellent job running the Friends of Silcox Hut.

In an endeavor made possible by Outing Committee chair Barbara Becker, who facilitated a grant from the Mazamas, Tom Bennett, Harvey Schmidt, Ph.D., and I, in conjunction with Dr. Mauri Pelto of Maine, participated in the North Cascades Glacial research project, which studies glacier ablation and global warming.

On April 25 and 26, Tom Bennett, Ian Wade and I are planning a Mazama conference entitled "Mountaineering Issues of Tibet" with historical and modern themes. The conference is co-sponsored by Barbra Brower, Ph.D., editor of the Himalayan Bulletin, with the Geography Department at Portland State University. The 25 proposed speakers include Khandgo Chazotang, the niece of His Holiness the Dali Lama, Stephen Venables, author of *Himalayan Alpine Style*, Lowell Thomas Jr., author of *Out of this World* and *Silent War in Tibet*, Edwin Bernbaum, author of *Sacred Mountains of the World*, AAC past president Lou Reichardt, and Oregon Section member Ian Wade as master of ceremony. For information contact Bob McGown at 2535 S.W. Palatine St., Portland, OR, 97219.

BOB MCGOWN, *Section Chair*

*AAC, Sierra Nevada Section.* 1997 brought the Sierra Nevada Section continued growth and success spiced with daunting new challenges. With the addition of western Nevada to our geographic region plus an increasing number of Southern Californians wanting to affiliate, our section now contains well over 400 members.

Six events sprinkled throughout the year brought us together. Our traditional Ski Weekend at Grover Hot Springs south of Lake Tahoe drew an enthusiastic crowd of skiers and soakers bent on late-winter fun. In April, a capacity crowd convened at the beautiful San Francisco peninsula home of Dr. Jim Fries for our spring Wine & Cheese party, which featured a lavish slide show by member David Keaton. Flowering dogwood forests and raging waterfalls formed the backdrop for our Yosemite Valley campout in May. More than 30 Sierra Nevadans, plus a family of party-crashing bears, came together to celebrate Allen Steck's birthday and enjoy the superb weather, perfect crack systems and huge friction slabs of the Valley.

Two other campouts, one in June at Lover's Leap near Lake Tahoe and one in September at the Owens River Gorge, completed our outdoor get-togethers for the year. At the Owens Gorge event, John Fischer, a well-known mountain guide and section member, gave an excellent presentation on the Leave No Trace organization and its philosophy. As a result, we have decided to help raise awareness in the climbing community of the ideas and activities of this organization by distributing literature and inviting representatives to speak at our events. We have also helped member Nick Shiestel promote community activities of the Sierra Mountain Guides, who offer excellent climbing safety instruction events free of charge under their Climb Smart! program.

Our Annual Section Dinner in November was beautifully planned by Jane Koski and our out-going Section Chairman Eric Brand. The City Rock Climbing Center in Emeryville (whose space was provided by owners Mark and Debra Melvin) boasted a lavish buffet and bar and was filled with oriental carpets loaned by art entrepreneur and member Gene White. More than 100 attendees lounged, feasted, hobnobbed and enjoyed a slide show about guiding in the Alps by Armin Fisher, a California native and the first non-Italian to become a certified UIAGM guide in Italy. With section enthusiasm running high, a contingent of almost 20 Sierra Nevadans shuttled up to Seattle in December for the AAC Annual Meeting.

The Sierra Nevada membership is greatly enriched by the many distinguished authors of mountain literature among us. Outstanding achievements this year included publication of *High Altitude Medicine*, a definitive work on high-altitude mountaineering and medicine by the late Dr. Herb Hultgren, who had long and illustrious careers in both fields. Prolific author

John Hart won his second Commonwealth Club Silver Medal in five years for his new book, *Storm Over Mono: The Mono Lake Battle and the California Water Future*. Also, to be published in the spring of 1998 is the third edition of John's *Walking Softly in the Wilderness: The Sierra Club Guide to Backpacking*. First published in 1977, the book's extensively rewritten *Third Edition* discusses just about everything one can think of in the line of techniques and gear, with a very strong low-impact emphasis. Chris Jones' ever popular *Climbing in North America* was reprinted as a paperback edition with a new foreword. Galen Rowell published a beautiful new book, *Bay Area Wild*, that highlights wildlife and wilderness around the San Francisco Bay Area. And readers throughout the world will be happy to know that Steve Roper and Allen Steck worked diligently all year to put together the next edition of their renowned publication Ascent, to be published by the AAC Press in 1999.

Of continuing concern to our section and the world climbing community are the changes being proposed by the National Park Service for Yosemite Valley. Instigated by devastating floods that struck the Valley at the start of 1997, these sweeping changes include the radical re-configuration of campgrounds, traffic patterns, day-use access, concessionaire-related housing and lodge units, and visitor controls. The efforts we have devoted to maximizing section communications have paid off in our ability to react quickly to these challenges. Many of our members attended on-site walk-throughs in the Valley, submitted extensive written comments, spoke out at open houses and workshops conducted by the National Park Service throughout California, and kept up a continual dialogue with park planners to lobby hard for our ideas and positions. As a result, the Park Service has amended some plans, allowed extensions on public-comment periods, and remained open to our suggestions for minimizing the impact of automobiles and people upon the quality of experience in Yosemite Valley.

Still, it's important to realize that changes proposed by the Park Service, which they want to begin implementing in 1998, could make climbing in Yosemite Valley logistically difficult or impossible for most of us. These changes would force any Valley visitors without pre-arranged reservations (up to six months in advance, credit-card payment required) for a campsite or hotel room to leave their private vehicles at gateway communities (30-60 minutes away) and take a regional bus into the park. It is unclear how often these buses would run, what their cost would be, or what the price or security levels would be for parking at the gateways. Visitors then would have to transfer to electric shuttle buses at a transit stop constructed somewhere at the El Capitan end of the Valley (various sites are being debated). Those visitors with reservations could drive directly to their accommodations, but then would be prohibited from driving anywhere else, except to exit the park. This obviously would severely limit climbers' ability to visit the Valley on a spontaneous basis, bring and store necessary gear and equipment, and get to the base of some of the most popular climbing cliffs. Similar changes are being considered for other national parks as well.

At this point, there are very few firm answers to the many major questions such a system poses. The Park Service is asking for ideas from the user public, and our section members are doing their utmost to ferret out ideas and represent all climbers in these issues. An ad-hoc committee consisting of Lou Reichardt, Nick Clinch, John Middendorf and Linda McMillan continues to communicate our needs to the Park Service planners. If you have questions or ideas relating to these issues, please contact the committee members directly.

During this year of Yosemite gloom and doom, there was, however, one resounding success. Stanley Albright, newly appointed Yosemite Park Superintendent, told us at the end of 1997 that after reading Steve Roper's popular book and listening to vigorous lobbying by our section members, he decided to start his term by setting at least one thing right after decades of neglect: He will change the lackluster name of Sunnyside Campground back to historic, traditional, and world-famous Camp 4.

ERIC BRAND AND LINDA MCMILLAN

*AAC, Northern Rockies Section.* After receiving word in late 1996 of the Board's decision to create this new section, we were not really sure what to do. The new section includes all of Montana, Idaho, Utah and Northeastern Nevada—quite a bit of wide open space! The idea we came up with was to start with creating chapters in some of the larger population areas throughout the section and let those chapters function as they wish. With input from the Club headquarters and other section chairs, we decided that Boise was a good place to start.

From February through April, several existing members of the club started meeting on a regular basis to discuss why we joined, what we wanted from our membership, how could we develop local activities and how we could create additional value to assist us in "marketing" the new chapter. Being the insurance guy, I had to get over the fact that our member benefit insurance coverage was not the reason everyone else joined! We decided that we should plan an event in conjunction with the local Boise Chapter members, Boise State University Climbing Club, local outdoor equipment retailers and local manufacturing reps for a combination climbing area clean-up day, equipment demo day, an interactive safety discussion, membership dinner and slide show.

Susan Bernatus, Bob Moseley, Scott MCleish, Brian and Karen Wright and I formed the nucleus of the Boise Chapter. Together with the B.S.U. Climbing Club, we had a successful clean-up day at the local Black Cliffs. The clean-up activities were followed by a demo day with equipment supplied by Five Ten, Metolius, La Sportiva, Scarpa and Black Diamond. More than 100 people of all ages, shapes and sizes participated with a smile on their face. During this time, several members and non-members discussed climbing communication techniques, belaying etiquette and general guidelines of safe cragging. Many people of all different skills levels were involved. This was followed by a membership dinner, at which we signed up several new members. Immediately following was an outstanding slide show graciously given by AAC Board Member Carlos Buhler. What a day! For the Boise Chapter, success was measured by the broad diversity of activities and skill levels of those participating.

In July, the Boise Chapter hosted the First Annual Northern Rockies Section Moondance at the City of Rocks in south-central Idaho. More than 50 people attended the non-host BBQ at a group campsite reserved by the chapter. Friends were made, lies were told and everyone agreed that we should do it again. Each year this event will occur as an annual gathering on the July weekend of or following the full moon. Everyone is invited.

Throughout these activities, many members commented that they enjoyed meeting fellow members in their area for the purpose of learning more of the local areas, hearing of new routes and meeting new climbing partners. Having just returned from a long weekend ice climbing in the Wind Rivers with several of the Boise Chapter folks I would not otherwise have known, I can personally attest to the value of meeting new people in my home town. Based on this success, I would like to see other chapters develop in Salt Lake City, Bozeman, Missoula and perhaps Eastern Idaho in conjunction with Jackson Hole. As the Section Chair, I offer my energy and assistance in organizing new activities or chapters and truly look forward to serving all members of the Northern Rockies Section. I can only do so with your input! Give me a call, e-mail me (dcol@rmci.net) or drop me a line with your comments, suggestions or ideas.

DOUG COLWELL, *Northern Rockies Section Chair*

*AAC, South Central Section.* The section held its annual meeting on October 27 in Houston at the Hilton Southwest Hotel. Past chairperson J. French Hill presided over the dinner and membership meeting, which were followed by a silent auction, slide show and lecture, and raffle. An AAC conservation grant of $500 was announced by Domestic Conservation Committee Chairperson Gail Billings for a volunteer trail project at Enchanted Rock State Natural Area in Texas. This grant was matched by another $500 from the South Central Section. These funds, along with $3,000 raised by local climbing clubs through the annual Gripper Climbing Competition, will be used in l998 to fund the trail project.

The silent auction after the dinner included a number of climbing equipment packages donated by manufacturers and retailers in the Houston area. Next, renowned climber Alex Lowe presented a retrospective of his many years in the mountains and adventures in the Himalaya, Russia, Antarctica and across the globe. A raffle concluded the evening's events, with new member Vonda Covington winning a Marmot tent. The event succeeded in generating 12 new members for the club and needed revenue for the section.

The section, in association with the El Paso Climbers Club and the Access Fund, has been in negotiation with the Texas Parks and Wildlife Department regarding the management of climbing at Hueco Tanks State Historical Park. In l997, the El Paso Climbers Club recommended improvements to the TPWD for the operation and protection of Hueco Tanks SHP. The TPWD used some of these recommendations for a draft Public Use Plan for Hueco. However, the draft plan contains several objectionable elements regarding climbing at Hueco. These are currently in negotiation with the TWPD and await additional public comment.

Planned activities for 1998 include a fall annual meeting in Oklahoma (Wichita Mountains), completion of the Enchanted Rock Trail Project, and a successful resolution of the Hueco Tanks situation. After completion of the current trail improvement project, the section will solicit applications for future conservation projects.

Officers elected at the October meeting were Michael Lewis (Chairperson), Michael Bradley (Vice Chairperson) and Jack Leebron (Secretary/Treasurer).

MICHAEL J. LEWIS, *Chairperson*

*AAC, New York Section.* The New York Section, in the interest of serving its rapidly growing membership, continued to expand the number and frequency of its activities in 1997. After hosting the December 1996 Annual Meeting of the Club, the section began the year with a January ice climbing outing in the Adirondacks, where good weather and excellent conditions prevailed. Winter activities continued through February with a cross-country ski weekend (also in the Adirondacks) organized by Duncan and Nancy Burke. Two more climbing events followed in June: the 20th Annual Spring Climbing Weekend at the Ausable Club in upstate New York and, in August, the Second Annual Indoor Speed Climbing Competition at Ralph Erenzo's ExtraVertical Climbing Center in mid-Manhattan. Strictly a fun event, the competition featured prizes according to gender and age group, followed by an awards dinner at Joey's Paesano Restaurant in Lincoln Center.

The section's social activities also provided members with the opportunity to meet, mingle and forge new friendships. In May, Alpinfilm '97, now in its eighth year of co-sponsorship by the section, attracted the usual capacity throng of 400 climbers and film buffs. Alpinfilm, the New York International Mountain Film Festival, is a juried competition offering cash awards to winning filmmakers. The Best of Festival Award went to Godfrey Reggio's *Anima Mundi* (with a score by Philip Glass) celebrating the planet's biodiversity. The Best Film on Climbing Award was won by *Diamonds in the Rough*, a humorous look at the world of bouldering, produced, directed and introduced by Todd Skinner. Finally, the People's Choice Award went to Bill Noble of Canada for his documentary on veteran British Columbia climber John Clarke. Other significant films included *Alison's Last Mountain,* the story of

Alison Hargreave's last climb on K2 and a subsequent visit by her family to base camp. The event helped benefit the *American Alpine Journal*.

In September, repeating a popular event held a few years before, Olaf Soot hosted a section cocktail party and barbecue at his home in Greenwich, Connecticut. On hand were demonstrations of the latest developments in portable satellite telephone as well as global positioning system technology.

Finally, in October, the section hosted its 18th Annual Dinner featuring Kurt Diemberger, the legendary Himalayan climber, as the special guest. Kurt's memorable show was on "K2: Mountain of Dreams and Destiny." A short talk was also given by Stephen Koch on his attempt to be the first person to snowboard all seven summits. The black-tie event raised more than $5,000 for the new clubhouse in Golden. At the Dinner, 17 new members, including four women, were introduced to the membership.

On the expedition front, section member William Rom, M.D., participated in an ascent of Mount Geladaintong (6621m) in Tibet's remote Kun Lun Range, the source of the Yangtze River. Finally, as of December, a group of 14 section members and their guests were busy planning a trekking and climbing expedition to New Zealand, details of which will appear in next year's *Journal*.

All in all, 1997 was a vintage year in every respect. Thanks to numerous volunteers, the section was able to do good and have fun.

PHILIP ERARD, *Chairman*

*AAC, New England Section.* The year began with our second Annual Dinner. Almost 90 New Englanders gathered once again to dress up, dine, socialize and travel back in time to vast and faraway mountains. Craigen Bowen assembled a graceful display of the stunning 19th century mountain photographs of Vittorio Sella, and Dick Tucker fielded a video of two of Kenneth Henderson's now-famous climbing films of the 1930s: Pinnacle Gully in winter and the Whitney-Gilman ridge on Cannon Cliff.

Section chair Barry Rugo opened the dinner program and then introduced Jed Williamson, who issued a call to support the American Mountaineering Center in Golden, Colarado. Festivities included the introduction of new members, drawings for Steve Weitzler's great door prizes, and the usual recognition of AAC notables in attendance: Bob and Gail Bates, Kenneth Henderson, Dr. Henry Kendall, Sam Streibert, Rick Wilcox and John Reppy among them.

After dinner, our eloquent guide, Mark Richey, transported us to India, where he led us "Fast and Light" on a second ascent of the East Pillar of Shivling with his partner, John Bouchard. Before evening's end, we had auctioned off an "historic jacket" (donated by Ann Carter, once owned by Henry Hall and worn by Ad), a sweeping Brad Washburn aerial of Huntington Ravine and a famed Sella print. The dinner proceeds have gone into the preservation of the motion pictures taken in the 1930s by Kenneth Henderson.

In April, we explored Nevada's Red Rocks with Al Stebbins, Fran Bennett, Dick Tucker and Pat Smith under the spectacular clear air display of Hale-Bopp during the early evening camping hours. Among the longer routes done: Tunnel Vision, Frogland, Olive Oil and Dark Shadows. The summer saw various members in Switzerland, the Tetons, British Columbia, the Karakoram and "just out west" like Al Stebbins, who visited his favorites: City of Rocks, Smith Rocks and Eldorado Canyon.

Paul Dale and Jim Van Buren shuttled back and forth between France and Switzerland to visit the Verdon Gorge at Orpierre, to climb the Dufourspitz of Monte Rosa via the West Ridge above Zermatt and to enjoy the Morgins route on the Saleve.

Dave Oka and Yuki Fujita concentrated efforts in Chamonix, where, when the conditions higher up frowned upon them, they enjoyed rock routes near d'Envers des Aguilles. They initiated the Chere Couloir and traversed from the Midi high station to the Aiguille Plan. A week or so later, Bill Atkinson arrived to do what could be safely climbed alone: the Petite Aiguille Verte and the Aiguille du Tour from Chamonix and the Breithorn from Zermatt. In Chamonix Bill encountered our own Alain Comeau, who was there for two weeks to guide his carefully attended clients on such routes as the Arête des Cosmiques and Il Gran Paradiso. Dick Tucker and Pat Smith chose Switzerland, climbing on the Tour d'Ai in Leysin and reaching the tops of the Freundenhorn and the Blumisalp and summits in Les Diablerets in the Bernese Oberland. Then, in the Oberengadine, they joined Bill Atkinson to climb the Piz Palu Ostgipfel—with a mini-crevasse rescue on the descent.

In the Bugaboos, Mark Bowen and Beverly Boynton, after climbing the other spires, completed the Beckey-Chouinard route on South Howser Tower, chopping the rappel anchors out of the ice on their descent. Mark also traveled to Bolivia, where, for Natural History, he spent several days atop 21,500-foot Nevado Sajama interviewing Lonnie Thompson, the leader of an Ohio State University paleoclimatological expedition that was taking summit ice cores from Bolivia's highest peak.

Eric Engberg and Nancy Savickas engaged themselves in Canada. Eric did the Cardiac Arête on the Grand Sentinel and the East Ridge of Mount Temple. Nancy climbed mounts Edith Cavell and Athabasca, following up with a fall foray to Yosemite Valley for Snake Dike on Half Dome.

Barry Rugo, Tom Nonis, Mark Richey and John Bouchard returned to the Karakoram, where they made significant progress in attempts on Baintha Brakk and Latok I, but were deterred by unseasonably bad weather and unexpected objective danger.

BILL ATKINSON, *Chairman*

*Mountaineering Club of Alaska.* The club's 1997 climbing activities included the following: On April 4, Elena Hinds, Cory Hinds and Jim Francis summitted Mount Marcus Baker (13,176') in the Chugach Mountains via the original (1938) Washburn route, the Northeast Ridge.

On May 4, Carlos Buhler and Charlie Sassara made the third ascent of University Peak in the Wrangell Mountains. At 8,500 feet, the east face was the tallest unexplored and unclimbed face in the range. Their seven-day alpine ascent of this extremely technical face was tentatively rated Alaska Grade VI-. During April 3-15, Kirk Towner, Paul Barry and Dave Hart made the third ascent of Mount Tressider (13,315') via the northern slopes (Alaska Grade I); the first ascent of Peak 12,610 (Mount Pandora), approaching its west ridge from the north (Alaska Grade II); and a one-day ski ascent of Mount Churchill (15,638') up its southeast slope (Alaska Grade I). Harry Hunt, Barry and Hart made the first ascent of Mount Riggs (11,738') via the south-southeast ridge (Alaska Grade IV-).

From May 4-30, Mark Flanum, Brad Gessner, Antonia Sparrow and David Harrison made a traverse from Kantishna to Kahiltna Base Camp, summitting Denali May 26. Walking from Kantishna to McGonagall Pass to get onto the Muldrow Glacier, they ascended Karsten's Ridge, then spent six days in a snow cave at the base of Browne's Tower awaiting better weather. They then traveled up the Harper Glacier and climbed the East Ridge to Denali's South Summit (20,320'), descending the West Ridge to Denali Pass and down the Harper Glacier to high camp at 16,800 feet. The next day they re-ascended Denali Pass and descended the West Buttress route to Kahiltna Base Camp. Bob Hempstead, Dawn Groth and Dave Hart climbed Mount Sanford (16,237') in the Wrangell Mountains May 15-25. Between May

31 and June 6, Peter Clifford, Dale LeTourneau, Stephanie Ruthven and Patrick Collins climbed Mount Spurr (11,070') in the Tordrillo Mountains west of Anchorage.

The club's training activities included Avalanche Transceiver and Ice Axe Self-Arrest in March; Glacier Travel/Crevasse Rescue at the Matanuska Glacier in May; and a Technical Ice Climbing School at the Matanuska Glacier in September.

MARK S. MIRAGLIA, *President*

*The Alpine Club of Canada.* For the Alpine Club of Canada, the year saw several major events. A re-enactment of the first ascent of Mount Lefroy and the commemoration of the Abbot Pass Hut took place August 2. A party composed of representatives of the ACC, Canadian Pacific Hotels, the Association of Canadian Mountain Guides, Parks Canada and the media re-enacted the first ascent to mark the 100th anniversary of the 1897 ascent. The commemoration of the Abbot Pass Hut (built in 1922 by mountain guides under the sponsorship of the Canadian Pacific Railway) as a National Heritage Site was celebrated at the Chateau Lake Louise.

The 30th anniversary of the Yukon Alpine Centennial Expedition was held in conjunction with the Mountain Guides' Ball in October. Dave Fisher, who played a major role in the organization of the YACE, was patron of the Guides' Ball and organized the reunion, which more than 60 original Expedition members attended.

In 1925, during the first ascent of Mount Alberta by a Japanese expedition, an ice axe was left on the summit. American members of the next successful climb of the peak in 1948 discovered the axe frozen into the ice at the summit. It was accidentally broken into two pieces when they tried to remove it. Then in 1965 another Japanese climbing group found the bottom part of the axe and took it home. It was not until the summer of 1997 that it was realized that both parts still existed—one piece in Canada at the Yellowhead Museum in Jasper, AB, and the other in Japan. In December, at the invitation of the Japanese Alpine Club, Mike Mortimer, ACC President, and Bob Sandford, VP for Publications, attended the Annual Meeting of the JAC, where the two pieces of the ice axe were fitted together. A 75th Anniversary Climb in the year 2000 is being planned, at which the two pieces of the ice axe will be rejoined on the summit.

These three events mark important milestones for the ACC and its members, and an initiative similar to the Mount Lefroy ascent is being planned for a centennial ascent of Mount Athabasca in 1998.

The club approved plans for the Heritage Club Program to recognize 350 longtime members. The Heritage Club will recognize three levels of membership service: 25-34 years, 35-49 years and 50 years. The ACC has 48 members with more than 50 years of service, who will be enrolled in the Heritage Club along with more than 300 others with 25-49 years.

The club approved the formation of a Whistler Section, bringing the number of sections across Canada to 17. Total membership stands at 6,000 members. A major membership drive is planned for 1998.

In the area of leadership, a major initiative has started to train leaders at both the national and sectional levels. The committee's report to the Board of Directors emphasized the development of a training syllabus using the 1986 syllabus as a foundation and aimed at meeting both national and section requirements. Initial summer and winter leadership training weeks at the national level are being established for 1998. Many sections, especially those in the Alberta Sections group, already offer similar courses to their members. A surcharge of up to $25 will be applied to national camps participants to support leadership development.

The ACC provided financial support through its Endowment Fund for several expeditions. These included two section expeditions: the Toronto Section expedition to the Slaggards area in Kluane and a Saskatchewan Section expedition to Cho Oyu. The 1997 International Expedition to Lhotse and the Royal Canadian Mounted Police Mount Logan Expedition to celebrate the 125th anniversary of the RCMP were supported as well.

1997 Awards: Distinguished Service Award—Ruth Oltmann; Silver Rope for Leadership—Robert Stirling, Phil Youwe and Marg Saul; A. O. Wheeler Legacy Award—Ken Hewitt, and Richard and Louise Guy.

BEVERLEY BENDELL

*The Mountaineers.* The Seattle Mountaineers climbing program, under the leadership of Barbara McCann, expanded its traditionally alpine program by adding an introductory class on sport climbing. Enrollment in the alpine climbing courses has remained high, with demand exceeding capacity. The basic climbing course is a one-year program that teaches knots, belaying, rappelling, crevasse rescue, ice axe use, rock climbing and glacier travel. It is targeted for people new to climbing and those with limited experience. Of the 220 students enrolled, 74 graduated. The intermediate climbing course is a more extended program that requires from two to five years to complete. This course teaches leading on 5th class rock, winter mountaineering skills and ice climbing. The program accepted 70 students, and 14 others graduated from the multi-year intermediate course in 1997.

The advanced climbing experiences (ACE) program was initiated during the 1995-1996 climbing season. During 1996-1997, under the leadership of Myrna Plum, this program offered a number of activities for the more experienced climber, including water ice climbing and aid climbing. Seminars on risk management, altitude and small-party rescue were available.

Club climbs in 1997 were predominately in the Washington Cascades and Olympics. Exceptions were a climb of the East Face of Mount Whitney and a week of climbing in Yosemite Valley. Two separate climbing parties attempted peaks in the Annapurna Himal (Tharpu Chuli and Singu Chuli), but were unsuccessful.

Two new seminar courses designed to enhance outdoor skills were presented by The Mountaineers. The first one, Fundamentals of Wilderness Travel, was aimed at the novice or aspiring backcountry traveler. Subjects covered were mountain weather, fitness, navigation, wilderness ethics, avalanche awareness, group dynamics, equipment, personal care and emergency response. About 25 volunteers taught or supported the course, including some of the most knowledgeable backcountry travelers in the region.

The second seminar course, Essentials of Leadership, focused on the soft skills of leadership. Some subjects included were leadership styles, team building, group dynamics and conflict resolution. Through applicable experiential activities and group discussion, participants explored the understanding of various types of leadership. Role playing in simulated outdoor group experiences encouraged a variety of different problem-solving methods.

In October, The Mountaineers Books published the sixth edition of *Mountaineering: Freedom of the Hills*, which is the standard textbook for rock, snow, ice and alpine climbing. During 1997 it also published *Denali's West Buttress: A Climber's Guide*, *Kilimanjaro & Mount Kenya: A Climbing Guide* and *Climbing California's Fourteeners*, as well as 48 other books about climbing. The Mountaineers Books is now the exclusive distributor for American Alpine Club Press, which includes their highly regarded *Journal* and *Accidents in North America*. Free catalogs for Mountaineers Books are available at 800-553-4453.

DONNA PRICE, *Trustee*

*The Mazamas.* The Climbing Committee, chaired by Susan Pyle Erickson, scheduled 288 climbs, which included 41 Basic School climbs, 23 winter climbs, 19 Explorer Post climbs, and six Ski Mountaineering climbs. The usual surly Northwest weather caused some of those scheduled climbs to fail or be canceled.

Recipients in the Mazama Awards Program numbered: (nine) Three Guardian Peaks (Hood, St. Helens, Adams); (four) Seven Oregon Cascades (Jefferson, Three Fingered Jack, Washington, Three Sisters); (11) 16 Major Peaks (all of the above, plus Olympus, Baker, Shuksan, Glacier, Stuart, Shasta); and (one) Leuthold Award (leading all 16 Major Peaks).

The Climber's Hot Line was used again to communicate climbs with vacancies and newly scheduled climbs. A numbering system for ropes was initiated to track the usage and need for change of the grade of worn or damaged ropes to less demanding service.

The Mazamas are in the middle of forest access problems, a dilemma shared by climbing and hiking clubs across the nation. USFS, state parks and national park areas are demanding smaller parties and stricter registration for use. Climbing fees are now being introduced in many of these areas, and it is often difficult to schedule training sessions on glaciers because of government regulations. To cope with this problem, the Climbing Committee instituted the Access Subcommittee to monitor the maze of regulations and deal with agencies. This, of course, is a strange position for a club like The Mazamas, which has conservation as one of its cornerstones.

The Basic Climbing Program enrolled 220 participants. These were divided into groups of nine students with about four instructors for each group. In addition to rock and snow training, the groups were required to add several training hikes, usually longer day trips into difficult terrain. The Intermediate Climbing Program graduated all of its 40 participants, despite uncooperative weather at Timberline on Mount Hood and Horsethief Butte in the Columbia River Gorge. The Advanced Rock Program enrolled 19, and the Advanced Snow and Ice Program had ten participants. The Leadership Training Program enrolled 19; five were approved as leaders. The backlog of leaders continues to diminish at a serious rate as more and more demands are made for additional training for leaders, some of whom have been established for many years.

The Outing Committee, chaired by Barbara Becker, sponsored trips to the Rogue River, Hart Mountain, the Tetons, Baja California, Ecuador, Peru, England, Norway and the Swiss Alps, where Barbara's husband lost his life.

The Swiss Alps party enjoyed a very successful climbing vacation until it ended in tragedy on August 4. Terry Becker, leading a climb on the Wetterhorn (Bernese Oberland), fell 1,500 feet to his death from a snow couloir while retrieving a rappel rope. The climbing party witnessed only a part of his tumble, several minutes after they had heard his muffled shouts from above. It is generally believed that natural, not climber's error, forces caused the accident. Terry Becker served as club President in 1994 and had a long record of difficult leads to his credit.

The Trail Trips Committee, chaired by Martin Hanson, continued its spiral upward in enthusiasm and participation, with 528 trips attracting 5,007 participant days. Besides a strong program of weekend hikes, the committee has built great interest in the "Street Rambles," which start at the clubrooms and cover parts of Portland's huge west side park areas. In 1997, other rambles were added for the Lake Oswego and Glendoveer areas. The Trail Tenders subcommittee of 11 members pushed forward in their program to improve trails of the area with pick, shovel, axe and pruning shears. Ray Sheldon's major effort on Mount Hood's Cathedral Ridge Trail, now officially named the Mazama Trail, has come to an end. Sheldon's project involved several hundred club members working on week outings and weekends. Rebuilding the trail required a vast amount of heavy work and untiring perseverance.

1997 was a salient year for the fiscal managers of The Mazamas, when the major assets of the club were placed into a separate trust. This significant move had been planned and suggested for two decades before President Robert Hyslop, Treasurer Howard Hanson and the Executive Council finally "took the bull by the horns."

JACK GRAUER, *Historian*

*Arizona Mountaineering Club.* The 300+ members of the Arizona Mountaineering Club enjoyed another successful year of climbing-based activities. The AMC meets monthly and, in 1997, featured such nationally known speakers as Kitty Calhoun, Paul Piana and Jeff Achey. Our series of climbing classes (basic, advanced and lead), offered twice during the year, were filled to capacity. Under the capable leadership of Wayne Schroeter, these classes emphasize safety and a strong commitment to the climbing ethic.

Club involvement continues on multiple access-related issues. We worked with the city of Scottsdale on park planning and trail layout for Pinnacle Peak Park, scheduled to re-open in 1998. This popular climbing area has been closed for nearly two years while the surrounding area undergoes development. From early in the planning process (and much to the chagrin of development interests), the city recognized that climbing is a viable activity in the park. The McDowell Mountains, bordering Scottsdale to the east, also face intense developmental pressure. The prime climbing area is ably represented on the McDowell-Sonoran Land Commission by AMC member Bill Berkley. Additionally, the AMC provides financial assistance to the Phoenix Bouldering Contest and strong fiscal support to the Access Fund.

Member activities of note included Michael Baker and Sally Borg's ongoing involvement as leaders of the Arizona Trail Association, a group working to build a continuous trail system across Arizona from north to south. Greg Opland published his long-awaited and sorely needed guidebook on central Arizona granite, *Phoenix Rock II*, and is scheduled to release a climbing guide to the Superstition Mountains in 1998. Blind climber Eric Weihenmayer, who has climbed Denali and Kilimanjaro, completed an Aconcagua expedition. In November, he was featured as the lead climber for Sarah Ferguson, Duchess of York, in the ABC television special "Adventures with the Duchess." He also helped with our club's "blind leading the blindfolded" outing, where members climbed blindfolded to simulate the conditions he climbs under. Even with Eric's guidance and support, this was very difficult (try it sometime). Although Eric led some of the climbs, the rest of us climbed on top ropes and politely declined his encouragement to try leading blindfolded.

TOM CONNOR, *President*

*The Colorado Mountain Club.* The year 1997 brought success and change to The Colorado Mountain Club. In January, John Juraschek became the CMC executive director and Chip Drumwright began his term as president. Their biggest challenge was finishing the $4.2 million fund-raising campaign for the creation of the American Mountaineering Center in Golden, Colorado. The AMC will be the home of the Colorado Mountain Club, the American Alpine Club (our partner in this venture) and other outdoor-related organizations. Those organizations include the American Mountain Guides Association, the Colorado Fourteeners Initiative, Climbing for Life, and the Colorado Trail Foundation. Under the strong and able leadership of Juraschek and Drumwright, club members rallied in support of the AMC. They contributed more than $530,000—twice the amount originally projected. By the end of 1997, the CMC and AAC reached their goal, and the AMC became a reality.

In the spring, the Club's board of directors held its first board retreat at the Snow Mountain Ranch in Fraser. The work done there became the foundation for board restructure. When approved by the requisite number of CMC groups, board size will be reduced from 35 to 20. A second tier of representation, the State Council, will be created to strengthen group relations and improve group communications.

Programs and services were a high priority of the volunteer leadership and staff. Kristy Judd, assistant director, managed the day-to-day operations while developing partnerships in the community at large. Scott Stebbins joined the CMC as publications manager in late 1996. His expertise in design and layout gave our monthly magazine, the *Trail & Timberline*, an exciting new look. The financial affairs of the club, as well as of the AMC, continued to be adeptly managed by Cathy McGuire. In September, Heide Anderson became conservation director. Her goal is to increase the CMC's visibility and participation in the environmental community.

Club members continued to enjoy the hundreds of activities offered throughout the year. We adopted the Leave No Trace principles, which are now an integral part of our school curriculums. The CMC also became a partner with the Colorado Fourteens Initiative to help mitigate environmental damage on Colorado's "loved-to-death" fourteeners. Many members took part in Adopt-A-Trail hikes, where they did both light trail maintenance and trail building. The High Altitude Mountaineering Section sponsored climbing trips to Ecuador, Bolivia, Chile, Mexico and Russia.

The Colorado Mountain Club looks forward to serving the mountain lovers of Colorado from its new headquarters in Golden. We invite you to visit the American Mountaineering Center. For information on the CMC, please call (303) 279-3080, or visit our website at http://www.entertain.com/cmc/.

SHERRY RICHARDSON, *President-Elect*

# In Memoriam, 1997

*With special thanks to David Harrah for his help in compiling this year's section*

## JOSEPH STETTNER
### 1901 - 1997

With the passing of Joe Stettner at age 95 on March 14, we must acknowledge the loss of one of the most remarkable figures in American mountaineering history. Joe and his inseparable younger brother, Paul, who predeceased him on May 26, 1994, were at the forefront of the great climbers of their time. But they deserve to be remembered for more than their incredible skill. Their strength of character, devotion to their companions and love of the mountain world are the Stettner hallmarks that will be remembered longer than their climbing accomplishments. Indeed, they eluded recognition and fame during the early years of their careers, but still became virtually legendary figures.

Until 1940, the Stettners climbed almost exclusively with each other. It was their close association with the Chicago Mountaineering Club from 1940 on that put them in touch with other climbers. Perhaps the most significant contribution I made to the Club as one of the co-founders was my success in bringing the Stettners into membership in that year. Both eventually served as president of the club, and were unquestionably its driving force.

Joe and Paul were born in Munich in 1901 and 1906, respectively. Joe immigrated in 1925 and Paul in 1926, settling in Chicago, where they worked in skilled trades until retirement. Joe was a metalsmith and coppersmith, and Paul was a photoengraver. Their climbing careers appear all the more remarkable when it is realized that they usually were limited to two-week vacations from Chicago.

The young Stettners were enthusiastic climbers and skiers in the Austrian Alps and Kaisergeberge, but were self-taught and did not arrive in this country as climbing aces. Their biggest climbs were all made in the United States. That for which they will forever be renowned was the first ascent of the Stettner Ledges on the East Face of Longs Peak in 1927, no doubt the most difficult climb in the country at that time. After a five-and-a-half day trip across the dirt roads of the Great Plains by motorcycle, they free climbed the sheer lower face of Longs Peak on-sight by a route that was repeated only twice in the next 19 years. The second of these repeats was led by Joe Stettner himself with Bob Ormes. Paul Stettner had led the entire first ascent in 1927.

On an outing of the Chicago Mountaineering Club based in the Needle Mountains of Colorado in 1947, Joe Stettner made his hardest climb, the first ascent of the East Face of Monitor Peak, with John Speck and me. This was probably the most difficult route in Colorado at that time. Typical of Joe's warm-hearted magnanimity were his remarks at the top: "Well, John, you will never climb it harder," and "Now, Jack, you have really done something!"

Other highlights in the climbing records of the Stettners included the North Ridge of the Grand Teton (fourth ascent), Beckey Couloir on the Grand Teton (first ascent) and new routes or variations on Mt. Owen, Nez Perce and the Rock of Ages in the Tetons. Joe and Paul made the first ascent of the North Face of Lone Eagle Peak in Colorado. Joe pioneered "Joe's Solo" on the East Face of Longs Peak by a line so bold that historians at first doubted its authenticity. Paul led the first ascent of the North Corner of Hallelujah in the Big Horns. Joe led two of the early ascents of the Devil's Tower (1948 and 1949) and Paul led another (1949).

The Stettner approach to climbing was spontaneous and lighthearted. They climbed primarily for the pure enjoyment of the sport and out of their love for the mountain environment. Records and fame meant nothing to them. They were as willing to spend a long day grinding up an easy climb with a string of neophytes as they were to tackle a tough climb with more experienced companions. The mountains provided fun and adventure to the Stettners and all who went with them. From their companions, they could draw the last breath and drain the last drop of energy, such was their ability to coax, encourage and inspire their struggling teammates. On a practice cliff, their advice to a perplexed rope-mate was often, "Now put your left foot in your right shoe!"

If climbing was fun for the Stettners and their companions, it was also adventurous. Serious falls, forced bivouacs and a narrow escape from a deep crevasse were prices paid for chances taken in the course of nearly 50 years of high-standard climbing. Turning back was not the Stettner way.

Both of the Stettner brothers served in the 10th Mountain Division during World War II, and Paul was decorated for valor in combat in Italy. The Stettner brothers were always the natural leaders of their ropes. After coming to the United States, neither of them ever climbed as second on the rope, except when they were climbing together. It is safe to say that they were placed in a class by themselves by everyone who saw them climb. For example, Paul Petzoldt, who followed Joe Stettner up the Devil's Tower, ascribed to him the agility of a circus acrobat. A final assessment of the place of the Stettner brothers in our climbing history was made by Chris Jones in Climbing in North America when he wrote, "A case can be made that the Stettner brothers formed the most powerful rope in the United States."

JACK FRALICK

ELIZABETH WOOLSEY
1908-1997

An enthusiastic member of the American Alpine Club for 62 years, Elizabeth D. "Betty" Woolsey, 88, died at her home on Trail Creek ranch above Wilson, Wyoming, on January 11. Her last glance was of the meadow, horses feeding on sparkling snow, with evening shadows approaching.

Betty was born December 28, 1908, in Albuquerque, New Mexico, where her father worked for the Forest Service. She spent her formative years living in a log house on the edge of a mesa. There, her bedroom faced the Sandia mountains, which, in her own words, "cast a spell on me." This spell lead to "a lifelong affair with the mountains." Following adventurous years spent in the southwest, the family, which now included five daughters, moved permanently to New Haven, Connecticut.

After graduating from Vassar, Betty was drawn to the European Alps, where she was accompanied by climbers who have since become legends. In the early 1930s, she went to Chamonix, France, where she ascended her first major peak, the Grepon. On this granite spire she was introduced to "awesome exposure." On another climb, she was exposed to the sight of an English climber, "sandwiched between two guides. The guides poked their client with an ice axe below and hauled from above like a piece of luggage," she remembered. In

Zermatt, Switzerland, guided by the noted Bernhardt Biner, Betty climbed her first high peak, Monte Rosa. From the summit, she looked down on the Matterhorn and other great peaks.

On her return to the United States, she explored the Big Horn Mountains with AAC members Bill House, Alan and Bill Wilcox. They climbed and named almost all the major peaks. One peak was named Mt. Woolsey in memory of her late father. In the Canadian Rockies, she climbed in the Banff area with Roger Whitney and Bradley Gilman. (The latter became president of the AAC in 1953.) The group enjoyed the climbs; however, she added, "they had no liking for the unstable rock."

All this mountain experience naturally led to exploration of the alpine world of ice and snow, beginning in Europe, where Betty first learned to ski. She credited her guides for teaching her how to deal with mountain emergencies in winter.

Betty was well-prepared for success when she entered international ski races in Europe, culminating in 1936 with what she called the "Nazi Olympics" in Germany. She was chosen as captain by her fellow team members. Betty, who delighted in being on the edge, excelled at downhill, and was the leading American skier in the Olympic event. She and her friend, Marian "Sis" McKean, entered major races that followed and they both compared favorably with the more-experienced Europeans.

Hitler intervened. The ski-racing scene came to America, and Betty's attention shifted to American mountains. In summer, she climbed in the Wind River mountains, the Tetons, and was a member of an expedition to Mount Waddington, which, at the time, was Canada's highest unclimbed peak.

Betty's ski-racing career climaxed when she won, handily, the 1939 U.S. National Downhill Championship at Mount Hood, Oregon. It was a high speed race. Sun Valley, a ski resort just three years old, became the focal point for American ski racing, and attracted a sprinkling of European racers and Hollywood luminaries. Betty naturally was drawn to the setting. She commented: "I settled down to a routine of skiing and partying, with emphasis on the latter."

Becoming disenchanted with resort life, Betty joined a trip with a group of friends headed for Jackson Hole, with its uncrowded slopes and light powder snow. "I discovered my piece of land the first time I skied down Teton Pass," she recalled. She acquired that land in 1943 and began the achievement of her life, creating Trail Creek Ranch.

On the "piece of land" stood a sturdy log house—lacking running water or electricity—and a few crumbling buildings, leftovers from the stage-stop days. At once, several friends were attracted to the scene and joyfully helped Betty put the place in order. An accomplished writer, she reluctantly left the ranch in winter to stay in New York City, where she was editor of *Ski Illustrated* magazine, the first of its kind in America. In three years, she resigned from the job and settled at Trail Creek permanently.

With improvements to the house, the addition of a barn, and more meadowland acquired, Betty began taking a few "paying guests." Following tradition, many guests found satisfaction assisting with ranch work.

Betty made sure that everyone would have the thrill of high-mountain adventures. Leading pack trips into the wilderness, she had only a map for a guide, and often relied on a catch of trout for the main course at dinner. She became acquainted with Gibb Scott, a rancher and hunting guide (he had even climbed the Grand Teton, which locals seldom did), and he became Betty's tutor for horseback travel in the mountains and ranching.

In winter, she shuttled skiers to the top of Teton Pass, and with knowledge gained from years of experience, led them safely down a variety of exhilarating runs. Those who had never skied powder before were just expected to follow. Somehow, the neophytes managed, and soon became proficient. Betty had an exceptional feel for snow, whether it was safe or unsafe. With her respect for avalanche danger, she hung a thermometer from a tree branch at the top of Telemark run to provide a clue. Betty would never ski the enormous open slopes of Glory Bowl in winter; rather, she waited for the consolidated spring snow. She undoubtedly holds the record for the number of runs made on Teton Pass, a record unlikely to be broken.

Trail Creek Ranch became well established, requiring wranglers, cooks, ranch hands and assorted chore boys. Betty always referred to employees as "the crew." The most important member, Margaret "Muggs" Schultz, expertly guided skiers down the slopes in winter, tended the hayfields and harvest in summer, and had inherent know-how to deal with most any problem on the ranch. She was assisted for many years by "Sis" McKean Wigglesworth, Betty's friend from ski racing days. Several crew members were influenced by Betty's enthusiasm and became successful dude ranchers, guides and outfitters.

Betty took delight in having a houseful of interesting people. She relished good food and good conversation. There was an intellectual side to her many-faceted personality. An insatiable reader, she was also devoted to opera, "Mozart in particular," she would add. An evening at the Met was a top priority when she visited New York.

As long as she was able, Betty refreshed her soul by irrigating the fields. Placing dams in the ditches, she would reverently watch as water flowed over the meadow, nourishing the hay ground and pasture for her animals. "Horses are the heart of a dude ranch," she asserted, and was justly proud of the herd she had put together and sustained.

A memorial service for Betty was held at Trail Creek Ranch on June 7, 1997, where her memorable words were recalled:

> I have seen the face of the land change in my lifetime. The wild uncrowded places are scarcer now, untracked snows harder to find, and ski racing has become big business. Time is running out. I would not have been born later.

All quotes are from Elizabeth Woolsey's autobiography, *Off the Beaten Track*, Wilson Bench Press, Box 104, Wilson, WY 83014.

VIRGINIA HUIDEKOPER

## WILLIAM P. HOUSE
### 1913 - 1997

Bill House grew up in Pittsburgh, attended Choate, and went on to Yale, where he became an outstanding leader of the Yale Mountaineering Club. He made some difficult local ascents and, in 1932, with Alan Willcox, made the second ascent of the Pinnacle Gully on Mt. Washington, an ice climb often regarded as the most difficult climb in the White Mountains. Two years later, he and Betty Woolsey made a new route up Jagged Mountain (13,836'), then considered by the *AAJ* to be "the most difficult peak yet ascended in the Colorado Rockies." This led to a trip with Betty Woolsey and Fritz Wiessner to Mt. Waddington in British Columbia. The mountain had turned back 16 previous expeditions, but Bill and Fritz climbed it. Their success also gained them permission to climb Devil's Tower, the great Wyoming monadnock, where they made the first regular ascent.

Bill by now had graduated from Yale and the Yale Forestry School, and had landed a job with the Society for the Protection of New Hampshire Forests. In 1936-37, jobs were scarce. Charlie Houston (leader), Dick Burdsall and I met Bill at the American Alpine Club in

New York and asked him to come on the First American Karakoram Expedition to K2 with us. This meant nearly a six-month commitment of his time: a month to get to India, a month to trek 350 miles in to the mountain, six weeks on the mountain and the same to return, with a little time for emergencies. He gave up his job and was told never to return.

Bill was a magnificent companion on the expedition. He solved the major problem on K2's Abruzzi Ridge by leading a route up a break in a great reddish rock buttress, now known in mountain circles as the House Chimney. The expedition went 4,000 feet higher on K2 than anyone had climbed before, but it did not reach the summit. Bill's climb of the House Chimney has been called by Messner and other major climbers to be the finest climb done at very high altitude before World War II.

In the fall of 1938, New England was struck by a tremendous hurricane that devastated miles of forests. Though Bill had been fired for leaving his job to go on the expedition, on his return he was eagerly welcomed back, and some years later became president of the society.

All his life, Bill was known for his honesty and sound judgment. He loved forestry but, like everyone else his age in 1941, he plunged into Army work, developing clothing and equipment at the Quartermaster General's Office for the 10th Mountain Division and other troops. The development of nylon climbing rope was one of his successes.

At the end of the war, he married Elaine Johnson, beginning a very happy marriage in the house they built in Chesham, New Hampshire, with its grand views of Mt. Monadnock. He died peacefully.

ROBERT H. BATES

## LYMAN SPITZER
### 1914 - 1997

On March 31, we lost a distinguished astrophysicist and an accomplished mountaineer when Lyman Spitzer died suddenly at his home in Princeton, New Jersey.

Lyman was born in Toledo, Ohio, and obtained a Bachelor's degree in physics from Yale in 1935. After spending a year at Cambridge University, he earned a Doctorate in Astrophysics from Princeton in 1938. Following a year at Harvard, he joined the Yale faculty. During World War II he worked for the U.S. Navy investigating the principles of underwater sound. In 1947, Princeton University invited him to become Chairman of the Department of Astronomy and Director of the Observatory. During the 32 years he held these positions, he joined with Martin Schwarzschild to build one of the country's leading graduate programs in astrophysics. He was elected to the National Academy of Sciences and earned the rare distinction of foreign membership in the Royal Society of London in 1990. He was awarded the National Medal of Sciences in 1980 and the prestigious Crafoord Prize of the Swedish Academy of Sciences in 1985.

His research covered many areas, including the dynamics of star clusters, the physical processes in the gas between stars, and plasma physics. He was a leader in developing magnetic confinement for controlled thermonuclear fusion, and founded the Princeton Plasma Physics Laboratory. In 1946, he published a stimulating paper on "Astronomical Advantages of an Extra-Terrestrial Observatory," which developed the concept of space-based telescopes. He brought these ideas to reality with the development of a 32-inch diameter telescope and associated spectrometer for the Copernicus satellite that NASA launched in 1972. He also led many preliminary studies for the Hubble Space Telescope, and provided much advice to

NASA on its operation.

Lyman began climbing on trips to the Alps and the Tetons. Then, around 1964, through association with colleagues, his climbing entered a more technical phase with weekends in the Shawangunks, trips to the White Sands Missile Range in New Mexico, and in winter on Huntington Ravine on Mt. Washington. In 1965 he participated in an Alpine Club of Canada expedition to Baffin Island. There he climbed Mt. Asgard and made the first ascent of Mt. Thor by the north ridge with Don Morton. Afterward, Lyman walked alone some 32 miles down the Weasel Valley and along the fjord to the town of Pangnirtung in order to return home ahead of the rest of the expedition. In 1967, he joined George Wallerstein and other astronomical colleagues in the Canadian Rocky Mountains east of Prince George, B.C. There he made first ascents of Mt. Walrus, Mt. Petrie, and Mt. Plaskett, the latter two named by the climbers after two prominent Canadian astronomers. Lyman returned to Canada with three Princeton colleagues in 1970 to climb Mt. Waddington from the Tiedemann Glacier.

His later climbing took him to the Dolomites and many places in the United States, including the Flat Irons, Eldorado Canyon, Lumpy Ridge and the Jackson-Johnson route on Hallet's Peak in Colorado, Seneca Rocks in West Virginia, the Needles in South Dakota, White Horse in New Hampshire, and Joshua Tree in California, as well as many routes in the Shawangunks. In 1976, Princeton University authorities were unsettled to find him climbing Cleveland Tower, the high point of the campus. He also climbed extensively with his wife, Doreen, and his four children and their children; to commemorate this bond, his family wore climbing slings at his memorial service. He was a member of the American Alpine Club and the Alpine Club. Lyman will be missed by his numerous colleagues, both astronomers and climbers.

DONALD C. MORTON

## HERBERT N. HULTGREN, M.D.
### 1917 - 1997

Herb Hultgren arguably made more important contributions to our understanding and management of mountain sickness than anyone in our lifetime. He was my friend and mentor for more than 30 years, and we did some interesting projects together. Herb had a delicious sense of humor not often revealed (though always appropriate). We argued often but usually agreed—and I learned far more than he did from me!

Herb was a giant in the field of mountain medicine and physiology. He knew mountains from his climbs and treks in the Himalayas, Andes, Alps, Rockies and Alaska. He was active in the American Alpine Club for 34 years and a past chairman of its medical committee. He was a dedicated researcher in the basic physiology and the clinical management of mountain sickness. His name is forever linked to High Altitude Pulmonary Edema (HAPE), a very serious problem that has killed many climbers, trekkers and others who went above a moderate altitude—and he knew more about this than anyone living.

He was widely known and respected as a practicing cardiologist and professor: He was Chief of Cardiology at Stanford for 12 years, and for 16 years at the Palo Alto Veterans Affairs Medical Center. In 1990, he was given the Albion W. Hewlett Award at Stanford for "the physician of care and skill who is committed to discovering and using biologic knowledge and wisdom and compassion to return patients to productive lives."

Herb wrote more than 300 medical articles and book chapters, and spoke at many medical meetings throughout the world. During his last five years, he collected all he knew about altitude in a textbook for doctors. Happil.y he saw the published book *High Altitude Medicine* before he died, at age 80, in October after struggling for a year with acute myelogenous leukemia. His book will be the ultimate authority on the subject.

Herb left many friends and family—and a large gap in medicine.

CHARLES S. HOUSTON, M.D.

## ARNOLD WEXLER
## 1918-1997

A rnold Wexler died in his sleep Sunday evening, November 16, of brain cancer. He was 79.

Arnold lived in a rarefied atmosphere—that of the research engineer at the National Institute of Standards and Technology and of the mountain climber. He is largely responsible for the Mountaineering Section as we know it. He co-invented the idea of dynamic belaying. He made nearly 50 first ascents of Canadian mountains, many of them requiring horrendous bushwhacking.

Arnold was born January 3, 1918, in Manhattan in New York City, but spent his early childhood in the Catskills until his family returned to New York City. He received a Bachelor's degree in chemical engineering from the City College of New York in 1940. In 1941, he joined the then-National Bureau of Standards to work in structural materials research and testing, eventually focusing on instrumentation and standards for measurement, primarily for determining the moisture content of gases. During Word War II, he tested climbing ropes and equipment so the military could undertake mountain operations. As an aside, his work on oxygen regulators for military pilots helped some climbing friends (inspired by Jacques Cousteau) to make their own underwater breathing apparatus to explore submerged passages in West Virginia caves.

He was one of a group of rock climbers that pioneered climbing in the Washington, D.C. area in the 1940s. When this group became the Mountaineering Section of the Potomac Appalachian Trail Club, Arnold served as its Chairman for five or six years, quietly leading it through its formative stage. Through his testing of ropes and climbing equipment at the National Bureau of Standards during WW II, Arnold met a west coast climber, (then Major) Richard Leonard. Together they made the first mathematical analysis of the forces on a falling climber, his anchors, the rope, and the belayer. They created the idea of dynamic belaying— a progressive snubbing of the rope around the belayer's body to mitigate the shock on the system. At Carderock, a local climbing area, Arnold encouraged the practice of dynamic belaying by using "Oscar," a 150-pound dummy, who could be dropped to simulate a falling climber. The ability to do a dynamic belay undermined the prevailing ethic that the leader should never fall because of the usual fatal consequences. Now the system need not fail. This was the first step toward today's new climbing ethic.

Even with dynamic belaying, Arnold was a cautious and competent climber. He believed in being able to climb down from a crux. Nevertheless, Arnold pioneered routes at Seneca Rocks in West Virginia such as *Simple J Malarkey* (5.7), *Ye Gods and Little Fishes* (5.8) in sneakers and driving pitons on sight—strong routes for 1953-54.

My strongest memories of Arnold are when we shared a little house at Seneca Rocks (now used by a guide service). It was furnished with local yard-sale furniture and a new wood stove. It was then that Arnold and I put up Prune (5.7). At a taxing moment on the first pitch, I clipped into a very old Army ring piton. As Arnold followed, he lifted it out with one finger.

Half of it had rusted away.

Arnold climbed almost every summer, either in the Canadian Rockies, the Interior Ranges or the Northwest Territories (at the Cirque of the Unclimbables, which his party named). There were also trips to the American Rockies, to the Alps in France and Italy, and to the Peruvian Andes. Altogether, Arnold made well over 100 ascents, of which nearly 50 were first ascents. His most notable climb was in 1946 to the Selkirks with Sterling Hendricks, who had been exploring the Canadian mountains. The Hendricks party made its way through one of the most inaccessible regions of British Columbia to make the second ascent of Mount Sir Sanford, a major peak which had been first climbed 32 years previously. Many of his subsequent trips involved horrendous bushwhacks, ferrying loads on pre-Kelty pack boards or in shapeless Army rucksacks, never finding air-dropped loads—all to get into those peaks that no one had ever climbed before. There is an excitement in this that is hard to duplicate now. For all of these things he had done, it was a pleasure to nominate him to be an Honorary Member of the Mountaineering Section.

Arnold had an ever-present curiosity about different ways of life and different cultures. It was only natural that he began folk dancing. He, and many of us climbers in the 1950s, would go each week to Dave Rosenberg's folk dances and afterward to his back-alley artist studio for beer. This curiosity about other peoples led him to trek several times in Nepal, to Kashmir and Ladakh at the western end of the Himalayas and to less rugged trips to other remote corners of the world.

Arnold was a gentle person, a patient teacher, and a trusted climbing partner.

JOHN CHRISTIAN

## HARRY CLAY MCDADE
## 1924-1997

A member of the American Alpine Club since 1965, Harry distinguished himself not so much by his alpinism, though he got around into a variety of mountain areas, but by the vigorous adherence to the Hippocratic Oath that he took with him wherever he went. Harry was born in Philadelphia and matriculated at the University of Pennsylvania and its Hahnemann Medical School. After a hitch in the U.S. Navy, he settled in to New Hampshire's North Country with a surgical residency at Mary Hitchcock Hospital in Hanover. In 1959, Harry joined the staff of the Littleton Regional Hospital, where he served for 26 years as Chief of Surgery. He was president of the Grafton County Medical Society and then that of the New Hampshire Medical Society before starting a six-year term as governor of the American College of Surgeons in 1987. Harry was widely honored by his peers in the medical field, receiving the Nathan Smith Award from the New England Surgical Society. But, for all his skill, Harry was unable to conquer the cancer that killed him after a long illness.

Recipient of the American Alpine Club's Sowles Award in 1992, Harry was beloved by a generation of mountain rescuers in the state of New Hampshire, starting with the undersigned and continuing almost until his death. He also got away from the North Country to make a new route on Mt. Foraker and a first ascent of Pacaraju. But it was his constant availability to the fish cops (game wardens) who had charge of all search and rescue operations in the state that won him the most admirers. Whenever there was a person lost in the hills of the Granite State, the first person to be alerted for potential need was Harry McDade. So much was this the case that he was made an honorary member of the Conservation Law Enforcement Division.

Harry was a man for all seasons, including among his non-mountaineering interests ornithology, ham radio, astronomy, and flying his own plane. Harry was also an active participant, almost from the start, in the Appalachian Mountain Club's Leadership Training Program, one of that organization's most valuable services to the public. The world, but particularly New Hampshire's mountain country, is a better place because of Dr. Harry McDade, who died on October 13. Harry was survived by his wife, Connie, and two children, one of whom is also a medical practitioner.

WILLIAM L. PUTNAM

## DONALD D. MCINTYRE
## 1946-1997

Those of us who were friends and family of Don McIntyre were shocked and profoundly saddened by the news that he suffered a fatal fall into a crevasse while descending from the summit of Mt. Ranier on July 29. Don and his climbing partner and close friend, Joel Koury, had ascended the difficult Liberty Ridge route the previous day. Joel was only slightly injured falling into the same crevasse.

Don had an infectious enthusiasm and love of mountaineering. All of us who climbed with him enjoyed the time we spent, whether it was stormbound in a tent or a beautiful day reaching the summit. Trading stories and laughs with Don was the best part of any trip.

Don was an accomplished and prolific mountaineer. During his 20-year career, he led or participated in 15 international expeditions to mountains in Alaska, Peru, Tibet, Mexico, Ecuador, Bolivia, Nepal, the Soviet Union, and the Swiss Alps. He reached the summits of Changtse, the north peak of Mt. Everest, Denali in Alaska, the Matterhorn and the Eiger in Switzerland, and Peak Communism in the Soviet Union, among many others. A long-time member of the American Alpine Club and more recently a professional member of the American Mountain Guides Association, he had started on a new career as a mountain guide after retiring from a distinguished career in service to his country. After serving a combat tour in Vietnam in the United States Air Force, he completed a Bachelor's degree at the University of Florida and then a Master's degree in education at Wayne State University. Over the next 27 years he held various security and investigative posts with the Department of Energy, working his way to Director of Counter Intelligence in charge of security for nuclear weapons, an extremely sensitive and important position.

Don was a devoted husband and father and is survived by his wife, Linda, in Reno, Nevada, his two children, Michael in San Francisco and Deanna in New York City, his mother, Sarah Jane, and two sisters, Lisa Houston and Kris Paul, all from Orlando, Florida.

JOHN G. CLEARY

## ALLAN BARD
## 1952-1997

Allan Bard died on July 5 from injuries sustained in a 200-foot fall while leading a climb of the Owen-Spalding Route on the Grand Teton in Wyoming.

A 20-year resident of the Eastern Sierra and 15-year resident of Bishop, Allan was a tremendously popular personality among the mountain sports communities throughout the nation. As an expert professional ski, mountain and river guide, he was truly a guide for all seasons. He was also a prolific professional writer and photographer, master carpenter and avid fly fisherman. His capacity for friendship and "can-do" enthusiasm was inspirational to all who knew him. It will be for his wonderful gift of storytelling that he will be most fondly remembered. Allan Bard was truly the bard of the High Sierra and will be most lovingly missed.

"Bardini here," was how Allan answered the phone. Soon you would hear tales of great things done and big plans in the making for the future. He achieved many of the goals for which he strove. He set very high standards for himself and others, whether that involved building a house in Bishop or stalking a big brown trout in Patagonia. Indeed, his accomplishments were many and varied, from Alaska to Chile, from Yosemite to Vermont. His feats are legendary, almost larger than life.

The treasure that Allan leaves us is not a check list of adventures but rather the spirit of how he ventured. In the stories he told and wrote he communicated who he was and how joyfully he lived. Here, then, is a brief story he wrote last year.

JOHN FISCHER

### The Backside of Beyond

Steve McQueen said, "I'd rather wake up in the middle of nowhere than in any city on earth." Edward Abbey referred to the urban scene as "syphilization." We read between the lines and suspect a cure for the most subtle of modern maladies, the condition caused by the nervous sense of urgency that seems to define life in the city.

In my job as a backcountry ski guide, I see people arrive at my door step from almost incomprehensibly busy lives in the city, ready to leave all the stress and schedules and meetings and freeway traffic alone for awhile. They need time to recreate, to recharge the old batteries, to think of nothing and reflect on everything, indeed to put life into perspective. Mostly they need to go skiing on the high and distant horizons. But skiing and mountains are only the medium for this revitalization, not the message. The message we receive is the importance of a quiet mind and satisfied soul.

Suddenly my job description is so much more than expert skier, tireless trail breaker, beast of burden, clever navigator, head chef and avalanche forecaster. In addition, I become confidant, confessor, entertainer, friend and perhaps even the Right Reverend Bardini, First Church of the Open Slopes. It is a job with great responsibility—and not just those related to hazard evaluation and risk management.

As a ski guide I have the pleasure of bringing the benefit of both. I notice that, when people have been touched by the wild lands, they are forever changed, forever more aware. They will never again see snow and mountain peaks and wind-sculpted tree trunks without being affected inside, differently than before they knew of such things, and they will return time and again to get in touch, to be touched. Certainly these are some of the deepest joys of skiing in wild places. It becomes important, then—in fact, essential—to savor and share these places and feelings. It is interesting that when we travel far afield to ski, what we often find is not just some intoxicating remote landscape but the convoluted topography of our own souls.

This is the value of skiing in, and being with, the lofty terrain of the mountains. These are the advantages of taking the high ground. I have been out into the great hinterlands beyond the backside of beyond, and my life is rich because of it. I am a wealthy man who just happens to be broke most of time, but I'm in good company. John Muir stated simply, "Go to the mountains and get their good tidings." Bill Koch once said, "The world would be a little better place to live if more folks went cross country skiing." I must agree with both of my learned colleagues.

Maybe world peace is just a few telemark turns away? Maybe it's worthy of being a movement? With bumper stickers! *Telemarking is Peace—Ski the Backside of Beyond.* Why not? I know of little else like a good day in the backcountry that gives me such incredible tranquility. This is especially true in times when life seems tediously short. But, as we know, life is short.

Which reminds me. I saw this rather interesting Sharper Image catalog item. It is a clock of sorts, but this time piece ticks off the time the average person has left to live. Standing and watching it is a little unnerving. A minute goes by and then another and then both are gone forever. Three hundred and sixty five days a year we get the opportunity to have a fresh start at life. A new day and fresh powder reminds those of us that slide over snow that skiing is life. Passion and vitality for living are some of the gifts we receive from skiing, particularly skiing in the great beyond. One need not travel to the North Pole or the Himalaya or the Andes or any of the high, hidden places of the world to know these things. Outback might simply mean skiing out back—out in the quiet woods behind the barn, or perhaps skiing through Central Park when the fist of winter grips the city in an icy gridlock. It could be skiing down a New England hillside or across the great expanse of a Heartland corn field. You are out on the backside of beyond when you feel the crisp bite of winter air in your lungs and the sting of wind-driven snow on your face and when you realize how insignificant you are in the face of such harsh adversity. That relativity that comes from knowing the wild places is essential to your well being, and yet we so often stay home, stay inside and insulate ourselves from it. I say, resist the urge to be complacent about experiencing the brutally beautiful joys of the backcountry skiing life. Go, my friends. Don't delay. Lose yourself and maybe you'll find yourself—on the backside of beyond.

## ANATOLI BOUKREEV
### 1958-1997

The last 15 months that have been left on my shoulders have given me three splendid successes, both personal and in sport. An ascent on Fitz Roy (3441m) in Patagonia via the west face in 25 hours round-trip, an ascent of the South Summit of Shishapangma (8008m) in Tibet in 28 hours round-trip with a partial descent on skis, and finally my second ascent of Lhotse (8516m) in Nepal. All this intensely moved and motivated me to continue my pursuit of and craving for alpinism.

The most beautiful thing that I remember, though, of these months was the start of a great friendship with the strongest alpinist of all time, Anatoli Boukreev, who had decided to continue his activities in my company.

Twenty-one times on the summits of the 8000-meter peaks in only eight years, the last four of these summits made within 80 days of each other, many with the fastest speed records for the 14 Himalayan giants, and 40 summits of more than 7000 meters to his credit—a veritable "tank" of high-altitude!

Little known in the international circles, Anatoli passed into the chronicles when, in 1996, he carried and saved from the hand of death some American alpinists who, bereft of oxygen, had been caught in a storm, beaten by wind and frozen by the temperatures on the flanks of Everest. On that occasion, Anatoli was capable of helping them in a situation where others could only stagger and hang on to their ice axes.

Ex-trainer of the National Russian Alpine skiing team, graduate of the "Army Sport Club" of Kazakstan, veteran of the Afgani War (special forces), Anatoli Boukreev showed me many things that revealed that he knew how to be a man before being an alpinist. I learned more things from him in one year than in all my 17 years of activity. Through the millions of circumstantial smiles and sneers that a great part of the world of alpinists gave, we communicated in November our intention to try the south face of Annapurna during the winter of 1997-98. There would only be the two of us, without Sherpas, without any other expeditions at base camp, deprived of any method of satellite or radio communication, and facing a mountain that counts more dead than alpinists on its summit and that, in winter, has been summited only once in more than 20 attempts.

We did not want to be disrespectful of a repeated invitation toward a more tranquil style of alpinism; we simply wanted to try an ascent of a mountain in a climatically difficult moment and with an old approach and style. Anatoli and I did not believe (and continue not to believe) in the "death of alpinism" that the sport has been sentenced to, often by illustrious persons who, due to their influence and the habit of wearing comfortable slippers, pretended that alpinism retired with them. Himalayan alpinism is alive and growing! And without a doubt changed, in respect to 15-20 years ago—but it is enough to have a pinch of imagination, some contrary ideas and no fear of eventual lack of success, to remember that there also are alternatives to the pilgrimages to high altitude. Without condemning sponsors and "intelligent" commercial expeditions, Anatoli knew how to marry his spirit of adventure with the sacrosanct need for making a living from alpinism. Extreme moralism, denigrating or defaming actions against other "colleagues" or other summits, never entered in the language or mind of Boukreev (even if it was part of interesting gossip. . . .)

All of this constitutes the testament that Anatoli has left me and that I leave to those who still have a passion, energy and desire to go to the mountains.

No one, ever, has seemed to me so human. No one, ever, has appeared to me so terribly strong. An abyss exists between him and the other champions and personalities of the Himalayas that I have had the good fortune (and with some, the misfortune) of having known. There remains now his imprint and the many lessons he has left me. There remain also the many ideas that he and I had in mind and that occupied also the last hours we spent together on that night, the 25th of December. . . .

SIMONE MORO

## DOUGLAS BYRON HALL
### 1969-1997

On January 25, the earth lost a most remarkable individual and a great creative spirit. Doug Hall was killed in a dramatic avalanche while climbing the notorious *Fang* route in Provo Canyon, Utah. He left behind a legacy of climbs and adventures by which his friends and family will remember him.

I had the good fortune of meeting Doug in 1992 and sharing many climbs and wonderful moments with him during our formative years as aspiring alpinists. He was attracted to the alpine regions of the world like snowfall to the mountains. Rarely in our short lives do we meet an energy as strong and constant as his. Always positive and seldom without his infectious smile, he touched many lives and added a sparkle of hope to the darkest situations.

Doug grew up in Pennsylvania, the son of Gerry and Nancy Hall. He was a talented young athlete who excelled in baseball and football, as well as being an excellent student and guitarist. He went on to graduate from Bucknell University with art and engineering degrees. He moved to Colorado in 1991 and soon became part of a close-knit group of Boulder adventure climbers. In just a few years, Doug had climbed extensively in such traditional areas as

Yosemite, Zion, Black Canyon of the Gunnison and Rocky Mountain National Park. I shared many of these climbs with Doug, and they remain some of my fondest memories.

Doug was an avid skier, spending several winters in the Colorado Rockies and Alta, Utah. He loved to tour in the backcountry with his friends and ski off the lovely summits of the Wasatch Range. Doug also was an avid photographer and was in the process of developing a productive professional career. His stunning images remain as a testament to his artistic genius. He was, no doubt, in position for a great shot when the white wave of energy surprised him from above.

When not climbing or skiing, Doug was the life of the party. His friends, many of whom were not climbers, will remember him as a warm, loving individual who gave his heart and soul to every friendship. He was a prolifically generous person, giving clothes and climbing gear he had accumulated during his tenure with Black Diamond to those in greater need than himself.

Doug was particularly intrigued with the allure of first ascents, and opened new climbs in the Wind River Range, Canyonlands, the Kichatna Spires of Alaska, the Cordillera Blanca and Cordillera Huayhuash in Peru. After Doug's death, his ashes were spread about a virgin summit in Tibet and the top of a fantastic rock spire in Kyrghyzstan so that his spirit may reside in the high and wild places that he loved so dearly. His dreams and aspirations will manifest themselves in those that he loved and those who loved him. . . .

Adios, brother. Until we meet again.

a whisper, a cry
the wind takes his hand
and leads him to the heavens
where he waits for his friends in peace

DOUGLAS J. BYERLY

# Appendices

## Appendix A: Expedition Regulations and Permits

Regulations and information for obtaining expedition permits to the countries listed below are available on request from the agencies noted.

ANTARCTICA
> National Science Foundation
> Office of Polar Programs
> Room 755
> 4201 Wilson Boulevard
> Arlington, VA 22230

BAFFIN ISLAND
> Superintendent of Auyuittuq National Park Reserve
> Parks Canada
> Eastern Arctic District
> P.O. Box 353 E.
> Pangnirtung, Northwest Territories
> XOA ORO
> CANADA

BHUTAN
> Trekking and Mountaineering Manager
> Bhutan Tourism Corporation
> P.O. Box 159
> Thimphu
> Bhutan

CHINA
> The Mountaineering Association of China
> Number 9 Tiyuguan Road
> Beijing
> The People's Republic of China

> The Mountaineering Association of Tibet, China
> Number 8 East Linkhor Road
> Lhasa
> Tibet, China

The Mountaineering Association of Xinjiang, China
Number 1 Renmin Road
Urumqi, Xinjiang
China

INDIA

Indian Mountaineering Foundation
Benito Juarex Road
Anand Niketan
New Delhi 100 021
India

NEPAL

HMG Ministry of Tourism and Civil Aviation
Mountaineering Division
Kathmandu
Nepal

(Trekking Peaks In Nepal:)
Nepal Mountaineering Association
P.O. Box 1435
Kathmandu
Nepal

PAKISTAN

Government of Pakistan
Ministry of Culture and Tourism
Tourism Division
Islamabad
Pakistan

C.I.S.: Georgia

Mountaineering and Climbing Association of Georgia
MCAG
P.O. Box 160
380008 Tbilisi
Georgia

Kyrgyzstan

Federation of Alpinism and Rock Climbing of the
        Republic of Kyrgyzstan
105 Panfilov Street
CIS-720035 Bishkek
Kyrgyzstan

Ukraine

Ukrainian Mountaineering Federation
Eksplanadna 42
252023 Kiev
Ukraine

C.I.S.: Other organizations
Euro Asian Association of Mountaineering and Climbing
Sokolnicheskaya pl. 9-1-134
107014 Moscow
Russia

# Appendix B: Meters to Feet

| meters | feet | meters | feet | meters | feet | meters | feet |
|--------|--------|--------|--------|--------|--------|--------|--------|
| 3300 | 10,827 | 4700 | 15,420 | 6100 | 20,013 | 7500 | 24,607 |
| 3400 | 11,155 | 4800 | 15,748 | 6200 | 20,342 | 7600 | 24,935 |
| 3500 | 11,483 | 4900 | 16,076 | 6300 | 20,670 | 7700 | 25,263 |
| 3600 | 11,811 | 5000 | 16,404 | 6400 | 20,998 | 7800 | 25,591 |
| 3700 | 12,139 | 5100 | 16,733 | 6500 | 21,326 | 7900 | 25,919 |
| 3800 | 12,467 | 4200 | 17,061 | 6600 | 21,654 | 8000 | 26,247 |
| 3900 | 12,795 | 5300 | 17,389 | 6700 | 21,982 | 8100 | 26,575 |
| 4000 | 13,124 | 5400 | 17,717 | 6800 | 22,310 | 8200 | 26,903 |
| 4100 | 13,452 | 5500 | 18,045 | 6900 | 22,638 | 8300 | 27,231 |
| 4200 | 13,780 | 5600 | 18,373 | 7000 | 22,966 | 8400 | 27,560 |
| 4300 | 14,108 | 5700 | 18,701 | 7100 | 23,294 | 8500 | 27,888 |
| 4400 | 14,436 | 5800 | 19,029 | 7200 | 23,622 | 8600 | 28,216 |
| 4500 | 14,764 | 5900 | 19,357 | 7300 | 23,951 | 8700 | 28,544 |
| 4600 | 15,092 | 6000 | 19,685 | 7400 | 24,279 | 8800 | 28,872 |

# Appendix C: Ratings

To help our readers in their research and to further the use of the *AAJ* as a reference tool, we offer the following explanations of the various systems of the world. Where appropriate (i.e., rock climbing grades), we compare the various systems. For snow, ice, mountaineering and aid, we describe the systems according to their individual merits.

| YDS | UIAA | French | Scandinavia | Poland | Romania | C.I.S. | Brazil | Australia | UK | UK |
|---|---|---|---|---|---|---|---|---|---|---|
| 5.0 | | | | I | | | | | | Diff |
| 5.1 | | | 3- | II | | III- | | | | |
| 5.2 | I | 1 | 3 | | 1A / 1B | III | | | 3a | VD |
| 5.3 | II | 2 | 3+ | III | 2A / 2B | III+ | | 11 | 3b | MS |
| 5.4 | III | 3 | 4 | IV | 3A / 3B | IV- | | 12 | 3c | S |
| 5.5 | IV | 4a | 4+ | | 4A / 4B | IV | | | 4a | HS |
| 5.6 | V- | 4b | 5- | V- | 5A | IV+ | | 13 | 4b | VS |
| 5.7 | V | 4c | 5 | V | 5B | | | 14 / 15 | | MVS |
| 5.8 | V+ / VI- | 5a | 5+ | V+ / VI- | 6A | V- | 4 / 4+ | 16 / 17 | 4c | HVS |
| 5.9 | VI | 5b | 6- | VI | | | 5 / 5+ | 18 | 5a | E1 |
| 5.10a | VI+ | 5c | | VI+ | | V | 6a | 19 | | |
| 5.10b | VII- | 6a | 6 | VI.1 | 6B | | 6b | 20 | 5b | E2 |
| 5.10c | | 6a+ | | VI.1+ | | | | | | |
| 5.10d | VII | 6b | 6+ | VI.2 | | V+ | 6c | 21 | 5c | E3 |
| 5.11a | VII+ | 6b+ | 7- | | | | 7a | 22 | | |
| 5.11b | | 6c | | VI.2+ | | | | 23 | | |
| 5.11c | VIII- | 6c+ | 7 | | | VI- | 7b | 24 | 6a | E4 |
| 5.11d | VIII | 7a | 7+ | VI.3 | | | 7c | 25 | | |
| 5.12a | VIII+ | 7a+ | 8- | VI.3+ | | | 8a | | | E5 |
| 5.12b | IX- | 7b | | VI.4 | | VI | 8b | 26 | | |
| 5.12c | | 7b+ | 8 | VI.4+ | | | 8c | 27 | | E6 |
| 5.12d | IX | 7c | 8+ | VI.5 | | | 9a | | 6b | |
| 5.13a | | 7c+ | 9- | | | VI+ | 9b | 28 | | |
| 5.13b | IX+ | 8a | | VI.5+ | | | 9c | 29 | | E7 |
| 5.13c | X- | 8a+ | 9 | | | | 10a | 30 | | |
| 5.13d | X | 8b | | VI.6 | | | 10b | 31 / 32 | 6c | E8 |
| 5.14a | | 8b+ | 9+ | | | | 10c | 33 | 7a | |
| 5.14b | X+ | 8c | | VI.6+ | | | | | | E9 |
| 5.14c | XI- | 8c+ | | VI.7 | | | | | 7b | E10 |
| 5.14d | XI | 9a | | | | | | | | |
| 5.15a | XI+ | | | | | | | | | |

# SNOW AND ICE GRADES

There are currently four major systems used to grade the severity of snow and ice climbs: Scottish Winter Grades, New England Ice Rating System, Canadian Ice Grading, and the Water Ice (WI) system developed by Jeff Lowe. Each is described below according to its own merits.

## SCOTTISH WINTER GRADES

The new two-tier system, which gives an overall grade based on an extended version of the previous I to V system (the new system extends to VIII), is in use. The overall difficulty is expressed by the Roman numeral. Technical grades apply to the hardest move or a short technical section of the route and are expressed by an Arabic numeral. It is the combination of the two that makes the system work.

The Scottish ethic is for ground-up leads in winter conditions. Pre-placed gear as employed in American mixed climbing is not considered good style. The defining character- istic of Scottish winter climbing is the weather—the humidity tends to produce hoar frost or rime on the rock, which makes progress more complex than movement over pure rock or pure ice.

Grade I: Climbs for which only one axe is required (e.g., snow gullies around 45° or easy ridges).

Grade II: Axe and hammer are required because of steep snow, a difficult cornice, or a short ice pitch. Difficulties are usually short. The ridges are more difficult but usually still scrambles in summer.

Grade III: Similarly technical but more sustained than Grade II. Sometimes short and tech- nical, particularly for mixed ascents of moderate rock climbs.

Grade IV: Steep ice from short vertical steps to long pitches of 60-70° that requires some arm strength. The mixed climbs require more advanced techniques such as torquing.

Grade V: Sustained steep ice (70-80°) or mixed climbs that require linking hard moves.

Grade VI: Vertical ice; mixed routes, either long and sustained, or, if short, sufficiently technical to require careful calculation.

Grade VII: Multi-pitch routes with long sections of vertical or thin ice. Mixed routes requiring fitness and experience to link many technical moves.

Grade VIII: At present, the hardest few routes in Scotland.

Technical grades on ice:
As a rough guideline, 3=60°, 4=70°, 5=80° or vertical steps, 6=vertical. It should be noted that the Scottish Grading System extends to 8.

## CANADIAN SYSTEM

The following description of the Canadian System is presented by Joe Josephson (all grades stated in this description are arrived at by comparisons between routes in the Rockies. Little or no thought is given to routes outside the range):

In the Canadian System, the grade of a route is the combination of its length, commitment required, technical difficulty and seriousness. Most people seem to focus solely upon the Technical Grade; however, ice climbing in the Rockies involves a number of variables, many of which are unique to the area.

*Commitment Grade* (Roman numerals I to VII): Also called Engagement Grade. The key factors here are the length and difficulty of approach and descent, length of the climb itself, the sustained nature of the climbing, and the objective hazard. The present modern routes are progressively thinner and on more fragile features. In some climbing areas, these qualities are included in the overall Commitment Grade. However, due to the added factor of severe remoteness of many Rockies routes, this notion is hard to include in a Rockies Commitment Grade. Thus, this system adds a Seriousness Grade to be discussed later. Commitment Grades given here are specific for frozen waterfalls and alpine routes that are considered as waterfall ice routes.

I. A very short and easy climb within minutes of the car with no avalanche hazard and easy descent by fixed anchors or walking off. Very little commitment.

II. A route of one or two pitches within easy reach of a vehicle or emergency facilities, and little or no objective hazard. A quick descent by rappel or walk off.

III. A multi-pitch route at low elevation or a one-pitch route with an involved approach (one hour or more and/or no trail) on foot or ski demanding good winter travel skills. The route may take from several hours to most of a day to complete. The approach and/or the climb are subject to occasional winter hazards including avalanche. Descent is usually by rappelling and may require you to make your own anchors.

IV. A multi-pitch route at higher elevations or remote regions and thus more subject to weather patterns and objective (primarily avalanche) hazards. May require several hours of approach on foot or ski with a greater knowledge of mountain travel and hazards. Descents may be over hazardous terrain and/or require construction of your own anchors.

V. A long climb that requires a full day to complete by a competent party. Usually on a high mountain face or gully ending above treeline. Subject to sustained climbing and/or avalanche hazards with a long involved approach on foot or ski. A high level of climbing experience and winter travel skills are needed to climb safely. Descent involves multiple rappels from your own anchors.

VI. A long waterfall with all the characteristics of a large alpine route. The climbing will be very sustained for its given technical grade. Only the best climbers will complete it in a day. Often requires a ski and/or glacier approach with a difficult and tiring descent. Objective hazards will be high, and may include: avalanche, falling seracs, high altitude, whiteout, crevasses and/or remoteness. An extraordinary degree of fitness and experience is required.

VII. A route that has every characteristic of a Grade VI but considerably longer and harder, both physically and emotionally. The climbing will be technically very difficult for many pitches and may take days to approach and climb. Objective hazards, such as large avalanche bowls and/or active seracs, will be very high. A 50-50 chance of getting the chop.

*Technical Grade* (Degree 1 to 8): This part accounts for the pure nature of the climbing on the single most sustained technical feature of a route. The predominate features contributing to this Technical Grade are length of a pitch, its overall steepness and the usual characteristics of the ice, which may include blue or plastic ice, chandelier mushrooms, thin plates, and/or overhanging bulges. In this description, it is designated by the acronym WI ("Water Ice"). In order to distinguish it from its Engagement Grade, the Technical Grade can also be summarized as the Degree of a route.

WI1: A frozen lake or stream bed. No one has had the audacity to yet claim a first ascent of a WI 1.

WI2: A pitch with short sections up to 80°. Good possibilities for protection and anchors.

WI3: Sustained ice up to 80°. Requires that parties be adept at placing protection and establishing belays. May have short sections of steeper ice but will have good resting places and the ice is usually good.

WI4: A sustained full pitch of off-vertical or a shorter length (10-25m) of vertical ice. The ice may have some technical features like chandeliers and may have long runouts between resting places.

WI5: A long strenuous pitch. May be a full ropelength of 88°-90° on good ice with few if any resting places, or a shorter (20-40m) pitch on bad featureless ice. Adequate protection will require excellent technique.

WI6: A full 50-meter pitch of dead-vertical ice or a shorter length of nasty proportions. Few if any resting sites. Protection will be put in while standing on frontpoints or in awkward situations. The ice quality is variable and the climbing is technical. Technique and efficiency are at a premium.

WI7: A full pitch of near-vertical or vertical ice that is very thin, or a long overhanging technical column of dubious adhesion. Requires diverse and creative techniques to climb and hopefully find protection. A very physically and emotionally draining pitch.

WI8. These routes do exist. We should never say that we have reached the pinnacle of technical possibility. All we need is the proper vision to see the lines and an adequate sense of the requirements needed, both technically and in terms of the hazards involved. Some time will be needed to establish and understand the WI7 grade and for people to learn how "to see" routes of such insane difficulty.

*Seriousness Grade*: R: Reserved for very thin routes, this is similar to the "runout" designation given in many rock climbing areas. Depending upon the season and the time of year, particularly early season, many routes may fall into this category and then fill out to a safer thickness later in the year. The "R" designation should be reserved for routes that are traditionally very thin even in the best of years. On these routes a party will be faced with long runouts with difficulty and/or creativity required to find adequate protection from the ice and/or the rock. Mixed routes may fall into this category.

X: These are very fragile routes that stand a possible chance of collapse while climbing them. By definition, these routes are usually runout as well. Therefore all the caution reserved for an "R" climb should be noted here. Again, an early season ascent can place a steep pillar into this category and then later in the year it may fill out to be quite solid.

*Rock Grades*: When a pitch is given a rock grading, this means the climbing is mostly on rock but may have sections of verglas, moss or snow. Rock climbing is graded on the YDS system from 5.0 to 5.10 and up. However, these pitches usually involve crampons so direct translation is very sticky indeed. The rock grade is generally how difficult the pitch "feels." With rock shoes and a chalk bag in the sun it will undoubtedly be easier, but it still means you must be competent at the stated grade.

*Length (in meters)*: Understanding the length of climb is important in estimating its overall difficulty and your ability to safely complete the route. Length means the total vertical gain from the bottom of the route to the top.

# NEW ENGLAND ICE RATING SYSTEM

This system was first described by Rick Wilcox in the early 1970s. It is used extensively in New England and was developed for the water ice found there. This system applies to a normal winter ascent of a route in moderate weather conditions. The system also incorporates a Commitment Rating, which indicates the time and logistical requirements of a climb.

NEI 1: Low-angle water ice of 40-50°, or long, moderate snow climbs requiring a basic level of technical expertise for safety.

NEI 2: Low-angle water ice routes with short bulges up to 60°.

NEI 3: Steeper water ice of 50-60° with 70-80° bulges.

NEI 4: Short, vertical columns, interspersed with rests on 50-60° ice; fairly sustained climbing.

NEI 5: Generally, multi-pitch ice climbs with sustained difficulties and/or strenuous vertical columns with little rest possible.

NEI 5+: Multi-pitch routes with a heightened degree of seriousness, long vertical sections, and extremely sustained difficulties. The hardest ice climbs in New England to date.

*Commitment Rating*

I: Up to several hours.

II: About half a day.

III: A full day (up to seven or eight hours).

IV: A substantial undertaking; a very long day, possibly including a bivouac.

V: A big-wall climb of one-and-a-half to two days. Could be done in a single day by a very fit team.

VI: Multi-day big-wall climbs requiring more than two days.

VII: Big-wall ascents in remote alpine situations.

# WATER ICE, ALPINE ICE, AND MIXED GRADES

Jeff Lowe began developing a system in the late 1970s for grading the technical difficulties of ice routes. It was meant to be used in conjunction with the Commitment Rating of the New England System. The type of ice to be found on a climb is designated by the letters AI, indicating alpine ice, or WI, indicating water ice, preceding the technical classification. When the primary difficulties of a climb are on mixed rock and ice climbed in crampons, the classification is proceeded by an M.

| Ice Classification<br>(AI, WI, or M) | Rock Classification |
| --- | --- |
| 1: Up to 50° snow or 35° ice | 1st to 3rd class |
| 2: Up to 60° snow or 40° ice | 4th class |
| 3: Up to 80° snow or 75° ice | 5.0-5.7 |
| 4: Up to vertical snow or 85° ice | 5.8-5.9 |
| 5: Overhanging cornices or 90° ice | 5.10 |
| 6: Very thin or technical 90°-plus ice | 5.11 |
| 7: 95° ice or overhanging mixed | 5.11+ |
| 8: Technical or overhanging mixed | 5.12 |
| 9: Technical overhanging mixed | 5.13 |
| 10: Sustained overhanging mixed | 5.14 |

# MOUNTAINEERING GRADES

There are currently four major systems used to grade the difficulty of mountaineering objectives. The French system pioneered the concept of grading. It has stood the test of time and is still in use. The National Climbing Classification System (NCCS), developed largely by Leigh Ortenburger in the United States, denotes grades for alpine objectives. The Russian system with its three-fold class structure is very applicable to high elevations. The Alaskan Grade, developed by Jonathan Waterman, is based on a 1966 Boyd J. Everett, Jr. paper, "The organization of an Alaskan Expedition." The quality and consistency of the routes used as standards in this system have led to its rapid acceptance. As with the ice ratings, each system is best described according to its own particular merits.

## FRENCH SYSTEM

The standard of the climb is assessed as a whole (based on normal conditions but taking into account altitude, length, objective dangers, liability of bad weather, difficulty of route finding, quality of rock, and technical difficulty), then combined with the technical standard of individual rock pitches. The overall standard is described as:

| | |
|---|---|
| Facile | (F) |
| Peu difficile | (PD) |
| Assez difficile | (AD) |
| Difficile | (D) |
| Tres Difficile | (TD) |
| Extrement Difficile | (ED1, ED2) |
| Abominable | (ABO) |

The technical difficulty of individual rock pitches are described by French rock grades.

## RUSSIAN

The Russian system is comprised of three different systems (Categories, Grades, and Classes) that, when combined, represent an accurate portrayal of a route.

*Grades.* There are 11 grades and sub-grades of difficulty in the Russian system. These range from 1B through 6A/B. These grades do not indicate whether a route is ice or rock or at a high or low altitude. Grades only take into account the ascent and not approaches and descents; they reflect the overall experience and knowledge necessary for a climber to adequately ascend a route. Thus an ascent of Shiprock and the West Buttress of Denali could both be classified as 3B. A route on the Eiger and on El Capitan could both be classified as 5A. The classification of 6B is reserved for the extraordinarily hard, top-level routes.

UIAA ratings are used to describe the difficulty of individual pitches on a route. These range from I to IV, with sub-grades of + and - between II and VI. A1-A4 are used to describe the difficulty of aid pitches. A lower case "e" is used to indicate if bolts were placed on the pitch.

1B: You may encounter rocks, with elements of II climbing on rocks, ice or snow. There is no need to use any gear to set up belay points or anchors.

2A: Contains one to two pitches of II+ category climbing. The rest (up to 10 pitches) will be easy II category climbing that may require use of a rope but does not require anchors or belay points.

2B: Normally contains one to two pitches of II+ category climbing with elements of III category climbing. The rest, up to 10 piches, can be II climbing.

3A: Contains one or one-and-a-half pitches of III or III+ climbing. Could be a rock, mixed or ice/snow route.

3B: A 3B route would have one to two crux pitches of III+ climbing with elements of IV category climbing. It normally takes six to 12 hours to complete the route, or it can be longer depending on the area and conditions.

4A: IV climbing routes normally contain two to three pitches of IVto IV+ climbing. The rest (up to 10 pitches or more) is III to III+ climbing. Normally, it takes one-half to one day to complete the route. It can be a rock, mixed or ice/snow route.

4B: Contains two to three pitches of IV+ climbing with elements of V (crux moves or overhangs) climbing. Total number of pitches is about five to 12. The rest of climbing is IV to IV. It would take one-half to two days to complete the route, depending on the area.

5A: Contains two to three pitches of V climbing. The rest of the pitches (up to 10 or more) are IV to IV+ climbing. There are rock, mixed and ice/snow 5A routes. It takes one to three days to complete the route, depending on the region of location.

5B: Significantly harder than 5A. Normally a two (or more) day route. It should contain at least two or three pitches of V climbing with elements of VI climbing. Normally, these routes are about 10 to 12 pitches long, so the rest of climbing is IV+ to V climbing. Can be either rock or mixed routes.

6A and 6B: The harder routes. They should include several pitches of VI climbing. They are normally about 20 or more pitch routes where the rest of climbing is V climbing.

*Classes*: Classes were developed under the old Soviet system of competition mountaineering. Of the eight classes, four would be chosen for a given competition.

High Altitude: Peaks above 6500 meters

High Altitude—Technical: Peaks between 5201 meters and 6500 meters

Technical: Peaks between 4200 meters and 5200 meters. Big walls usually fall into this class.

Rock: Peaks less than 4200 meters.

Ice-Snow: This class was implemented to raise the technical ice climbing skills of Soviet climbers, which were lacking due to inferior equipment.

Traverse: The linking of two or more mountains, climbed one after another, with descent by a different route.

Winter: This class relies entirely on the temporal aspect of the season. Ascents must fall within certain dates in each region.

NCCS GRADES

The National Climbing Classification System (NCCS) describes the overall difficulty of a multi-pitch alpine climb in terms of time and technical rock difficulty. It takes the following factors into account: length of the climb, number of hard pitches, average pitch difficulty, difficulty of the hardest pitch, commitment, route-finding problems, ascent time, rockfall, icefall, weather problems, approach, and remoteness of an area. It should be emphasized that an increase in grade mandates an increasing level of psychological preparation and commitment.

Grade I: Normally requires only several hours to do the technical portion; can be of any technical difficulty.

Grade II: Normally requires half a day for the technical portion; can be of any technical difficulty.

Grade III: Normally requires a full day for the technical portion; can be of any technical difficulty.

Grade IV: Expected to take one long hard day of technical climbing (longer on the first ascent); the hardest pitch is usually no less than 5.7.

Grade V: Expected to take an average of one-and-a-half days; the hardest pitch is rarely less than 5.8.

Grade VI: Usually takes two or more days; generally includes considerably difficult free climbing and/or aid climbing.

Grade VII: Big walls in very remote locations that are climbed in an alpine style. These are long climbs that are exposed to severe weather with complex approaches.

ALASKA GRADE

A grading system unique to Alaska is needed because of the severe storms, the cold, the altitude, and the extensive cornicing. Each ascending grade has all the elements of the previous grade.

Grade 1: An easy glacier route.

Grade 2: Moderate, with no technical difficulties aside from knife-edges, high altitude, and weather problems.

Grade 3: Moderate to hard; a mildly technical climb with occasional cornicing and short steep sections.

Grade 4: Hard to difficult; involves more sustained climbing.

Grade 5: Difficult, with sustained technical climbing requiring a high level of commitment. Scant bivouac sites.

Grade 6: Severe, with poor retreat options (generally long, corniced ridges), hanging bivouacs subjected to spindrift avalanches, or offering the highest standards of sustained technical climbing for over 4,000 feet.

# AID CLIMBING

(The following explanation of the A1 to A5 grading system for aid climbing pitches is given by John Middendorf.) Climbing sections of rock that are impassable free but accept gear to allow progress is considered aid climbing. Aid climbing's greatest value is that it allows climbers to ascend the long awesome rock walls and faces in the world's wild places that would otherwise be unclimbable. Special techniques, skills, and equipment are required. Aid climbing, though more cumbersome and complex than free climbing, is an essential technique for a climber's ability to ascend the vertical and overhanging milieu of his or her pursuit.

The scope of this description is to define the A1 to A5 system of grading individual aid pitches. First a note on the overall grading system of a particular big-wall climb. A climb rated Grade VI 5. 10 A4 indicates the length (Grade VI indicates a greater than two-day climb), the maximum free difficulty (5.10), and the hardest aid pitch (A4). The overall grading system, however, never tells the full story. The same Grade VI 5.10 A4 rating could apply to an eight-pitch, three-day route with only one pitch of A4 and a short, well-protected section of 5.10, or it could represent a horrendous 30-pitch, 10-day nail-up, with multiple horror-show A4 pitches and bold unprotected pitches of 5.10. Big-wall climbing is such, however, that the general difficulty of a route becomes apparent once you see the climb in question, and the intimidation that one feels when looking up at a massive chunk of stone is roughly proportional to the effort and skill that will be required to climb it.

*Ratings*

A0: Also known as "French-free." Uses gear to make progress, but generally no aiders required. Examples: Half Dome Regular route, sections of the *Nose* route on El Cap, the first two pitches of the West Face (either a quick 5.10 A0 with three points of aid, or tricky 5.11c).

A1: Easy aid. Placements are straightforward and solid. No risk of any piece pulling out. Aiders generally required. Fast and simple for C1, the hammerless corresponding grade, but not necessarily fast and simple for nailing pitches. Examples (clean): the non-5.12 version of the *Salathé* Headwall, *Prodigal Son* on Angel's Landing and *Touchstone Wall* in Zion.

A2: Moderate aid. Placements generally solid but possibly awkward and strenuous to place. Maybe a tenuous placement or two above good pro with no fall danger. Examples: the right side of E1 Cap Tower (nailing), *Moonlight Buttress* and *Space Shot* in Zion (clean).

A2+: Like A2, but with possibly several tenuous placements above good pro. Twenty- to 30-foot fall potential but with little danger of hitting anything. Route finding abilities may be required. Examples: the new-wave grades of *Mescalito* and the *Shield* on El Cap, the Kor route on the Titan in the Fisher Towers area.

A3: Hard aid. Testing methods required. Involves many tenuous placements in a row. Generally, solid placements that could hold a fall found within a pitch. Long fall potential up to 50 feet (six to eight placements ripping), but generally safe from serious danger. Usually requires several hours to complete a pitch due to complexity of placements. Examples: The *Pacific Ocean Wall* lower crux pitches (30 feet between original bolts on manky fixed copperheads), Standing Rock in the desert (the crux being a traverse on the first pitch with very marginal gear and 30-foot swing potential into a corner).

A3+: Like A3, but with dangerous fall potential. Tenuous placements (such as marginal tied-off pins or a hook on a fractured edge) after long stretches of body-weight pieces (here body-weight placements are considered for all practical purposes as any piece of gear not solid enough to hold a fall). Potential to get hurt if good judgement is not exercised. Time required generally exceeds three hours for experienced aid climbers. Example: Pitch three of *Days of No Future* on Angel's Landing in Zion, with a crux of 50 feet of birdbeaks and tied-off blades in soft sandstone followed by a blind, marginal Friend placement in loose rock that is hard to test properly, all above a ledge.

A4: Serious aid. Lots of danger. Sixty- to 100-foot fall potentials common, with uncertain landings far below. Examples: pitches on the *Kaliyuga* on Half Dome and the *Radiator* on Abraham in Zion.

A4+: More serious than A4. These leads generally take many hours to complete and require the climber to endure long periods of uncertainty and fear, often requiring a ballet-like efficiency of movement in order not to upset the tenuous integrity of marginal placements. Examples: the "Welcome to Wyoming" pitch (formerly the "Psycho Killer" pitch) on the *Wyoming Sheep Ranch* on E1 Cap, which requires 50 feet of climbing through a loose, broken, and rotten diorite roof with very marginal, scary placements like stoppers wedged in between two loose, shifting, rope-slicing slivers of rock, all over a big jagged loose ledge that would surely break bones and maim the climber. The pitch is then followed by 100 feet of hooking interspersed with a few rivets to the belay.

A5: Extreme aid. Nothing really trustworthy of catching a fall for the entire pitch. Rating should be reserved only for pitches with no bolts or rivets (holes) for the entire pitch. Examples: pitches on the *Jolly Roger* and the *Wyoming Sheep Ranch* on El Cap, Jim Beyer routes in Arches National Park and the Fisher Towers.

A6: A theoretical grade. A5 climbing with marginal belays that would not hold a fall.

# Contributors' Guidelines

The *American Alpine Journal* records the significant climbing accomplishments of the world in an annual volume. We encourage climbers to submit brief (250-500 words), factual accounts of their climbs and expeditions. While we welcome submissions in a variety of forms, contributors are encouraged to follow certain guidelines when submitting materials. Accounts should be submitted by e-mail. Alternatively, submit accounts by regular post both as a hard copy and on disk; both Mac and PC disks are acceptable. When submitting an account on disk, please save it as a text file. Please include your club affiliation when submitting accounts.

Deadlines for all accounts are February 1 for the preceding calendar year of January 1 to December 31. For Patagonian climbs, the deadline is extended to February 15.

We encourage contributors to submit relevant photographs; we accept both black-and-white and color slides and prints. When submitting an image to show a route line, we ask that you submit the image along with a photo- or laser-copy and draw the lines in on the copy. Alternatively, submit two copies of the same image (a virgin copy and a copy with the route line drawn in), or draw the line of the route on a vellum or similar tracing paper overlay. Please do not draw directly on the photograph.

Photographic duplicates should be reproduction quality. Please send all images via registered mail. *The American Alpine Journal* is not responsible for images lost or damaged in the mail. Topos and maps are also encouraged; camera-ready original copies are necessary for quality reproduction.

While we do not pay for accounts or lead articles, those accounts from which we publish a photograph will receive a complimentary copy of the *Journal*. Authors of lead articles and the photographer of the cover photo will receive a one-year complimentary membership to The American Alpine Club.

Please address all correspondences to:

The American Alpine Journal
710 Tenth Street, Suite 140
Golden, Colorado 80401
tel.: (303) 384-3515
fax: (303) 384-3573
e-mail:aaj@americanalpineclub.org
http://www.americanalpineclub.org

# Index

COMPILED BY JESSICA KANY

VOLUME 72 • 1998